MATH TEACHING SERIES
STUDENTS • TEACHERS • PARENTS

A step-by-step
MATH TEACHING SERIES
for
Students, Teachers, **AND** Parents

GRADE LEVEL

7

ABOUT THE AUTHOR:
Nicholas Aggor is a parent and an ex-senior engineer with a master's degree
in engineering, fully trained in the prestigious Six Sigma Blackbelt
of Problem Solving, and a National Dean's List Scholar

www.MathTeachingSeries.com
Published by Nicholas Aggor Publisher, LLC.

Welcome to the Math Teaching Series

IF YOU ARE AN EDUCATOR...

This text and every text in the Math Teaching Series provide new "tools" designed to assist you in teaching mathematics. After listening and working with educators to assist all students, even those who struggle with math, we were able to build a step-by-step method to improve the delivery of effective instruction.

IF YOU ARE A PARENT...

We will guide your student to build skills and they will become competent. Study will progress with less stress and more peace as the student and you are able to work together toward success. Pride in accomplishment can come early and stay during the study effort with the system.

IF YOU ARE A STUDENT...

These texts were built to assist all students and allow them to earn respect for their efforts. Those who struggle can get the help they need in a process built to avoid becoming lost and stuck. You are guided and the course is designed to allow you to build competence in skills, which will allow you to feel confident!

Nicholas Aggor, an Author, an Engineer, a Parent

This series of texts is dedicated to making the playing field a more fair and equal process to all students with a well-constructed platform to deliver the lessons.

I believe there are always at least three parties to the success of education. With the student supported with a text built to this level of support, we are confident that the educators of the world will now receive "hands on" help as well for the student with parents, relatives, and others who are dedicated to the journey that can use this text.

I wish to thank all the teachers who help in the real life struggle to teach.

We have designed a new set of tools for students, teachers, and parents.

Nicholas Aggor

Texas Instruments images used with permission of the copyright owner.

Material extracted from TI-Nspire™ Math and Science Learning Technology and TI-Nspire™ Learning Handheld Quick Reference with permission of the publisher Copyright (2007), Texas Instruments Incorporated

ISBN: 978-0-9840609-2-4

School to Home Connection

You promise to work and I promise you will not get lost.

Math Teaching Series Lesson One

LEARN WHY TO WORK AND YOU WILL SUCCEED

- You are as rich and as intelligent as anyone while studying this book.
- Stay with me and work daily and you will see improved results.
- This is all about effort, so follow the pathways and you will improve.

LEARN HOW TO WORK AND YOU WILL SUCCEED

- Peace and quiet will allow focus. NO radio, television, games, and phones.
- Expect to win, to progress and keep score daily and results will improve.
- Your teachers are there to help and teach, so show them your work daily.

Daily Score Card

1. Students grade parents for providing scheduled studies time, homework time, bed time, quiet place to study, quiet place to do homework, and food.
2. Parents grade students for the effort the students make during the scheduled studies time, homework time, and bed time.
3. Teachers grade students during quizzes, homework, and tests.

| Days | Studies Time | Quality Control at Home | | Quality Control at School | Steps to Improve |
		Students' Grading	Parents' Grading	Teachers' Grading	Improvement
Mon					
Tue					
Wed					
Thu					
Fri					
Sat					
Sun					

- Students earn good results with good work habits. Take pride in your efforts.
- Share your daily effort with your parents, guardians, your family, and friends.
- Seek advice and help from your math teachers on your journey to success.
- Parents should make copies of the score card for monitoring progress.

How to Use This Book Most Effectively

There is a consistent teaching method in the text to follow.

Your book contains Examples, with step-by-step demonstration of "how to" do the math problems. As you study, focus on learning the "how to" properly and the solutions offered throughout your text will teach you the methods to use.

Practice the Examples and come to know how to do the work. The Examples section will "teach you" the process in a step-by-step manner. This way, learning the correct methods will prevent you from getting lost or stuck. You will find each step to be connected and the pace will allow you to progress with confidence.

After following the Examples offered with understanding, work the chapter Exercise Problems. As you do the Exercise Problems, use the "hints" provided, as you need them, sending you back to the Examples. This will allow you to advance, and as you learn the steps properly, your confidence will strengthen.

Challenge questions are designed for you to excel in the area of study. Allow yourself time to work the Challenge Questions as they will strengthen your skills.

Word Problems provide Real World applications of the methods you are learning. You are provided with the "how to" method again, showing the step-by-step solutions to solve these questions properly. This will help to improve your math reasoning skills.

Learn to use the Table of Contents (front) and the Index of Terms (back) in this book. These are reference aids to quickly direct you to solutions.

TABLE OF CONTENTS - Grade 7

Chapter 24: Scatter Plots

Chapter 25: Congruent Triangles

Chapter 26: Similar Triangles

STEM-AND-LEAF PLOT

Cumulative Review

1. Mary said that to divide by a fraction is the same as multiplying by the reciprocal of the fraction. Is her statement correct? Hint: Review the section on the Division of Fractions in the Math Teaching Series for grade 6 or grade 7.

2. Divide, multiply, subtract, or add. Hint: Review the section on the Division of Fractions in the Math Teaching Series for grade 6 or grade 7.

   a. $\dfrac{2}{5} \div \dfrac{4}{15} =$ **b.** $\dfrac{2}{5} \times \dfrac{4}{15} =$ **c.** $\dfrac{2}{5} + \dfrac{4}{15} =$ **d.** $\dfrac{2}{5} - \dfrac{4}{15} =$

3. Find the value of each expression. Hint: Review the chapter on the Order of Operations in the Math Teaching Series for grade 6 or grade 7.

   a. $12 + 3 \cdot 4 - 8$ **b.** $16 - 20 \div 4$ **c.** $7 \cdot 2 - 2$ **d.** $9 \div 3 \cdot 2$

New Terms
Stem-and-leaf plot, **stem**, **leaf**

A stem-and-leaf plot is a table that shows groups of data arranged by **place value**. (Review the section on **Place Value** in the Math Teaching Series for grade 5 if needed.)
A stem-and-leaf plot is used to display and compare data.

How to Make a Stem-and-Leaf Plot
Example 1
Using the data values, (a) make a stem-and-leaf plot.
               (b) explain how the stem-and-leaf plot is made.
   Ages of people in a club.
   Data values

28	34	16	50	12	13
34	14	7	16	25	19
16	9	28	50	55	19
74	36	8			

Solution
a). The tens digit of each number is its **stem**. The **stems** are listed from the least to the greatest. The **leaf** of each data value is written to the right of its stem, and they are written in order from the least to the greatest. The stem-and-leaf plot is shown below:

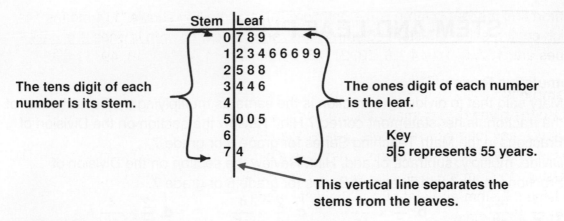

Stem	Leaf
0	7 8 9
1	2 3 4 6 6 6 6 9 9
2	5 8 8
3	4 4 6
4
5	0 0 5
6
7	4

The tens digit of each number is its stem.

The ones digit of each number is the leaf.

Key
5|5 represents 55 years.

This vertical line separates the stems from the leaves.

b). The stem-and-leaf plot is made from data values using the four items listed below:

1. Under the stems column, list the tens digit of every number in order from the least to the greatest and these tens digits becomes the stems. The data values contain one-digit numbers which are ones, so the stem column begins with zero because the ones has no place value for tens. The highest data is 74, and therefore, the tens digits under the stem column range from 0 to 7, and therefore, choose 0 to 7 as stems also.

2. Under the leaves column and beside each ten digit, write the ones digits of each number in order from least to greatest, and these ones digits become the leaves. For example, the data values for the stem-and-leaf plot:

2|5 8 8 are 25, 28, and 28.

tens   ones

3. The ones digits are written under the leaf column to the right of its stem, and they are written from the least to the greatest.

4. The "key" helps us to confirm the place values of the stem and leaf columns. For example, the key "5|5" means 55 years" and it confirms that the stem column is tens and the leaf column is ones.

Example 2

List the data values in the stem-and-leaf plot.

Stem	Leaf
0	1 7 9
1	4 4 8
2	0 1 6
3	0 0 9
4	4 5 6 8 9
5	1 4

Key
1|4 means 14

Solution

Using the information in Example 1, regarding the fact that the stem column is the tens column and the leaf column is the ones column and the key shows "1|4 means 14", which confirms that the stem column is tens and the leaf column is ones, the data values are: 1, 7, 9, 14, 14, 18, 20, 21, 26, 30, 30, 39, 44, 45, 46, 48, 49, 51, 54.

Example 3

a. Use the given data to make a stem-and-leaf plot.
b. How many teams have scores greater than 65?
c. How many leaves are in the stem-and-leaf plot?
d. Using the stem-and-leaf plot, what is the median?
e. Using the stem-and-leaf plot, what is the mode?
f. What is the range?

Teams	A	B	C	D	E	F	G	H	I	J	K	L	M	N
Scores per year	24	30	30	48	56	29	70	72	27	32	30	44	50	48

Solution

a. The scores range from 24 to 72, so the stems are from 2 to 7, and the ones digits are written under the leaf column to the right of the stems, and they are written from the least to the greatest as shown:

```
Stem   |Leaf
      2|4 7 9
      3|0 0 0 2
      4|4 8 8
      5|0 6
      6|
      7|0 2
```
key,
7|0   means 70.

b. There are two teams which have scores greater 65 and the scores are:

$$7|0\ 2 \quad \text{which are 70 and 72.}$$

c. There are 14 leaves in the stem-and-leaf plot. The number of leaves is the same as the number of the scores.

d. The middle score is the median, however, since there are 14 scores, the middle score is the average of the 7th and the 8th scores.
The 7th leaf = 32 and the 8th leaf = 44.
Therefore, the average of the 7th and 8th scores

$$= \frac{\text{7th score} + \text{8th score}}{2}$$

$$= \frac{32 + 44}{2} = \frac{76}{2} = 38 \text{ scores.}$$

In order to find the median, the data needs to be arranged in order from the least to the greatest. **Note** that the stem-and-leaf plot already arranges the numbers in order from the least to the greatest.

e. The score that occurs the most is the mode. From the stem-and-leaf plot, the mode is:

$3|0\ 0\ 0$ which is 30, 30, and 30 because 30 occurs the most.

f. The **range is the largest score minus the smallest score** which is 72 - 24 = 48

Example 4

a. Use the data to make a stem-and-leaf plot. The weights are given to the nearest whole number.

b. Explain what

$7|0\ 8$ mean

c. What does

$1\ 2|0\ 0$ mean?

d. What is the mean?

People	A	B	C	D	E	F	G	H	I	J	K	L	M
Weight in lbs.	145	85	94	142	100	68	140	120	85	100	70	78	120

Solution

a. The numbers range from 68 to 145, and therefore, the stem should range from 6 to 14, and from the key the numbers under the leaf column are ones. The stem and leaf plot is shown as shown:

```
Stem | Leaf
   6 | 8
   7 | 0 8
   8 | 5 5
   9 | 4
  10 | 0 0
  11 |
  12 | 0 0                  key
  13 |                      14|0  means 140 lbs.
  14 | 0 2 5
```

b. $7|0\ 8$ means 70 lbs. and 78 lbs. (See similar explanation in Examples 1 and 2).

c. $1\ 2|0\ 0$ means 120 lbs. and 120 lbs. (See similar explanation in Examples 1 and 2).

d. The mean is the same as the average.

$$\text{Mean} = \frac{\text{Sum of all the numbers}}{\text{Total number of the numbers}}$$

4

$$= \frac{68 + 70 + 78 + 85 + 85 + 94 + 100 + 100 + 120 + 120 + 140 + 142 + 145}{13}$$

$$= \frac{1347}{13}$$

$= 103.6$ lbs. You may use a calculator to obtain the answer.

Back-to-Back Stem-and-Leaf Plot
Example 5
a. What is a back-to-back stem-and-leaf plot?
b. What is the back-to-back stem-and-leaf plot used for?
Solution
a. A back-to-back stem-and-leaf plot is simply two stem-and-leaf plots joined together.
b. A back-to-back stem-and-leaf plot is used to compare two related sets of data.

How to Make a Back-to-Back Stem-and-Leaf Plot
Example 6
Describe how a back-to-back stem-and-leaf plot is made. Give an example.
A back-to-back stem-and-leaf plot is made as shown:
Record the stems in the center of the plot.
Record one set of the leaf at the left side of the stem and record the other set of the leaf at the right side of the stem as shown:

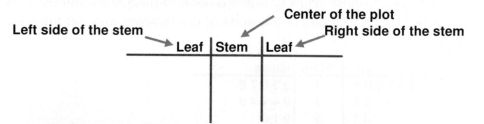

The key to the back-to-back stem-and-leaf plot can be written in two forms, (**a**) and (**b**).
Use back-to-back stem-and-leaf plot of the weights of boys and girls shown below as an example.

Girls (weights in lbs.)	Stem	Boys (weights in lbs)
9 6 5	1	7 9
9 8 4	2	0 5
6 5 3 0	3	
8 7 2 1	4	3 6 8

The keys are:

(a) means 24 lbs. ←——— 4|2|0 ———→ means 20 lbs.
    (Note that this key is
    written in the reverse form).

(b) | 4|3 means 43 lbs.
                               0| 3| means 30 lbs.
                                      (Note that this key is written in the
                                      reverse form).

Example 7

a. Use the given data to make a back-to-back stem-and-leaf plot.

Ages of males and females entering a certain library												
Females (years)	44	22	10	19	34	40	17	10	22	31	45	19	10
Males (years)	24	30	17	20	29	10	24	24	31	36	18	15	16

b. Find the median and the mode of the ages of the females.

c. What is the median and the mode of the ages of the males?

d. What is the range of the ages of the females?

e. What is the range of the ages of the males?

f. Comparing the ages of the females and the males, which range is smaller?

g. Which median is greater? Is this difference shown by the stem-and-leaf plot? How is this difference shown by the stem-and-leaf plot?

Solution

a. Using the information under "How to make a back-to-back stem-and-leaf plot" the back-to-back stem-and-leaf plot of the ages of the females and the males are drawn as shown:

Female	Stem	Males
9 9 7 0 0 0	1	0 5 6 7 8
2 2	2	0 4 4 4 9
4 1	3	0 1 6
5 4 0	4	

key:
Means 31 years ←——1|3|0 ———→ Means 30 years

b. The median is the middle leaf of the ages of the females, which is 22 years. (Count the ages under the leaf column to get to the middle age). The leaf that occurs the most is the mode. From the back-to-back stem-and-leaf plot, the age that occurs most is 10 years, and therefore, the mode is 10 years.

Note that 0 0 0 |1| means 10, 10, and 10.

c. The median is the middle leaf of the ages of the males, which is 24 years. (Count the ages under the leaf column to get the middle age). The leaf that occurs the most is the mode. From the back-to-back stem-and-leaf plot, the age that occurs the most is 24 years, so the mode is 24 years.

6

Note that | 2|4 4 4   means 24, 24, and 24.

d. The range of the ages of the females is the greatest age minus the least age which is 45 - 10 = 35 years.

e. The range of the ages of the males is the greatest age minus the least age which is 36 - 10 = 26 years.

f. From the solution **d**, the range of the ages of the females is 35 years. From the solution **e**, the range of the males is 26 years. The range of the females' ages is greater than the range of the males' ages and this difference can be shown in the stem and leaf plot because the females' ages are spread more than the males' ages.

g. From solution **b**, the median age of the females is 22 years and from the solution **c**, the median age of the males is 24 years. Therefore, the median age of the males is greater than the median age of the females. The ages of the females are too close together to show any significant difference in the spread of the data (ages) on the stem-and-leaf plot.

Example 8

Use the back-to-back stem-and-leaf plot to answer the following questions.
   (**a**) Find the median for each set of data. Which median is greater? How is this difference shown by the stem-and-leaf plot?
   (**b**) Find the mode for each set of data.
   (**c**) Find the mean for each set of data.
   (**d**) What is the range for each set of data?
   (**e**) Which range is greater? How is this difference shown by the stem and leaf plot?

The time people use to find library books.
(Time to the nearest tenth of a minute).

Females	Stem	Males
9 8 7 5 1 0	7	2 4
6 5 3 1 1 0	8	5 7
7 5 4 3	9	2 3 5
8 6 4 3 3	10	2 3 4
2	11	0 2 5
	12	1
	13	3 7
	14	5 8
	15	
	16	3 8 9

key:
| 10|2   means 10.2 minutes
3| 9| means 9.3 minutes

Solution

Note that the key shows that the data under the leaf are not ones but rather tenths of a minute.

(**a**) The median age of the females' data is the middle leaf of the females' data. Since there are 22 data for the females, the middle terms are the 11th and the 12th terms of the data, which are 8.6 and 8.5 minutes. The average of the 11th and

7

the 12th terms of the female data is the median of the females' data. So the

median of the females' data $= \dfrac{8.6 + 8.5}{2} = \dfrac{17.1}{2} = 8.55$ minutes.

(Hint: See the chapter/section on Median.)

The median of the males' data is the middle leaf of the males' data.

Since there are 21 data for the males, the 11th data is the middle data which is 11.0 minutes. The median of the males' data is greater than the median of the females' data. The difference in the median between the females' and the males' data is shown by the stem-and-leaf plot because the females' data is clustered near the top.

(**b**) The leaf that occurs the most in each set of the data is the mode for the data. Considering the females' data, two numbers occur most which are 8.1 minutes and 10.3 minutes.

> **Note that 1 1 | 8 | means 8.1 and 8.1**
> **Note that 3 3 | 10 | means 10.3 and 10.3**

Considering the males' data, no data in the males' leaf occurs most, so the male data has no mode.

(**c**) Mean $= \dfrac{\text{Sum of all the data}}{\text{Total number of the data}}$

Considering the females' ages:

Mean $=$ (7.0 + 7.1 + 7.5 + 7.7 + 7.8 + 7.9 + 8.1 + 8.1 + 8.3 + 8.5 + 8.6 + 9.3 + 9.4 + 9.5 + 9.7 + 10.3 + 10.3 + 10.4 + 10.6 + 10.8 + 11.2) ÷ 21

$= \dfrac{188.1}{21} = 8.96 = 9.0$ minutes.

Considering the males' ages:

Mean $= \dfrac{\text{Sum of all the data}}{\text{Total number of the data}}$

$=$ 7.2 + 7.4 + 8.5 + 8.7 + 9.2 + +9.3 + 9.5 + 10.2 + 10.3 +10.4 + 11.0 + 11.2 + 11.5 + 12.1 + 13.3 + 13.7 + 14.5 + 14.8 + 16.3 + 16.8 + 16.9) ÷ 21

$= \dfrac{242.8}{21} = 11.56 = 11.6$ minutes   (You may use a calculator.)

(**d**) The range of each set of data is the largest time minus the smallest time. Considering the females, the largest time is 11.2 minutes and the smallest time is 7.0 minutes, and therefore, the range is:

11.2 - 7.0 = 4.2 minutes.

Considering the males, the largest time is 16.9 minutes and the smallest time is 7.2 minutes, and therefore, the range = 16.9 - 7.2 = 9.7 minutes.

(**e**) From solution (**d**), the range of the females' data is 4.2 minutes and the range for the males' data is 9.7 minutes, and therefore, the males' range is greater than the females' range and this difference is shown by the stem-and-leaf plot because the females' data is clustered to the top while the males' data is spread.

Exercises

1. What is a stem-and-leaf plot?

2. What is a stem-and-leaf plot used for?

3. Use the data values to:

(**a**) make a stem-and-leaf plot.

(**b**) explain how the stem-and-leaf plot is made.

Hint: See Example 1.

Ages of people in a book club (ages in years).

15	17	34
22	38	34
34	45	62
40	60	28
15	65	29

4. Use the data values to make a stem-and-leaf plot.

(**a**). Weight of people in lbs.

25	44	55	20
68	37	34	16
34	62	47	20
16	20	59	37
77	32	25	32

(**b**). Number of books per shelf

44	69	30
19	30	20
36	40	40
30	62	36
27	31	44

Hint: See Example 1.

5. List the data values in the following stem-and-leaf plots. Hint: See Example 2.

(a)
```
0 | 2 8 9
1 | 3
2 | 5 8 9
3 | 0 0 0 5 8
4 | 0 1 8 9
```
key: 4 | 0   means 40

(b)
```
0 | 1 4 8 9
1 | 7 8 9
2 | 0 0 3 8
3 | 4 9
4 | 0 3 7 9
5 | 0 0 9
```
key: 1 | 7   means 17

©
```
0 | 0 3 5
1 | 0 0 4
2 | 3
3 | 4 8
4 | 0 0 0 1
5 | 1 3 6 8
```
key: 3 | 4   means 34.

6a. Use the given data in tables 1 and 2 to make two separate stem-and-leaf plots.

Table 1

Teams	A	B	C	D	E	F	G	H	I	J
Scores per year	16	10	25	16	16	34	48	25	40	37

Table 2

Teams	A	B	C	D	E	F	G	H	I	J	K	L
Scores per year	9	27	17	35	27	17	30	34	27	35	42	30

6b. From each stem-and-leaf plot, how many teams have scored above 40 points per year?

6c. How many leaves are there in each stem-and-leaf plot?

6d. Find the median from each stem-and-leaf plot.

6e. Find the mode and the range of each stem-and-leaf plot.
   Hint: See Example 3.

7a. Use the data to make a stem-and-leaf plot. The weights are given to the nearest whole number in lbs.

Animals	A	B	C	D	E	F	G	H	I	J	K	L
Weight in lbs.	77	30	29	37	30	48	44	56	70	54	61	48

7b. Explain the meaning of 3|007.

7c. Explain the meaning of 4|88.

7d. What is the mean of the data?
   Hint: See Example 4.

8a. What is a back-to-back stem-and-leaf plot?

8b. What is a back-to-back stem-and-leaf plot used for?
   Hint: See Example 5.

9. Describe how a back-to-back stem-and-leaf plot is made.
   Hint: See Example 6.

10a. Use the given data to make a back-to-back stem-and-leaf plot.

Ages in years of people entering the library												
Females	29	20	50	42	20	32	19	21	50	32	20	20
Males	36	41	32	36	30	14	30	44	48	36	40	30

10b. Find the median and the mode of the ages of the females.

10c. Find the median and the mode of the ages of the males.

10d. What is the range of the ages of the males?

10e. What is the range of the ages of the females?

10f. Which range is smaller? How is the difference shown by the stem-and-leaf plot?
   Hint: See Example 7.

11a. Use the given data to make a back-to-back stem-and-leaf plot.

Miles per gallon ratings of 4-cylinder and 6-cylinder cars.											
Model type	A	B	C	D	E	F	G	H	I	J	K
4-Cylinder	16	18	20	35	42	18	28	32	28	32	18
6-Cylinder	10	15	17	25	29	15	21	24	19	25	15

11b. Find the median and the mode of the 4-cylinder cars.

11c. Find the median and the mode of the 6-cylinder cars.

11d. What is the range of the 4-cylinder car data?

11e. What is the range of the 6-cylinder car data?
   Hint: See Example 7.

12. Use the back-to-back stem-and-leaf plot to answer the questions:
   a. Find the median for each set of data. Which median is greater? How is this

difference shown by the stem and leaf plot?

b. Find the mode for each set of data.

c. Find the mean for each set of data.

d. What is the range for each set of data?

Ratings of miles per gallon for 4-cylinder and 6-cylinder cars.
Ratings to the nearest tenth of a mile per gallon.

4-Cylinder		6-Cylinder
	14	0 4
	15	3 5 7 9
	16	4 1
	17	
	18	0 0 1
	19	5 8
	20	
	21	
8 7 4 0 0	22	
9 7 6	23	
4 2 1 0	24	

key: 15|3 means 15.3 mpg.
6|23 means 23.6 mpg.
mpg means miles per gallon.

Hint: See Example 8

13. Create a stem-and-leaf plot of the data values.

a. 54, 36, 48, 88, 93, 48, 50, 36, 50, 72, 61. Hint: See Example 3**a**

b. 6.6, 9.4, 6.0, 7.4, 10.0, 8.7, 10.0, 6.0

Hint: Although this problem is not a back-to-back stem-and-leaf plot, it is similar to Example 8 because the data values are in decimals (see the key of Example 8).

Challenge Questions

14. List the data values in the following stem-and-leaf plots.

(a)	0	2 3 4
	1	0 0 1
	2	8 9
	3	
	4	4 8 9
	5	0 0 0 2

key: 2|8 means 28.

(b)	1	0 0 0
	2	4 8 9
	3	2
	4	7 8
	5	0 5 8
	6	1 1 14

key: 4|7 means 47.

©	1	7 9
	2	0 0 4
	3	4
	4	
	5	1 3 8 9
	6	4 7

key: 6|4 means 6.4

15. Use the data values to make stem-and-leaf plots.

a. Age of people in years.

17	25	23
25	17	23
18	19	18
20	23	17
24	24	19
38	39	42

b. Weight of people in lbs.

65	60	50
72	78	63
78	84	78
50	80	71
55	50	55

11

c. From the stem-and-leaf plot of **a** and **b**, find the median, mode, and range.

d. What does 1 | 99 mean?

e. What does 5 | 000 mean?

16a. Use the given data to make a back-to-back stem-and-leaf plot.

Ages of teachers in a certain school.						
Male (years)	24	36	55	47	50	36
Females (years)	23	41	28	32	30	23

16b. Find the mode, range, median, and mean of the ages of the male teachers.

16c. Find the mode, range, median, and mean of the ages of the female teachers.

17. Use the back-to-back stem-and-leaf plot to answer the following question.
What is the mode, range, median, and mean for the data set?

```
    8 6│ 10 │0 1 4
      9│ 11 │4
       │ 12 │5 6
  2 0 0│ 13 │            key:  6│10│   means 10.6
    4 2│ 14 │3 1              │14│3   means 14.3
```

18. Find the mode, range, median, and mean of the following stem-and-leaf plot.

(a) Stem	Leaf
2	0 0
3	1 2
4	2 3

key: 3 | 1 means 31.

(b) Stem	Leaf
5	2 3
6	2 4
7	0 0 1

key: 7 | 0 means 7.0

© Stem	Leaf
13	2 4
14	0 0 2

key: 13 | 2 means 132.

CHAPTER 2

BOX-AND-WHISKER PLOTS

Now Terms

box-and-whiskers plot, quartile, interquartile range

A **box-and-whisker plot** shows sets of distribution of data into four groups, and each of the four groups contains about the same number of data. The **box-and-whisker plot is used to compare sets of data**. The **quartiles** separate or divide a data set into about four equal parts. The **interquartile range** is the upper quartile minus the lower quartile.

How to Make a Box-and-Whisker Plot

Example 1

(c) Mean $= \dfrac{\text{Sum of the data items}}{\text{Number of data items}}$

$= \dfrac{79 + 86 + 88 + 88 + 89 + 90 + 95}{7}$

$= \dfrac{615}{7}$

$= 87.857$ You may use a calculator to find $\dfrac{615}{7}$.

$= 88\%$ to the nearest whole number.

Range = Greatest data item - Least data item

$= 95 - 79$

$= 16\%$

The mode is the data item that occurs most.

$= 88$

Group Exercises
(a). Use the **stem-and-leaf plot** of the ages of students in a math club to draw a **box-and-whisker plot**.

```
0 2 2 3 4
1 0 0 1 1 2 3 9
```

(b) Find the median by using the **stem-and-leaf plot** and also by using a **box-and-whisker plot**.

(c) Considering the spread of the data items, explain why the upper whisker is longer than the upper portion of the box.

(d) Find the percent of the data items that are represented by the **entire box portion** of the box-and-whisker plot. Does your answer agree with the description of the box-and-whisker plot? Hint: The data is divided into **4 groups** by the box and whisker plot.

(e) Find the percent of the data items that fall into each region of the **box-and-whisker plot**? Does your answer agree with the description of the **box-and-whisker plot**. Hint: The data is divided into **4** groups by the box-and-whisker plot.

Example 6
Find the range, the first, and the third quartiles of the data set. Find the median of the data set.

93 84 78 88 91 88 89
Solution

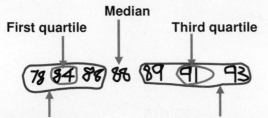

Median

First quartile   Third quartile

Lower half of the data.   Upper half of the data

Order the data from the least to the greatest.

Range = Largest data item - Smallest data item.
   = 93 - 78 (Largest data item = 93 and the smallest data item = 78.
   = 15
First quartile = Median of the lower half of the data.
        = 84
Third quartile = Median of the upper half of the data.
        = 91
Median is the number that divides the data into two equal parts.
Median = 88.

Example 7

Find the range, median, the first, and third quartiles for the data set.
15 13 14 17 15 16 17 19 15 20 21 17
Solution
Order the data items from the smallest to the largest as shown:
                13 14 15 15 15 16 17 17 17 19 20 21
Range = Largest value - Smallest value
   = 21 - 13
   = 8
We may group the data as follows to help us with the quartiles:

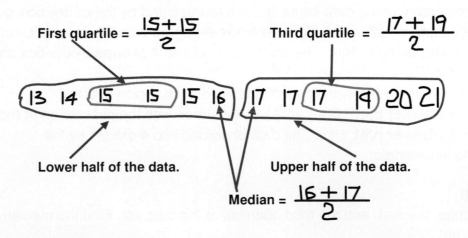

First quartile = $\dfrac{15+15}{2}$ Third quartile = $\dfrac{17+19}{2}$

13 14 15 15 15 16   17 17 17 19 20 21

Lower half of the data.   Upper half of the data.

Median = $\dfrac{16+17}{2}$

The median is the average of the two middle numbers that divide the data into two equal parts when the total number of the data is an even number. (The data has a total of 12 numbers and 12 is an even number).

$$\text{Median} = \frac{16 + 17}{2}$$

$$= 16\frac{1}{2}$$

First quartile = Median of the lower half of the data.

$$= \frac{15 + 15}{2}$$

$$= \frac{30}{2}$$

$$= 15$$

Third quartile = Median of the upper half of the data.

$$= \frac{17 + 19}{2}$$

$$= \frac{36}{2}$$

$$= 18$$

Example 8
Find the smallest value, median, first quartile, third quartile, and the largest value for the data set.
50 22 17 23 56 21 23 64 23 17 19 44 42 49 39 36 45
Solution
Order the data items from the smallest to the largest as shown:
17 17 19 21 22 23 23 23 36 39 42 44 45 49 50 56 64
The smallest value = 17   See the order of the data items.
Group the ordered data as follows in order to identify the quartiles:

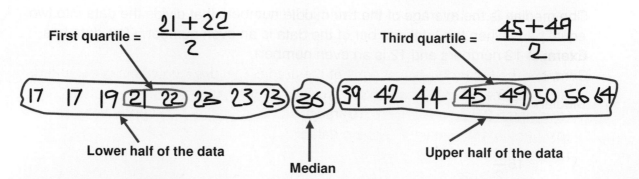

First quartile = $\dfrac{21+22}{2}$

Third quartile = $\dfrac{45+49}{2}$

Lower half of the data

Median

Upper half of the data

Median is the number that divides the data into two equal parts. So, the median is the number in the middle.

Median = 36

The first quartile is the median (middle number) of the lower half of the data.

First quartile = $\dfrac{21+22}{2}$ There is no middle number. Find the average of the two middle numbers.

$$= \dfrac{43}{2}$$

$$= 21.5$$

The third quartile is the median (middle number) of the upper half of the data.

Third quartile = $\dfrac{45+49}{2}$ There is no middle number. Find the average of the two middle numbers.

$$= \dfrac{94}{2} = 47$$

The largest value = 64.   See the order of the data items.

Example 9

(a) Select the values that can be found using a stem-and-leaf plot.

    1. upper quartile   **2.** median   **3.** range   **4.** mean

    5. mode   **6.** lower quartile   **7.** upper extreme   **8.** lower extreme

(b) Select the values that **cannot** be found using a box-and-whisker plot.

    1. upper quartile   **2.** interquartile range   **3.** range

    4. mean   **5.** mode   **6.** median

Solution

(a) All the values from 1 to 8 can be found using a stem and leaf plot.

(b) The mean and the mode cannot be found from the box-and-whisker plot.

Comparing Data Sets Using Box-and-Whisker Plot.

Example 10
Compare the box-and-whisker plots of the grades that the students in class A and class B obtained in geography. Which class has the higher

   (**a**) median   (**b**) range   (**c**) upper extreme
   (**d**) range of the middle half of the data
   (**e**) lower extreme

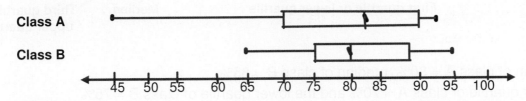

Solution
Use the scale in the diagram from 45 to 100 to compare the two box-and-whisker plots of the class A and the class B.

(**a**) Class A has the higher median.   See the diagram.

(**b**) Class A has the higher range because the distance between the upper extreme
     value and the lower extreme value is longer for class A.
     (We can subtract the lower extreme value from the upper extreme value of each
     set of the class (data) to find the class that has the higher range.)

(**c**) Class B has the higher upper extreme value because the extreme value of
     class B has bigger value than the extreme value of class A.

(**d**) The range of the middle half of the data is the length of the box which is greater
     for class A

(**e**) Class B has the higher "lower extreme" value.   See the diagram.

Example 11
For each box-and-whisker plot, find the values listed.

a. median   **b.** lower quartile   **c.** upper quartile
d. interquartile range   **e.** lower extreme   **f.** upper extreme   **g.** range

History test scores of students in class A and class B.

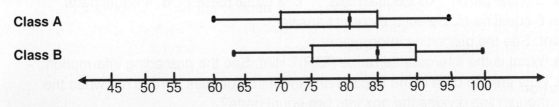

Solution
Redraw the box-and-whisker plots and link all the values to a position on the number line.

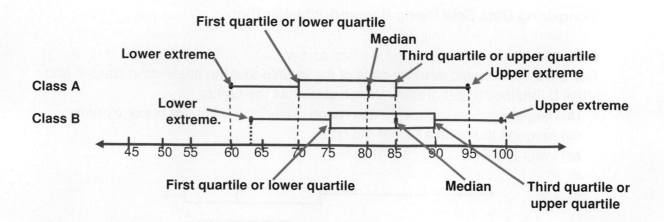

a. Median of class A = 80%, median of class B = 85%

b. Lower quartile of class A = 70% and the lower quartile of class B = 75%

c. Upper quartile of class A = 85% and the upper quartile of class B = 90%

d. Interquartile range of class A = Upper quartile - lower quartile
   = 85% - 70% = 15%

   Interquartile range of class B = Upper quartile - lower quartile
   = 90% - 75% = 15%

e. Lower extreme of class A = 60% and lower extreme of class B = 63%

f. Upper extreme of class A = 95% and upper extreme of class B = 100%

g. Range of class A = Largest value - Smallest value = 95% - 60% = 35%
   Range of class B = Largest value - Smallest value = 100% - 63% = 37%

Exercises

1. Select the correct answer. The box-and-whisker plot shows the distribution of data into:

   a. two groups.   b. three groups.   c. four groups.   d. five groups.
      Hint: See Group Exercises, item (d), or see the preceding information.

2. Select the correct answer. Each group described in Exercise 1 contains about:

   a. twice the data.   b. three times the data.   c. the same number of data.
      Hint: See the preceding information.

3. The quartile separates or divides a data into about

   a. 5 equal parts.   b. 2 equal parts.   c. 3 equal parts.   d. 4 equal parts.

   e. 6 equal parts. Select the correct answer.

   Hint: See the preceding information.

4. a. What is the interquartile range (IQR)? Hint: See the preceding information.

   b. How are the data in the second and the third quartiles spread out when the median line divides the box into two equal parts?
      Hint: See the information/section under "Critical Thinking."

   c. Describe the range of a data that has a long whisker or box. Hint: See the information/section under "Critical Thinking."

   d. Complete the statement. A long whisker or box shows that the data in that quartile or quartiles have a _____ range. Hint: See the information/section under "Critical Thinking."

5. Describe how you would make a box-and-whisker plot and list all the data name that you would use in making the box-and-whisker plot.
   Hint: See Example 1.

6. Use the given data to make a box-and-whisker plot. Find the interquartile range, the mode, and the mean.
   a. 9, 6, 10, 11, 8, 7, 12, 9, 5, 8, 7
   b. 15, 14, 7, 10, 9, 6, 13, 8, 9, 7, 6
   c. 2, 7, 8, 3, 4, 5, 9, 3, 7, 8, 8
   Hint: See Example 2.

7. Describe in **your own words** how the median is found in the stem-and-leaf plot and the box-and-whisker plot. Hint: See Example 3.

8. Describe **in your own words** how the smallest and the largest data items are found in the stem-and-leaf plot and the box-and-whisker plot. Hint: See Example 4.

9 a. Use the stem-and-leaf plots A, B, and C of the grades of students in percent to make a box-and-whisker plot.
   b. Find the interquartile range of each set of data.
   c. Find the mean and the range of each set of data.
   d. Find the mode of each set of data.

A Stem	Leaf
7	5 8
8	0 0 3
9	1 8

Key: 7|5 means 75%.

B Stem	Leaf
6	8
7	8 9
8	0 1 3 7

Key: 6|8 means 68%

C Stem	Leaf
6	9
7	5 6
8	8 9
9	0 5

Key: 7|5 means 75%

Hint: See Example 5.

10. Find the range, the first, and the third quartiles of each set of data. Find the median of each set of data.
   a. 65, 35, 72, 56, 60, 59, 45.
   b. 98, 42, 38, 79, 82, 88, 56.
   c. 77, 85, 23, 57, 48, 61, 68.
   Hint: See Example 6.

11. Find the range, the median, the first, and the third quartiles for each data set.
   a. 11, 14, 17, 10, 28, 18, 39, 44, 35, 12, 14, 15.
   b. 19, 24, 3, 29, 13, 16, 9, 7, 13, 14, 7, 14.
   c. 10, 8, 6, 4, 12, 8, 5, 6, 9, 12, 11, 7.
   Hint: See Example 7.

12. Find the smallest value, median, first quartile, third quartile, and the largest value for each data set.
   a. 7, 8, 9, 18, 9, 14, 17, 22, 27, 19, 11, 12, 10, 12, 13, 9, 26
   b. 40, 32, 11, 16, 18, 21, 27, 12, 17, 13, 15, 14, 13, 9, 10, 16, 14

c. 13, 2, 7, 8, 2, 15, 11, 11, 12, 13, 14, 10, 8, 9
   Hint: See Example 8.
13. The mean and mode cannot be found from the box-and-whisker plot.
    True or False? Hint: See Example 9.
14. Compare the box-and-whisker plots (A) and (B) for the grades in percent that
    students in class Y and class Z obtained in chemistry. Which class has the
    higher:
    a. range.   **b.** range of the middle half of the data.
    c. median.   **d.** lower quartile.   **e.** lower extreme.
    f. upper quartile.   **g.** upper extreme.

(A)

Chemistry test scores in percent of students in classes Y and Z.

Class Y

Class Z

45 50 55   60 65   70 75   80 85   90   95 100

(B)

Chemistry test scores in percent of students in classes Y and Z.

Class Y

Class Z

45 50 55   60 65   70 75   80 85   90   95 100

Hint: See Example 10 and the notes on lower quartile and upper quartile.
15. For each set of the box-and-whisker plot X and Y, find the values listed.
    a. median.   **b.** range.   **c.** interquartile range.
    d. upper quartile.   **e.** lower quartile.   **f.** lower extreme.
    g. upper extreme.

(The box-and-whisker plots X and Y are located on the next page.)

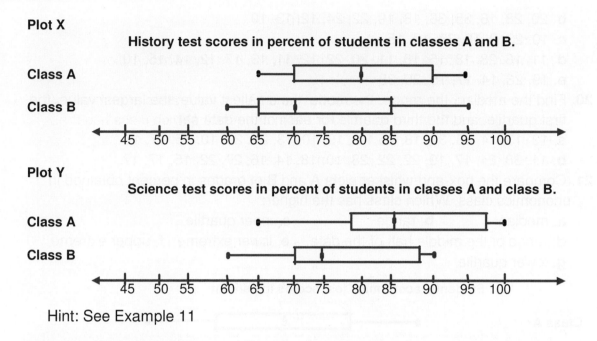

Plot X

History test scores in percent of students in classes A and B.

Class A

Class B

45 50 55 60 65 70 75 80 85 90 95 100

Plot Y

Science test scores in percent of students in classes A and class B.

Class A

Class B

45 50 55 60 65 70 75 80 85 90 95 100

Hint: See Example 11

Challenge Questions

16. Use each given data to make a box-and-whisker plot. Find the interquartile range, range, mean, median, and mode.

    a. 10, 12, 7, 15, 11, 10, 13, 9, 12, 11, 14.

    b. 5, 8, 9, 12, 7, 13, 9, 7, 13, 10, 13.

17. Find the range, the first quartile, the third quartile, and the median of each of the data sets.

    a. 4, 10, 12, 14, 8, 11, 9

    b. 13, 19, 22, 14, 19, 10, 19

    c. 27, 21, 32, 18, 38, 18, 21

18. Use the stem-and-leaf plots A, B, and C of the grades of physics students in percent to:

    a. make a box-and-whisker plot.

    b. find the interquartile range.

    c. find the mean and the range.

    d. find the mode.

A

Stem	Leaf
6	0 8 8
7	7 9
8	5
9	8

Key: 7|7 means 77%.

B

Stem	Leaf
8	8 9
9	5 7 8 9
10	0

Key: 10|0 means 100%.

C

Stem	Leaf
8	0 0 6 8
9	5 7 8

Key: 8|0 means 80%.

19. Find the range, the median, the first, and the third quartiles of each data set.

    a. 5, 11, 17, 16, 9, 7, 18, 22, 28, 11, 15, 12

25

b. 20, 28, 16, 35, 36, 18, 19, 22, 24, 12, 13, 10

c. 10, 23, 9, 16, 28, 13, 15

d. 11, 18, 28, 18, 15, 16, 11, 20, 22, 12, 11, 13, 17, 12, 14, 15, 10

e. 19, 28, 14, 17, 15, 26, 38

20. Find the median, the range, the mode, the smallest value, the largest value, the first quartile, and the third quartile for each of the data set.

a. 12, 13, 14, 28, 36, 18, 45,1 6, 19, 10, 13, 24, 26, 10, 15, 17, 16

b. 11, 38, 24, 17, 19, 22, 22, 28, 10, 18, 14, 16, 27, 22, 15, 17, 17

21. Compare the box-and-whisker plots A and B of grades in percent obtained in economics class. Which class has the higher:

a. median **b.** range **c.** upper quartile

d. range of the middle half of the data **e.** lower extreme **f.** upper extreme

g. lower quartile

Students' economics test scores in percent

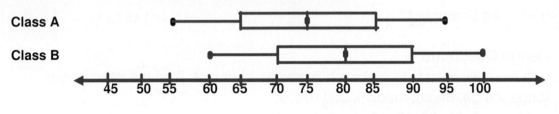

CHAPTER 3

ORDER OF OPERATIONS

Quick Cumulative Review

1. Mary said that to divide by a fraction is the same as to multiply by the reciprocal of the fraction. Is her statement correct? Hint: Review the section of the Math Teaching Series on Dividing by a Fraction.

2. Explain what is meant by the reciprocal of a number. Hint: Review the section of the Math Teaching Series on the Reciprocal of Numbers.

3. John said that $\frac{2}{3} \div \frac{1}{6} = 8$. Is this statement correct? Give reasons for your answer.

4. Evaluate:

a. $\frac{3}{4} \div \frac{1}{4} =$ **b.** $10 \div \frac{1}{5} =$ **c.** $\frac{3}{5} \times \frac{2}{3} =$ **d.** $\frac{3}{5} + \frac{2}{3} =$

Hint: Review the sections on Fractions in the Math Teaching Series.

5. The measure of a side of a square is 3 m.

a. What is the perimeter of the square?

b. What is the area of the square?

Hint: Review the sections on Perimeter and Area in the Math Teaching Series.

6. If the product of two numbers is zero, then the value of at least one of the numbers is _____. Give reasons for your answer. Hint: Review the chapter/section on the "Multiplication of Whole Numbers."

New Terms
order of operations, **"PERMDAS"**, **exponents**, **square root**

Order of Operations
The order of operations is the sequence to follow in solving expressions involving parentheses, exponents, roots, multiplication, division, addition, and subtraction.

➤ **What have I learnt so far?**

Explaining the Order of Operations
Example 1
Explain the order of operations by:

a. Finding the total number of balls by addition only

b. Finding the total number of balls by using additions and multiplication. Show that the answer in **a** is the same as the answer in **b**.

c. Showing that if the addition operation is done before the multiplication operation in equation $[A]$ of solution **b**, a wrong answer is obtained.

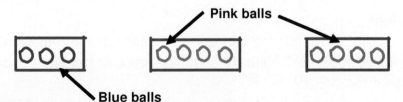

Pink balls

Blue balls

Solution
a The total number of balls by addition only = 3 blue balls + 4 pink balls + 4 pink balls.

$$= 11 \text{ balls.}$$

b. Alternate method:

Since there are 2 sets of 4 pink balls the total number of pink balls = 2 × 4 pink balls. There are 3 blue balls also, therefore, the total number of balls

$$= 3 + 2 \times 4 \underline{\hspace{3cm}} [A]$$

$$= 3 + 8$$

$$= 11 \text{ balls.}$$

27

Therefore, the answer in the solution **a** is the same as the answer in solution **b**.

c. Note that in the solution **b**, the answer 11 is obtained because the multiplication operation was done before the addition operation in equation $[A]$. If the addition operation is done first before the multiplication operation in equation $[A]$, a different and a wrong answer is obtained as shown:

$3 + 2 \times 4$

$5 \times 4 = 20$ **(This is a different and a wrong answer).**

Conclusion

We can conclude from Example 1 that the expression $3 + 2 \times 4$ could result in more than one value as the solution but only one value is the correct answer. Therefore, mathematicians have agreed on an order to follow when performing operations and this order is known as the **order of operations**.

The order of operations may be simplified as **PERMDAS** where:

Rule 1: **P** = Parentheses: Do the operations within the ( ) first if there are any.

Rule 2: **E** = Exponents: Do exponents second if there are any.

Rule 3: **R** = Roots: Do roots third if there are any. The roots refers to all types of roots.
(Examples of types of roots are: $\sqrt{}$, $\sqrt[3]{}$, $\sqrt[4]{}$, ...)

Rule 4: **M** = Multiplication and **D** = Divide from left to right: Do multiplication and division from left to right if there are any.

Rule 5: **A** = Add and **S** = Subtract from left to right: Do multiplication and division from left to right if there are any.

_____
_____   I can solve the problems too if only
I understand the concepts.

Addition and Subtraction
Example 2
Find the value of each expression.

a. $3 + 2 - 1$ **b.** $22 - 2 + 4$ **c.** $10 - 2 - 3$

Solution

PERMDAS, specifically Rule 5 which states "**A** = Add and **S** = Subtraction from left to right" should be used to find the values of **a**, **b**, and **c**.

a. Using Rule 5 from left to right, we have to do the addition first before the subtraction step-by-step as shown:

$$3 + 2 - 1 = 5 - 1 \qquad (3 + 2 = 5)$$
$$= 4$$

b. Using Rule 5 from left to right, we have to subtract first before the addition step-by-step as shown:

$$22 - 2 + 4 = 20 + 4 \qquad (22 - 2 = 20)$$

$$= 24 \qquad (20 + 4 = 24)$$

c. Using Rule 5 from left to right, we have to do the subtraction on the left first and then do the second subtraction step-by-step as shown:

$$10 - 2 - 3 = 8 - 3 \qquad (10 - 2 = 8)$$
$$= 5 \qquad (8 - 3 = 5)$$

Multiplication and Division
Example 3
Find the value of each expression

a. $9 \cdot 2 \div 3$ **b.** $24 \div 3 \cdot 2$ **c.** $60 \div 10 \div 2$

Solution
PERMDAS, specifically Rule 4, which states "**M** = Multiplication and **D** = Division from left to right" should be used to find the values of questions **a**, **b**, and **c**.

a. Using Rule 4 from left to right, we should do the multiplication before the division step-by-step as shown:

$$9 \cdot 2 \div 3 = 18 \div 3 \qquad (9 \cdot 2 = 18)$$
$$= 6 \qquad (18 \div 3 = 6)$$

b. Using Rule 4 from left to right, we should do the division before multiplication step-by-step as shown:

$$24 \div 3 \cdot 2 = 8 \cdot 2 \qquad (24 \div 3 = 8)$$
$$= 16 \qquad (8 \cdot 2 = 16)$$

c. Using Rule 4 from left to right, we should do the division at the left side first before doing the second division step-by-step as shown:

$$60 \div 10 \div 2 = 6 \div 2 \qquad (60 \div 10 = 6)$$
$$= 3 \qquad (6 \div 2 = 3$$

Addition, Subtraction, Multiplication, and Division
Example 4
Find the value of each expression.

a. $5 \cdot 3 - 4$ **b.** $24 - 4 \cdot 2$ **c.** $60 \div 10 + 5$

d. $7 - 60 \div 10$ **e.** $10 - 2 \cdot 3 + 4$ **f.** $10 + 2 \cdot 3 - 4$

g. $20 - 3 \cdot 4 + 6 \div 3$ **h.** $20 \div 5 \cdot 2 + 6 - 2$ **i.** $2 \cdot 8 \div 4$

j. $16 \div 4 \cdot 2$ **k.** $21 \div 3 + 3 \cdot 10$ **l.** $9 + 6 - 4 \cdot 2$ **m.** $2 + 4 \cdot 6$

Solution
PERMDAS, specifically Rule 4 which states, **M** = Multiplication and **D** = Division from left to right" and Rule 5 which states, "**A** = Add and **S** = Subtract from left to right" should be used to find the values of questions **a, b, c, d, e, f, g, h, i, j, k, l, and m** as shown:

a. Using **PERMDAS**, the multiplication should be done before subtraction step-by-step as shown:

$$5 \cdot 3 - 4 = 15 - 4 \qquad (5 \cdot 3 = 15)$$
$$= 11 \qquad (15 - 4 = 11)$$

b. Using **PERMDAS**, multiplication should be done before subtraction step-by-step as shown:

$$24 - 4 \cdot 2 = 24 - 8 \qquad\qquad (4 \cdot 2 = 8)$$
$$= 16 \qquad\qquad (24 - 8 = 16)$$

c. Using **PERMDAS**, division should be done before the addition step-by-step as shown:

$$60 \div 10 + 5 = 6 + 5 \qquad\qquad (60 \div 10 = 6)$$
$$= 11 \qquad\qquad (6 + 5 = 11)$$

d. Using **PERMDAS**, division should be done before subtraction step-by-step as shown:

$$7 - 60 \div 10 = 7 - 6 \qquad\qquad (60 \div 10 = 6)$$
$$= 1 \qquad\qquad (7 - 6 = 1)$$

e. Using **PERMDAS**, do multiplication, subtraction, and then addition step-by-step as shown:

$$10 - 2 \cdot 3 + 4 = 10 - 6 + 4 \qquad\qquad (2 \cdot 3 = 6)$$
$$= 4 + 4 \qquad\qquad (10 - 6 = 4)$$
$$= 8 \qquad\qquad (4 + 4 = 8)$$

f. Using **PERMDAS**, do multiplication, addition, and then subtraction step-by-step as shown:

$$10 + 2 \cdot 3 - 4 = 10 + 6 - 4 \qquad\qquad (2 \cdot 3 = 6)$$
$$= 16 - 4 \qquad\qquad (10 + 6 = 16)$$
$$= 12 \qquad\qquad (16 - 4 = 12)$$

g. Using **PERMDAS**, do the multiplication, division, subtraction, and then addition step-by-step as shown:

$$20 - 3 \cdot 4 + 6 \div 3 = 20 - 12 + 6 \div 3 \qquad\qquad (3 \cdot 4 = 12)$$
$$= 20 - 12 + 2 \qquad\qquad (6 \div 3 = 2)$$
$$= 8 + 2 \qquad\qquad (20 - 12 = 8)$$
$$= 10 \qquad\qquad (8 + 2 = 10)$$

h. Using **PERMDAS**, do the division, multiplication, addition, and then subtraction step-by-step as shown:

$$20 \div 5 \cdot 2 + 6 - 2 = 4 \cdot 2 + 6 - 2 \qquad\qquad (20 \div 5 = 4)$$
$$= 8 + 6 - 2 \qquad\qquad (4 \cdot 2 = 8)$$
$$= 14 - 2 \qquad\qquad (8 + 6 = 14)$$
$$= 12 \qquad\qquad (14 - 2 = 12)$$

i. Using **PERMDAS**, do the multiplication, and then the division step-by-step as shown:

$$2 \cdot 8 \div 4 = 16 \div 4 \qquad\qquad (2 \cdot 8 = 16)$$
$$= 4 \qquad\qquad (16 \div 4 = 4)$$

j. Using **PERMDAS**, do the division, and then the multiplication step-by-step as shown:

$$16 \div 4 \cdot 2 = 4 \cdot 2 \qquad\qquad (16 \div 4 = 4)$$
$$= 8 \qquad\qquad (4 \cdot 2 = 8)$$

k. Using **PERMDAS**, do the division, multiplication, and then the addition step-by-step as shown:

$$21 \div 3 + 3 \cdot 10 = 7 + 3 \cdot 10 \qquad (21 \div 3 = 7)$$
$$= 7 + 30 \qquad (3 \cdot 10 = 30)$$
$$= 37 \qquad (7 + 30 = 37)$$

l. Using **PERMDAS**, do multiplication, addition, and then subtraction step-by-step as shown:

$$9 + 6 - 4 \cdot 2 = 9 + 6 - 8 \qquad (4 \cdot 2 = 8)$$
$$= 15 - 8 \qquad (9 + 6 = 15)$$
$$= 7 \qquad (15 - 8 = 7)$$

m. Using **PERMDAS**, do multiplication before addition step-by-step as shown:

$$2 + 4 \cdot 6 = 2 + 24 \qquad (4 \cdot 6 = 24)$$
$$= 26 \qquad (2 + 24 = 26)$$

━━━━━━━━━━━━━━ It is not difficult, if I make the time
to practise, I can become a "MathMaster".

Addition, Subtraction, Multiplication, Division, and Parentheses
Example 5
Find the value of each expression.

a. $2 \cdot (4 + 2)$ **b.** $(5 - 3) \cdot 3$ **c.** $24 \div (10 + 2)$ **d.** $(25 - 5) \div 4$
e. $(11 + 4) \cdot 2 + 3$ **f.** $6 + (10 - 3)$ **g.** $12 \div 3 \cdot (6 - 2)$ **h.** $3 \cdot (7 + 3) \div 5$
i. $6 \cdot 2 \div (8 - 6)$ **j.** $(16 + 4) \times (7 - 2)$ **k.** $13 + 8 \div (18 - 16)$ **l.** $(4 + 2 \cdot 5) \div 2$
m. $3 \cdot (11 - 2 \cdot 3 \div 6) \div (20 \div 4 - 3)$ **n.** $15 - (7 + 2)$ **o.** $(36 + 4) \times (5 - 2)$
p. $(19 - 9) - (7 - 5)$ **q.** $(23 - 19) + (7 + 3)$

Solution

PERMDAS is used to find the values of questions **a** to **q** as follows:

a. Do the addition inside of the parenthesis, and then multiply step-by-step as shown:

$$2 \cdot (4 + 2) = 2 \cdot 6 \qquad (4 + 2) = 6$$
$$= 12 \qquad (2 \cdot 6 = 12)$$

b. Do the subtraction inside of the **parenthesis**, and then multiply step-by-step as shown:

$$(5 - 3) \cdot 3 = 2 \cdot 3 \qquad (5 - 3) = 2$$
$$= 6 \qquad (2 \cdot 3 = 6)$$

c. Do the addition inside of the **parenthesis**, and then divide step-by-step as shown:

$$24 \div (10 + 2) = 24 \div 12 \qquad (10 + 2) = 12$$
$$= 2 \qquad (24 \div 12 = 2)$$

d. Do the subtraction inside of the **parenthesis**, and then divide step-by-step as shown:

$$(25 - 5) \div 4 = 20 \div 4 \qquad (25 - 5) = 20$$
$$= 5 \qquad (20 \div 4 = 5)$$

e. Do the addition inside of the **parenthesis**, multiply, and then add step-by-step as shown:

$$(11 + 4) \cdot 2 + 3 = 15 \cdot 2 + 3 \qquad (11 + 4) = 15$$
$$= 30 + 3 \qquad (15 \cdot 2 = 30)$$
$$= 33 \qquad (30 + 3 = 33)$$

f. Do the subtraction inside of the **parenthesis**, and then add step-by-step as shown:

$$6 + (10 - 3) = 6 + 7 \qquad (10 - 3) = 7$$
$$= 13 \qquad (6 + 7 = 13)$$

g. Do the subtraction inside of the **parenthesis**, do the division, and then multiply step-by-step as shown:

$$12 \div 3 \cdot (6 - 2) = 12 \div 3 \cdot 4 \qquad (6 - 2 = 4)$$
$$= 4 \cdot 4 \qquad (12 \div 3 = 4)$$
$$= 16 \qquad (4 \cdot 4 = 16)$$

h. Do the addition inside of the **parenthesis**, do the multiplication, and then do the division step-by-step as shown:

$$3 \cdot (7 + 3) \div 5 = 3 \cdot 10 \div 5 \qquad (7 + 3) = 10$$
$$= 30 \div 5 \qquad (3 \cdot 10 = 30)$$
$$= 6 \qquad (30 \div 5 = 6)$$

i. Do the subtraction inside the **parenthesis**, do the multiplication, and then do the division step-by-step as shown:

$$6 \cdot 2 \div (8 - 6) = 6 \cdot 2 \div 2 \qquad (8 - 6) = 2$$
$$= 12 \div 2 \qquad (6 \cdot 2 = 12)$$
$$= 6 \qquad (12 \div 2 = 6)$$

j. Do the addition inside of the **parenthesis** on the left side, do the subtraction in the **parenthesis** on the right side, and then multiply step-by-step as shown:

$$(16 + 4) \times (7 - 2) = 20 \times (7 - 2) \qquad (16 + 4 = 20)$$
$$= 20 \times 5 \qquad (7 - 2 = 5)$$
$$= 100 \qquad (20 \times 5 = 100)$$

k. Do the subtraction inside of the **parenthesis**, do the division, and then do the addition step-by-step as shown:

$$13 + 8 \div (18 - 16) = 13 + 8 \div 2 \qquad (18 - 16) = 2$$
$$= 13 + 4 \qquad (8 \div 2 = 4)$$
$$= 17 \qquad (13 + 4 = 17)$$

l. Do the multiplication inside the **parenthesis**, do the addition inside of the **parenthesis**, and then do the division step-by-step as shown:

$$(4 + 2 \cdot 5) \div 2 = (4 + 10) \div 2 \qquad (2 \cdot 5 = 10)$$
$$= 14 \div 2 \qquad (4 + 10 = 14)$$
$$= 7 \qquad (14 \div 2 = 7)$$

m. Do the operations inside of the **parenthesis** on the left side according to PERMDAS by multiplying, dividing, and then subtracting, then do the operations inside of the **parenthesis** on the right side according to PERMDAS by dividing, and then subtract. Finally, multiply and divide as shown step-by-step:

$$3 \cdot (11 - 2 \cdot 3 \div 6) \div (20 \div 4 - 3) =$$

$$3 \cdot (11 - 2 \cdot 3 \div 6) \div (20 \div 4 - 3)$$

$$= 3 \cdot (11 - 6 \div 6) \div (20 \div 4 - 3) \qquad\qquad (2 \cdot 3 = 6)$$

$$= 3 \cdot (11 - 1) \div (20 \div 4 - 3) \qquad\qquad (6 \div 6 = 1)$$

$$= 3 \cdot 10 \div (20 \div 4 - 3) \qquad\qquad (11 - 1 = 10)$$

$$= 3 \cdot 10 \div (5 - 3) \qquad\qquad (20 \div 4 = 5)$$

$$= 3 \cdot 10 \div 2 \qquad\qquad (5 - 3 = 2)$$

$$= 30 \div 2 \qquad\qquad (3 \cdot 10 = 30)$$

$$= 15 \qquad\qquad (30 \div 2 = 15)$$

n. Do the addition inside of the **parenthesis**, and then do the subtraction step-by-step as shown:

$$15 - (7 + 2) = 15 - 9 \qquad\qquad\qquad (7 + 2 = 9)$$
$$= 6 \qquad\qquad\qquad (15 - 9 = 6)$$

o. Do the addition inside of the **parenthesis** at the left side, do the subtraction inside of the **parenthesis** at the right side, and then multiply step-by-step as shown:

$$(36 + 4) \times (5 - 2) = 40 \times (5 - 2) \qquad\qquad (36 + 4 = 40)$$
$$= 40 \times 3 \qquad\qquad (5 - 2 = 3)$$
$$= 120 \qquad\qquad (40 \times 3 = 120)$$

p. Do the subtraction inside of the **parenthesis** at the left side, do the subtraction inside of the **parenthesis** at the right side, and then do the subtraction step-by-step as shown:

$$(19 - 9) - (7 - 5) = 10 - (7 - 5) \qquad\qquad (19 - 9 = 10)$$
$$= 10 - 2 \qquad\qquad (7 - 5 = 2)$$
$$= 8 \qquad\qquad (10 - 2 = 8)$$

q. Do the subtraction inside of the **parenthesis** at the left side, do the addition inside of the **parenthesis** at the right side, and then do the addition step-by-step as shown:

$$(23 - 19) + (7 + 3) = 4 + (7 + 3) \qquad\qquad (23 - 19 = 4)$$
$$= 4 + 10 \qquad\qquad (7 + 3 = 10)$$
$$= 14 \qquad\qquad (4 + 10 = 14)$$

Addition, Subtraction, Multiplication, Division, Parentheses, Exponents, and Roots

Quick Review
Exponents show repeated multiplication. Therefore, an exponent tells how many times a base is used as a factor as shown:

(a).

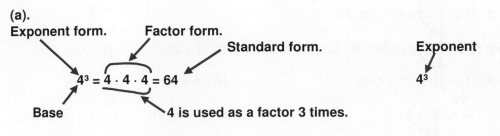

(b). $2^3 = 2 \cdot 2 \cdot 2 = 8$

In this section, "**Roots**" are actually referred to as **square roots**.

If $A = x^2$, then x is the square root of A. The square root of x^2 is written as $\sqrt{x^2} = x$ where $\sqrt{}$ is the symbol for square root. (**Note**: Finding the square root is similar to finding the length of a side of a square when the area of the square is known.) Review the section on the Area of a Square. Review the section on Square Root also.

For examples:

a. $\sqrt{4} = \sqrt{2^2} = 2$

b. $\sqrt{9} = \sqrt{3^3} = 3$

c. $\sqrt{16} = \sqrt{4^2} = 4$

d. $\sqrt{25} = \sqrt{5^2} = 5$

e. $\sqrt{36} = \sqrt{6^2} = 6$

f. $\sqrt{49} = \sqrt{7^2} = 7$

g. $\sqrt{64} = \sqrt{8^2} = 8$

h. $\sqrt{81} = \sqrt{9^2} = 9$

i. $\sqrt{100} = \sqrt{10^2} = 10$

Example 6

Find the value of each expression.

a. $(3^2 - \sqrt{9}) - \sqrt{16} + 2^2$

b. $2^2 \times \sqrt{25} + \sqrt{16}$

c. $\sqrt{36} + 4^2 - \sqrt{9}$

d. $(2^3 + \sqrt{25}) - (3^2 - \sqrt{36})^2$

e. $(\sqrt{81} - 2^2 + \sqrt{16}) \times (6^2 - 4^2 - 3^2) \div 2$

Solution

PERMDAS is used to find the values of questions **a** to **e** as shown:

a. Do the **exponent** and the **root** inside of the **parenthesis**, and then subtract inside of the **parenthesis**, do the **exponent outside the parenthesis**, do the **root outside the parenthesis**, subtract, and then add step-by-step as shown:

$$(3^2 - \sqrt{9}) - \sqrt{16} + 2^2 = (9 - \sqrt{9}) - \sqrt{16} + 2^2 \qquad 3^2 = 9$$
$$= (9 - 3) - \sqrt{16} + 2^2 \qquad \sqrt{9} = 3$$
$$= 6 - \sqrt{16} + 2^2 \qquad 9 - 6 = 3$$
$$= 6 - \sqrt{16} + 4 \qquad 2^2 = 4$$
$$= 6 - 4 + 4 \qquad \sqrt{16} = 4$$
$$= 2 + 4 \qquad 6 - 4 = 2$$
$$= 6 \qquad 2 + 4 = 6$$

b. Do the **exponent**, do the **roots**, multiply, and then add step-by-step as shown:

$$2^2 \times \sqrt{25} + \sqrt{16} = 4 \times \sqrt{25} + \sqrt{16} \qquad 2^2 = 4$$
$$= 4 \times 5 + 4 \qquad \sqrt{25} = 5, \sqrt{16} = 4$$

34

$$= 20 + 4 \qquad\qquad 4 \times 5 = 20$$
$$= 24 \qquad\qquad 20 + 4 = 24$$

c. Do the **exponent**, do the **roots**, add, and then subtract step-by-step as shown:

$$\sqrt{36} + 4^2 - \sqrt{9} = \sqrt{36} + 16 - \sqrt{9} \qquad\qquad 4^2 = 16$$
$$= 6 + 16 - 3 \qquad\qquad \sqrt{36} = 6, \sqrt{9} = 3$$
$$= 22 - 3 \qquad\qquad 6 + 16 = 22$$
$$= 19 \qquad\qquad 22 - 3 = 19$$

d. Do the **exponent** and the **root** inside of the **parenthesis** on the left side, and then add, do the **exponent** and the **root** inside of the **parenthesis** on the right side, and then subtract, do the **exponent** inside of the **parenthesis** on the right side, and finally subtract as shown step-by-step:

$$(2^3 + \sqrt{25}) - (3^2 - \sqrt{36})^2 = (8 + \sqrt{25}) - (3^2 - \sqrt{36})^2 \qquad\qquad 2^3 = 2 \cdot 2 \cdot 2 = 8$$
$$= (8 + 5) - (3^2 - \sqrt{36})^2 \qquad\qquad \sqrt{25} = 5$$
$$= 13 - (3^2 - \sqrt{36})^2 \qquad\qquad (8 + 9) = 13$$
$$= 13 - (9 - \sqrt{36})^2 \qquad\qquad 3^2 = 9$$
$$= 13 - (9 - 6)^2 \qquad\qquad \sqrt{36} = 6$$
$$= 13 - 3^2 \qquad\qquad (9 - 6)^2 = 3^2$$
$$= 13 - 9 \qquad\qquad 3^2 = 9$$
$$= 4 \qquad\qquad 13 - 9 = 4$$

e. Do the **operations** inside of the **parenthesis** at the left side according to **PERMDAS**, do the **operations** inside of the **parenthesis** at the right side according to **PERMDAS**, multiply the results, and then divide as shown step-by-step:

$$(\sqrt{81} - 2^2 + \sqrt{16}) \times (6^2 - 4^2 - 3^2) \div 2$$
$$= (\sqrt{81} - 4 + \sqrt{16}) \times (6^2 - 4^2 - 3^2) \div 2 \qquad\qquad 2^2 = 4$$
$$= (9 - 4 + 4) \times (6^2 - 4^2 - 3^2) \div 2 \qquad\qquad \sqrt{81} = 9, \sqrt{16} = 4$$
$$= (5 + 4) \times (6^2 - 4^2 - 3^2) \div 2 \qquad\qquad 9 - 4 = 5$$
$$= 9 \times (6^2 - 4^2 - 3^2) \div 2 \qquad\qquad 5 + 4 = 9$$
$$= 9 \times (36 - 16 - 9) \div 2 \qquad\qquad 6^2 = 36, 4^2 = 16, 3^2 = 9$$
$$= 9 \times (20 - 9) \div 2 \qquad\qquad 36 - 16 = 20$$
$$= 9 \times 11 \div 2 \qquad\qquad 20 - 9 = 11$$
$$= 99 \div 2 \qquad\qquad 9 \times 11 = 99$$
$$= 49\frac{1}{2} \qquad\qquad 99 \div 2 = 49\frac{1}{2}$$

The notes and the generous worked examples have provided me with the conceptual understanding and the computational fluency to do my homework.

Exercises

1. What is meant by the order of operations?
2. What does PERMDAS stands for?
3. Find the value of each expression. Hint: See Example 2.
   Match similar exercises with similar examples.

   a. 8 + 4 - 3   **b.** 16 - 7 + 3   **c.** 16 - 5 - 8
   d. 32 - 10 + 5   **e.** 13 + 2 - 7   **f.** 24 - 6 - 10

4 Find the value of each expression. Hint: See Example 3.
   Match similar exercises with similar examples.

   a. 10 · 2 ÷ 4   **b.** 15 ÷ 5 · 3   **c.** 36 ÷ 6 ÷ 6
   d. 28 ÷ 7 · 3   **e.** 24 ÷ 4 ÷ 3   **f.** 8 · 2 ÷ 4

5. Find the value of each expression. Hint: See Example 4.
   Match similar exercises with similar examples.

   a. 6 · 4 - 3   **b.** 36 - 5 · 2   **c.** 30 ÷ 3 + 4
   d. 8 - 30 ÷ 5   **e.** 12 - 4 · 2 + 6   **f.** 5 + 3 · 4 - 2
   g. 16 - 2 · 5 + 4 ÷ 2   **h.** 14 ÷ 7 · 3 + 8 - 3   **i.** 4 · 6 ÷ 3
   j. 12 ÷ 3 · 4   **k.** 18 ÷ 6 + 2 · 6   **l.** 6 + 12 - 3 · 4   **m.** 7 + 2 · 4

6. Find the value of each expression. Hint: See Example 5.
   Match similar exercises with similar examples.

   a. 4 · (7 + 3)   **b.** (7 - 5) · 2   **c.** 36 ÷ (4 + 2)
   d. (18 - 3) ÷ 5   **e.** (13 + 2) · 2   **f.** 8 + (24 - 9)
   g. 16 ÷ 4 · (8 - 6)   **h.** 2 · (5 + 4) ÷ 6   **i.** 8 · 3 ÷ (12 - 8)
   j. (12 + 6) × (9 - 7)   **k.** 11 + 3 ÷ (4 - 2)   **l.** (5 + 3 · 5) ÷ 2
   m. 4 · (12 - 3 · 4 ÷ 3)   **n.** 8 - (3 + 5)   **o.** (14 + 2) × (6 - 4)
   p. (9 - 3) - (13 - 7)   **q.** (15 - 8) + (4 + 8)

7. Find the value of each expression. Hint: See Example 6.
   Match similar exercises with similar examples.

   a. $(2^2 - \sqrt{4}) - \sqrt{4} + 3^2$ **b.** $3^2 \times \sqrt{16} + \sqrt{9}$ **c.** $\sqrt{64} + 3^2 - \sqrt{9}$
   d. $(3^3 + \sqrt{9}) - (2^3 - \sqrt{25})^2$ **e.** $(\sqrt{100} - 3^2 + \sqrt{25}) \times (5^2 - 3^2 - 2^2)$

Challenge Questions

8 Find the value of each expression.

   a. 10 - 3 - 4   **b.** 17 - 8 + 2   **c.** 18 + 3 - 9   **d.** 36 ÷ 6 ÷ 3
   e. 9 · 2 ÷ 3   **f.** 15 ÷ 3 · 3   **g.** 10 - 4 ÷ 2   **h.** 8 - 2 · 4 + 5
   i. 18 - 11 · 2   **j.** 12 ÷ 4 + 3   **k.** 8 · 4 - 5   **l.** 5 · 4 ÷ 2
   m. 12 - 3 · 2 + 4 ÷ 2   **n.** 24 ÷ 6 · 2 + 9 - 7   **o.** 16 ÷ 4 · 3
   p. 24 ÷ 4 + 3 · 4   **q.** 8 + 3 · 5   **r.** 10 + 4 - 2 · 4   **s.** 3 · 4 ÷ 2

9. Find the value of each expression.

   a. 6 · 3 ÷ (9 - 6)   **b.** (8 + 3) · 4   **c.** 24 ÷ (5 + 3)   **d.** 3 · (5 + 6)
   e. 15 ÷ 3 · (7 - 3)   **f.** 3 · (4 + 3) ÷ 3   **g.** (12 - 3) - (10 - 4)

h. $(10 - 4) \times (7 + 3)$ **i.** $(8 + 4 \div 2) \div 5$ **j.** $6 \cdot (14 - 3 \times 4 \div 3)$
k. $(14 - 8) + (3 + 7)$ **l.** $3 \cdot (16 - 4 \cdot 2 \div 8)$ **m.** $(7 + 5 \cdot 5) \div 4$
10. Find the value of each expression.

    a. $\sqrt{81} - 2^3 + \sqrt{4}$ **b.** $3^2 \cdot \sqrt{4} - \sqrt{9}$ **c.** $4^2 - \sqrt{100} \div 2$

    d. $(4^2 + \sqrt{81}) - (2^3 - \sqrt{9})^2$ **e.** $(3^3 - \sqrt{16}) - \sqrt{16} + 3^2$

    f. $\sqrt{81} + 3^2 - \sqrt{16}$ **g.** $(4^2 - \sqrt{16}) - \sqrt{9} + 3^2$ **h.** $3^3 \cdot \sqrt{25} + \sqrt{36}$

Answers to Selected Questions
3a. 9   **4a.** 5   **5a.** 21   **6a.** 40   **7a.** 9

Extension of the Order of Operations Using PERMDAS
(A). Fraction Bar

The order of operations using PERMDAS can be **extended** to include **a fraction bar**. A fraction bar indicates that the operations in the numerator are done separately using PERMDAS, the operations in the denominator are also done separately using PERMDAS, and finally, the numerator is divided by the denominator.

Example 7
Find the value of each expression.

  a. $\dfrac{24 \div (7 - 3)}{9 - 3}$ **b.** $\dfrac{(16 - 4) - 2}{5 - 12 \div 4}$ **c.** $\dfrac{(15 - 7) \cdot 4}{16 - 4 \cdot 3}$ **d.** $\dfrac{3 \cdot 4 + 10}{12 \div 3 - 1}$

Solution

a. Considering the **numerator** and using PERMDAS, do the subtraction inside of the **parenthesis**, and then do the division. Considering the **denominator** and using PERMDAS, do the subtraction, and then divide the **numerator** by the **denominator** as shown step-by-step:

$$\frac{24 \div (7 - 3)}{9 - 3} = \frac{24 \div 4}{9 - 3} \qquad\qquad (7 - 3) = 4$$

$$= \frac{6}{9 - 3} \qquad\qquad 24 \div 4 = 6$$

$$= \frac{6}{6} \qquad\qquad 9 - 3 = 6$$

$$= 1 \qquad\qquad 6 \div 6 = 1$$

b. Considering the **numerator** and using PERMDAS, do the subtraction inside of the **parenthesis**, and then do the subtraction outside the parenthesis. Considering the **denominator** and using PERMDAS, do the division, and then the subtraction. Finally divide the **numerator** by the **denominator** as shown step-by-step:

$$\frac{(16 - 4) - 2}{5 - 12 \div 4} = \frac{12 - 2}{5 - 12 \div 4} \qquad\qquad (16 - 4) = 12$$

$$= \frac{10}{5 - 12 \div 4} \qquad\qquad 12 - 2 = 10$$

$$= \frac{10}{5 - 3} \qquad\qquad 12 \div 4 = 3$$

$$= \frac{10}{2} \qquad\qquad 5 - 3 = 2$$

$$= 5 \qquad\qquad 10 \div 2 = 5$$

c. Considering the **numerator** and using **PERMDAS**, do the subtraction inside the **parenthesis**, and then multiply. Considering the **denominator** and using PERMDAS, do the multiplication and subtraction, and finally, divide the **numerator** by the **denominator** step-by-step as shown:

$$\frac{(15 - 7) \cdot 4}{16 - 4 \cdot 3} = \frac{8 \cdot 4}{16 - 4 \cdot 3} \qquad\qquad (15 - 7) = 8$$

$$= \frac{32}{16 - 4 \cdot 3} \qquad\qquad 8 \cdot 4 = 32$$

$$= \frac{32}{16 - 12} \qquad\qquad 4 \cdot 3 = 12$$

$$= \frac{32}{4} \qquad\qquad 16 - 12 = 4$$

$$= 8 \qquad\qquad 32 \div 4 = 8$$

d. Considering the **numerator** and using PERMDAS, multiply, and then add. Considering the **denominator** and using PERMDAS, divide, and then subtract. Finally, divide the numerator by the denominator step-by-step as shown:

$$\frac{3 \cdot 4 + 10}{12 \div 3 - 1} = \frac{12 + 10}{12 \div 3 - 1} \qquad\qquad 3 \cdot 4 = 12$$

$$= \frac{22}{12 \div 3 - 1} \qquad\qquad 2 + 10 = 22$$

$$= \frac{22}{4 - 1} \qquad\qquad 12 \div 3 = 4$$

$$= \frac{22}{3}$$ $$4 - 1 = 3$$

$$= 7\frac{1}{3}$$ $$22 \div 3 = 7\frac{1}{3}$$

(B). Parentheses, Parenthesis, and Brackets

Parentheses is the plural form of parenthesis.

The symbol for a parenthesis is ( ) and the symbol for a bracket is [ ]. The brackets may be considered as another type of parentheses, and that the operations inside of the **parentheses** are done first according to PERMDAS **before** the operations inside of the **brackets** are done according to PERMDAS, and then we should do the remaining operations according to PERMDAS. The parentheses and brackets are used in expressions when further groupings of the numbers in the expression are necessary. Note that the operations should always be done within the **innermost grouping** symbols first.

Example 8

Find the value of each expression.

a. $[(9 - 5) + 3] \cdot 2$ **b.** $[(19 - 4) \div (12 - 9)] \cdot 3$

Solution

a. Do the subtraction inside of the **parentheses**, do the addition inside of the **bracket** next, and then multiply step-by-step as shown:

$$[(9 - 5) + 3] \cdot 2 = [4 + 3] \cdot 2 \qquad\qquad (9 - 5) = 4$$
$$= 7 \cdot 2 \qquad\qquad\qquad [4 + 3] = 7$$
$$= 14 \qquad\qquad\qquad 7 \cdot 2 = 14$$

b. Do the subtractions inside of **both parentheses**, do the division inside of the **bracket** next, and then multiply step-by-step as shown:

$$[(19 - 4) \div (12 - 9)] \cdot 3 = [15 \div 3] \cdot 3 \qquad (19 - 4) = 15, (12 - 9) = 3$$
$$= 5 \cdot 3 \qquad\qquad\qquad [15 \div 3] = 5$$
$$= 15 \qquad\qquad\qquad 5 \cdot 3 = 15$$

Example 9

Find the value of each expression.

a. $[(7 - 5)^2 + 3] \cdot 3$ **b.** $[(10 - 8)^3 \div (9 - 7)^2] \cdot 3$ **c.** $[(11 - 9)^2 \times (24 - 23)^2]^2 \cdot 2$

Solution

a. Do the operation inside of the **parenthesis**, do the operation in the **bracket**, and then multiply step-by-step as shown:

$$[(7 - 5)^2 + 3] \cdot 3 = [2^2 + 3] \cdot 3 \qquad\qquad (7 - 5)^2 = 2^2$$
$$= [4 + 3] \cdot 3 \qquad\qquad\qquad 2^2 = 4$$
$$= 7 \cdot 3 \qquad\qquad\qquad [4 + 3] = 7$$
$$= 21 \qquad\qquad\qquad 7 \cdot 3 = 21$$

b. Do the operations inside of both **parentheses**, do the operations in the **bracket**, and then multiply step-by-step as shown:

$$[(10 - 8)^3 \div (9 - 7)^2] \cdot 3 = [2^3 \div 2^2] \cdot 3 \qquad (10 - 8)^3 = 2^3, (9 - 7)^2 = 2^2$$
$$= [8 \div 4] \cdot 3 \qquad 2^3 = 2 \cdot 2 \cdot 2 = 8, 2^2 = 2 \cdot 2 = 4$$
$$= 2 \cdot 3 \qquad [8 \div 4] = 2$$
$$= 6 \qquad 2 \cdot 3 = 6$$

c. Do the operations inside of both **parentheses**, do the operations in the bracket, square the simplification inside the bracket, and then multiply step-by-step as shown:

$$[(11 - 9)^2 \times (24 - 23)^2]^2 \cdot 2 = [2^2 \times 1^2]^2 \cdot 2 \qquad (11 - 9)^2 = 2^2, (24 - 23)^2 = 1^2$$
$$= [4 \times 1]^2 \cdot 2 \qquad 2^2 = 4, 1^2 = 1$$
$$= 4^2 \cdot 2 \qquad [4 \times 1]^2 = 4^2$$
$$= 16 \cdot 2 \qquad 4^2 = 4 \times 4 = 16$$
$$= 32 \qquad 16 \cdot 2 = 32$$

▬▬▬▬▬▬▬▬▬ The notes and the generous worked examples have provided me with the conceptual understanding and the computational fluency to do my homework.

Exercises

1. Find the value of each expression. Hint: See Example 7. Match similar exercises with similar examples.

a. $\dfrac{18 \div (11 - 9)}{17 - 14}$ b. $\dfrac{(19 - 3) - 4}{6 - 9 \div 3}$ c. $\dfrac{(27 - 23) \cdot 4}{18 - 7 \cdot 2}$ d. $\dfrac{5 \cdot 3 + 5}{9 - 20 \div 5}$

2. Find the value of each expression. Hint: See Example 8. Match similar exercises with similar examples.

a. $[(12 - 7) + 4] \cdot 3$ **b.** $[(14 - 6) \div (16 - 12)] \cdot 2$

3. Find the value of each expression. Hint: See Example 9.
Match similar exercises with similar examples.

a. $[(9 - 7)^2 + 6] \cdot 2$ **b.** $[(5 - 1)^2 \div (11 - 9)^2] \cdot 2$ **c.** $[(18 - 16)^2 \times (7 - 5)^2]^2 \cdot 2$

Challenge Questions

4. Find the value of each expression.

a. $\dfrac{4 \cdot 3 + 8}{11 - 36 \div 6}$ b. $\dfrac{(7 - 4) \cdot 5}{9 - 4}$ c. $[(7 - 3) + 2] \cdot 4$

d. $[(6 - 4)^3 \div (5 - 3)^2] \cdot 2$ **e.** $[(14 + 10) \div (8 - 2)] \cdot 2$ **f.** $[(3 + 1)^2 \times (13 - 11)^2] \cdot 2$

Answers to Selected Questions.

1a. 3   **2b.** 27   **3a.** 20

PERCENT

Percent Concept

The word **percent** means per one hundred. Percent may also be explained as a certain number out of 100. For example, 40 out of 100 students went to the zoo, means 40 percent went to the zoo and the 40 percent can be written as 40%. The 40% or 40 out of 100 can also be expressed as the fraction $\frac{40}{100}$.

The word percent is replaced by the symbol %. Note also that any common fraction that has a denominator of 100 can be expressed as a percent as shown:

(a) $\frac{12}{100} = 12\%$ (b) $\frac{8}{100} = 8\%$ (c) $\frac{99.9}{100} = 99.9\%$

(d) $\frac{300}{100} = 300\%$ (e) $\frac{100}{100} = 100\%$ (f) $\frac{2\frac{1}{2}}{100} = 2\frac{1}{2}\%$

(g) $\frac{\frac{1}{2}}{100} = \frac{1}{2}\%$ (h). $\frac{.8}{100} = .8\%$ (i) $\frac{1}{100} = 1\%$

Let us use the grid that has 100 squares to explain the concept of percent.

A									
A	B								
A					B				
A									
A									
A		B							
A									
A									
A			B						
A									

(a). Each square represents 1 out of 100 squares of the grid which can be expressed as one percent or 1%.

(b). There are 10 squares that contain the letter A, out of the 100 squares of the grid, and this can be expressed as 10 percent (10%) of the squares of the grid contain the letter A.

(c). There are 4 squares that contain the letter B, out of the 100 squares of the grid. This can be expressed as 4 percent (4%) of the squares of the grid contain the letter B.

Team Exercise

The class should be divided into four groups. Each group should use the grid to answer the following questions, and then report the answers to the class. The grid has a total of 100 squares.

What percent of the squares contain:

(a). Q   (b). P   (c). X   (d). M   (e). K

K		Q	X	K	P			P	
	M						M		
P		Q					Q		
P				K					
					P				
	K		K						Q
P									
P			X		P	M		Q	

Example 1

70 out of 100 is what percent?

Solution

Step 1: Express 70 out of 100 as a percent.

$$70 \text{ out of } 100 = \frac{70}{100} = 70\%$$

Therefore, 70 out of 100 is 70% .

Exercises

Express the following as a percent. Hint: See Example 1.

(1) 2 out of 100   (2) 28 out of 100   (3) 23 out of 100

(4) 100 out of 100   (5) $78\frac{1}{2}$ out of 100   (9) 48.5 out of 100

Answers to Selected Exercises

(1) 2%   (2) 28%

Express Percent as a Fraction

1. If we count 33 squares out of 100 squares of a grid, then we can represent the 33 squares out of the 100 squares as 33% or $\frac{33}{100}$.

2. **Team Exercise**: Each team should sketch a grid that contains 100 squares. The grid should have a total of ten columns and ten rows. Each column and each row should contain ten squares. Each team should shade five columns which are joined together from one edge of the grid blue. Compare the five columns which are shaded blue, to the whole grid. Is the size of the five columns which are shaded blue about half the size of the whole grid? The five columns which are shaded blue contain 50 squares out of the 100 squares of the grid, and this can be expressed as $\frac{50}{100}$ or 50%, but the five columns which are shaded blue are half of the whole grid, so we can say:

$$\frac{50}{100} = 50\% = \frac{1}{2}$$

Rule: To express a percent as a fraction, put the percent number as a numerator over 100, and then reduce the fraction to the lowest term if possible.

Example 1
Change 37% to a fraction.
Solution
Using the rule to express a percent as a fraction, put the percent number as the numerator over 100, and then reduce the fraction to the lowest term if possible.

$$37\% = \frac{37}{100}$$

Example 2
Change 25% to a fraction.
Solution
Using the rule to express a percent as a fraction, put the percent number as the numerator over 100, and then reduce the fraction to the lowest term if possible.

$$25\% = \frac{25}{100} = \frac{\overset{1}{\cancel{25}}}{\underset{4}{\cancel{100}}} \quad \text{Reduce to the lowest term by dividing by 5.}$$

$$= \frac{1}{4}$$

Example 3
Change 125% to a fraction.
Solution
Using the rule to express a percent as a fraction, put the percent number as the numerator over 100, and then reduce the fraction to the lowest term if possible.

$$125\% = \frac{125}{100}$$

$$= \frac{\overset{5}{\overset{25}{\cancel{\cancel{125}}}}}{\underset{20}{\underset{4}{\cancel{\cancel{100}}}}}$$ Reduce to the lowest term by dividing by 5.

$$= \frac{5}{4}$$

Example 4

Express $22\frac{1}{2}$ % as a fraction.

Solution
Using the rule to express a percent as a fraction, put the percent number as the numerator over 100, and then reduce to the lowest term if possible.

$$22\frac{1}{2}\% = \frac{22\frac{1}{2}}{100}$$

$\dfrac{22\frac{1}{2}}{100}$ can be written as $22\frac{1}{2} \div 100$

$= \dfrac{45}{2} \div \dfrac{100}{1}$ (**Note**: $22\frac{1}{2} = \dfrac{45}{2}$ and $100 = \dfrac{100}{1}$. Refer to the chapter on Fractions).

$= \dfrac{45}{2} \times \dfrac{1}{100}$ (**Note**: 100 is inverted which is the reciprocal of 100 and the division

symbol changes to a multiplication symbol because to divide by a fraction is the same as to multiply by the reciprocal of the fraction. Review the chapter on the Division of Fractions).

44

$$= \frac{\overset{9}{\cancel{45}}}{2} \times \frac{1}{100} \qquad \text{Reduce to the lowest term by dividing by 5.}$$
$$\phantom{=\frac{45}{2}\times\frac{1}{100}}{\underset{20}{}}$$

$$= \frac{9}{2} \times \frac{1}{20} = \frac{9}{40}$$

Example 5

Change .4% to a fraction.

Solution

Using the rule to express a percent as a fraction, put the percent number as the numerator over 100, and then reduce the fraction to the lowest term if possible.

$$4\% = \frac{.4}{100}$$

$$= .4 \times \frac{1}{100} \qquad \text{Rearrange } \frac{.4}{100} \text{ as } .4 \times \frac{1}{100}.$$

$$= \frac{4}{10} \times \frac{1}{100} \qquad .4 = \frac{4}{10}, \text{ review the chapter on Decimals.}$$

$$.4 \text{ is in a decimal form, and } \frac{4}{10} \text{ is in a fraction form.}$$

$$= \frac{\overset{1}{\cancel{4}}}{10} \times \frac{1}{\underset{25}{\cancel{100}}} \qquad \text{Divide by 4.}$$

$$= \frac{1}{10} \times \frac{1}{25}$$

$$= \frac{1}{250} \qquad 25 \times 10 = 250$$

The required fraction is $\frac{1}{250}$.

Example 6

Change .12% to a fraction.

Solution

Using the rule to express a percent as a fraction, put the percent number as the numerator over 100, and then reduce to the lowest term if possible.

$$.12\% = \frac{.12}{100}$$

$$= .12 \times \frac{1}{100} \qquad \text{Rearrange } \frac{.12}{100} \text{ as } .12 \times \frac{1}{100}$$

$$= \frac{12}{100} \times \frac{1}{100} \qquad .12 = \frac{12}{100}, \text{ review the chapter on Decimals.}$$

.12 is in a decimal form, and $\frac{12}{100}$ is in a fraction form.

$$= \frac{\overset{3}{\cancel{12}}}{\underset{25}{\cancel{100}}} \times \frac{1}{100} \qquad \text{Divide by 4.}$$

$$= \frac{3}{25} \times \frac{1}{100}$$

$$= \frac{3}{2500} \qquad 25 \times 100 = 2500$$

The required fraction is $\dfrac{3}{2500}$

Example 7

Change .124% to a fraction.

Solution

Using the rule to express a percent as a fraction, put the percent number as the numerator over 100, and then reduce to the lowest term if possible.

$$.124\% = \frac{.124}{100}$$

$$= .124 \times \frac{1}{100} \qquad \text{Rearrange } \frac{.124}{100} \text{ as } .128 \times \frac{1}{100}.$$

$$= \frac{124}{1000} \times \frac{1}{100} \qquad .124 = \frac{124}{1000}, \text{ review the chapter on Decimals.}$$

.124 is in a decimal form, and $\frac{124}{1000}$ is in a fraction form.

$$= \frac{\overset{31}{\cancel{124}}}{1000} \times \frac{1}{\underset{25}{\cancel{100}}} \qquad \text{Divide by 4.}$$

$$= \frac{31}{1000} \times \frac{1}{25}$$

$$= \frac{31}{2500} \qquad 25 \times 100 = 2500$$

The required fraction is $\frac{31}{2500}$.

Exercises

1. Express the following percents as fractions and reduce the answers to the lowest terms if possible. Hint: See Examples 1, 2, and 3.
   (a) 27% (b) 20% (c) 135% (d) 90% (e) 110%

2. Express the following percents as fractions and reduce the answers to the lowest term if possible. Hint: See Example 4.
   (a) $32\frac{1}{2}$% (b) $4\frac{2}{3}$% (c) $6\frac{3}{4}$% (d) $17\frac{1}{3}$% (e) $1\frac{1}{9}$%

3. Express the following percents as fractions and reduce the answers to the lowest term if possible. Hint: See Example 5.
   (a) .2% (b) .7% (c) .5% (d) .3% (e) .8%

4. Express the following percents as fractions and reduce the answers to the lowest terms if possible. Hint: See Example 6.
   (a) .14% (b) .11% (c) .15% (d) .31% (e) .70%

5. Express the following percents as fractions and reduce the answers to the lowest terms if possible. Hint: See Example 7.
   (a) .114% (b) .133% (c) .115% (d) .131% (e) .105%

Challenge Exercises

6. Express the following percents as fractions and reduce the answers to the lowest terms if possible.
   (a) .6% (b) 75% (c) $7\frac{3}{5}$% (d) .215% (e) 135%

   (f) 10% (g) 6% (h) .12% (i) $6\frac{1}{2}$% (j) 110%

Answers to Selected Exercises

1(a) $\frac{27}{100}$ 1(b) $\frac{1}{5}$ 2(a) $\frac{13}{40}$ 2(b) $\frac{7}{150}$

3(a) $\frac{1}{50}$ 3(b) $\frac{7}{100}$ 4(a) $\frac{7}{5000}$ 4(b) $\frac{11}{10,000}$

5(a) $\dfrac{57}{50,000}$ **5(b)** $\dfrac{133}{100,000,}$

REAL WORLD APPLICATIONS - WORD PROBLEMS
Express Percent as Fraction

Example 1
Yesterday, 2% of the students in a school were absent. What fraction of the students were absent?
Solution
Using the rule to express a percent as a fraction, write the percent number as the numerator over 100, and then reduce to the lowest term if possible.

$$2\% = \frac{2}{100}$$

$$= \frac{\overset{1}{\cancel{2}}}{\underset{50}{\cancel{100}}} \quad \text{Reduce to the lowest term by dividing by 2.}$$

$$= \frac{1}{50}$$

The fraction of the students that were absent was $\dfrac{1}{50}$.

Example 2
A television set was reduced by 15%. What fraction of the price is the reduction?
Solution
Using the rule to express a percent as a fraction, write the percent number as the numerator over 100, and then reduce the fraction to the lowest term if possible.

$$15\% = \frac{15}{100}$$

$$= \frac{\overset{3}{\cancel{15}}}{\underset{20}{\cancel{100}}} \quad \text{Reduce to the lowest term by dividing by 5.}$$

$$= \frac{3}{20}$$

The fraction of the price that was the reduction is $\dfrac{3}{20}$

Example 3

In a school, 65% of the students like soccer, what fraction of the students like soccer?

Solution

Using the rule to express a percent as a fraction, write the percent number as the numerator over 100, and then reduce the fraction to the lowest term if possible.

$$65\% = \frac{65}{100}$$

$$= \frac{\overset{13}{\cancel{65}}}{\underset{20}{\cancel{100}}} \qquad \text{Reduce to the lowest term by dividing by 5.}$$

$$= \frac{13}{20}$$

The fraction of the students that like soccer is $\dfrac{13}{20}$.

Example 4

A computer system was on sale at 10% off the regular price. What fraction of the regular price was the reduction?

Solution

Using the rule to express a percent as a fraction, write the percent number as the numerator over 100, and then reduce to the lowest term if possible.

$$10\% = \frac{10}{100} \qquad \text{The reduction was 10\%.}$$

$$= \frac{\overset{1}{\cancel{10}}}{\underset{10}{\cancel{100}}} \qquad \text{Reduce to the lowest term by dividing by 10.}$$

$$= \frac{1}{10}$$

The fraction of the regular price that was on sale is $\dfrac{1}{10}$.

Exercises

1. 25% of the students in a class went to the zoo. What fraction of the students went

to the zoo? Hint: See Example 1.
2. A television set was reduced by 10%. What fraction of the price is the reduction? Hint: See Example 2.
3. 75% of the students in a class like science. What fraction of the students like science? Hint: See Example 3.
4. A car is on sale at 6% off the regular price. What fraction of the regular price is the the reduction? Hint: See Example 4.
5. A house was sold at 8% off the original selling price. What is the fraction of the reduction of the price of the house? Hint: See Example 4.
6. 16% of the students in a class went to medical schools. What is the fraction of the students that went to medical schools? Hint: See Example 3.

Challenge Questions
7. 55% of the students at the Peki Secondary School are girls. What is the fraction of the girls in the school?
8. A printer was sold at 25% off the original price. What is the fraction of the reduction of the price of the computer?

Answers to Selected Exercises
1. $\dfrac{1}{5}$ **2.** $\dfrac{1}{10}$ **3.** $\dfrac{3}{4}$

Express Fractions as Percents
Recall that we already discussed the grid at the beginning of this chapter (Percent). One square out of the 100 squares in the grid can be written as 1% and this can be expressed as $\dfrac{1}{100}$. This means that if we have a fraction such as $\dfrac{1}{100}$ and we want to change the fraction which is $\dfrac{1}{100}$ to a percent, we have to multiply the fraction by 100, and then attach the % sign.

$$\dfrac{1}{100} \times 100$$

$$= \dfrac{1}{\cancel{100}} \times \cancel{100}^{\,1} \qquad \text{Do the division}$$

$$= 1\%$$

Rule: To express a fraction as a percent multiply the fraction by 100, and then attach the % sign to the answer.

Example 1

Express $\frac{1}{10}$ as a percent.

Solution

Using the rule express the fraction as a percent by multiplying the fraction by 100, and then attach the % sign to the answer.

$$\frac{1}{10} \text{ as a percent} = \frac{1}{10} \times 100$$

$$= \frac{\overset{10}{\cancel{100}}}{\underset{1}{\cancel{10}}} \qquad \text{Reduce to the lowest term by dividing by 10.}$$

$$= 10\%$$

Example 2

Change $\frac{2}{15}$ to a percent.

Solution

Using the rule express the fraction as a percent by multiplying the fraction by 100, and then attach the % sign to the answer.

$$\frac{2}{15} \text{ as percent} = \frac{2}{15} \times 100$$

$$= \frac{2}{\underset{3}{\cancel{15}}} \times \overset{20}{\cancel{100}} \qquad \text{Reduce to the lowest term by dividing by 5.}$$

$$= \frac{40}{3} = 13\frac{1}{3}\% \qquad \text{Review the section on Mixed Numbers.}$$

Example 3

Change $\frac{3}{7}$ to a percent.

Solution

Using the rule express the fraction as a percent by multiplying the fraction by 100, and then attach the % sign to the answer.

$$\frac{3}{7} \text{ as a percent} = \frac{3}{7} \times 100$$

$$= \frac{300}{7}$$

$$= 42\frac{6}{7} \qquad \text{Review the section on Mixed Numbers.}$$

$\frac{3}{7}$ as a percent $= 42\frac{6}{7}\%$.

Exercises

1. Express the following fractions as percents. Hint: See Example 1.

    a) $\frac{1}{2}$ **b)** $\frac{1}{4}$ **c)** $\frac{1}{5}$ **d)** $\frac{1}{15}$ **e)** $\frac{1}{25}$ **f)** $\frac{1}{50}$

2. Express the following fractions as percents. Hint: See Example 2.

    a) $\frac{2}{5}$ **b)** $\frac{3}{10}$ **c)** $\frac{4}{5}$ **d)** $\frac{4}{15}$ **e)** $\frac{1}{25}$ **f)** $\frac{7}{25}$

3. Change the following fractions to percents. Hint: See Example 3.

    a). $\frac{2}{3}$ **b)**. $\frac{2}{7}$ **c)**. $\frac{2}{9}$ **d)**. $\frac{3}{8}$ **e)**. $\frac{3}{11}$ **f)**. $\frac{5}{12}$

Challenge Questions

4. Change the following fractions to percents.

    a) $\frac{4}{15}$ **b)**. $\frac{1}{3}$ **c)**. $\frac{1}{20}$ **d)**. $\frac{7}{30}$ **e)**. $\frac{7}{8}$ **f)**. $\frac{4}{9}$

Answers to Selected Exercises

    1(a) 50%   **1(b)** 25%   **2(a)** 40%   **2(b)** 30%

    3(a) $66\frac{2}{3}\%$ **3(b)** $28\frac{4}{7}\%$

REAL WORLD APPLICATIONS – WORD PROBLEMS
Express Fractions as Percents

Example 1

Given that $\frac{4}{5}$ of the students in a high school like soccer. What percent of

the students like soccer?

Solution

Using the rule express the fraction as a percent by multiplying the fraction by 100,
and then attach the % sign to the answer.

Percent of the student population $= 100\%$

Note: There is an imaginary decimal point behind the last digit of all whole numbers. (Review the chapter on Decimal Fractions).

Rule: To express a percent as a decimal fraction, move the decimal point in the percent number two places or two digits to the left of the decimal point, and ignore the percent sign.

Example 1

Express 25.5% as a decimal fraction.

Solution

Using the rule, to express a percent as a decimal fraction, move the decimal point in the percent number two places or two digits to the left of the decimal point, and ignore the percent sign as shown:

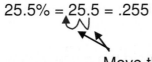

$$25.5\% = 25.5 = .255$$

Move the decimal point two places or two digits to the left.

Therefore, 25.5% = .255

Example 2

Express 25% as a decimal fraction.

Solution

Using the rule, to express a percent as a decimal fraction, move the decimal point in the percent number two places or two digits to the left of the decimal point, and ignore the percent sign as shown:

$$25\% = .25 = .25$$

Move the imaginary decimal point behind 25 two places or two digits to the left.

Therefore, 25% = .25

Note: There is an imaginary decimal point behind the last digit of every whole number.

Example 3

Express 2.55% as a decimal fraction.

Solution

Using the rule, to express a percent as a decimal fraction, move the decimal point in the percent number two places or two digits to the left of the decimal point, and ignore the percent sign.

Write a 0 here to hold the place value.

$$2.55\% = 2.55 = .0255$$

Move the decimal point two places or two digits to the left.

Therefore, $2.55\% = .0255$

Example 4

Express .255% as a decimal fraction.

Solution

Using the rule, to express a percent as a decimal fraction, move the decimal point in the percent number two places or two digits to the left of the decimal point, and ignore the percent sign.

Write two 0 here to hold the place values

$$.255\% = .255 = .00255$$

Move the decimal point two places or two digits to the left.

Therefore, $.255\% = .00255$

Exercises

1. Express the following percents as decimals. Hint: See Example 1.

(a) 28.1%	(b) 95.5%	(c) 64.9%	(d) 75.5%	(e) 95.3%
(f) 12.4%	(g) 17.7%	(h) 55.6%	(i) 49.9%	(j) 99.9%
(k) 39.8%	(l) 16.6%	(m) 11.1%	(n) 36.7%	(o) 57.8%

2. Express the following percents as decimals. Hint: See Example 2.

(a) 26%	(b) 27%	(c) 99%	(d) 35%	(e) 64%
(f) 75%	(g) 38%	(h) 45%	(i) 17%	(j) 19%
(k) 11%	(l) 34%	(m) 17%	(n) 88%	(o) 96%

3. Express the following percents as decimals. Hint: See Example 3.

(a) 3.22%	(b) 4.45%	(c) 7.1%	(d) 9.61	(e) 1.1%
(f) 2.1%	(g) 9.9%	(h) 8.5%	(i) 6.25%	(j) 7.9%

4. Express the following percent as decimal. Hint: See Example 4.

(a) .234%	(b) .641%	(c) .111%	(d) .2%	(e) .12%
(f) .75%	(g) .35%	(h) .99%	(i) .1%	(j) .4%

Challenge Questions

5. Express the following percents as decimal fractions.

(a) 72%	(b) 33.4%	(c) .01%	(d) 1.71%	(e) .09%

(f) .3%   (g) 4.2%   (h) 13.1%   (i) 95%   (j) .88%

Answers to Selected Questions.
(1)(a) .281   **2(a)** .26   **3(a)** .0322   **4(a)** .00234

REAL WORLD APPLICATIONS – WORD PROBLEMS
Percent to Decimal Fractions

Example 1
Given that 12.32% of the items in a store are on sale, what decimal fraction of the items is on sale?

Solution

Using the rule to express a percent as a decimal fraction, move the decimal point in the percent number two places or two digits to the left of the decimal point, and ignore the percent sign.

$$12.32\% = 12.32 = .1232$$

Move the decimal point two places or two digits to the left.

The decimal fraction of the items on sale = .1232

Example 2
There are 7% of the boys at the Peki High School who work at the Peki Super Market. What is the decimal fraction of the boys that work at the Peki Super Market?

Solution

Using the rule to express a percent as a decimal fraction, move the decimal point in the percent number two places or two digits to the left of the decimal point, and ignore the percent sign.

Write a 0 here to hold the place value.

$$7\% = 7 = .07$$

Move the imaginary decimal point behind 7 to two places or two digits to the left.

Therefore, .07 is the decimal fraction of the boys.

Example 3
.64% of a certain concentration of orange drink is water. What is the decimal fraction of the concentration made of water?

Solution

Hint: Orange drink is made by mixing pure orange juice with water.

Using the rule to express a percent as a decimal fraction, move the decimal point in the percent number two places or two digits to the left of the decimal point, and ignore the percent sign.

Write two 0 here to hold the place values.

$$.64\% = .64 = .0064$$

Move the decimal point two places or two digits to the left.

The decimal fraction of the concentration of the orange drink is .0064.

Exercises

1. Given that 17.2% of the computers in a certain store are on sale, what decimal fraction of the computers are on sale? Hint: See Example 1.
2. In a certain elementary school, 3% of the girls like soccer. What is the decimal fraction of the girls that like soccer? Hint: See Example 2.
3. The concentration of a certain orange drink is made up of .95% water. What is the decimal fraction of the concentration of water in the orange drink? Hint: See Example 3.

Challenge Questions

4. Given that the concentration of a certain drink is .5% water, what is the decimal fraction of the concentration of the water in the drink?
5. If 1% of the employees in a certain company prefer to take their vacation in the summer, what is the decimal fraction of the employees that prefer to take their vacation in the summer?
6. Mrs. Aggor went to the store to buy a shirt because 46.8% of the shirts were on sale. What is the decimal fraction of the shirts that are on sale?

Express Decimal Fractions as Percents

Note that expressing decimal fractions as percents is the opposite of expressing percents as decimal fractions, and therefore, the method of expressing decimal fractions as percents is the opposite of the method of expressing the percents as decimal fractions. Review the rule for expressing percents as decimal fractions in the preceding rule.

Rule: To express decimal fractions as percent, move the decimal point two places or two digits to the right, and then attach the % sign.

Example 1

Express .92 as a percent.

Solution

Using the rule to express decimal fractions as percents, move the decimal point two places or two digits to the right, and then attach the % sign.

Attach the % sign.

$$.92 = .92 = 92\%$$

Move the decimal point two places or two digits to the right.

Therefore, .92 = 92%

Example 2

Change the following decimal fractions to percents:

(a) 1.87   (b) 1.8

Solution

(a). Using the rule to express decimal fractions as percents, move the decimal point two places or two digits to the right, and then attach the % sign:

Attach the % sign.

$$1.87 = 1.87 = 187\%$$

Move the decimal point two places or two digits to the right.

Therefore, 1.87 = 187%

(b). Using the rule to express decimal fractions as percents, move the decimal point two places or two digits to the right, and then attach the % sign.

Write a 0 here to hold the place value.

$$1.8 = 1.8 = 180\% \longleftarrow \text{Attach the \% sign.}$$

Move the decimal point two places or two digits to the right.

Example 3

Change the following decimal fractions to percents.

(a) .001   (b) .275   (c) 1.00

Solution

(a). Using the rule to express decimal fractions as percents, move the decimal point two places or two digits to the right, and then attach the % sign.

Attach the % sign.

.001 = .001 = .1%

Move the decimal point two places or two digits to the right.

Therefore, .001 = .1%

(**b**). Using the rule to express decimal fractions as percents, move the decimal point two places or two digits to the right, and then attach the % sign.

Attach the % sign.

.275 = .275 = 27.5%

Move the decimal point two places or two digits to the right.

Therefore, .275 = 27.5%

(**c**). Using the rule to express decimal fractions as percents, move the decimal point two places or two digits to the right, and then attach the % sign.

Attach the % sign.

1.00 = 1.00 = 100%

Move the decimal point two places or two digits to the right.

Therefore, 1.00 = 100%

Exercises

1. Change the following decimal fractions to percents. Hint: See Example **1**.
   (**a**) .79   (**b**) .34   (**c**) .07   (**d**) .12   (**e**) .11

2. Change the following decimal fractions to percents. Hint: See Example **2(a)**.
   (**a**) 2.94   (**b**) 9.99   (**c**) 3.40   (**d**) 7.75   (**e**) 1.25

3. Change the following decimal fractions to percents. Hint: See Example **3(a)**.
   (**a**) 3.9   (**b**) 9.9   (**c**) 28.1   (**d**) 44.6   (**e**) 7.8

4. Change the following decimal fractions to percents. Hint : See Example **3(a)**.
   (**a**) .002   (**b**) .009   (**c**) .004   (**d**) 2.001   (**e**) 10.002

5. Change the following decimal fractions to percents. Hint: See Example **3(b)**.
   (**a**) .298   (**b**) .444   (**c**) .891   (**d**) .658   (**e**) .481

6. Change the following decimal fractions to percents. Hint: See Example **3(c)**.
   (**a**) 9.00   (**b**) 6.00   (**c**) 4.00   (**d**) 8.00   (**e**) 2.00

Challenge Questions

7. Express the following decimal fractions as percents.

(a) .3   (b) 4.2   (c) 13.1   (d) 95   (e) .88

8. Express the following decimal fractions as percents.

   (a) 1.1   (b) .001   (c) 1.78   (d) 7.0   (e) .09
   (f) .90   (g) 3.0   (h) 1   (i) .21   (j) .01

Answers to Selected Exercises

1(a) 79%   **2(a)** 294%   **3(a)** 390%

4(a) 0.2%   **5(a)** 29.8%   **6(a)** 900%

REAL WORLD APPLICATIONS – WORD PROBLEMS
Express Decimal Fractions as Percents

Example 1

Given that .65 of the students in a certain school are girls, what percent of the students are girls?

Solution

Using the rule to express decimal fractions as percents, move the decimal point two places or two digits to the right, and then attach the % sign.

Attach the % sign.

.65 = .65 = 65%

Move the decimal point two places or two digits to the right.

The percent of the girls = 65%.

Example 2

John will make 1.9 profit in his investment.
Express his profit as a percent.

Solution

Using the rule to express decimal fractions as percents, move the decimal point two places or two digits to the right, and then attach the % sign.

Write a 0 here to hold the place value.

1.9 = 1.9 = 190% ⟵ Attach the % sign.

Move the decimal point two places or two digits to the right.

The percent profit = 190%.

Example 3

Given that .268 of the computers in a certain store were sold at a discount. What

61

percent of the computers were sold at a discount ?

Solution

Using the rule to express decimal fractions as percents, move the decimal point two places or two digits to the right, and then attach the % sign:

Attach the % sign.

.268 = .268 = 26.8%

Move the decimal point two places or two digits to the right.

The percent of the computers sold at a discount was 26.8%

Example 4

Given that .022 of the students in a certain class study history, what is the percent of the students that study history?

Solution

Using the rule, to express decimal fractions as percents, move the decimal point two places or two digits to the right, and then attach the % sign.

Attach the % sign.

.022 = .022 = 2.2%

Move the decimal point two places or two digits to the right.

The percent of the students that study history is 2.2%

Exercises

1. Given that .75 of the students in a certain class are boys, what percent of the students are boys? Hint: See Example 1.

2. Eric made .078 profit on his investment. What is his percent profit? Hint: See Example 2 .

3. Given that .289 of the people who go to the zoo are children, what percent of the people who go to the zoo are children? Hint: See Example 3.

4. Given that .501 of the students in a certain class study chemistry, what percent of the students study chemistry? Hint: See Example 4.

Challenge Questions

5. Given that .018 of the animals in a certain zoo are lions, what percent of the animals are lions?

6. Given that .684 of the books in a certain library involve science, what is the percent of the books that involves science?

Percents (%)	Fractions	Decimals or Decimal Fractions
5%	$\dfrac{5}{100}$	.05
65%		
16%		
	$\dfrac{17}{100}$	
	$\dfrac{73}{100}$	
		.008
		.08
		.8
2.1%		
.33%		

2. Complete the table by filling in the columns for decimal fractions, percents, and fractions. Hint: See examples under the sections in decimal fractions, percents, common fractions, and also see the two examples in the second and the third rows of the table in this question.

(The table is on the next page.)

Decimal fractions	Percent (%)	Common fractions
.8	$\dfrac{8}{10} \times 100 = 80\%$	$\dfrac{8}{10} = \dfrac{4}{5}$
.004	$\dfrac{4}{1000} \times 100 = .4\%$	$\dfrac{4}{1000} = \dfrac{1}{250}$
2.67		
85.8		
.561		
.018		
.o8		
.7		
9.49		
72.004		
.47		
.15		
$\dfrac{35}{100} = .35$	35%	$\dfrac{35}{100} = \dfrac{7}{20}$
	60%	
	160%	
	74.5%	
	9.8%	
	2%	
	13.11%	
12.5% = .125	$\dfrac{1}{8} \times 100 = 12.5\%$	$\dfrac{1}{8}$
		$\dfrac{272}{100}$
		$\dfrac{6}{12}$
		$\dfrac{9.7}{100}$
		$\dfrac{24\frac{1}{3}}{60}$
		$\dfrac{100}{100}$

3. Copy and complete the table by filling in the columns for common fractions,

decimal fractions, and percents. Hint: See separate examples under the sections on decimal fractions, percents, and common fractions.

Common fraction	Decimal fraction	%
$\frac{57}{100}$		
$\frac{8}{24}$		
$\frac{7}{9}$		
$\frac{9.7}{100}$		
$\frac{5645}{100}$		
$\frac{18}{65}$		
	.358	
	.019	
	75.45	
	38.01	
	3.2	
	.6	
		2.5%
		275%
		1%
		60%
		4700.8%
		26.15%

Understanding 100%

(**1**) 100% means $\frac{100}{100} = \frac{1}{1} = 1$. 100% therefore means one whole of anything or the total of anything.

(**2**) If 100% of the employees at a certain company are women, it means that no men work at the company.

(**3**). If 100% of the students in grade 5B are boys, it means that all the students in grade 5B are boys.

(**4**) If 100% of the students visited the zoo yesterday, it means that all the students visited the zoo.

Understanding Percent

(1) If 70% of the students in a certain school are girls, it means that
100% – 70% = 30% are boys since the whole student population should be 100%.

(2) If 55% of the doctors in a certain hospital are women, then the percent of the male
doctors is 100% – 55% = 45% since the whole doctor population in the hospital
should be 100%.

(3) If 5% of a class is absent, it means that 100% – 5% = 95% of the students are
present since the whole class should be 100%.

REAL WORLD APPLICATIONS – WORD PROBLEMS
Understanding Percent

Example 1
There are 48% of boys in a school. What is the percent of the girls?
Solution
The percent of the girls = 100% – 48% = 52%

Example 2
An advance school consists of students studying chemistry, physics, and biology. A
student may study only one subject. Given that 25% of the students study chemistry
and 30% of the students study biology, what is the percent of the students that study
physics?
Solution
Total student population = 100%
Percent of students that study chemistry and biology = 25% + 30% = 55%.
Percent of students that study physics = 100% – 55% = 45%.

Example 3
A school has 800 students. If 55% of the student population are boys,
(a) what is the percent of girls in the school?
(b) how many girls are in the school?
Solution
(a) Total student population = 100%
　　Percent of the boys = 55%
　　Percent of the girls = 100% - 55% = 45%
(b) From solution (a), the percent of the girls = 45%
　　The number of the girls in the school = 45% of 800
$$\downarrow\ \ \downarrow\ \downarrow$$
$$= \frac{45}{100} \times 800 \qquad \text{Note: } 45\% = \frac{45}{100}, \text{ "of" is} \times.$$

$$= \frac{45}{\overset{}{\underset{1}{100}}} \times \overset{8}{800} \qquad \text{Divide by 100.}$$

$$= 45 \times 8$$
$$= 360 \text{ girls}$$

Therefore, the number of the girls in the school is 360.

Example 4

A school has a population of 1,200 students. If 5 percent of the students are absent,

(**a**) what is the percent of the students present?

(**b**) what is the number of the students present?

(**c**) what is the number of the students absent?

Solution

(**a**) The percent of the whole student population = 100%

The percent of the students that are absent = 5%

The percent of the students that are present = 100% - 5% = 95%

(**b**) From the solution of (**a**), the percent of the students that are present = 95%

Student population of the school = 1,200

The number of the students present = 95% of the student population.

$$= 95\% \text{ of } 1,200$$
$$\downarrow \quad \downarrow \quad \downarrow$$
$$= \frac{95}{100} \times 1,200 \quad \text{Note: } 95\% = \frac{95}{100}, \text{ "of" is } \times.$$

$$= \frac{95}{\underset{1}{100}} \times \overset{12}{1,200} \quad \text{Divide by 100.}$$

$$= 95 \times 12$$
$$= 1140 \text{ students.}$$

Therefore, 1140 students were present.

(**c**) The number of students absent

$$= \text{Student population} - \text{Number of students present.}$$
$$= 1,200 - 1140$$
$$= 60 \text{ students.}$$

Therefore, 60 students were absent.

Fractional Parts of Percents

The fractional part of a percent such as $\frac{1}{5}\%$ means $\frac{1}{5}$ out of 100. Recall that,

for example, 2% means 2 out of 100. Recall that $2\% = \frac{2}{100}$, and therefore, $\frac{1}{5}\% = \frac{\frac{1}{5}}{100}$.

Rule: To express a fraction of a percent as a decimal fraction, write the fraction over 100, and then divide, ignoring the % sign.

Example 1

Express $\frac{1}{5}\%$ as a decimal fraction

Solution

Using the rule to express a fraction of a percent as a decimal fraction, write the fraction over 100, and then divide, ignoring the % sign.

$$\frac{1}{5}\% = \frac{\frac{1}{5}}{100}$$

$$= \frac{\frac{1}{5}}{\frac{100}{1}} \qquad \text{Change 100 to a fraction by writing 100 as } \frac{100}{1} = 100.$$

$$= \frac{1}{5} \times \frac{1}{100} \qquad \text{Recall that to divide a fraction by another fraction, the}$$

top fraction $(\frac{1}{5})$ is multiplied by the inverted bottom

fraction $(\frac{1}{100})$. The inverted bottom fraction is called the

reciprocal.

$$= \frac{1 \times 1}{5 \times 100} = \frac{1}{500}$$

$$500\overline{)1} = 500\overline{)1.000}$$

$$\begin{array}{r} .002 \\ 500\overline{)1.000} \\ -\underline{1\,000} \\ 0\,000 \end{array}$$

(Review the chapter on Dividing a Smaller Number by a Bigger Number).

Therefore, $\frac{1}{5}\% = .002$

70

Example 2

Change $\frac{6}{8}$% to a decimal fraction.

Solution

Using the rule to express a fraction of a percent as a decimal fraction, write the fraction over 100, and then divide, ignoring the % sign.

$$\frac{6}{8}\% = \frac{\frac{6}{8}}{100}$$

$$= \frac{\frac{6}{8}}{\frac{100}{1}} \qquad \text{Change 100 to a fraction by writing 100 as } \frac{100}{1} = 100.$$

$$= \frac{6}{8} \times \frac{1}{100} \qquad \text{Recall that to divide a fraction by another fraction, the top}$$

fraction $(\frac{6}{8})$ is multiplied by the inverted bottom

fraction $(\frac{1}{100})$. The inverted bottom fraction is called the

reciprocal.

$$= \frac{\overset{3}{\cancel{6}}}{\underset{4}{\cancel{8}}} \times \frac{1}{100} \qquad \text{Divide the numerator and the denominator by 2.}$$

$$= \frac{3}{4} \times \frac{1}{100} = \frac{3 \times 1}{4 \times 100} = \frac{3}{400}$$

$$400\overline{)3} = 400\overline{)3.0000} \quad \begin{array}{r} .0075 \\ \hline 3.0000 \\ -\ 2800\downarrow \\ \hline 2000 \\ -\ 2000 \\ \hline 0000 \end{array}$$

(Review the chapter on Dividing a Smaller Number by a Bigger Number).

Therefore, $\frac{6}{8}\% = .0075$

Example 3

Change $2\frac{1}{2}\%$ to decimal fraction.

Solution

Using the rule to express a fraction of a percent as a decimal fraction, write the fraction over 100, and then divide, ignoring the % sign.

$$2\frac{1}{2}\% = \frac{2\frac{1}{2}}{100}$$

$$= \frac{\frac{5}{2}}{100} \qquad \text{Change } 2\frac{1}{2} \text{ to an improper fraction of } \frac{5}{2}.$$

$$= \frac{\frac{5}{2}}{\frac{100}{1}} \qquad \text{Change 100 to a fraction by writing 100 as } \frac{100}{1} = 100.$$

$$= \frac{5}{2} \times \frac{1}{100} \qquad \text{Recall that to divide a fraction by another fraction,}$$

the top fraction ($\frac{5}{2}$) is multiplied by the inverted

bottom fraction ($\frac{1}{100}$), which is the reciprocal.

$$= \frac{\overset{1}{\cancel{5}}}{2} \times \frac{1}{\underset{20}{\cancel{100}}} \qquad \text{Divide numerator and denominator by 5.}$$

$$= \frac{1}{2} \times \frac{1}{20} = \frac{1 \times 1}{2 \times 20} = \frac{1}{40}$$

$$40\overline{)1} \quad = \quad 40\overline{)\begin{array}{l} .025 \\ 1.000 \\ -\ 80 \\ \hline 200 \\ -200 \\ \hline 000 \end{array}}$$

(Review the chapter on Dividing a Smaller Number by a Bigger Number.)

Therefore, $2\frac{1}{2}\% = .025$

Exercises

1. Express the following fractions of percents as decimal. Round your answer
   to 3 decimal places. Hint: See Example 1.

   (a) $\frac{1}{2}\%$ (b) $\frac{1}{4}\%$ (c) $\frac{1}{3}\%$ (d) $\frac{1}{10}\%$ (e) $\frac{1}{12}\%$

   (f) $\frac{1}{7}\%$ (g) $\frac{1}{9}\%$ (h) $\frac{1}{15}\%$ (i) $\frac{1}{11}\%$ (j) $\frac{1}{20}\%$

2. Change the following fractions of percents to decimals. Round your answer
   to 3 decimal places. Hint: See Example 2.

   (a) $\frac{2}{10}\%$ (b) $\frac{2}{5}\%$ (c) $\frac{3}{7}\%$ (d) $\frac{2}{7}\%$ (e) $\frac{3}{5}\%$

   (f) $\frac{3}{5}\%$ (g) $\frac{3}{11}\%$ (h) $\frac{4}{15}\%$ (i) $\frac{5}{8}\%$ (j) $\frac{9}{10}\%$

3. Change the following mixed numbers of percents to decimals. Round
   your answer to 3 decimal places. Hint: See Example 3.

   (a) $2\frac{1}{4}\%$ (b) $1\frac{1}{2}\%$ (c) $2\frac{2}{5}\%$ (d) $1\frac{3}{5}\%$ (e) $4\frac{3}{4}\%$

   (f) $5\frac{2}{5}\%$ (g) $6\frac{5}{6}\%$ (h) $10\frac{2}{3}\%$ (i) $8\frac{2}{5}\%$ (j) $3\frac{3}{4}\%$

Challenge Questions

4. Change the following mixed numbers and fractions from percents to decimals.

   (a) $2\frac{3}{4}\%$ (b) $\frac{1}{6}\%$ (c) $\frac{2}{9}\%$ (d) $2\frac{3}{5}\%$ (e) $\frac{1}{10}\%$

   (f) $\frac{3}{8}\%$ (g) $5\frac{5}{6}\%$ (h) $\frac{1}{8}\%$ (i) $7\frac{1}{7}\%$ (j) $\frac{5}{7}\%$

Answers to Selected Exercises

1(a) 0.005   2(a) 0.002   3(a) 0.023

REAL WORLD APPLICATIONS - WORD PROBLEMS
Express Fractions of Percents as Decimals

Example 1

Given that $\frac{3}{4}$% of the goods in a certain store are on sale, what is the decimal fraction of the goods that are on sale?

Solution

Using the rule, to express a fraction of a percent as a decimal fraction, write the fraction over 100, and then divide, ignoring the % sign.

$$\frac{3}{4}\% = \frac{\frac{3}{4}}{100}$$

$$= \frac{\frac{3}{4}}{\frac{100}{1}} \qquad \text{Change 100 to a fraction by writing 100 as } \frac{100}{1} = 100.$$

$$= \frac{3}{4} \times \frac{1}{100} \qquad \text{Recall that to divide a fraction by another fraction, the top}$$

fraction ($\frac{3}{4}$) is multiplied by the inverted bottom

fraction ($\frac{1}{100}$). The inverted bottom fraction is called the

reciprocal.

$$= \frac{3 \times 1}{4 \times 100} = \frac{3}{400}$$

$$400\overline{)3} = 400\overline{)3.0000} \\ \underset{}{\overset{.0075}{}} \\ -2800 \\ 2000 \\ -2000 \\ 0000$$

(Review the chapter on Dividing a Smaller Number by a Bigger Number).

Therefore, $\frac{3}{4}\% = .0075$.

Example 2

Agbeko Fish Pond has a lot of fish. Mr. Johnson owns $22\frac{1}{2}$% of the fish in the pond. What is the decimal fraction of the fish that is owned by Mr. Johnson?

Solution

Using the rule, to express a fraction of a percent as a decimal fraction, write the fraction over 100, and then divide, ignoring the % sign.

$$22\frac{1}{2}\% = \frac{22\frac{1}{2}}{100}$$

$$= \frac{\frac{45}{2}}{100} \qquad \text{Change } 22\frac{1}{2} \text{ to an improper fraction } (\frac{45}{2}).$$

$$= \frac{\frac{45}{2}}{\frac{100}{1}} \qquad \text{Change 100 to fraction by writing 100 as } \frac{100}{1} = 100.$$

$$= \frac{45}{2} \div \frac{100}{1} \qquad \text{Review division of fractions.}$$

$$= \frac{45}{2} \times \frac{1}{100} \qquad \text{Recall that to divide a fraction by another fraction,}$$

the top fraction is multiplied by the inverted

bottom fraction ($\frac{1}{100}$). The inverted bottom fraction

is called the reciprocal.

$$= \frac{\overset{9}{\cancel{45}}}{2} \times \frac{1}{\underset{20}{\cancel{100}}} \qquad \text{Divide the numerator and the denominator by 5.}$$

$$= \frac{9 \times 1}{2 \times 20} = \frac{9}{40}$$

$$40\overline{)9} \quad = \quad 40\overline{)9.000} \\ \overset{.225}{} \\ -8\,0 \\ 1\,00 \\ -80 \\ 2\,00 \\ -2\,00 \\ 000$$

(Review the chapter on dividing a smaller number by a bigger number).

Therefore, $22\frac{1}{2}\% = .225$.

Exercises

1. A bank rate was increased by $\frac{3}{10}$%, what is the decimal fraction of the increase? Hint: See Example 1.

2. The population of a certain country increased by $8\frac{1}{3}$% last year. What is the decimal fraction of the increase? Hint: See Example 2.

Challenge Questions

3. Eric's academic performance has improved by $5\frac{1}{3}$% . What is the decimal fraction of his improvement?

4. The number of books at the library has been reduced by $\frac{7}{10}$%. What is the decimal fraction of the reduction of the books?

FRACTIONAL PARTS OF PERCENTS - Alternative Method

The preceding sections show how to change the fractional parts of percents to decimals. This section shows an alternative method of changing the fractional parts of percent to decimals.

Rule: **To express a fraction of a percent as a decimal, change the common fraction to a decimal fraction by dividing the numerator by the denominator, and then dividing the result by 100 by moving the decimal point two places or digits to the left, and then ignore the % sign.**

Example 1

Express $\frac{2}{5}$% as a decimal.

Solution

Use the rule which states, to express a fraction of a percent as a decimal, change the common fraction to a decimal fraction by dividing the numerator by the denominator, and then divide the result by 100 by moving the decimal point two places or two digits to the left, and then ignore the % sign.

Step 1: Change the common fraction to a decimal fraction by dividing the numerator by the denominator.

$$\frac{2}{5} = 5\overline{)\begin{array}{c} .4 \\ 2.0 \\ -\underline{20} \\ 00 \end{array}}$$

$$\frac{2}{5}\% = .4\%$$

Step 2: Divide the result in Step 1 by 100 by moving the decimal point two places or two digits to the left.

Write two 0 here to hold the place value.

$$.4\% = \frac{4}{100} = .4 = .004$$

Move the decimal point two places or two digits to the left.

Therefore, $\frac{2}{5}\% = .004$

Exercises
Use the preceding alternative method in Example 1 for "changing a fractional part of a percent to a decimal" to solve the exercises under the section, "Fractional Parts of Percent."

Find the Percent of a Number
Rule 1: To find the percent of a number, multiply the given percent by the given number.

Example 1
Find 5% of 80
Solution
Using the rule to find the percent of a number, multiply the given percent by the given number.

$$5\% \text{ of } 80 = 5\% \times 80 \qquad \text{Note: "of" means to multiply.}$$

$$= \frac{5}{100} \times 80 \qquad \text{Note: } 5\% = \frac{5}{100}.$$

$$= \frac{\overset{1}{\cancel{5}}}{\underset{20}{\cancel{100}}} \times 80 \qquad \text{Divide by 5.}$$

$$= \frac{1}{\underset{1}{\cancel{20}}} \times \overset{4}{\cancel{80}} \qquad \text{Divide by 20.}$$

$$= \frac{4}{1} = 4$$

Therefore, 5% of 80 = 4

Rule 2: **To find the percent of a number**, **change the percent to a decimal fraction, and then multiply the decimal fraction equivalent of the percent by the number**.

Note: Rule 2 is an alternative method of finding the percent of a number.

Example 2
Find 5% of 80. Hint: Use Rule 2 in solving this problem. This problem is the same as Example 1.

Solution
Using Rule 2 to find the percent of a number, change the percent to a decimal fraction, and then multiply the decimal fraction equivalent of the percent by the number as shown:

Step 1: Change the percent to a decimal fraction.

Write a 0 here as a place holder.

$$5\% = \frac{5}{100} = .05$$

Move the imaginary decimal point behind 5 two places or two digits to the left.

Note: There is an imaginary decimal point behind the last digit of any whole number. (Review the chapter on Decimals).

Step 2: Multiply the decimal fraction equivalent of the percent by the number as shown:

```
        80
    ×  .05      Review decimal multiplication.
       400
    + 000  ←  Write this 0 as a place holder.
      4.00
```

Therefore, 5% of 80 is 4.
Note that the methods used in Examples 1 and 2 give the same answer of 4.

Example 3
What is 1.7% of $50?
Solution
Using Rule 2 to find the percent of a number, change the percent to a decimal fraction, and then multiply the decimal fraction equivalent of the percent by the number as shown:

Step 1: Change the percent to a decimal fraction.

Write a 0 here as a place holder.

$$1.7\% = \frac{1.7}{100} = .017 = .017$$

Move the decimal point two places or .

Step 2: Multiply the decimal fraction equivalent of the percent by the number ($50) as shown:

```
        $50
    ×  .017
       350
       500   ←   Write a 0 here as a place holder.
    + 0000   ←   Write two 0s here as place holders
      0.850
```

Move the decimal point three decimal places or 3 digits to the left. Review decimal multiplication.

Therefore, 1.7% of $50 is $.85

Example 4

Find $6\frac{1}{4}\%$ of $28.14.

Solution

Using Rule 2 to find the percent of a number, change the percent to a decimal fraction, and then multiply the decimal fraction equivalent of the percent by the number as shown:

Step 1: Change the percent to a decimal fraction.

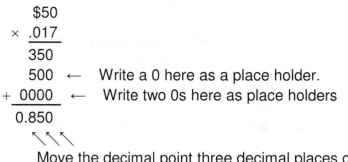

Write a 0 here as a place holder.

$$6\frac{1}{4}\% = \frac{6\frac{1}{4}}{100} = \frac{6.25}{100} = .\ 6.25 = .0625 \qquad \text{Note: } 6\frac{1}{4} = 6.25$$

Move the decimal point two decimal places or two digits to the left.

79

Step 2: Multiply the decimal fraction equivalent of the percent by the number ($28.14) as shown:

$$
\begin{array}{r}
\$28.14 \\
\times\ .0625 \\
\hline
14070 \\
56280 \\
+\ 1688400 \\
\hline
1.758750 \\
\end{array}
$$

56280 ← Write a 0 here as a place holder.

+ 1688400 ← Write two 0s here as place holders.

↑ Move the decimal point 6 decimal places or 6 digits to the left.

Therefore, $6\dfrac{1}{4}$ of $28.14 is $1.76 to the nearest hundredth or cent.

Exercises

1. Find 7% of the following numbers. Hint: See Example 1. Give your answer to three decimal places.
   (**a**) 160　　　(**b**) 16.4　　　(**c**) 58.2　　　(**d**) 142.1

2. Find 15% of the following numbers. Hint: See Example 2. Give your answer to 3 decimal places.
   (**a**) 35　　　(**b**) 46.2　　　(**c**) 10　　　(**d**) 242

3. Find 26% of the following numbers. Hint See Example 2. Give your answer to 3 decimal places.
   (**a**) 24　　　(**b**) 78.51　　　(**c**) .01　　　(**d**) .8

4. Find 3.8% of the following amounts. Hint: See Example 3.
   (**a**) $70　　　(**b**) $75　　　(**c**) $115　　　(**d**) $275

5. Find 35.8% of the following amounts. Hint: See Example 3.
   (**a**) $48　　　(**b**) $12　　　(**c**) 28　　　(**d**) $36

6. Find $8\dfrac{1}{2}$% of the following amounts. Hint: See Example 4.
   (**a**) $50.25　　　(**b**) $12.78　　　(**c**) $78.17　　　(**d**) 124.48

7. Find $16\dfrac{1}{4}$% of the following amounts. Hint: See Example 4.
   (**a**) $24.25　　　(**b**) 47.34　　　(**c**) $66.48　　　(**d**) $164.28

8. Find $12\dfrac{1}{5}$% of the following numbers. Hint: See Example 4. Give your answer to 3 decimal places.
   (**a**) 72　　　(**b**) 36.3　　　(**c**) 46.32　　　(**d**) 147.18

Challenge Questions

9. Find $\frac{1}{4}$% of 100. Hint : Review the section on "Fractional Parts of Percent." Give your answer to 3 decimal places.

10. Find .8% of 64.12. Hint: Review the section on "Fractional Parts of Percent." Round your answer to 3 decimal places.

11. Find 7.8% of $36.87.

12. Find 8% of 1348. Round your answer to 3 decimal places.

13. Find $\frac{4}{5}$% of 125. Hint: Review the section on "Fractional Parts of Percent." Round your answer to 3 decimal places.

14. Find $24\frac{1}{4}$% of $78.36

Answers to Selected Questions

1(a) 11.200   **4(a)** $2.66   **6(a)** $4.27

REAL WORLD APPLICATIONS – WORD PROBLEMS
To Find the Percent of a Number

Example 1

There are 20 students in a class. If 45% of the students are boys, how many boys are in the class?

Solution

Using Rule 2 to find the percent of a number, change the percent to a decimal fraction, and then multiply the decimal fraction equivalent of the percent by the number as shown:

Step 1: Change the percent to a decimal fraction

$$45\% = \frac{45}{100} = .45 = .45$$

$$\uparrow$$

Move the imaginary decimal point
2 decimal places to the left.

Step 2: Multiply the decimal fraction equivalent of the percent by the number (20)
    as shown:

81

$$\begin{array}{r} 20 \\ \times\ .45 \\ \hline 100 \\ +\ 800 \\ \hline 9.00 \end{array}$$ ← Write a 0 here as a place holder.

Move the decimal point two decimal or two digits to the left.
Review the section on Decimal Multiplication.

The number of boys in the class is 9.

Example 2

An employee earns $9\frac{1}{2}$% commission. What is the commission earned on a sale of $3,580.28?

Solution

Using Rule 2 to find the percent of a number, change the percent to a decimal fraction, and then multiply the decimal fraction equivalent of the percent by the number as shown:

Step 1: Change the percent to a decimal fraction.

Need to fill this digit position with
a zero as a place holder.
↓

$$9\frac{1}{2}\% = 9.5\% = \frac{9.5}{100} = 9.5 = .095$$

↑↑

Move the decimal point two decimal places or two digits
to the left.

Step 2: Multiply the decimal fraction equivalent of the percent by the number (3,580.28) as shown:

$$\begin{array}{r} \$3,580.28 \\ \times\ \quad .095 \\ \hline 1790140 \\ 32222520 \\ +\ 00000000 \\ \hline \$340.12660 \end{array}$$

← Write a 0 here as a place holder.
← Write two 0s here as place holders.

Move the decimal point 5 places to the left.
Review the section on Decimal Multiplication.

Therefore, $9\frac{1}{2}$% of $3,580.28 is $340.13 to the nearest cent.

Example 3

George's salary was $45,200. If his salary is increased by 12%,
(**a**) what is the increase in his salary?
(**b**) what is his new salary?

Solution

Using Rule 2 to find the percent of a number, change the percent to a decimal fraction, and then multiply the decimal fraction equivalent of the percent by the number as shown:

(**a**) **Step 1**: Change the percent to a decimal fraction.

$$12\% = \frac{12}{100} = .12 = .12$$

⇈

Move the imaginary decimal point two decimal places or two digits to the left.

Step 2: Multiply the decimal fraction equivalent of the percent by the number (45,200) as shown:

$$
\begin{array}{r}
\$45,200 \\
\times\quad .12 \\
\hline
90400 \\
+\ 452000 \\
\hline
\$5424.00
\end{array}
$$

← Write a 0 here as a place holder.

⇈

Move the decimal point two decimal places or digits to the left.

Therefore, the increase in George's salary is $5424.00

(**b**) George's new salary = current salary + Increase in salary
$$= \$45,200.00 + \$5,424.00$$
$$= \$50,624.00$$

Example 4

Mr. Benson needs a 15% down payment on a new house. If the new house costs $200,000, how much of a down payment does Mr. Benson need?

Solution

Using Rule 2 to find the percent of a number, change the percent to a decimal fraction, and then multiply the decimal fraction equivalent of the percent by the number.

Step 1: Change the percent to a decimal fraction.

$$15\% = \frac{15}{100} = .15 = .15$$

⇈

Move the imaginary decimal point two decimal places or two digits to the left.

Step 2: Multiply the decimal fraction equivalent of the percent by the number (200,000).

$$
\begin{array}{r}
\$200{,}000 \\
\times \quad\quad .15 \\
\hline
1000000 \\
+ \quad 2000000 \\
\hline
\$30{,}000.00
\end{array}
$$

← Write a 0 here as a place holder.

⇈

Move two decimal places or
two digits to the left.

Therefore, the down payment is $30,000.00.

Exercises

1. In a school, 55% of the students are boys. If there are 500 students in the school,
   (**a**) how many boys are in the school?
   (**b**) how many girls are in the school? Hint: See Example 1.

2. An employee earns $13\frac{1}{4}$% commission. What is the commission earned on a sale of $6,258? Hint: See Example 2.

3. Ama's salary was $55,436.19. If her salary is increased by 5%,
   (**a**) what is the increase in her salary?
   (**b**) what is her new salary?
   Hint: See Example 3.

4. Seth bought a new house for $175,000. If he paid 8% down payment on the new house, how much did he pay for the new house? Hint: See Example 4.

Challenge Questions

1. Mr. Albert has to pay 14% down payment on a new house. If the new house cost $225,000, what is the down payment of Mr. Albert?

2. Elizabeth's current salary is increased by $12\frac{1}{2}$%. If her current salary is $55,200.78, what is the increment in her salary?

3. An employee earns $8\frac{1}{2}$% commission. What is the commission earned on a sale of $3,648.37?

4. The population of a school is 650 students. If 40% of the students are girls,
   (**a**) how many girls are in the school?
   (**b**) how many boys are in the school?

Percent of One Number Compared to Another Number

In mathematics, it is possible to find what percent a number is of another number, and this is really a ratio expressed in percent.

Rule: To find what percent a number is of another number, divide the first number by the second number, and then move the decimal point two places or two digits to the right in the quotient, and then attach the % sign.

Special note: Some students who may find it difficult in setting up the solution of the percent problems can use the "is of" ($\frac{is}{of}$) method. The facts in the rule can be stated as "a number is what percent of another number?" and this can be expressed generally as:

$$\frac{is}{of} = \frac{a\ number}{another\ number}$$

Example 1

Express 3 as a percent of 5.

Solution

The facts in the question can be stated as: "3 **is** what percent **of** 5?" and this can be expressed as:

$$\frac{is}{of} = \frac{3}{5}$$

Using the rule to find what percent of a number is of another number, divide 3 by 5 and then move the decimal point two places or two digits to the right in the quotient, and then attach the % sign.

Step 1: Divide the first number by the second number as shown:

$$\frac{3}{5} = 5\overline{)3} = 5\overline{)\begin{array}{r} .6 \\ 3.0 \\ -30 \\ \hline 00 \end{array}}$$

Step 2: Change the .6 to a percent by moving the decimal point two places or two digits to the right, and then adding the percent sign, which is the same as multiplying .6 by 100.

Write a 0 here as a place holder.
↓
.6 = .6 = 60%
↑↑

Move the decimal point two places or two digits to the right.

(Review the chapters on Decimal Fraction and Percent.)

Therefore, 3 is 60% of 5.

Example 2

Express the ratio 2 out of 10 as a percent to the nearest whole number.
Solution
The facts in the question can be stated as: "2 **is** what percent **of** 10?" and this can be expressed as:

$$\frac{is}{of} = \frac{2}{10}$$

Using the rule to find what percent a number is of another number, divide 2 by 10, and then move the decimal point two places or two digits to the right in the quotient, and then attach the % sign.

Step 1: " 2 out of 10 " is $\frac{2}{10}$ or simply divide 2 by 10.

$$\frac{2}{10} = 10\overline{)2} = 10\overline{)2.0}$$
$$\underline{-2\ 0}$$
$$0\ 0$$

Step 2: Change .2 to a percent by moving the decimal point two places or two digits to the right, and then attach the percent sign.

Write a 0 here as a place holder.

$$.2 = .2\ \ = 20\%$$

Move the decimal point two places or two digits to the right.

Therefore, 2 is 20% of 10.

Exercises. Round all answers to the nearest whole number.
1. Express the following ratios as percents. Hint: See Example 2.

(a) 1 out of 5	(b) 3 out of 10	(c) 3 out of 20
(d) 4 out of 12	(e) 3 out of 9	(f) 2 out of 8
(g) 2 out of 20	(h) 4 out of 100	(i) 20 out of 50
(j) 12 out of 60	(k) 3 out of 15	(l) 8 out of 64

2. Express 2 as a percent of 8. Hint: See Example 1.
3. Express 10 as a percent of 100. Hint: See Example 1.
4. Express 5 as a percent of 25. Hint: See Example 1.
5. Express 6 as a percent of 24. Hint: See Example 1.
6. Express 40 as a percent of 90. Hint: See Example 1.
7. 15 is what percent of 125? Hint: See Example 1.

Challenge Questions

8. Express the following ratios as percents. Round your answers to the nearest whole number.

(a) 25 out of 75   (b) 5 out of 65   (c) 6 out of 36

(d) 35 out of 100   (e) 15 out of 100   (f) 50 out of 150

9. 25 is what percent of 125? Round your answer to the nearest whole number.

10. Express 4 as a percent of 48. Round your answer to the nearest whole number.

REAL WORLD APPLICATIONS – WORD PROBLEMS
Percent of One Number Compared to Another Number

Example 1

There are 8 girls and 12 boys in a class. What percent of the class is boys?

Solution

Total number of the students = 8 + 12 = 20 students.

The facts in the question can be stated as: "12 **is** what percent **of** 20?" and this can be expressed as:

$$\frac{is}{of} = \frac{12}{20}$$

Using the rule to find what percent a number is of another number, divide the number of boys by the total number of the students, and then move the decimal point two places or two digits to the right in the quotient, and then attach the % sign.

Step 1: Divide the number of boys by the total number of students as shown:

$$\frac{\text{Number of boys}}{\text{Total number of students}} = \frac{12}{20}$$

$$= \frac{\overset{3}{\cancel{12}}}{\underset{5}{\cancel{20}}} \qquad \text{Reduce to the lowest terms by dividing by 4.}$$

$$= \frac{3}{5}$$

$$\frac{3}{5} = 5\overline{)3} = 5\overline{)3.0}^{.6} \\ \qquad\qquad -\underline{30} \\ \qquad\qquad\quad 0$$

Step 2: Change .6 to a percent by moving the decimal point 2 places to the right, and then attach the percent sign which is the same as multiplying by 100.

$$= \$20 \times \frac{\frac{100}{10}}{10}$$

Review Division by Fractions.

$$= \$20 \times \frac{\overset{10}{\cancel{100}}}{\underset{1}{\cancel{10}}}$$

$$= \$20 \times 10 = \$200$$

Therefore, the original price is $200.

b. Using the Proportion Method

Hint: Review the chapter on Proportion.
Let us now use proportion to solve Example 1.
Let the original price be x.
Write a proportion as shown:

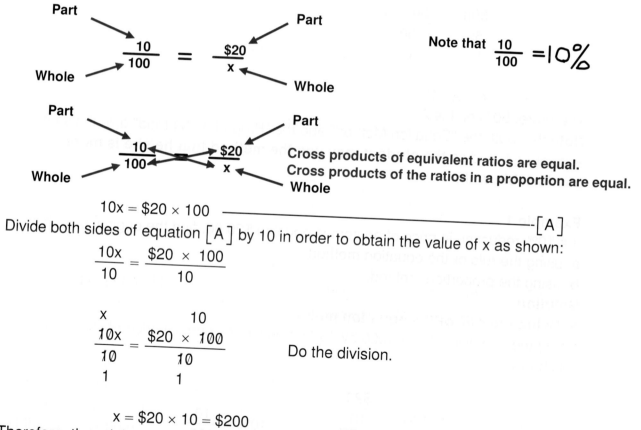

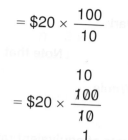

Note that $\frac{10}{100} = 10\%$

Cross products of equivalent ratios are equal.
Cross products of the ratios in a proportion are equal.

$$10x = \$20 \times 100 \qquad\qquad\qquad\text{[A]}$$

Divide both sides of equation [A] by 10 in order to obtain the value of x as shown:

$$\frac{10x}{10} = \frac{\$20 \times 100}{10}$$

$$\frac{\overset{x}{\cancel{10x}}}{\underset{1}{\cancel{10}}} = \frac{\$20 \times \overset{10}{\cancel{100}}}{\underset{1}{\cancel{10}}} \qquad \text{Do the division.}$$

$$x = \$20 \times 10 = \$200$$

Therefore, the original price is $200.

Example 2

25% of what number is 100?

a. Find the number by using the rule or the equation method.

b. Find the number by using the proportion method.

Solution

a. Using the rule or the equation method

Using the rule, divide 100 by 25% as shown:

$$\frac{100}{25\%} = \frac{\frac{100}{25}}{100} \qquad \textbf{Note: } 25\% = \frac{25}{100}$$

$$\frac{\frac{100}{25}}{100} = 100 \div \frac{25}{100}$$

$$= 100 \times \frac{100}{25} \qquad \text{Review Division by Fractions.}$$

$$= 100 \times \frac{\overset{4}{\cancel{100}}}{\underset{1}{\cancel{25}}}$$

$$= 100 \times 4 = 400$$

The number is 400. Therefore, 25% of 400 is 100.

b. Using the proportion method

Hint: Review the chapter on proportion.

Let us now use proportion to solve Example 2.

Let the number be x.

Write a proportion as shown:

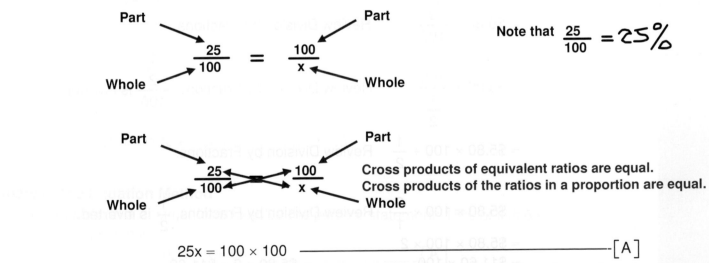

$$25x = 100 \times 100 \hspace{1cm}\text{------------------------------------}[A]$$

Divide both sides of equation $[A]$ by 25 in order to obtain the value of x as shown:

2. Write an equation in a decimal form to solve the percent statement: 25% of 90 is n.
The required equation is:

$$0.25 \cdot 90 = n$$

Hint: n can be found if 0.25 is multiplied by 90.

3. Write an equation for x of 36 is 24 in a form so that you can solve for x.
The required equation is:

$$x \cdot 36 = 24 \underline{\hspace{4cm}} [A]$$

Hint: x can be found if both sides of the equation $[A]$ are divided by 36.

The value of x can be expressed in decimal or in percent by multiplying by 100.

Summary of the Proportion Method

1. Write a proportion to solve the equation: 10% of 64 is x.
The required proportion is:

$$\frac{10}{100} = \frac{x}{64} \qquad \text{Notice that } 10\% = \frac{10}{100}.$$

Hint: When writing a proportion, the order of the ratios that form the proportion are very important, otherwise the solution of the proportion will not be correct. Review the chapter on proportion. In this case, the order of the ratios are formed by using "part divided by whole" as shown:

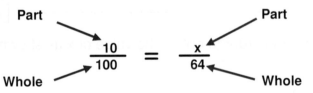

Hint: x can be found by cross multiplying the ratios of the proportion and then dividing both sides of the equation formed by 100.

2. Write a proportion to solve the equation: 28% of x is 49.
The required proportion is:

$$\frac{28}{100} = \frac{49}{x} \qquad \text{Notice that } 28\% = \frac{28}{100}.$$

Hint: When writing a proportion, the order of the ratios that form the proportion are very important, otherwise the solution of the proportion will not be correct. Review the chapter on proportion. In this case, the order of the ratios are formed by using "part divided by whole." as shown:

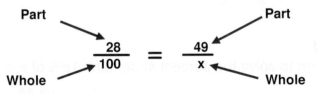

Hint: x can be found by cross multiplying the ratios of the proportion and then dividing both sides of the equation formed by 28.

3. Write a proportion to solve the equation: x% of 85 is 25.

The required proportion is:

$$\frac{x}{100} = \frac{25}{85}$$ Notice that x% = $\frac{x}{100}$.

Hint: When writing a proportion, the order of the ratios that form the proportion are very important, otherwise the solution of the proportion will not be correct. Review the chapter on proportion. In this case, the order of the ratios are formed by using "part divided by whole," as shown:

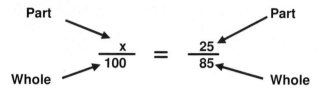

Hint: x can be found by cross multiplying the ratios of the proportion, and then dividing both sides of the equation formed by 85.

Exercises

You may setup similar equations as shown under the "Summary of the Equation Method" and the "Summary of the Proportion Method" in solving Exercises 1 to 12 as needed.

1. If a 15% reduction in the price of an item is equal to $45.00, find the original price. Hint: See Example 1.

2. 22% of what number is 48? Round your answer to the nearest whole number. Hint: See Example 2.

3. $4.50 is $\frac{1}{5}$% of what amount? Hint: See Example 3.

4. $\frac{1}{4}$% of what number is 28? Hint: See Example 3.

5. $7.75 is 5% of what amount? Hint: See Example 2.

6. $28.45 is 45% of what amount? Hint: See Example 2.

7. 65% of what number is 160? Hint: See Example 2.

8. Write a proportion to solve each of the following equations:

   a. 30% of x is 40.   **b.** 54% of n is 72.   **c.** 15% of x is 65.

   d. 2% of k is 64.   **e.** 5% of x is 60.   **f.** 70% of p is 35.

   Hint: See the "Summary of the Proportion Method," item 2.

9. Solve each proportion in exercise 8.

   Hint: See the "Summary of the Proportion Method," item 2.

Challenge Questions

10. 30% of what number is 90?

11. 15% of what number is 125?

12. $10.25 is $\frac{1}{4}$% of what amount?

13. If a 6% reduction in the price of an item is $16.25, what is the cost of the item?
14. $6.75 is 5% of what amount?
15. 34% of what number is 24?
16. Write a proportion to solve each of the following equations:
    a.60% of p is 9.   **b.** 20% of n is 80.   **c.** 4% of x is 36.

Answers to Selected Exercises

1. $300   **2**. 218.18   **8a.** $\dfrac{30}{100} = \dfrac{4}{x}$ **8d.** $\dfrac{2}{100} = \dfrac{64}{k}$

REAL WORLD APPLICATIONS - WORD PROBLEMS
Finding a Number When a Percent of it is Known

Example 1
A shirt was sold on a sale at 20% reduction. If the amount of the reduction was $10. what was the original price of the shirt?
Solution
Using the rule, the original price of the shirt can be found by dividing the reduction amount by the percent of the reduction, as shown:

$$\frac{\$10}{20\%} = \frac{\$10}{\frac{20}{100}} \qquad \text{Note that } 20\% = \frac{20}{100}$$

$$= \$10 \div \frac{20}{100} \qquad \text{Review Division by Fractions.}$$

$$= \$10 \times \frac{100}{20} \qquad \text{Review Division by Fractions, } \frac{20}{100} \text{ is inverted.}$$

To divide by a fraction is the same as multiplying by the reciprocal of the fraction.

$$= \$10 \times \frac{\overset{5}{\cancel{100}}}{\underset{1}{\cancel{20}}} \qquad \text{Divide by 20.}$$

$$= \$10 \times 5 = \$50$$

Therefore, the original price of the shirt is $50.

Example 2

Mr. Apreaku earns a commission of 10.2% on sales. If he earns $98.65 in commission, find the amount of his sales.

Solution

Using the rule, the amount of the sale can be found by dividing the commission earned by the percent of the commission, as shown:

$$\frac{\$98.65}{10.2\%} = \frac{\$98.65}{\dfrac{10.2}{100}} \qquad \text{Note that } 10.2\% = \frac{10.2}{100}$$

$$= \$98.65 \div \frac{10.2}{100} \qquad \text{Review Division by Fractions.}$$

$$= \$98.65 \times \frac{100}{10.2} \qquad \text{Review Division by Fractions, } \frac{10.2}{100} \text{ is inverted.}$$

$$= \$967.156 \qquad \text{Once you setup the solution, you may use a calculator to calculate the final answer.}$$

Therefore, the amount of his sale was $967.16 to the nearest cent.

Example 3

If 45% of the students in a school are girls, and there are 490 girls, find the total number of students.

Solution

Using the rule, divide the number of girls by the percent of the girls to obtain the total number of students.

$$\frac{490}{45\%} = \frac{490}{\dfrac{45}{100}} \qquad \text{Note that } 45\% = \frac{45}{100}$$

$$= 490 \div \frac{45}{100}$$

$$= 490 \times \frac{100}{45} \qquad \text{Review Division by Fractions, } \frac{45}{100} \text{ is inverted.}$$

$$\qquad\qquad\qquad \text{To divide by a fraction is the same as to multiply by the reciprocal of the fraction.}$$

$$= 490 \times \frac{\overset{20}{\cancel{100}}}{\underset{9}{\cancel{45}}}$$

$$= \frac{490 \times 20}{9} = 1088.8 \qquad \text{(You may use a calculator)}$$

The total number of students is 1089 to the nearest whole number

Exercise

1. A computer part was on sale at a 15% reduction. If the amount of the reduction was $30.00, what was the original price of the computer part? Hint: See Example 1.
2. Mr. Wilson earns a commission of 8.5% of sales. If he earns $425.00 in commission, find the amount of his sales. Hint: See Example 2.
3. If 60% of the students in a school are girls and there are 300 girls in the school, what is the total number of students in the school? Round your answer to the nearest whole number. Hint: See Example 3.

Challenge Questions

4. If 35% of the students in a school study geography, and there are 275 students who study geography, how many students are in the school? Round your answer to the nearest whole number.
5. Mrs. Collins earns a commission of 12.5% on sales. If she earns $65.75 in commission, find the amount of her sales.
6. An advanced calculator was on sale at a 5% reduction. If the amount of the reduction was $15.25, what was the original price of the calculator?

REAL WORLD APPLICATIONS - WORD PROBLEMS
Percent of Increase or Decrease

The percent of increase or decrease is the increase or decrease expressed as a percent.

Percent of Increase
Example 1
Mary was making $5.00 per hour for baby–sitting and her earnings has been increased to $6.0 per hour. What is the percent of the increase?
Solution
Step 1: Her increase per hour can be calculated by subtracting her original earning per hour from her new earning per hour as shown:

Increase per hour = New earnings per hour – original earning per hour
$$= \$6.00 - \$5.00$$
$$= \$1.00$$

Step 2: Fraction of the increase per hour is calculated by dividing the increase per hour by the original earning per hour as shown:

Fraction of increase per hour $= \dfrac{\textbf{Increase per hour}}{\textbf{Original earning per hour}}$

$$= \frac{\$1.00}{\$5.00} = \frac{1}{5}$$

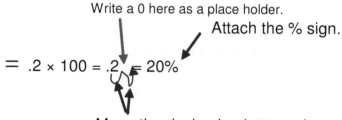

Therefore, the decimal fraction of increase = .2

Step 3: Change the fraction of increase to percent by moving the decimal point of the decimal fraction of the increase 2 places or two digits to the right which is the same as multiplying the decimal fraction of the increase by 100.

Percent increase = decimal fraction of increase × 100

$$= .2 \times 100$$

Write a 0 here as a place holder.

Attach the % sign.

$$= .2 \times 100 = .2 = 20\%$$

Move the decimal point two places or two digits to the right.

Therefore, the percent increase = 20%

Rule 1: To find the percent of increase, divide the increase by the original number, and then move the decimal point 2 places to the right or multiply the quotient by 100, and attach the % sign.

Example 2

What are the 3 major steps in finding the percent of increase?

Solution

The 3 major steps in finding percent of increase are:

Step 1: Find the increase by subtracting the original number from the new number.

Step 2: Find the fraction of the increase by dividing the increase by the original number.

Step 3: Change the fraction of the increase to percent by moving the decimal point 2 places or two digits to the right or by multiplying the quotient by 100.

Example 3

The weekly allowance of George was increased from $10 to $12. What is the percent of increase?

Solution

Step 1: Find the increase in his allowance by subtracting the original allowance from the new allowance.

$$\text{Increase} = \textbf{New allowance} - \textbf{Original allowance}$$
$$= \$12 - \$10$$
$$= \$2$$

Step 2: Find the fraction of the increase by dividing the increase by the original allowance as shown:

$$\textbf{Fraction of the increase} = \frac{\textbf{Increase}}{\textbf{Original allowance}}$$

$$= \frac{\$2}{\$10} = \frac{2}{10}$$

$$\frac{2}{10} = 10\overline{)2.0}$$
$$\underline{-2\,0}$$
$$00$$

$$= .2 \quad \text{This is the decimal fraction of the increase.}$$

Step 3: Change the decimal fraction of the increase to a percent by moving the decimal point of the decimal fraction of the increase two places or two digits to the right, and then attach the % sign, which is the same as multiplying the decimal fraction of the increase by 100.

Write a 0 here as a place holder.

Attach the % sign.

$$.2 = .2\,0 = 20\%$$

Move the decimal point two places or two digits to the right.

The percent of increase = 20 %.

Alternative method: Shortcut method for percent of increase.

When the students understand the steps for finding the percent of increase, the students may use shortcut in solving the problems. The formula is:

$$\textbf{Percent of increase} = \frac{\textbf{Increase}}{\textbf{Original number}} \times \textbf{100}$$

Let us solve Example 3 using the shortcut method.

$$\textbf{Percent of increase} = \frac{\textbf{Increase}}{\textbf{Original number}} \times \textbf{100}$$

$$= \frac{2}{10} \times 100$$

$$= \frac{2}{\underset{1}{\cancel{10}}} \times \overset{10}{\cancel{100}} \qquad \text{Divide by 10.}$$

$$= 2 \times 10 = 20\%$$

Therefore, the percent of increase = 20%.

Note that the shortcut method is useful when the numerators can be divided by the denominators evenly so that there will be no decimal fractions involved.

Group Exercise

The class should be divided into four groups and each group should solve Example 1 using the shortcut method, and then report their solution to the whole class.

Rule 2: The formula for finding the percent of increase is:

$$\textbf{Percent of increase} = \frac{\textbf{Increase}}{\textbf{Original number}} \times \textbf{100}$$

Percent of Decrease

Example 4

Joyce was making $5.00 per hour for baby-sitting. Her earnings were decreased to $3.00 per hour. What is the percent of decrease in her earnings per hour?

Solution

Step 1: The decrease in her payment can be calculated by subtracting her original earnings per hour from her new earnings per hour.

$$\textbf{Decrease} = \textbf{New payment per hour} - \textbf{Original payment per hour}$$
$$= \$5.00 - \$3.00 = \$2.00$$

Step 2: The fraction of the decrease is calculated by dividing the decreased amount per hour by the original earnings per hour.

$$\textbf{Fraction of the decrease} = \frac{\textbf{Decrease amount per hour}}{\textbf{Original payment per hour}}$$

$$= \frac{\$2.00}{\$5.00} = \frac{2}{5}$$

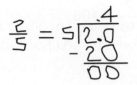

$$\frac{2}{5} = 5\overline{)2.0}$$

Fraction of the decrease = .4   Note that .4 is the decimal fraction of the decrease.

Step 3: Change the decimal fraction of the decrease to a percent by moving the decimal point of the decimal fraction two places or two digits to the right, and then attach the % sign, which is the same as multiplying the decimal fraction of the decrease by 100.

Write a 0 here as a place holder.

Attach the % sign.

.4 = .4 = 40%

Move the decimal point two places or two digits to the right.

Therefore, the percent of decrease in her earnings per hour is 40%.

Rule 3: To find the percent of decrease, divide the decrease by the original number, and move the decimal point two places or two digits to the right, and then attach the % sign, which is the same as multiplying the quotient by 100.

Example 5
What are the 3 major steps in finding the percent of a decrease?

Solution
The 3 major steps for finding the percent of the decrease are:

Step 1: Find the decrease by subtracting the original number from the new number.

Step 2: Find the fraction of the decrease by dividing the decreased amount by the original number.

Step 3: Change the decimal fraction of the decrease to a percent by moving the decimal point two places or two digits to the right, which is the same as multiplying the decimal fraction of the decrease by 100.

Shortcut method for percent decrease - Group exercise
When the students understand the steps for finding the percent of decrease, the student may use the shortcut in solving the problems. The formula is:

$$\text{Percent of decrease} = \frac{\text{Decrease}}{\text{Original number}} \times 100$$

Rule 4: The formula for finding the percent of decrease is:

$$\text{Percent of decrease} = \frac{\text{Decrease}}{\text{Original number}} \times 100$$

Divide the class into four groups and each group should solve Example 4 using the shortcut method and then report their solution to the class.

Example 6

The weekly allowance of Grace was reduced from $15.00 to $12.00. What is the percent of reduction in her weekly allowance?

Solution

Step 1: Find the reduction in her allowance by subtracting the new allowance from the original allowance.

Reduction in allowance = Original allowance − New allowance

$$= \$15.00 - \$12.00$$
$$= \$3.00$$

Step 2: Find the fraction of the reduction by dividing the reduction in allowance by the original allowance.

$$\textbf{Fraction of the reduction} = \frac{\textbf{Reduction}}{\textbf{Original allowance}}$$

$$= \frac{\$3.00}{\$15.00} = \frac{3}{15}$$

$$\frac{3}{15} = 15\overline{)3.0} \quad \begin{array}{r} .2 \\ -30 \\ \hline 00 \end{array}$$

The fraction of the reduction = .2. **Note** that .2 is the decimal fraction of the reduction.

Step 3: Change the decimal fraction of the reduction to a percent by moving the decimal point of the decimal fraction of the reduction two places or two digits to the right, and then attach the % sign, which is the same as multiplying the decimal fraction of the reduction by 100.

Write a 0 here as a place holder

Attach the % sign.

$$.2 = .2 = 20\%$$

Move the decimal point two places or two digits to the right.

The percent of reduction is 20%

Alternative Method - Shortcut Method.

Let us solve Example 6 using the shortcut method.

$$\text{Percent of reduction} = \frac{\text{Reduction}}{\text{Original number}} \times 100$$

$$= \frac{\$3.00}{\$15.00} \times 100$$

$$= \frac{\overset{1}{\cancel{\$3.00}}}{\underset{1}{\cancel{\$15.00}}} \times \overset{20}{\cancel{100}} \qquad \text{Divide by 3 and then by 5.}$$

$$= 20\%$$

Therefore, the percent of reduction = 20%.

Note that the shortcut method is useful when the numerator can be divided by the denominator evenly so that the quotient will not be a decimal fraction.

Group Project

The class should be divided into four groups. Each group should cut four sale coupons from the newspaper and bring them to school. Each group should use the sale coupons to make the table below. Each group should calculate the percent of decrease in price.

Items	Original price	Amount saved by coupon	Percent of decrease
Bread			
Cereal			
Medicine			
Kool–Aid			

Which group found the highest percent of reduction? Compare the group exercise to Examples 1 to 6. Each group should list the similarities and differences between the group exercise and the Examples 1 to 6.

Exercises

1. $20 is increased to $24, what is the percent of increase? Hint: See Examples 1, 2, and 3.
2. $45 is increased to $54, what is the percent of increase? Hint: See Examples 1, 2, and 3.
3. Two weeks ago, John was given 6 oranges. Last week, he was given 8 oranges. What is the percent of increase of the oranges? Hint: See Examples 1, 2, and 3.
4. Two months ago, Mr. Johnson was paid $230 and last month, he was paid $245. What is the percent of increase in his payment? Hint: See Examples 1, 2, and 3.
5. Maggie earned $16,500 last year, and this year she will earn $17,000. What is the

percent of increase? Hint: See Examples 1, 2, and 3.

6. The population of a school last year was 535 students. This year, the enrollment is 643 students. What is the percent of increase? Hint: See Examples 1, 2, and 3.

7. Mrs. Jackson bought a car for $10,000 and she sold it for $12,000. What was the percent of profit? Hint: Percent profit is the same as percent of increase. See Examples 1, 2, and 3.

8. Rebecca's rent was increased from $595 to $610. What was the percent of increase? Hint: See Examples 1, 2, and 3.

9. What is the percent of decrease if:
   (a) $12 is decreased to $7? Hint: See Example 4 and 5.
   (b) $15 is decreased to $9? Hint: See Example 4 and 5.
   (c) $150 is decreased to $140? Hint: See Example 4 and 5.
   (d) $348 is decreased to $292? Hint: See Example 4 and 5.

10. Last year, Samuel was paid $6 per hour for baby-sitting. This year, he is being paid $4 per hour for baby-sitting. What is the percent of decrease? Hint: See Examples 4 and 5.

11. Mr. Collins weighed 190 pounds and after dieting for nine months, his weight was 175 pounds. What percent of his weight did he lose? Hint: See Examples 4 and 5.

12. A computer part selling for $120.00 was reduced to $100.00. What was the percent of decrease? Hint: See Examples 4, 5, and 6.

Challenge Questions

13. The enrollment of the students in a school decreased from 455 students to 395 students. What is the percent of decrease?

14. Mr. Watson bought a car for $15,440 and sold it for $16,000. What is the percent of increase?

15. Nick's rent was $725 last year. This year, his rent is $750. What is the percent of increase in his rent?

16. A furniture set, which was selling for $1,250, was reduced to $1,200. What is the percent of the reduction?

17. Two years ago, Amanda saved $400, and last year she saved $425. What is the percent of increase?

Answers to Selected Exercises

1. 20%   5. 3.03%   9(a) 41.67%   11. 7.89%

Cumulative Review

1. Find: (Round your answer to 2 decimal places).
   (a) 2 out of 125   (b) 5% of 100   (c) 15% of 52.50

2. Change each percent to a decimal. Round the answer to 2 decimal places.

(a) 1% (b) $8\frac{1}{2}$% (c) 120%

(d) 15% (e) 12% (f) 45%

3. Write the following ratios as percents. Round your answer to 2 decimal places.
   (a) 2 out of 5 (b) 9 out of 10 (c) 8 out of 20
   (d) 7 out of 49 (e) 15 out of 125 (f) 3 out of 12

4. Change each decimal to a percent. Round your answer to 2 decimal places.
   (a) .5 (b) .48 (c) .34
   (d) 4.98 (e) .08 (f) .002
   (g) .7 (h) 1.25 (i) .041

5. Round the following answers to 2 decimal places.
   (a) 25 is what percent of 125?
   (b) Find what percent 15 is of 100?
   (c) 12% of what amount is $150?
   (d) If 45% of a number is 200, find the number.
   (e) $\frac{2}{5}$% of what number is 75?

6. Find the percent of increase or decrease. Round off to 1 decimal place.
   (a) A school's enrollment of 425 students increased to 475 students.
   (b) John's expenses increased from $225 per week to $310 per week .
   (c) Gertrude's weight decreased from 170 pounds to 140 pounds.

More Cumulative Review

1. Change the following to decimal fractions. Round off each answer to the nearest hundredth.

   (a) $\frac{1}{5}$ (b) $\frac{9}{10}$ (c) $\frac{4}{7}$ (d) $\frac{3}{8}$ (e) $\frac{5}{12}$

   (f) $\frac{4}{9}$ (g) $\frac{5}{14}$ (h) $\frac{5}{9}$ (i) $\frac{2}{7}$ (j) $\frac{13}{15}$

2. $120 \div .24 =$ 3. $5.04 \times .09 =$ 4. $.91 + 784.1 =$

5. $91 - 7.989 =$ 6. $45.381 - 2.492 =$ 7. $.41 \times .98 =$

8. $\frac{1}{2} \div \frac{1}{2} =$ 9. $\frac{3}{4} \div \frac{3}{8} =$ 10. $\frac{5}{7} \times \frac{14}{2} =$

11. $.4 \div 10 =$ 12. $18.7 \times 100 =$ 13. $78 \times 10 =$

(c) From the chapter on prime factorization, Example 2, the prime factors of 60 are:
$$2 \cdot 2 \cdot 3 \cdot 5.$$
Therefore, the exponential form of 60 is:
$$60 = 2 \cdot 2 \cdot 3 \cdot 5 = 2^2 \cdot 3 \cdot 5$$

Standard form.   Exponential form

Example 3
(a) Find the value of 4^3
(b) Find the value of 3^4
(c) Find the value of $2 \cdot 3^2$
(d) $2 \cdot 3^2 \cdot 4^2 =$
(e) Find the value of $2^2 \cdot 3 \cdot 5^2$

Solution
(a) $4^3 = 4 \times 4 \times 4 = 64$
(b) $3^4 = 3 \times 3 \times 3 \times 3 = 81$
(c) $2 \cdot 3^2 = 2 \times 3 \times 3 = 18$
(d) $2 \cdot 3^2 \cdot 4^2 = 2 \times 3 \times 3 \times 4 \times 4 = 288$
(e) $2^2 \cdot 3 \cdot 5^2 = 2 \times 2 \times 3 \times 5 \times 5 = 300$

Example 4
(a) Find the value of 6^1
(b) Find the value of 4^0
(c) Find the value of $6^1 \cdot 4^0 \cdot 2^2$
(e) Find the value of $3^0 \cdot 20^0 \cdot x^0$

Solution
(a) $6^1 = 6$
(b) $4^0 = 1$ **Notice that any number to the power of 0 is equal to 1, therefore, $4^0 = 1$.**
(c) $6^1 \cdot 4^0 \cdot 2^2 = 6 \times 1 \times 2 \times 2 = 24$ Note $4^0 = 1$
(d) $2^0 \cdot 5^1 \cdot 6^2 = 1 \times 5 \times 6 \times 6 = 180$ Note $2^0 = 1$
(e) $3^0 \cdot 20^0 \cdot x^0 = 1 \times 1 \times 1 = 1$ Note $3^0 = 1$, $20^0 = 1$, $x^0 = 1$

Example 5
Complete each equation:
(a) $a \cdot a \cdot b \cdot b \cdot b = a^2?$

(b) $2 \cdot 2 \cdot 3 \cdot 5 \cdot 5 = 2^2 \cdot 3$?

(c) $2 \cdot x \cdot 4 \cdot y \cdot x = 8x^2$?

(d) $3 \cdot x \cdot y \cdot 2 \cdot y = ?x?$

(e) $a^0 \cdot 4 = ? \cdot 4$

(f) $a^0 \cdot b^0 \cdot 3 \cdot 3 \cdot 4 = ? ? 3^2 \cdot 4$

Solution
(a) $a \cdot a \cdot b \cdot b \cdot b = a^2 b^3$ (b^3 because there are 3 bases of b).

113

(a² because there are 2 bases of a).

(b) $2 \cdot 2 \cdot 3 \cdot 5 \cdot 5 = 2^2 \cdot 3 \cdot 5^2$ (5² because there are 2 bases of 5).

(2² because there are 2 bases of 2).

(3 because there is 1 base of 3).

(c) $2 \cdot x \cdot 4 \cdot y \cdot x = 8x^2y$ (y because there is 1 base of y).

(x² because there are 2 bases of x).

(8 because 2 · 4 = 8).

(d) $3 \cdot x \cdot y \cdot 2 \cdot y = 6xy^2$ (6 and y² because 3 × 2 = 6 and there are 2 bases of y).

(x because there is 1 base of x).

(e) $a^0 \cdot 4 = 1 \cdot 4$ (Note: $a^0 = 1$)

(f) $a^0 \cdot b^0 \cdot 3 \cdot 3 \cdot 4 = 1 \cdot 1 \cdot 3^2 \cdot 4$ (Note: $a^0 = 1$, and $b^0 = 1$)

(3² because there are 2 bases of 3).

Exercises

1. Explain what is meant by the base and the exponent of a number in the exponential form.

2. How do you read the following: Hint: See Example 1.

(a) 2^5 (b) 3^4 (c) 10^3 (d) 100^2

(e) 9^1 (f) 12^3 (g) 5^3 (h) 2^6

3. Write the following in the exponential form. Hint: See Example 2.

(a) 9   (b) 12   (c) 16   (d) 18   (e) 20

(f) 32   (g) 45   (h) 25   (i) 36   (j) 27

(k) 21   (l) 27   (m) 35   (n) 99   (o) 64

4. Find the following values. Hint: See Example 3.

(a) 2^4 (b) 8^2 (c) $2^3 \cdot 3^2$ (d) $3^2 \cdot 4^2$

(e) $2 \cdot 3^2 \cdot 5^2$ (f) $2^2 \cdot 4 \cdot 5^2$ (g) $2 \cdot 3^2 \cdot 4$ (h) $2^3 \cdot 3 \cdot 4^2$

(i) $3 \cdot 4 \cdot 5^2$ (j) $2 \cdot 3^2 \cdot 6$ (k) $2 \cdot 2 \cdot 4^2$ (l) $2^2 \cdot 3^2 \cdot 4$

(m) 10^2 (n) 9^2 (o) $2 \cdot 10^3$ (p) $3^2 \cdot 8^2$

5. Find the following values. See Example 4.

(a) 100^0 (b) 9^1 (c) $2^0 \cdot 3^2$ (d) $2^2 \cdot 4^0 \cdot 5^1$

(e) $2^2 \cdot 3 \cdot 4^2$ (f) $2^3 \cdot 3^0 \cdot 4^2$ (g) $3^2 \cdot 5^0 \cdot 6^2$ (h) $4^0 \cdot 2^2 \cdot 3^2$

(i) $2^0 \cdot 3^1 \cdot 5^0$ (j) $6^0 \cdot 10^0 \cdot 15^0$ (k) $2^0 \cdot 3^0 \cdot 5^0$ (l) $2^2 \cdot 6^2 \cdot 9^0$

(m) $3^2 \cdot 5^0 \cdot 8^0$ (n) $2^3 \cdot 3^2 \cdot 4^0$ (o) $100^0 \cdot 200^0 \cdot 300^0$ (p) $10^2 \cdot 4^2$

6. Complete each equation. See Example 5.

(a) $a \cdot a \cdot b \cdot b = a^2$?   (b) $2 \cdot 3 \cdot 3 \cdot 5 = 2 \cdot ? \cdot 5$ (c) $2 \cdot 2 \cdot 2 \cdot x \cdot x = ? \, x^2$

(d) $3 \cdot x \cdot 2 \cdot y \cdot x = ? \cdot x^2 \cdot y$ (e) $2 \cdot a \cdot b \cdot 3 \cdot a \cdot = 6 \, ? \, b$ (f) $4 \cdot x \cdot y \cdot 2 \cdot y = 8 \, x$?

(g) $a \cdot a \cdot a \cdot b = ? \, b$ (h) $3 \cdot a \cdot x \cdot 4 \cdot a \cdot x = ? \, a^2$?   (i) $a^0 \cdot b^0 \cdot 2 \cdot 2 = 1 \, ? \, 2^2$

(j) $2 \cdot 2 \cdot 4^0 \cdot a^0 = 2^2 \cdot ? \cdot 1$ (k) $x^0 \cdot y^0 \cdot z^0 = ? \, ? \, ?$ (l) $4 \cdot y \cdot x \cdot b \cdot 2 \cdot y \cdot b = ? \, ? \, x \, y^2$

Challenge Questions

7. Find the value.

    (a) $7^2 \cdot 9^0 =$ (b) 150^0 (c) $2^0 \cdot 5^2 \cdot 7^0 =$ (d) $5^2 \cdot a^0 \cdot b^2$

8. Complete the equation.

   (a) $3 \cdot a \cdot b \cdot a \cdot b = 3a^2$?   (b) $4 \cdot a \cdot b \cdot 3 \cdot a \cdot b = ? \, a^2 b^2$

Answers to Selected Questions

  3(a). 3^2 4(a). 16   5(a). 1

EXPONENTS

An exponent shows how many times a base is used as a factor. For example,

$$1000 = 10 \cdot 10 \cdot 10 = 10^3$$

exponent

10 is the base
3 is the exponent

base

The exponent of 3 shows that the base which is 10 is used as a factor of 1000 three times. "10^3" is read as "10 to the third power or "10 cubed."

Multiplying Powers With the Same Base

The factors of any power such as 5^4 may be grouped in different ways as shown:

$5 \cdot 5 \cdot 5 \cdot 5 = 5^4$ —————————————————————[A]

$(5 \cdot 5 \cdot 5) \cdot 5 = 5^3 \cdot 5^1 = 5^4$ ——————————————[B]

$(5 \cdot 5) \cdot (5 \cdot 5) = 5^2 \cdot 5^2 = 5^4$ ———————————[C]

$5 \cdot (5 \cdot 5 \cdot 5) = 5^1 \cdot 5^3 = 5^4$ ——————————————[D]

By observing equation [A], we can write:

$5 \cdot 5 \cdot 5 \cdot 5 = 5^1 \cdot 5^1 \cdot 5^1 \cdot 5^1 = 5^{1+1+1+1} = 5^4$

By observing equation [B], we can write:

$(5 \cdot 5 \cdot 5) \cdot 5 = 5^3 \cdot 5^1 = 5^{3+1} = 5^4$

By observing equation [C], we can write:

$(5 \cdot 5) \cdot (5 \cdot 5) = 5^2 \cdot 5^2 = 5^{2+2} = 5^4$

By observing equation [D], we can write:

$5 \cdot (5 \cdot 5 \cdot 5) = 5^1 \cdot 5^3 = 5^{1+3} = 5^4$

Therefore, observing equations [A], [B], [C], and [D], to multiply powers with the same base, use the same base, and then add the exponents such that in general,

$\mathbf{b}^m \cdot \mathbf{b}^n = \mathbf{b}^{m+n}$

Example 1

Multiply and write each product as one power.

a. $6^2 \cdot 6^7$ **b.** $7^3 \cdot 3^2$ **c.** $8^3 \cdot 8$ **d.** $4^2 \cdot a^2 \cdot 4^3 \cdot a^5$ **e.** $7^2 \cdot 7^6 \cdot 7^4$

Solution

a. $6^2 \cdot 6^7 = 6^{2+7}$ Add the exponents since the bases 6 and 6 are the same.

$\qquad\qquad\qquad\qquad$ Generally, $\mathbf{b}^m \cdot \mathbf{b}^n = \mathbf{b}^{m+n}$

$\qquad\quad = 6^9$ $2 + 7 = 9$

b. $7^3 \cdot 3^2 = 7^3 \cdot 3^2$ The bases 7 and 3 are not the same so their exponents cannot be combined.

c. $8^3 \cdot 8 = 8^3 \cdot 8^1$ 8 is the same as 8^1

$\qquad\quad = 8^{3+1}$ Add the exponents since the bases 8 and 8 are the same.

$\qquad\qquad\qquad\qquad$ Generally, $\mathbf{b}^m \cdot \mathbf{b}^n = \mathbf{b}^{m+n}$

$\qquad\quad = 8^4$ $3 + 1 = 4$

d. $4^2 \cdot a^2 \cdot 4^3 \cdot a^5 = (4^2 \cdot 4^3) \cdot (a^2 \cdot a^5)$ Grouping the like bases together.

$\qquad\qquad\qquad\quad = 4^{2+3} \cdot a^{2+5}$ Add the exponents of the like bases.

$\qquad\qquad\qquad\quad = 4^5 \cdot a^7$ $2 + 3 = 5$ and $2 + 5 = 7$. The bases **4** and **a** are not the same so we cannot combine them.

e. $7^2 \cdot 7^6 \cdot 7^4 = 7^{2+6+4}$ Add the exponents because the bases 7, 7, and 7 are the same.

$\qquad\qquad\quad = 7^{12}$ $2 + 6 + 4 = 12$.

Example 2

Multiply using exponents.

a. $9^3 \cdot x^4 \cdot 2^4 \cdot 9 \cdot x^3 \cdot 2^n$

b. $n^2 \cdot k^3 \cdot n^4 \cdot k^2 \cdot n$

Solution

a. $9^3 \cdot x^4 \cdot 2^4 \cdot 9 \cdot x^3 \cdot 2^n = (9^3 \cdot 9) \cdot (x^4 \cdot x^3) \cdot (2^4 \cdot 2^n)$ Grouping the like bases.

$\qquad\qquad\qquad\qquad\quad = (9^3 \cdot 9^1) \cdot (x^4 \cdot x^3) \cdot (2^4 \cdot 2^n)$ **Note**: 9 is the same as 9^1.

$\qquad\qquad\qquad\qquad\quad = 9^{3+1} \cdot x^{4+3} \cdot 2^{4+n}$ Add the exponents of the like bases.

$\qquad\qquad\qquad\qquad\quad = 9^4 \cdot x^7 \cdot 2^{4+n}$ We can no longer combine the exponents because the bases 9, x, and 2 are not the same.

b. $n^2 \cdot k^3 \cdot n^4 \cdot k^2 \cdot n = (n^2 \cdot n^4 \cdot n) \cdot (k^3 \cdot k^2)$ Grouping the like bases of n and k.

$\qquad\qquad\qquad\qquad = (n^2 \cdot n^4 \cdot n^1) \cdot (k^3 \cdot k^2)$ **Note**: n is the same as n^1.

$$= n^{2+4+1} \cdot k^{3+2} \qquad \text{Add the exponents of the like bases.}$$
$$= n^7 \cdot k^5 \qquad \text{We can no longer combine the exponents}$$
because the bases n and k are not the same.

Dividing Powers With the Same Base

Let us observe what happens when we divide powers with the same base as shown:

$$\frac{4^6}{4^4} = \frac{4 \cdot 4 \cdot 4 \cdot 4 \cdot 4 \cdot 4}{4 \cdot 4 \cdot 4 \cdot 4} = \frac{\cancel{4} \cdot \cancel{4} \cdot \cancel{4} \cdot \cancel{4} \cdot 4 \cdot 4}{\cancel{4} \cdot \cancel{4} \cdot \cancel{4} \cdot \cancel{4}} = 4 \cdot 4 = 4^2 \qquad \underline{\qquad}[A]$$

It should then be observed from equation $[A]$ that $\dfrac{4^6}{4^4} = 4^{6-4} = 4^2$

Therefore, to divide powers with the same base, use the same base, and then subtract the exponents, such that in general $\dfrac{b^m}{b^n} = b^{m-n}$, and $b \neq 0$. The symbol $\neq$ means "is not equal to." Note that $b \neq 0$ because if $b = 0$, then $\dfrac{b^m}{b^n} = \dfrac{0^m}{0^n}$, but it is impossible to divide by 0.

Example 3

Divide and write each quotient as one power.

a. $\dfrac{6^5}{6^3}$ b. $\dfrac{n^5}{n^2}$ c. $\dfrac{m^6}{n^4}$

Solution

a. $\dfrac{6^5}{6^3} = 6^{5-3} = 6^2$ Subtract the exponents since the bases 6 and 6 are the same. Generally, $\dfrac{b^m}{b^n} = b^{m-n}$, $b \neq 0$.

b. $\dfrac{n^5}{n^2} = n^{5-2} = n^3$ Subtract the exponents since the bases n and n are the same. Generally, $\dfrac{b^m}{b^n} = b^{m-n}$, $b \neq 0$.

c. $\dfrac{m^6}{n^4}$ Cannot combine the exponents because the bases m and n are not the same.

Example 4

Simplify each expression. Your answer should be in exponents.

a. $\dfrac{3^4 \cdot n^6}{n^2 \cdot 3^2}$ **b.** $\dfrac{x^7 \cdot y^8 \cdot 2^8}{y^6 \cdot 2^5 \cdot x^3}$ **c.** $\dfrac{12^7 \cdot n^6 \cdot y^5 \cdot x^4}{12^4 \cdot y^2 \cdot x \cdot k^2}$

Solution

a. $\dfrac{3^4 \cdot n^6}{n^2 \cdot 3^2} = 3^{4-2} \cdot n^{6-2}$ 　　　Subtract the exponents of the like bases.

$$\dfrac{3^4}{3^2} = 3^{4-2}, \dfrac{n^6}{n^2} = n^{6-2}. \text{ Generally, } \dfrac{b^m}{b^n} = b^{m-n}, b \neq 0.$$

$$= 3^2 \cdot n^4 \qquad\qquad 4 - 2 = 2 \text{ and } 6 - 2 = 4.$$

b. $\dfrac{x^7 \cdot y^8 \cdot 2^8}{y^6 \cdot 2^5 \cdot x^3} = x^{7-3} \cdot y^{8-6} \cdot 2^{8-5}$ 　　　Subtract the exponents of the like bases.

$$\dfrac{x^7}{x^3} = x^{7-3}, \dfrac{y^8}{y^6} = y^{8-6}, \dfrac{2^8}{2^5} = 2^{8-5}$$

$$= x^4 \cdot y^2 \cdot 2^3 \qquad\qquad 7 - 3 = 4, \, 8 - 6 = 2 \text{ and } 8 - 5 = 3.$$

c. $\dfrac{12^7 \cdot n^6 \cdot y^5 \cdot x^4}{12^4 \cdot y^2 \cdot x \cdot k^2} = \dfrac{12^{7-4} \cdot n^6 \cdot y^{5-2} \cdot x^{4-1}}{k^2}$ 　　　Subtract the exponents of

the like bases.

$$= \dfrac{12^3 \cdot n^6 \cdot y^3 \cdot x^3}{k^2} \qquad \text{For example: } \dfrac{12^7}{12^4} = 12^{7-4} = 12^3$$

$$\dfrac{y^5}{y^2} = y^{5-2} = y^3$$

$$\dfrac{x^4}{x} = \dfrac{x^4}{x^1} = x^{4-1} = x^3$$

Note that $x = x^1$.

Zero Power

It can be shown that 1 can be expressed as a fraction with the numerator and the denominator of the fraction having the same base and the same exponents and subtracting the exponents will result in a zero exponent as follows:

$$1 = \dfrac{3^2}{3^2} = 3^{2-2} = 3^0$$

Therefore, $1 = 3^0$

Therefore, the zero power of any number except 0 equals 1 such that in general **$b^0 = 1$ and $b \neq 0$.**

Example 5

Evaluate

a. 7^0 **b.** $5^6 \, 5^{-6}$ **c.** $\dfrac{10^4}{10^4}$ **d.** $\dfrac{n^5}{n^5}$

e. $\dfrac{12^7 \cdot y^5 \cdot 4^3}{12^7 \cdot y^5 \cdot 4^2}$ **f.** $\dfrac{4^5 \cdot 3^4 \cdot n^9 \cdot 3^{-4}}{4^5 \cdot n^9}$

Solution

a. $7^0 = 1$ The zero power of any number except 0 equals 1.

b. $5^6 \cdot 5^{-6} = 5^{6 + (-6)}$ To multiply powers with the same base, use the same base, and then add the exponents such that in general, $\mathbf{b}^m \cdot \mathbf{b}^n = \mathbf{b}^{m+n}$.

$5^6 \cdot 5^{-6} = 5^{6-6}$ Note: $+ (- = -$, therefore, $6 + (-6) = 6 - 6$.

$\quad\quad\quad\quad = 5^0$ $6 - 6 = 0$.

$\quad\quad\quad\quad = 1$ The zero power of any number except 0 is 1.

c. $\dfrac{10^4}{10^4} = 10^{4-4}$ To divide powers with the same base, use the same base and then subtract the exponents such that in general $\dfrac{b^m}{b^n} = b^{m-n}$ and $b \neq 0$.

$\quad\quad\quad = 10^0$ $4 - 4 = 0$

$\quad\quad\quad = 1$ The zero power of any number except 0 is 1

d. $\dfrac{n^5}{n^5} = n^{5-5}$ To divide powers with the same base, use the same base and then subtract the exponents such that in general $\dfrac{b^m}{b^n} = b^{m-n}$, and $b \neq 0$.

$\quad\quad\quad = n^0$ $5 - 5 = 0$.

$\quad\quad\quad = 1$ The zero power of any number except 0 is 1.

e. $\dfrac{12^7 \cdot y^5 \cdot 4^3}{12^7 \cdot y^5 \cdot 4^2} = 12^{7-7} \cdot y^{5-5} \cdot 4^{3-2}$ To divide powers with the same base, use the same base and then subtract the exponents such that in general

$$\frac{b^m}{b^n} = b^{m-n} \text{ and } x \neq 0.$$

$= 12^0 \cdot y^0 \cdot 4^1$ 　　　　$7 - 7 = 0, 5 - 5 = 0, \text{ and } 3 - 2 = 1.$

$= 1 \cdot 1 \cdot 4$ 　　　　　　$12^0 = 1, y^0 = 1, \text{ and } 4^1 = 4.$

$= 4$

f. $\dfrac{4^5 \cdot 3^4 \, n^9 \cdot 3^{-4}}{4^5 \cdot n^9} = 4^{5-5} \cdot 3^{4+(-4)} \cdot n^{9-9}$　To divide powers with the same base, use

the same base, and then subtract the

exponents such that in general $\dfrac{b^m}{b^n} = \mathbf{b}^{m-n}$

and $b \neq 0$. For examples: $\dfrac{4^5}{4^5} = 4^{5-5}$

$$\frac{n^9}{n^9} = n^{9-9}$$

To multiply powers with the same base, use
the same base, and then add the exponents
such that in general $b^m \cdot b^n = b^{m+n}$.
For example: $3^4 \cdot 3^{-4} = 3^{4+(-4)}$.

$= 4^0 \cdot 3^{4-4} \cdot n^0$ 　　　Note: $+ \, (- = -$, for example: $\quad 3^{4+(-4)} = 3^{4-4}$.

$= 4^0 \cdot 3^0 \cdot n^0$ 　　　　$5 - 5 = 0, 4 - 4 = 0, \text{ and } 9 - 9 = 0.$

$= 1 \cdot 1 \cdot 1$ 　　　　　　The zero power of any number except 0 is 1.

$= 1$

Negative Exponents and Dividing With Exponent.

We can show that $10^{-1} = \dfrac{1}{10}$ as shown:

$$\frac{10^2}{10^3} = \frac{10 \cdot 10}{10 \cdot 10 \cdot 10}$$

$$\frac{10^2}{10^3} = \frac{\overset{1}{\cancel{10}} \cdot \overset{1}{\cancel{10}}}{\underset{1}{\cancel{10}} \cdot \underset{1}{\cancel{10}} \cdot 10} \qquad\qquad \text{Divide by 10}$$

$$\frac{10^2}{10^3} = \frac{1}{10} \rule[0.5ex]{4cm}{0.4pt}[\text{A}]$$

But $\dfrac{10^2}{10^3} = 10^{2-3}$ $\qquad$ To divide powers with the same base, use the same

base, and then subtract the exponents such that in

general $\dfrac{b^m}{b^n} = b^{m-n}$ and $b \neq 0$. For example,

$$\dfrac{10^2}{10^3} = 10^{2-3}.$$

$\dfrac{10^2}{10^3} = 10^{-1}$ $\rule{4cm}{0.4pt}$ [B]

Note: 2 - 3 = -1.

Comparing equation [A] and equation [B], it can be written that:

$10^{-1} = \dfrac{1}{10^1} = \dfrac{1}{10}$ $\qquad$ Note that equation [A] is the same as equation [B].

Therefore, in general, $b^{-n} = \dfrac{1}{b^n}$ for all real numbers and $b \neq 0$. It can therefore, be

stated in general that: **A base with a negative exponent is equal to I divided by that base with a positive exponent.**

Example 6
Evaluate.

a. 4^{-3} $\quad$ **b.** $(-4)^{-3}$ $\quad$ **c.** $\dfrac{(-4)^2}{(-4)^3}$ $\quad$ **d.** $\dfrac{(6-4)^3}{(9-7)^6}$ $\quad$ **e.** $(4 \cdot 3)^4 \cdot (2 \cdot 6)^{-6}$ $\quad$ **f.** $2^3 \cdot 2^{-2} \cdot 2^{-3}$

Solution

a. $4^{-3} = \dfrac{1}{4^3}$ $\qquad$ In general, $b^{-n} = \dfrac{1}{b^n}$, $b \neq 0$.

$\qquad = \dfrac{1}{4 \cdot 4 \cdot 4}$ $\qquad 4^3 = 4 \cdot 4 \cdot 4$

$\qquad = \dfrac{1}{64}$ $\qquad 4 \cdot 4 \cdot 4 = 64$

b. $(-4)^{-3} = \dfrac{1}{(-4)^3}$ $\qquad$ In general, $b^{-n} = \dfrac{1}{b^n}$, and $b \neq 0$.

$\qquad = \dfrac{1}{(-4) \cdot (-4) \cdot (-4)}$ $\qquad (-4)^3 = (-4) \cdot (-4) \cdot (-4)$

$$= \frac{1}{-64} = -\frac{1}{64}$$

Note: $(-4) \cdot (-4) = +16 = 16$, but $(-4) \cdot (-4) \cdot (-4) = -64$

because the product of odd number negative signs is negative. Therefore, $(-) \cdot (-) \cdot (-) = -$. Hint: Review multiplication involving negative numbers.

c. $\frac{(-4)^2}{(-4)^3} = (-4)^{2-3}$

To divide powers with the same base, use the same base

and then subtract the exponents, such that in general $\frac{b^m}{b^n} = b^{m-n}$ and $b \neq 0$.

 $\frac{(-4)^2}{(-4)^3} = (-4)^{-1}$

Note: $2 - 3 = -1$

$$= \frac{1}{(-4)^1}$$

In general, $b^{-n} = \frac{1}{b^n}$, and $b \neq 0$.

$$= \frac{1}{-4}$$

Note: $\frac{1}{(-4)^1} = \frac{1}{(-4)} = \frac{1}{-4}$ Any number with exponent 1 is

the same number.

d. $\frac{(6-4)^3}{(9-7)^6} = \frac{2^3}{2^6}$

Do the operations inside the parentheses first.

Hint: See the section on the Order of Operations.
$6 - 4 = 2$ and $9 - 7 = 2$.

$$= 2^{3-6}$$

To divide powers with the same base, use the same base, and then subtract the exponents, such that in general $\frac{b^m}{b^n} = b^{m-n}$, and $b \neq 0$.

$$= 2^{-3}$$

$3 - 6 = -3$

$$= \frac{1}{2^3}$$

In general, $b^{-n} = \frac{1}{b^n}$, $b \neq 0$

$$= \frac{1}{2 \cdot 2 \cdot 2}$$

$2^3 = 2 \cdot 2 \cdot 2$

$$= \frac{1}{8}$$

$2 \cdot 2 \cdot 2 = 8$.

e. $(4 \cdot 3)^4 \cdot (2 \cdot 6)^{-6}$ $= 12^4 \cdot 12^{-6}$ Do the operations inside the parentheses first.

$= 12^{4 + (-6)}$

Hint: See the section on order of operations. To multiply powers with the same base, use the same base, and then add the exponents, such that in general, $b^m \cdot b^n = b^{m+n}$

$= 12^{4-6}$

Note: $+ (- = -$, for example, $12^{4 + (-6)} = 12^{4-6}$.

$= 12^{-2}$

$4 - 6 = -2$

$= \dfrac{1}{12^2}$

In general, $b^{-n} = \dfrac{1}{b^n}$, and $b \neq 0$.

$= \dfrac{1}{12 \cdot 12}$

$12^2 = 12 \cdot 12 = 144$.

$= \dfrac{1}{144}$

f. $2^3 \cdot 2^{-2} \cdot 2^{-3} = 2^{3 + (-2) + (-3)}$

To multiply powers with the same base, use the same base, and then add the exponents, such that in general, $b^m \cdot b^n = b^{m+n}$.

$= 2^{3-2-3}$

Note: $+(- = -$, such that $+ (-2) = -2$ and $+ (-3) = -3$.

$= 2^{3-5}$

$-2 - 3 = -5$

$= 2^{-2}$

$3 - 5 = -2$

$= \dfrac{1}{2^2}$

In general, $b^{-n} = \dfrac{1}{b^n}$, and $b \neq 0$.

$= \dfrac{1}{2 \cdot 2}$

$2^2 = 2 \cdot 2$

$= \dfrac{1}{4}$

$2 \cdot 2 = 4$

Example 7

Simplify

$$\dfrac{5}{3^{-2}}$$

Solution

$\dfrac{5}{3^{-2}} = \dfrac{5}{\dfrac{1}{3^2}}$

In general, $b^{-n} = \dfrac{1}{b^n}$, and $b \neq 0$. Therefore, $3^{-2} = \dfrac{1}{3^2}$.

$= 5 \div \dfrac{1}{3^2}$

$$= 5 \times \frac{3^2}{1}$$

To divide by a fraction, multiply by the reciprocal of the fraction. Hint: Review Division by Fractions.

$$= 5 \times 3 \times 3 \qquad 3^2 = 3 \times 3$$
$$= 45$$

Example 8

Simplify. $\dfrac{15x^5y^3}{5x^2y}$

Solution

$$\frac{15x^5y^3}{5x^2y} = \frac{\overset{3}{\cancel{15}}x^5y^3}{\underset{1}{\cancel{5}}x^2y} = \frac{3x^5y^3}{x^2y}$$

Divide the numerical coefficients by 5.

$$= \frac{3x^5y^3}{x^2y} = 3x^{5-2}y^{3-1}$$

Subtract the exponents of the powers

of the denominator from the exponents of the powers with the same base in the numerator. Note that $y = y^1$.

$$= 3x^3y^2$$

Example 9

Simplify. **a.** $\dfrac{-36a^5bc^4}{6a^2bc^3}$ **b.** $\dfrac{18p^5k^9}{-6p^2k^6}$

Solution

a. $\dfrac{-36a^5bc^4}{6a^2bc^3} = \dfrac{\overset{-6}{\cancel{-36}}a^5bc^4}{\underset{1}{\cancel{6}}a^2bc^3} = \dfrac{-6a^5bc^4}{a^2bc^3}$

Divide the numerical coefficients by 6.

$$= \frac{-6a^5bc^4}{a^2bc^3} = -6a^{5-2}b^{1-1}c^{4-3}$$

Subtract the exponents of the powers of the denominator from the exponents of the powers with the same base in the numerator. Note that $b = b^1$.

$$= -6a^3b^0c^1$$
$$= -6a^3 \cdot 1 \cdot c^1 \qquad\qquad b^0 = 1.$$
$$= -6a^3c \qquad\qquad\qquad c^1 = c.$$

b. $\dfrac{18p^5k^9}{-6p^2k^6} = \dfrac{\overset{3}{\cancel{18}}p^5k^9}{\underset{-1}{\cancel{-6}}p^2k^6} = \dfrac{3p^5k^9}{-p^2k^6}$ Divide the numerical coefficients by 6.

$$= -3p^{5-2}k^{9-6}$$

Subtract the exponents of the powers of the denominator from the exponents of the powers with the same base in the numerator. Note that in general, $\dfrac{a}{-b}$ = a certain negative number and $b \neq 0$.

$$= -3p^3k^3$$

Example 10

Simplify $\dfrac{-24p^7k^5}{-8p^3k^2}$

Solution

$\dfrac{-24p^7k^5}{-8p^3k^2} = \dfrac{\overset{3}{\cancel{-24}}p^7k^5}{\underset{1}{\cancel{-8}}p^3k^2} = \dfrac{3p^7k^5}{p^3k^2}$ Divide the numerical coefficients by -8.

$$= \dfrac{3p^7k^5}{p^3k^2} = 3p^{7-3}k^{5-2}$$

Subtract the exponents of the powers of the denominator from the exponents of the powers with the same base in the numerator. Note $-8 \div (-8) = 1$, $-24 \div (-8) = 3$.

$$= 3p^4k^3 \qquad 7 - 3 = 4 \text{ and } 5 - 2 = 3.$$

Exercises

1. What is an exponent?

2. What is a base?

3. Multiply and write each product as one power. Hint: See Examples 1a, 1c, and 1e.

   a. $3^4 \cdot 3^7$ **b.** $9^5 \cdot 9$ **c.** $5^4 \cdot 5^6 \cdot 5^3$

   d. $4^4 \cdot 4^2$ **e.** $5^4 \cdot 5^6 \cdot 5^3$ **f.** $6^2 \cdot 6 \cdot 6^4$

4. Multiply and write each product as one power. Hint: See Example 1b and 1d.

   a. $3^4 \cdot n^5$ **b.** $5^3 \cdot 4^6$ **c.** $a^4 \cdot b^3$

5. Multiply using exponents. Hint: See Example 2a.

   a. $4^3 \cdot n^5 \cdot 3^4 \cdot n^2 \cdot 4^2$ b. $k^4 \cdot 7^2 \cdot k^3 \cdot 7^4 \cdot k^5$

6. Multiply using exponents. Hint: See Example 2a.

a. $b^4 \cdot w^4 \cdot n \cdot b^2 \cdot n^3 \cdot w^2$ **b.** $x^4 \cdot v \cdot k^2 \cdot v^2 \cdot x^2$

c. $p^4 \cdot n^7 \cdot d^2 \cdot p^2 \cdot n^2$ **d.** $a^2 b^4 \cdot c^3 \cdot a^3 \cdot c^2$

7. Divide and write each quotient as one power. Hint: See Example 3a.

a. $\dfrac{4^7}{4^2}$ **b.** $\dfrac{9^{14}}{9^6}$ **c.** $\dfrac{7^4}{7^3}$ **d.** $\dfrac{6^6}{6^4}$

8. Divide and write each quotient as one power. Hint: See Example 3b.

a. $\dfrac{n^9}{n^4}$ **b.** $\dfrac{w^5}{w^2}$ **c.** $\dfrac{k^8}{k^5}$ **d.** $\dfrac{b^5}{b^3}$

9. Divide and write each quotient as one power. Hint: See Example 3c.

a. $\dfrac{k^4}{m^3}$ **b.** $\dfrac{12^5}{11^4}$ **c.** $\dfrac{x^7}{b^5}$ **d.** $\dfrac{7^5}{6^4}$

10. Simplify each expression. Hint: See Example 4a and 4b.

a. $\dfrac{5^8 \cdot k^5}{k^3 \cdot 5^4}$ **b.** $\dfrac{4^4 \cdot x^5 \cdot y^6}{y^2 \cdot x^3 \cdot 4^2}$ **c.** $\dfrac{w^7 \cdot u^5 \cdot x^4 \cdot 3^3}{x^2 \cdot u^3 \cdot 3^2 \cdot w^7}$

11. Simplify each expression. Hint: See Example 4c.

a. $\dfrac{11^6 \cdot w^9 \cdot y^5 \cdot 6^5}{y^3 \cdot w^6 \cdot 11^4 \cdot 6^3 \cdot v^2}$ **b.** $\dfrac{k^6 \cdot 2^2 \cdot 10^3}{10^9 \cdot 2^4 \cdot k^3 \cdot x}$

12. Evaluate. Hint: See Example 5a.

     a. 10^0 **b.** 1^0 **c.** 29^0 **d.** 100^0

13. Evaluate. Hint: See Example 5b.

     a. $2^7 \cdot 2^{-7}$ **b.** $6^{10} \cdot 6^{-10}$ **c.** $8^5 \cdot 8^{-5}$ **d.** $9^8 \cdot 9^{-8}$

14. Evaluate. Hint: See Example 5c.

a. $\dfrac{3^4}{34}$ **b.** $\dfrac{8^7}{8^7}$ **c.** $\dfrac{5^9}{5^9}$ **d.** $\dfrac{2^{10}}{2^{10}}$

15. Evaluate. Hint: See Example 5d.

a. $\dfrac{k^8}{k^8}$ **b.** $\dfrac{n^{10}}{n^{10}}$ **c.** $\dfrac{p^5}{p^5}$ **d.** $\dfrac{j^8}{j^8}$

16. Evaluate. Hint: See Example 6a.

     a. 5^{-2} **b.** 4^{-2} **c.** 6^{-3} **d.** 3^{-3}

17. Evaluate. Hint: See Example 6b.

     a. $(-3)^{-2}$ **b.** $(-2)^{-3}$ **c.** $(-5)^{-3}$ **d.** $(-4)^{-4}$

18. Evaluate. Hint: See Example 6c.

a. $\dfrac{(-3)^2}{(-3)^3}$ **b.** $\dfrac{(-3)^2}{(-3)^4}$ **c.** $\dfrac{(-5)^2}{(-5)^4}$ **d.** $\dfrac{(-4)^2}{(-4)^4}$

19. Evaluate. Hint: See Example 6d.

a. $\dfrac{(5-3)^2}{(6-4)^3}$ **b.** $\dfrac{(7-5)^3}{(8-6)^5}$ **c.** $\dfrac{(9-6)^2}{(7-4)^4}$ **d.** $\dfrac{(5-1)^2}{(9-5)^4}$

20. Evaluate. Hint: See Example 6e.

   a. $(3 \cdot 2)^3 \cdot (6 \cdot 1)^{-5}$ **b**. $(4 \cdot 4)^4 \cdot (8 \cdot 2)^{-6}$

   c. $(2 \cdot 2)^4 \cdot (4 \cdot 1)^{-6}$ **d**. $(2 \cdot 6)^{-6} \cdot (4 \cdot 3)^4$

21. Evaluate. Hint: See Example 6f.

   a. $2^4 \cdot 2^{-6} \cdot 2^{-2}$ **b**. $3^{-2} \cdot 3^4 \cdot 3^{-3}$ **c**. $4^2 \cdot 4^{-3} \cdot 4^2 \cdot 4^{-2}$

22. Simplify. Hint: See Example 7.

   a. $\dfrac{4}{3^{-2}}$ **b**. $\dfrac{3}{2^{-4}}$ **c**. $\dfrac{12}{3^{-3}}$ **d**. $\dfrac{5}{4^{-2}}$

23. Simplify. Hint: See example 8

   a $\dfrac{16x^4y^5}{4x^2y}$ **b** $\dfrac{25x^6y^3}{5x^2y^2}$ **c** $\dfrac{9p^7k^3}{3p^2k}$ **d** $\dfrac{12x^{15}y^3}{4x^{12}y}$

24. Simplify. Hint: See Example 9

   a. $\dfrac{-12a^9bc^{14}}{6a^3bc^6}$ **b**. $\dfrac{30w^{15}x^{11}}{-10w^2x^6}$ **c**. $\dfrac{-18a^5b^3c^{10}}{2a^2bc^6}$ **d**. $\dfrac{36wp^{12}x^{13}}{-9wp^2x^6}$

25. Simplify. Hint: See Example 10

   a. $\dfrac{-24p^7k^5}{-8p^3k^2}$ **b**. $\dfrac{-21x^9k^7}{-7x^5k^2}$ **c**. $\dfrac{-36s^{17}k^8}{-9s^3k^2}$ **d**. $\dfrac{-22x^7k^5}{-11x^3k^5}$

Challenge Questions

26. Multiply using exponents.

   a. $n^4 \cdot 3^3 \cdot 4^2 \cdot 3^2 \cdot 4^2$ **b**. $x^6 \cdot y^4 \cdot x^2 \cdot y$

27. Evaluate

   a. 17^0 **b**. 10^{-2} **c**. $11^{-12} \cdot 11^{-12}$ **d**. $\dfrac{2}{3^{-2}}$

   e. $\dfrac{4}{3^{-2}}$ **f**. $k^4 \cdot k^{-4}$ **g**. $\dfrac{(-2)^2}{(-2)^4}$ **h**. $(4 \cdot 3)^2 \cdot (2 \cdot 6)^{-4}$

   i. $2^{-3} \cdot 2^{-2} \cdot 2^3$ **j**. $3^{-3} \cdot 3^2 \cdot 3^{-3}$ **k**. $4^4 \cdot 4^{-6}$ **l**. $(3 \cdot 2)^2 \cdot (2 \cdot 3)^{-4}$

   m. $\dfrac{v^5}{v^2}$ **n**. $\dfrac{9^7}{9^5}$ **o**. $(-3)^{-3}$ **p**. 3^{-3}

   q. $\dfrac{2^3}{2^3}$ **r**. $\dfrac{2}{4^{-2}}$ **s**. $\dfrac{m^n}{m^x}$ **t**. $\dfrac{9^0 \cdot n^{-7} \cdot w^5 \cdot k^{-4}}{n^{-2} \cdot w^{-2} \cdot k^2 \cdot 7^0}$

28. Simplify

   a. $4^6 \cdot y^4 \cdot x^5$ **b**. $\dfrac{(7-6)^3}{(8-6)^2}$ **c**. $\dfrac{(9-7)^2}{(7-5)^4}$ **d**. $\dfrac{(5-2)^2}{(9-6)^3}$

e. $\dfrac{5^0 \cdot n^3 \cdot p^5}{n^{-4} \cdot w^2}$ f. $\dfrac{t^{-3}}{t^3}$ g. $\dfrac{t^3}{t^{-3}}$ h. $(2 \cdot 6)^{-6} \cdot (4 \cdot 3)^6$

i. $x^3 \cdot x^5 \cdot x^0 \cdot x$ j. $x^4 \cdot c^9 \cdot y^3 \cdot c^9 \cdot y^0$ k. $y \cdot y^0$

29. Simplify.

a $\dfrac{24x^8y^9}{4x^3y}$ b. $\dfrac{42w^{12}x^7}{-6w^5x^3}$ c. $\dfrac{18x^{10}y^4}{3x^4y^2}$ d. $\dfrac{-28x^7k^9}{-7x^4k^2}$

e. $\dfrac{-15x^5k^8}{-3x^5k^2}$ f. $\dfrac{-18a^6b^7c^{10}}{3a^2bc^8}$ g. $\dfrac{-32s^{11}k^7}{-8s^3k^5}$ h. $\dfrac{28x^{18}y^9}{4x^{10}y^6}$

Answers to Selected Questions.

3a. 3^{11} **4a.** Cannot combine as one power because the bases are different.

6a. $b^6 \cdot w^6 \cdot n^4$

9a. Quotient cannot be written as one power because the bases are different.

13a. 1   **18a.** $-\dfrac{1}{3}$ **22a.** 36

SCIENTIFIC NOTATION

Scientific notation can be used to write large numbers in the standard form **more easily**. A large number written in scientific notation is a mathematical statement expressed as **a product of two factors** as follows:

The first factor is a number that is at least 1 but less than 10 and the second factor is a power of 10.

So, to change the standard form of a number to scientific notation, multiply the first factor (that is at least 1 but less than 10) by the second factor (that is a power of 10) as shown:

Standard form = Scientific notation

= (**first factor that is at least 1 but less than 10**) × (**second factor that is a power of 10.**)

128

Example 1

Write 640,000,000 in scientific notation.

Solution

Step 1: Find the first factor of 640,000,000 by counting the number of places the decimal point in the standard form must be moved to the left to form a number that is at least 1 but less than 10 as shown:

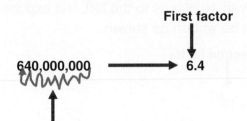

Move the decimal point 8 places to the left.

      Note that there is an imaginary decimal point after every whole number, review the chapter on decimals.

Step 2: Find the second factor of 640,000,000 by using the fact that since the decimal point in step 1 is moved 8 places to the left, the exponent of 10 is 8. The exponent of 10 is 8 can be written as shown:

Second factor

Exponent of 10 is 8 = 10^8

Step 3: Write the number (640,000,000) in the scientific notation as the product of the two factors of 6.4 and 10^8 as shown:

$$640,000,000 = 6.4 \times 10^8$$

Example 2

Write 72,000,000,000 in the scientific notation.

Solution

Step 1: Find the first factor of 72,000,000,000 by counting the number of places the decimal point in the standard form must be moved to the left to form a number that is at least 1 but less than 10 as shown:

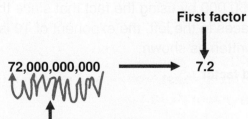

Move the decimal point 10 places to the left.

Note that there is an imaginary decimal point after every whole number, review the chapter on Decimals.

Step 2: Find the second factor of 72,000,000,000 by using the fact that since the decimal point in step 1 is moved 10 places to the left, the exponent of 10 is 10. The exponent of 10 is 10 can be written as shown:

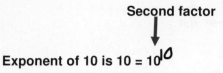

Second factor

Exponent of 10 is 10 = 10^{10}

Step 3: Write the number (72,000,000,000) in the scientific notation as the product of the two factors of 7.2 and 10^{10} as shown:

$$72,000,000,000 = 7.2 \times 10^{10}$$

Example 3

Write 3,960,000 in the scientific notation.

Solution

Step 1: Find the first factor of 3,960,000 by counting the number of places the decimal point in the standard form must be moved to the left to form a number that is at least 1 but less than 10 as shown:

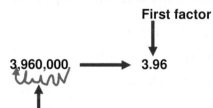

First factor

$$3,960,000 \longrightarrow 3.96$$

Move the decimal point 6 places to the left.

Note that there is an imaginary decimal point after every whole number, review the chapter on decimals.

Step 2: Find the second factor of 3,960,000 by using the fact that since the decimal point in step 1 is moved 6 places to the left, the exponent of 10 is 6. The exponent of 10 is 6 can be written as shown:

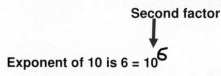

Second factor

Exponent of 10 is 6 = 10^{6}

Step 3: Write the number (3,960,000) in the scientific notation as the product of the two factors of 3.96 and 10^6 as shown:

$$3,960,000 = 3.96 \times 10^6$$

Example 4

Write 59,738,100,000,000 in the scientific notation.

Solution

Step 1: Find the first factor of 59,738,100,000,000 by counting the number of places the decimal point in the standard form must be moved to the left to form a number that is at least 1 but less than 10 as shown:

First factor

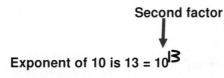

59, 738,100,000,000 $\longrightarrow$ 5.97381

Move the decimal point 13 places to the left.

Note that there is an imaginary decimal point after every whole number, review the chapter on decimals.

Step 2: Find the second factor of 59,738,100,000,000 by using the fact that since the decimal point in step 1 is moved 13 places to the left, the exponent of 10 is 13. The exponent of 10 is 13 can be written as shown:

Second factor

Exponent of 10 is 13 = 10^{13}

Step 3: Write the number 59,738,100,000,000 in the scientific notation as the product of the two factors of 5.97381 and 10^{13} as shown:

$$59,738,100,000,000 = 5.97381 \times 10^{13}$$

Example 5

Explain why each of the numbers is not written in the scientific notation.

a. $7.5 + 10^6$ **b.** 15×10^7 **c.** 6.2×8^5 **d.** 0.876×10^9

Solution

a. The scientific notation is written as the product of two factors but $7.5 + 10^6$ is not a product, but rather an addition.

b. The scientific notation is written as the product of two factors such that the first factor must be at least 1 but less than 10, but in 15×10^7, the first factor which is 15 is rather more than 10.

c. The scientific notation is written as the product of two factors such that the second factor is an exponent or power of 10, but in 6.2×8^5, the second factor is 8^5 but 8^5 is not an exponent or power of 10.

d. The scientific notation is written as the product of two factors such that the first factor must be at least 1 but less than 10, but in 0.876×10^9, the first factor which is 0.876 is less than 1.

How to Write Scientific Notations of Numbers Less Than 1

In order to write the scientific notation of numbers that are less than 1, the decimal point in the number **must be moved to the right and must be placed behind the first non-zero digit so as to obtain a number that is at least 1.**

Since the decimal point is moved to the right, **the exponent must be negative.** Recall that a scientific notation is still a mathematical statement expressed as the product of two factors such that the first factor is at least 1 but less than 10 and the second factor is a power of 10.

Example 6

Write 0.0000004 in the scientific notation.

Solution

Step 1: Find the first factor of 0.0000004 by counting the number of places the decimal point in the decimal notation **must be moved to the right** to form a number that is at least 1 but less than 10 as shown:

First factor

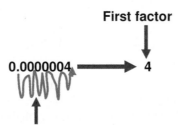

$$0.0000004 \longrightarrow 4$$

Move the decimal point 7 places to the right.

Step 2: Find the second factor of 0.0000004 by using the fact that since the decimal point in step 1 is moved 7 places to the **right**, the exponent of 10 is **-7**. The exponent of 10 is -7 can be written as shown:

Second factor

Exponent of 10 is -7 = 10^{-7}

Step 3: Write the number 0.0000004 in the scientific notation as the product of the two factors 4 and 10^{-7} as shown:

$$0.0000004 = 4 \times 10^{-7}$$

Example 7

Write 0.000001426 in the scientific notation.

Solution

Step 1: Find the first factor of 0.000001426 by counting the number of places the decimal point must be **moved to the right** to form a number that is at least 1 but less than 10 as shown:

First factor

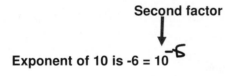

0.000001426 $\longrightarrow$ 1.426

Move the decimal point 6 places to the right.

Step 2: Find the second factor of 0.000001426 by using the fact that since the decimal point in step 1 is moved 6 places to the right, the exponent or the power of 10 is -6. The exponent of 10 is -6 can be written as shown:

Second factor

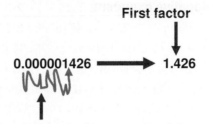

Exponent of 10 is -6 = 10^{-6}

Step 3: Write the number 0.000001426 in the scientific notation as the product of the two factors 1.426 and 10^{-6} as shown:

$$0.000001426 = 1.426 \times 10^{-6}$$

How to Write Scientific Notation in the Standard Notation

In order to write the scientific notation as the standard notation, two rules should be followed:

Rule 1: If the exponent of the base of the scientific notation is positive, it means that the decimal point in the scientific notation should be moved to the **right** according to the magnitude of the exponent. Hint: See Example 8a.

Example of the scientific notation with positive exponent is:

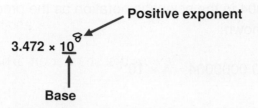

Positive exponent

3.472×10^8

Base

Rule 2: If the exponent of the base of the scientific notation is negative, it means that the decimal point in the scientific notation should be moved to the **left** according to the magnitude of the exponents. Hint: See Example 8b.

Example of the scientific notation with negative exponent is:

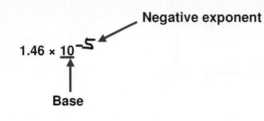

Negative exponent

1.46×10^{-5}

Base

Example 8
Write each scientific notation in the standard notation.

a. 3.472×10^8 **b.** 1.46×10^{-5} **c.** -6.3×10^6

Solution
a. $3.472 \times 10^8 = 3.472 \times 100{,}000{,}000$ $10^8 = 100{,}000{,}000$

$= 3.472$

**Move the decimal point 8 places to the right.
See rule 1.**

**Write the zeros here as place holders.
Review the chapter on decimals.**

$= 3.472\,00\,00\,00\,0$

**Move the decimal point 8 places to the right.
See rule 1.**

$347{,}200{,}000$

Note that a detailed explanation is provided for the understanding of the concept, however, the detailed explanation may not be necessary in solving your homework exercises. The student should understand and apply how the decimal point may be moved to the right or left as needed in order to solve their exercises.

b. $1.46 \times 10^{-5} = 1.46 \times \dfrac{1}{10^5}$

In general, $b^{-n} = \dfrac{1}{b^n}$ and $b \neq 0$.

Review the chapter on exponents.

$$= 1.46 \times \dfrac{1}{100,000}$$

$$= \dfrac{1.46}{100,000}$$

$$= \underset{\text{1.46}}{}$$

Move the decimal point 5 places to the left.
See rule 2.

Write the zeros here as place holders.
Review the chapter on decimals.

$= 0\,0\,0\,0\,0\,1.46$

Move the decimal point 5 places to the left.
See rule 2.

$$= 0.0000146$$

Note that the detailed explanation is provided for the understanding of the concept, however, the detailed explanation may not be necessary in solving your homework exercises. The student should understand and apply how the decimal point may be moved to the right or left as needed in order to solve their exercises.

c. $-6.3 \times 10^6 = -6.3 \times 1,000,000$

$10^6 = 1,000,000$

$= -6.3$

Move the decimal point 6 places to the right.
See rule 1.

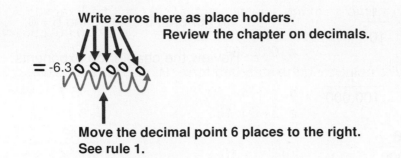

Write zeros here as place holders.
Review the chapter on decimals.

$= -6.3\,0\,0\,0\,0\,0$

Move the decimal point 6 places to the right.
See rule 1.

$= -6300000$

Note that the detailed explanation is provided for the understanding of the concept, however, the detailed explanation may not be necessary in solving your homework exercises. The student should understand and apply how the decimal point may be moved to the right or left as needed in order to solve their exercises.

Exercises

1. Describe how you would write 4.8969×10^7 in the standard notation. Hint: See the preceding notes.

2. Describe how you would write 0.00038 in the scientific notation. Hint: See Example 6.

3. The scientific notation can be used to write large numbers in standard form more easily. True or False? Hint: See the preceding notes.

4. The scientific notation is made up of two factors. True or False?
   Hint: See the preceding notes.

5. Write the following numbers in the scientific notation. Hint: See Example 1.
   a. 530,000,000   **b.** 720,00   **c.** 480,000,000
   d. 940,000,000,000   **e.** 670,00   **f.** 110,000,000

6. Write the following numbers in the scientific notation. Hint: See Example 2.
   a. 64,000,000   **b.** 55,000,000   **c.** 78,000
   d. 12,000,000   **e.** 99,000   **f.** 84,000,000,000

7. Write the following numbers in the scientific notation. Hint: See Example 3.
   a. 5,870,000   **b.** 7,250,000   **c.** 6,740,000
   d. 2,940,000,000   **e.** 4,390,000,000   **f.** 8,390,000

8. Write the following numbers in the scientific notation. Hint: See Example 4.
   a. 47,891,200,000   **b.** 98,147,300,000   **c.** 57,284,000
   d. 64,734,300,000,000   **e.** 38,234,400,000   **f.** 49,195,000

9. Explain why each number is not written in the scientific notation. Hint: See Example 5.
   a. $2.9 + 10^7$ **b.** 12×10^4 **c.** 4.5×9^{10}
   d. 0.491×10^8 **e.** $5.7 + 10^8$ **f.** 0.34×10^7

10. Write the following numbers in the scientific notation. Hint: See Example 6.
    a. 0.000006   **b.** 0.00009   **c.** 0.000002
    d. 0.0008   **e.** 0.0003   **f.** 0.0000007

11. Write the following numbers in the scientific notation. Hint: See Example 7.
   a. 0.00004135
   b. 0.000741
   c. 0.000000148
   d. 0.00000278
   e. 0.00389
   f. 0.0091

12. Write each scientific notation in the standard form. Hint: See Example 8.
   a. 4.731×10^5
   b. 1.246×10^{-7}
   c. -5.71×10^4
   d. 9.81×10^7
   e. 3.46×10^{-5}
   f. 8.1×10^8
   g. 1.2×10^{-6}
   h. -5.7×10^4
   i. 3.481×10^9
   j. 4.793×10^6
   k. -7.4×10^7
   l. 7.34×10^{-4}
   m. -9.31×10^7
   n. 5.712×10^5
   o. 6.341×10^{-7}

Answers to Selected Questions
   5a. 5.3×10^8 **6a.** 6.4×10^7 **7a.** 5.87×10^6 **8a.** 4.78912×10^{10}
   10a. 6×10^{-6} **11a.** 4.135×10^{-5} **12a.** 473100

Challenge Questions
13. Write each number in the scientific notation.
   a. 72,000,000
   b. 0.000002
   c. 0.0000192
   d. 94,000,000
   e. 1,000,000,000
   f. 4000,000,000
   g. 77,000,000
   h. 142,000,000
   i. 298,000
   j. 8,000,000,000
   k. 272,000
   l. 0.00078
   m. 0.00000418
   n. 0.0009
   o. 22,000,000,000

14. Explain why each of the following is not in scientific notation.
   a. 0.491×10^4
   b. $3.7 + 10^{16}$
   c. 38×10^4
   d. 4.81×6^5
   e. 4.9×7^8
   f. 50×10^6

15. Write each number in the standard notation.
   a. 3.12×10^6
   b. 1.7×10^9
   c. 1.48×10^{-4}
   d. -2.4×10^5
   e. 3.6×10^4
   f. -4.8×10^4
   g. 7.1×10^{-5}
   h. 4.2×10^{-4}
   i. -2.2×10^6

AVERAGE, MEAN, RANGE, MODE, AND MEDIAN

Average

Explanation 1
In its simplest form, an average is to share or divide anything equally. For example,

how can we share or divide 6 oranges equally between 2 girls? We can share the 6 oranges equally such that each girl will receive 3 oranges as follows:

Six oranges to be shared equally.

Equal share of 3 oranges   **Equal share of 3 oranges**

From the above picture, we are able to divide 6 oranges equally between 2 girls by dividing the total number of the oranges by the number of people who are to receive the share. Similarly, **an average is the total number divided by the number of the numbers**, and in this case the number of the numbers involves 2 girls which can be written as follow:

$$\text{Average} = \frac{\text{Total number of oranges}}{\text{Number of people}} = \frac{6}{2} = 3 \text{ oranges}$$

Explanation 2

Assume that a girl has 2 oranges and another girl has 4 oranges and they are requested to share the oranges equally, then they have to add the oranges together and then divide the total number of the oranges or the sum of the oranges by 2 or the number of the girls. Similarly, sharing the oranges equally is the same as finding the average which can be stated as follows: **an average is the sum of numbers divided by the number of the numbers**. This average can be written as follows:

$$\text{Average} = \frac{\text{Sum of oranges}}{\text{Number of people}} = \frac{2+4}{2} = \frac{6}{2} = 3$$

Conclusion from Explanations 1 and 2.

In Explanation 1, we find the average by dividing "Total number of oranges" by "Number of people," but in Explanation 2, the average is found by dividing the

"Sum of oranges" by "Number of people." We can then combine Explanations 1 and 2 together to write that **an average is the total or the sum of the numbers divided by the number of the numbers**. Therefore, there are two methods of finding averages as explained by Examples 1 and 2, and stated in the rule below:

Rule: An average can be found by dividing the total number by the number of the numbers if the total number is given in the question, otherwise the average can be found by dividing the sum of the numbers by the number of the numbers if the individual numbers are given in the question.

Understanding Average

When students from schools take part in the external examinations, the schools are rated by the average performance of the students in each school by dividing the sum of the test scores of all the students in a specific school by the number of students who took the test. The average test score can be written as shown:

$$\text{Average test score} = \frac{\text{Sum of the test scores}}{\text{Number of the students who took the test}} \qquad [A]$$

Group Exercise

The class should be divided into four groups and without using any students' names, each group should be given the test scores of the last weekly test. Each group should find the average test score of the last weekly test by completing the tables as shown and using the average equation, which is equation $[A]$.

Test scores :

Student #	1	2	3	4	5	6	7	8	. . .	N
Test score	?	?	?	?	?	?	?	?	. . .	?

Each group should report out the average test score to the whole class.
Each group should discuss the following 4 questions and to list and report out their answer with reasons to the whole class.
1. Are the average test score from the 4 groups the same?
2. How could the average test score be improved? When each student's test score is increased by 2, what happens to the average test score? Is the average test score higher when the individual test score is increased by 2?
3. Could you name some external tests that your school participates in?
4. What factors will lower the average test score? When the individual test score is lowered by 2, does the average test score becomes lower?

Example 1
(**a**). The test scores of five students out of a maximum score of 10 are 8, 7, 9, 10, and 6.

Find the average test score of the students.

(**b**). The total age of 5 boys is 20 years. What is their average age?

Solution

(**a**). Using the formula, the average test score is:

$$\text{Average test score} = \frac{\text{Sum of the test scores}}{\text{Number of the students that took the test}} \qquad [A]$$

Sum of the test scores $= 8 + 7 + 9 + 10 + 6 = 40$

Number of the students that took the test $= 5$

$$\text{Average test score} = \frac{40}{5} \qquad \text{See equation } [A]$$

$$= \frac{\overset{8}{\cancel{40}}}{\underset{1}{\cancel{5}}} \qquad \text{Divide by 5.}$$

Therefore, the average test score is 8.

(**b**). The total age of the 5 boys $= 20$ years

The number of the boys $= 5$

Using the formula:

$$\text{Average} = \frac{\text{Total number (ages)}}{\text{Number of people}} = \frac{20}{5}$$

$$= \frac{\overset{4}{\cancel{20}}}{\underset{1}{\cancel{5}}} \qquad \text{(Divide by 5).}$$

Therefore, the average age of the 5 boys is 4 years.

Example 2

Find the average of the following numbers:

$$1\frac{1}{2}, \, 2\frac{3}{4}, \, 3\frac{2}{3}, \, 2\frac{1}{2}$$

Solution

Using the formula, the average of the numbers is:

$$\text{Average number} = \frac{\text{Sum of the numbers}}{\text{Number of the numbers}} \qquad [A]$$

Sum of the numbers $= 1\dfrac{1}{2} + 2\dfrac{3}{4} + 3\dfrac{2}{3} + 2\dfrac{1}{2}$

Number of the numbers $= 4$ (There are 4 numbers involved.)

Add the numbers as follow: (Review the Addition of Mixed Numbers).

$$1\dfrac{1}{2} = 1\dfrac{1}{2} \times \dfrac{6}{6} = 1\dfrac{6}{12}$$

$$2\dfrac{3}{4} = 2\dfrac{3}{4} \times \dfrac{3}{3} = 2\dfrac{9}{12}$$

$$3\dfrac{2}{3} = 3\dfrac{2}{3} \times \dfrac{4}{4} = 3\dfrac{8}{12}$$

$$2\dfrac{1}{2} = 2\dfrac{1}{2} \times \dfrac{6}{6} = 2\dfrac{6}{12}$$

$$8\dfrac{29}{12} = 8 + 2\dfrac{5}{12} = 10\dfrac{5}{12} \quad \text{(Review Division of Fractions)}$$

Sum of the numbers $= 10\dfrac{5}{12}$

Using equation $[A]$:

Average number $= \dfrac{10\dfrac{5}{12}}{4}$ (There are 4 numbers.)

$= 10\dfrac{5}{12} \div 4$

$= 10\dfrac{5}{12} \times \dfrac{1}{4}$ (Review the Division of Fractions - multiply by reciprocal of 4.)

Note: The reciprocal of any number $= 1 \div$ the number

$= \dfrac{125}{12} \times \dfrac{1}{4}$ (Review the Multiplication of Mixed Fractions.)

$= \dfrac{125}{48} = 2\dfrac{29}{48}$

Therefore, the average number is $2\dfrac{29}{48}$

Example 3
The average age of 8 children is 9 years. If the ages of seven of the children are 6,

141

$8\dfrac{1}{2}$, 4, 10, 11, 12, and 9, how old is the 8th child?

Solution

Sum of the ages of the 7 children $= 6 + 8\dfrac{1}{2} + 4 + 10 + 11 + 12 + 9 = 60\dfrac{1}{2}$ years.

Total ages of the 8 children $= 8 \times$ average age of the 8 children.
$$= 8 \times 9 \text{ years}$$
$$= 72 \text{ years.}$$

Age of 8th child = Total age of the 8 children − Sum of the ages of the 7 children
$$= 72 \text{ years} - 60\dfrac{1}{2} \text{ years}$$
$$= 11\dfrac{1}{2} \text{ years.}$$

Therefore, the age of the 8th child is $11\dfrac{1}{2}$ years.

Mean, Range, Mode, and Median.

The **mean** is the same as the average.

The **range** is the difference between the biggest number and the smallest number in a data.

Example 4

The table shows the ages of 9 students.

Students #	1	2	3	4	5	6	7	8	9
Ages	16	14	13	14	17	15	14	12	11

a. Find the range of the ages of the students.

b. Find the mean age of the students.

c. By conducting a group exercise, find the range of the data by using a line plot.

d. Find the mode of the data.

e. By using the line plot in Example 4c, how would you find the mode of the data?

f. Find the median age of the students.

g. By using the line plot of Example 4c, how would you find the median age of the students?

Solution

a. From the table, the student # 5 has the highest age of 17 years and the student #9 has the lowest age of 11 years.

Therefore, the range = Highest age - Lowest age
$$= 17 \text{ years} - 11 \text{ years} = 6 \text{ years.}$$

b. Let us find the mean age of the students as follows:

Sum of the ages of the students = 16 + 14 13 + 14 + 17 + 15 + 14 + 12 + 11
$$= 126 \text{ years}$$

The number of students = 9   From the table, 9 students are listed.

The mean of the ages of the students $= \dfrac{\text{Sum of the ages of the students}}{\text{Number of the students}}$

$$= \dfrac{126 \text{ years}}{9}$$

= 14 years   Review the division of integers.

Therefore, the mean age of the students is 14 years.

c. Group Exercise
The class should be divided into four groups. Each group should complete the line plot of the ages of all the 9 students, using x for each mark as started below.

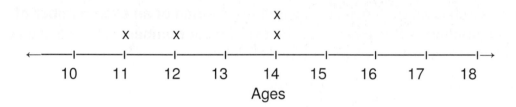

Ages

How could the range be determined from the line plot?
Answer: The x at the extreme left side of the line plot indicates the lowest age and the x at the extreme right side of the line plot indicates the highest age.
Subtract the lowest age from the highest age to obtain the range.

d. The **mode** is the number that occurs most often. From the table, the age 14 years occurs 3 times which is the age that occurs most often, and therefore, 14 is the mode.

e. Group Exercise
From the completed line plot, how could you find the mode?
Answer: **The age column which has the most "x" indicates the mode.** Which age column has the most "x"? What is then the mode from the line plot? The mode is the data that appears most.

f. The **median** is the middle number when data is listed in numerical order.
Numerical order means to list the data from the least number to the greatest number, in order without omission. We can write the ages of the 9 students in numerical order as shown:

$$11,\ 12,\ 13,\ 14,\ 14,\ 14,\ 15,\ 16,\ 17$$
$$\uparrow$$

This 14 is the middle number when the data is listed in numerical order, and therefore, this 14 is the median.

g. Group Exercise

From the completed line plot, how could you find the median?
Answer: The x's on the line plot are already in numerical order, and therefore, by counting the x from left to right on the line plot, **we should be able to locate the x which is at the middle of the data and this middle x is the median**.
What is the median from the line plot?

Special Method for Finding Median

The median is the middle number when data is listed in numerical order. However, if the data is an even number of numbers, there will be no middle number as the median as shown:

$$6,\ 8,\ 12,\ 14$$

The numbers 6, 8, 12, and 14 have no middle number because the number of the numbers is 4 which is an even number. **To find the median of an even number of numbers, the median is the average of the two middle numbers**. The two middle numbers of 6, 8, 12, and 14 are 8 and 12, and therefore,

$$\text{the average of 8 and 12} = \frac{8 + 12}{2} = \frac{20}{2} = 10.$$

Therefore, the median of 6, 8, 12, and 14 is 10.

How to Solve Multi-Step Problems Involving Mean.

Example 5

The mean of the ages of 3 boys is 5 years. How old should the fourth boy be such that the mean of the 4 boys will be 8 years?
Solution

The method of solving this problem involves finding the total ages of the 3 boys and then let x represents the age of the fourth boy. We can then find the sum of the ages of all the 4 boys, we can also find the mean of the ages of all the four boys. Finally, we can equate the mean of the ages of the 4 boys to 8 years and then solve for x which is the age of the fourth boy as follow:

Total ages of the 3 boys = 3 × Mean age of the 3 boys.

$$= 3 \times 5 \text{ years} \qquad \text{Mean age of the 3 boys} = 5 \text{ years.}$$
$$= 15 \text{ years}$$

Let the age of the fourth boy = x years
Total age of all the 4 boys = 15 years + x years

$$\text{Mean of the ages of the 4 boys} = \frac{\text{Sum of the ages of the 4 boys}}{\text{Total number of boys}}$$

$$= \frac{15 + x}{4}$$

Since the question gives us the mean of the 4 boys is 8 years, we can equate $\frac{15 + x}{4}$ to 8 and then solve for x which is the age of the fourth boy as follows:

$$\frac{15 + x}{4} = 8$$

$$\frac{15 + x}{4} = \frac{8}{1} \qquad \text{8 is the same as } \frac{8}{1}.$$

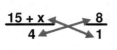

Cross products of a proprotion are equal. A proportion is a statement that two ratios are equal. Review the chapter on proportion.

$(15 + x) \times 1 = 4 \times 8$ Review the chapter on Proportion.

$15 \times 1 + x \times 1 = 4 \times 8$ Multiply to eliminate the bracket.

$15 + x = 32$ $4 \times 8 = 32$.

$15 - 15 + x = 32 - 15$ Subtract 15 from both sides of the equation $15 + x = 32$ in order to obtain x.

$0 + x = 17$ $15 - 15 = 0$ and $32 - 15 = 17$.

$x = 17$

Therefore, the fourth boy should be 17 years.

_____

The notes and the generous worked examples have provided me with conceptual understanding and computational fluency to do my homework.

Exercises

1. (a) Explain what is meant by average, mean, range, mode, and median.

   (b) Six boys are given $24. What is the average amount each boy will receive? Hint: See Example **1(a)**.

   (c). If 8 students are to share 16 apples, what is the average number of the apples will each student receive? Hint: See Example **1(b)**.

2. What is the average of 4, 5, 2, and 1? Hint: See Example **1(a)**.

3. Find the average of the following numbers: Hint: See Examples **1(a)** and **2**.

(a) 2.1, 6.4, 2.8, 1.2, 2.5

(b) $1\frac{1}{2}$, $6\frac{2}{3}$, $1\frac{5}{6}$

(c) 22, 5, 14, 6, 8

(d) 4, 7, 8, 11, 2, 6, 3, 9, 13

(e) 14, 16, 8, 10, 7, 5

(f) 77, 43

(g) $2\frac{2}{3}$, $1\frac{3}{4}$, $3\frac{1}{4}$, $\frac{1}{3}$

(h) 1, 3, 9, 11, 4, 3, 12

(i) 14, 24, 31, 16

(j) 5, 10, 12, 14, 6

(k) 8, 5, 2

(l) 10, 6, 8, 4

(m) 2, 7, 5, 1, 10

4. From the given data, find the range. Hint: See the section under Range. See Example **4a**.

(a) 3, 4, 7, 28

(b) 101, 7, 2, 94

(c) 38, 49, 86, 99, 31, 2

(d) 2, 8, 4, 35, 44

(e) 39, 98, 401, 30, 11

(f) 15, 25, 7, 5

5. Find the median. Hint: See the section on Median. See Example **4f**.

(a) 4, 8, 1, 6, 4

(b) 9, 5, 8

(f) 7, 12, 3

(g) 4.2, 3.1, 6.4, 1.8, 6.2

(h) $7\frac{1}{2}$, $6\frac{1}{3}$, $8\frac{3}{4}$, $6\frac{2}{3}$, $7\frac{1}{4}$

(i) 6.3, 4.7, 8.4

6. Find the median. Hint: See the section on the Special Method of Finding the Median.

(a) 2, 8, 5, 3

(b) 3, 7, 8, 1

(c) 12, 2, 4, 6, 1, 3

(d) 12, 4

(e) 4, 6

(f) 3, 4, 8, 2, 7, 9

(g) 110, 112, 100, 98

(h) 2.4, 2.8, 4.2, 6.4

(i) $7\frac{1}{2}$, $6\frac{2}{3}$, $2\frac{2}{3}$, $1\frac{3}{4}$

7. Find the mode. Hint: See the section on Mode. See Example 4d.

(a) 2, 3, 7, 8, 2, 9, 3, 2

(b) 4, 1, 6, 9, 4, 2, 4, 1

(c) 9, 11, 6, 7, 9, 4, 9

(d) 1, 4, 6, 1, 7, 1, 2, 6, 4

(e) 4, 1, 5, 1, 6, 5, 8, 5

(f) 2, 6, 9, 4, 6, 2, 6

8. Find the mode and the range. Hint: See the section on Mode and Range. See Examples **4a** and **4d**.

(a) 12, 14, 4, 12, 3, 1, 12, 14

(b) 19, 24, 6, 19, 4, 2

(c) 3, 6, 9, 10, 6, 24, 4

(d) 1, 4, 5, 6, 5, 13, 5

(e) 2.5, 6.8, 4.1, 3, 6.8, 7.2

(f) $4\frac{1}{2}$, $1\frac{7}{8}$, $6\frac{4}{5}$, $1\frac{7}{8}$, 2

(g) $2\frac{3}{4}$, $1\frac{1}{2}$, $8\frac{3}{7}$, $2\frac{3}{4}$, 6, $2\frac{3}{4}$

(h) 1.5, 7.5, 2.5, 2.5, 1.5, 2.5, 1.5

9. The mean of 3 numbers is 2. What is the fourth number such that the mean of all the four numbers should be 5. Hint: See Example **5**.

10. The mean age of 2 girls is 4 years. What should be the age of the third girl such that the mean of all three girls should be 6 years? Hint: See Example **5**.

11. The mean of 5 numbers is 7, what should be the sixth number for the mean of all the 6 numbers to be 4? Hint: See Example **5**.

12. The mean of the ages of 3 girls is 14 years, what should be the age of the fourth

girl such that the mean age of all the 4 girls should be 12 years old? Hint: See Example **5**.

Challenge Questions
13. Find the average. Round off your answer to the nearest whole number.
   (a) 2, 6, 14   (b) 14, 28, 31, 43   (c) 2.4, 6.9, 1.3
   (d) 1.6, 10.4   (e) 36, 54, 104, 64   (f) 3, 7, 8, 4, 9
   (g) $2\frac{3}{4}$, 3, $4\frac{1}{2}$, $2\frac{1}{4}$ (h) $10\frac{3}{4}$, $11\frac{1}{4}$ (i) 4.4, 6.9, 3.3

14. Find the range and the mode.
   (a) 1, 7, 6, 1, 4, 1, 9   (b) 14, 2, 8, 1.4   (c) 2.2, 4.8, 2.2, 4
   (d) 8, 10, 17, 10, 34, 10   (e) 2, 2, 4, 8, 4, 9, 4   (f) 6, 7, 11, 14, 7

15. Find the mean.
   (a) 2, 3, 4   (b) 10, 22   (c) 1.2, 4.3, 3.5
   (d) $14\frac{2}{6}$, $82\frac{2}{3}$, 2   (e). 31, 3   (f). 12, 6, 12

16. Find the mean.
   (a) 2, 9, 7, 1, 4   (b) 1, 6, 8, 2, 10, 3   (c) 2, 4, 1, 8
   (d) 2.2, 4.2, 6.8, 1.8   (e) $1\frac{1}{4}$, $6\frac{1}{2}$, $2\frac{1}{4}$ (f) 7, 9

17. The mean of 3 numbers is 6. What should be the fourth number such that the mean of all the four numbers should be 10?

Answers to Selected Questions
1(b) $4.00   **3**(a) 3   **4**(a) 25   **9**. 14

REAL WORLD APPLICATIONS - WORD PROBLEMS

1. The average test score of 5 students is 12. If the test score of 4 students are 10, 13, 10, and 14, what is the test score of the 5th student? Hint: See Example **3** under the chapter Average.
2. The ages of three students are 9, 10, and 11 years. Find their average age. Hint: See Example **1** under chapter Average.

Challenge Questions
3. The average age of 6 employees is 25 years. If the ages of 4 of the employees

are 20, 21, 30, and 23 years, what is the total ages of the 2 remaining employees?

4. The weekly test scores of 6 students are 90%, 78%, 89%, 98%, 86%, and 65%. What is the average test score of the students?

5. Make a line plot of the following data and using the line plot explain how you would obtain the mode, range, mean, and the median. Hint: Number the number line from 0 to 30.

8, 12, 16, 28, 2, 18, 12, 4, 8, 12, 10, 12, 2, 2, 28.

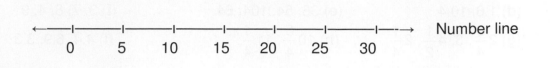

Number line

0   5   10   15   20   25   30

ALGEBRAIC EXPRESSIONS

An algebraic expression is formed by numbers, variables and the operations of addition, subtraction, division, multiplication, powers, and roots as shown in Table 1:

Table 1

Word Phrases	Operations needed	Examples of expressions
1. A number **plus** 2. 2. A number **increased** by 2. 3. 2 **more** than a number. 4. **Add** 2 to a number.	+	Let x be the number, and therefore, the expression is **x + 2.**
1. **Subtract** 3 from a number. 2. A number **decreased** by 3. 3. 3 **less** than a number. 4. A number **minus** 3. 5. **Difference** of a number and 3.	—	Let n be the number, and therefore, the expression is **n - 3.**
1. 4 **divided** into a number. 2. A number **divided** by 4. 3. **Quotient** of a number and 4.	÷	Let k be the number, and therefore, the expression is **k ÷ 4.**
1. **Product** of 5 and a number. 2. 5 **multiplied** by a number. 3. 5 **times** a number.	×	Let y be the number, and therefore, the expression is **5 × y = 5y.**
1. A number to the **power** a.	Power	Let 2 be the number, and therefore, the expression is **2^a.**
1. **Root** of a number x.	√	Let x represent the number, and therefore, the expression is **$\sqrt{x}$.**

Key point: Understand and know the relationship between the words in **bold** under the "word phrase" column and the corresponding "operations needed" column in Table 1. For example, **more** means addition and **less** means subtraction.

Exercises or Group Exercises

1. Write an algebraic expression for each word phrase. Hint: See examples of the expressions in table 1.

a. 10 more than k.	**b**. 8 less than x.	**c**. P minus 6.
d. w decreased by 15.	**e**. the quotient of 6 and p.	**f**. Product of 2 and k.
g. 7 multiplied by v.	**h**. Difference of 9 and b.	**i**. Subtract 1 from n.
j. 5 times k.	**k**. Add 11 to y.	**l**. Increase 12 by x.
m. z to the power 6.	**n**. Root of k.	**o**. 8 to the power w.

Complex Word Phrases

It is possible to combine some of the word phrases in Table 1 to form complex word phrases as shown in Table 2:

(Table 2 is located on the next page.)

Table 2

Key Words	Word Phrases	Examples of expressions
more, products	2 **more** than the **product** of 4 and k.	4k is the **product** of 4 and k, and therefore, the expression is 4k + 2.
less, product	4 **less** than the **product** of 6 and k.	6k is the **product** of 6 and k, and therefore, the expression is 6k - 4.
less, divide	10 **less** than m **divided** by 7.	m **divided** by 7 is m ÷ 7, and therefore, the expression is m ÷ 7 - 10.
more, divide	10 **more** than m **divided** by 7.	m **divided** by 7 is m ÷ 7, and therefore, the expression is m ÷ 7 + 10.
times, sum	3 **times** the **sum** of n and 5.	The **sum** of n and 5 is n + 5, and therefore, the expression is 3(n + 5).
times, difference	8 **times** the **difference** of x and 6.	The **difference** of x and 6 is x - 6, and therefore, the expression is 8(x - 6).
times, product	2 **times** the **product** of k and 5.	The **product** of k and 5 is 5k, and therefore, the expression is 2 × 5k = 10k.
times, quotient	**Twice** the **quotient** of p and 58.	The **quotient** of p and 58 is p ÷ 58, and therefore, the expression is 2(p ÷ 58).
plus, product	2 **plus** the **product** of 3 and y.	The **product** of 3 and y is 3y, and therefore, the expression is 3y + 2.
minus, product	2 **minus** the **product** of 3 and y.	The **product** of 3 and y is 3y, and therefore, the expression is 2 - 3y.
fraction, sum	**Five-sixth** the **sum** of k and 3.	The **sum** of k and 5 is k + 5, and therefore, the expression is $\frac{5}{6}$(k + 3).

Key Points: 1. Understand and know the relationship among the "key words" column the "word phrase column," and the "examples of expressions column."

2. **Note** that each complex word phrase has at least two operations and it is important that the student should know which operation should be done first. In Table 2, the operations to be done first are in bold under the column "examples of expressions."

Exercises

1. Write an algebraic expression for each word phrase. Hint: See the examples in

Table 2 and also watch for the key words in Table 2.

a. 10 more than the product of 7 and w.   **b**. 1 less than the product of 8 and k.

c. 3 less than k divided by 6.   **d**. 6 times the sum of w and 10.

e. 4 times the difference of y and 2.   **f**. 7 plus the product of 6 and k.

g. 20 minus the product of 5 and w.   **h**. 2 more than k divided by 6.

i. 8 times the product of m and 10.   **j**. Twice the quotient of 60 and w.

k. Four times the quotient of 100 and p.   **l**. One-third the sum of w and 12.

m. One-third the difference between 32 and p.

Challenge Questions

2. Write the expression for the following word phrases.

a. w more than 5 times k.   **b**. 11 more than p times n.

c. n less than 4 times b.   **d**. 100 decreased by 3 times w.

e. w less than twice n.   **f**. Half the quotient of w and k.

g. 6 times the product of p and k.   **h**. Half the difference between k and 3.

(Once you understand how to write expressions, you can then write and solve equations in the chapter on equations using an "equal to" symbol to show that two expressions are equal.)

Evaluation of Expressions
Example 1

Evaluate each expression for $a = 2$, $b = 3$, $c = 2.1$, and $d = 4$.

a. $a + d$ **b**. $\dfrac{b}{a}$ **c**. $(ac) + 10$ **d**. $\dfrac{14}{a} - 3$

e. $\dfrac{d}{a} + c$ **f**. $3bc$ **g**. $(d - c) - a$ **h**. $b + \dfrac{d}{a}$

Solution

a. Substitute 2 for a and 4 for d into the expression $a + d$ as shown:

$$a + d = 2 + 4$$
$$= 6$$

b. Substitute 3 for b and 2 for a into the expression $\dfrac{b}{a}$ as shown:

$$\frac{b}{a} = \frac{3}{2}$$
$$= 1\frac{1}{2}$$

c. Substitute 2 for a and 2.1 for c into the expression $(ac) + 10$ as shown:

$$(ac) + 10 = (2 \times 2.1) + 10$$
$$= 4.2 + 10$$
$$= 14 \cdot 2$$

d. Substitute 2 for a into the expression $\dfrac{14}{a}$ - 3 as shown:

$$\dfrac{14}{a} - 3 = \dfrac{14}{2} - 3$$
$$= 7 - 3 \qquad\qquad 14 \div 2 = 7$$
$$= 4$$

e. Substitute 4 for d, 2 for a, and 2.1 for c into the expression $\dfrac{d}{a}$ + c as shown:

$$\dfrac{d}{a} + c = \dfrac{4}{2} + 2.1$$
$$= 2 + 2.1$$
$$= 4.1$$

f. Substitute 3 for b and 2.1 for c into the expression 3bc as shown:

$$3bc = 3 \times 3 \times 2.1$$
$$= 9 \times 2.1 \qquad\qquad 3 \times 3 = 9$$
$$= 18.9$$

g. Substitute 4 for d, 2.1 for c, and 2 for a into the expression (d - c) - a as shown:

$$(d - c) - a = (4 - 2.1) - 2$$
$$= 1.9 - 2 \qquad\qquad 4 - 2.1 = 1.9$$
$$= -.1 \qquad\qquad\quad 1.9 - 2 = -.1$$

h. Substitute 3 for b, 4 for d, and 2 for a into the expression b $+\dfrac{d}{a}$ as shown:

$$b + \dfrac{d}{a} = 3 + \dfrac{4}{2}$$
$$= 3 + 2 \qquad\qquad 4 \div 2 = 2$$
$$= 5$$

Exercises

1. Evaluate each expression for a = 8, b = 2, c = 1, and d = 4. Hint: Match similar exercises with the similar examples in Example 1.

a. db

b. $\dfrac{a}{d}$ + b

c. d + c

d. (ab) + 4

e. $\dfrac{12}{b}$ + 4

f. $\dfrac{d}{c}$ + b

g. (a - d) - b

h. c + $\dfrac{d}{b}$

Challenge Questions

2. Evaluate each expression for m = 9, n = 2, w = 3, and p = 4.

a. mn

b. $\dfrac{18}{w}$ - p

c. (m - p) - w

d. n + $\dfrac{m}{w}$

e. $\dfrac{p}{n}$ + m

f. $\dfrac{24}{p}$ + m

g. p + nw

h. mp + n

EQUATIONS

New words: **equations, variable, solution, and solve**

An **equation** uses an "equal to" symbol to show that two expressions are equal. The examples of equations are:

$2x + 1 = 4 - x$, $w + 4 = 10$, $5n = 15$, and $\dfrac{25}{5} = 5$.

An equation is therefore, similar to a seesaw such that the weight of the people on one side of the seesaw **is equal to** the weight of the people at the other side of the seesaw when the beam of the seesaw is horizontal or balanced.

Beam of the seesaw

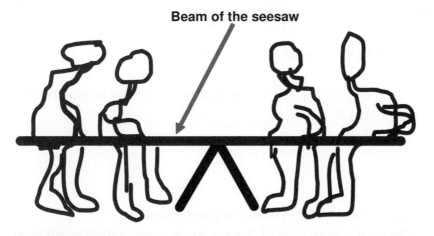

Group Exercise
The class may be divided into four groups and under the supervision of the teacher, and other adults, the students should balance the beam of a seesaw to demonstrate that an equation is similar to a balanced beam of a seesaw.

The **variable** in an equation is the unknown value in an equation. For example, x is the variable in the equation $2x + 1 = 4 - x$.
The **solution** to an equation is the value of the variable in the equation. To **solve** an equation means that we should **find the value of the variable**.

Solving Equations Using Addition
We can simply state the "**addition property of equality**" as shown:

When the same number is added to both sides of an equation, the resulting equation still has equal values at both sides of the equation.

Addition Property of Equality

Adding the same number to both sides of an equation.	Algebra
Add 4 to both sides of the equation 3 + 6 = 9 as shown: $\begin{array}{r} 3 + 6 \ = 9 \\ \underline{+\,4 \quad +4} \\ 3 + 10 = 13 \end{array}$ Note that the resulting value of both sides of the equation after adding 4 to both sides of the equation is the same, which is 13	$x = w$ $x + z = w + z$

Example 1
Solve for n in the equation n - 6 = 12. Check your answers.

Solution

The basic method of solving for n is to isolate the variable n.

$n - 6 = 12$

$n - 6 + 6 = 12 + 6$ Add 6 to both sides of the equation in order to isolate the variable n.

      $n = 18$ -6 + 6 = 0

Check Your Answer

$n - 6 = 12$

$18 - 6 = 12$ Substitute 18 for n in the original equation.

      $12 = 12$ Since the right side of the equation is equal to the left side, the answer is correct.

Example 2
Solve for t in the equation 8 = t - 4. Check your answer.

Solution

The basic method for solving for t is to isolate t.

$8 = t - 4$

$8 + 4 = t - 4 + 4$ Add 4 to both sides of the equation in order to isolate t.

$12 = t + 0$ 8 + 4 = 12 and -4 + 4 = 0

$12 = t$

Check Your Answer

$8 = t - 4$

8 = 12 - 4   Substitute 12 for t in the original equation.

8 = 8   Since the left side of the equation is equal to the right
                                    side of the equation, the answer is correct.

Example 3

Solve for w in the equation 10 = -2 - w. Check your answer.

Solution

The basic method for solving for w is to isolate w.

10 = -2 - w

10 + 2 = -2 + 2 - w   Add 2 to both sides of the equation in order to isolate w.

12 = 0 - w   -2 + 2 = 0

12 = -w

12(-1) = -w(-1)   Multiply both sides of the equation by -1 in order to
                                    change -w to w because we are asked to solve for w but
                                    not -w.

-12 = w   **Note**: 12(-1) = -12 and -w(-1) = +w = w.

Check Your Answer

10 = -2 - w

10 = -2 - (-12)   Substitute w = -12, into the original equation.

10 = -2 + 12   -(-12) = +12

10 = 10   -2 + 12 = 10

                                    Since the left side of the equation is equal to the right side
                                    of the equation, the answer is correct.

Solving Equations Using Subtraction

We can simply state the "**subtraction property of equality**" as follows:

When the same number is subtracted from both sides of an equation, the resulting
equation still has equal values at both sides of the equation.

Subtraction Property of Equality

Subtract the same number from both sides of an equation.	Algebra
Subtracting 4 from both sides of the equation 10 + 8 = 18 as shown: 10 + 8 = 18 　- 4　　- 4 10 + 4 = 14 Note that the resulting value of both sides of the equation after subtracting 4 from both sides of the equation is the same which is 14.	x = w x - z = w - z

Example 4
Solve for x in the equation $x + 3 = 16$. Check your answer.
Solution
The basic method for solving for x is to isolate x.

$x + 3 = 16$

$x + 3 - 3 = 16 - 3$ Add 3 to both sides of the equation in order to isolate x.

$x + 0 = 13$ $+3 - 3 = 0$

$x = 13$

Check Your Answer
$x + 3 = 16$

$13 + 3 = 16$ Substitute $x = 13$ into the original equation.

$16 = 16$ Since the left side of the equation is equal to the right side of the equation, the answer is correct.

Example 5
Solve for y in the equation $12 = 3 + y$. Check your answer.
Solution
The basic method for solving for y is to isolate y.

$12 = 3 + y$

$12 - 3 = 3 - 3 + y$ Subtract 3 from both sides of the equation in order to isolate y.

$9 = 0 + y$ $12 - 3 = 9$ and $3 - 3 = 0$.

$9 = y$

Check Your Answer
$12 = 3 + y$

$12 = 3 + 9$ Substitute $y = 9$ into the original equation.

$12 = 12$ Since the left side of the equation is equal to the right side of the equation, the answer is correct.

Applications

Example 6
The sum of two numbers is 19. One of the numbers is 11. What is the other number?
Solution
Let the other number be n.

The sum of the two numbers is 19, therefore:

$n + 11 = 19$

$n + 11 - 11 = 19 - 11$ Subtract 11 from both sides of the equation in order to isolate n.

$$n + 0 = 8 \qquad +11 - 11 = 0 \text{ and } 19 - 11 = 8.$$
$$n = 8$$

Example 7

When 2 is subtracted from a number the difference is 13. What is the number?

Solution

Let the number be n.

When 2 is subtracted from the number the difference is 13, therefore:

$$n - 2 = 13$$
$$n - 2 + 2 = 13 + 2 \qquad \text{Add 2 to both sides of the equation to isolate n.}$$
$$n + 0 = 15 \qquad -2 + 2 = 0 \text{ and } 13 + 2 = 15.$$
$$n = 15$$

Exercises

1. What is a variable in an equation?

2. What is meant by the solution of an equation?

3. Solve for the variable in each equation. Check your answer.
   Hint: See Example 1 and Example 2.

   a. x - 4 = 10   **b.** w - 3 = 11   **c.** 15 = y - 5

   d. p - 7 = -3   **e.** 8 = 6 + y   **f.** w - 6 = 14

4. Solve for the variable in each equation. Check your answer.
   Hint: See Example 3.

   a. 14 = 2 - k   **b.** 8 = 6 - w   **c.** 4 - w = 12

   d. 3 - p = 9   **e.** 12 = w + 4   **f.** 7 + w = 14

5. Solve for the variable in each equation. Check your answer.
   Hint: See Example 4 and Example 5.

   a. x + 2 = 6   **b.** x + 14 = 14   **c.** 11 = p + 10

   d. 13 = 14 + t   **e.** 12 = w + 4   **f.** 7 + w = 14

6. The sum of two numbers is 25. One of the numbers is 15. What is the other number? Hint: See Example 6.

7. When 4 is subtracted from a number, the difference is 29. What is the number? Hint: See Example 7

Challenge Questions

8. Solve for the variable in each equation.

   a. n + 14 = 16   **b.** 12 - p = 14   **c.** x - 5 = 9   **d.** 12 - t = 4

   e. 2 - e = 7   **f.** w + 2 = 6   **g.** 6 + w = 10   **h.** 9 + t = 11

9. When 13 is subtracted from a number, the difference is 24. What is the number?

10. The sum of two numbers is 55. One of the numbers is 27. What is the other number?

11. Mary's age in years minus 8 is 29. How old is Mary. Hint: Let x = Mary's age in

years.

Solving Equations by Dividing

To solve for the variable in an equation where the variable forms a multiplication equation, use the "**division property of equality**" to obtain the solution.

We can simply state **the division property of equality** as:

When the same non-zero number is used to divide both sides of an equation, the resulting equation still has equal values on both sides of the equation.

Division Property of Equality

Divide both sides of the equation by the same non-zero number.	Algebra
Dividing both sides of the equation 5 × 4 = 20 by the same non-zero number of 2 as shown: $$\frac{5 \times 4}{2} = \frac{20}{2}$$ $$10 = 10$$ Note that the resulting value of both sides of the equation after dividing both sides of the equation by 2 is the same which is 10	$$w = p$$ $$\frac{w}{x} = \frac{p}{x}$$ x is a non-zero number.

Example 8

Solve and check your answer.

a. $5n = 25$ **b.** $21 = 3x$

Solution

a. The basic method to solve for n is to isolate n.

$5n = 25$

$$\frac{5n}{5} = \frac{25}{5}$$ Divide both sides of the equation by 5 in order to isolate n.

$$\frac{\overset{n}{\cancel{5n}}}{\underset{1}{\cancel{5}}} = \frac{\overset{5}{\cancel{25}}}{\underset{1}{\cancel{5}}}$$

n = 5.

Check Your Answer

5n = 25

$5 \cdot 5 = 25$ Substitute 5 for n in the original equation.

25 = 25   Since the left side of the equation is equal to the right side of the equation, the answer is correct

b. The basic method to solve for x is to isolate x.

21 = 3x

$$\frac{21}{3} = \frac{3x}{3}$$ Divide both sides of the equation by 3 in order to isolate x.

$$\frac{\overset{7}{\cancel{21}}}{\underset{1}{\cancel{3}}} = \frac{\overset{x}{\cancel{3x}}}{\underset{1}{\cancel{3}}}$$

7 = x

Check Your Answer

21 = 3x

$21 = 3 \cdot 7$ Substitute 7 for x in the original equation.

21 = 21   Since the left side of the equation is equal to the right side of the equation, the answer is correct.

Solving Equations by Multiplication

To solve for the variable in an equation where the variable forms a division equation, use the "**multiplication property of equation**," to obtain the solution.

We can simply state the **multiplication property of equality** as:

when the same number is used to multiply both sides of an equation, the resulting equation still has equal values on both sides of the equation.

Multiplication Property of Equality

(The table for the Multiplication Property of Equality is shown on the next page.)

$$\frac{\overset{1}{5}}{\underset{2}{10}} = \frac{1}{2}$$

$$\frac{1}{2} = \frac{1}{2}$$

Since the left side of the equation is equal to the right side of the equation, the answer is correct.

Applications
Hint: Review the chapter on "Algebraic Expressions."

Example 10
A number divided by 4 equals 8. What is the number? Hint: See Example **9a**.
Solution

Let the number be x. The number divided by 4 equals 8, therefore, $\frac{x}{4} = 8$.

The basic method for obtaining x **is to isolate the x**.

$$\frac{x}{4} \cdot 4 = 8 \cdot 4$$

Multiply both sides of the equation by 4 in order to isolate the x when the 4 cancels out on the left side of the equation as shown:

$$\frac{x}{\underset{1}{4}} \cdot \overset{1}{4} = 8 \cdot 4$$

x = 32

Example 11
a. John scored 3 times as many points as Nick. If John scored 24 points, how many points did Nick score? Hint: See Example 8.

b. A CD cost 3 times as much as an LP. If the CD cost $18.00, how much did the LP cost? Hint: See Example 8.

Solution

a. Step 1: Set up the equation.

Let the number of the points scored by Nick = x.

John scored 3 times as many points as Nick and John scored 24 points. Therefore:

$$3x = 24$$

Step 2: Solve the equation. The basic method for solving for x is to isolate the x.

$$\frac{3x}{3} = \frac{24}{3}$$ Divide both sides of the equation by 3 in order to isolate the x.

$$\frac{\overset{x}{\cancel{3x}}}{\underset{1}{\cancel{3}}} = \frac{\overset{8}{\cancel{24}}}{\underset{1}{\cancel{3}}}$$

x = 8 points.

b. Step 1: Set up the equation. Hint: Review the chapter on the "Algebraic Expressions."
Let the cost of the LP = x.
A CD cost 3 times as much as an LP and the CD cost $18.00, therefore:
18 = 3x

Step 2: Solve the equation.
The basic method for solving for x is to isolate the x by dividing both sides of the equation by 3 as follows:
18 = 3x

$$\frac{18}{3} = \frac{3x}{3}$$ Divide both sides of the equation by 3 in order to isolate the x.

$$\frac{\overset{6}{\cancel{18}}}{\underset{1}{\cancel{3}}} = \frac{\overset{x}{\cancel{3x}}}{\underset{1}{\cancel{3}}}$$

6 = x
x = $6.00

Exercises

1. Solve and check your answer. Hint : See Example 8.

 a. 3x = 15   **b.** 12 = 4x   **c.** 36 = 9y

 d. 4p = 28   **e.** 3y = 27   **f.** 5w = 45

2. Solve and check your answer. Hint : See Example 9.

 a. $\dfrac{x}{3} = 10$ **b.** $\dfrac{y}{5} = 2$ **c.** $\dfrac{p}{4} = 3$ **d.** $\dfrac{w}{5} = 6$

 e. $\dfrac{3}{x} = \dfrac{1}{3}$ **f.** $\dfrac{2}{y} = \dfrac{1}{5}$ **g.** $\dfrac{1}{4} = \dfrac{3}{w}$ **h.** $\dfrac{p}{3} = 6$

3. A number divided by 3 equals 21.
 What is the number? Hint: See Example 10.

163

4. Elizabeth has 3 times as many CD's as Nancy.
   If Elizabeth has 9 CD's how many CD's does Nancy have? Hint: See Example 11.
5. A number divided by 5 equals 9. What is the number? Hint: See Example 10.

Challenge Questions
6. Solve for the variable and check your answer.

   a. $6x = 42$ **b.** $\dfrac{p}{5} = 3$ **c.** $64 = 4x$ **d.** $\dfrac{4}{p} = \dfrac{1}{3}$

7. A number divided by 4 equals 6. What is the number?
8. Samuel made 4 times as much money this week for baby-sitting as George.
   If Samuel made $36.00, how much did George make?

Solving Two-Step Equations
Example 12
Solve $2x + 1 = 9$.
Solution
Step 1: Isolate 2x by subtracting 1 from both sides of the equation.

   $2x + 1 = 9.$

   $2x + 1 - 1 = 9 - 1$ Subtract 1 from both sides of the equation in order to isolate the term with x in it which is 2x.

   $2x = 8$

Step 2: Isolate x by dividing both sides of the equation by 2.

   $\dfrac{2x}{2} = \dfrac{8}{2}$ Divide both sides of the equation by 2 in order to isolate the x.

   $\dfrac{\overset{x}{\cancel{2x}}}{\underset{1}{\cancel{2}}} = \dfrac{\overset{4}{\cancel{8}}}{\underset{1}{\cancel{2}}}$

   $x = 4$

Example 13
Solve: **a.** $3y - 5 = -20$ **b.** $\dfrac{w}{8} + 6 = 2$ **c.** $12 = \dfrac{n}{3} - 4 \cdot 2$ **d.** $28 = 10n - 12$

Solution
a. $3y - 5 = -20$
Step 1: Isolate 3y.

   $3y - 5 + 5 = -20 + 5$ Add 5 to both sides of the equation in order to isolate the term with y which is 3y.

   $3y + 0 = -15$ $-5 + 5 = 0$ and $-20 + 5 = -15$.

   $= -15$

Step 2: Isolate y

$$3y = -15$$

$$\frac{3y}{3} = -\frac{15}{3}$$

Divide both sides of the equation by 3 in order to isolate the y.

$$\frac{\overset{y}{\cancel{3y}}}{\underset{1}{\cancel{3}}} = -\frac{\overset{5}{\cancel{15}}}{\underset{1}{\cancel{3}}}$$

$$y = -5$$

b. $\dfrac{w}{8} + 6 = 2$

Step 1: Isolate $\dfrac{w}{8}$.

$$\frac{w}{8} + 6 - 6 = 2 - 6$$

Subtract 6 from both sides of the equation in order to isolate the term with w which is $\dfrac{w}{8}$.

$$\frac{w}{8} + 0 = -4$$

6 - 6 = 0 and 2 - 6 = -4

$$\frac{w}{8} = -4$$

Step 2: Isolate w.

$$\frac{w}{8} \times 8 = -4 \times 8$$

Multiply both sides of the equation by 8 in order to eliminate the 8 as a denominator, and then isolate w.

$$\frac{w}{\underset{1}{\cancel{8}}} \times \overset{1}{\cancel{8}} = -4 \times 8$$

Divide by 8.

$$w = -32$$

c. $12 = \dfrac{n}{3} - 4 \cdot 2$

Step 1: Isolate $\dfrac{n}{3}$.

$$12 + 4 \cdot 2 = \frac{n}{3} - 4 \cdot 2 + 4 \cdot 2$$

Add $4 \cdot 2$ to both sides of the equation in order to isolate the term with n which is $\frac{n}{3}$.

$$12 + 8 = \frac{n}{3} + 0$$

$4 \cdot 2 = 8$ and $-4 \cdot 2 + 4 \cdot 2 = 0$ or $-8 + 8 = 0$.

$$20 = \frac{n}{3}$$

Step 2: Isolate n.

$$20 \times 3 = \frac{n}{3} \times 3$$

Multiply both sides of the equation by 3 in order to eliminate the 3 as a denominator, and then isolate n.

$$20 \times 3 = \frac{n}{\overset{3}{\underset{1}{3}}} \times \overset{1}{3}$$

$$60 = n$$

d. $28 = 10n - 12$

Step 1: Isolate 10n.

$$28 + 12 = 10n - 12 + 12$$

Add 12 to both sides of the equation in order to isolate the term with n which is 10n.

$$40 = 10n$$

$28 + 12 = 40$ and $-12 + 12 = 0$.

Step 2: Isolate n.

$$\frac{40}{10} = \frac{10n}{10}$$

Divide both sides of the equation by 10 in order to isolate n.

$$\frac{\overset{4}{\underset{1}{40}}}{\underset{1}{\overset{}{10}}} = \frac{\overset{n}{\underset{1}{10n}}}{\underset{1}{\overset{}{10}}}$$

$$4 = n$$

REAL WORLD APPLICATIONS - WORD PROBLEMS
Applications and Solving Two-Step Equations

Hint: Review the chapter on "Algebraic Expression."

Example 14

Gertrude wants to buy a DVD for $45.00. She already has $5.00. If she earns $4.00 an hour for baby-sitting, how many hours must she work to earn the money she needs?

Solution

Step 1: Let n be the number of hours that Gertrude must work.

Step 2: Write an equation based on the information.

She earns $4.00 an hour for baby-sitting and from Step 1, she must work for n hours, and therefore, the total money that she makes baby-sitting is:

4n dollars.

But she already has $5.00, therefore, the total money that she needs is 4n + 5 dollars. The total money that she needs which is 4n + 5 dollars must be equal to the cost of the DVD which is $45.00. Therefore:

4n + 5 = 45

Step 3: Solve the equation by isolating the n.

(Note that once the equation is set up, we can then use the two-step equation solving method such as in Example 12 and Example 13 to find n.)

$$4n + 5 = 45$$

$$4n + 5 - 5 = 45 - 5$$ Subtract 5 from both sides of the equation in order to isolate the term with n, which is 4n.

$$4n = 40$$ +5 - 5 = 0 and 45 - 5 = 40.

$$\frac{4n}{4} = \frac{40}{4}$$ Divide both sides of the equation by 4 in order to isolate n.

$$\frac{\overset{n}{\cancel{4n}}}{\underset{1}{\cancel{4}}} = \frac{\overset{10}{\cancel{40}}}{\underset{1}{\cancel{4}}}$$

$$n = 10 \text{ hours.}$$

Example 15

If a number is divided by 5 and then 3 is subtracted, the result is 2. What is the number?

Solution

Step 1: Let x be the number

Step 2: Write an equation based on the information in the question.

The number is divided by 5 and from step 1, the number is x, and therefore,

the number divided by $5 = \frac{x}{5}$.

If 3 is subtracted from the number divided by 5, the result is 2, and therefore,

$$\frac{x}{5} - 3 = 2$$

Step 3: Solve the equation by isolating the x.

(**Note** that once the equation is set up, we can then use the two-step equation solving method such as in Example 12 and Example 13 to find x.)

$$\frac{x}{5} - 3 = 2$$

$$\frac{x}{5} - 3 + 3 = 2 + 3 \qquad$$ Add 3 to both sides of the equation in order to isolate the term in x which is $\frac{x}{5}$.

$$\frac{x}{5} = 5 \qquad -3 + 3 = 0 \text{ and } 2 + 3 = 5.$$

$$\frac{x}{5} \times 5 = 5 \times 5 \qquad$$ Multiply both sides of the equation by 5 in order to isolate x.

$$x = 25$$

Example 16

If you divide a number by 4 and 5 is added to the result, you get 11. What is the number?

Solution

Step 1: Let p be the number.

Step 2: Write an equation based on the information in the question. The number is divided by 4 and from Step 1, the number is p, and therefore, the number divided by $4 = \frac{p}{4}$.

If 5 is added to the number divided by 4, the result is 11, and therefore,

$$\frac{p}{4} + 5 = 11$$

Step 3: Solve the equation by isolating the p.

(**Note** that once the equation is set up, we can then use the two-step equation solving method such as in Example 12 and Example 13 to find p.)

$$\frac{p}{4} + 5 = 11$$

$$\frac{p}{4} + 5 - 5 = 11 - 5 \qquad$$ Subtract 5 from both sides of the equation in order to isolate the term in p which is $\frac{p}{4}$.

$$\frac{p}{4} = 6 \qquad +5 - 5 = 0 \text{ and } 11 - 5 = 6.$$

$$\frac{p}{4} \times 4 = 6 \times 4 \qquad \text{Multiply both sides of the equation by 4 in order to isolate p.}$$

$$\frac{\overset{1}{\cancel{p}}}{\underset{1}{\cancel{4}}} \times 4 = 6 \times 4$$

$$p = 24$$

Example 17

Four more than the product of 8 and a number is 36. What is the number?

Solution

Step 1: Let the number be m.

Step 2: Write an equation based on the information in the question.

The product of 8 and the number is 8m because, from Step 1, the number is m. Therefore, 4 more than the product of 8 and the number is 8m + 4. Then if 4 more than the product of 8 and the number is 36, this statement can be written as:

8m + 4 = 36

Step 3: Solve the equation by isolating the m.

(**Note** that once the equation is set up, we can then use the two-step equation solving method such as in Example 12 and Example 13 to find m.)

8m + 4 = 36

8m + 4 - 4 = 36 - 4   Subtract 4 from both sides of the equation in order to isolate the term with m, which is 8m.

8m = 32   +4 - 4 = 0 and 36 - 4 = 32

$$\frac{8m}{8} = \frac{32}{8} \qquad \text{Divide both sides of the equation by 8 in order to isolate m.}$$

$$\frac{\overset{1}{\cancel{8}m}}{\underset{1}{\cancel{8}}} = \frac{\overset{4}{\cancel{32}}}{\underset{1}{\cancel{8}}}$$

$$m = 4$$

Example 18

Five less than the product of 6 and a number is 31. What is the number?

Solution

Step 1: Let the number be x.

Step 2: Write an equation based on the information in the question.

The product of 6 and the number will be 6 · x or 6x because, from Step 1, the number is x. Therefore, 5 less than the product of 6 and the number will be 6x - 5. Then, if five less than the product of 6 and the number is 31, the statement will be:

$$6x - 5 = 31$$

Step 3: Solve the equation by isolating the x.

(**Note** that once the equation is set up, we can then use the two-step equation solving method such as in Example 12 and Example 13 to find x.)

$$6x - 5 = 31$$

$$6x - 5 + 5 = 31 + 5$$ Add 5 to both sides of the equation in order to isolate the term in x which is 6x.

$$6x = 36$$ -5 + 5 = 0 and 31 + 5 = 36

$$\frac{6x}{6} = \frac{36}{6}$$ Divide both sides of the equation by 6 in order to isolate x.

$$\frac{\overset{x}{\cancel{6x}}}{\underset{1}{\cancel{6}}} = \frac{\overset{6}{\cancel{36}}}{\underset{1}{\cancel{6}}}$$

$$x = 6$$

Example 19

John earned $30.00 washing cars. He earned $6.00 less than 3 times what Mary earned. How much did Mary earn?

Solution

Step 1: Let k be the money that Mary earned.

Step 2: Write an equation based on the information in the question.

3 times what Mary earned = 3k because from Step 1, k is the money that Mary earned. The expression $6.00 less than 3 times what Mary earned can be stated as: 3k - 6.

$30.00 is $4.00 less than 3 times what Mary earned and this statement can be written as: 3k - 6 = 30

Step 3: Solve the equation by isolating the k.

$$3k - 6 = 30$$

$$3k - 6 + 6 = 30 + 6$$ Add 6 to both sides of the equation in order to isolate the term in k which is 3k.

$$3k = 36$$ -6 + 6 = 0 and 30 + 6 = 36.

$$\frac{3k}{3} = \frac{36}{3}$$

Divide both sides of the equation by 3 in order to isolate the k.

$$\begin{array}{cc} k & 12 \\ \dfrac{3k}{3} = \dfrac{36}{3} \\ 1 & 1 \end{array}$$

$$k = \$12$$

Exercises

1. Solve for x, y, w, or p in each equation.
  Hint: See Example 12.

  a. $4x + 3 = 15$ **b.** $2y + 4 = 12$ **c.** $5 + 3p = 20$
  d. $2p + 6 = 18$ **e.** $4w + 4 = 24$ **f.** $5w + 6 = 26$

2. Solve for x, y, w, or p in each equation.
  Hint: See Examples **13a** and **13d**.

  a. $4x - 3 = 9$ **b.** $3p - 6 = 24$ **c.** $5y - 3 = 12$
  d. $6p - 5 = 19$ **e.** $4w - 4 = 16$ **f.** $-4 + 3y = 11$
  g. $-3 + 3w = 12$ **h.** $-5 + 4x = 15$ **j.** $3p - 3 = 18$

3. Solve for x or w. Hint: See Examples **13b** and **13c**.

  a. $24 = \dfrac{x}{3} + 4.1$ **b.** $\dfrac{w}{5} - 2 = 7$ **c.** $13 = \dfrac{w}{2} - 7$ **d.** $8 = \dfrac{x}{3} + 6.3$

4. Solve for w or p. Hint: See Example **13d**.

  a. $12 = 3w - 3$ **b.** $9 = 4p - 1$ **c.** $7 = 5p - 8$ **d.** $6 = 3w - 3$

5. Mary wants to buy a camera for \$64. She already has \$14. If she earns \$5 an hour for baby-sitting, how many hours must she work to earn the money she needs? Hint: See Example 14.

6. If a number is divided by 4 and then 5 is subtracted the result is 4. What is the number? Hint: See Example 15.

7. If you divide a number by 3 and add 6 to the result, you get 16. What is the number? Hint: See Example 16.

8. Seven more than the product of 6 and a number is 31. What is the number? Hint: See Example 17.

9. Three less than the product of 5 and a number is 22. What is the number? Hint: See Example 18

10. Judith earned \$24 baby-sitting. She earned \$4 less than twice what Mary earned. How much did Mary earned? Hint: See Example 19.

Challenge Questions

11. Solve for x, y, w, or p in each equation.

a. 3w - 7 = 23   **b.** 4x + 5 = 41   **c.** 6x - 2 = 22
d. -4 + 4p = 28   **e.** 6 + 7p = 27   **f.** 4y + 3 = 27

g. $9 = \dfrac{w}{4} + 8$ **h.** $\dfrac{y}{4} - 2.4 = 3$ **j.** 8 = 4p - 8

12. Five less than the product of 8 and a number is 27. What is the number?
13. Nine more than the product of 4 and a number is 19. What is the number?
14. If you divide a number by 4 and add 11 to the result, you get 15.
    What is the number?
15. Nick earned $36 baby-sitting. He earned $18 less than three times what John
    earned. How much did John earned?
16. George wants to buy a copy of the "Mathmasters series" book for $37. He
    already has $17. If he earns $6 an hour baby-sitting, how many hours does
    he have to work to earn the money he needs?

Answers to Selected Questions

2f.   -4 + 3y = 11
    -4 + 4 + 3y = 11 + 4   Add 4 to both sides of the equation to isolate 3y.
          3y = 15

$$\dfrac{3y}{3} = \dfrac{15}{3}$$ Divide both sides of the equation by 3 in order to isolate y.

          y = 5

MULTI-STEP EQUATION SOLVING

Equations With Like Terms or Variables

Equations with like terms are equations with the same types of variables. For example
in the equation 6x + 2x = 24, the terms 6x and 2x have the same type of variable
in x, and therefore, we say that the equation 6x + 2x = 24 has like terms in x. The
general method for solving equations with like terms is to isolate all the like terms to
one side of the equation add or subtract the like terms, then divide to isolate the
variable.

Example 1

Solve for x, k, or w.

a. 6x + 2x = 24   **b.** 5k - 2k = 9   **c.** 3w + 12 = 5w

Solution

a. 6x + 2x = 24

Step 1: Add the like terms.

$$8x = 24 \qquad\qquad 6x + 2x = 8x$$

Step 2: Divide both sides of the equation by 8 to isolate x.

$$\frac{8x}{8} = \frac{24}{8}$$

$$\frac{\overset{x}{\cancel{8x}}}{\underset{1}{\cancel{8}}} = \frac{\overset{3}{\cancel{24}}}{\underset{1}{\cancel{8}}}$$

$$x = 3$$

b. 5k - 2k = 9

Step 1: Subtract the like terms.

$$3k = 9 \qquad\qquad 5k - 2k = 3k.$$

Step 2: Divide both sides of the equation by 3 to isolate k.

$$\frac{3k}{3} = \frac{9}{3}$$

$$\frac{\overset{k}{\cancel{3k}}}{\underset{1}{\cancel{3}}} = \frac{\overset{3}{\cancel{9}}}{\underset{1}{\cancel{3}}}$$

$$k = 3$$

c. 3w + 12 = 5w

Step 1: Isolate all the like terms to one side by subtracting 3w from both sides of the equation.

$$3w - 3w + 12 = 5w - 3w$$

$$12 = 2w \qquad\qquad 3w - 3w = 0 \text{ and } 5w - 3w = 2w.$$

Step 2: Divide both sides of the equation by 2 in order to isolate w.

$$\frac{12}{2} = \frac{2w}{2}$$

$$\frac{\overset{6}{\cancel{12}}}{\underset{1}{\cancel{2}}} = \frac{\overset{w}{\cancel{2w}}}{\underset{1}{\cancel{2}}}$$

$$6 = w$$

Example 2

Solve for x, k, or w.

a. $8x - 1 - 3x = 24$ **b.** $9w + 3 = 6w + 15$ **c.** $-8k - 5 = 4k - 29$

Solution

a. $8x - 1 - 3x = 24$

Step 1: Isolate the like terms to one side of the equation by adding 1 to both sides of the equation.

$$8x - 1 + 1 - 3x = 24 + 1$$
$$8x - 3x = 25 \qquad\qquad -1 + 1 = 0$$

Step 2: Combine the like terms by subtracting 3x from 8x.

$$5x = 25 \qquad\qquad 8x - 3x = 5x$$

Step 3: Isolate x by dividing both sides of the equation by 5.

$$\frac{5x}{5} = \frac{25}{5}$$

$$\frac{\overset{x}{\cancel{5x}}}{\underset{1}{\cancel{5}}} = \frac{\overset{5}{\cancel{25}}}{\underset{1}{\cancel{5}}}$$

$$x = 5$$

b. $9w + 3 = 6w + 15$

Step 1: Isolate the like terms to one side of the equation by subtracting 6w from both sides of the equation and also subtracting 3 from both sides of the equation.

$$9w + 3 - 3 - 6w = 6w - 6w + 15 - 3$$
$$9w - 6w = 12 \qquad\qquad 3 - 3 = 0,\ 6w - 6w = 0,\ \text{and}\ 15 - 3 = 12.$$

Step 2: Combine the like terms by subtracting 6w from 9w.

$$3w = 12 \qquad\qquad 9w - 6w = 3w$$

Step 3: Isolate w by dividing both sides of the equation by 3.

$$\frac{3w}{3} = \frac{12}{3}$$

$$\frac{\overset{1}{\cancel{3w}}}{\underset{1}{\cancel{3}}} = \frac{\overset{4}{\cancel{12}}}{\underset{1}{\cancel{3}}}$$

$$w = 4$$

c. -8k - 5 = 4k - 29

Step 1: Isolate the like terms to one side of the equation by adding 8k to both sides of the equation and also by adding 29 to both sides of the equation.

-8k + 8k -5 + 29 = 4k + 8k -29 + 29

$$24 = 4k + 8k \qquad\qquad \text{-8k + 8k = 0, -5 + 29 = 24,}$$
$$\text{and -29 + 29 = 0.}$$

Step 2: Combine the like terms by adding 4k to 8k.

$$24 = 12k$$

Step 3: Isolate k by dividing both sides of the equation by 12.

$$\frac{24}{12} = \frac{12k}{12}$$

$$\frac{\overset{2}{\cancel{24}}}{\underset{1}{\cancel{12}}} = \frac{\overset{k}{\cancel{12}}}{\underset{1}{\cancel{12}}}$$

$$2 = k \text{ or } k = 2$$

Example 3

Solve for x, y, or w.

a. $\dfrac{4}{5} = x + \dfrac{3}{4}$ **b.** $y - 1\dfrac{1}{2} = 2\dfrac{1}{3}$ **c.** $\dfrac{6}{7} = w - \dfrac{2}{3}$

Solution

a. $\dfrac{4}{5} = x + \dfrac{3}{4}$ **Type of equation: Addition type**

Step 1: Isolate x by subtracting $\dfrac{3}{4}$ from both sides of the equation.

$$\frac{4}{5} - \frac{3}{4} = x + \frac{3}{4} - \frac{3}{4}$$

$$\frac{4}{5} - \frac{3}{4} = x \qquad\qquad \frac{3}{4} - \frac{3}{4} = 0$$

Step 2: Subtract $\frac{3}{4}$ from $\frac{4}{5}$ to obtain the value of x.

$$\frac{4}{5} - \frac{3}{4} = x$$

$$\frac{16 - 15}{20} = x \qquad\qquad \text{LCD (least common denominator)} = 20.$$

$$\frac{1}{20} = x \qquad\qquad 16 - 15 = 1$$

b. $y - 1\frac{1}{2} = 2\frac{1}{3}$ **Type of equation: Subtraction type**

Step 1: Isolate y to one side of the equation by adding $1\frac{1}{2}$ to both sides of the equation.

$$y - 1\frac{1}{2} + 1\frac{1}{2} = 2\frac{1}{3} + 1\frac{1}{2}$$

$$y = 2\frac{1}{3} + 1\frac{1}{2} \qquad\qquad -1\frac{1}{2} + 1\frac{1}{2} = 0$$

Step 2: Add $2\frac{1}{3}$ to $1\frac{1}{2}$ to obtain the value of y.

$$y = 2\frac{1}{3} + 1\frac{1}{2}$$

$$2\frac{1}{3} \cdot \frac{2}{2} = \frac{2}{6} \swarrow \text{LCD} \qquad\qquad \text{Review Addition of Fractions.}$$

$$+ 1\frac{1}{2} \cdot \frac{3}{3} = \frac{3}{6} \swarrow \text{LCD} \qquad\qquad \text{Review Addition of Fractions.}$$

$$3\frac{5}{6} \qquad\qquad\qquad 2 + 1 = 3 \text{ and } \frac{2}{6} + \frac{3}{6} = \frac{5}{6}$$

$$y = 3\frac{5}{6}$$

c. $\frac{6}{7} = w - \frac{2}{3}$ **Type of equation: Subtraction type**

Step 1: Isolate w to one side of the equation by adding $\frac{2}{3}$ to both sides of the equation.

$$\frac{6}{7} + \frac{2}{3} = w - \frac{2}{3} + \frac{2}{3}$$

$$\frac{6}{7} + \frac{2}{3} = w \qquad\qquad -\frac{2}{3} + \frac{2}{3} = 0$$

Step 2: Add $\frac{6}{7}$ to $\frac{2}{3}$ in order to obtain the value of w.

$$\frac{6}{7} + \frac{2}{3} = w$$

$$\frac{18 + 14}{21} = w \qquad\qquad\qquad LCD = 21$$

$$\frac{32}{21} = w \qquad\qquad\qquad \text{Review Addition of Fractions.}$$

$$1\frac{11}{21} = w$$

Example 4

Solve for m and w.

a. $2.4 = m - 0.17$ **b**. $w + 1.5 = 3.16$

Solution

a. $2.4 = m - 0.17$ **Type of equation: Subtraction type**

Step 1: Isolate m to one side of the equation by adding 0.17 to both sides of the equation.

$$2.4 + 0.17 = m - 0.17 + 0.17$$
$$2.4 + 0.17 = m \qquad\qquad -0.17 + 0.17 = 0$$

Step 2: Add 2.4 to + 0.17 in order to obtain the value of m.

$$\begin{array}{r} 2.4 \\ + 0.17 \\ \hline 2.57 \end{array}$$

Therefore, $2.57 = m$ or $m = 2.57$

b. $w + 1.5 = 3.16$ **Type of equation: Addition type**

Step 1: Isolate w to one side of the equation by subtracting 1.5 from both sides of the equation.

$$w + 1.5 - 1.5 = 3.16 - 1.5$$

$$w = 3.16 - 1.5 \qquad\qquad 1.5 - 1.5 = 0$$

Step 2: Subtracting 1.5 from 3.16 to obtain the value of w.

$$\begin{array}{r} 3.16 \\ -\ 1.5 \\ \hline 1.66 \end{array}$$

$$w = 1.66$$

Exercises

1. What is meant by like terms?

2. Solve for x, y, or k in each equation. Hint: See Example 1.

    a. $4x + 3x = 21$ **b**. $7y - 2y = 25$ **c**. $2k + 18 = 5k$

    d. $3y + 27 = 12y$ **e**. $6k + 2k = 32$ **f**. $5x - 2x = 30$

3. Solve for x, k, or w. Hint: See Example 2.

    a. $7x - 2 - 4x = 31$ **b**. $4w + 4 = 2w$ **c**. $-5k - 3 = 3k - 27$

    d. $6w + 12 = 3w$ **e**. $-6k - 4 = 2k - 20$ **f**. $3w + 4 - 2x = 23$

4. Solve for w, x, or y. Hint: See Example 3.

    a. $\dfrac{4}{5} = x + \dfrac{1}{2}$ **b**. $y - 1\dfrac{1}{3} = 2\dfrac{1}{4}$ **c**. $\dfrac{4}{5} = w - \dfrac{1}{2}$

    d. $w - 1\dfrac{1}{4} = 3\dfrac{1}{2}$ **e**. $\dfrac{3}{4} = y + \dfrac{1}{3}$ **f**. $\dfrac{2}{3} = x - \dfrac{2}{3}$

5. Solve for m or w. Hint: See Example 4.

    a. $3.8 = m - 0.24$ **b**. $w + 1.7 = 4.19$ **c**. $w + 1.5 = 3.21$

    d. $4.2 = w - 0.33$ **e**. $m + 2.8 = 3.18$ **f**. $5.3 = w - 0.12$

Challenge Questions

6. Solve for x, y, or w in each equation.

    a. $5y - 7 - 3y = 10$ **b**. $6.7 = x - 2.4$ **c**. $4w - 2w = 6$

    d. $-4y - 2 = 3y - 16$ **e**. $8.4 = x - 2.33$ **f**. $\dfrac{3}{4} = w + \dfrac{1}{2}$

    g. $x - 2\dfrac{1}{2} = 1\dfrac{3}{4}$ **h**. $3y + 16 = 7y$ **i**. $\dfrac{4}{5} = w - \dfrac{1}{3}$

Distributive Property with Equations.

The distributive property states that for any number a, b, and c:

$a(b + c) = ab + ac$

$a(b - c) = ab - ac$.

This distributive property is used in simplifying expressions.

Distributive Law with a Positive on the Outside

Example 1
Simplify each expression.

a. 2(x + 4)   **b.** 2(x - 4)   **c.** 3(2n + 6)   **d.** 6(4 - 2g)

Solution

a. 2(x + 4)

$$2(x + 4) = 2 \cdot x + 2 \cdot 4$$ Distributive property; $a(b + c) = ab + ac$.
$$= 2x + 8$$

b. 2(x - 4)

$$2(x - 4) = 2 \cdot x - 2 \cdot 4$$ Distributive property; $a(b - c) = ab - ac$.
$$= 2x - 8$$

c. 3(2n + 6)

$$3(2n + 6) = 3 \cdot 2n + 3 \cdot 6$$ Distributive property; $a(b + c) = ab + ac$
$$= 6n + 18$$

d. 6(4 - 2g)

$$6(4 - 2g) = 6 \cdot 4 - 6 \cdot 2g$$ Distributive property; $a(b - c) = ab - ac$.
$$= 24 - 12g.$$

Exercises
Simplify each expression. Hint: See Example 1.

1. 4(a + 2)   **2.** 3(2x - 6)   **3.** 6(y + 2)   **4.** 8(2w - 5)

5. 4(10 - 3a)   **6.** 3(w - 1)   **7.** 5(3g - 4)   **8.** 3(a + 5)

9. 7(2x + 4)   **10.** 4(3y - 5)   **11.** 6(2 - 46)   **12.** 4(3 + 2x)

13. 5(2a + 1)   **14.** 6(a + b)   **15.** 2(3c - 2)   **16.** 3(2y - 8)

Distributive Law with a Negative on the Outside
During multiplication or division (see Example 2):

1. If all the symbols are positive the answer is positive.

2. If the number of negative symbols is an even number, then the answer is positive.

3. If the number of negative symbols is an odd number, then the answer is negative.

Example 2

Simplify each expression.

  a. -2(3 + 4x)   **b.** -3(-4 + 2a)   **c.** -4(-2x - 6)

  d. -(-2a - 4)   **e.** -(2a + 6)   **f.** -(-3x + 5)

Solution

  a. -2(3 + 4x)

  $-2(3 + 4x) = -2 \cdot 3 + (-2)(4x)$ Distribution property; $-a(b + c) = -ab + (-a)c$.

  $\qquad\qquad = -6 - 8x$ Note, odd number of negative symbols = -

  $\qquad$ (-)(+) = -, therefore, $-2 \cdot 3 = -6$

  $\qquad\qquad\qquad \downarrow \quad \downarrow$

  $\qquad\qquad\qquad$ (-) (+) = -

  Note, odd number of negative symbols = -

  $\qquad$ +(-)(+) = -, therefore, + (-2)(4x) = -8

  $\qquad\qquad\qquad \downarrow \downarrow \quad \downarrow$

  $\qquad\qquad\qquad$ + (-) (+) = -

  b. -3(-4 + 2a)

  $-3(-4 + 2a) = (-3)(-4) + (-3)(2a)$ Distributive property; $-a(-b + c) = (-a)(-b) + (-a)(c)$.

  $\qquad\qquad = 12 - 6a$ Note, even number of negative symbols = +

  $\qquad$ (-)(-) = +, therefore, (-3)(-4) = +12 = 12.

  Note, odd number of negative symbols = -

  $\qquad$ +(-)(+) = -, therefore, + (-3)(2a) = -6.

  $\qquad\qquad\qquad \downarrow \downarrow \quad \downarrow$

  $\qquad\qquad\qquad$ + (-) (+) = -

  c. -4(-2x - 6)

  $-4(-2x - 6) = (-4)(-2x) - (-4)(6)$ Distributive property; $-a(-b - c) = (-a)(-b) - (-a)(c)$.

  $\qquad\qquad = 8x + 24$ Note, even number of negative symbols = +

  $\qquad$ (-)(-) = +, therefore, (-4)(-2x) = +8x = 8x.

  $\qquad\qquad\qquad \downarrow \quad \downarrow$

  $\qquad\qquad\qquad$ (-) (-) = +

  Note, even number of negative symbols = +

  $\qquad$ (-)(-)(+) = +, therefore,   -(-4)(6) = 24

  $\qquad\qquad\qquad \downarrow \downarrow \downarrow$

  $\qquad\qquad\qquad$ - (-)(+) = -

  d. -(-2a - 4)

  $-(-2a- 4) = -2(-a) - (-4)$ Distributive property; $-(-b - c) = -(-b) - (-c)$

  $\qquad\qquad = 2a + 4$ Note, even number of negative symbols = +

  $\qquad$ (-)(-) = +, therefore, -(-a) = +a = a.

  $\qquad\qquad\qquad \downarrow \downarrow$

  $\qquad\qquad\qquad$ (-)(-) = +

  Note, even number of negative symbols = +

  $\qquad$ (-)(-) = +, therefore, - (-4) = +4 = 4.

  $\qquad\qquad\qquad \downarrow \downarrow$

  $\qquad\qquad\qquad$ (-)(-) = +

e. -(2a + 6)

-(2a + 6) = -(2a) + (-)(6)   Distributive property; -(**b** + **c**) = -**b** + (-)(**c**).

= -2a - 6   Note, odd number of negative symbols = -

Hint: See Example 2a.

f. -(-3x + 5)

-(-3x + 5) = -(-3x) + (-)(5)   Distributive property

= 3x - 5   See the preceding examples.

Exercises

1. Simply each expression. Hint: See Example **2a**.

   a. -2(4 + 5a)   **b**. -4(3 + 4x)   **c**. -3(4x + 2)

   d. -5(3y + 6)   **e**. -6(2 + 3w)   **f**. -3(2w + 4)

2. Simplify each expression. Hint: See Example **2b**.

   a. -2(-2 + 2w)   **b**. -3(-4 + 6a)   **c**. -4(-5 + 3w)

   d -5(-6 + 3a)   **e** -2(-3 + 2x)   **f**. -3(-3 + 4a)

3. Simplify each expression. Hint: See Example **2c**.

   a. -3(-3x - 2)   **b**. -2(-6x - 4)   **c**. -5(-7a - 6)

   d. -4(-4y - 3)   **e**. -6(-2w - 5)   **f**. -3(-5w - 5)

4. Simplify each expression. Hint: See Example **2d**.

   a. -3(3a - 3)   **b**. -(-4w - 5)   **c**. -(-6y - 7)

   d. -(-5x - 4)   **e**. -(-7a - 6)   **f**. -(4x - 5)

5. Simplify each expression. Hint: See Example **2e**.

   a. -(3x + 4)   **b**. -4(w + 7)   **c**. -(3a + 6)

   d -(-4y + 5)   **e**. -4(a + 6)   **f**. -(5w + 3)

6. Simplify each expression. Hint: See Example **2f**.

   a. -(-4a + 2)   **b**. -(-3y + 4)   **c**. -(-5w + 3)

   d. -(-3x + 4)   **e**. -(-6y + 2)   **f**. -(-2x + 8)

Challenge Questions

7. Simplify each expression.

   a. -(-3a - 4)   **b**. -2(-4 - 3y)   **c**. -4(6 + 7w)

   d. -(-3w + 6)   **e**. -3(-2w - 3)   **f**. -2(-5 + 3a)

Answers to Selected Questions

1a. -8 - 10a   **2a**. 4 - 4w   **3a**. 9x + 6

4a. -9 + 9a   **5a**. -3x - 4   **6a**. 4a - 2.

Distributive Law with Equations.
Example 1
Solve for y.   2(4 + y) = 12

Solution

$2(4 + y) = 12$

Step 1: Simplify the equation.

$2 \cdot 4 + 2 \cdot y = 12$ Distributive property

$8 + 2y = 12$ $2 \cdot 4 = 8$

Step 2: Isolate 2y by subtracting 8 from both sides of the equation.

$8 - 8 + 2y = 12 - 8$

$2y = 4$ $8 - 8 = 0$ and $12 - 8 = 4$.

Step 3: Isolate y by dividing both sides of the equation by 2.

$$\frac{2y}{2} = \frac{4}{2}$$

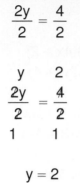

$$y = 2$$

Rules

Two rules are needed when dividing as shown:

Rule 1: If the symbols $(+, -)$ of the numerator and the denominator are the same, the symbol of the answer is **positive**.

For example, $\dfrac{-a}{-a} = +1 = 1$ and $\dfrac{+a}{+a} = \dfrac{a}{a} = 1$.

Rule 2: If the symbols $(+, -)$ of the numerator and the denominator are different, the symbol of the answer is **negative**.

For example, $\dfrac{-a}{a} = -1$ and $\dfrac{a}{-a} = -1$

Example 2

Solve for x. $-3(2x + 3) = -15$

Solution

$-3(2x + 3) = -15$

Step 1: Simplify the equation.

$-3 \cdot (2x) -3 \cdot (+3) = -15$ Distributive property.

$-6x - 9 = -15$ Note, odd number of negative symbols = -

Step 2: Isolate -6x to one side of the equation by adding 9 to both sides of the equation.

$-6x - 9 + 9 = -15 + 9$

$-6x = -6$ $-9 + 9 = 0$ and $-15 + 9 = -6$.

Step 3: Isolate x to one side of the equation by dividing both sides of the equation by -6.

$$\frac{-6x}{-6} = \frac{-6}{-6}$$

$$\frac{\overset{x}{\cancel{-6}x}}{\underset{1}{\cancel{-6}}} = \frac{\overset{1}{\cancel{-6}}}{\underset{1}{\cancel{-6}}}$$

Hint: Rule 1 is used here.

$$x = 1$$

Example 3

Solve for w. $-2(2w - 3) = 12$

Solution

$-2(2w - 3) = 12$

Step 1: Simplify the equation.

   $-2 \cdot 2w - 2 \cdot (-3) = 12$ Distributive property.

   $-4w + 6 = 12$ Note, odd number of negatives = -

            $-(+) = -$, therefore, $-2 \cdot (2w) = -4w$.

               $\downarrow$ $\downarrow$

              $-$ $(+) = -$

        Note, even number of negatives = +.

         $-(-) = +$, therefore, $-2 \cdot (-3) = +6 = 6$.

            $\downarrow$ $\downarrow$

           $-$ $(-) = +$.

Step 2: Isolate -4w to one side of the equation by subtracting 6 from both sides of the equation.

   $-4w + 6 - 6 = 12 - 6$

    $-4w = 6$ $+6 - 6 = 0$ and $12 - 6 = 6$.

Step 3: Isolate w to one side of the equation by dividing both sides by -4.

$$\frac{-4w}{-4} = \frac{6}{-4}$$

$$\frac{\overset{w}{\cancel{-4}w}}{\underset{1}{\cancel{-4}}} = \frac{\overset{3}{\cancel{6}}}{\underset{-2}{\cancel{-4}}}$$

Hint: Rule 1 is used for $\dfrac{-4w}{-4}$ and Rule 2 is used for $\dfrac{6}{-4}$.

$$w = \frac{3}{-2}$$

$$w = -1\frac{1}{2}$$

Example 4

Solve for w. $\qquad -(2w - 4) = -14$

Solution

$-(2w - 4) = -14$

Step 1: Simplify the equation.

$\qquad -(2w - 4) = -14$

$\qquad (-)2w - (-)4 = -14 \qquad$ Distributive property.

$\qquad -2w + 4 = -14 \qquad$ Note, odd number of negative numbers = -.

$\qquad\qquad\qquad\qquad\qquad -(+) = -$, therefore, $-(2w) = -2w$.

$$\downarrow \downarrow$$
$$-(+) = -$$

Note, even number of negatives = +

$-(-) = +$, therefore, $-(-4) = +4 = 4$

$$\downarrow \downarrow$$
$$-(-) = +$$

Step 2: Isolate -2w to one side of the equation by subtracting 4 from both sides of the equation.

$\qquad -2w + 4 - 4 = -14 - 4$

$\qquad -2w = -18 \qquad\qquad\qquad +4 - 4 = 0$ and $-14 - 4 = -18$.

Step 3: Isolate w to one side of the equation by dividing both sides of the equation by -2.

$$\frac{-2w}{-2} = \frac{18}{-2}$$

$$\frac{\overset{w}{\cancel{-2w}}}{\underset{1}{\cancel{-2}}} = \frac{\overset{-9}{\cancel{18}}}{\underset{1}{\cancel{-2}}} \qquad$$ Hint: Rule 1 is used for $\frac{-2w}{-2}$ to obtain $+w = w$ and

$\qquad\qquad\qquad\qquad$ Rule 2 is used for $\frac{18}{-2}$ to obtain -9.

$$w = -9$$

Example 5

Solve for b. $\qquad 2b + 3(b - 4) = 4$

Solution

$2b + 3(b - 4) = 4$

Step 1: Simplify the equation.

$2b + 3 \cdot 2b - 3 \cdot 4 = 4$ Distributive property

$2b + 6b - 12 = 4$

Step 2: Combine the like terms.

$8b - 12 = 4$ $2b + 6b = 8b.$

Step 3: Isolate 8b to one side of the equation by adding 12 to both sides of the equation.

$8b - 12 + 12 = 4 + 12$

     $8b = 16$ $-12 + 12 = 0$ and $4 + 12 = 16$

Step 4: Isolate b to one side of the equation by dividing both sides of the equation by 8.

$$\frac{8b}{8} = \frac{16}{8}$$

$$\frac{\overset{b}{\cancel{8b}}}{\underset{1}{\cancel{8}}} = \frac{\overset{2}{\cancel{16}}}{\underset{1}{\cancel{8}}}$$

$$b = 2$$

Example 6

Solve for x. $9x + 5 - 2(3x + 6) = 14$

Solution

$9x + 5 - 2(3x + 6) = 14$

Step 1: Simplify the equation.

$9x + 5 - 2(3x) + (-2)(6) = 14$ Distributive property

    $9x + 5 - 6x - 12 = 14$

Step 2: Combine the like terms.

$3x - 7 = 14$ $9x - 6x = 3x$ and $5 - 12 = -7$

Step 3: Isolate 3x to one side of the equation by adding 7 to both sides of the equation.

$3x - 7 + 7 = 14 + 7$

     $3x = 21$ $-7 + 7 = 0$ and $14 + 7 = 21$

Step 4: Isolate x by dividing both sides of the equation by 3.

$$\frac{3x}{3} = \frac{21}{3}$$

$$\frac{\overset{x}{\cancel{3x}}}{\underset{1}{\cancel{3}}} = \frac{\overset{7}{\cancel{21}}}{\underset{1}{\cancel{3}}}$$

$x = 7$

Example 7

Solve for n. $2(3 - n) = 16 - 2(3 + 2n)$

Solution

$2(3 - n) = 16 - 2(3 + 2n)$

Step 1: Simplify the equation.

$2 \cdot 3 - 2 \cdot n = 16 - 2 \cdot 3 + (-2)(2n)$ Distributive property.

$6 - 2n = 16 - 6 - 4n$ $+ (-2)(2n) = -2(2n) = -2 \cdot 2n = -4n$

Step 2: Isolate the like terms to the left side of the equation by adding 4n to both sides of the equation and also subtracting 6 from both sides of the equation.

$6 - 6 - 2n + 4n = 16 - 6 - 6 - 4n + 4n$

$-2n + 4n = 4$ $6 - 6 = 0$, $16 - 6 - 6 = 4$, and $-4n + 4n = 0$

$2n = 4$

Step 3: Isolate n to one side of the equation by dividing both sides of the equation by 2.

$$\frac{2n}{2} = \frac{4}{2}$$

$$\frac{\overset{n}{\cancel{2n}}}{2} = \frac{\overset{2}{\cancel{4}}}{\underset{1}{\cancel{2}}}$$

$$n = 2$$

Example 8

Solve for n. $8n - 3(4 - 2n) = 6(n + 1)$

Solution

$8n - 3(4 - 2n) = 6(n + 1)$

Step 1: Simplify the equation.

$8n - 3 \cdot 4 - (-3)(2n) = 6 \cdot n + 6 \cdot 1$ Distributive property.

$8n - 12 + 6n = 6n + 6$ Hint: See previous examples.

Step 2: Isolate the like terms to the left side of the equation by subtraction 6n from both sides of the equation and also by adding 12 to both sides of the equation.

$8n - 12 + 12 + 6n - 6n = 6n - 6n + 6 + 12$

$8n = 6 + 12$ $-12 + 12 = 0$ and $6n - 6n = 0$.

$8n = 18$

Step 3: Isolate n by dividing both sides of the equation by 8.

$$\frac{8n}{8} = \frac{18}{8}$$

$$\frac{\overset{n}{\cancel{8n}}}{\underset{1}{\cancel{8}}} = \frac{18}{8}$$

$$n = 2\frac{2}{8} = 2\frac{1}{4}$$ Review the reduction of fractions to the lowest terms.

Group Exercises

1. Using Rule 1, give the correct answer.

   a. $\dfrac{-6}{-2} =$ **b.** $\dfrac{-10}{-5} =$ **c.** $\dfrac{8}{4} =$ **d.** $\dfrac{-64}{-8} =$

2. Using Rule 2, give the correct answer:

   a. $\dfrac{-8}{-2} =$ **b.** $\dfrac{10}{-5} =$ **c.** $\dfrac{-8}{4} =$ **d.** $\dfrac{64}{-8} =$

Exercises.

1. Solve for x, y, or w. Hint: See Example 1.

   a. $3(2 + x) = 12$ **b.** $4(5 + w) = 28$ **c.** $2(3 + y) = 15$

2. Solve for x, y, or w. Hint: See Example 2.

   a. $-2(3x + 3) = -12$ **b.** $-4(3y + 2) = -32$ **c.** $-5(2w + 1) = -15$

3. Solve for x, y, or w. Hint: See Example 3.

   a. $-3(2w - 4) = 24$ **b.** $-4(3y - 2) = 32$ **c.** $-5(2x - 2) = 30$

4. Solve for x, y, or w. Hint: See Example 4.

   a. $-(3w - 3) = -15$ **b.** $-(4y - 5) = -29$ **c.** $-(5x - 6) = -31$

5. Solve for y. Hint: See Example 5.

   a. $3y + 3(3y - 4) = 12$ **b.** $2y + 4(2y - 5) = 10$ **c.** $5y + 3(4y - 2) = 11$

6. Solve for w, x, or y. Hint: See Example 6.

   a. $10w + 7 - 3(2w + 3) = 14$ **b.** $14x + 10 - 4(3x + 2) = 6$ **c.** $15y - 3(4y + 4) + 8 = 8$

7. Solve for w, x, or y. Hint: See Example 7.

   a. $3(4 - w) = 30 - 4(2 + w)$ **b.** $2(5 - 3x) = 28 - 3(3 + 3x)$ **c.** $4(2 - 2y) = -2(4 + 5y) + 28$

8. Solve for w, x, or y. Hint: See Example 8.

   a. $5w - 2(3 - 2w) = 4(w + 1)$ **b.** $2y - 2(8 - 3y) = 3(4 - 2y)$ **c.** $4x - 3(4 - 2x) = 2(2x + 2)$

Challenge Questions

9. Solve for w, x, or y.

   a. $-(3x + 16) = 1$ **b.** $-2(2w - 3) = -10$ **c.** $6y + 2(2y - 3) = 14$

   d. $2(3 - 2w) = 20 - 3(2 + 4w)$ **e.** $6w - 3(1 - w) = 3(w + 3)$

REAL WORLD APPLICATIONS - WORD PROBLEMS

Review the section on "**Algebraic Expressions**" first so that you may be able to write the equations correctly.

Group Review

Write the following phrases in mathematical terms.

1. 8 less than three times **a** is: 3**a** - 8

2. x decreased by 4 times a number is: x - 4n where n is the number.

3. y more than 3 times k is: 3k + y

4. 4 less than 10 times a number is: 10n - 4 where n is the number.

Example 1

If 4 is increased by twice a number, the result is 20.
What is the number?

Solution

Setup: Let the number be x, and therefore, twice the number = 2x. We can write 4 increased by 2x as 4 + 2x.

The result of 4 increased by 2x is 20, therefore,

$$4 + 2x = 20$$

Step 1: Isolate 2x to one side of the equation by subtracting 4 from both sides of the equation.

$$4 - 4 + 2x = 20 - 4 \qquad\qquad 4 - 4 = 0 \text{ and } 20 - 4 = 16.$$
$$2x = 16$$

Step 2: Isolate x to one side of the equation by dividing both sides of the equation by 2.

$$\frac{2x}{2} = \frac{16}{2}$$

$$\frac{\overset{1}{\cancel{\underset{1}{2x}}}}{} = \frac{\overset{8}{\cancel{\underset{1}{16}}}}{}$$

$$x = 8$$

Example 2

3 times a number is subtracted from 8 more than 5 times the number the result is 48.

a. What is the number?

b. Check your answer.

Solution

a. **Setup**: Let the number be n. Therefore, 3 times the number is 3n. We can write 8 more than 5 times the number as $5n + 8$. We can write 3n subtracted from $5n + 8$ as $5n + 8 - 3n$, and therefore, we can write that the result of $5n + 8 - 3$ is 48 as:

$$5n + 8 - 3n = 48$$

Step 1: Isolate the like terms to one side of the equation by subtracting 8 from both sides of the equation.

$$5n + 8 - 8 - 3n = 48 - 8$$
$$5n - 3n = 40$$

Step 2: Combine like terms by subtracting 3n from 5n.

$$2n = 40$$

Step 3: Isolate n to one side of the equation by dividing both sides of the equation by 2.

$$\frac{2n}{2} = \frac{40}{2}$$

$$\frac{\overset{n}{\cancel{2n}}}{\underset{1}{\cancel{2}}} = \frac{\overset{20}{\cancel{40}}}{\underset{1}{\cancel{2}}}$$

$$n = 20$$

b. To check the answer n = 20 substitute 20 for n in the original equation $5n + 8 - 3n = 48$ to see if the result will be 48 or not. If the result is 48 then the answer n = 20 is correct but if the result is not 48 then the answer n = 20 is not correct.

$5n + 8 - 3n = 48$ then becomes $5 \times 20 + 8 - 3 \times 20 = 48$
$$100 + 8 - 60 = 48$$
$$108 - 60 = 48 \quad \text{Review Order of Operations.}$$
$$48 = 48$$

The answer n = 20 is correct.

Example 3

If 4 times Mary's age is increased by 10 more than 3 times her age the result is 59.

a. How old is Mary?

b. Check your answer.

Solution

189

a. **Setup**: Let Mary's age be x, and therefore, 4 times Mary's age = 4x. We can write 10 more than 3 times her age as $3x + 10$. The result of 4x increased by $3x + 10$ is 59 can be written as:

$$4x + 3x + 10 = 59$$

Step 1: Isolate the like terms to one side of the equation by subtracting 10 from both sides of the equation.

$$4x + 3x + 10 - 10 = 59 - 10$$
$$4x + 3x = 49 \qquad 10 - 10 = 0 \text{ and } 59 - 10 = 49.$$

Step 2: Combine the like terms by adding 4x and 3x together.

$$7x = 49$$

Step 3: Isolate x to one side of the equation by dividing both sides of the equation by 70.

$$\frac{7x}{7} = \frac{49}{7}$$

$$\frac{\overset{x}{\cancel{7x}}}{\underset{1}{\cancel{7}}} = \frac{\overset{7}{\cancel{49}}}{\underset{1}{\cancel{7}}}$$

$$x = 7 \text{ years.}$$

b. To check the answer x = 7 years, substitute 7 for x in the original equation $4x + 3x + 10 = 59$ to see if the result will be 59 or not. If the result is 59 then the answer x = 7 years is correct, but if the result is not 59, then the answer x = 7 years is not correct.

$$4x + 3x + 10 = 59 \text{ then becomes } 4 \times 7 + 3 \times 7 + 10 = 59$$
$$28 + 21 + 10 = 59$$
$$59 = 59$$

The answer x = 7 years is correct.

Exercises

1. If 6 is increased by twice a number, the result is 40. Find the number.
Hint: See Example 1.

2. If 8 is increased by 4 times a number, the result is 24. Find the number.
Hint: See Example 1.

3. If 4 times a number is subtracted from 12 more than 6 times the number, the result is 36.
   a. Find the number.   **b**. Check your answer.
Hint: See Example 2.

4. If 3 times John's age is increased by 10 more than 5 times his age, the result is 74.
   a. How old is John?   **b**. Check your answer.
Hint: See Example 3.

Challenge Questions

5. If 2 is increased by twice a number, the result is 20. Find the number.

6. If 4 times Chase's age is increased by 8 more than twice his age, the result is 44.

a. How old is Chase?   **b**. Check your answer.

7. If twice Samuel's age is increased by 4 more than 4 times his age, the result is 48.

   a. How old is Samuel?   **b**. Check your answer.

Cumulative Review

1. Write 13,000,000 in the scientific notation.

2. Write 935,000,000 in the scientific notation.

3. The formula for the area of a rectangle is A = L × W, where A = area, L = length, and W = width. Find L in terms of A and W. Hint: Divide both sides of the equation by W.

4. What is the formula for finding the area of:

   a. A parallelogram?   **b**. A triangle?

5. Find the measure of the angle for x in each triangle.

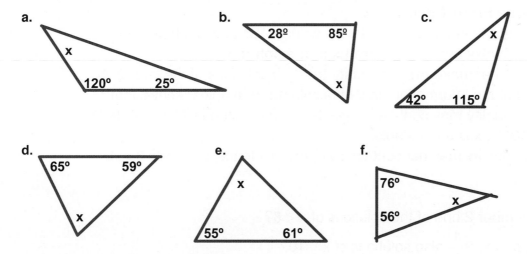

6. Find the value of x in each diagram.

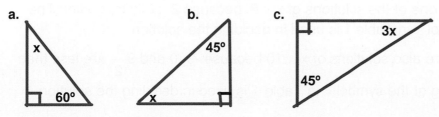

INEQUALITY

The statement that uses > and < to show that two quantities are not equal is an **inequality**. The symbols for inequalities, their meanings, examples, and their solutions are shown in the table below:

Table 1

Symbols	Meaning	Examples	Solutions
<	is less than.	x < 10 means x is less than 10.	Every number less than 10 is a solution.
>	is greater than	x > -3 means x is greater than -3.	Every number greater than -3 is a solution.
≤	is less than or equal to.	x ≤ 6 means x is less than or equal to 6.	Every number less than 6 or equal to 6 is a solution.
≥	is greater than or equal to.	y ≥ -2 means y is greater or equal to -2.	Every number greater than -2 or equal to -2 is a solution.

Conclusions From Table 1

1. Notice that the information under the column "Solutions" shows that:
   a. An inequality may have **more than one solution**.
   b. Values that make **the inequality true** are solutions of the inequality.
2. Notice that the information under the column "Examples" shows that:
   a. An inequality may contain a variable, as in the inequality x < 10. In this inequality, x is the variable.
   b. An inequality may not contain a variable, as in the inequality 3 > -3.

Example 1

a. Is the number 2 one of the solutions of x < 8?

b. Are -9, 0, and $9\frac{1}{2}$ also solutions of x < 10?

Solution

a. Yes, the number 2 is one of the solutions of x < 8, because 2 < 8 is true. Hint: The meaning of the symbol < in Table 1 is used in deciding the solution.

b. Yes, -9, 0, and $9\frac{1}{2}$ are also solutions of x < 10 because -9, 0 and $9\frac{1}{2}$ are less than 10. Hint: The meaning of the symbol < in Table 1 is used in deciding the solution.

Example 2

Are $-2\frac{1}{2}$, 0, and 100 also solutions of x > -3?

Solution

Yes, $-2\frac{1}{2}$, 0, and 100 are also solutions of x > -3 because $-2\frac{1}{2}$, 0, and 100 are greater than -3. Hint: The meaning of the symbol > in Table 1 is used in deciding the solution.

Example 3

Are -99, 0, and $\frac{1}{4}$ also solutions of $x \le \frac{1}{3}$?

Solution

Yes, -99, 0, and $\frac{1}{4}$ are also solutions of $x \le \frac{1}{3}$ because -99, 0, and $\frac{1}{4}$ are less than $\frac{1}{3}$. Hint: The meaning of the symbol $\le$ in Table 1 is used in deciding the solution.

Example 4

a. Are $\frac{1}{8}$, 0, and 50 also solutions of $y \ge -\frac{1}{4}$?

b. Are -10, −1, and $-\frac{3}{4}$ also solutions of $y \ge -\frac{1}{4}$?

Solutions

a. Yes, $\frac{1}{8}$, 0, and 50 are also solutions of $y \ge -\frac{1}{4}$ because $\frac{1}{8}$, 0, and 50 are greater than $-\frac{1}{4}$. Hint: The meaning of the symbol $\ge$ in Table 1 is used in deciding the solution.

b. No, -10, −1, and $-\frac{3}{4}$ are not also solutions of $y \ge -\frac{1}{4}$ because -10, −1, and $-\frac{3}{4}$ are less than $-\frac{1}{4}$. Hint: The meaning of the symbol $\ge$ in Table 1 is used in deciding the solution, additionally, the graphical solution of inequalities on a number line (which is the next section) may help more in the understanding of the solution of example 4b.

How to Graph the Solutions of Inequalities on the Number Line

There are three main steps in graphing all the solutions of inequalities as follows:
Step 1: Draw a number line as shown:

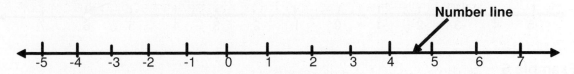

Number line

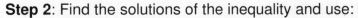

Step 2: Find the solutions of the inequality and use:

    a. a hollow dot to show that a specific number is not a solution as shown:

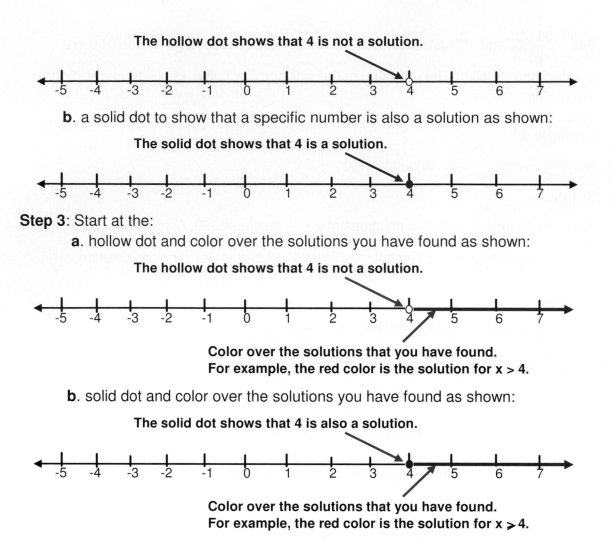

The hollow dot shows that 4 is not a solution.

b. a solid dot to show that a specific number is also a solution as shown:

The solid dot shows that 4 is a solution.

Step 3: Start at the:

    a. hollow dot and color over the solutions you have found as shown:

The hollow dot shows that 4 is not a solution.

Color over the solutions that you have found.
For example, the red color is the solution for x > 4.

    b. solid dot and color over the solutions you have found as shown:

The solid dot shows that 4 is also a solution.

Color over the solutions that you have found.
For example, the red color is the solution for x ≥ 4.

Note: **1.** You may combine Step 1, Step 2, and Step 3 in solving problems.

      2. The red color arrow on the number line shows that the solutions go on forever.

Example 5

Graph the solution of $x < 6$ on a number line.

Solution

Every number less than 6 is a solution of $x < 6$. Let us graph the solution as shown:

The hollow dot shows that 6 is not a solution

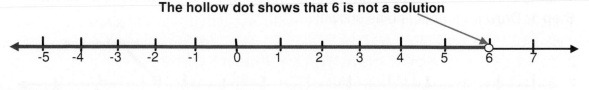

Example 6

Graph the solution of $x > 3$ on a number line.

Solution

Every number greater than 3 is a solution to x > 3. Let us graph the solution as shown:

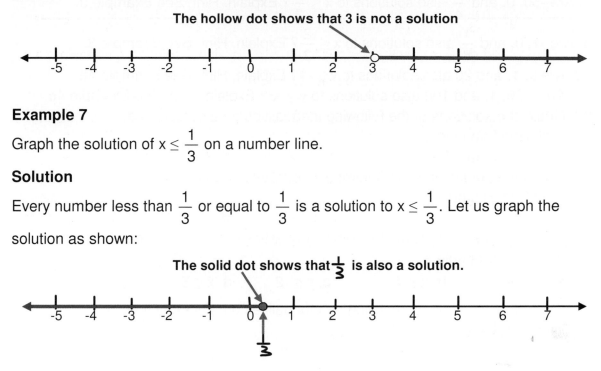

The hollow dot shows that 3 is not a solution

Example 7

Graph the solution of $x \le \dfrac{1}{3}$ on a number line.

Solution

Every number less than $\dfrac{1}{3}$ or equal to $\dfrac{1}{3}$ is a solution to $x \le \dfrac{1}{3}$. Let us graph the solution as shown:

The solid dot shows that $\dfrac{1}{3}$ is also a solution.

Example 8

Graph the solution of $y \ge -\dfrac{1}{4}$ on a number line.

Solution

Every number that is greater than or equal to $-\dfrac{1}{4}$ are solutions to $y \ge -\dfrac{1}{4}$. Let us graph the solution as shown:

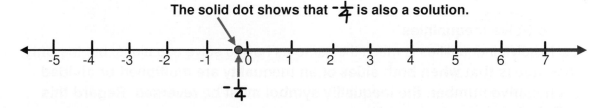

The solid dot shows that $-\dfrac{1}{4}$ is also a solution.

Exercises or Group Exercises

1. List the four symbols of inequality and state what each symbol means.
   Hint: See the Table 1.
2. If x < 6, is 5 a solution? Explain. Hint: See Example 1.
3. If x < 3, are -11 and 0 also solutions? Hint: See Example 1.
4. If x < 8, is 10 a solution? Explain. Hint: See Example 1.
5. If x > 2, is 10 a solution? Explain. Hint: See Example 2.
6. If x > 2, is 0 a solution? Explain. Hint: See Example 2.

7. If $y > 14$, is 13 a solution? Explain. Hint: See Example 4b.

8. Are -50, 0, and $\dfrac{1}{4}$ also solutions to $x \le \dfrac{1}{2}$? Explain. Hint: See Example 3.

9. Are -1, 0, and $\dfrac{1}{8}$ also solutions to $x \le \dfrac{2}{3}$? Explain. Hint: See Example 3.

10. Are 0, 1, and 20 also solutions to $y \ge -1$? Explain. Hint: See Example 4**a**.

11. Are -2, 0, 1, and 100 also solutions to $y \ge -3$? Explain. Hint: See Example 4**a**.

12. Graph the solutions of the following inequalities on a number line.
   Hint: See Example 5.
   a. $x < 4$ **b.** $x < 7$ **c.** $y < 2$ **d.** $x < -3$

13. Graph the solutions of the following inequalities on a number line.
   Hint: See Example 6.
   a. $x > 2$ **b.** $x > 5$ **c.** $x > -2$ **d.** $y > 0$

14. Graph the solutions of the following inequalities on a number line.
   Hint: See Example 7.
   a. $x \le \dfrac{1}{2}$ **b.** $x \le 4$ **c.** $y \le -2$ **d.** $x \le 5$

15. Graph the solutions of the following inequalities on a number line.
   Hint: See Example 8.
   a. $y \ge -\dfrac{1}{2}$ **b.** $y \ge 3$ **c.** $x \ge -2$ **d.** $y \ge 1$

Challenge Questions

16. Graph the solutions of the following inequalities on a number line.
   a. $x \ge 0$ **b.** $x \le 0$ **c.** $x \ge -1$ **d.** $x < -2$
   e. $y \le -5$ **f.** $y < -6$ **g.** $y > 6$ **h.** $x > -4$

17. Explain why -2 is one of the solutions of $x \ge -3$

18. Explain why -4 is not a solution of $x \ge -3$

How to Solve Inequalities

How to solve inequalities is much the same as how to solve equations, but the **only difference is that when both sides of an inequality are multiplied or divided by a negative number, the inequality symbol must be reversed. Regard this as Rule 1**.

Example 1
Solve for x.
$x + 7 \le 3$
Solution
$x + 7 \le 3$
$x + 7 - 7 \le 3 - 7$ Subtract 7 from both sides of the inequality in order to eliminate the 7 at the left side of the equation so

$x + 0 \leq -4$

$\quad x \leq -4$

that x alone will remain at the left side of the inequality.
7 - 7 = 0 and 3 - 7 = -4.

Example 2
Solve for x.

$x - 5 \leq -6$

Solution

$x - 5 \leq -6$

$x - 5 + 5 \leq -6 + 5$

Add 5 to both sides of the inequality in order to eliminate the -5 from the left side of the inequality so that only x remains at the left side of the inequality.
-5 + 5 = 0 and -6 + 5 = -1.

$x + 0 \leq -1$

$x \leq -1$

Example 3
Solve for n

$n + 6 \geq -4$

Solution

$n + 6 \geq -4$

$n + 6 - 6 \geq -4 - 6$

Subtract 6 from both sides of the inequality so that only n remains at the left side of the inequality.
6 - 6 = 0 and -4 - 6 = -10

$n + 0 \geq -10$

$n \quad \geq -10$

Example 4
Solve for t.

$\dfrac{t}{4} \geq -8$

Solution

$\dfrac{t}{4} \geq -8$

$\dfrac{t}{4} \times 4 \geq -8 \times 4$

Multiply both sides of the inequality by 4 in order to eliminate the denominator of 4 from the left side of the inequality so that only t should remain at the left side of the inequality.

$\overset{1}{\underset{1}{\dfrac{t}{4}}} \times 4 \geq -32$

Divide by 4 and also -8 × 4 = -32

$t \geq -32$

197

Example 5

Solve for y. $-2y \leq -5$

Solution

$-2y \leq -5$

$$\frac{-2y}{-2} \geq \frac{-5}{-2}$$

↑

(Reverse the symbol).

Divide both sides of the inequality by -2 and **reverse** the inequality symbol so that only y should remain at the left side of the equation. **See Rule 1.**

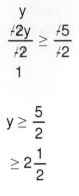

Note: The negative symbols attached to the numerators and the denominators cancel out each other.

$$y \geq \frac{5}{2}$$

$$\geq 2\frac{1}{2}$$

Example 6

Solve for k.

$$\frac{k}{-3} > 6$$

Solution

$$\frac{k}{-3} > 6$$

$$\frac{k}{-3} \times (-3) < 6 \times (-3)$$

↑

(Reverse the symbol).

Multiply both sides of the inequality by -3 in order to eliminate the denominator on the left side of the inequality so that only k remains at the left side of the inequality. **See Rule 1.**

$$\frac{k}{\cancel{-3}} \times (\cancel{-3}) < -18$$

Note: The negative symbols at the left side of the inequality cancel out and also $6 \times (-3) = -18$.

$k < -18$

Example 7

Solve for p.

- 4p ≥ 12
Solution
-4p ≥ 12

$$\frac{-4p}{-4} \leq \frac{12}{-4}$$

↑
(Reverse the symbol).

Divide both sides of the inequality by -4 in order to eliminate the -4 from the left side of the inequality so that only p should remain at the left side of the inequality, and then **reverse** the inequality symbol. **See Rule 1**.

$$\frac{\overset{p}{\cancel{-4p}}}{\underset{1}{\cancel{-4}}} \leq -3$$

Note: The negative symbols that are attached to the inequality cancel out to give positive p which is simply written as p, also 4p ÷ 4 = p and 12 ÷ (-4) = -3.

p ≤ -3

Exercises

1. Judith said that when both sides of an inequality are multiplied or divided by a negative number, the symbol of the inequality is reversed.
Is her statement true or false?

2. Solve for x, n, and k. Hint: See Example 1, 2, and 3.

    a. x + 10 ≤ 12   **b**. n + 2 ≥ 3   **c**. k - 4 ≤ -3

    d. n + 11 ≥ - 3   **e**. x - 3 ≤ 4   **f**. k + 3 < -5

3. Solve for x, n, and k. Hint: See Example 4.

    a. $\frac{k}{6} \geq -2$ **b**. $\frac{n}{4} \leq 3$ **c**. $\frac{x}{2} > 4$

    d. $\frac{n}{3} < -6$ **e**. $\frac{k}{3} > -4$ **f**. $\frac{x}{5} \leq 4$

4. Solve for x, n, and k. Hint: See Examples 5 and 7.

    a. -2y < -8   **b**. -3n < 12   **c**. -4k ≥ 16

    d. -3x ≥ -2   **e**. -5y > 25   **f**. -6k ≤ 36

    g. - 4k ≥ 8   **h**. -2n ≤ -24   **i**. -7x > -21

5. Solve for x, n, and k. Hint: See Example 6.

    a. $\frac{k}{-4} < 2$ **b**. $\frac{n}{-3} \geq 3$ **c**. $\frac{n}{-5} \leq -2$

    d. $\frac{n}{-5} > -3$ **e**. $\frac{x}{-4} < -12$ **f**. $\frac{n}{-2} > 0$

Challenge Questions

6. Solve for x, n, and k.

a. $\dfrac{x}{3} > 5$ **b.** $\dfrac{k}{-2} \le -1$ **c.** $\dfrac{n}{-5} \ge -2$

d. $k + 4 \ge -7$ **e.** $n - 6 < 3$ **f.** $x - 8 \le -4$

Answers to Selected Questions

2a. $x \le 2$ **3a.** $k \ge -12$ **4a.** $y > 4$ **5a.** $k > -8$

Cumulative Review

1. Solve for w in each equation.

a. $2w = 12$ **b.** $\dfrac{w}{5} = 4$ **c.** $\dfrac{2}{3} \times w = 6$

2. The average age of two boys is 8 years. What is their total ages? Hint: You may use the formula for finding averages.

3. $25 \times 5 =$ **4.** $2.5 \times 5 =$ **5.** $2.5 \times .5 =$

4. Find the measure of the angles for b and x in each parallelogram.

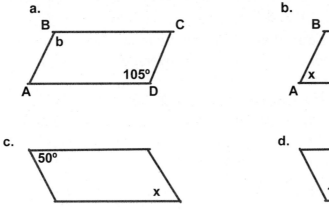

5. By considering each right angle, find the measure of x.

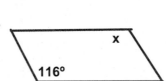

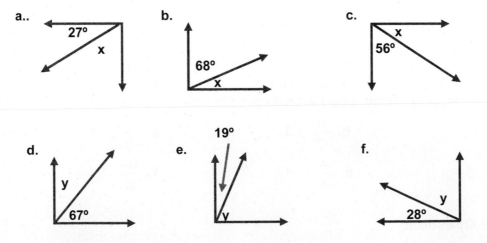

200

SOLVING MULTI-STEP INEQUALITY

Solving Two-step Inequalities

Solving two-step inequalities is much like solving two-step equations, but the symbol of the inequality is reversed when both sides of the inequality are multiplied or divided by a negative number. Regard this statement again as **Rule 1**.

Example 1

Solve and graph $2x - 4 > 2$.

Solution

$2x - 4 > 2$

$2x - 4 + 4 > 2 + 4$ Add 4 to both sides of the inequality in order to eliminate -4 from the left side of the inequality so that only $2x$ should remain at the left side of the inequality.

$2x + 0 > 6$ $-4 + 4 = 0$, and $2 + 4 = 6$

$2x > 6$

$$\frac{2x}{2} > \frac{6}{2}$$ Divide both sides of the inequality by 2 in order to obtain only x at the left side of the inequality.

$$\frac{\overset{x}{\cancel{2x}}}{2} > \frac{\overset{3}{\cancel{6}}}{2}$$
$$1 \qquad 1$$

$x > 3$

This is the graph of $x > 3$.

The hollow dot shows that 3 is not a solution

Example 2

Solve and graph $-8 < 4x + 4$

Solution

$-8 < 4x + 4$

$-8 - 4 < 4x + 4 - 4$ Subtract 4 from both sides of the inequality in order to eliminate the 4 at the right side of the inequality so that only 4x should remain at the right side of the inequality.

$-8 - 4 = -12$, and $4 - 4 = 0$

$$-12 < 4x + 0$$

$$\frac{-12}{4} < \frac{4x}{4}$$

Divide both sides of the inequality by 4 so that only x remains at the right side of the inequality.

$$\frac{\overset{-3}{\cancel{-12}}}{\cancel{4}} < \frac{\overset{x}{\cancel{4x}}}{\cancel{4}}$$
$$1 \qquad 1$$

Note that the inequality symbol is not reversed because the inequality is not divided by a negative number.

$-3 < x$

The graph of $x > -3$ is shown below.

The hollow dot shows that -3 is not a solution

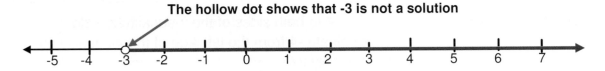

Example 3

Solve and graph $-3x + 7 \leq 4$

Solution

$-3x + 7 \leq 4$

$-3x + 7 - 7 \leq 4 - 7$

Subtract 7 from both sides of the inequality in order to eliminate the 7 on the left side of the inequality so that only -3x should remain at the left side of the inequality.

$-3x + 0 \leq -3$

$7 - 7 = 0, 4 - 7 = -3$.

$-3x \leq -3$

$$\frac{-3x}{-3} \geq \frac{-3}{-3}$$

↑
(Reverse the symbol).

Divide both sides of the inequality by -3 so that only x should remain at the left side of the inequality, and then **reverse** the inequality symbol. Hint: **See Rule 1**.

$$\frac{\overset{x}{\cancel{-3x}}}{\cancel{-3}} \geq \frac{\overset{1}{\cancel{-3}}}{\cancel{-3}}$$
$$1 \qquad 1$$

Note: The negative symbols cancel out so that the answer becomes positive.

$x \geq 1$

The graph of $x \geq 1$ is shown below.

The solid dot shows that 1 is also a solution.

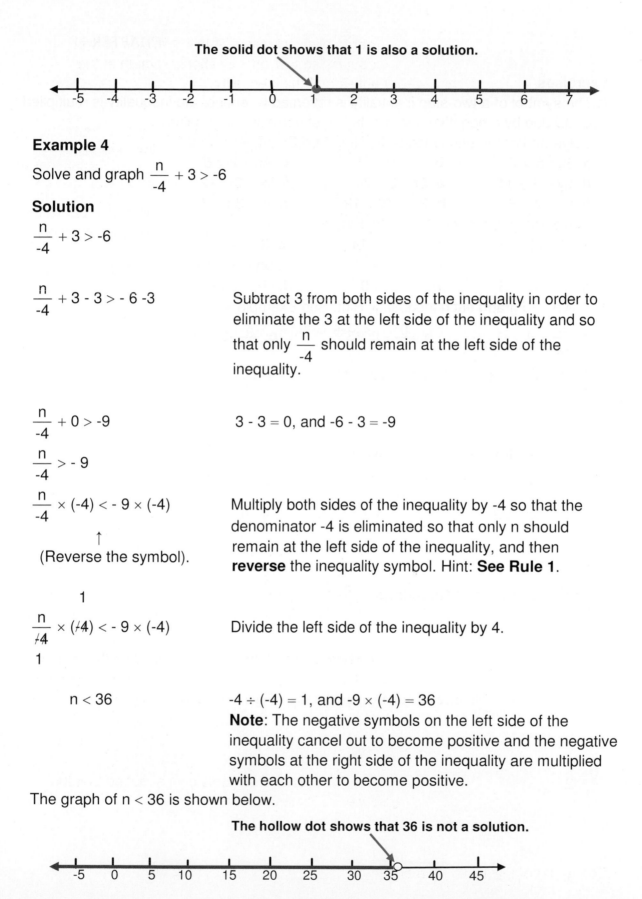

Example 4

Solve and graph $\dfrac{n}{-4} + 3 > -6$

Solution

$\dfrac{n}{-4} + 3 > -6$

$\dfrac{n}{-4} + 3 - 3 > -6 - 3$ Subtract 3 from both sides of the inequality in order to eliminate the 3 at the left side of the inequality and so that only $\dfrac{n}{-4}$ should remain at the left side of the inequality.

$\dfrac{n}{-4} + 0 > -9$ $3 - 3 = 0$, and $-6 - 3 = -9$

$\dfrac{n}{-4} > -9$

$\dfrac{n}{-4} \times (-4) < -9 \times (-4)$ Multiply both sides of the inequality by -4 so that the denominator -4 is eliminated so that only n should remain at the left side of the inequality, and then **reverse** the inequality symbol. Hint: **See Rule 1**.

↑
(Reverse the symbol).

$\overset{1}{\underset{1}{\dfrac{n}{\cancel{-4}}}} \times (\cancel{-4}) < -9 \times (-4)$ Divide the left side of the inequality by 4.

$n < 36$ $-4 \div (-4) = 1$, and $-9 \times (-4) = 36$
Note: The negative symbols on the left side of the inequality cancel out to become positive and the negative symbols at the right side of the inequality are multiplied with each other to become positive.

The graph of $n < 36$ is shown below.

The hollow dot shows that 36 is not a solution.

203

Exercises

1. The symbol of a two-step inequality is reversed whenever the inequality is multiplied or divided by a negative number. Is this statement true or false?

2. Solve and graph each inequality. Hint: See Examples 1 and 2.

    a. $3x - 5 > 7$ **b.** $-5 < 2x - 9$ **c.** $4n + 2 < 6$

    d. $5y + 1 \leq 11$ **e.** $2n - 3 \geq 7$ **f.** $3x + 6 \geq 12$

    g. $6n - 4 > 8$ **h.** $3n + 16 < 12$ **i.** $-6 \geq 3n + 3$

3. Solve and graph each inequality. Hint: See Example 3.

    a. $-2x + 5 \leq 9$ **b.** $8 + 3x < 14$ **c.** $3x - 4 > 8$

    d. $-4x - 6 \geq 10$ **e.** $-6 - 2x \leq -2$ **f.** $5n + 3 < 13$

    g. $4n + 6 > -6$ **h.** $5 - 3x > 8$ **i.** $-7n - 20 \leq -27$

4. Solve and graph each inequality. Hint: See Example 4.

    a. $\dfrac{x}{-2} + 4 > -1$ **b.** $\dfrac{n}{-3} - 2 \leq 3$ **c.** $\dfrac{k}{-4} - 5 < -4$

    d. $-2 + \dfrac{k}{-3} > -4$ **e.** $6 + \dfrac{n}{-4} \leq 7$ **f.** $\dfrac{x}{-6} + 7 > 9$

Challenge Questions

5. Solve and graph each inequality.

    a. $-3n + 2 > -4$ **b.** $\dfrac{n}{-3} - 2 \leq 4$ **c.** $7x - 4 > 3$

    d. $4x + 3 \leq 11$ **e.** $4 + \dfrac{k}{-2} \geq 6$ **f.** $\dfrac{n}{3} - 4 \leq -2$

Answers to Selected Questions

(The answers to the selected questions are located on the next page.)

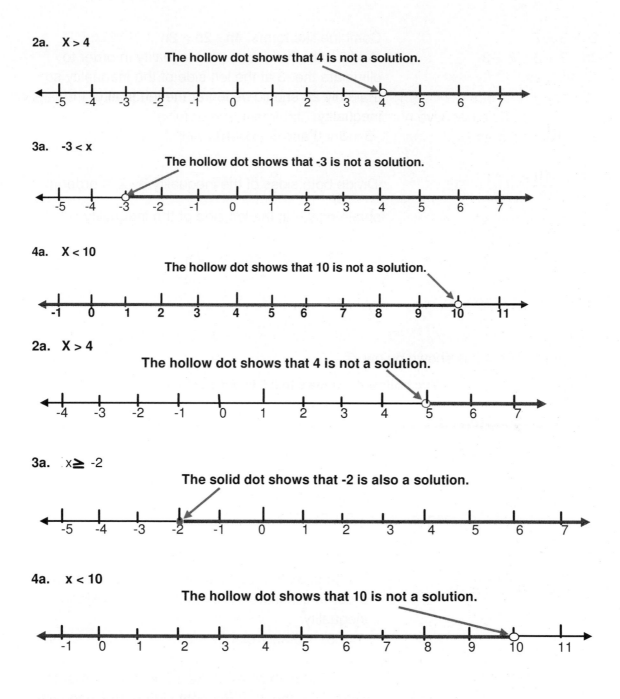

2a. X > 4

The hollow dot shows that 4 is not a solution.

3a. -3 < x

The hollow dot shows that -3 is not a solution.

4a. X < 10

The hollow dot shows that 10 is not a solution.

2a. X > 4

The hollow dot shows that 4 is not a solution.

3a. x ≥ -2

The solid dot shows that -2 is also a solution.

4a. x < 10

The hollow dot shows that 10 is not a solution.

How to Solve Multi-step Inequalities

Solving multi-step inequalities is much like solving an equation but the symbols of the inequalities must be reversed whenever both sides of the inequalities are multiplied or divided by a negative number. Regard this statement as **Rule 1**.

Example 1

Solve and graph $4n - 3 - 2n > 7$

Solution

$4n - 3 - 2n > 7$

205

2n - 3 > 7

Combine like terms. 4n - 2n = 2n

2n - 3 + 3 > 7 + 3

Add 3 to both sides of the inequality in order to eliminate the -3 at the left side of the inequality so that only 2n should be left at the left side of the inequality.

2n > 10

-3 + 3 = 0 and 7 + 3 =10.

$\dfrac{2n}{2} > \dfrac{10}{2}$

Divide both sides of the inequality by 2 in order to obtain only n at the left side of the inequality.

$\dfrac{\overset{1}{\cancel{2}n}}{\underset{1}{\cancel{2}}} > \dfrac{\overset{5}{\cancel{10}}}{\underset{1}{\cancel{2}}}$

n > 5

The graph of n > 5 is shown below.

The hollow dot shows that 5 is not a solution.

Example 2

Solve and graph the inequality 3x + 2 ≤ 6x - 7

Solution

3x + 2 ≤ 6x - 7

3x -3x + 2 ≤ 6x -3x -7

Subtract 3x from both sides of the inequality in order to eliminate the 3x at the left side of the inequality.

0 + 2 ≤ 3x - 7

3x - 3x = 0 and 6x - 3x = 3x.

2 ≤ 3x -7

2 + 7 ≤ 3x - 7 + 7

Add 7 to both sides of the inequality in order to eliminate the -7 at the right side of the inequality so that only 3x should remain at the right side of the inequality.

9 ≤ 3x

2 + 7 = 9 and -7 + 7 = 0.

$\dfrac{9}{3} \le \dfrac{3x}{3}$

Divide each side of the inequality by 3 in order to obtain only x at the right side of the inequality.

$$\frac{9}{3} \leq \frac{3x}{3}$$

$$\frac{3 \quad x}{1 \quad 1}$$

$3 \leq x$

The graph of $3 \leq x$ is shown below.

The solid dot shows that 3 is also a solution.

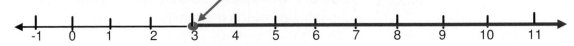

Example 3

Solve and graph the inequality $4 - 6x \geq 8 - 4x$

Solution

$4 - 6x \geq 8 - 4x$

$4 - 6x + 4x \geq 8 - 4x + 4x$ Combine like terms by adding 4x to both sides of the inequality in order to eliminate -4x at the right side of the inequality.

$4 - 2x \geq 8$ $-4x + 4x = 0$ and $-6x + 4x = -2x$.

$4 - 4 - 2x \geq 8 - 4$ Subtract 4 from both sides of the inequality in order to eliminate the 4 at the left side of the inequality and so that only -2x should remain at the left side of the inequality.

$-2x \geq 4$ $4 - 4 = 0$ and $8 - 4 = 0$.

$$\frac{-2x}{-2} \leq \frac{4}{-2}$$

$\uparrow$

(Reverse the symbol).

Divide both sides of the inequality by -2 in order to obtain only x at the left side of the inequality and then **reverse** the inequality symbol.

Hint: See Rule 1.

$$\frac{x \quad -2}{\frac{\cancel{-2}x}{\cancel{-2}} \leq \frac{4}{-2}}$$

$$1 \quad 1$$

Note: The negative symbols on the left side of the inequality cancel out and also $4 \div (-2) = -2$.

$x \leq -2$

The graph of $x \leq -2$ is as shown:

The solid dot shows that -2 is also a solution.

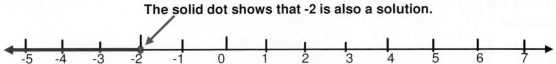

Example 4

Solve and graph the inequality -2n + 3 < -7 - 4n

Solution

-2n + 3 < -7 - 4n

-2n + 2n + 3 < -7 - 4n + 2n   Move or combine all the "ns" to the right side of the inequality by adding 2n to both sides of the inequality in order to eliminate the -2n at the left side of the inequality so that only 3 remains at the left side of the inequality.

3 < -7 - 2n   -2n + 2n = 0 and -4n + 2n = -2n

3 + 7 < -7 + 7 - 2n   Add 7 to both sides of the inequality in order to eliminate the -7 at the right side of the inequality so that only -2n should remain at the right side of the inequality.

10 < -2n   3 + 7 = 10 and -7 + 7 = 0.

$$\frac{10}{-2} > \frac{-2n}{-2}$$

Divide both sides of the inequality by -2 in order to obtain only n at the right side of the inequality and **reverse** the inequality symbol. **Hint: See Rule 1.**

↑
(Reverse the symbol).

$$\frac{\overset{-5}{\cancel{10}}}{-2} > \frac{\overset{n}{\cancel{-2n}}}{\cancel{-2}}$$
$$1 \qquad 1$$

Note: The negative symbols at the right side of the inequality cancel out and also 10 ÷ (-2) = -5.

-5 > n

The graph of -5 > n is as shown:

The hollow dot shows that -5 is not a solution.

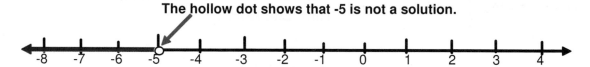

Example 5

Solve and the graph the inequality $\frac{1}{3} \geq \frac{n}{2} - \frac{5}{6}$.

Note how the LCD (least common denominator) is used to solve this problem. Review the LCD.

Solution

$$\frac{1}{3} \geq \frac{n}{2} - \frac{5}{6}$$

208

$\frac{1}{3} \times 6 \geq (\frac{n}{2} - \frac{5}{6})6$

Multiply both sides of the inequality by the LCD of the fractions $\frac{1}{3}$, $\frac{n}{2}$, and $\frac{5}{6}$ which is 6 in order to change the fractions to whole numbers.

$\frac{6}{3} \geq (\frac{n}{2})6 - (\frac{5}{6})6$

Distributive property, for an example, $a(b - c) = ab - ac$.

$\overset{2}{\underset{1}{\frac{6}{3}}} \geq (\frac{n}{2})\overset{3}{\underset{1}{6}} - (\frac{5}{6})\overset{1}{\underset{1}{6}}$

$\frac{6}{3} = 2$, $(\frac{n}{2})6 = 3n$, and $(\frac{5}{6})6 = 5$

$2 \geq 3n - 5$

$2 + 5 \geq 3n - 5 + 5$

Add 5 to both sides of the inequality in order to eliminate the -5 at the right side of the inequality and also to obtain only 3n at the right side of the inequality.

$7 \geq 3n$

$2 + 5 = 7$ and $-5 + 5 = 0$.

$\frac{7}{3} \geq \frac{3n}{3}$

Divide both sides of the inequality by 3 in order to obtain only n at the right side of the inequality.

$2\frac{1}{3} \geq \frac{\overset{n}{\cancel{3n}}}{\underset{1}{\cancel{3}}}$

$2\frac{1}{3} \geq n$

The graph of $2\frac{1}{3} \geq n$ is as shown:

The solid dot shows that $2\frac{1}{3}$ is also a solution.

Example 6

Solve and graph the inequality $-\frac{3x}{4} + \frac{2}{3} > -\frac{x}{2} + \frac{7}{8}$

Note how the LCD (least common denominator) is used to solve the problem.

Solution

$$-\frac{3x}{4} + \frac{2}{3} > -\frac{x}{2} + \frac{7}{8}$$

$$(-\frac{3x}{4} + \frac{2}{3})24 > (-\frac{x}{2} + \frac{7}{8})24$$

Multiply both sides of the inequality by the LCD of the fraction $\frac{3x}{4}$, $\frac{2}{3}$, $\frac{x}{2}$, and $\frac{7}{8}$ which is 24 in order to change the fractions into whole numbers.

$$(-\frac{3x}{4})24 + (\frac{2}{3})24 > (-\frac{x}{2})24 + (\frac{7}{8})24$$

Distributive property, for example, $a(b + c) = ab + ac$.

$$\overset{6}{(-\frac{3x}{4})}24 + \overset{8}{(\frac{2}{3})}24 > \overset{12}{(-\frac{x}{2})}24 + \overset{3}{(\frac{7}{8})}24$$

$$(-3x)6 + (2)8 > (-x)12 + (7)3$$
$$-18x + 16 > -12x + 21$$
$$-18x + 12x + 16 > -12x + 12x + 21$$

Combine like terms of x by adding 12x to both sides of the inequality in order to eliminate the -12x at the right side of the inequality.
$-18x + 12x = -6x$, and $-12x + 12x = 0$.

$$-6x + 16 > 0 + 21$$
$$-6x + 16 > 21$$
$$-6x + 16 - 16 > 21 - 16$$

Subtract 16 from both sides of the inequality in order to eliminate the 16 at the left side of the inequality so that only -6x should remain on the left side of the inequality.
$16 - 16 = 0$, and $21 - 16 = 5$.

$$-6x + 0 > 5$$
$$-6x > 5$$

$$\frac{-6x}{-6} < \frac{5}{-6}$$
$$\uparrow$$
(Reverse the symbol).

Divide both sides of the inequality by -6 so that only x remains at the right side of the inequality and then **reverse** the inequality symbol because you are dividing by a negative number.
Hint: See Rule 1

$$\overset{x}{\frac{\cancel{-6}x}{\cancel{-6}}} < \frac{5}{-6}$$
$$1$$

Note: The negative symbols at the left side of the inequality cancel out.

$x < -\dfrac{5}{6}$

The graph of $x < -\dfrac{5}{6}$ is as follows:

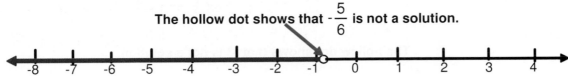

The hollow dot shows that $-\dfrac{5}{6}$ is not a solution.

Exercises

1. Whenever both sides of an equality are multiplied or divided by a negative number, the inequality symbol must be_____.

2. Solve and graph the following inequalities. Hint: See Examples 1 and 2.

a. $4x - 2 - 2x > 6$ **b.** $4x - 2 - 3x < 5$ **c.** $2x + 2 \le 5x - 7$

d. $3 + 6n \ge 3n - 15$ **e.** $4n + n - 3 > 12$ **f.** $4 - 2n < 3n - 6$

3. Solve and graph the following inequalities. Hint: See Example 4.

a. $-2x + 8 > -5x - 1$ **b.** $-6n + 5 \ge -2n + 21$

c. $3k - 5k + 7 \le -1$ **d.** $-1 - 3n < 15 - 7n$

4. Solve and graph the following inequalities. Hint: See Examples 5 and 6.

a. $\dfrac{1}{4} \le \dfrac{n}{-3} - \dfrac{1}{6}$ **b.** $\dfrac{n}{4} - \dfrac{3}{8} > \dfrac{1}{2}$ **c.** $\dfrac{1}{2} + \dfrac{2n}{3} > \dfrac{5}{6}$

d. $\dfrac{-3n}{4} + \dfrac{1}{2} \ge \dfrac{n}{2} - \dfrac{3}{4}$ **e.** $\dfrac{2}{3} - \dfrac{5n}{9} \le -\dfrac{n}{3} + \dfrac{4}{9}$ **f.** $-\dfrac{n}{6} - \dfrac{2}{3} < \dfrac{2}{3} - \dfrac{5n}{6}$

Challenge Questions

5. Solve and graph the following inequalities.

a. $5x + 2 < 2x + 8$ **b.** $6 - 2n > 5n - 8$ **c.** $\dfrac{3x}{4} - \dfrac{3}{8} \ge \dfrac{1}{4} + \dfrac{x}{8}$

d. $5k + 5 < 13 + k$ **e.** $\dfrac{4}{5} - \dfrac{3x}{5} \le -\dfrac{4}{5} - \dfrac{x}{10}$ **f.** $9 - 6n - 1 > -2n$

Answers to Selected Questions

(The answers to the selected questions are located on the next page.)

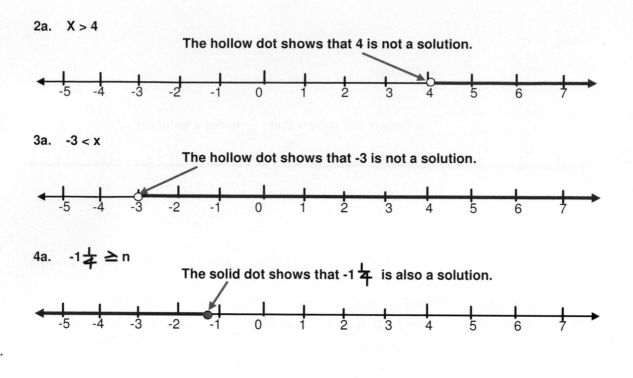

2a. X > 4

The hollow dot shows that 4 is not a solution.

3a. -3 < x

The hollow dot shows that -3 is not a solution.

4a. $-1\frac{1}{4} \geq n$

The solid dot shows that $-1\frac{1}{4}$ is also a solution.

SQUARE ROOTS

The square root of a number x is a number y such that when y is multiplied by itself, equals the original number x. The symbol for square root is $\sqrt{}$.

$$\text{If } x = y \cdot y,$$
$$\text{then } \sqrt{x} = \sqrt{y \cdot y}$$
$$= y$$

Example 1

Find the square root of 4.

Solution

Step 1: To find the square root of 4, find the factors of 4 such that when the factor is multiplied by itself, equals 4. This factor is the square root of 4.

The factors of 4 are: 4×1

2×2

Step 2: Select the factor that, when multiplied by itself equals 4.

The factors $2 \times 2 = 4$, therefore, the square root of 4 is 2.

We can write the square root of 4 is 2 mathematically as $\sqrt{4} = 2$.

212

Example 2

Find the $\sqrt{25}$.

Solution

Step 1: To find the $\sqrt{25}$, find the factors of 25 such that the factor multiplied by itself equals 25 is the square root.

The factors of 25 are: 25×1 and 5×5

Step 2: Select the factor that, when multiplied by itself equals 25.

The factor $5 \times 5 = 25$, therefore,

$$\sqrt{25} = \sqrt{5 \times 5}$$
$$= 5$$

Important Rules

For any number represented by x and y:

Rule 1: If $x = y \cdot y = y^2$, then

$$\sqrt{x} = \sqrt{y \cdot y} = \sqrt{y^2}$$
$$= y$$

Rule 2: If $x = y \cdot y = y^2$, then

$$-\sqrt{x} = -\sqrt{y \cdot y} = -\sqrt{y^2}$$
$$= -y$$

Rule 3: If $x = y \cdot y = y^2$ then

$$\pm\sqrt{x} = \pm\sqrt{y \cdot y} = \pm\sqrt{y^2}$$

Rule 4: $\sqrt{0} = 0$ and $\sqrt{1} = 1$

Example 3

Find the $\sqrt{11^2}$.

Solution

Using Rule 1, $\sqrt{11^2} = 11$

Example 4

Find the $-\sqrt{25}$.

Solution

Using Rule 2, $-\sqrt{25} = -\sqrt{5 \times 5} = -\sqrt{5^2}$
$$= -5$$

Example 5

Find the $\pm\sqrt{100}$.

Solution

Using Rule 3, $\pm\sqrt{100} = \pm\sqrt{10 \times 10} = \pm\sqrt{10^2}$

$$= \pm 10$$

Exercises

1. Describe how you can find the square root of a number.
2. Find the value. Hint: See Examples 1, 2, and Rule 1.

   a. $\sqrt{9}$ **b.** $\sqrt{16}$ **c.** $\sqrt{36}$ **d.** $\sqrt{49}$ **e.** $\sqrt{64}$

3. Find the value. Hint: See Example 3 and Rule 1.

   a. $\sqrt{3^2}$ **b.** $\sqrt{6^2}$ **c.** $\sqrt{p^2}$ **d.** $\sqrt{9^2}$ **e.** $\sqrt{12^2}$

4. Find the value. Hint: See Examples 4.

   a. $-\sqrt{9}$ **b.** $-\sqrt{36}$ **c.** $-\sqrt{4^2}$ **d.** $-\sqrt{81^2}$ **e.** $-\sqrt{100}$

5. Find the value. Hint: See Example 5 and Rule 3.

   a. $\pm\sqrt{25}$ **b.** $\pm\sqrt{25}$ **c.** $\pm\sqrt{25}$ **d.** $\pm\sqrt{25}$ **e.** $\pm\sqrt{25}$

Challenge Questions

6. Find the value.

   a. $\sqrt{81}$ **b.** $-\sqrt{132}$ **c.** $\pm\sqrt{64}$ **d.** $\sqrt{100}$ **e.** $\pm\sqrt{16}$

Notes

1. The symbol $\sqrt{}$ is the square root and it is also called the radial symbol.

2. $\sqrt{2}$ for an example is known as the radical number.

3. $\sqrt{4}$ for an example is read as the positive square root of 4.

4. $-\sqrt{4}$ for an example is read as the negative square root of 4.

5. $\pm\sqrt{4}$ for an example is read as positive or negative square root of 4.

6. The square roots of numbers that can be found easily without decimals such as
$\sqrt{4} = 2$, $\sqrt{9} = 3$, and $\sqrt{25} = 5$ are called **perfect squares**. Therefore, any number
that is the square of an integer is called a **perfect square**.

How to Solve Expressions Involving the Square Root Symbol

To solve for the expression involving the square root symbol such as $\sqrt{x^2 + y^2}$,

Step 1: Find the square root of each number, and then add the squares of the numbers together. Let's assume that $x^2 + y^2 = z$, then,

$$\sqrt{x^2 + y^2} = \sqrt{z}$$

Step 2: Find the value of $\sqrt{z}$.

Example 6

Find the value of $\sqrt{8^2 + 6^2}$

Solution

Step 1: Find the square of each number, and then add the squares of each of the numbers together.

$$\sqrt{8^2 + 6^2} = \sqrt{8 \cdot 8 + 6 \cdot 6}$$
$$= \sqrt{64 + 36}$$
$$= \sqrt{100}$$

Step 2: Find the value of $\sqrt{100}$.

$$\sqrt{100} = \sqrt{10 \cdot 10} = \sqrt{10^2}$$
$$= 10 \qquad \text{Rule 1 is used.}$$

Example 7

Find the value of $\sqrt{3^2 + 1^2 + 1^2 + 2^2 + 1^2}$.

Solution

Step 1: Find the square of each number, and then add the squares of the numbers together.

$$\sqrt{3^2 + 1^2 + 1^2 + 2^2 + 1^2} = \sqrt{3 \cdot 3 + 1 \cdot 1 + 1 \cdot 1 + 2 \cdot 2 + 1 \cdot 1}$$
$$= \sqrt{9 + 1 + 1 + 4 + 1}$$
$$= \sqrt{16}$$

Step 2: Find the value of $\sqrt{16}$.

$$\sqrt{16} = \sqrt{4 \cdot 4} = \sqrt{4^2}$$
$$= 4 \qquad \text{Rule 1 is used.}$$

Exercises

1. Find the values. Hint: See Example 6.

   a. $\sqrt{4^2 + 3^2}$ **b.** $\sqrt{12^2 + 5^2}$ **c.** $\sqrt{6^2 + 8^2}$

2. Find the values. Hint: See Example 7.

   a. $\sqrt{6^2 + 3^2 + 2^2}$ **b.** $\sqrt{2^2 + 1^2 + 4^2 + 2^2}$

REAL WORLD APPLICATIONS - WORD PROBLEMS
Square Roots

Example 1

Find the perimeter of a square which has an area of 25 ft^2

Solution

Setup: Area of a square = side × side.

Therefore, 25 ft^2 = side × side.

25 ft^2 = s × s   Let a side of the square = s ft.

25 ft^2 = s^2 _____ [A].

Step 1: Find the value of the side or s.

To find s, find the square root of both sides of equation [A].

$$\sqrt{25 \text{ ft}^2} = \sqrt{s^2}$$

$$\sqrt{5^2 \text{ ft}^2} = \sqrt{s^2}$$

5 ft = s   Hint: See Rule 1.

$$\sqrt{5^2 \text{ ft}^2} = 5 \text{ ft. and } \sqrt{s^2} = s.$$

Therefore, the side of the square is 5 ft. long.

Step 2: Find the perimeter of the square.

The perimeter is the distance around the square.

The square has 4 equal sides therefore:

Perimeter of the square = 4 × s   where s = length of a side of the square.

= 4 × 5 ft   s = 5 ft

= 20 ft

Exercises - Applications

1. The area of a square is 16 cm^2. Find the perimeter of the square. Hint: See Example 1.

2. Find the perimeter of a square which has an area of 49 m^2 Hint: See Example 1.

3. A square swimming pool has an area of 100 m^2. Find the perimeter of the swimming pool. Hint: See Example 1.

4. Find the perimeter of each of the **square** diagrams.

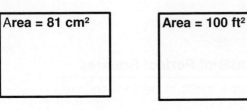

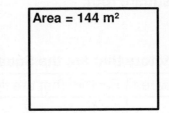

Area = 81 cm²   Area = 100 ft²   Area = 144 m²

Note: All the diagrams in this book are not drawn to scale.

Hint: See Example 1.

5. Find the perimeter of a square which has an area of 36 m². Hint: See Example 1.

Answer to a Selected Question

1. 16 cm.

Cumulative Review

1. Simplify:

   a. $4^2 - 3^2 =$ **b.** $5^2 + 2^2 =$ **c.** $4^2 \div 2^2 =$

   d. $6^2 \div 2^2 =$ **e.** $3^2 \cdot 3^2 =$ **f.** $50 \div 5^2 =$

2. Find each square root.

   a. $\sqrt{16} =$ **b.** $\sqrt{25} + 6 =$ **c.** $\sqrt{36} + \sqrt{9} =$

3. What is the sum of the measures of the angles on a line?

4. Simplify: $\sqrt{49} + 4^2 - 20 =$

SQUARE ROOT OF PERFECT SQUARES

Review

A **perfect square** is a number that has an integer as its square root.

For an example: $\sqrt{25} = \sqrt{5 \times 5} = \sqrt{5^2} = 5$. So 25 is a perfect square. Note that the **square root** of the square of a number is the number itself. (**Integers** are a set of whole numbers including their opposites and zero such as ..., -5, -4, -3, -2, -1, 0, 1, 2, 3, 4, 5, ...) The square root of a perfect square is the factor of a number that can be multiplied by itself to obtain the perfect square.

Some perfect squares are 1, 4, 9, 16, 25, 36, 48, 64, 81, and 100. The factor of each perfect square that can be multiplied by itself to obtain the perfect square are listed as shown:

   $25 = 5 \cdot 5$, $36 = 6 \cdot 6$, $49 = 7 \cdot 7$, $64 = 8 \cdot 8$, $81 = 9 \cdot 9$, and $100 = 10 \cdot 10$.

Notice that 1, 4, 9, 16, 25, 36, 48, 64, 81, and 100 are called perfect squares because they are **squares of integers**. Notice also that the opposite of squaring a number is

finding its square root.

Some Factors that are the Square Roots of Perfect Squares

Perfect squares	Factors that are the square roots of perfect squares
1	$1 \cdot 1 = 1$
4	$2 \cdot 2 = 4$
9	$3 \cdot 3 = 9$
16	$4 \cdot 4 = 16$
25	$5 \cdot 5 = 25$
36	$6 \cdot 6 = 36$
49	$7 \cdot 7 = 49$
64	$8 \cdot 8 = 64$
81	$9 \cdot 9 = 81$
100	$10 \cdot 10 = 100$

How to find the Positive and Negative Square Roots of a Number

The symbol $\sqrt{}$ is used to indicate the positive or principal square root, and the symbol $-\sqrt{}$ is used to indicate the negative square root.

Both the positive and the negative square roots may be combined and written as $\pm\sqrt{}$.

Example 1

Find the two square roots of:

a. 25   **b.** 1

Solution

a. $\sqrt{25} = \sqrt{5 \times 5}$ The factors of 25 that can be multiplied by itself to obtain 25 is 5. For example, $5 \times 5 = 25$.

$= \sqrt{5^2}$ $5 \times 5 = 5^2$

$= 5$ Recall that the square root of the square of a number is the number itself.

Also, $-\sqrt{25} = -\sqrt{5 \times 5}$ $25 = 5 \times 5$

$= -\sqrt{5^2}$ $5 \times 5 = 5^2$

$= -5$ Recall that the square root of the square of a number is the number itself.

Since $5 \times 5 = 25$ and $-5 \times (-5) = 25$, then both 5 and -5 are the two square roots of 25.

218

b. $\sqrt{1} = \sqrt{1 \cdot 1}$ The factors of 1 that can be multiplied by itself to obtain 1 is 1. For example, $1 \times 1 = 1$.

$\sqrt{1} = \sqrt{1^2}$ $1 \cdot 1 = 1^2$

     $= 1$ Recall that the square root of the square of a number is the number itself.

Also, $-\sqrt{1} = -\sqrt{1 \times 1}$ $1 = 1 \times 1$

     $= -\sqrt{1^2}$ $1 \times 1 = 1^2$

     $= -1$ Recall that the square root of the square of a number is the number itself.

Since $1 \times 1 = 1$ and $-1 \times (-1) = 1$, then both 1 and -1 are the two square roots of 1.

How to Evaluate Expressions Involving Square Roots

Example 2

Evaluate $3\sqrt{4} - 1$

Solution

$3\sqrt{4} - 1 = 3 \cdot 2 - 1$ Use the order of operations (PERMDAS) to solve this problem. See the section on the Order of Operations. Do the square root first, $\sqrt{4} = 2$.

     $= 6 - 1$ Do the multiplication second. See the section or the chapter on PERMDAS, $3 \cdot 2 = 6$

     $= 5$ Do the subtraction last. See PERMDAS. $6 - 1 = 5$

Example 3

Evaluate $\sqrt{9 + 16} + 3$

Solution

$\sqrt{9 + 16} + 3 = \sqrt{25} + 3$ Do the operation (addition) under the square root first. $\sqrt{9 + 16} = \sqrt{25}$ see PERMDAS.

     $= 5 + 3$ $\sqrt{25} = 5$. Find the square root second.

     $= 8$ $5 + 3 = 8$. Do the addition last.

Example 4

Evaluate $3\sqrt{16 + 9} - 8$

Solution

$3\sqrt{16 + 9} - 8 = 3\sqrt{25} - 8$ Do the operation (addition) under the square root first. Review the Order of Operations. See PERMDAS.

$= 3 \cdot 5 - 8$ $\sqrt{25} = 5$. Find the square root second, see PERMDAS.

$= 15 - 8$ $3 \cdot 5 = 15$. Do the multiplication third, see PERMDAS.

$= 7$ $15 - 8 = 7$. Do the subtraction last, see PERMDAS.

Example 5

Find the square root of $\dfrac{25}{4}$.

Solution

The square root of $\dfrac{25}{4} = \sqrt{\dfrac{25}{4}}$ Use the square root symbol, $\sqrt{}$.

$= \dfrac{\sqrt{25}}{\sqrt{4}}$ The square root of the numerator and the denominator of a fraction can be found separately if the fraction does not reduce to to a whole number.

$= \dfrac{5}{2}$ Do the square root operation first. $\sqrt{25} = 5$, and $\sqrt{4} = 2$. See PERMDAS.

$= 2\dfrac{1}{2}$ Do the division last. See PERMDAS.

Example 6

Evaluate $3\sqrt{\dfrac{32}{2}} + 12$

Solution

$3\sqrt{\dfrac{32}{2}} + 12 = 3\sqrt{16} + 12$ Note that the square root of the numerator of 32 and the denominator of 2 cannot be found separately and easily, but the fraction $\dfrac{32}{2}$ reduces to a whole number of 16. So we do the operation under the square root first. $\dfrac{32}{2} = 16$. See PERMDAS.

$= 3 \cdot 4 + 12$ Complete the operation involving the square root. $\sqrt{16} = 4$.

$= 12 + 12$ Do the multiplication second. $3 \cdot 4 = 12$. See PERMDAS.

$= 24$ Do the addition last. See PERMDAS, $12 + 12 = 24$.

Example 7

Evaluate $-(\sqrt{81} - \sqrt{16})$.

Solution

$-(\sqrt{81} - \sqrt{16}) = -(9 - 4)$ Do the operations (square roots) in the parenthesis first, See PERMDAS. $\sqrt{81} = 9$ and $\sqrt{16} = 4$.

$= -(5)$ Complete doing the operation (subtraction) in the parenthesis. $9 - 4 = 5$. See PERMDAS.

$= -5$

Example 8

Evaluate $-(\sqrt{9} \cdot \sqrt{100})$.

Solution

$-(\sqrt{9} \cdot \sqrt{100}) = -(3 \cdot 10)$ Do the operations (square roots) in the parenthesis first. See PERMDAS. $\sqrt{9} = 3$ and $\sqrt{100} = 10$.

$= -(30)$ Complete the operation (multiplication) in the parenthesis next. $3 \cdot 10 = 30$. See PERMDAS.

$= -30$

REAL WORLD APPLICATIONS - WORD PROBLEMS
Square Root of Perfect Squares

Example 9

A cocoa farm in Ghana is in the form of a square. If the area of the farm is 4 square miles, find how long is a side of the farm.

Solution

The formula for finding the area of the square cocoa farm is:

    Area = Side · Side

    Area = S · S   Let S = Side = Length of a side

    Area = S^2 _____[A]

Substitute Area = 4 square miles into equation [A] as follows:

    $4 \text{ mi}^2 = S^2$ _____[B]

Find the square root of both sides of equation [B] as shown:

$$\sqrt{4 \text{ mi}^2} = \sqrt{S^2}$$

$$\sqrt{2^2 \text{ mi}^2} = \sqrt{S^2} \qquad 4 = 2^2$$

2 mi = S   Recall that the square root of the square of a number is the number itself.

Therefore, the side of the squared cocoa farm is 2 miles.

Example 10

A school's swimming pool is in the shape of a square. If a side of the square is 2 kilometers, what is the area of the swimming pool?

Solution

A side of the square swimming pool = 2 km

The formula for the area of the square swimming pool is:

Area = Side · Side

Area = S · S   Let S = Side.

Area = S^2 _____[A]

Substitute S = 2 km in equation [A] as follows:

Area = $(2 \text{ km})^2$

   = 2 km · 2 km $(2 \text{ km})^2 = 2 \text{ km} \cdot 2 \text{ km}$

   = 4 km^2.

Therefore, the area of the squared swimming pool is 4 km^2.

Example 11

Evaluate: **a.** $\pm\sqrt{16}$ **b.** $\pm\sqrt{36}$

Solution

a. $\pm\sqrt{16} = \pm\sqrt{4^2}$ $16 = 4^2$

   = ±4 because both the positive and negative roots are indicated. Recall that the square root of the square of a number is the number itself.

b. $\pm\sqrt{36} = \pm\sqrt{6^2}$ $36 = 6^2$

   = ±6 because both the positive and negative roots are indicated. Recall that the square root of the square of a number is the number itself.

Example 12

Solve each equation.

a. $n^2 = 9$ **b.** $16 = t^2$ **c.** $y^2 = \dfrac{4}{25}$ **d.** $0.16 = w^2$

Solution

a. $n^2 = 9$ Given in the question.

$\sqrt{n^2} = \pm\sqrt{9}$ Equations with squares can be solved by taking the square root of both sides of the equation. This is because the square root of the number that is squared (or raised to the second power) equals the number itself.

$n = \pm 3$ The square root of the number that is squared (or raised to the second power) equals the number itself. So, $\sqrt{n^2} = n$, and $\pm\sqrt{9} = \pm\sqrt{3^2} = \pm 3$. Recall that every positive number has both a positive and a negative square roots.

b. $16 = t^2$ Given in the question.

$\pm\sqrt{16} = \sqrt{t^2}$ Equations with squares can be solved by taking the square root of both sides of the equation. This is because the square root of the number that is squared (or raised to the second power) equals the number itself.

$\pm 4 = t$ The square root of the number that is squared (or raised to the second power) equals the number itself. So, $\sqrt{t^2} = t$, and $\pm\sqrt{16} = \pm 4$. Recall that every positive number has both a positive and a negative square roots.

c. $y^2 = \dfrac{4}{25}$ Given in the question.

$\sqrt{y^2} = \pm\sqrt{\dfrac{4}{25}}$ Equations with squares can be solved by taking the square root of both sides of the equation. This is because the square root of the number that is squared (or raised to the second power) equals the number itself.

$y = \pm\dfrac{2}{5}$ The square root of the number that is squared (or raised to the second power) equals the number itself. So, $\sqrt{y^2} = y$, and $\pm\sqrt{\dfrac{4}{25}} = \pm\sqrt{\dfrac{2^2}{5^2}} = \pm\dfrac{2}{5}$. Recall that every positive number has both a positive and a negative square roots.

d. $0.16 = w^2$ Given in the question.

$\pm\sqrt{0.16} = \sqrt{w^2}$ Equations with squares can be solved by taking the square root of both sides of the equation. This is because the square root of the number that is squared (or raised to the second power) equals the number itself.

$\pm 0.4 = w$ The square root of the number that is squared (or raised to the second power) equals the number itself. So, $\sqrt{w^2} = w$, and $\pm\sqrt{0.16} = \pm\sqrt{0.4^2} = \pm 0.4$. We can also find $\sqrt{0.16}$ on the calculator by depressing $.16\sqrt{} =$ on the calculator to obtain 0.4. Recall that every positive number has both a positive and a negative square roots. Hint: See page 239 about how to use a calculator to find the square root of a number.

Exercises

1. Complete the statements:
   a. A perfect square is _____
   b. The opposite of squaring a number is finding a _____
2. Find the two square roots of each number.
   a. 9   **b.** 36   **c.** 81   **d.** 16   **e.** 4
   Hint: See Example 1.
3. Evaluate each expression. Hint: See Example 2.
   a. $2\sqrt{4} + 10$ **b.** $3\sqrt{36} - 4$ **c.** $2\sqrt{100}$
   d. $4\sqrt{81} + 6$ **e.** $2\sqrt{144} - 8$ **f.** $4\sqrt{25} + 11$
4. Evaluate each expression. Hint: See Example 3.
   a. $\sqrt{5 + 20} + 9$ **b.** $\sqrt{6 + 30} - 5$ **c.** $\sqrt{59 + 5} + 9$
   d. $\sqrt{4 + 12} - 3$ **e.** $\sqrt{29 - 4} + 3$ **f.** $\sqrt{92 - 11} - 4$
5. Evaluate each expression. Hint: See Example 4.
   a. $3\sqrt{27 - 2} + 5$ **b.** $2\sqrt{45 - 9} - 8$ **c.** $3\sqrt{17 + 8} + 8$
   d. $2\sqrt{74 + 7} + 12$ **e.** $23\sqrt{1 + 99} + 4$ **f.** $4\sqrt{16 + 20} - 9$
6. Evaluate each expression. Hint: See Example 5.
   a. $\sqrt{\dfrac{36}{16}}$ **b.** $\sqrt{\dfrac{9}{4}}$ **c.** $\sqrt{\dfrac{81}{25}}$ **d.** $\sqrt{\dfrac{81}{16}}$ **e.** $\sqrt{\dfrac{4}{9}}$ **f.** $\sqrt{\dfrac{9}{16}}$
7. Evaluate each expression. Hint: See Example 6.
   a. $4\sqrt{\dfrac{50}{2}} + 10$ **b.** $3\sqrt{\dfrac{72}{2}} + 3$ **c.** $4\sqrt{\dfrac{27}{3}} - 7$ **d.** $5\sqrt{\dfrac{16}{4}} - 8$
8. Evaluate each expression. Hint: See Example 7.
   a. $-(\sqrt{25} - \sqrt{9})$ **b.** $-(\sqrt{36} - \sqrt{25})$ **c.** $-(\sqrt{16} - \sqrt{4})$
   d. $-(\sqrt{81} + \sqrt{25})$ **e.** $-(\sqrt{25} + \sqrt{4})$ **f.** $-(\sqrt{16} - \sqrt{9})$
9. Evaluate each expression. Hint: See Example 8.
   a. $-(\sqrt{4} \cdot \sqrt{9})$ **b.** $-(\sqrt{81} \cdot \sqrt{16})$ **c.** $\sqrt{25} \cdot \sqrt{9}$

d. $-(\sqrt{25} \cdot \sqrt{25})$ **e.** $-(\sqrt{4} \cdot \sqrt{4})$ **f.** $-(\sqrt{36} \cdot \sqrt{25})$

10. The length of a side of a square classroom is 100 m. Find the area of the classroom.
Hint: See Example 10.

11. A square garden has an area of 81 m^2. Find the length of a side of the garden.
Hint: See Example 9.

12. Evaluate:

a. $\pm\sqrt{4}$ **b.** $\pm\sqrt{49}$ **c.** $\pm\sqrt{100}$ **d.** $\pm\sqrt{81}$

Hint: See Example 11.

13. Solve each equation.

a. $t^2 = 4$ **b.** $m^2 = 25$ **c.** $k^2 = 144$ **d.** $36 = p^2$

Hint: See Examples 12a and 12b.

14. Solve each equation.

a. $c^2 = \dfrac{9}{25}$ **b.** $p^2 = \dfrac{9}{64}$ **c.** $r^2 = \dfrac{81}{100}$ **d.** $\dfrac{4}{81} = p^2$

Hint: See Example 12c.

15. Solve each equation.

a. $y^2 = 0.25$ **b.** $w^2 = 0.36$ **c.** $p^2 = 0.81$ **d.** $0.0121 = k^2$

Hint: See Example 12d.

Challenge Questions

16. Evaluate each expression.

a. $4\sqrt{39 - 3} + 4$ **b.** $\sqrt{\dfrac{81}{4}}$ **c.** $6\sqrt{25}$ **d.** $\sqrt{\dfrac{100}{4}}$

e. $-(\sqrt{4} \cdot \sqrt{4})$ **f.** $3\sqrt{13 - 4} + 15$ **g.** $-(\sqrt{64} - \sqrt{36})$ **h.** $4\sqrt{100}$

i. $\sqrt{26 - 10}$ **j.** $\sqrt{25} - \sqrt{4}$ **k.** $\sqrt{81} + \sqrt{16}$ **l.** $\sqrt{36} \cdot \sqrt{9}$

m. $(\sqrt{81} \cdot \sqrt{4})$

17. Evaluate:

a. $\pm\sqrt{9}$ **b.** $\pm\sqrt{64}$ **c.** $\pm\sqrt{25}$ **d.** $\pm\sqrt{144}$

Answers to Selected Questions

2a. 3 and -3   **3a.** 14   **4a.** 14   **5a.** 20

6a. $1\dfrac{1}{2}$ **7a.** 30   **8a.** -2   **9a.** -6

12a. ±2 **13a.** ±2 **14a.** $\pm\dfrac{3}{5}$ **15a.** ±0.5

Special Properties of Square Roots

The square roots have the following properties:
  a. $\sqrt{a} \cdot \sqrt{a} = a$, **where a $\geq$ 0.**
  b. $(-\sqrt{a})(-\sqrt{a}) = a$, **where a $\geq$ 0.**

Example 12
a. Show that $\sqrt{9} \cdot \sqrt{9} = 9$.
b. Show that $(-\sqrt{25})(-\sqrt{25}) = 25$.

Solution

a. $\sqrt{9} \cdot \sqrt{9} = \sqrt{3^2} \cdot \sqrt{3^2}$ $9 = 3^2$

$= 3 \cdot 3$ Recall that the square root of the square of a number is the number itself.

$= 9$ This is the required answer.

b. $(-\sqrt{25})(-\sqrt{25}) = (-\sqrt{5^2})(-\sqrt{5^2})$ $25 = 5^2$

$= (-5)(-5)$ $\sqrt{5^2} = 5$, recall that the square root of the square of a number is the number itself.

$= 25$ $(-5)(-5) = 25$
This is the required answer.

Special Note
The solution to Example 12a confirms the special property of square roots, which is:

  $\sqrt{a} \cdot \sqrt{a} = a$, **where a $\geq$ 0.**

The solution to Example 12b confirms the special property of square roots, which is:

  $(-\sqrt{a})(-\sqrt{a}) = a$, **where a $\geq$ 0.**

Exercises
Use the following special properties of the square root to answer the exercises.
  a. $\sqrt{a} \cdot \sqrt{a} = a$, **where a $\geq$ 0.**
  b. $(-\sqrt{a})(-\sqrt{a}) = a$, **where a $\geq$ 0.**

Evaluate:

1. $\sqrt{3} \cdot \sqrt{3}$ **2.** $(-\sqrt{11})(-\sqrt{11})$ **3.** $\sqrt{13} \cdot \sqrt{13}$ **4.** $(-\sqrt{6})(-\sqrt{6})$

5. $\sqrt{10} \cdot \sqrt{10}$ **6.** $(-\sqrt{10})(-\sqrt{10})$ **7.** $\sqrt{101} \cdot \sqrt{101}$ **8.** $(-\sqrt{6558})(-\sqrt{6558})$

Answers to Selected Questions
1. 3   **8.** 6558

SIMPLIFYING RADICALS - MORE ON SQUARE ROOTS

How to Add or Subtract Expressions that Contain Radicals

In order to add or subtract expressions that contain radicals, the number or the expression under the radical sign must be equal. The number or the expression under the radical sign then becomes the common factor. In this case, we have to find the common factor of the whole expression and then simplify as needed.
(Hint: Review the chapter/section on Common Factors. Recall that the number or the expression under the radical sign is called the **radicand**.)

Example 1
Simplify.

a. $3\sqrt{10} + 2\sqrt{10}$　　　　**b.** $7\sqrt{3} - 4\sqrt{3}$

Solution

a. $3\sqrt{10} + 2\sqrt{10} = (3+2)\sqrt{10}$　　　Notice that $\sqrt{10}$ is a common factor.

　　　　　　　　$= 5\sqrt{10}$　　　　　　Simplify, $(3+2) = 5$.

b. $7\sqrt{3} - 4\sqrt{3} = (7-4)\sqrt{3}$　　　　Notice that $\sqrt{3}$ is a common factor.

　　　　　　　$= 3\sqrt{3}$　　　　　　　Simplify, $(7-4) = 3$.

Example 2
Simplify.

a. $9\sqrt{3} - 5\sqrt{2} + \sqrt{3} + 7\sqrt{2}$　　　　　　**b.** $6\sqrt{11} - 9 - 4\sqrt{11} + 13$

Solution

a. $9\sqrt{3} - 5\sqrt{2} + \sqrt{3} + 7\sqrt{2} = 9\sqrt{3} + 1\sqrt{3} + 7\sqrt{2} - 5\sqrt{2}$　Rearrange in order to group the like radicands together.
Notice that $\sqrt{3}$ can be written as $1\sqrt{3}$ to make factoring understandable later.

　　　　　　　　$= (9+1)\sqrt{3} + (7-5)\sqrt{2}$　Notice that $\sqrt{3}$ and $\sqrt{2}$ are common factors. Hint: Review the chapter/section on factoring.

　　　　　　　　$= 10\sqrt{3} + 2\sqrt{2}$

b. $6\sqrt{11} - 9 - 4\sqrt{11} + 13 = 6\sqrt{11} - 4\sqrt{11} + 13 - 9$　　　Rearrange in order to group the like radicands together.

$$= (6 - 4)\sqrt{11} + 4$$

Notice that $\sqrt{11}$ is a common factor. Hint: Review the chapter/section on factoring. Simplify, $13 - 9 = 4$.

$$= 2\sqrt{11} + 4$$

Simplify, $(6 - 4) = 2$.

Example 3

Simplify.

a. $4\sqrt{27} - 2\sqrt{48}$ **b.** $6\sqrt{18} - 7 - 3\sqrt{98}$

Solution

a. $4\sqrt{27} - 2\sqrt{48} = 4\sqrt{9 \times 3} - 2\sqrt{16 \times 3}$

The radicands are not equal, so we cannot factor.

In this case, we should make sure that no factors of the radicands are perfect squares other than 1.

$27 = 9 \times 3$, and 9 is a perfect square.

$48 = 16 \times 3$, and 16 is a perfect square.

$$= 4\sqrt{9} \cdot \sqrt{3} - 2\sqrt{16} \cdot \sqrt{3}$$

$\sqrt{9 \times 3}$ can be written as $\sqrt{9} \cdot \sqrt{3}$ so that we can find the square root of the perfect square of 9.

$\sqrt{16 \times 3}$ can be written as $\sqrt{16} \cdot \sqrt{3}$ so that we can find the square root of the perfect square of 16.

$$= 4 \times 3\sqrt{3} - 2 \times 4\sqrt{3}$$

$\sqrt{9} = 3$, and the square root of $\sqrt{16} = 4$.

$$= 12\sqrt{3} - 8\sqrt{3}$$

Simplify, $4 \times 3 = 12$, and $2 \times 4 = 8$.

$$= (12 - 8)\sqrt{3}$$

Notice that $\sqrt{3}$ is a common factor.

$$= 4\sqrt{3}$$

Simplify, $(12 - 8) = 4$.

Special Note: Notice that in the solution to Example 3a,

$$\sqrt{27} = \sqrt{9 \cdot 3} = \sqrt{9} \cdot \sqrt{3} = 3\sqrt{3}$$

$3\sqrt{3}$ is known as the simplest radical form of $\sqrt{27}$.

$$\sqrt{48} = \sqrt{16 \cdot 3} = \sqrt{16} \cdot \sqrt{3} = 4\sqrt{3}$$

$4\sqrt{3}$ is known as the simplest radical form of $\sqrt{48}$.

b. $6\sqrt{18} - 7 - 3\sqrt{98} = 6\sqrt{9 \times 2} - 7 - 3\sqrt{49 \times 2}$ The radicands are not equal, so we

cannot factor.
In this case, we should make sure that no factors of the radicands are perfect squares other than 1.
$18 = 9 \times 2$, and 9 is a perfect square.
$98 = 49 \times 2$, and 49 is a perfect square.

$= 6\sqrt{9}\sqrt{2} - 7 - 3\sqrt{49}\sqrt{2}$ $\sqrt{9 \times 2}$ can be written as $\sqrt{9} \cdot \sqrt{2}$ so that we can find the square root of the perfect square of 9.
$\sqrt{49 \times 2}$ can be written as $\sqrt{49} \cdot \sqrt{2}$ so that we can find the square root of the perfect square of 49.

$= 6 \times 3\sqrt{2} - 7 - 3 \times 7\sqrt{2}$ $\sqrt{9} = 3$, and $\sqrt{49} = 7$.

$= 18\sqrt{2} - 7 - 21\sqrt{2}$ Simplify, $6 \times 3 = 18$, and $3 \times 7 = 21$.

$= 18\sqrt{2} - 21\sqrt{2} - 7$ $\sqrt{2}$ is a common factor, rearrange the terms so that we can factor $\sqrt{2}$.

$= (18 - 21)\sqrt{2} - 7$ Notice that $\sqrt{2}$ is a factor.

$= -3\sqrt{2} - 7$ Simplify, $(18 - 21) = 3$.

Example 4
Simplify.
$2\sqrt{90y} - 3\sqrt{10y} + \sqrt{40y}$
Solution
$2\sqrt{90y} - 3\sqrt{10y} + \sqrt{40y} = 2\sqrt{9 \times 10y} - 3\sqrt{10y} + \sqrt{4 \times 10y}$

The radicands are not equal, so we cannot factor.
In this case, we should make sure that no factors of the radicands are perfect squares other than 1.
$90y = 9 \times 10y$, and 9 is a perfect square.
$40y = 4 \times 10y$, and 4 is a perfect square.

$= 2\sqrt{9} \cdot \sqrt{10y} - 3\sqrt{10y} + \sqrt{4} \cdot \sqrt{10y}$

$\sqrt{9 \times 10y}$ can be written as $\sqrt{9} \cdot \sqrt{10y}$ so that we can find the square root of the perfect square of 9.
$\sqrt{4 \times 10y}$ can be written as $\sqrt{4} \cdot \sqrt{10y}$ so

229

that we can find the square root of the perfect square of 4.

$$= 2 \times 3\sqrt{10y} - 3\sqrt{10y} + 2\sqrt{10y}$$

$$\sqrt{9} = 3, \text{ and } \sqrt{4}.$$

$$= 6\sqrt{10y} - 3\sqrt{10y} + 2\sqrt{10y}$$

Simplify, $2 \times 3 = 6$.

$$= (6 - 3 + 2)\sqrt{10y} \quad \text{Notice that } \sqrt{10y} \text{ is a factor.}$$

$$= 5\sqrt{10y} \qquad \text{Simplify, } (6 - 3 + 2) = 5$$

Example 5
Simplify.

$$3x\sqrt{45xy^2} - \sqrt{80x^3y^2}$$

Solution

$$3x\sqrt{45xy^2} - \sqrt{80x^3y^2} = 3x\sqrt{9 \cdot 5xy^2} - \sqrt{16 \cdot 5x^3y^2}$$

The radicands are not equal, so we cannot factor.
In this case, we should make sure that no factors of the radicands are perfect squares other than 1.
$45 = 9 \cdot 5$, and 9 is a perfect square.
$80 = 16 \cdot 5$, and 16 is a perfect square.

$$= 3x\sqrt{9} \cdot \sqrt{5x} \cdot \sqrt{y^2} - \sqrt{16 \cdot 5x \, x^2 y^2} \qquad x^3 = x \, x^2$$

$$= 3x\sqrt{9} \cdot \sqrt{5x} \cdot \sqrt{y^2} - \sqrt{16} \cdot \sqrt{5x} \cdot \sqrt{x^2} \cdot \sqrt{y^2}$$

$$\sqrt{16 \cdot 5x \, x^2 y^2} = \sqrt{16} \cdot \sqrt{5x} \cdot \sqrt{x^2} \cdot \sqrt{y^2}$$

$$= 3x \cdot 3\sqrt{5x} \cdot y - 4\sqrt{5x} \cdot xy$$

$$\sqrt{9} = 3, \sqrt{y^2} = y, \sqrt{16} = 4,$$
$$\sqrt{x^2} = x, \text{ and } \sqrt{y^2} = y$$

$$= 9xy\sqrt{5x} - 4xy\sqrt{5x}$$

Simplify: $3x \cdot 3 \cdot y = 9xy$, and $4 \cdot x \cdot y = 4xy$

230

$$= (9xy - 4xy)\sqrt{5x} \qquad \text{Notice that } \sqrt{5x} \text{ is a factor.}$$
$$= 5xy\sqrt{5x} \qquad \text{Simplify: } (9xy - 4xy) = 5xy.$$

Example 6

Use a shortcut method to solve Example 5. Example 5 shows the detailed method of solving the problem in order to provide understanding. Once the detailed method is understood, the student can use shortcut method in solving homework and during tests.

Simplify.

$$3x\sqrt{45xy^2} - \sqrt{80x^3y^2}$$

Solution

$$3x\sqrt{45xy^2} - \sqrt{80x^3y^2} = 3x\sqrt{9 \cdot 5xy^2} - \sqrt{16 \cdot 5x^3y^2}$$
$$= 3x \cdot 3y\sqrt{5x} - 4xy\sqrt{5x}$$
$$= 9xy\sqrt{5x} - 4xy\sqrt{5x}$$
$$= (9xy - 4xy)\sqrt{5x}$$
$$= 5xy\sqrt{5x}$$

Special Note: Shortcut method can be used to solve Examples 3 and 4, which should be similar to Example 6.

Exercises

1. Simplify:

    a. $5\sqrt{5} + 6\sqrt{5}$ **b.** $8\sqrt{11} - 4\sqrt{11}$ **c.** $4\sqrt{10} - 2\sqrt{10}$

    d. $10\sqrt{3} - 4\sqrt{3}$ **e.** $3\sqrt{7} + 2\sqrt{7}$ **f.** $2\sqrt{2} + 7\sqrt{2}$

    Hint: See Example 1.

2. Simplify:

    a. $4\sqrt{5} - 7\sqrt{2} + 2\sqrt{5} + 10\sqrt{2}$ **b.** $5\sqrt{3} - 4 + 2\sqrt{3} + 6$

    c. $12\sqrt{7} + 9 - 3\sqrt{7} - 6$ **d.** $8 + 9\sqrt{11} - 5\sqrt{11} + 2$

    Hint: See Example 2.

3. Express in simplest radical form:

    a. $\sqrt{27}$ **b.** $\sqrt{48}$ **c.** $\sqrt{12}$

    d. $\sqrt{18}$ **e.** $\sqrt{300}$ **f.** $\sqrt{200}$

    Hint: See the Special Note for the solution to Example 3a.

4. Simplify:

    a. $10\sqrt{27} - 3\sqrt{48}$ **b.** $2\sqrt{20} + 3\sqrt{80}$ **c.** $\sqrt{40} + 2\sqrt{10}$

    d. $8\sqrt{90} - 3\sqrt{10}$ **e.** $\sqrt{45} - 2\sqrt{20}$ **f.** $\sqrt{98} + 2\sqrt{18}$

g. $4\sqrt{48} - 15 - 2\sqrt{27}$

Hint: See Example 3.

5. Simplify:

a. $3\sqrt{40y} + 2\sqrt{10y} + 2\sqrt{90y}$ **b.** $2\sqrt{20x} + 4\sqrt{45x} - \sqrt{80x}$

c. $3\sqrt{80y} - \sqrt{20y} + 2\sqrt{45y}$ **d.** $2\sqrt{12x} + 3\sqrt{27x} - \sqrt{48x}$

e. $3\sqrt{27y} - 6\sqrt{48y} - 2\sqrt{27y}$

Hint: See Example 4.

6. Simplify:

a. $4x\sqrt{45x^3y^2} - \sqrt{80x^3y^2}$ **b.** $3\sqrt{80x^3y^2} + 2\sqrt{20x^3y^2}$

c. $6x\sqrt{20x^2y^3} - 2\sqrt{45x^2y^3}$ **d.** $5x\sqrt{20x^3y^2} - \sqrt{45x^3y^2} + \sqrt{80x^3y^2}$

Hint: See Example 5.

7. Use the shortcut method to solve Exercises 5 and 6.

Hint: See Example 6.

Answers to Selected Questions

1a. $11\sqrt{5}$ **2a.** $6\sqrt{5} + 3\sqrt{2}$ **3a.** $3\sqrt{3}$ **4a.** $18\sqrt{3}$

Multiplication Property of Square Roots

The multiplication property of square roots states,

$$\sqrt{ab} = \sqrt{a} \cdot \sqrt{b}, \text{ where } a \geq 0 \text{ and } b \geq 0.$$

How to write radical expressions in the simplest radical form:

1. Look for perfect-square factors in each radicand.
2. Apply the Multiplication Property of Square Roots.

$$\sqrt{ab} = \sqrt{a} \cdot \sqrt{b}, \text{ where } a \geq 0 \text{ and } b \geq 0.$$

3. Find the square roots of the perfect squares.
4. Leave the non-perfect factors in the radical form.

Example 1

Simplify:

a. $\sqrt{6} \cdot \sqrt{3}$ **b.** $\sqrt{7} \cdot \sqrt{14}$ **c.** $(\sqrt{5})^2$

Solutions

a. $\sqrt{6} \cdot \sqrt{3} = \sqrt{6 \cdot 3}$ The Multiplication Property of Square Roots permit us to multiply separate radicals.

$$\sqrt{ab} = \sqrt{a} \cdot \sqrt{b}, \text{ where } a \geq 0 \text{ and } b \geq 0$$

$= \sqrt{18}$ Simplify: $6 \cdot 3 = 18$

$= \sqrt{9 \cdot 2}$ $\qquad$ $18 = 9 \cdot 2$, notice that 9 is a factor.

$= \sqrt{9} \cdot \sqrt{2}$ $\qquad$ No factor of the radicand should be a perfect square other than 1. Notice that 9 is both a factor and a perfect square.

$= 3\sqrt{2}$ $\qquad$ $\sqrt{9} = \sqrt{3 \cdot 3} = \sqrt{3^2} = 3$ Notice that 2 is left in the radical form because it is not a perfect square.

The square root of any number to the second power equals the number itself. $\sqrt{a^2} = a$, where $a \geq 0$

b. $\sqrt{7} \cdot \sqrt{14} = \sqrt{7} \cdot \sqrt{7 \cdot 2}$ $\qquad$ $14 = 7 \cdot 2$ (factor 14 into 7 and 2)

$= \sqrt{7} \cdot \sqrt{7} \cdot \sqrt{2}$ $\qquad$ $\sqrt{7 \cdot 2} = \sqrt{7}\sqrt{2}$ because the Multiplication Property of Square Roots permit us to multiply separate radicals.

$\sqrt{ab} = \sqrt{a}\sqrt{b}$, where $a \geq 0$ and $b \geq 0$

$= 7\sqrt{2}$ $\qquad$ $\sqrt{7} \cdot \sqrt{7} = \sqrt{7 \cdot 7} = \sqrt{7^2} = 7$

The square root of any number to the second power is the number itself. $\sqrt{a^2} = a$, where $a \geq 0$.

Notice that 7^2 forms a perfect square.

c. $(\sqrt{5})^2 = (\sqrt{5})(\sqrt{5})$ $\qquad$ The second power means the product of two identical factors. Hint: See the section/chapter on exponents.

$= \sqrt{5 \cdot 5}$ $\qquad$ $(\sqrt{5})(\sqrt{5}) = \sqrt{5} \cdot \sqrt{5} = \sqrt{5 \cdot 5}$

The Multiplication Property of Square Roots permit us to multiply separate radicals.

$\sqrt{ab} = \sqrt{a} \cdot \sqrt{b}$, where $a \geq 0$ and $b \geq 0$

$= \sqrt{5^2}$ $\qquad$ $5 \cdot 5 = 5^2$ $\qquad$ Notice that 5^2 forms a perfect square.

$= 5$ $\qquad$ The square root of any number to the second power is the number itself. $\sqrt{a^2} = a$, where $a \geq 0$

Example 2

Simplify: $(3\sqrt{6})^2$

Solution

$(3\sqrt{6})^2 = (3\sqrt{6})(3\sqrt{6})$ $\qquad$ The second power means the product of two identical factors. Hint: See the section/chapter on exponents.

$= (3 \cdot 3)\sqrt{6} \cdot \sqrt{6}$ $\qquad$ Rearrange the factors.

$= 9\sqrt{6 \cdot 6}$ $\qquad$ $3 \cdot 3 = 9$, and $\sqrt{6}\sqrt{6} = \sqrt{6 \cdot 6}$

The Multiplication Property of Square Roots permit us to multiply separate radicals.

$$\sqrt{ab} = \sqrt{a} \cdot \sqrt{b}, \text{ where } a \geq 0 \text{ and } b \geq 0$$

$= 9\sqrt{6^2}$ $6 \cdot 6 = 6^2$ Notice that 6^2 forms a perfect square.

$= 9 \cdot 6$ The square root of any number to the second power equals the number itself. $\sqrt{a^2} = a$, where $a \geq 0$

$= 54$ $9 \cdot 6 = 54$

Example 3

Simplify:

$$\sqrt{2}\,(3 + \sqrt{8})$$

Solution

$\sqrt{2}\,(3 + \sqrt{8}) = \sqrt{2} \cdot 3 + \sqrt{2} \cdot \sqrt{8}$ Multiply $\sqrt{2}$ by the numbers in the parenthesis. Hint: Review Distributive Property.

$= \sqrt{2} \cdot 3 + \sqrt{2} \cdot \sqrt{4 \cdot 2}$ $8 = 4 \cdot 2$

$= \sqrt{2} \cdot 3 + \sqrt{2} \cdot \sqrt{4} \cdot \sqrt{2}$ $\sqrt{4 \cdot 2} = \sqrt{4} \cdot \sqrt{2}$

The Multiplication Property of Square Roots permit us to multiply separate radicals.

$\sqrt{ab} = \sqrt{a} \cdot \sqrt{b}$, where $a \geq 0$ and $b \geq 0$.

$= \sqrt{2} \cdot 3 + \sqrt{2} \cdot \sqrt{2} \cdot \sqrt{4}$ Rearrange: $\sqrt{2} \cdot \sqrt{4} \cdot \sqrt{2} = \sqrt{2} \cdot \sqrt{2} \cdot \sqrt{4}$

$= \sqrt{2} \cdot 3 + \sqrt{2 \cdot 2} \cdot \sqrt{4}$ $\sqrt{2} \cdot \sqrt{2} = \sqrt{2 \cdot 2}$

The Multiplication Property of Square Roots permit us to multiply separate radicals.

$\sqrt{ab} = \sqrt{a} \cdot \sqrt{b}$, where $a \geq 0$ and $b \geq 0$.

$= \sqrt{2} \cdot 3 + \sqrt{4} \cdot \sqrt{4}$ $2 \cdot 2 = 4$

$= \sqrt{2} \cdot 3 + \sqrt{2^2} \cdot \sqrt{2^2}$ $4 = 2^2$

$= \sqrt{2} \cdot 3 + 2 \cdot 2$ $\sqrt{2^2} = 2$ Notice that 2^2 forms a perfect square. The square root of any number to the second power equals the number itself. $\sqrt{a^2} = a$, where $a \geq 0$.

$= 3\sqrt{2} + 4$ Rearrange: $\sqrt{2} \cdot 3 = 3\sqrt{2}$, and $2 \cdot 2 = 4$.

Special Note - Square-Root Expression Simplification Conditions

In order to simplify a square-root expression, the following three conditions must be met:

1. No factor of the radicand should be a perfect square other than 1.

2. No radical should be in the denominator of a fraction.

3. The radicand must contain no fraction.

Notice that all the examples under the section, Multiplication Property of Square Roots, satisfy the three Square-Root Expression Simplification Conditions.

Example 4

Simplify:

$(5 - \sqrt{2})(4 + \sqrt{2})$

Solution

$(5 - \sqrt{2})(4 + \sqrt{2}) = 5 \cdot 4 + 5 \cdot \sqrt{2} - \sqrt{2} \cdot 4 - \sqrt{2} \cdot \sqrt{2}$

Multiply each number in the first parenthesis by each number in the second parenthesis. Hint: Review Distributive Property.

$= 20 + 5\sqrt{2} - 4\sqrt{2} - \sqrt{2} \cdot \sqrt{2}$ Simplify

$= 20 + 5\sqrt{2} - 4\sqrt{2} - \sqrt{2 \cdot 2}$

$\sqrt{2} \cdot \sqrt{2} = \sqrt{2 \cdot 2}$

The Multiplication Property of Square Roots permit us to multiply separate radicals.

$\sqrt{ab} = \sqrt{a} \cdot \sqrt{b}$, where $a \geq 0$ and $b \geq 0$.

$= 20 + 5\sqrt{2} - 4\sqrt{2} - \sqrt{2^2}$ $2 \cdot 2 = 2^2$

$= 20 + 5\sqrt{2} - 4\sqrt{2} - 2$ $\sqrt{2^2} = 2$

The square root of any number to the second power equals the number itself. $\sqrt{a^2} = a$, where $a \geq 0$.

Notice that 2^2 forms a perfect square.

$= 20 - 2 + (5 - 4)\sqrt{2}$ Rearrange the numbers. Notice that $\sqrt{2}$ is a common factor for $5\sqrt{2}$ and $4\sqrt{2}$.

$= 18 + \sqrt{2}$ Simplify: $20 - 2 = 18$, and $5 - 4 = 1$.

$1\sqrt{2} = \sqrt{2}$

Exercises

1. State the multiplication property of square roots.

2. Mary said, "The square root of any number to the second power equals the number itself. $\sqrt{a^2} = a$, where $a \geq 0$." Is her statement correct?

3. Simplify:

    a. $\sqrt{5} \cdot \sqrt{5}$ **b.** $\sqrt{3} \cdot \sqrt{6}$ **c.** $\sqrt{5} \cdot \sqrt{15}$ **d.** $\sqrt{2} \cdot \sqrt{8}$ **e.** $\sqrt{32} \cdot \sqrt{2}$

f. $\sqrt{3} \cdot \sqrt{24}$ **g.** $\sqrt{18} \cdot \sqrt{2}$ **h.** $(\sqrt{7})^2$ **i.** $(\sqrt{11})^2$ **j.** $\sqrt{3} \cdot \sqrt{12}$

Hint: See Example 1.

4. Simplify:

  a. $(2\sqrt{8})^2$ **b.** $(3\sqrt{8})^2$ **c.** $(6\sqrt{5})^2$ **d.** $(x\sqrt{7})^2$ **e.** $2\sqrt{3} \cdot 4\sqrt{3}$

  f. $3\sqrt{6y} \cdot 4\sqrt{6y}$ **g.** $\sqrt{3} \cdot 3\sqrt{3}$ **h.** $(2\sqrt{2})^2$ **i.** $(2\sqrt{11})^2$

Hint: See Example 2.

5. Simplify:

  a. $\sqrt{2}(4 + \sqrt{8})$ **b.** $\sqrt{3}(2 + \sqrt{12})$ **c.** $3\sqrt{2}(3\sqrt{2} - \sqrt{6})$ **d.** $2\sqrt{3}(\sqrt{3} + 2\sqrt{12})$

Hint: See Example 3.

6. What are the three square-root expression simplification conditions?

7. Simplify:

  a. $(6 + \sqrt{3})(6 + \sqrt{3})$ **b.** $(\sqrt{3} - 4)(\sqrt{3} + 6)$

  c. $(4 - \sqrt{2})(4 + \sqrt{2})$ **d.** $(3\sqrt{2} + 4\sqrt{3})(3\sqrt{2} - 4\sqrt{3})$

  e. $(2\sqrt{5} + 2\sqrt{2})(\sqrt{5} - \sqrt{2})$ **f.** $(2\sqrt{2} - \sqrt{12})(5\sqrt{2} - 3\sqrt{12})$

Hint: See Example 4.

Answers to Selected Questions

3a. 5   **4a.** 32   **5a.** $4\sqrt{2} + 4$

Division Property of Square Roots

The Division Property of Square Roots states:

$$\sqrt{\frac{a}{b}} = \frac{\sqrt{a}}{\sqrt{b}}, \text{ where } a \geq 0, \text{ and } b \geq 0.$$

Example 1

Simplify:

a. $\sqrt{\dfrac{9}{16}}$ **b.** $\sqrt{\dfrac{5}{36}}$ **c.** $\sqrt{\dfrac{9}{7}}$

Solution

a. $\sqrt{\dfrac{9}{16}} = \dfrac{\sqrt{9}}{\sqrt{16}}$ The Division Property of Square Roots permits us to

                separate square roots. $\sqrt{\dfrac{a}{b}} = \dfrac{\sqrt{a}}{\sqrt{b}}$, **where** $a \geq 0$, **and** $b \geq 0$.

      $= \dfrac{3}{4}$ Simplify the numerator and the denominator: $\sqrt{9} = 3$, and

           $\sqrt{16} = 4$.

b. $\sqrt{\dfrac{5}{36}} = \dfrac{\sqrt{5}}{\sqrt{36}}$ The Division Property of Square Roots permits us to

separate square roots. $\sqrt{\dfrac{a}{b}} = \dfrac{\sqrt{a}}{\sqrt{b}}$, **where a $\geq$ 0, and b $\geq$ 0.**

$= \dfrac{\sqrt{5}}{6}$ We cannot simplify the numerator. Simplify the denominator.

$\sqrt{36} = 6$

c. $\sqrt{\dfrac{9}{7}} = \dfrac{\sqrt{9}}{\sqrt{7}}$ The Division Property of Square Roots permits us to

separate square roots. $\sqrt{\dfrac{a}{b}} = \dfrac{\sqrt{a}}{\sqrt{b}}$, **where a $\geq$ 0, and b $\geq$ 0.**

$= \dfrac{3}{\sqrt{7}}$ Simplify the numerator, $\sqrt{9} = 3$. Notice that the denominator

cannot be easily simplified. Notice also that a radical remains in the denominator of $\sqrt{7}$. Recall from the three conditions for square-root expressions in the simplest radical form, one of the conditions is that no radical should be in the denominator of the fraction.

$= \dfrac{3}{\sqrt{7}} \cdot \dfrac{\sqrt{7}}{\sqrt{7}}$ $\dfrac{3}{\sqrt{7}}$ can be changed to the simplest radical form by

multiplying by $\dfrac{\sqrt{7}}{\sqrt{7}}$, which is equivalent to multiplying by 1.

This process of removing a radical expression from the denominator is known as **rationalizing the denominator.**

$= \dfrac{3\sqrt{7}}{7}$ Simplify: $3 \cdot \sqrt{7} = 3\sqrt{7}$, and $\sqrt{7} \cdot \sqrt{7} = 7$

Exercises

1a. State the Division Property of Square Roots.
1b. Explain what is meant by **rationalizing the denominator.**
2. Simplify:

   a. $\sqrt{\dfrac{4}{9}}$ **b.** $\sqrt{\dfrac{4}{25}}$ **c.** $\sqrt{\dfrac{9}{25}}$ **d.** $\sqrt{\dfrac{49}{64}}$

   Hint: See Example 1a.

3. Simplify:

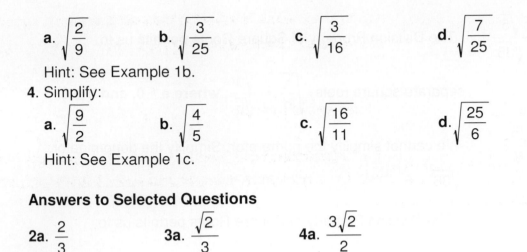

a. $\sqrt{\dfrac{2}{9}}$ **b.** $\sqrt{\dfrac{3}{25}}$ **c.** $\sqrt{\dfrac{3}{16}}$ **d.** $\sqrt{\dfrac{7}{25}}$

Hint: See Example 1b.

4. Simplify:

a. $\sqrt{\dfrac{9}{2}}$ **b.** $\sqrt{\dfrac{4}{5}}$ **c.** $\sqrt{\dfrac{16}{11}}$ **d.** $\sqrt{\dfrac{25}{6}}$

Hint: See Example 1c.

Answers to Selected Questions

2a. $\dfrac{2}{3}$ **3a.** $\dfrac{\sqrt{2}}{3}$ **4a.** $\dfrac{3\sqrt{2}}{2}$

SQUARE ROOTS OF NON-PERFECT SQUARES

How to Estimate the Square Roots of Non-perfect Squares

One way to estimate the square root of non-perfect squares is to find two perfect squares which are closest to the non-perfect number such that one of the perfect squares should be greater than the non-perfect number and the other perfect square should be less than the non-perfect number. The square root of the non-perfect number is between the two factors of the two perfect squares such that if the factor of the greater perfect square is multiplied by itself, the product will give the perfect square of the larger perfect square. Similarly, if the factor of the smaller perfect square is multiplied by itself, the product will give the perfect square of the smaller perfect square.

Example 1

a. Find the two integers that $\sqrt{5}$ is between.

b. Find the **best whole number estimate** of $\sqrt{5}$.

Solution

a. Think of two perfect squares that are closest to $\sqrt{5}$ such that one of the perfect squares is greater than 5 and the other perfect square is less than 5 as follows:

$3^2 = 9$ $9 > 5$

$2^2 = 4$ $4 < 5$

Therefore, $\sqrt{5}$ is between 2 and 3,

or $9 > 5 > 4$ _____[A]

Find the square root of equation [A] as follows:

$\sqrt{9} > \sqrt{5} > \sqrt{4} = 3 > \sqrt{5} > 2$

Therefore, $\sqrt{5}$ is between 2 and 3.

b. From Equation $[A]$, since 5 is closer to 4 than 9, the **best whole number estimate (or the nearest whole number estimate)** for $\sqrt{5}$ is 2.

Example 2
Find the two integers that $-\sqrt{29}$ is between.
Solution
Think of the two perfect squares that are closest to $-\sqrt{29}$ such that one of the perfect squares is greater than 29 and the other perfect square is less than 29 as follows:

$(-5)^2 = 25 \qquad 25 < 29$
$(-6)^2 = 36 \qquad 36 > 29$

Therefore, $-\sqrt{29}$ is between -5 and -6,

or $25 < 29 < 36$ _____$[A]$

Find the square root of equation $[A]$ as follows:

$\pm\sqrt{25} < \pm\sqrt{29} < \pm\sqrt{36}$

$-5 < -\sqrt{29} < -6$ The question involves only the negative square root.

               Note: The square root of any positive number can be + or -.

Therefore, $-\sqrt{29}$ is between -5 and -6.

How to Use the Calculator to Estimate the Value of a Square Root

Note: Different calculators use different methods in finding square roots. Refer to your calculator manual for the correct method that your calculator uses. For example, to find $\sqrt{4}$, the method can be: Press $\sqrt{\ }$ 4 =, Press 2nd $\sqrt{\ }$ 4 =, or Press 4 $\sqrt{\ }$ = on your calculator, depending on the type of calculator.

Example 3
Use a calculator to estimate $\sqrt{17}$. Round your answer to the nearest tenth.
Solution
$\sqrt{17} \approx 4.1231056...$ Press 17$\sqrt{\ }$ on your calculator.

$\sqrt{17} \approx 4.1$ Rounded to the nearest tenth. Hint: Review decimal fractions.

Example 4
Use a calculator to find $\sqrt{108}$. Round your answer to the nearest tenth.
Solution
$\sqrt{108} \approx 10.392304...$ Press 108$\sqrt{\ }$ on your calculator.

     ≈ 10.4 Rounded to the nearest tenth. Note that the hundredth position digit is 9 which is greater than 5, and therefore, the tenth position digit which is 3 is rounded up to 4.
                        Hint: Review Decimal Fractions.

Example 5

Use a calculator to find $\sqrt{300.95}$. Round your answer to the nearest tenth.

Solution

$\sqrt{300.95} \approx 17.34791...$ Press 300.95 $\sqrt{}$ on your calculator.

≈ 17.3 Rounded to the nearest tenth.

            Hint: Review decimal fractions (rounding of numbers).

Example 6

Evaluate the expression. Round your answer to two decimal places.

$\sqrt{10} \cdot (-\sqrt{36})$

Solution

$\sqrt{10} \cdot (-\sqrt{36}) = \sqrt{10} \cdot -6$ Do the operation in the parenthesis first.

            See the chapter on the Order of Operations.

$\approx -18.9736...$ Depress 10 $\sqrt{x}$ × 6 = on your calculator in order to obtain 1.8 9736..., and then attach the negative sign which is attached to 6 to obtain -1.89736...

            Note: Some calculators may have just $\sqrt{}$ instead of $\sqrt{x}$ as the symbol for square root.

≈ -18.97 Rounded to 2 decimal places.

Example 7

Find the values of $\sqrt{2}$, $\sqrt{3}$, and π. Round each number to the nearest tenth.

Indicate $\sqrt{3}$ and π on a number line.

Solution

$\sqrt{2} \approx 1.4142135...$ Depress 2 $\sqrt{}$ = on your calculator to obtain 1.4142135...

≈ 1.4 Rounded to the nearest tenth. (Review "Place Values").

$\sqrt{3} \approx 1.7320508...$ Depress 3 $\sqrt{}$ = on your calculator to obtain 1.7320508...

≈ 1.7 Round to the nearest tenth. (Review "Place Values").

$\pi = \dfrac{22}{7}$ The standard value of π is $\dfrac{22}{7}$.

$= 3.1428571...$ Depress 22 ÷ 7= on the calculator to obtain 3.1428571...

$= 3.1$ Rounded to the nearest tenth.

Locate 1.4, 1.7, and 3.1 on a number line as shown:

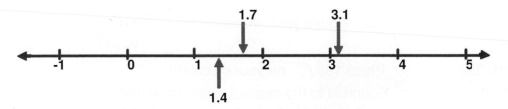

1. Find the two integers that each square root number is between.
Find the best estimate to the nearest whole number.
Hint: See Example 1.

   a. $\sqrt{6}$ **b.** $\sqrt{55}$ **c.** $\sqrt{98}$ **d.** $\sqrt{120}$

2. Find the integers that each square root number is between. Hint: See
Example 2.

   a. $-\sqrt{6}$ **b.** $-\sqrt{13}$ **c.** $-\sqrt{27}$ **d.** $-\sqrt{99}$

3. Use a calculator to estimate each square root number. Round your answer
to the nearest tenth. Hint: See Example 3.

   a. $\sqrt{11}$ **b.** $\sqrt{51}$ **c.** $\sqrt{91}$ **d.** $\sqrt{101}$

4. Use the calculator to find the value of each square root number.
Hint: See Example 4. Round your answer to the nearest tenth.

   a. $\sqrt{79}$ **b.** $\sqrt{24}$ **c.** $\sqrt{62}$ **d.** $\sqrt{112}$

5. Use the calculator to find the value of each square root number.
Hint: See Example 5.
Round your answer to the nearest tenth.

   a. $\sqrt{400.8}$ **b.** $\sqrt{92}$ **c.** $\sqrt{37}$ **d.** $\sqrt{15}$

6. Evaluate each expression. Round your answer to 2 decimal places.
Hint: See Example 6.

   a. $\sqrt{8}\cdot(-\sqrt{9})$ **b.** $\sqrt{7}\cdot(-\sqrt{16})$ **c.** $\sqrt{10}\cdot(-\sqrt{64})$ **d.** $\sqrt{8}\cdot\sqrt{100}$

7. Find the values of $\sqrt{5}$, $\sqrt{11}$, and $\sqrt{13}$. Round your answers to the nearest tenth.
Locate your answers on a number line. Hint: See Example 7.

Challenge Questions

8. Use a calculator to find the value of each square root number.
Round your answer to the nearest tenth.

   a. $\sqrt{9}$ **b.** $\sqrt{89.4}$ **c.** $\sqrt{5}$ **d.** $\sqrt{39}$ **e.** $\sqrt{40}$

9. Locate $\sqrt{7}$, $\sqrt{12}$, and $\sqrt{17}$ on a number line. Round each number to the
nearest tenth.

10. Evaluate each expression. Round your answer to the nearest tenth.

   a. $\sqrt{10}\cdot(-\sqrt{49})$ **b.** $\sqrt{17}\cdot(-\sqrt{9})$ **c.** $\sqrt{7}\cdot\sqrt{36}$

11. Find the two integers that each square root number is between.

   a. $\sqrt{10}$ **b.** $\sqrt{67}$ **c.** $\sqrt{101}$ **d.** $\sqrt{120}$

Answers to Selected Questions

1a. 2 and 3   **2a.** -2 and -3   **3a.** 3.3
4a. 8.9   **5a.** 20.0   **6a.** -8.49

CUBE ROOT

$\sqrt[3]{b}$ is called the "cube root of b". If $\sqrt[3]{b} = k$, it means that $b = k \cdot k \cdot k = k^3$.
Substitute k^3 for b in the expression $\sqrt[3]{b}$.

$$\sqrt[3]{b} = \sqrt[3]{k^3} = k$$

In general, $\sqrt[n]{b}$, the "nth root of b" is k such that $k \cdot k \cdot k......k = b$.　　　　(n factors of k).

$$\sqrt[n]{b} = \sqrt[n]{k^n} = k$$

Since we have shown that $\sqrt[3]{k^3} = k$, we can conclude that the cube root of any number raised to the third power is the number itself. Similarly, the nth root of any number raised to the nth power is the number itself.

Example 1
Find $\sqrt[3]{8}$.
Solution

$\sqrt[3]{8} = 2$ because $2 \cdot 2 \cdot 2 = 8$, such that $\sqrt[3]{8} = \sqrt[3]{2 \cdot 2 \cdot 2} = \sqrt[3]{2^3} = 2$.

$\sqrt[3]{2^3} = 2$ because the cube root of any number raised to the third power is the number itself.

Example 2
Find $\sqrt[3]{64}$.
Solution
Find the factor of 64 that can be multiplied by itself three times in order to obtain 64 by using the factor tree as shown:

(The factor tree is located on the next page.)

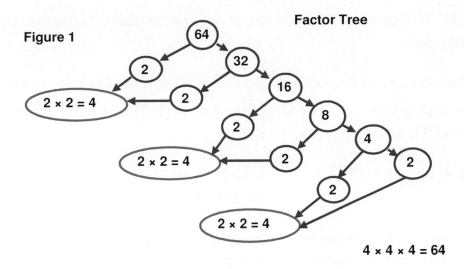

Figure 1　　　　　　　　　　　　**Factor Tree**

$4 \times 4 \times 4 = 64$

From the factor tree, $4 \cdot 4 \cdot 4 = 64$. (Hint: Review the topic on factorization and simply multiply each factor by itself three times until you get a factor that can be multiplied by itself three times to give 64, and this factor is the cube root of 64.)

Therefore, $\sqrt[3]{64} = \sqrt[3]{4 \cdot 4 \cdot 4} = \sqrt[3]{4^3} = 4$　　　(The cube root of any number which is to the third power is the number itself.)

Example 3

Find $\sqrt[3]{-125}$.

Solution

Find the factor of -125 that can be multiplied by itself three times in order to obtain -125 by using the factor tree as shown:

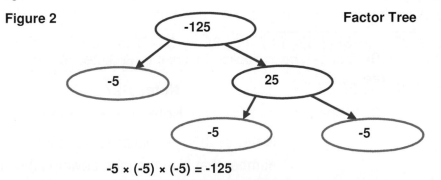

Figure 2　　　　　　　　　　　　**Factor Tree**

$-5 \times (-5) \times (-5) = -125$

From the factor tree, $(-5) \cdot (-5) \cdot (-5) = -125$. (Hint: Review the topic on factorization and simply multiply each factor by itself three times until you get a factor that can be multiplied by itself three times to give -125, and this factor is the cube root of -125.)

Therefore, $\sqrt[3]{-125} = \sqrt[3]{(-5) \cdot (-5) \cdot (-5)} = \sqrt[3]{-5^3} = -5$　(The cube root of any number which is to the third power is the number itself.)

Note: $\sqrt[3]{(-5)^3} = -5$ because the cube root of any number that is to the third power is the number itself.

Notice that we can find the root of a negative number when the index or the power of the root is odd: $\sqrt[3]{-125} = \sqrt[3]{(-5)\cdot(-5)\cdot(-5)} = \sqrt[3]{-5^3} = -5$. The index or the power of the root is 3 and 3 is an odd number.

Example 4

Find $-\sqrt[3]{-27}$

Solution

Find the factor of -27 that can be multiplied by itself three times in order to obtain -27 by using the factor tree as shown:

Figure 3   **Factor Tree**

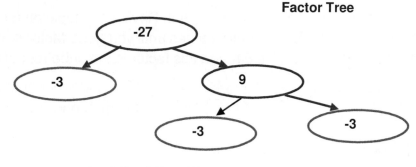

$$-3 \times (-3) \times (-3) = -27$$

From the factor tree, $(-3)\cdot(-3)\cdot(-3) = -27$. (Hint: Review the topic on factorization and simply multiply each factor by itself three times until you get a factor that can be multiplied by itself three times to give -125, and this factor is the cube root of -27.)

Therefore, $\sqrt[3]{-27} = \sqrt[3]{(-3)\cdot(-3)\cdot(-3)} = \sqrt[3]{(-3)^3} = -3$ (The cube root of any number which
                                                                                             is to the third power is the number itself.)

Therefore $-\sqrt[3]{-27} = -(-3)$ **Note:** $\sqrt[3]{-27} = -3$.

          $= 3$ Answer.   **Note:** -(- = +, therefore, -(-3) = +3 = 3.

                              Note: $\sqrt[3]{(-3)^3} = -3$ because the cube root of any
                              number that is to the third power is the number itself.

Table of Powers Involving Square and Cube

The table 1 of powers involving **square** and **cube** of numbers may provide more understanding of the structure of the factors and powers of numbers.

244

Table 1   Powers Involving Square and Cube of Numbers

Number	Square	Cube	Cube Root
2	$2 \cdot 2 = 2^2 = 4$	$2 \cdot 2 \cdot 2 = 2^3 = 8$	$\sqrt[3]{8} = \sqrt[3]{2^3} = 2$
3	$3 \cdot 3 = 3^2 = 9$	$3 \cdot 3 \cdot 3 = 3^3 = 27$	$\sqrt[3]{27} = \sqrt[3]{3^3} = 3$
4	$4 \cdot 4 = 4^2 = 16$	$4 \cdot 4 \cdot 4 = 4^3 = 64$	$\sqrt[3]{64} = \sqrt[3]{4^3} = 4$
5	$5 \cdot 5 = 5^2 = 25$	$5 \cdot 5 \cdot 5 = 5^3 = 125$	$\sqrt[3]{125} = \sqrt[3]{5^3} = 5$
6	$6 \cdot 6 = 6^2 = 36$	$6 \cdot 6 \cdot 6 = 6^3 = 216$	$\sqrt[3]{216} = \sqrt[3]{6^3} = 6$
7	$7 \cdot 7 = 7^2 = 49$	$7 \cdot 7 \cdot 7 = 7^3 = 343$	$\sqrt[3]{343} = \sqrt[3]{7^3} = 7$
8	$8 \cdot 8 = 8^2 = 64$	$8 \cdot 8 \cdot 8 = 8^3 = 512$	$\sqrt[3]{512} = \sqrt[3]{8^3} = 8$
9	$9 \cdot 9 = 9^2 = 81$	$9 \cdot 9 \cdot 9 = 9^3 = 729$	$\sqrt[3]{729} = \sqrt[3]{9^3} = 9$
10	$10 \cdot 10 = 10^2 = 100$	$10 \cdot 10 \cdot 10 = 10^3 = 1000$	$\sqrt[3]{1000} = \sqrt[3]{10^3} = 10$
11	$11 \cdot 11 = 11^2 = 121$	$11 \cdot 11 \cdot 11 = 11^3 = 1331$	$\sqrt[3]{1331} = \sqrt[3]{11^3} = 11$
12	$12 \cdot 12 = 12^2 = 144$	$12 \cdot 12 \cdot 12 = 12^3 = 1728$	$\sqrt[3]{1728} = \sqrt[3]{12^3} = 12$

Note carefully that Table 1 can be read forward and backward. For example, 2 cubed is 8 but the cube root of 8 is 2.

Exercises

1. Find: **a.** $\sqrt[3]{27}$ **b.** $\sqrt[3]{125}$ **c.** $\sqrt[3]{216}$

   Hint: Use the method in Example 1 or Example 2.

2. Using Example 1, find $\sqrt[3]{1000}$.

3. Find the following cube roots. Hint: See Example 3.

   a. $\sqrt[3]{-27}$ **b.** $\sqrt[3]{-64}$ **c.** $\sqrt[3]{-8}$ **d.** $\sqrt[3]{-216}$

4. Evaluate the following. Hint: See Example 4.

   a. $-\sqrt[3]{-64}$ **b.** $-\sqrt[3]{-125}$ **c.** $-\sqrt[3]{-8}$ **d.** $-\sqrt[3]{-216}$

Answers to Selected Questions

1a. 3   **3a.** -3   **4a.** 4

Volume of a Cube

The cube of any number is the number to the third power. Therefore, the cube of 5 is 5^3. The cube also refers to a solid figure that has equal length, width, and height.

The formula for finding the volume of a cube is:

Volume = Length × Width × Height

But all the sides of a cube figure are **equal** and if we let a side of the cube be S, then the volume of the cube becomes:

Volume = S × S × S
$$= \mathbf{S}^3$$

Therefore, the cube of any number may be considered as the volume of a cube if the number were to be the sides of a cube.

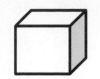 **This figure is a cube with all the sides equal.**

Example 5

The length of a side of a cube is 10 cm. Find the volume of the cube.

Solution

The formula for finding the volume of a cube is:

$$\text{\textbf{Volume}} = \mathbf{S}^3$$
$$= (10 \text{ cm})^3 \qquad\qquad S = 10 \text{ cm.}$$
$$= 10 \text{ cm} \times 10 \text{ cm} \times 10 \text{ cm}$$
$$= 1000 \text{ cm}^3.$$

Example 6

Find the length of a side of a cube which has a volume of 8 m^3.

Solution

The formula for the volume of a cube is:

$$\text{\textbf{Volume}} = \mathbf{S}^3 \qquad\qquad S \text{ is the length of a side of the cube.}$$
$$8 \text{ m}^3 = S^3 \underline{\hspace{6cm}} \text{[A]}$$

It is given in the problem that the volume is 8 m^3.

Find the cube root of both sides of the equation [A] in order to obtain the value of S as follows:

$$\sqrt[3]{8 \text{ m}^3} = \sqrt[3]{S^3}$$
$$\sqrt[3]{2 \text{ m} \times 2 \text{ m} \times 2 \text{ m}} = \sqrt[3]{S^3} \qquad 8 \text{ m}^3 = 2 \text{ m} \times 2 \text{ m} \times 2 \text{ m}$$
$$\sqrt[3]{(2 \text{ m})^3} = \sqrt[3]{S^3} \qquad 2 \text{ m} \times 2 \text{ m} \times 2 \text{ m} = (2 \text{ m})^3$$
$$2 \text{ m} = S \qquad \text{The cube root of any number to the third power is the number itself.}$$

Exercises

1. Find the volume of a cube which has a length of a side of 2 m. Hint: See Example 5.

2. Find the volume of each cube which has a length of a side as follows.
Hint: See Example 1.

    a. 3 m   **b**. 5 cm   **c**. 4 ft

3. Find the length of a side of each cube which has the following volumes.
Hint: See Example 6.

    a. 64 m^3 **b**. 27 ft^3 **c**. 125 cm^3

Answers to Selected Questions.

    2a. 27 m^3 **3a**. 4 m

RATIOS

Kofi and Ama have 12 pencils. They have agreed to divide the pencils such that Kofi will have 8 pencils and Ama will have the remaining 4 pencils. To find out how many times more pencils Kofi has than Ama, divide 8 by 4.

$$8 \div 4 = 2$$

Therefore, Kofi has twice as many pencils as Ama. In the above statement we are comparing two quantities which are the number of Kofi's pencils and the number of Ama's pencils by division. Similarly, **a ratio is the comparison of two quantities by division**. The ratio of the number of Kofi's pencils to Ama's pencils can be expressed in three ways as shown:

        1). Using "to" method (8 to 4).

        2). Using fraction method ($\frac{8}{4}$).

        3). Using a colon(:) method (8 : 4).

The ratio $\frac{8}{4}$ can be reduced to the simplest form as $\frac{2}{1}$ by dividing both the numerator and the denominator by 4. Note carefully that a ratio should always have a denominator, and therefore, if the denominator is 1, we must always write the denominator as 1.

Rule 1: To find the ratio of one number to another number, write the first number as the numerator and the second number as a denominator, and then reduce to the

lowest term if possible. For example, the ratio of x to y is $\frac{x}{y}$ or x : y and y is a non-zero number.

More Ratio Concepts

Recall from the section on fractions that reducing a fraction to the lowest terms, the value of the fraction is not changed, and similarly, reducing a ratio to the lowest term does not change the value of the ratio.

REAL WORLD APPLICATIONS - WORD PROBLEMS

Example 1

A class consists of 13 girls and 12 boys.

(a) What is the ratio of the girls to the boys?

(b) What is the ratio of the boys to the girls?

(c) What is the ratio of the boys to the whole class?

(d) What is the ratio of the girls to the whole class?

(e) What is the ratio of the total class to the number of girls?

(f). What is the ratio of the total class to the number of boys?

Solution

(a) The number of girls = 13

The number of boys = 12

Using Rule 1, which states, " To find the ratio of one number to another number, write the first number as the numerator and the second number as the denominator and then reduce to the lowest term if possible," the ratio of the girls to the boys is:

$$\frac{\text{Number of girls}}{\text{Number of boys}} = \frac{13}{12} \text{ or } 13:12$$

(b) Using Rule 1, the ratio of the boys to the girls is:

$$\frac{\text{Number of boys}}{\text{Number of girls}} = \frac{12}{13} \text{ or } 12:13$$

(c) The total number of students in the whole class = 12 + 13 = 25

Using Rule 1, the ratio of the number of boys to the whole class is:

$$\frac{\text{Number of boys}}{\text{Total number of students}} = \frac{12}{25} \text{ or } 12:25$$

(d) The total number of students in the whole class = 12 + 13 = 25.

Using Rule 1, the ratio of the number of the girls to the whole class is:

$$\frac{\text{Number of girls}}{\text{Total number of students}} = \frac{13}{25} \text{ or } 13:25$$

(e) The total number of students in the whole class is 12 + 13 = 25.

Using Rule 1, the ratio of the whole class to the number of girls is:

$$\frac{\text{Total number of students}}{\text{Number of girls}} = \frac{25}{13} \quad \text{or} \quad 25 : 13$$

(f). The total number of students in the whole class is 12 + 13 = 25.

Using Rule 1, the ratio of the whole class to the number of boys is:

$$\frac{\text{Total number of students}}{\text{Number of boys}} = \frac{25}{12} \quad \text{or} \quad 25 : 12$$

Example 2

The ratio of rabbits to birds in a small zoo is 7 : 3.

If the total population of the rabbits and the birds at the zoo is 30,

(a) how many rabbits are in the zoo?

(b) how many birds are in the zoo?

Solution

Step 1: Find the total ratio.

Total ratio = 7 + 3 = 10

Step 2: Find the fractions of the rabbits and the birds.

$$\text{The fraction of the rabbits} = \frac{\text{The ratio of the rabbits}}{\text{Total ratio}} = \frac{7}{10}$$

$$\text{The fraction of the birds} = \frac{\text{The ratio of the birds}}{\text{Total ratio}} = \frac{3}{10}$$

(a)

Step 3: To find the number of rabbits in the zoo, multiply the fraction for the rabbits by the total population of the zoo.

Therefore, the number of rabbits at the zoo $= \dfrac{7}{10} \times 30$

$$= \frac{7}{\overset{1}{\underset{}{10}}} \times \overset{3}{30} \quad \text{Divide the numerator and the denominator by 10.}$$

$$= 7 \times 3 = 21 \text{ rabbits}$$

(b)

Step 4: To find the number of birds at the zoo, multiply the fraction for birds by the total population of the zoo.

Therefore, the number of birds at the zoo $= \dfrac{3}{10} \times 30$

$$= \dfrac{3}{\underset{1}{\cancel{10}}} \times \overset{3}{\cancel{30}} = 9 \text{ birds.} \qquad \text{Divide the numerator and the denominator by 10.}$$

$$= 3 \times 3 = 9 \text{ birds}$$

Example 3

Mr. Jones is 45 years old. His son is 10 years old.

What is the ratio of Mr. Jones age to his son's age?

Solution

Using Rule 1, the ratio of Mr. Jones' age to his son's age is:

$$\dfrac{45}{10} \quad \text{or} \quad 45 : 10$$

$$= \dfrac{\overset{9}{\cancel{45}}}{\underset{2}{\cancel{10}}} \qquad \text{Reduce } \dfrac{45}{10} \text{ to the lowest term by dividing by 5.}$$

$$= \dfrac{9}{2}$$

Therefore, the ratio of Mr. Jones' age to his son's age is $\dfrac{9}{2}$ or $9 : 2$

Example 4

What is the ratio of 7 days to 3 weeks?

Solution

Before a ratio can be written, make sure that both the numerator and the denominator of the ratio have the same unit. In this example, the units are days and weeks. We cannot express days as a ratio of weeks. Convert 7 days to 1 week by dividing 7 days by 7 because 7 days = 1 week .

Solution

Using Rule 1, the ratio of 7days to 3 weeks is :

Hint: See Example 1.

6. Judith scored 100% on a test, John scored 95% on the same test. What is the ratio of the test score of Judith to that of John? Reduce your answer to the lowest terms. Hint: See Example 3.

7. What is the ratio of 10 minutes to 1 hour? Hint: The units of a ratio must be the same, 60 minutes =1 hour, see Example 4.

8. What is the ratio of 2 feet to 6 inches? Hint: The unit of a ratio must be the same, 12 inches = 1 foot, see Example 4.

9. What is the ratio of 3 weeks to 3 months? Hint: The unit of a ratio must be the same, 4 weeks = 1 month, see Example 4 .

10 Nick, Jones, and George shared $250 in the ratio 5 : 12 : 8, respectively.
   (a) What is the total ratio?
   (b) What is the fraction of the money that Nick received?
   (c) What is the fraction of the money that Jones received?
   (d) What is the fraction of the money that George received?
   (e) What is the money that Nick received?
   (f) What is the money that Jones received?
   (g) What is the money that George received?
   Hint: See Example 5.

Challenge Questions

1. What is the ratio of 2 hours to 30 minutes?

2. What is the ratio of 6 feet to 10 inches?

3. A woman is 35 years old and her son is 5 years old. What is the ratio of the woman's age to the son's age?

4. There are 600 students in a certain school. The ratio of the girls to the boys at the school is 6 : 4.
   (a) Find the fraction of the student population that are girls?
   (b) Find the fraction of the student population that are boys?
   (c) How many students are girls in the school?
   (d) How many students are boys in the school?

5. What is the ratio of 2 weeks to 2 months?

6. Three students shared $100.00 in the ratio 6 : 3 : 1. How much did each student receive?

7. What is the ratio of 6 inches to 2 feet?

EQUIVALENT RATIOS

Equivalent ratios are ratios that represent the same thing or the same value. For example the ratios $\dfrac{1}{2}$, $\dfrac{2}{4}$, and $\dfrac{4}{8}$ are equivalent ratios because all of them represent

the same value of $\dfrac{1}{2}$ when all the ratios are reduced to the lowest term.

Understanding the Concept of Equivalent Ratios

The concept of the equivalent ratios can further be explained by observing the equal areas of the squares of figure 1, figure, 2 and figure 3. In figure 1, the square

is divided into two parts and the area of the triangle BCD represents $\dfrac{1}{2}$ of the area of

the square ABCD. The square ABCD in figure 2 is divided into 4 parts and the same area triangle BCD is now represented by 2 parts(areas of triangles BCE and CDE)

which can be written as $\dfrac{2}{4}$ parts of the same square ABCD which can be reduced to

the lowest term to obtain $\dfrac{1}{2}$. The square ABCD in figure 3 is divided into 8 parts and

the same triangle BCD is now represented by 4 parts which can be written as $\dfrac{4}{8}$ parts

of the same square ABCD which can be reduced to the lowest term to obtain $\dfrac{1}{2}$.

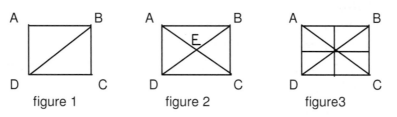

figure 1   figure 2   figure3

The logic is the fact that the same area of triangle BCE is represented as $\dfrac{1}{2}$ in

figure 1 and it is represented as $\dfrac{2}{4}$ in Figure 2 and it is represented as $\dfrac{4}{8}$ in Figure 3,

and therefore, all the ratios of $\dfrac{1}{2}$, $\dfrac{2}{4}$, and $\dfrac{4}{8}$ represent the same area of the triangle

BCD, similarly equivalent ratios are ratios that represent the same thing or value. Equivalent ratios can be expressed or written as equivalent fractions. Cross products of equivalent fractions are equal and this will help us to solve many problems as illustrated in the following examples.

Rule 1: **Equivalent ratios can be expressed or written as equivalent fractions and the cross products of equivalent fractions are equal**.

Example 1

a). There are 205 animals and 37 birds at a certain zoo. Write the ratio of the number of the birds to the number of the animals in 3 different ways.

b). Complete to get equivalent or equal ratios: $\dfrac{3}{2} = \dfrac{12}{?}$

c). Complete to get equivalent or equal ratios: 4 : 1 and ? : 4

Solution

The number of birds = 37, the number of animals = 205.

Ratios can be written in three different ways by using "to," a fraction bar, or a colon.

The ratio of the birds to the animals is: 37 to 205, $\dfrac{37}{205}$, or 37 : 205.

b). There are two methods to solve this problem. They are by "cross products," or by inspection.

Cross Products Method

$\dfrac{3}{2} = \dfrac{12}{?}$ can be written as $\dfrac{3}{2} = \dfrac{12}{y}$ so that we can solve for y.

Cross products of equivalent ratios or fractions are equal, and therefore,

$$\dfrac{3}{2} \diagdown\diagup \dfrac{12}{y} \quad \text{is } 3 \times y = 2 \times 12$$

$$3y = 24 \quad\text{——————————}\quad [A]$$

Divide each side of equation $[A]$ by 3 to obtain y as shown:

$$\dfrac{3y}{3} = \dfrac{24}{3}$$

$$\dfrac{\overset{y}{\cancel{3}y}}{\underset{1}{\cancel{3}}} = \dfrac{\overset{8}{\cancel{24}}}{\underset{1}{\cancel{3}}}$$

$$y = 8$$

Therefore, the equivalent ratios of $\dfrac{3}{2} = \dfrac{12}{?}$ are $\dfrac{3}{2} = \dfrac{12}{8}$.

Inspection Method

Let us inspect the ratio $\dfrac{3}{2}$ and $\dfrac{12}{?}$ and find out how the numerator 3 can be changed to the numerator 12. We should find that the numerator 3 is multiplied by 4 to obtain the numerator of 12 and similarly we have to multiply the denominator of 2 by the same number 4 to give us a denominator of 8.

$$\diagup \text{ multiply by the same number.}$$

$$\dfrac{3}{2} = \dfrac{3 \times ?}{2 \times ?} = \dfrac{3 \times 4}{2 \times 4} = \dfrac{12}{8}$$

$$\diagdown \text{ multiply by the same number.}$$

Therefore, the equivalent ratio $\dfrac{3}{2} = \dfrac{12}{?}$ should be $\dfrac{3}{2} = \dfrac{12}{8}$

c). In order for 4 : 1 and ? : 4 to be equal ratios , then 4 : 1 = ? : 4 and the ratio

can be written in a fraction form as $\dfrac{4}{1} = \dfrac{?}{4}$

There are two methods to solve this problem which is by "cross products " or by inspection.

Cross Products Method

The cross product of equivalent ratios or fractions are equal, and therefore:

$$\dfrac{4}{1} \diagup\!\!\!\!\diagdown \dfrac{?}{4} \quad \text{is } 4 \times 4 = 1 \times ?$$

$$16 = ?$$

Therefore, the equivalent ratio of $\dfrac{4}{1} = \dfrac{?}{4}$ is $\dfrac{4}{1} = \dfrac{16}{4}$

Inspection Method

Let us inspect the equivalent ratio $\dfrac{4}{1} = \dfrac{?}{4}$ to find out how the denominator 1 in the first ratio changes to the denominator 4 in the second ratio. The denominator 1 is multiplied by 4 to get the denominator 4 in the second ratio and similarly, the numerator 4 of the first ratio should be multiplied by the same number 4 to obtain the numerator of 16 in the second ratio as shown:

$$\dfrac{4}{1} = \dfrac{?}{4} \quad , \qquad \dfrac{4}{1} = \dfrac{4 \times ?}{1 \times ?} = \dfrac{4 \times 4}{1 \times 4} = \dfrac{16}{4}$$

↑ multiply by the same number.

↑   ↑

↘ multiply by the same number.

1st ratio   2nd ratio

Therefore, the equivalent ratio is $\dfrac{4}{1} = \dfrac{16}{4}$.

Example 2

a). State four ways to show that one ratio is equivalent to the other?

b). Show that $\dfrac{2}{4}$ and $\dfrac{4}{8}$ are equivalent ratios.

Solution

a). The four ways to show that one ratio is equivalent to another ratio are:
by multiplying each term in the smaller ratio by the same number that will be equal to the bigger ratio, by dividing each term of the bigger ratio by the same number that will be equal to the smaller ratio, by reducing each ratio to the lowest term

or by finding the cross products of the ratios. The cross product of equivalent ratios are equal.

b). Let us use each of the four methods in solution (a) to solve the problem.

Method 1:

What same number can multiply the terms of the smaller ratio (the smaller ratio is $\frac{2}{4}$) in order to obtain the bigger ratio (the bigger ratio is $\frac{4}{8}$)? This can be expressed as shown:

what number that can multiply 2 to obtain 4?

$$\frac{2}{4} = \frac{2 \times \ ?}{4 \times \ ?} = \frac{4}{8}$$

smaller ratio ↗   ↖ bigger ratio

what number can multiply 4 to obtain 8?

Since the terms of the smaller ratio can be multiplied by the same number, which is 2 to obtain the bigger ratio, the two ratios are equivalent.

Note: Recall that when the terms of a ratio are multiplied by the same number, the value of the ratio does not change, and that equivalent ratios have equivalent fractions.

Method 2:

What same number can divide the terms of the bigger ratio (the bigger ratio is $\frac{4}{8}$) in order to obtain the smaller ratio. This can be expressed as shown:

what number can divide 4 to obtain 2?

$$\frac{4}{8} = \frac{4 \div \ ?}{8 \div \ ?} = \frac{2}{4}$$ smaller ratio

bigger ratio ↗   what number can divide 8 to obtain 4?

$$\frac{4}{8} = \frac{4 \div 2}{8 \div 2} = \frac{2}{4}$$

Since the terms of the bigger ratio can be divided by the same number, which is 2 to obtain the smaller ratio, the two ratios are equivalent.

Note: Recall that when the terms of a ratio are divided by the same number, the value of the ratio does not change, and that equivalent ratios have equivalent fractions.

Method 3:

Reduce each ratio to the lowest term, and if the lowest terms are equal, then the ratios are equivalent.

257

Reduce $\dfrac{2}{4}$ to the lowest term by dividing the term by 2.

Therefore, $\dfrac{2}{4} = \dfrac{\overset{1}{\cancel{2}}}{\underset{2}{\cancel{4}}} = \dfrac{1}{2}$

Reduce $\dfrac{4}{8}$ to the lowest term by dividing the term by 4.

Therefore, $\dfrac{4}{8} = \dfrac{\overset{1}{\cancel{4}}}{\underset{2}{\cancel{8}}} = \dfrac{1}{2}$

Since $\dfrac{2}{4} = \dfrac{1}{2}$ and $\dfrac{4}{8} = \dfrac{1}{2}$, both ratios are equivalent.

Method 4:
The cross products of equivalent fractions are equal, and therefore,

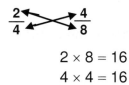

$$2 \times 8 = 16$$
$$4 \times 4 = 16$$

Since the cross products of the fractions are equal, the fractions are equivalent fractions, and therefore, the ratios are equivalent ratios.

Example 3
It is a fact that equivalent ratios can be written as equivalent fractions. Show that the ratio 15 : 6 is equivalent to 5 : 2.
Solution
The ratios 15 : 6 and 5 : 2 can be written as fractions as shown:

$$15 : 6 = \dfrac{15}{6} \quad \text{and} \quad 5 : 2 = \dfrac{5}{2}$$

The fractions $\dfrac{15}{6}$ and $\dfrac{5}{2}$ are equivalent because the terms in $\dfrac{15}{6}$ can be divided by

3 to obtain $\dfrac{5}{2}$ as shown:

$$\frac{\overset{5}{\cancel{15}}}{\underset{2}{\cancel{6}}} = \frac{5}{2} \quad \text{or} \quad \frac{15}{6} = \frac{15 \div ?}{6 \div ?} = \frac{5}{2}$$

Therefore, the ratio 15 : 6 is equivalent to 5 : 2. Note that the style of the solution to Example 2(b) Method 2 is used to solve this problem.

Alternative Method

This problem can simply be solved by using Rule 1, which states that the equivalent ratios can be written as equivalent fractions and the cross products of equivalent fractions are equal.

Let us check if the cross products of the equivalent fractions are equal or not, as shown:

$$\frac{15}{6} = \frac{5}{2}, \text{ and the cross products are:}$$

Therefore, $15 \times 2 = 30$, $6 \times 5 = 30$

Since the cross products are equal the ratios are equivalent.

Example 4

Are the ratios $\frac{1}{6}$ and $\frac{5}{31}$ equivalent?

Solution

The ratios $\frac{1}{6}$ and $\frac{5}{31}$ are already written in the fraction form, and therefore, let us find out if the two fractions $\frac{1}{6}$ and $\frac{5}{31}$ are equivalent or not. We should find what same number that can multiply the term of $\frac{1}{6}$ in order to obtain the ratio $\frac{5}{31}$ as shown:

$$1 \times 5 = 5$$

$$\frac{1}{6} = \frac{1 \times ?}{6 \times ?} = \frac{5}{31}$$

$$6 \times 5 = 30. \text{ Note that 30 is not 31.}$$

Since 5 can not be multiplied by the terms of $\frac{1}{6}$ which are 1 and 6 in order to obtain

5 and 31, $\frac{1}{6}$ and $\frac{5}{31}$ are not equivalent fractions, and therefore, the ratios $\frac{1}{6}$ and $\frac{5}{31}$ are not equivalent ratios.

Alternative Method

This problem can simply be solved by using Rule 1 which states that " Equivalent ratios can be written as equivalent fractions and the cross products of equivalent fractions are equal." Let us check if the cross products of the equivalent fractions are equal or not, as shown:

$$\frac{1}{6} = \frac{5}{31}$$

$1 \times 31 = 31$
$6 \times 5 = 30$ Note that 30 is not equal to 31.

Since the cross products are 31 and 30, and $31 \neq 30$, the ratios $\frac{1}{6}$ and $\frac{5}{31}$ are not

equivalent. Note that the symbol $\neq$ means "is not equal to."

Example 5

Find a ratio that is equivalent to $\frac{6}{9}$ and explain your reasons.

Solution

There are two ways to solve this problem. One way is to divide the numerator and the

denominator of $\frac{6}{9}$ by the same number and the quotient will give us the solution to

the problem as shown:

$$\frac{6}{9} = \frac{6 \div 3}{9 \div 3} = \frac{2}{3}$$

Therefore, the equivalent of $\frac{6}{9}$ is $\frac{2}{3}$

Alternative Method

Another way to solve the problem is to multiply the numerator and the denominator

of $\frac{6}{9}$ by the same number as shown:

$$\frac{6}{9} = \frac{6 \times ?}{9 \times ?} = \frac{6 \times 2}{9 \times 2} = \frac{12}{18}$$ Note: Both the numerator and the denominator

are multiplied by the same number 2.

Therefore, the equivalent of $\dfrac{6}{9}$ is $\dfrac{12}{18}$

Exercises

1. Ratios can be written in three ways using "to," "colons," or fractions. Write each of the following ratio statements in three ways. Hint: See Example 1.
   (a) A class consists of 11 boys and 13 girls. What is the ratio of boys to girls?
   (b) There are 2 oranges and 6 apples in a room. What is the ratio of apples to oranges?
   (c) There are 4 vans and 9 cars at the school. What is the ratio of the vans to the cars?

2. State the four ways by which it can be shown that one ratio is equivalent to another ratio. Hint: See Example 2(a).

3. Complete the following statement:
   Equivalent ratios can be written as ————————————— Hint: See Rule 1.

4. Explain what is meant by equivalent ratios.

5. Explain what is meant by equivalent fractions.

6. Show that the following ratios are equivalent, use the cross products method. Hint: See Examples 2 and 3.
   (a) 1 : 2 and 2 : 4   (b) 2 : 4 and 4 : 8   (c) 2 : 4 and 8 : 16

   (d) 3 : 6 and 9 : 18   (e) 3 : 9 and 9 : 27   (f) 6 : 12 and 12 : 24

   (g) $\dfrac{9}{15}$ and $\dfrac{3}{5}$ (h) $\dfrac{3}{5}$ and $\dfrac{12}{20}$ (i) $\dfrac{1}{6}$ and $\dfrac{2}{12}$

   (j) $\dfrac{3}{4}$ and $\dfrac{9}{12}$ (k) $\dfrac{12}{16}$ and $\dfrac{3}{4}$ (l) $\dfrac{5}{15}$ and $\dfrac{10}{30}$

7. Are the ratios $\dfrac{1}{2}$ and $\dfrac{2}{5}$ equivalent? Hint: See Example 4.

8. Determine if the following ratios are equivalent or not. Hint: See Examples 3 and 4.
   (a) $\dfrac{1}{2}$ and $\dfrac{8}{16}$ (b) $\dfrac{1}{3}$ and $\dfrac{3}{8}$ (c) $\dfrac{3}{2}$ and $\dfrac{9}{6}$

   (d) 6 : 2 and 12 : 4   (e) 1 : 3 and 2 : 6   (f) 2 :3 and 5 : 6

   (g) 1 : 5 and 2 : 10   (h) 4 : 1 and 16 : 3   (i) 4 : 2 and 8 : 4

   (j) $\dfrac{2}{3}$ and $\dfrac{4}{6}$ (k) $\dfrac{5}{2}$ and $\dfrac{25}{10}$ (l) $\dfrac{7}{2}$ and $\dfrac{21}{3}$

Challenge Questions

9. A class has 6 girls and 5 boys.

   (a) What is the ratio of the boys to the girls?

   (b) What is the ratio of the girls to the boys?

   (c) What is the ratio of the boys to the number of students in the whole class?

10. Show that the following ratios are equivalent:

   (a) $\dfrac{5}{1}$ and $\dfrac{25}{5}$ (b) $\dfrac{1}{4}$ and $\dfrac{4}{16}$ (c) $\dfrac{2}{7}$ and $\dfrac{6}{21}$

   (d) $8 : 2$ and $16 : 4$ (e) $3 : 7$ and $9 : 21$ (f) $\dfrac{4}{3}$ and $\dfrac{12}{9}$

11. Determine which ratios are equivalent or not:

   (a) $\dfrac{1}{3}$ and $\dfrac{2}{7}$ (b) $\dfrac{8}{1}$ and $\dfrac{64}{8}$ (c) $\dfrac{2}{3}$ and $\dfrac{1}{2}$

   (d) $\dfrac{2}{9}$ and $\dfrac{6}{27}$ (e) $4 : 3$ and $12 : 9$ (f) $2 : 1$ and $6 : 3$

12. Complete the equations to obtain equivalent or equal ratios:

   (a) $\dfrac{2}{4} = \dfrac{?}{8}$ (b) $\dfrac{4}{3} = \dfrac{8}{?}$ (c) $\dfrac{?}{2} = \dfrac{5}{6}$

   (d) $\dfrac{3}{8} = \dfrac{9}{?}$ (e) $\dfrac{4}{?} = \dfrac{12}{15}$ (f) $\dfrac{1}{3} = \dfrac{?}{9}$

PROPORTION

A **proportion** is an equation stating that two ratios are equal.

For example, $\dfrac{30}{10} = \dfrac{15}{5}$ is a proportion because when each ratio $\dfrac{30}{10}$ and $\dfrac{15}{5}$ are reduced to the lowest terms, it can be seen that both ratios are equal as shown:

$$\dfrac{30}{10} = \dfrac{\overset{3}{\cancel{30}}}{\underset{1}{\cancel{10}}} = 3, \quad \text{the ratio } \dfrac{30}{10} \text{ is reduced to the lowest term by dividing by 10.}$$

$$\dfrac{15}{5} = \dfrac{\overset{3}{\cancel{15}}}{\underset{1}{\cancel{5}}} = 3, \quad \text{the ratio } \dfrac{15}{5} \text{ is reduced to the lowest term by dividing by 5.}$$

By reducing $\dfrac{30}{10}$ and $\dfrac{15}{5}$ to the lowest terms, it can be seen that each ratio is equal

to 3, and therefore, both ratios are equal and we can then conclude that $\dfrac{30}{10} = \dfrac{15}{5}$ is a

proportion. In fact we have written a proportion by writing that $\dfrac{30}{10} = \dfrac{15}{5}$ or

30 : 15 = 15 : 5, and in each equation we are showing that the relationship of the numbers 30 to 10 is the same as the relationship of the numbers 15 to 5.
Note that the ratio 30 : 10 has the same value as the ratio 15 : 5 because when ratios are reduced to the lowest terms, their values are not changed.

Property of Proportion

Rule 1: The cross products of a proportion are equal, such that if $\dfrac{a}{b} = \dfrac{c}{d}$ then ad = bc,

and that b and d are non-zero numbers.

If $\dfrac{a}{b} = \dfrac{c}{d}$, then the cross products are:

   which is ad = bc   and b ≠ 0 and d ≠ 0
where ≠ means "not equal to".

Cross product means to multiply diagonally as shown above.
Note: To make sure that ratios are **equal**, or are **a proportion**, we multiply the cross products and compare the value of each cross product, and if the cross products are equal, then the ratios are equal or are a proportion. We can also show that two ratios are equal by reducing each ratio to the lowest term. If the lowest terms are equal, then the two ratios are equal.

Summary
The two methods used to identify proportions are:
1. cross products.
2. lowest terms.

Example 1

Are the ratios $\dfrac{2}{3} = \dfrac{3}{4}$ a proportion?

Solution
Using the rule, the cross products of a proportion are equal.
The cross products are shown:

$$\dfrac{2}{3} = \dfrac{3}{4}$$

$$2 \times 4 \neq 3 \times 3$$

$$8 \neq 9 \quad \text{The sign} \neq \text{means not equal to.}$$

Since 8 is not equal to 9, the ratio $\dfrac{2}{3} = \dfrac{3}{4}$ is not a proportion.

Example 2
Mr. Johnson drove 60 miles in 2 hours. On the next day, he drove 90 miles in 3 hours. Write a proportion and determine if the proportion is true or false.
Solution
The proportion can be written as:
$$60 : 2 = 90 : 3 \quad \text{or} \quad \dfrac{60}{2} = \dfrac{90}{3}$$
Using Rule 1, the cross products of a proportion are equal, and therefore, we can use cross products to determine if the proportion is true or false.

$$\dfrac{60}{2} \diagdown\diagup \dfrac{90}{3}$$

$$60 \times 3 = 2 \times 90$$
$$180 = 180$$
Since the cross products of the ratios are equal, the proportion is true.

Example 3
Last year, Blengo Middle School was cleaned by 6 people in 10 days. This year, the school was cleaned by 4 people in 12 days working at the same rate as that of last year. Write a proportion and determine if the proportion is true or false.
Solution
The proportion can be written as:
$$6 \text{ people} : 10 \text{ days} = 4 \text{ people} : 12 \text{ days} \quad \text{or} \quad \dfrac{6}{10} = \dfrac{4}{12}$$
Using the Rule 1, the cross product of a proportion are equal, determine if the proportion is true or false.

$$\dfrac{6}{10} \diagdown\diagup \dfrac{4}{12}$$

$$6 \times 12 \neq 10 \times 4 \quad (\neq \text{ means not equal}).$$
$$72 \neq 40$$
Since the cross products are not equal, the proportion is false.

Rule 2
To find a missing number (y) in a proportion, find the cross products, and then divide as needed.

Example 4
Find the value of y in the proportion $\dfrac{y}{4} = \dfrac{5}{2}$

Solution

Using Rule 2, which states that, "to find a missing number (y) in a proportion, find the cross products, and then divide as needed," solve the problem as shown:

$$\frac{y}{4} \diagdown\diagup \frac{5}{2} \qquad \text{or } y \times 2 = 4 \times 5$$

$$2y = 20 \quad\text{——————} [A]$$

Divide each side of equation $[A]$ by 2 to obtain y.

$$\frac{2y}{2} = \frac{20}{2}$$

$$\begin{array}{cc} y & 10 \\ \dfrac{\cancel{2y}}{\cancel{2}} = \dfrac{\cancel{20}}{\cancel{2}} \\ 1 & 1 \end{array} \qquad \text{Divide by 2.}$$

$$y = 10$$

Example 5

Solve the proportions:

(a) $\dfrac{2}{5} = \dfrac{y}{100}$ $\qquad$ (b) $\dfrac{2}{1.8} = \dfrac{4}{y}$

Solution

(a) Using Rule 2,

$$\frac{2}{5} \diagdown\diagup \frac{y}{100} \qquad \text{or } 2 \times 100 = 5 \times y$$

$$200 = 5y \quad\text{——————} [A]$$

Divide each side of equation $[A]$ by 5 to obtain y.

$$\frac{200}{5} = \frac{5y}{5}$$

$$\begin{array}{cc} 40 & y \\ \dfrac{\cancel{200}}{\cancel{5}} = \dfrac{\cancel{5y}}{\cancel{5}} \\ 1 & 1 \end{array}$$

$$40 = y, \text{ or } y = 40.$$

(b) Using Rule 2,

$$\frac{2}{1.8} \diagdown \frac{4}{y} \qquad \text{or } 2 \times y = 1.8 \times 4$$

$$2y = 7.2 \quad\text{————}\quad [B]$$

Divide each side of equation $[B]$ by 2 in order to obtain the value of y.

$$\frac{2y}{2} = \frac{7.2}{2}$$

$$\frac{\overset{y}{\cancel{2y}}}{\underset{1}{\cancel{2}}} = \frac{\overset{3.6}{\cancel{7.2}}}{\underset{1}{\cancel{2}}}$$

$$y = 3.6$$

Example 6
Solve the proportions:

(a) $\dfrac{y+2}{5} = \dfrac{y}{4}$

(a) $\dfrac{y+3}{y} = \dfrac{8}{6}$

Solution
(a) Using Rule 2,

$$\frac{y+2}{5} \diagdown\diagup \frac{y}{4} \qquad \text{or } (y+2) \times 4 = 5 \times y$$

$$y \times 4 + 2 \times 4 = 5 \times y$$

$$4y + 8 = 5y \quad\text{————}\quad[A]$$

Subtract 4y from each side of equation $[A]$ in order to obtain the value of y as shown:

$$4y + 8 - 4y = 5y - 4y$$

$$8 = y \qquad\qquad \text{(Note: } 4y - 4y = 0, \ 5y - 4y = y)$$

$$y = 8$$

(b) Using Rule 2,

$$\frac{y+3}{y} \diagdown\diagup \frac{8}{6} \qquad \text{or } (y+3) \times 6 = y \times 8$$

$$y \times 6 + 3 \times 6 = y \times 8$$

$$6y + 18 = 8y \quad\text{————}\quad[B]$$

Subtract 6y from each side of equation $[B]$ in order to eliminate the 6y at the left side of the equation $[B]$ as shown:

$$6y + 18 - 6y = 8y - 6y \qquad \text{(Note: } 6y - 6y = 0 \text{, and } 8y - 6y = 2y)$$
$$18 = 2y \rule{4cm}{0.4pt} [C]$$

Divide each side of equation $[C]$ by 2 to obtain the value of y as shown:

$$\frac{18}{2} = \frac{2y}{2}$$

$$\frac{\overset{9}{\cancel{18}}}{\underset{1}{\cancel{2}}} = \frac{\overset{y}{\cancel{2y}}}{\underset{1}{\cancel{2}}}$$

$$9 = y, \text{ or } y = 9$$

Example 7

Find the value of y in the following proportions.

(a) $\dfrac{4}{y-2} = \dfrac{5}{y+5}$
(b) $\dfrac{y-6}{y+8} = \dfrac{2}{3}$

Solution

(a) Using Rule 2,

$$\frac{4}{y-2} \bowtie \frac{5}{y+5} \qquad \text{or} \quad 4 \times (y+5) = (y-2) \times 5$$

$$4 \times y + 4 \times 5 = y \times 5 - 2 \times 5$$
$$4y + 20 = 5y - 10 \rule{2cm}{0.4pt} [A]$$

Subtract from each side of the equation $[A]$ in order to eliminate 4y from the left side of equation $[A]$ as shown:

$$4y + 20 - 4y = 5y - 10 - 4y \quad \text{(Note: } 4y - 4y = 0 \text{ , } 5y - 4y = y)$$
$$20 = y - 10 \rule{2cm}{0.4pt} [B]$$

Add 10 to each side of equation $[B]$ in order to obtain y at the right side of equation $[B]$ as shown:

$$20 + 10 = y - 10 + 10 \qquad \text{(Note: } -10 + 10 = 0)$$
$$30 = y, \text{ or } y = 30$$

(b) Using Rule 2,

$$\frac{y-6}{y+8} \bowtie \frac{2}{3} \qquad \text{or} \quad (y-6) \times 3 = (y+8) \times 2$$

$$y \times 3 - 6 \times 3 = y \times 2 + 8 \times 2 \qquad \text{Multiply}$$
$$3y - 18 = 2y + 16 \rule{2cm}{0.4pt} [C]$$

Add 18 to each side of equation $[C]$ in order to eliminate 18 from the left side of equation $[C]$ as shown:

$$3y - 18 + 18 = 2y + 16 + 18 \qquad \text{(Note: } -18 + 18 = 0\text{)}$$
$$3y \qquad\quad = 2y + 34 \;\underline{\hspace{4cm}}\;[D]$$

Subtract 2y from each side of equation $[D]$ in order to eliminate 2y at the right side of equation $[D]$ as shown:

$$3y - 2y = 2y + 34 - 2y \qquad \text{(Note: } 3y - 2y = y, \; 2y - 2y = 0\text{)}$$
$$y = 34$$

Exercises

1. What is a ratio?

2. What is a proportion?

3. Comparing a ratio and a proportion, what is the difference between a ratio and a proportion?

4. Write a ratio that forms a proportion, and then write another ratio that does not form a proportion, and explain your reasoning. Hint: See Examples 1 to 3.

5. Determine which proportions are true or false: Hint: See Examples 1 to 3.

  (a) $\dfrac{1}{2} = \dfrac{3}{7}$ (b) $\dfrac{1}{3} = \dfrac{1}{4}$ (c) $\dfrac{1}{2} = \dfrac{3}{6}$ (d) $\dfrac{1}{3} = \dfrac{4}{12}$

6. Solve each proportion for the missing number. Hint: See Examples 4 and 5.

  (a) $\dfrac{y}{2} = \dfrac{3}{4}$ (b) $\dfrac{2}{y} = \dfrac{1}{8}$ (c) $\dfrac{2}{3} = \dfrac{y}{6}$ (d) $\dfrac{5}{y} = \dfrac{3}{6}$

  (e) $\dfrac{6}{y} = \dfrac{2}{7}$ (f) $\dfrac{3}{4} = \dfrac{y}{8}$ (g) $\dfrac{3}{2} = \dfrac{5}{y}$ (h) $\dfrac{2.5}{5} = \dfrac{y}{3}$

  (i) $\dfrac{3}{y} = \dfrac{2.1}{1}$ (j) $\dfrac{4}{y} = \dfrac{4}{7}$ (k) $\dfrac{2}{7} = \dfrac{?}{49}$ (l) $\dfrac{2}{c} = \dfrac{20}{48}$

  (m) $2 : 5 = n : 4$ (n) $4 : 3 = 5 : a$ (o) $y : 8 = 1 : 32$ (p) $c : 2 = 3.6 : 6$

7. Solve the proportions. Hint: See Example 6a.

  (a) $\dfrac{y + 1}{2} = \dfrac{y}{4}$ (b) $\dfrac{2 + y}{3} = \dfrac{y}{6}$ (c) $\dfrac{y + 3}{4} = \dfrac{y}{2}$

  (d) $\dfrac{3 + y}{4} = \dfrac{y}{8}$ (e) $\dfrac{y + 2}{3} = \dfrac{y}{6}$ (f) $\dfrac{4 + y}{4} = \dfrac{y}{3}$

8. Find y in the proportion. Hint: See Example 6b.

  (a) $\dfrac{y + 2}{y} = \dfrac{2}{3}$ (b) $\dfrac{y + 1}{y} = \dfrac{2}{3}$ (c) $\dfrac{y + 3}{y} = \dfrac{1}{4}$

  (d) $\dfrac{y + 4}{y} = \dfrac{4}{3}$ (e) $\dfrac{y + 4}{y} = \dfrac{3}{4}$ (f) $\dfrac{y + 2}{y} = \dfrac{2}{4}$

9. Solve the proportion. Hint: See Example 7a.

(a) $\dfrac{3}{y-2} = \dfrac{5}{y+5}$

(b) $\dfrac{2}{y-2} = \dfrac{3}{y+1}$

(c) $\dfrac{2}{y-1} = \dfrac{4}{y+2}$

(d) $\dfrac{1}{y-1} = \dfrac{2}{y+2}$

(e) $\dfrac{4}{y-3} = \dfrac{2}{y+3}$

(f) $\dfrac{1}{y-1} = \dfrac{3}{y+4}$

10. Find y in the proportions. Hint: See Example 7b.

(a) $\dfrac{y-1}{y+2} = \dfrac{1}{4}$

(b) $\dfrac{y-2}{y+4} = \dfrac{3}{4}$

(c) $\dfrac{y-2}{y+5} = \dfrac{1}{5}$

(d) $\dfrac{y-3}{y+5} = \dfrac{2}{5}$

(e) $\dfrac{y-5}{y+4} = \dfrac{5}{2}$

(f) $\dfrac{4+y}{y+3} = \dfrac{2}{3}$

Challenge Questions.

11. Find the value of y in the proportions.

(a) $\dfrac{y-5}{y+2} = \dfrac{1}{4}$

(b) $\dfrac{6}{y-3} = \dfrac{3}{y+6}$

(c) $\dfrac{y+4}{y} = \dfrac{3}{4}$

(d) $\dfrac{6+y}{6} = \dfrac{y}{4}$

(e) $2 : 7 = 4 : y$

(f) $\dfrac{y}{4} = \dfrac{1}{16}$

(g) $\dfrac{3}{y} = \dfrac{3}{4}$

(h) $\dfrac{3}{16} = \dfrac{y}{32}$

(i) $y : 6 = 3 : 18$

12. Find the missing number.

(a) $\dfrac{2}{3} = \dfrac{\$10}{?}$

(b) $\dfrac{\$15}{y} = \dfrac{3}{4}$

(c) $\dfrac{6 \text{ feet}}{y} = \dfrac{4}{6}$

(d) $\dfrac{12}{3} = \dfrac{y}{4 \text{ days}}$

General Order of a Proportion for Solving Word Problems

Recall that a proportion is an equation stating that two ratios are equal, and in solving word problems, it **is critical to set the terms of the two ratios in order**, otherwise the solution of the problem will not be correct. For example, let us write the proportion for the following information. If 3 packages of pencils cost $8, what is the cost of 7 packages of pencils. The required proportion can be written as shown:

First ratio   Second ratio

3 packages : $8 = 7 packages : y

First   Second   First   Second
term   term   term   term

Let y be the cost of 7 packages of pencils. The general order of the above proportion can be written as shown:

$$\text{packages} : \$ = \text{packages} : \$ \quad\text{—————— } [A]$$

Note that the left side of the ratio of equation $[A]$ has "packages" followed by the $ symbol and the **same order** "packages" followed by the $ symbol occurs at the right side of equation $[A]$. In order to solve word problems in proportion, the **ratios must be written in the same order**.

Note carefully, that if the two ratios are written as a proportion without the correct order of the terms of the ratios as shown:

$$\text{packages} : \$ = \$: \text{packages},$$

the proportion will not be correct, and therefore, the answer will not be correct. **It is strongly suggested that in order to solve word problems involving proportions the terms of the ratios must be written in the correct order**.

REAL WORLD APPLICATIONS - WORD PROBLEMS
Proportion

Example 1

Mr. Johnson drove 60 miles in 2 hours. How long will he take to travel 180 miles if he is traveling at the same speed?

Solution

The proportion can be written as:

$$60 \text{ miles} : 2 \text{ hours} = 180 \text{ miles} : y \quad\text{or}\quad \frac{60 \text{ miles}}{2} = \frac{180 \text{ miles}}{y} \quad\text{where } y \text{ is}$$

the time taken to travel 180 miles.

Using Rule 2, which states that, "to find a missing number (y) in a proportion, **find the cross products and divide as needed**," solve the problem as shown:

$$\frac{60}{2} \diagdown \frac{180}{y} \qquad\text{or}\quad 60 \times y = 2 \times 180$$

$$60y = 360 \quad\text{—————— } [A]$$

Divide each side of equation $[A]$ by 60 to obtain the value of y as shown:

$$\frac{60y}{60} = \frac{360}{60}$$

$$\frac{\overset{y}{\cancel{60}y}}{\underset{1}{\cancel{60}}} = \frac{\overset{6}{\cancel{360}}}{\underset{1}{\cancel{60}}}$$

$$\frac{y}{1} = \frac{6}{1} \text{ , or } y = 6 \text{ hours}$$

Therefore, it takes 6 hours to travel 180 miles.

Example 2

If 2 packages of pens cost $6.40, how many packages can be bought for $38.40?

Solution

Let y be the number of the packages of pens that can be bought for $38.40.

The proportion can be written as:

2 packages: $6.40 = y : $38.40   or $\dfrac{2 \text{ packages}}{\$6.40} = \dfrac{y \text{ packages}}{\$38.40}$

Using Rule 2, **find the cross product**, **and solve the problem** as shown:

$$\frac{2}{6.40} \diagup\!\!\!\!\diagdown \frac{y}{38.40}$$ or 2 × 38.40 = 6.40 × y

$$2 \times 38.40 = 6.40 \times y \quad\text{————}[A]$$

Divide each side of equation [A] by 6.40 in order to obtain the value of y as shown:

$$\frac{2 \times 38.40}{6.40} = \frac{6.40 \times y}{6.40}$$

$$\frac{2 \times 38.40}{6.40} = \frac{\overset{1}{\cancel{6.40}} \times y}{\underset{1}{\cancel{6.40}}}$$

$$\frac{2 \times \overset{6}{\cancel{38.40}}}{\underset{1}{\cancel{6.40}}} = y \qquad \text{You may use a calculator to divide by 6.40.}$$

$$2 \times 6 = y$$
$$12 = y$$

Therefore, 12 packages of the pens can be bought for $38.40.

Example 3

Three shirts cost $10 and 7 shirts cost $25. Is this proportion false or true?

Solution

The proportion can be written as:

$$3 \text{ shirts} : \$10 = 7 \text{ shirts} : \$25 \quad \text{or} \quad \frac{3}{10} = \frac{7}{25}$$

Using Rule 2, find the cross products, and note that **the cross products of a proportion are equal**, therefore,

$$\frac{3}{10} \diagup\!\!\!\!\!\diagdown \frac{7}{25} \qquad \text{or} \quad 3 \times 25 \neq 10 \times 7$$

$$75 \neq 70,$$

≠ means not equal to. Since 75 ≠ 70, the cross products are not equal, and therefore, the proportion is false.

Example 4

A store sold 7 oranges for $3, how many similar oranges would be bought for $5.14? Give your answer to the nearest whole number.

Solution

The proportion can be written as:

$$7 \text{ oranges} : \$3 = y : \$5.14 \quad \text{or} \quad \frac{7 \text{ oranges}}{\$3} = \frac{y}{\$5.14}$$

Let y be the number of oranges that can be bought for $5.14.

Using Rule 2, the **cross products of a proportion are equal**, and solve the problem as shown:

$$\frac{7 \text{ oranges}}{\$3} \diagup\!\!\!\!\!\diagdown \frac{y}{\$5.14} \qquad \text{or} \quad 7 \text{ oranges} \times \$5.14 = \$3 \times y$$

$$7 \text{ oranges} \times \$5.14 = \$3 \times y \quad \text{——————} \quad [A]$$

Divide each side of equation [A] by $3 in order to obtain the value of y as shown:

$$\frac{7 \text{ oranges} \times \$5.14}{\$3} = \frac{\$3 \times y}{\$3}$$

$$\frac{7 \text{ oranges} \times \$5.14}{\$3} = \frac{\overset{1}{\cancel{\$3}} \times y}{\underset{1}{\cancel{\$3}}}$$

$$\frac{35.98 \text{ oranges}}{3} = y \qquad \text{Divide by 3}$$

$$11.9 \text{ oranges} = y$$

Therefore, 12 oranges (to the nearest whole number) can be bought for $5.14.

Example 5

Red peppers are on sale for $.72 a dozen. What is the price of 32 peppers?

Solution

The proportion can be written as:

$$\text{peppers} : \$ = \text{peppers} : \$ \qquad \text{(general order of the proportion.)}$$
$$12 \text{ peppers} : \$.72 = 32 \text{ peppers} : y \qquad \text{(a dozen} = 12)$$
$$\text{or}$$

$$\frac{12 \text{ peppers}}{\$.72} = \frac{32 \text{ peppers}}{y}$$

Let y be the cost of 32 peppers.

Using Rule 2, **find the cross products, divide as needed**, and solve the problem as shown:

$$\frac{12 \text{ peppers}}{\$0.72} \bowtie \frac{32 \text{ peppers}}{y} \qquad \text{or } 12 \text{ peppers} \times y = \$.72 \times 32 \text{ peppers}$$

$$12 \text{ peppers} \times y = \$.72 \times 32 \text{ peppers} \quad \text{————————————} \quad [A]$$

Divide each side of the equation $[A]$ by 12 peppers in order to obtain the value of y as shown:

$$\frac{\overset{1}{\cancel{12 \text{ peppers}}} \times y}{\underset{1}{\cancel{12 \text{ peppers}}}} = \frac{\$.72 \times \overset{\$.06}{\cancel{32 \text{ peppers}}}}{\underset{1}{\cancel{12 \text{ peppers}}}} \qquad \text{You may use a calculator.}$$

$$y = \$.06 \times 32 = \$1.92$$

Therefore, 32 peppers will cost $1.92.

Example 6

If some special peanuts are priced at $1.80 per kg., how many kg. of the same type of the peanut can be bought for $12.60?

Solution

The proportion can be written as:

$$\$: \text{kg.} = \$: \text{kg} \qquad \text{(general order of the proportion).}$$

$$\$1.80 : 1 \text{ kg} = \$12.60 : y \quad \text{or} \quad \frac{\$1.80}{1 \text{ kg}} = \frac{\$12.60}{y}$$

Let y be the number of kg. that will cost $12.60.
Using Rule 2, **find the cross products, then divide as needed**, and solve the proportion as shown:

$$\frac{\$1.80}{1 \text{ kg.}} \;\;\diagdown\!\!\!\!\diagup\;\; \frac{\$12.60}{y} \qquad \text{or} \quad \$1.80 \times y = 1 \text{ kg.} \times \$12.60.$$

$$\$1.80 \times y = 1 \text{ kg} \times \$12.60 \quad\text{————————}\; [A]$$

Divide each side of equation $[A]$ by $1.80 in order to obtain the value of y as shown:

$$\frac{\overset{1}{\cancel{\$1.80}} \times y}{\underset{1}{\cancel{\$1.80}}} = \frac{1 \text{ kg} \times \overset{7}{\cancel{\$12.60}}}{\underset{1}{\cancel{\$1.80}}} \qquad \text{You may use a calculator to divide.}$$

$$y = 1 \text{ kg} \times 7 = 7 \text{ kg.}$$
Therefore, 7 kg will cost $12.60.

Example 7

Elizabeth earned $20 for 4 hours of baby-sitting. At this rate, what would she earn for 3 hours of baby-sitting?

Solution

The proportion can be written as:
$$\$: \text{hours} = \$: \text{hours} \quad \text{(general order of the proportion).}$$

$$\$20 : 4 \text{ hours} = y : 3 \text{ hours} \qquad \text{or} \quad \frac{\$20}{4} = \frac{y}{3}$$

Let y be the amount earned in 3 hours.
Using Rule 2, **find the cross products, then divide as needed,** and solve the problem as shown:

$$\frac{\$20}{4 \text{ hrs.}} \;\;\diagdown\!\!\!\!\diagup\;\; \frac{y}{3 \text{ hrs.}} \qquad \text{or} \quad \$20 \times 3 \text{ hrs.} = 4 \text{ hrs.} \times y$$

$$\$20 \times 3\text{hr.} = 4\text{hr.} \times y \quad\text{————————}\; [A]$$

Divide each side of equation $[A]$ by 4 hr. in order to obtain the value of y as shown:

274

$$\frac{\overset{\$5}{\cancel{\$20}} \times 3\cancel{hr.}}{\underset{1}{\cancel{4\ hr.}}} = \frac{\overset{1}{\cancel{4\ hr.}} \times y}{\underset{1}{\cancel{4\ hr.}}}$$

$$\$5 \times 3 = y \quad \text{or } y = \$15$$

Therefore, Elizabeth will earn $15 in 3 hours.

Example 8

A certain machine can print 3000 pages in 2 hours. At this rate, how many minutes would it take to print 600 pages?

Solution

The proportion can be written as:

pages : hours = pages : hours   (general order of the proportion.)

$$3000 \text{ pages} : 2 \text{ hours} = 600 \text{ pages} : y \quad \text{or} \quad \frac{3000 \text{ pages}}{2 \text{ hr.}} = \frac{600 \text{ pages}}{y}$$

Let y be the time taken to print 600 pages.

Using Rule 2, **find the cross products, and then divide as needed**, and solve the proportion as shown:

$$\frac{3000 \text{ pages}}{2 \text{ hrs.}} \underset{\longleftrightarrow}{\times} \frac{600 \text{ pages}}{y}$$

$$3000 \text{ pages} \times y = 600 \text{ pages} \times 2 \text{ hr.} \quad\text{——————————} [A]$$

Divide each side of equation $[A]$ by 3000 pages in order to obtain the value of y as shown:

$$\frac{\overset{1}{\cancel{3000 \text{ pages}}} \times y}{\underset{1}{\cancel{3000 \text{ pages}}}} = \frac{600 \text{ pages} \times 2 \text{ hr.}}{3000 \text{ pages}}$$

$$y = \frac{600 \text{ pages} \times 2 \text{ hr.}}{3000 \text{ pages}}$$

$$y = \frac{600 \text{ pages} \times 120 \text{ minutes}}{3000 \text{ pages}} \qquad (\ 60 \text{ minutes} = 1 \text{ hr}$$

$$2 \text{ hrs} = 60 \times 2 = 120 \text{ minutes})$$

$$y = \frac{\overset{1}{\cancel{600}} \text{ pages} \times 120 \text{ minutes}}{\underset{\underset{5}{30}}{\cancel{3000}} \text{ pages}} \quad \text{(Divide by 100, and then by 6)}$$

$$y = \frac{1 \times 120 \text{ minutes}}{\cancel{5}} = 24 \text{ minutes}.$$

Therefore, it will take 24 minutes to print 600 pages.

Example 9

Grace hit 6 home runs in 97 times at bat. At this rate, how many times at bat would she need to hit 9 home runs? Round your answer to the nearest whole number.

Solution

The proportion can be written as :

   home runs : # of times at bat = home runs : # of times at bat   (General order)

   6 home runs : 97 times at bat = 9 home runs : y,

or

$$\frac{6 \text{ home runs}}{97 \text{ times at bat}} = \frac{9 \text{ home runs}}{y}$$

Let y be the number of times at bat that would be needed to produce 9 home runs. Using Rule 2, **find the cross products**, **and then divide as needed** and solve the problem as shown:

$$\frac{6 \text{ home runs}}{97 \text{ times at bat}} \underset{\times}{} \frac{9 \text{ home runs}}{y}$$

or 6 home runs × y = 97 times at bat × 9 home runs   ————————————— [A]

Divide each side of equation [A] by 6 home runs in order to obtain the value of y as shown:

$$\frac{6 \text{ home runs} \times y}{6 \text{ home runs}} = \frac{97 \text{ times at bat} \times 9 \text{ home runs}}{6 \text{ home runs}}$$

$$\frac{\overset{1}{\cancel{6 \text{ home runs}}} \times y}{\underset{1}{\cancel{6 \text{ home runs}}}} = \frac{97 \text{ times at bat} \times 9 \text{ home runs}}{6 \text{ home runs}}$$

$$y = \frac{97 \text{ times at bat} \times \overset{3}{\cancel{9}} \text{ home runs}}{\underset{2}{\cancel{6}} \text{ home runs}} \qquad \text{(Divide by 3)}$$

$$y = \frac{97 \text{ times at bat} \times 3}{2} = \frac{291 \text{ times at bat}}{2} \qquad (97 \times 3 = 291)$$

$y = 145.5$ times at bat   (Review decimal fractions).

$y = 146$ times at bat to the nearest whole number. (Review decimal fractions).

Therefore, 146 times at bat would be needed to hit 9 home runs.

Exercises

1. Eric drove 45 miles in 3 hours. How long will he take to travel 135 miles if he travels at the same rate? Hint: See Example 1.

2. If 3 packages of candy cost $12.00, how many packages can be bought for $28.00. Hint: See Example 2.

3. Determine which proportions are false and which are true. Hint: See Example 3.

   (a) $\dfrac{2}{3} = \dfrac{6}{9}$ (b) $\dfrac{2}{3} = \dfrac{4}{7}$ (c) $\dfrac{3}{5} = \dfrac{1}{4}$ (d) $\dfrac{1}{2} = \dfrac{6}{12}$

4. A store sold 5 mangoes for $4.00, how many similar mangoes can be bought for $24.00? Hint: See Example 4.

5. Oranges are on sale for $1.60 per dozen. What is the price of 4 oranges? Hint: See Example 5.

6. Red peppers are on sale for $.64 a dozen. What is the price of 30 peppers? Hint: See Example 5.

7. If some special apples are priced at $1.20 per pound, how many pounds of the same type of the of the apples can be bought for $3.00? Hint: See Example 6.

8. Mary earned $63.00 for 7 hours of baby-sitting. At this rate, what would she earn for 2 hours of baby-sitting? Hint: See Example 7.

9. A special machine can print 250 pages in 2 hours. At this rate, how many minutes would it take to print 95 pages? Hint: See Example 8.

10. Judith hit 2 home runs in 13 times at bat. At this rate, how many times at bat will she need to hit 5 home runs? Round off your answer to the nearest whole number. Hint: See Example 9.

Challenge Questions

11. A train covers 80 miles in 2 hours. How long will it take the train to travel 240 miles at the same speed?

12. Five oranges cost $2.00 and three of the same type of oranges cost $4.00. Is the proportion true or false?

13. John earned $30.00 for 5 hours of baby-sitting. At this rate, how much will he earn for 7 hours of baby-sitting?

Answers to Selected Questions
1. 9 hours   **6.** $1.60

Cumulative Review
1. Find the area of each figure. The figures are triangles and a rectangle.

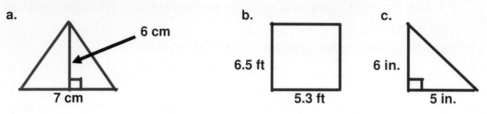

a.   6 cm   7 cm

b.   6.5 ft   5.3 ft

c.   6 in.   5 in.

RATES

Joshua can ride 5 miles in 2 hours on his bicycle. The 5 miles in 2 hours can be written as a ratio as follows:

$$\frac{5 \text{ miles}}{2 \text{ hours}}$$

Note that the ratio above compares two quantities which are 5 and 2 which are measured in two different units which are miles and hours.

Ratios that compare two quantities measured in different units are called rates.

Group Exercise
The class should be divided into four groups. Each group should select 3 students who can represent them in running 100 yards. Each group should have their own stop watch.

Each group should time and record how long it takes each of the selected 3 students to run the 100 yards. Each group should complete the chart that follows and also find the speed of each student in 100 yards per __ minutes.

Chart

Group 1, 2, 3, or 4.

Student #	Distance	Time to run 100 yards	Speed = $\dfrac{\text{Distance}}{\text{Time}}$
1	100 yards	____ minutes	$\dfrac{100\ \text{yards}}{\_\_\_\ \text{minutes}}$
2	100 yards	____ minutes	$\dfrac{100\ \text{yards}}{\_\_\_\ \text{minutes}}$
3	100 yards	____ minutes	$\dfrac{100\ \text{yards}}{\_\_\_\ \text{minutes}}$

Each group should report to the whole class about their best speed. Note that the speed which compares distance to time is a rate, and this can be expressed as yards per minute or miles per hour. Similarly, rates can also be expressed as 100 miles in 6 hours, 8 mangoes for $6.00 and printing of 200 pages in 15 minutes.

Complete the Table

Suppose from the group exercise, a student ran 100 yards in 4 minutes, complete the table below that predicts how far the same student can run in 8 and 12 minutes if the student runs at the same rate.

Time in minutes	4	8	12
Distance in yards	100	?	?

Explain how you can predict the distances the student runs in 8 and 12 minutes. The prediction is based on the fact that 8 minutes is twice 4 minutes, 12 minutes is 3 times 4 minutes such that the following rates can be written as shown in (a) and (b).

(a) 4 is multiplied by 2 to obtain 8, therefore, 100 should also be multiplied by 2 to obtain 200.

$$\frac{100}{4} : \frac{?}{8} = \frac{100}{4} : \frac{200}{8}$$

(b) 4 is multiplied by 3 to obtain 12, therefore, 100 should also be multiplied by 3 to obtain 300.

$$\frac{100}{4} : \frac{?}{12} = \frac{100}{4} : \frac{300}{12}$$

The table becomes:

Time in minutes	4	8	12
Distance in yards	100	200	300

The table that we have created is obtained by using the idea of equivalent ratios.
Equivalent ratios are ratios which have equivalent fractions.
Equivalent fractions means fractions that are the same in value or equal and
equivalent ratios means ratios that are the same in value or equal.
For example,

$$\frac{100 \text{ yards}}{4 \text{ minutes}} \text{ is equivalent to } \frac{200 \text{ yards}}{8 \text{ minutes}} \text{ because each term of}$$

$$\frac{200 \text{ yards}}{8 \text{ minutes}} \text{ can be divided by 2 to obtain } \frac{100 \text{ yards}}{4 \text{ minutes}}.$$

Similarly, $\frac{100 \text{ yards}}{4 \text{ minutes}}$ is equivalent to $\frac{300 \text{ yards}}{12 \text{ minutes}}$ because the terms of

$$\frac{300 \text{ yards}}{12 \text{ minutes}} \text{ can be divided by 3 to obtain } \frac{100 \text{ yards}}{4 \text{ minutes}}.$$

Rule 1 :
Equivalent ratios can be written as equivalent fractions and the cross product of
equivalent fractions are equal.

Distance-Time Graph
A distance-time graph is a graph that shows the distance on the y axis and the time
on the x-axis. From the distance-time graph, we can tell the time it takes to cover a
certain distance and also, we can tell the distance covered in a certain time as
shown in Example 1.

Example 1
Using the distance-time graph of a man who is walking slowly,
a. Find the distance walked in 2 hours.
b. How long does it take to walk 3.5 miles?

c. What is the distance walked in $3\frac{1}{2}$ hours?

d. How long did he take to walk 3 miles? Select one of the answers.

(Answers: **1**. 6 hrs.   **2**. 4 hrs.   **3**. $5\frac{1}{5}$ hrs.).

e. What distance did he walk in 1 hr.?

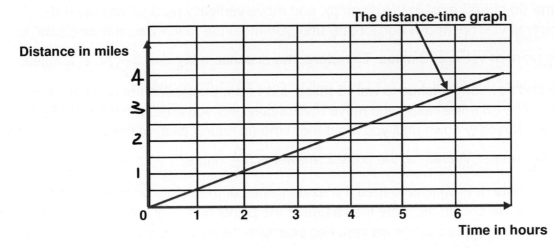

The distance-time graph

Distance in miles

Time in hours

Solution

The important features of the distance-time graph are as shown and this features will help us in understanding how to solve the problem.

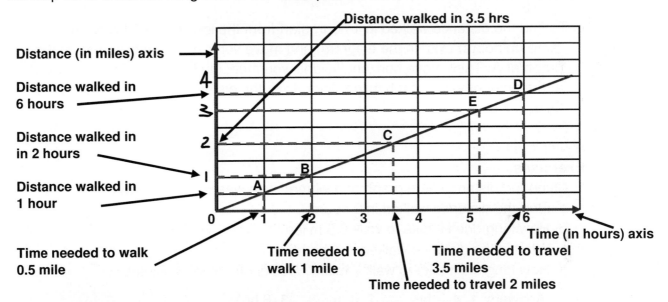

Distance walked in 3.5 hrs

Distance (in miles) axis

Distance walked in 6 hours

Distance walked in in 2 hours

Distance walked in 1 hour

Time (in hours) axis

Time needed to walk 0.5 mile

Time needed to walk 1 mile

Time needed to travel 3.5 miles

Time needed to travel 2 miles

a. To find the distance walked in 2 hr., start from the location of 2 hr. on the "time (in hours) axis" in the diagram, and move vertically up until you meet the graph at point A. Then move horizontally to the "distance (in miles) axis" to meet the "distance (in miles) axis" at the point of value of 1 mile. Therefore, the distance walked in 2 hr. is 1 mile.

b. To find how long it takes to walk 3.5 miles, start from the location of 3.5 miles on the "distance (in miles) axis" in the diagram, and move horizontally until you meet the graph at point D. Then move vertically down until you meet the "time (in hours) axis" at the point of value of 6 hr. Therefore, the time needed to walk 3.5 miles 6 hr.

c. To find the distance walked in $3\frac{1}{2}$ hr., start from the location of $3\frac{1}{2}$ hr. on the

281

"time (in hours) axis" in the diagram, and move vertically up until you meet the graph at C. Then move horizontally until you meet the "distance (in miles) axis" at the point of value of 2 miles. Therefore, the distance walked in $3\frac{1}{2}$ hr. is 2 miles.

d. To find how long it takes to walk 3 miles, start from the location of 3 miles on the "distance (in miles) axis" and move horizontally until you meet the graph at E. Then move vertically down until you meet the "time (in hours) axis" at the point of location of $5\frac{1}{5}$ hours. Therefore, the correct answer is $5\frac{1}{5}$ hours.

Special note: It is difficult to read the exact values of the points on a graph at times. Therefore, we should estimate the values of the points on the graph as the required answers at times as best as we can. For example, the best answer that we obtained in Example 1d is $5\frac{1}{5}$ hr., but $5\frac{1}{5}$ hr. may not be the exact answer, but luckily in this case, $5\frac{1}{5}$ hr. is one of the answers provided.

e. To find the distance walked in 1 hour, start from the location of 1 hr. on the "time (in hours) axis" in the diagram, and move vertically up until you meet the graph at A. Then move horizontally until you meet the "distance (in miles) axis" at the point of value of 0.5 miles. Therefore, the distance walked in 1 hr. is 0.5 mile.

Exercises
1. Using the distance-time graph of a woman who was walking slowly,
    a. Find the distance walked in 2 hours.
    b. How long does it take to walk 6.5 miles?
    c. What is the distance walked in 1 hour?
    d. How long did it take to walk 7 miles? Select one of the answers.

    (Answers: **1**. $4\frac{1}{3}$ hr.   **2**. 4 hr.   **3**. 6 hr.).

    e. What distance did she walk in 3.5 hr.?

    (The distance-time graph is located on the next page.)

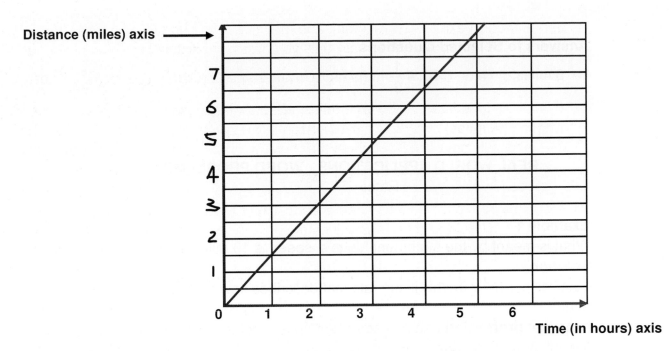

Distance (miles) axis →

Time (in hours) axis

Challenge Question

2. Using the distance-time graph of a girl who was walking slowly,

    a. Find the distance walked in 3 hours.

    b. How long does it take to walk 2 miles?

    c. What is the distance walked in 4 hours?

    d. How long did it take to walk 5 miles? Select one of the answers.

      (Answers: **1**. $4\frac{1}{3}$ hr.   **2**. $2\frac{1}{2}$ hr.   **3**. 4 hr.)

    e. What distance did she walk in 1 hr.?

Distance (miles) axis →

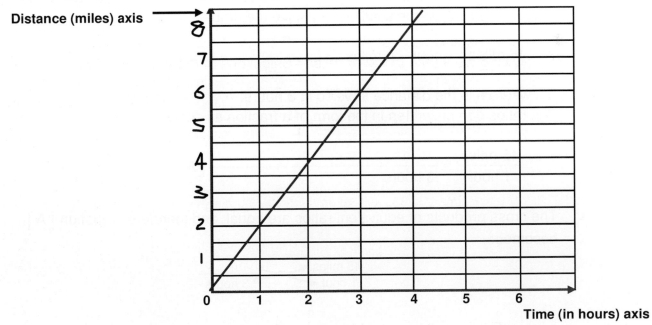

Time (in hours) axis

283

REAL WORLD APPLICATIONS - WORD PROBLEMS
Rates

Example 1
What is meant by the statement "John's speed is 10 miles per hour?"
Solution
10 miles per hour (mi/hr) is the rate that describes how fast John can travel in one hour.
Note that **proportion** can be used to set up and solve rate problems as shown in the following examples.

Example 2
Joshua drove his car at a speed of 45 miles per hour.
(a) How far did he travel in 3 hours at that rate?
(b) If he traveled 225 miles at that rate, how many hours did he take to complete the trip.
Solution
(a) We are given in the problem that Joshua traveled 45 miles in every 1 hour, and we are required to find how long did he take to travel 225 miles. We can use a proportion to set up the solution and solve the problem as shown:

45 miles : 1 hour = n miles : 3 hours,

where n is the distance traveled in 3 hours.
The ratios can be written in the form of a fraction as shown:

$$\frac{45\text{ miles}}{1\text{ hour}} = \frac{n}{3\text{ hours}} \underline{\hspace{3cm}} [\text{A}]$$

The cross products of equivalent ratios are equal, and therefore, equation $[\text{A}]$ becomes:

$$45\text{ miles} \times 3\text{ hours} = 1\text{ hour} \times n\text{ miles} \underline{\hspace{3cm}} [\text{B}]$$

Divide each side of equation [B] by 1 hour in order to obtain the value of n as shown:

$$\frac{45 \text{ miles} \times 3 \text{ hours}}{1 \text{ hour}} = \frac{1 \text{ hour} \times n}{1 \text{ hour}}$$

$$\frac{45 \text{ miles} \times 3 \text{ hours}}{1 \text{ hour}} = \frac{1 \text{ hour} \times n}{1 \text{ hour}}$$

$$45 \text{ miles} \times 3 = n$$
$$135 \text{ miles} = n$$

Therefore, Joshua traveled 135 miles in 3 hours.

(b) We are given in the problem that Joshua traveled 45 miles in every hour and we are required to find how many hours he took to travel 225 miles. We can use proportion to set up the solution and solve the problem as shown:

$$45 \text{ miles} : 1 \text{ hour} = 225 \text{ miles} : n,$$

where n is the number of hours taken to travel 225 miles. The ratios can be written in the form of fractions as shown:

$$\frac{45 \text{ miles}}{1 \text{ hour}} = \frac{225 \text{ miles}}{n} \quad\text{————————— [C]}$$

The cross products of equivalent ratios are equal, and therefore, equation [C] then becomes:

$$\frac{45 \text{ miles}}{1 \text{ hour}} \times\!\!\!\!\times \frac{225 \text{ miles}}{n}$$

$$45 \text{ miles} \times n = 1 \text{ hour} \times 225 \text{ miles} \quad\text{————————— [D]}$$

Divide each side of equation [D] by 45 miles in order to obtain the value of n as shown:

$$\frac{45 \text{ miles} \times n}{45 \text{ miles}} = \frac{1 \text{ hour} \times 225 \text{ miles}}{45 \text{ miles}}$$

$$\frac{\overset{1}{\cancel{45 \text{ miles}}} \times n}{\underset{1}{\cancel{45 \text{ miles}}}} = \frac{1 \text{ hour} \times \overset{\overset{5}{\cancel{45}}}{\cancel{225}} \text{ miles}}{\underset{\underset{1}{\cancel{9}}}{\cancel{45}} \text{ miles}} \qquad \text{Divide by 5 and then by 9}$$

$$\uparrow$$
Divide by 45

$$n = 1 \text{ hour} \times 5$$
$$= 5 \text{ hours}$$

Therefore, Joshua used 5 hours to travel 225 miles.

Example 3

If Eric paid $6.24 for 3 gallons of gasoline, at this price,

(a) how much will he pay for 5 gallons of gasoline?

(b) how many gallons can he buy for $12.48?

(c) how much would 7 gallons cost?

Solution

(a) A proportion can be used to set up the solution as follows:

$6.24 : 3 gallons = ? : 5 gallons

where ? represents the cost for 5 gallons of gasoline.

(Always remember to set the terms of a proportion in order.)

The proportion can be written in a fraction form as shown:

$$\frac{\$6.24}{3 \text{ gallons}} = \frac{?}{5 \text{ gallons}}$$

Cross products of equivalent ratios are equal, and therefore:

$$\frac{\$6.24}{3 \text{ gallons}} \bowtie \frac{?}{5 \text{ gallons}}$$

$$\$6.24 \times 5 \text{ gallons} = 3 \text{ gallons} \times ? \quad\text{————————}\ [A]$$

Divide each side of equation [A] by 3 gallons in order to obtain the value for ?

Equation [A] then becomes:

$$\frac{\$6.24 \times 5 \text{ gallons}}{3 \text{ gallons}} = \frac{3 \text{ gallons} \times ?}{3 \text{ gallons}}$$

$$\frac{\overset{\$2.08}{\cancel{\$6.24} \times 5 \cancel{\text{ gallons}}}}{\underset{1}{\cancel{3 \text{ gallons}}}} = \frac{\overset{1}{\cancel{3 \text{ gallons}} \times ?}}{\underset{1}{\cancel{3 \text{ gallons}}}}$$

$$\$2.08 \times 5 = ?$$
$$\$10.40 = ?$$

Therefore, 5 gallons of gasoline = $10.40

(b) Proportion can be used to set up the solution as shown:

286

$6.24 : 3$ gallons $= \$12.48 : n$ gallons ———————————— $[B]$

where n represents the number of gallons of gasoline that can be bought with $12.48. Equation $[B]$ can be written in a fraction form as shown:

$$\frac{\$6.24}{3 \text{ gallons}} = \frac{\$12.48}{n}$$

Cross products of equivalent ratios are equal, and therefore:

$$\frac{\$6.24}{3 \text{ gallons}} \quad\nearrow\!\!\!\searrow\quad \frac{\$12.48}{n}$$

Therefore, $\$6.24 \times n = 3$ gallons $\times \$12.48$ ———————— $[C]$

Divide each side of equation $[C]$ by $6.24 in order to obtain the value for n gallons of gasoline as shown:

$$\frac{\$6.24 \times n}{\$6.24} = \frac{3 \text{ gallons} \times \$12.48}{\$6.24}$$

$$\frac{\overset{1}{\cancel{\$6.24}} \times n}{\underset{1}{\cancel{\$6.24}}} = \frac{3 \text{ gallons} \times \overset{2}{\cancel{\$12.48}}}{\underset{1}{\cancel{\$6.24}}}$$

$$n = 3 \text{ gallons} \times 2$$
$$n = 6 \text{ gallons}$$

Therefore, 6 gallons can be bought for $12.48.

(c) A proportion can be used to set up the solution as shown:

$$\$6.24 : 3 \text{ gallons} = n : 7 \text{ gallons}$$

where n is the cost for 7 gallons of gasoline.
The ratios can be written in the form of a fraction as shown:

$$\frac{\$6.24}{3 \text{ gallons}} = \frac{n}{7 \text{ gallon}} \qquad\qquad\text{———————} [D]$$

The cross products of equivalent ratios are equal, and therefore, equation $[D]$ becomes:

$$\$6.24 \times 7 \text{ gallons} = 3 \text{ gallons} \times n \quad\rule{3cm}{0.4pt}\quad [E]$$

Divide each side of equation [E] by 3 gallons in order to obtain the value of n as shown:

$$\frac{\overset{\$2.08}{\cancel{\$6.24}} \times 7 \text{ gallons}}{\underset{1}{3 \text{ gallons}}} = \frac{\underset{1}{\cancel{3 \text{ gallons}}} \times n}{\cancel{3 \text{ gallons}}}$$

$$\$2.08 \times 7 = n$$
$$\$14.56 = n$$

Therefore, 7 gallons of gasoline will cost $14.56.

Example 4

During the first 2 days of her vacation, Elizabeth spent $5.12 on breakfast.
At this rate,

(a) how much did she spend on breakfast for 7 days?

(b) how many days of breakfast could she buy with $23.04?

Solution

(a) We are given in the problem that in 2 days Elizabeth spent $5.12 on breakfast and we are requested to find how much she spent on breakfast in 7 days. We can use a proportion to set up and solve the problem as shown:

$$2 \text{ days} : \$5: 12 = 7 \text{ days} : n,$$

where n is how much money Elizabeth spent on the breakfast for 7 days. The ratios can be written in the form of a fraction as shown:

$$\frac{2 \text{ days}}{\$5.12} = \frac{7 \text{ days}}{n} \quad\rule{3cm}{0.4pt}\quad [A]$$

The cross products of equivalent ratios are equal, and therefore, equation [A] then becomes:

$$2 \text{ days} \times n = \$5.12 \times 7 \text{ days} \quad\rule{3cm}{0.4pt}\quad [B]$$

Divide each side of equation $\left[B\right]$ by 2 days in order to obtain the value of n as shown:

$$\frac{2\ days\ \times\ n}{2\ days} = \frac{\$5.12\ \times\ 7\ days}{2\ days}$$

$$\frac{\overset{1}{2\ days}\ \times\ n}{\underset{1}{2\ days}} = \frac{\$5.12\ \times\ 7\ days}{2\ days}$$

$$n = \frac{\$5.12\ \times\ 7}{2} = \frac{\$35.84}{2}$$

$$= \$17.92$$

(b) We are given in the problem that in 2 days Elizabeth spent $5.12 on breakfast and we are requested to find how many days of breakfast she could buy for $23.04. We can use a proportion to set up and solve the problem as shown:

2 days : $5.12 = n : $23.04,

where n represents the number of days of breakfast that could be bought with $23.04. The ratios can be written in the form of fractions as shown:

$$\frac{2\ days}{\$5.12} = \frac{n}{\$23.04} \quad\rule{3cm}{0.4pt}\ \left[C\right]$$

The cross products of equivalent ratios are equal, and therefore, equation $\left[C\right]$ then becomes:

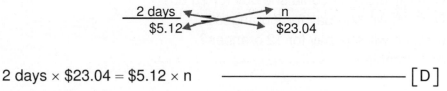

$$2\ days \times \$23.04 = \$5.12 \times n \quad\rule{3cm}{0.4pt}\ \left[D\right]$$

Divide each side of equation $\left[D\right]$ by $5.12 in order to obtain the value of n as shown:

$$\frac{2\ days\ \times\ \$23.04}{\$5.12} = \frac{\$5.12\ \times\ n}{\$5.12}$$

$$\frac{2 \text{ days} \times \$23.04}{\$5.12} = \frac{\overset{1}{\$5.12} \times n}{\underset{1}{\$5.12}}$$

$$\frac{2 \text{ days} \times \$23.04}{\$5.12} = n \qquad \text{(You may use a calculator).}$$

$$9 \text{ days} = n$$

Therefore, Elizabeth can buy breakfast for 9 days with $23.04.

Exercises

1. Explain what is meant by a rate.
2. Explain the statement that Eric's car uses a gallon of gasoline per 18 miles.
   Hint: See Example 1.
3. A bus covers 60 miles in 3 hours, and at this rate:
   (a) How many miles will the bus cover in 10 hours?
   (b) How many hours will the bus take to cover 100 miles?
   (c) How many hours will the bus take to cover 45 miles?
   Hint: See Example 2, you may use a calculator. Round your answer to 2 decimal places.
4. Judith can walk 5 miles in 3 hours, and at this rate:
   (a) How long does she take to walk 15 miles?
   (b) How long does she take to walk 25 miles?
   (c) How many miles can she walk in 10 hours?
   (d) How many miles can she walk in 12 hours?
   Hint : See Example 2. Round your answer to 1 decimal place.
5. Hope bought 3 oranges for $.90.
   (a) How many oranges could she buy for $3.60?
   (b) How much will she pay for 9 oranges?
   (c) How much will she pay for 12 oranges?
   Hint: See Example 4.

Challenge Questions

6. Samuel bought 6 apples for $1.00.
   (a) How many apples could he buy for $3.50?
   (b) How many apples could he buy for $2.25?
   (c) How much will he pay for 10 apples?
   (d) How much will he pay for 24 apples?
   (e) How much will he pay for 36 apples?
   (f) How many apples could he buy for $4.00?
7. Given that Joseph can run 5 miles in 2 hours and at that rate:

(a) How long does he take to run 20 miles?
(b) How many miles does he cover in 8 hours?
(c) How long does he take to run 12 miles?
(d) How many miles does he cover in 14 hours?
(e) How long does he take to run 50 miles?

Answers to Selected Questions
3a. 200 miles   **4a**. 9 hr.

Cumulative Review
1. Explain mean, median, and mode.
2. Explain ratio, equivalent ratio, proportion, and rate.
3. Divide:

    a. $\dfrac{3}{5} \div \dfrac{4}{15} =$ **b.** $\dfrac{6}{7} \div \dfrac{3}{14} =$ **c.** $\dfrac{8}{9} \div 4 =$

4. Multiply:

    a. $\dfrac{3}{5} \times 20 =$ **b.** $\dfrac{3}{4} \times \dfrac{4}{15} =$ **c.** $9 \times \dfrac{5}{6} =$

5. The sum of the measures of two angles of a rectangle is 100^0. Find the measure of the third angle of the triangle.
6. Add or subtract:

    a. 9.01 - 2.44 =   **b.** 73.64 + 6. 33 =   **c.** 10.79 - 3.88 =

CHAPTER 15

VARIATIONS

DIRECT VARIATION

In a direct variation, two variables are related proportionally by a constant positive ratio. The constant positive ratio is called the constant of proportionality.
If Joshua can travel 5 miles in every 1 hour, then we expect that his speed which is $\dfrac{\text{distance}}{\text{time}}$ can be represented as follows:

$$\text{Speed} = \frac{\text{distance}}{\text{time}} = \frac{5 \text{ mi}}{1 \text{ hr}} = \frac{10 \text{ mi}}{2 \text{ hr}} = \frac{15 \text{ mi}}{3 \text{ hr}} = \frac{20 \text{ mi}}{4 \text{hr}} = 5 \text{ mph}$$

$$= \text{a constant positive ratio.}$$

291

The distance traveled by Joshua varies directly with the time and it can be represented by the equation y = kx, where the constant ratio k is 5.

In general: **If y varies directly as x then y = kx or $\dfrac{y}{x}$ = k where k is the constant.**

How to Determine Whether a Data Set Varies Directly
Example 1
Determine whether the data set shows direct variation in (**a**) table 1 and (**b**) table 2 using a graph, and then using algebra.

Table 1

Time (hr)	1	2	3	4
Distance (mi)	5	10	15	20

Table 2

Time (hr)	1	2	3	4
Distance (mi)	3	5	2	8

Solution
(**a**). **Considering Table 1**
Graphical method
Make a graph that shows the relationship between the time and the distance by plotting the data given in Table 1 on a graph paper as shown:

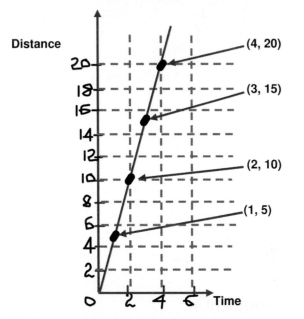

From the graph, the points lie in a straight line, and so the graph is linear and it passes through the point (0, 0). **A graph that is linear and passes through the point (0, 0) shows direct variation.**

Algebraic Method
Compare the ratios of the data in Table 1 to see if a direct variation occurs or not as shown:

$$\frac{5}{1} = \frac{10}{2} = \frac{15}{3} = \frac{20}{4} = 5 = \text{constant value.}$$

The ratios give a constant value of 5, and therefore, the relationship is a direct variation. Note also that the ratios are proportional and for any direct variation, the cross products of any of the ratios is equal as shown:

$$\frac{5}{1} = \frac{10}{2}$$

A proportion is an equation that states that two ratios are equal.

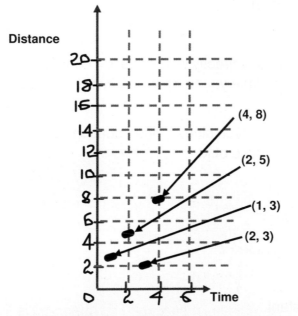

Cross multiply

$5 \cdot 2 = 1 \cdot 10$ In a proportion, the cross product of ratios are equal.

$10 = 10$ Confirms cross products of ratios are equal because the left side of the equation equals to the right side of the equation.

(b). Considering Table 2

Graphical Method

Make a graph that shows the relationship between the time and the distance by plotting the data in Table 2 on graph paper as shown:

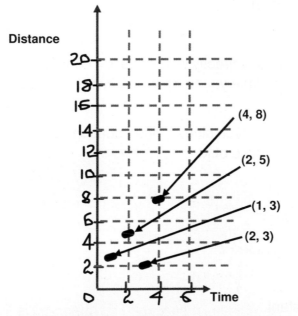

From the graph, the points do not lie in a straight line, and therefore, the graph is not linear. **A graph that is not linear does not show direct variation.**

Algebraic Method

Compare the ratios of the data in table 2 to see if a direct variation occurs or not as follows:

$$\frac{3}{1} \neq \frac{5}{2} \neq \frac{2}{3} \neq \frac{8}{4} \neq \text{a constant value.}$$

The symbol $\neq$ means not equal to.

The ratios do not give a constant value, and therefore, the relationship is not a direct variation. Note also that the ratios are not proportional, and therefore, the cross products of any of the two ratios are not equal as shown:

$$\frac{3}{1} \neq \frac{5}{2}$$

Cross multiplication of unequal ratios.

$3 \cdot 2 \neq 5 \cdot 1$ The cross products are not equal.

$6 \neq 5$ Confirms cross products of the ratios are not equal because the left side of the equation $6 = 5$ is not equal to the right side of the equation.

How to Find the Constant of Variation and How to Write an Equation of Direct Variation

Example 2

If y varies directly as x and y = 12 when x = 3, find the constant of the variation and write an equation of direct variation.

Solution

Step 1: Find the value of k.

    $y = kx$ y varies directly with x and k = constant.

    $12 = k \cdot 3$ Substitute y = 12 and x = 3 into the equation y = kx.

    $\dfrac{12}{3} = \dfrac{k \cdot 3}{3}$ Divide both sides of the equation 12 = k · 3 by 3 to find the value of k.

$$\frac{\overset{4}{\cancel{12}}}{\underset{1}{\cancel{3}}} = \frac{\overset{k}{\cancel{k \cdot 3}}}{\underset{1}{\cancel{3}}}$$

    $4 = k$ and k is the constant.

Step 2: Write the equation of the direct variation.

    From step 1, k = 4.

    Substitute k = 4 into the original equation y = kx to obtain the equation of the direct variation as follows:

    $y = kx$

    $y = 4x$ Substitute k = 4.

    Therefore, the equation of the direction variation is y = 4x.

Example 3
Find the equation of the direct variation given that y varies directly with x and x = 4 when y = 18.
Solution
Step 1: Find the value of k.

$y = kx$ — y varies directly with x, where k is the constant.

$18 = k \cdot 4$ — Substitute y = 18 and x = 4 into the equation y = kx.

$\dfrac{18}{4} = \dfrac{k \cdot 4}{4}$ — Divide both sides of the equation 18 = k · 4 by 4 in order to obtain the value of k.

$\dfrac{\overset{9}{\cancel{18}}}{\underset{2}{4}} = \dfrac{k \cdot \overset{1}{\cancel{4}}}{\underset{1}{4}}$

$\dfrac{9}{2} = k$

Step 2: Write the equation of the direct variation.

From step 1, $k = \dfrac{9}{2}$

Substitute $k = \dfrac{9}{2}$ into the original equation y = kx to obtain the equation of the direct variation as shown:

$y = kx$

$y = \dfrac{9}{2}x$ — Substitute $k = \dfrac{9}{2}$ into the equation y = kx.

Therefore, the equation of the direct variation is $y = \dfrac{9}{2}x$.

How to Find the Unknown Variable in Direct Variations

Example 4
If y varies directly as x and y = 25 when x = 10, find x when y = 75.
Solution

In direct variations, all the ratios or all the values of $\dfrac{y}{x}$ are equal to a certain constant, k. Therefore, all the ratios or all the values of $\dfrac{y}{x}$ must be equal. We can therefore, setup and solve a proportion to find x as shown:

$$\frac{y_1}{x_1} = \frac{y_2}{x_2}$$ A proportion is a statement showing that 2 ratios are equal.

$$\frac{25}{10} = \frac{75}{x}$$ Substitute $y_1 = 25$, $x_1 = 10$, $y_2 = 75$, and $x_2 = x$.

$$\frac{25}{10} \diagup \frac{75}{x}$$ **Cross multiply because the cross products of a proportion are equal.**

$$25 \cdot x = 10 \cdot 75$$ Cross product of a proportion are equal.

$$\frac{25 \cdot x}{25} = \frac{10 \cdot 75}{25}$$ Divide both sides of the equation $25 \cdot x = 10 \cdot 75$

by 25 in order to obtain the value of x.

$$\frac{\overset{x}{\cancel{25} \cdot x}}{\underset{1}{\cancel{25}}} = \frac{10 \cdot \overset{3}{\cancel{75}}}{\underset{1}{\cancel{25}}}$$

$$x = 10 \cdot 3$$
$$x = 30$$

Example 5

If y varies directly as x and $y = 9$ when $x = 4$ find y when $x = 28$.

Solution

In direct variations, all the ratios or all the values of $\frac{y}{x}$ are equal to a certain constant, k.

Therefore all the ratios or all the values of $\frac{y}{x}$ must be equal. We can therefore set up

and solve a proportion to find y as shown:

$$\frac{y_1}{x_1} = \frac{y_2}{x_2}$$ A proportion is a statement showing that two ratios are equal.

$$\frac{9}{4} = \frac{y}{28}$$ Substitute $y_1 = 9$, $x_1 = 4$, $y_2 = y$, and $x_2 = 28$.

   **Cross multiply because the cross products of a proportion are equal.**

$$4 \cdot y = 9 \cdot 28$$ Cross products of a proportion are equal.

$$\frac{4 \cdot y}{4} = \frac{9 \cdot 28}{4}$$ Divide both sides of the equation $4 \cdot y = 9 \cdot 28$ by 4 to obtain the value of y.

$$\frac{4 \cdot \overset{y}{y}}{\underset{1}{4}} = \frac{9 \cdot \overset{7}{28}}{\underset{1}{4}}$$

$$y = 9 \cdot 7$$
$$y = 63.$$

Exercises

1. Explain a direct variation.
2. Explain in one sentence how you could tell from a graph that:
    a. a data set is a direct variation.
    b. a data set is not a direct variation.
       Hint: See Example 1.
3. Explain in one sentence how you could tell from a table using algebra that a data set is:
    a. a direct variation.
    b. not a direct variation.
       Hint: See Example 1.
4. The table shows the distance covered per hour by Mrs. Brown.

Time (hr)	1	2	3	4	5
Distance (mi)	2	4	6	8	10

   a. Explain graphically that the data set is a direct variation.
   b. Using algebra, explain why the data set is a direct variation.
      Hint: See Example 1.
5. Find each constant and each equation of direct variation, given that y varies directly with x. Hint: See Example 1.
   a. y is 14 when x is 7.   **b**. y is 93 when x is 3.   **c**. y is 84 when x is 12.
   d. y is 10 when x is 50.   **e**. y is 3 when x is 24 f.   **f**. y is 3 when x is 21.
   g. y is 128 when x is 2.   **h**. y is 100 when x is 10.   **i**. y is 15 when x is 12.
   j. y is 4 when x is 15   **k**. y is 4 when x is 48.   **l**. y is 3 when x is 63.
6. For each of the following values of x and y, y varies directly as x. Find the value of x. Hint; See Example 4.
   a. y is 15 when x is 3. Find x when y is 75
   b. y is 56 when x is 16. Find x when y = 7
   c. y is 16 when x is 36. Find x when y = 4
   d. y is 24 when x is 8. Find x when y = 4

e. y is 3 when x is 7. Find x when y = 36

f. y is 18 when x is 24. Find x when y = 6.

7. For each of the following values of x and y, y varies directly as x. Find the value of y.
   Hint: See example 5.

   a. y is 5 when x is 8. Find y when x is 32.

   b. y is 64 when x is 4. Find y when x is 1.

   c. y is 100 when x is 5. Find y when x is 20.

   d. y is 21 when x is 35. Find y when x is 7.

   e. y is 4 when x is 28. Find y when x is 7.

   f. y is 7 when x is 3. Find y when x is 24.

Answers to Selected Questions

5a. Constant is 2 and the equation of the direct variation is y = 2x.

6a. x = 15   **7a.** y = 20.

INVERSE VARIATION

In the direct variation, the variables x and y either increase together or decrease together. **In the inverse variation**, **as one variable quantity increases, the other variable quantity decreases**. This is written as $\mathbf{y = \dfrac{k}{x}}$ or yx = k where k is a constant of the variation, k ≠ 0 and x ≠ 0. Note that a constant is a number that will not change for a specific relation. **It is important to note that in the inverse variation, the product of the variables is a constant.**

If it takes 50 days to build a new soccer stadium by 200 people, then if we increase the number of workers, then the number of days to complete a similar new stadium will decrease. Therefore, as the number of the workers increases, the number of days needed to build the new stadium decreases. This is an example of inverse variation.

How to Tell if Each Relationship From a Table is an Inverse or Not, and How to Write an Equation of the Relation

Example 1

The table shows the number of days needed to drive new cars from lot A to lot B based on the size of the work crew.

   a. Tell whether each relationship is an inverse variation.

   b. Write the equation of the relationship.

Crew size	10	20	25	40	50
Days of driving	100	50	40	25	20

Solution

a. Let the "crew size" be the variable y.

Let the "days of driving" be the variable x.

For an **inverse variation**, the product of the variables is a constant, therefore:

$xy = k$ where k is a constant or a constant number.

Let us find the value of k in each relation to see if the value of k is the same or constant as shown:

$xy = k$, $10 \cdot 100 = 1000$, $20 \cdot 50 = 1000$, $25 \cdot 40 = 1000$

$40 \cdot 25 = 1000$, $50 \cdot 20 = 1000$.

Since the products of the variables are always the same, which is 1000, the relation is an inverse variation, and therefore, $k = 1000$.

b. From the solution of Example **1a**, $k = 1000$. From the solution of Example **1a**, the relation is an inverse variation, and therefore, the products of the variations are constant as shown:

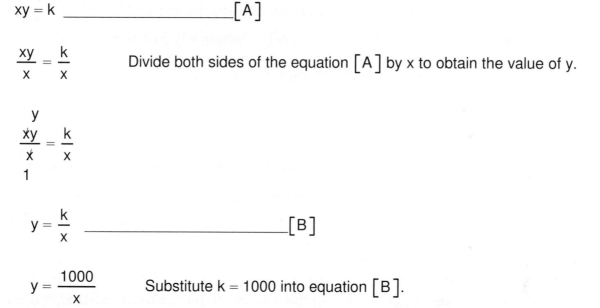

$xy = k$ _____[A]

$\dfrac{xy}{x} = \dfrac{k}{x}$ Divide both sides of the equation [A] by x to obtain the value of y.

$\dfrac{\overset{y}{\cancel{x}y}}{\underset{1}{\cancel{x}}} = \dfrac{k}{x}$

$y = \dfrac{k}{x}$ _____[B]

$y = \dfrac{1000}{x}$ Substitute $k = 1000$ into equation [B].

Therefore, the equation of the relation is $y = \dfrac{1000}{x}$.

Example 2

The table shows the number of toys produced in a given amount of time. Tell whether the relation is an inverse variation.

Toys produced	28	36	48	55	60
Time (hr)	2	3	4	5	6

Solution

Let the number of the toys produced be the variable x.

Let the number of hours required to produce the toys be the variable y.

In an inverse variation, the product of the variables is a constant or a constant number.

Therefore, if the relation is an inverse variation, then $xy = k$ where k is a constant or a constant number, so let us check if the products of the variables are constants or constant numbers as follows:

$$xy = k, \quad 28 \cdot 2 = 56, \quad 36 \cdot 3 = 108.$$

The product is not the same, and therefore, the relation is not an inverse variation.

How to Write an Equation That Shows How y is Related to x When Given That y Varies Inversely as x and the Values of x and y are Given

Example 3

If y varies inversely as x and y = 5 when x = 10 write an equation that shows how y is related to x.

Solution

Step 1: Find k.

y = 5 when x = 10.

The equation for an inverse variation can also be written as:

$$y = \frac{k}{x} \text{_____} [A] \qquad \text{where k is a constant.}$$

$$5 = \frac{k}{10} \text{_____} [B] \qquad \text{Substitute } y = 5 \text{ and } x = 10 \text{ into the}$$

equation [A].

$$10 \cdot 5 = \frac{k}{10} \cdot 10 \qquad \text{Multiply both sides of the equation } [B] \text{ by 10 in}$$

order to eliminate the denominator 10 at the right side of the equation [B] to obtain the value of k.

$$50 = \frac{k}{\overset{\cancel{10}}{\cancel{10}}} \times \overset{1}{\cancel{10}}$$

$$50 = k$$

Step 2: Write an equation to show how y is related to x.

It is already given in the question that y varies inversely as x, so let us use the equation for inverse variation to write the equation that relates y to x as shown:

$$y = \frac{k}{x} \text{_____} [C] \qquad \qquad \text{Equation for inverse variation.}$$

$$y = \frac{50}{x}$$ Substitute k = 50 in equation [C].

The equation that relates y to x is:

$$y = \frac{50}{x}$$

How to Graph Inverse Variation Functions

Example 4

a. Graph the inverse variation function of $f(x) = \frac{1}{x}$.

b. What are the special features of the graph $f(x) = \frac{1}{x}$?

c. What value of x makes the function or the graph undefined? Explain why the graph did not cross neither the x-axis nor the y-axis.

d. Label the graph with the four quadrants.

Solution

Step 1: Create a table for x and y.

Create a table for x and y by assigning numbers to x and finding the corresponding values of y as shown:

(The table for x and y is located on the next page.)

x	$y = f(x) = \dfrac{1}{x}$	y	(x, y)
-4	$y = f(-4) = \dfrac{1}{-4} = -\dfrac{1}{4}$	$-\dfrac{1}{4}$	$(-4, -\dfrac{1}{4})$
-3	$y = f(-3) = \dfrac{1}{-3} = -\dfrac{1}{3}$	$-\dfrac{1}{3}$	$(-3, -\dfrac{1}{3})$
-2	$y = f(-2) = \dfrac{1}{-2} = -\dfrac{1}{2}$	$-\dfrac{1}{2}$	$(-2, -\dfrac{1}{2})$
-1	$y = f(-1) = \dfrac{1}{-1} = -1$	-1	(-1,-1)
$-\dfrac{1}{2}$	$y = f(-\dfrac{1}{2}) = \dfrac{1}{-\dfrac{1}{2}} = 1 \times (\dfrac{-2}{1}) = -2$	-2	$(-\dfrac{1}{2}, -2)$
0	$y = f(0) = \dfrac{1}{0} =$ Not defined	Not defined	(0, Not defined)
$\dfrac{1}{2}$	$y = f(\dfrac{1}{2}) = \dfrac{1}{\dfrac{1}{2}} = 1 \times \dfrac{2}{1} = 2$	2	$(\dfrac{1}{2}, 2)$
1	$y = f(1) = \dfrac{1}{1} = 1$	1	(1, 1)
2	$y = f(2) = \dfrac{1}{2}$	$\dfrac{1}{2}$	$(2, \dfrac{1}{2})$
3	$y = f(3) = \dfrac{1}{3}$	$\dfrac{1}{3}$	$(3, \dfrac{1}{3})$
4	$y = f(4) = \dfrac{1}{4}$	$\dfrac{1}{4}$	$(4, \dfrac{1}{4})$

Step 2: Plot the points (x, y) in the table on graph paper and connect the points with a smooth curve as shown:

(The graph is located on the next page.)

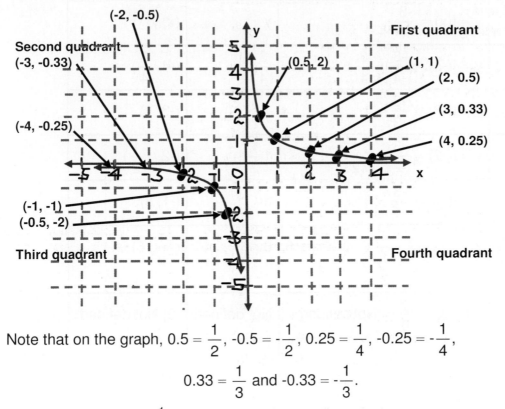

Note that on the graph, $0.5 = \dfrac{1}{2}$, $-0.5 = -\dfrac{1}{2}$, $0.25 = \dfrac{1}{4}$, $-0.25 = -\dfrac{1}{4}$,

$$0.33 = \dfrac{1}{3} \text{ and } -0.33 = -\dfrac{1}{3}.$$

b. The function $f(x) = \dfrac{1}{x}$ creates two graphs. One graph is in the first quadrant and the other graph is in the third quadrant. Both graphs cross neither the x-axis nor the y-axis.

c. When $x = 0$, the function $f(x) = \dfrac{1}{x} =$ becomes $f(0) = \dfrac{1}{0} =$ undefined, and this is the reason why the graphs could not cross neither the x-axis nor the y-axis.

d. The four quadrants are shown on the graph.

Example 5

a. Graph the inverse variation function $f(x) = \dfrac{-3}{x}$.

b. What are the special features of the graph of $f(x) = \dfrac{-3}{x}$?

c. What value of x makes the function or the graph undefined? Explain why the graph did not cross neither the x-axis nor the y-axis.

Solution

a. Step 1: Create a table for x and y.

Create a table for x and y by assigning numbers to x and then finding the corresponding values of y as shown:

303

x	$y = f(x) = \dfrac{-3}{x}$	y	(x, y)
-4	$y = f(-4) = \dfrac{-3}{-4} = \dfrac{3}{4}$	$\dfrac{3}{4}$	$(-4, \dfrac{3}{4})$
-3	$y = f(-3) = \dfrac{-3}{-3} = 1$	1	(-3, 1)
-2	$y = f(-2) = \dfrac{-3}{-2} = 1\dfrac{1}{2}$	$1\dfrac{1}{2}$	$(-2, 1\dfrac{1}{2})$
-1	$y = f(-1) = \dfrac{-3}{-1} = 3$	3	(-1, 3)
$-\dfrac{1}{2}$	$y = f(-\dfrac{1}{2}) = \dfrac{-3}{-\dfrac{1}{2}} = -3(-\dfrac{2}{1}) = 6$	6	$(-\dfrac{1}{2}, 6)$
0	$y = f(0) = \dfrac{-3}{0} = $ Not defined	Not defined	(0, Not defined)
$\dfrac{1}{2}$	$y = f(\dfrac{1}{2}) = \dfrac{-3}{\dfrac{1}{2}} = -3(\dfrac{2}{1}) = -6$	-6	$(\dfrac{1}{2}, -6)$
1	$y = f(1) = \dfrac{-3}{1} = -3$	-3	(1, -3)
2	$y = f(2) = \dfrac{-3}{2} = -\dfrac{3}{2} = -1\dfrac{1}{2}$	$-1\dfrac{1}{2}$	$(2, -1\dfrac{1}{2})$
3	$y = f(3) = \dfrac{-3}{3} = -1$	-1	(3, -1)
4	$y = f(4) = \dfrac{-3}{4} = -\dfrac{3}{4}$	$-\dfrac{3}{4}$	$(4, -\dfrac{3}{4})$

Step 2: Plot the points (x, y) in the table on graph paper and connect the points with a smooth curve as shown:

(The graph is located on the next page.)

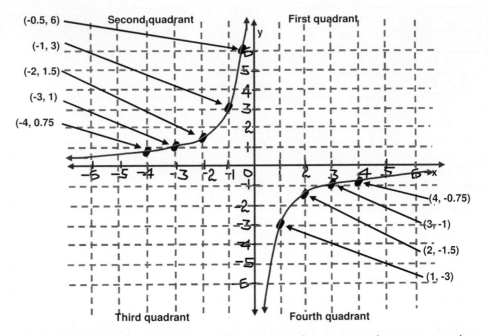

Notice on the graph that $0.75 = \dfrac{3}{4}$, $1.5 = 1\dfrac{1}{2}$, $-0.5 = -\dfrac{1}{2}$, $-1.5 = -1\dfrac{1}{2}$, and $-0.75 = -\dfrac{3}{4}$.

b. The function $f(x) = \dfrac{-3}{x}$ creates two graphs. One graph is in the second quadrant and the other graph is in the fourth quadrant. Both graphs cross neither the x-axis nor the y-axis.

c. When $x = 0$, the function $f(x) = \dfrac{-3}{x}$ becomes $f(0) = \dfrac{-3}{0}$ = undefined, and this is the reason why the graphs could not cross neither the x-axis nor the y-axis.

How to Find x or y in an Inverse Variation

Example 6
If y is 4 when x is 7 and y varies inversely as x, explain how to find y when x is 2.
Find y when x is 2.
Solution
In an inverse variation, the product of the variables is a constant. This means that:

$xy = k$ Where x and y are variables and k is a constant.

$xy = $ constant

Therefore, $x_1 y_1 = x_2 y_2$ Where $x_1 = 7$, $y_1 = 4$, $x_2 = 2$, and y_2 is the unknown.

$7 \cdot 4 = 2 \cdot y_2$ Substitute $x_1 = 7$, $y_1 = 4$, $x_2 = 2$, and y_2 into the equation $x_1 y_1 = x_2 y_2$.

$\dfrac{7 \cdot 4}{2} = \dfrac{2 \cdot y_2}{2}$ Divide both sides of the equation $7 \cdot 4 = 2 \cdot y_2$ by 2 in order to obtain the value of y_2.

$$\frac{\overset{2}{7 \cdot 4}}{\underset{1}{2}} = \frac{\overset{y_2}{2 \cdot y_2}}{\underset{1}{2}}$$

$$7 \cdot 2 = y_2$$
$$14 = y_2$$

Therefore, when $y = 14$, $x = 2$.

Example 7

If y is $\frac{2}{5}$ when x is -30, find x when y is 2.

Solution

In an inverse variation, the products of the variables is a constant. This means that:

$\qquad xy = k \qquad\qquad$ Where x and y are variables and k is a constant.

$\qquad xy = \text{constant}$

Therefore, $x_1 y_1 = x_2 y_2 \qquad$ Where $x_1 = -30$, $y_1 = \frac{2}{5}$, $x_2 = $ unknown and $y_2 = 2$.

$$(-30) \cdot \frac{2}{5} = x_2 \cdot 2 \qquad$$ Substitute $x_1 = -30$, $y_1 = \frac{2}{5}$, $x_2 = $ unknown and $y_2 = 2$ into the equation $x_1 y_1 = x_2 y_2$.

$$\frac{(-30) \cdot \frac{2}{5}}{2} = \frac{x_2 \cdot 2}{2} \qquad$$ Divide both sides of the equation $(-30) \cdot \frac{2}{5} = x_2 \cdot 2$ by 2 in order to obtain the value of x_2.

$$\frac{\overset{-6}{\cancel{(-30)}}}{\underset{1}{\cancel{2}}} \cdot \frac{\overset{1}{\cancel{2}}}{\underset{1}{5}} = \frac{x_2 \cdot \overset{1}{\cancel{2}}}{\underset{1}{\cancel{2}}} \qquad$$ Rewrite the left side of the equation and then divide as shown.

$$-3 \cdot 2 = x_2$$
$$-6 = x_2$$

Therefore, when $y = 2$, $x = -6$.

Exercises

1. Explain what is meant by inverse variation. Hint: See the preceding explanations.
2. What is the difference between direct variation and inverse variation?
   Hint: See the preceding explanations.
3. In each table, tell whether x varies inversely as y. Write the equation of the

relationship. Hint: See Example 1.

a.
x	y
1	36
2	18
4	9
6	6

b.
x	y
1	12
2	6
3	4
4	3

c.
x	y
2	12
3	8
4	6

d.
x	8	10	20	40	80
y	5	4	2	1	0.5

4. The table shows the cleaning time of a school based on the number of workers.
   a. Tell whether the relationship is an inverse variation.
   b. Write the equation of the relationship. Hint: See Example 1.

Time (hr)	6	3	10	5	10
Number of workers	5	10	3	6	3

5. In each table, tell whether x varies inversely as y. Hint: See Example 2.

a.
x	y
1	8
2	10
3	4
4	6

b.
x	y
1	4
2	10
3	8
4	9

c.
x	y
2	22
3	34
5	40
7	14

6. The table shows the distance covered by a student in a given time. Tell whether the relationship is an inverse variation. Hint: See Example 2.

Distance (mi)	1	2	3	4	5	6
Time (min)	12	25	30	38	42	56

7. Find each constant of each inverse variation equation, given that x and y vary inversely. Hint: See Example 3.
   a. $y = 10$ when $x = 2$ b. $y = 3$ when $x = 4$ c. $y = 12$ when $x = 5$
   d. $y = 11$ when $x = 8$ e. $y = 7$ when $x = 3$ f. $y = 2$ when $x = 3$
   g. $y = 16$ when $x = 3$ h. $y = 6$ when $x = 11$

8. Graph each inverse variation function. What are the special features of the graph? Explain why the graph did not cross neither the x-axis nor the y-axis.
   Hint: See Example 4.

   a. $f(x) = \dfrac{1}{2x}$ b. $f(x) = \dfrac{1}{3x}$ c. $f(x) = \dfrac{2}{x}$

9. Graph each inverse variation function.
   What are the special features of the graph?
   What value of x makes the function or the graph undefined?
   Explain why the graph did not cross neither the x-axis nor the y-axis.
   Hint: See Example 5.

   a. $f(x) = -\dfrac{1}{x}$ b. $f(x) = -\dfrac{2}{x}$ c. $f(x) = -\dfrac{1}{2x}$

10. If y is 4 when x is 12 and y varies inversely as x, explain how to find y when x is 3.

Find y when x is 3. Hint: See Example 6.

11. Given that y varies inversely as x;
    a. If y is 6 when x is 8, find y when x is 3.
    b. If y is 4 when x is 10, find y when x is 5.
    c. If y is 7 when x is 12, find y when x is 3.
    d. If y is 16 when x is 12, find x when y is 8.
    e. If y is 3 when x is 32, find x when y is 4.
    f. If y is 6 when x is 11, find y when x is 3.
    Hint: See Example 6.

12. Given that y varies inversely as x:
    a. If y is 6 when x is -11, find x when y is 2.
    b. If y is $\frac{3}{4}$ when x is -24, find y when x is 4.
    c. If y is 3 when x is -8, find x when y is -4.
    d. If y is $\frac{2}{5}$ when x is -40, find y when x is 4.
    e. If y is $\frac{5}{6}$ when x is 24, find y when x is 12.
    f. If y is $\frac{3}{4}$ when x is 24, find y when x is 27.
    Hint: See Example 7.

Challenge Questions

13. If y varies inversely as x, write an equation that shows how y is related to x for each situation.
    a. y is 8 when x is 2.   **b.** y is 12 when x is 36.
    c. y is 3 when x is 9   **d.** y is 3 when x is 7.

14. Given that y varies inversely as x,
    a. If y is 7 when x is -12, find x when y is 35.
    b. If y is 15 when x is 4, find y when x is 3.

15. If y varies inversely with x and y = 27 when x = 9, find the constant of variation.

Answers to Selected Questions

7a. constant is 20 and y = $\frac{20}{x}$.   **11a.** y = 16   **12a.** x = -33.

REAL WORLD APPLICATIONS OF VARIATIONS - WORD PROBLEMS

Example 1

The height of a triangle with an area 60 cm² varies inversely with the length of its base.
If the base = 30 cm when the height = 4 cm, find the base when the height = 10 cm.

Solution

Let the length of the base $= b$ and let the height $= h$. It is given in the question that the height of the triangle varies inversely with the length of the base. In the inverse variation, the product of the variables is a constant. Therefore, $b \cdot h = k$ where k is a constant. Since $b \cdot h = k$ for any set of b and h we can write:

$$b_1 h_1 = b_2 h_2$$ where $b_1 = 30$ cm, $h_1 = 4$ cm, $b_2 =$ unknown length of the base, and $h_2 = 10$ cm.

$$30 \cdot 40 = b_2 \cdot 10 \underline{\hspace{4cm}}[A]$$

Substitute $b_1 = 30$ cm, $h_1 = 4$ cm, and $h_2 = 10$ cm into the equation $b_1 h_1 = b_2 h_2$.

Divide both sides of the equation $[A]$ by 10 in order to obtain the value of b_2 as shown:

$$\frac{30 \cdot 4}{10} = \frac{b_2 \cdot 10}{10}$$

$$\frac{\overset{3}{\cancel{30}} \cdot 4}{\underset{1}{\cancel{10}}} = \frac{b_2 \cdot \overset{1}{\cancel{10}}}{\underset{1}{\cancel{10}}}$$

$$3 \cdot 4 = b_2$$
$$12 = b_2$$

Therefore, when the height is 10 cm the base is 12 cm.

Boyle's Law

Physics is a higher level science subject. In physics, Bolye's law shows that when the volume of a gas decreases, the pressure increases. The relationship between the volume and the pressure is an inverse variation, where the variables are volume and pressure. Since the product of the variables of an inverse relation is a constant, we can write:

$VP = K$ where $V =$ volume, $P =$ pressure, and $K =$ a constant.

Therefore, for any set of variables of volume and pressure, we can write:

$V_1 P_1 = V_2 P_2 = V_3 P_3 = V_4 P_4 =...$, and this is known as the Boyle's Law.

Example 2

Using Boyle's law, when the volume of a gas decreases the pressure increases.

a. Find the inverse variation function of the data in the table.

b. Use the inverse variation function to find the pressure of the gas if the volume is decreased to 4 liters.

Volume (L)	5	6	10	12	15
Pressure (atm)	12	10	6	5	4

Solution

a. Step 1: Find K.

In an inverse variation, the product of the variables is a constant.
Therefore, we can write:

VP = K   Where V = volume, P = pressure and K = a constant.

Therefore: 5 · 12 = K   Substitute a set of the data from the table, for example, V = 5 L and P = 12 atm into the equation VP = K.

60 = K

Step 2: Write the inverse variation function.

In general, the inverse function of two variables x and y is written as shown:

$$y = \frac{K}{x} \text{ and } f(x) = \frac{K}{x}$$ where f(x) is the function form of y.

Similarly:

$$f(V) = \frac{K}{V}$$ where f(v) is the function.

$$f(V) = \frac{60}{V}$$ Substitute K = 60 into the equation $f(V) = \frac{K}{V}$.

From step 1, K = 60.

Therefore, the inverse variation function of the data is $f(V) = \frac{60}{V}$.

b. The inverse variation function is:

$$f(V) = \frac{60}{V}$$

Therefore, if V = 4 L, then,

$$f(4) = \frac{60}{4}$$ Substitute V = 4 L into the equation $f(V) = \frac{60}{V}$.

$$f(4) = \frac{\overset{15}{\cancel{60}}}{4}$$

f(4) = 15

Therefore, the pressure of the gas if the volume is decreased to 4 liters is 15 atm.

Exercises

1. The height of a triangle varies inversely with the length of its base. If the length of the base = 45 cm when the height is 5 cm, find the length of the base when the height is 9 cm. Hint: See Example 1.

2. When the volume of a gas decreases, the pressure increases.

a. Find the inverse variation function of the data in the table.

b. Use the inverse variation function to find the pressure of the gas when the volume is 2 liters.

Hint: See Example 2.

Volume (L)	3	6	9	10
Pressure (atm)	30	15	10	9

3. The mass of an object varies inversely with its acceleration if a constant force of 60 N is applied to it. Using the table:

   a. Write an inverse variation function.

   b. What is the mass of an object if its acceleration is 20 m/s^2?

Hint: See Example 2.

Mass (kg)	2	4	5	6	10
Acceleration (m/s^2)	30	15	12	10	6

Challenge Questions

4. The table shows the number of weeks needed to clean a hospital based on the size of the work crew.

Work crew size	2	3	4	10
Weeks of cleaning	45	30	22.5	9

a. Write an inverse variation function

b. What is the size of the work crew needed to clean the hospital in 8 weeks?

CHAPTER 16

INTEGERS

Cumulative Review

1. $44 + 17 =$ **2.** $33 - 4 =$ **3.** $54 + 8 =$ **4.** $16 - 7 =$

5. $23 - 17 =$ **6.** $12 \div 4 =$ **7.** $18 \times 2 =$ **8.** $15 \div 3 =$

9. $\begin{array}{r} 12 \\ \times\ 3 \\ \hline \end{array}$ **10.** $\begin{array}{r} 9 \\ \times\ 3 \\ \hline \end{array}$ **11.** $72 \div 3 =$ **12.** $7 + 8 =$

13. $15 + 8 =$ **14.** $18 \div 3 =$ **15.** $16 - 8 =$ **16.** $9 \times 2 =$

17. $35 \div 5 =$ **18.** $21 - 15 =$ **19.** $30 \div 6 =$ **20.** $17 - 8 =$

| **21.** 25 | **22.** 18 | **23.** 37 | **24.** 17 |
| $\times$ 3 | + 19 | - 13 | $\times$ 4 |

25. $42 \div 3 =$ **26.** $24 \div 8 =$ **27.** $12 + 38 =$ **28.** $44 - 18 =$

New Terms: integer, negative integer, positive integer, opposites, and absolute values.

An **integer** is any negative or positive whole number or zero. We can show integers on the number line as:

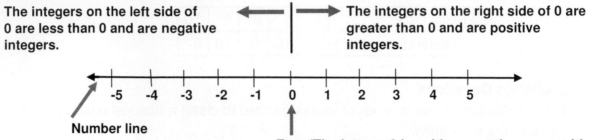

The integers on the left side of 0 are less than 0 and are negative integers.

The integers on the right side of 0 are greater than 0 and are positive integers.

Number line

Zero (The integer 0 is neither negative nor positive).

Negative integers are always written with a – sign, however, positive integers can be written with or without a + sign. Positive and negative integers can be used to represent actual life situations as shown:

a. The temperature 40 degrees below zero can be written as -40^0F.

b. The temperature 52 degrees above zero can be written as $+52^0$F or 52^0F.

Example 1
a. Express twenty feet below sea level using integers.
b. Express thirty feet above sea level using integers.
Solution
Hint: The sea level is at 0 ft. such that any measurement above the sea level is a positive number and any measurement below the sea level is a negative number.
a. Twenty feet below sea level can be written as –20 ft.
b. Thirty feet above sea level can be written as +30 ft or 30 ft.

Team Project
The class should be divided into four teams and each team should write about two situations that negative or positive integers could be used such as scoring a football game by losing 10 yards or gaining 12 yards. Each team should report to the class about their real life situations with integers.

Graph Integers
Integers can be graphed on a number line by drawing a dot.

Example 2

Graph –4 on the number line.

Solution

Draw a number line and then draw a dot at the position of –4.

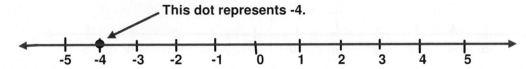

Example 3

Graph +3 on the number line.

Solution

Draw a number line and then draw a dot at the position of +3.

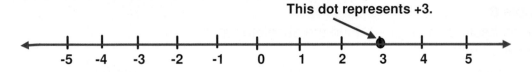

Opposite Integers

The opposite of saving $4.00 in the bank is withdrawing $4.00 from the bank. In both cases, the same amount of $4.00 is involved. Every integer has an opposite and **opposite integers** are at the same distances from 0 on a number line, but in opposite directions.

Example 4

Write the opposite of +3.

Solution

The opposite integers are at the same distance from 0 on a number line, but in the opposite direction as shown:

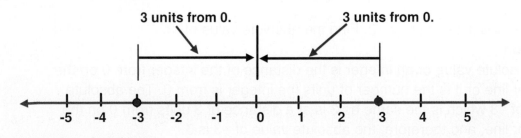

The opposite of +3 is –3.

Example 5

Write the opposite of –4.

313

Solution

The opposite integers are at the same distance from 0 on a number line, but in the opposite direction.

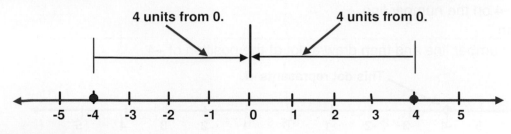

The opposite of –4 is +4 or 4.

Absolute Value

The **absolute value** of an integer is the distance of the integer from 0 on the number line or it is the number of units the integer is from 0 on the number line.

Example 6

Find the absolute value of –4. Find the absolute value of +4.

Solution

The absolute value of an integer is the distance of the integer from 0 on the number line or the number of units the integer is from 0 on the number line. The absolute value of –4 is at a distance of 4 units from 0, and therefore, the absolute value of –4 is +4 or 4.

The absolute value of +4 which is the same as 4 is at a distance of 4 units from 0, and therefore, the absolute value of +4 is 4.

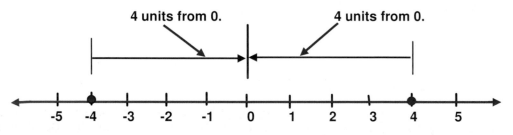

Example 7

Find the absolute value of +3. Find the absolute value of -3.

Solution

The absolute value of an integer is the distance of the integer from 0 on the number line or it is the number of units the integer is from 0. The absolute value of +3 which is the same as 3 is at a distance of 3 units from 0 on the number line, and therefore, the absolute value of +3 is 3.

The absolute value of -3 is at a distance of 3 units from 0 on the number line, and therefore, the absolute value of -3 is 3.

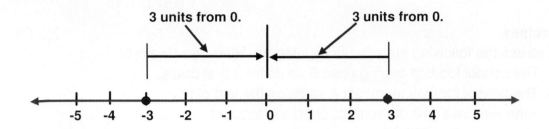

3 units from 0.   3 units from 0.

Conclusion

The absolute value of any number **is the same number without any sign in front of the number** as shown:

a. The absolute value of –4 is 4.

b. The absolute value of +4 is 4.

c. The absolute value of –3 is 3.

d. The absolute value of +3 is 3.

| | is the symbol for the absolute value.

|–6| means the absolute value of –6 which is 6.

|–2| means the absolute value of –2 which is 2.

We can conclude that the absolute value of any number is the same number without any sign in front of the number.

Example 8

Find |–5|

Solution

The absolute value of any number is the value of the same number without any sign in front of the number. Therefore, |–5| = 5.

Example 9

Find |–10| + |–8| + |+2|

Solution

The absolute value of any number is the value of the same number without any sign in front of the number. Therefore, |–10| + |– 8| + |+2|

$$= 10 + 8 + 2 \qquad (|-10| = 10, |-8| = 8, |+2| = 2)$$
$$= 20$$

Example 10

Evaluate: |+2| – |–9| + 4 + |+2| – |–1|

Solution

The absolute value of any number is the same number without any sign in front of the number. Therefore,

$$|+2| - |-9| + 4 + |+2| - |-1|$$
$$= 2 - 9 + 4 + 2 - 1 \qquad (|+2| = 2, |-9| = 9, |+2| = 2, |-1| = 1)$$
$$= -2 \qquad (2 \cdot 9 = -7, -7 + 4 = -3, -3 + 2 = -1, -1 \cdot 1 = -2)$$

315

Exercises

1. Express the following statements as integers. Hint: See Example 1.

   a. The school football team gained 5 yards for a first down.

   b. The school football team lost 4 yards on the last play.

   c. John withdrew $10.00 from his checking account.

   d. Mary deposited $20.00 in her checking account.

2. Graph the following on a number line. Hint: See Examples 2 and 3.

   a. –2   **b**. +5   **c**. –6   **d**. +1   **e**. –1

3. Identify the integers graphed. Hint: See Examples 1, 2, and 3.

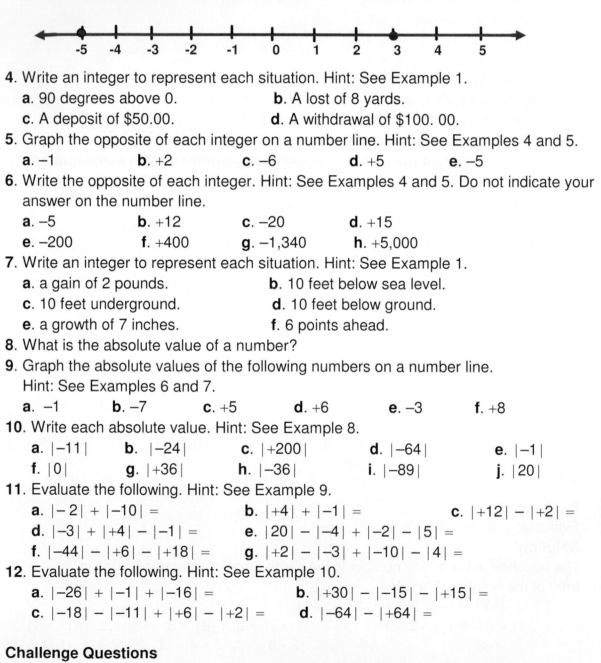

4. Write an integer to represent each situation. Hint: See Example 1.

   a. 90 degrees above 0.   **b**. A lost of 8 yards.

   c. A deposit of $50.00.   **d**. A withdrawal of $100. 00.

5. Graph the opposite of each integer on a number line. Hint: See Examples 4 and 5.

   a. –1   **b**. +2   **c**. –6   **d**. +5   **e**. –5

6. Write the opposite of each integer. Hint: See Examples 4 and 5. Do not indicate your answer on the number line.

   a. –5   **b**. +12   **c**. –20   **d**. +15

   e. –200   **f**. +400   **g**. –1,340   **h**. +5,000

7. Write an integer to represent each situation. Hint: See Example 1.

   a. a gain of 2 pounds.   **b**. 10 feet below sea level.

   c. 10 feet underground.   **d**. 10 feet below ground.

   e. a growth of 7 inches.   **f**. 6 points ahead.

8. What is the absolute value of a number?

9. Graph the absolute values of the following numbers on a number line. Hint: See Examples 6 and 7.

   a. –1   **b**. –7   **c**. +5   **d**. +6   **e**. –3   **f**. +8

10. Write each absolute value. Hint: See Example 8.

   a. $|-11|$ **b**. $|-24|$ **c**. $|+200|$ **d**. $|-64|$ **e**. $|-1|$

   f. $|0|$ **g**. $|+36|$ **h**. $|-36|$ **i**. $|-89|$ **j**. $|20|$

11. Evaluate the following. Hint: See Example 9.

   a. $|-2| + |-10| =$ **b**. $|+4| + |-1| =$ **c**. $|+12| - |+2| =$

   d. $|-3| + |+4| - |-1| =$ **e**. $|20| - |-4| + |-2| - |5| =$

   f. $|-44| - |+6| - |+18| =$ **g**. $|+2| - |-3| + |-10| - |4| =$

12. Evaluate the following. Hint: See Example 10.

   a. $|-26| + |-1| + |-16| =$ **b**. $|+30| - |-15| - |+15| =$

   c. $|-18| - |-11| + |+6| - |+2| =$ **d**. $|-64| - |+64| =$

Challenge Questions

13. Evaluate the following.

    a. $|-100| - |-100| =$ **b.** $|+58| - |+48| =$ **c.** $16 + |-16| =$

14. Graph the opposite of 10.

15. Graph $-7, -8, 0, 2,$ and 6 on the same number line.

16. Write an integer to describe each situation.

    a. A helicopter rises 100 feet.

    b. A submarine is 20 feet below the surface of the water.

Answers to Selected Questions

10a. 11   **11a.** 12   **12a.** 43   **16a.** +100ft or 100ft

Compare and Order Integers

A time line can be used to show the events of the day. For example, a student's daily time line may include the following:

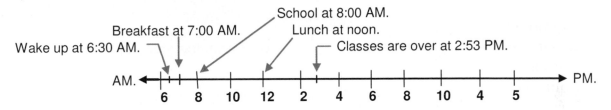

On the above number line, the student wakes up at 6:30 A.M. before having breakfast at 7:00 A.M., Similarly, you can use number lines to compare and order numbers. The numbers to the right on a number line are always greater than the numbers to the left. Alternatively, the numbers to the left on a number line are always less than the numbers to the right. **Notice** that on the number line that follows, –4 is to the left of 0, therefore, –4 is less than 0, and also, 0 is greater than –4 since 0 is to the right of –4 on the number line.

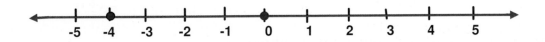

Team Exercise

The class should be divided in to teams and each team should make a typical Monday time line for a student within the team starting from the time the student wakes up to the time that the student goes to bed. The time line should include dinner time, play time, and homework time. Each team should report their time line to the whole class.

  1. From your time line, could you say that a time line can help you to order events?

  2. Each team should make a time line for a typical Thanksgiving Day and then report the time line to the whole class.

Example 1

Use the number line to order –4, +3, –5, +4, and –2 from the least to the greatest.

Solution

The number line is drawn with the integers –4, +3, –5, +4, and –2 indicated on it as shown:

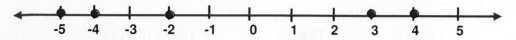

The number to the left on the number line is always less than the number to the right, and therefore, using the number line, the order of the numbers from the least to the greatest is:

$$-5, -4, -2, 3, \text{ and } 4.$$

Example 2

Use the number line to order +5, –1, 0, –4, and +3 from the greatest to the smallest.

Solution

The number line is drawn with the integers +5, –1, 0, –4, and +3 indicated on it as shown:

The number to the right on the number line are always greater than the numbers on the left, and therefore, using the number line, the order of the numbers from the greatest to the least is:

$$+5, +3, 0, -1, \text{ and } -4.$$

Using "greater than" and "less than" symbols

The symbol > means greater than.
The symbol < means less than.

Example 3

Using the number line, replace ? with <, > or =.

a. –3 ? –1   **b.** 0 ? –3   **c.** +1 ? –1

Solution

a. Graph -3 and –1 on a number line.

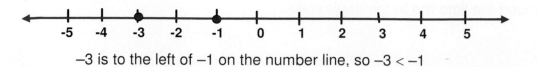

−3 is to the left of −1 on the number line, so −3 < −1

318

b. Graph 0 and –3 on a number line.

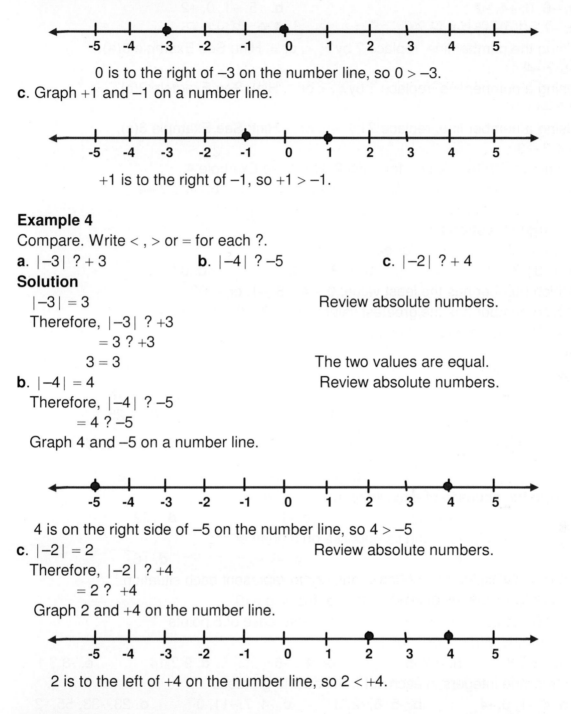

0 is to the right of –3 on the number line, so 0 > –3.

c. Graph +1 and –1 on a number line.

+1 is to the right of –1, so +1 > –1.

Example 4

Compare. Write < , > or = for each ?.

a. $|-3|$? + 3   **b**. $|-4|$? –5   **c**. $|-2|$? + 4

Solution

$|-3| = 3$ Review absolute numbers.

Therefore, $|-3|$? +3

       = 3 ? +3

     3 = 3   The two values are equal.

b. $|-4| = 4$ Review absolute numbers.

Therefore, $|-4|$? –5

     = 4 ? –5

Graph 4 and –5 on a number line.

4 is on the right side of –5 on the number line, so 4 > –5

c. $|-2| = 2$ Review absolute numbers.

Therefore, $|-2|$? +4

     = 2 ? +4

Graph 2 and +4 on the number line.

2 is to the left of +4 on the number line, so 2 < +4.

Exercises

1. Use the number line to order the following numbers from the least to the greatest. Hint: See Example 1.

     a. –3, +5, –4, –1, 0, +2   **b**. +6, 0, –4, –2,

     c. –1, 0, –6, +4, +1,   **d**. +4, –3, 0, +5

2. Use the number line to order the following numbers from the greatest to the least. Hint: See Example 2.

   a. −6, 0, +4, −2   **b.** +5, −1, 0, +2

   c. −1, +1, 0, +5, −4   **d.** 0, +2, −2, +5

3. Using the number line, replace ? by >, <, or =. Hint: See Example 3(a).

   −5 ? −4

4. Using a number line, replace ? by >, < or =. Hint: See Example 3(b).

   0 ? −1

5. Using a number line, replace ? by >, < or =. Hint: See Example 3(c).

   + 4 ? − 3

6. Compare. Write >, < or = for each ?. Hint: See Example 4.

   a. $|-5|$? +4   **b.** $|-1|$? −6   **c.** $|+2|$? −4

Challenge Questions

Compare. Write >, < or = for each?

7. a. $|-3|$? $|+3|$ **b.** $|-2|$? −2   **c.** 0 ? −1

8. Which number has the least value: 0, −4, +8, −1, or −10?

9. Which number has the greatest value: −14, −2, +9, +100, or −200?

10. What is the absolute value of −1000?

Mixed Review

1. 20% of $100.00 =   **2.** $\frac{2}{3}$ of 18 =   **3.** $\frac{1}{6} \times \frac{18}{25} =$

4. The inverse of $\frac{3}{4}$ =   **5.** The opposite of −6 =   **6.** Absolute of -7 =

7. $2 + 4 \div 2 - 1 =$ **8.** 6901 − 5999 =   **9.** 25 × 6 =

10. Write the opposite of each integer.

   a. -99   **b.** +12   **c.** -1   **d.** +32

11. Graph each integer and its opposite on a number line.

   a. -4   **b.** +5   **c.** -6   **d.** +6

12. Name a positive or a negative number to represent each situation.

   a. 13 feet above sea level   **b.** Earning $10

   c. 15^0 below 0   **d.** A decrease of 5 points

13. Compare. Write < or > for ?.

   a. -8 ? 8   **b.** 0 ? -5   **c.** -4 ? -6   **d.** 9 ? 14   **e.** -8 ? 1

14. Order the integers in each set from least to greatest.

   a. 4, -1, 0, -4   **b.** -5, 8, -2, 3   **c.** -4, 7, -11, 0   **d.** 23, -33, 55, -2

ADDITION OF INTEGERS

I can solve the problems too if only I understand the concepts.

New Term
Zero pair

Playing a Board Game - Group Exercises

Example 1
John and Mary decide to play a board game.
- John starts at 0 and rolls a 4.
- The fourth square tells him to roll again. His token lands on a square that tells him to move back 4 spaces.

How many spaces from the start is John's token?

Solution
Use red counters to represent negative integers and blue counters to represent positive integers.

> Let (-) represent red counters, which then represent negative integers.
> Let (+) represent blue counters, which then represent positive integers.

Step 1: Use 4 positive (blue) counters to represent John's first roll which can be represented as +4. Place all of the counters on a table.

$$(+) (+) (+) (+)$$

Step 2: Use 4 negative (red) counters to represent John's 4 spaces backwards. Place the 4 negative (red) counters on the table with the 4 positives (blue) counters from Step 1.

$$(+) (+) (+) (+)$$
$$(-) (-) (-) (-) \quad = +4 + (-4)$$

Step 3: Make as many pairs of one positive and one negative counters. The sum of each pair is zero, and so remove each **zero pair** since it does not change the value on the table.

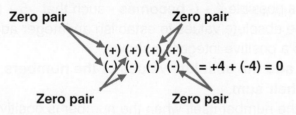

There are no counters left on the table. John's token is 0 spaces from the start which means that John is back to the starting point.

Let us establish an integer addition rule for adding a negative integer to a positive integer. From Example 1, note that +4 + (-4) = 0 is possible if + (- **becomes** - such that +4 + (-4) can be written as +4 - 4 = 0. It is important to note that + (- **becomes** -. We can use absolute values to establish an integer addition rule for adding a negative integer to a positive integer as shown:

> **Adding a negative integer to a positive integer (or adding a positive integer to a negative integer), subtract the smaller absolute value from the larger, and then use the sign of the number with larger absolute value as the sign of the sum. If the two integers are equal, their sum is zero.**

The absolute value of a number is the number itself when the number is positive or zero, and the absolute value of a number is the opposite of the number when the number is negative. (Review the chapter/section on Absolute Values.)

Example 1 can be written as: +4 + (-4) = 0. The absolute of +4 is 4 and the absolute of -4 is 4 (the opposite of -4 is 4), so that 4 - 4 = 0.

Hint: See how Example 1 is solved using a shortcut method in Example 6.

Zero pairs means equal numbers of positive and negative integers such that the addition of each pair is zero.

Example 2

Use counters to find -5 + (-2)

Solution

Use red counters to represent negative integers.

Let (-) represent red counters, which then represent negative integers.

Step 1: Place 5 negative counters on the table to represent -5.
Place 2 more negative counters on the same table to represent adding -2.

(-) (-) (-) (-) (-)
(-) (-)

Step 2: There are no positive counters, and therefore, we cannot remove any zero pairs. Count the total number of counters on the table.

Step 3: There are a total of 7 negative counters on the table and this represents -7.
Therefore, -5 + (-2) = -7.

Let us establish an integer addition rule for adding two negative integers. From Example 2, note that -5 + (-2) = -7 is possible if + (- **becomes** - such that -5 + (-2) can be written as -5 - 2 = -7. We can use absolute values to establish an integer addition rule for adding a negative integer to a positive integer as shown:

> **Adding two negative numbers, add the absolute values of the numbers, and then attach a negative sign to their sum.**

The absolute value of a number is the number itself when the number is positive or zero, and the absolute value of a number is the opposite of the number when the number is negative. (Review the chapter/section on Absolute Values.)

Example 2 can be written as: -5 + (-2) =. The absolute of -5 is 5 (the opposite of -5 is 5), and the absolute of -2 is 2 (the opposite of -2 is 2), so that 5 + 2 = 7. Using the rule, attach a negative sign to this sum, so that the sum becomes -7. Therefore, -5 + (-2) = -7.

Hint: See how Example 2 is solved using a shortcut method in Example 7.

Example 3
Use counters to find -3 + (+4)

Solution

Use red counters to represent negative integers and blue counters to represent positive integers.

Let (+) represent blue counters, which then represent positive integers.
Let (-) represent red counters, which then represent negative integers.

Step 1: Place 3 negative counters on a table
Place 4 positive counters on the same table representing adding +4.

(-) (-) (-)
(+) (+) (+) (+)

Step 2: Make as many pairs of the positive and negative counters. The sum of each pair is zero and so remove each zero pair since it does not change the value on the table.

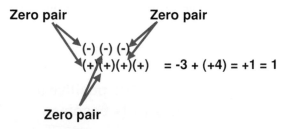

Count the total number of counters left on the table.

Step 3: There is 1 positive counter left on the table. Therefore, -3 + (+4) = +1 = 1.
Let us establish an integer addition rule for adding a negative integer to a positive integer. From Example 3, note that -3 + (+4) = +1 is possible if + (+ **becomes** + such that -3 + (+4) = +1 can be written as -3 + 4 = +1 = 1. In mathematics, positive signs are not generally attached to a number to indicate that the number is positive, so +1 is written as 1. We can use absolute values to establish an integer addition rule for adding a positive integer to a negative integer as shown:

Adding a positive integer to a negative integer (or adding a negative integer to a positive integer), subtract the smaller absolute value from the larger, and then use the sign of the number with larger absolute value as the sign of the sum. If the two integers are equal, their sum is zero.

The absolute value of a number is the number itself when the number is positive or zero, and the absolute value of a number is the opposite of the number when the number is negative. (Review the chapter/section on Absolute Values.)

Example 3 can be written as: -3 + (+4) =. The absolute of -3 is 3 (the opposite of -3 is 3) and the absolute of +4 is 4 (the absolute value of a number is the number itself when the number is positive), so that 4 - 3 = 1. Using the rule, use the sign of the number with larger absolute value as the sign of the sum, and in this case, the larger absolute number is 4, and the sign of 4 is positive. In general, we do not attach a positive sign to an answer, so that 4 - 3 = +1 = 1.

Hint: See how Example 3 is solved using a shortcut method in Example 8.

Example 4
Use counters to find +1 + (+4)
Solution
Use blue counters to represent positive integers.

Let (+) represent blue counters, which then represent positive integers.

Step 1: Place 1 positive counter on the table to represent +1
Place 4 positive counters on the table to represent +4

(+)
(+) (+) (+) (+)

Step 2: Since there are no negative counters, we cannot remove any zero pair numbers.

Step 3: Count the total number of counters on the table, which is +5.
Therefore, +1 + (+4) = +5.

Let us establish an integer addition rule for adding two positive integers.
From Example 4, note that +1 + (+4) = +5 is possible if + (+ **becomes** + such that +1 + (+4) = +5 can be written as +1 + 4 = 5.

From Example 4, note that +1 + (+4) = +5 means that **to add any two positive integers, add the two integers and attach the positive sign after the addition, which is called the sum.** In this particular case, add 1 to 4 which is 5, and then attach a positive sign to the 5 which is +5. In mathematics, positive signs are not generally attached to a number to indicate that the number is positive, so +5 is written as 5. The rule for adding two positive integers is as shown:

To add any two positive integers, add the two integers and attach the positive sign after the addition, which is called the sum.

Hint: See how Example 4 is solved using a shortcut method in Example 9.

Example 5
Find -6 + (+4)
Solution
Use red counters to represent negative integers and blue counters to represent

positive integers.

Let (+) represent blue counters, which then represent positive integers.
Let (-) represent red counters, which then represent negative integers.

Step 1: Place 6 negative counters on the table to represent -6.
Place 4 positive counters on the table to represent +4.

(-) (-) (-) (-) (-) (-)
(+) (+) (+) (+)

Step 2: Make as many pairs of one positive and one negative counters. The sum of each pair is zero, and so remove each zero pair since it does not change the value on the table.

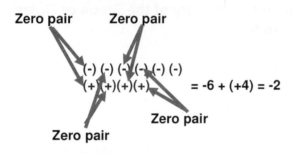

Count the total number of counters left on the table. There are a total of 2 negative counters left on the table, therefore: -6 + (+4) = -2

Let us establish a rule for integer addition of positive and negative integers.
From Example 5, note that -6 + (+4) = -2 is possible if + (+ **becomes** + such that -6 + (+4) = -2 can be written as -6 + 4 = -2.

Notice how the negative sign is attached to the final answer because 6 (not -6) is larger than 4, and 6 has the negative sign. Notice also that, if the question were to be -3 + 4 = , the solution is -3 + 4 = +1 = 1. In this case, there is no negative sign attached to 1 because 3 is less then 4, and although 3 has a negative sign. Notice that the absolute value of -6 is 6 (-6 is the opposite of 6), and the absolute value of +4 is 4, so that 6 - 4 = 2. In example 5, the larger absolute value is 6 and the smaller absolute value is 4, so that 6 - 4 = 2, and the sign of the larger absolute number is -, so that -6 + 4 = -2. We can use absolute values to establish an integer addition rule for adding a positive integer to a negative integer as shown:

Adding a positive integer to a negative integer (or adding a negative integer to a positive integer), subtract the smaller absolute value from the larger, and then use the sign of the number with larger absolute value as the sign of the sum. If the two integers are equal, their sum is zero.

Hint: See how Example 5 is solved using a shortcut method in Example 10.

Summary of the Steps or Rules for Adding Integers

1. Addition of two integers with like signs

    a. Find the absolute values of the integers.

    b. Find the sum of the absolute values

    c. Attach the sign common to both integers to the answer.

2. Addition of two integers with unlike signs.

    a. Find the absolute values of the integers.

    b. Find the difference of the absolute values.

    c. Attach the sign of the integer with the greater absolute value to the answer.

       If the absolute values of both integers are the same, then their sum is zero.

Let us Use the information Under the Section "Summary of the Steps or Rules for Adding Integers" to Solve Examples 1 to 5.

Example 6

Find the sum.

+4 + (-4)   **This is the same as Example 1**.

Solution

Find the absolute values of +4 and -4. See "Addition of two integers with unlike signs."

      $|+4| = 4$

      $|-4| = 4$

Find the **difference** of the absolute values. Hint: Find the **difference** of the absolute values of the integers with **unlike signs**

      $4 - 4 = 0$ Since the two integers have unlike signs, and their absolute values are the same, their sum is zero. Hint: "See Addition of Two Integers With Unlike Signs."

Example 7

Find the sum.

-5 + (-2)   **This is the same as Example 2**.

Solution

Find the absolute values of -5 and -2. See "Addition of Two Integers With Like Signs."

      $|-5| = 5$

      $|-2| = 2$

Find the **sum** of the absolute values. Hint: Find the **sum** of the absolute values of the integers with **like signs**. See "Addition of Two Integers With Like Signs."

      $5 + 2 = 7$

Attach the sign common to both integers to the answer. So,

      $-5 + (-2) = -7$ Note: The - sign is common to both 5 and 2.

                        Hint: See the information under the section "Addition of Two Integers With Like Signs."

Example 8
Find the sum.

-3 + (+4)   **This is the same as Example 3.**
Solution
Find the absolute values of -3 and +4. See "Addition of two integers with unlike signs."

$$|-3| = 3$$
$$|+4| = 4$$

Find the **difference** of the absolute values. Hint: Find the **difference** of the absolute values of the integers with **unlike signs. Subtract the smaller absolute integer from the larger absolute integer.**

$$4 - 3 = 1$$

Attach the sign of the integer with the greater absolute value to the answer. So,

-3 + (+4) = +1 = 1   Note: +1 is the same as 1.
                         Hint: See Addition of Two Integers With Unlike
                         Signs.

Example 9
Find the sum.

+1 + (+4)   **This is the same as Example 4.**
Solution
Find the absolute values of +1 and +4. See "Addition of Two Integers With Like Signs."

$$|+1| = 1$$
$$|+4| = 4$$

Find the **sum** of the absolute values. Hint: Find the **sum** of the absolute values of the integers with **like signs.** See "Addition of Two Integers With Like Signs."

$$1 + 4 = 5$$

Attach the sign common to both integers to the answer. So,

+1 + (+4) = +5 = 5   Note: The + sign is common to both 1 and 4.
                       Hint: See the information under the section
                       Addition of Two Integers With Like Signs.

Example 10
Find the sum.

-6 + (+4)   **This is the same as Example 5.**
Solution
Find the absolute values of -6 and +4. See "Addition of two integers with unlike signs."

$$|-6| = 6$$
$$|+4| = 4$$

Find the **difference** of the absolute values. Hint: Find the **difference** of the absolute values of the integers with **unlike signs. Subtract the smaller absolute integer from the larger absolute integer.**

$$6 - 4 = 2$$

Attach the sign of the integer with the larger absolute value to the answer. So,

$$-6 + (+4) = -2$$ Notice that the integer with the larger absolute value is 6. The 6 has a - sign, so attach a - sign to the answer. Hint: "See Addition of Two Integers With Unlike Signs."

═══════════════════════════════════════

The notes and the generous worked examples have provided me with conceptual understanding and computational fluency to do my homework.

Exercises

1. Explain what is meant by zero pairs.

2. Group exercise:

   Mary and John decided to play a board game. Mary started at 0 and rolled 5. The fifth square tells her to roll again. Her token lands on a square that tells her to move back 3 spaces. How many spaces back is Mary's token? Hint: See Examples 1 and 6. You may use the integer addition rule for Examples 1 and 6.

3. Group exercise:

   Use counters to find the following: Hint: See Examples 2.

a. -3 + (-2) =	**b.** -7 + (-2) =	**c.** -1 + (-1) =
d. -10 + (-7) =	**e.** -5 + (-4) =	**f.** -6 + (-4) =
g. -3 + (-5) =	**h.** -5 + (-4) =	**i.** -7 + (-7) =

4. Solve Exercise 3 without using counters. Use the rule for adding integers.
   Hint: See the rule for Examples 2 and 7. Note that + (- is -.

5. Use counters to find the following: Hint: See Example 3.

a. -4 + (+8) =	**b.** -7 + (+2) =	**c.** -1 + (+1) =
d. -2 + (+6) =	**e.** -9 + (+1) =	**f.** -6 + (+4) =
g. -4 + (+8) =	**h.** -5 + (+6) =	**j.** -7 + (+7) =

6. Solve Exercise 5 without using counters. Use the rule for adding integers.
   Hint: See Examples 3 and 8. Note that + (+ is +.

7. Use counters to find the following: Hint: See Example 4.

a. +2 + (+6) =	**b.** +1 + (+9) =	**c.** +7 + (+3) =
d. +4 + (+7) =	**e.** +8 + (+4) =	**f.** +3 + (+11) =
g. +6 + (+5) =	**h.** +5 + (+8) =	**j.** +3 + (+7) =

8. Solve Exercise 7 without using counters. Use the rule for adding integers in Examples 4 and 9.
   Hint: See Example 4.

9. Use counters to solve the following. Hint: See Example 5.

a. -5 + (+4) =	**b.** -6 + (+2) =	**c.** -6 + (+1) =	**d.** -8 + (+4) =
e. -7 + (+5) =	**f.** -5 + (+2) =	**g.** -4 + (+3) =	**h.** -2 + (+1) =

10. Solve Exercise 9 without using counters. Use the rule for adding integers in Examples 5 and 10. Hint: See Example 5.

Challenge Questions

11 Solve the following problems.

a. +6 + (-4) =   **b.** -3 + (-5) =   **c.** -4 + (+) 2 =   **d.** -6 + 0 =

e. -7 + (-7) =   **f.** +4 + (-6) =   **g.** +7 + (+) 3 =   **h.** +2 - 6 =

12 Compare and write <, > or = for ? Hint: Use Examples 1 to 5 to simplify first before comparing. To solve **a**, simplify +2 + (-4) as -2 first, and then compare -2 to -3. Since -2 is greater than -3, the correct answer to **a** is +2 + (-4) > -3.

a. +2 + (-4) ? -3   **b.** -2 + (+8) ? +5   **c.** +4 + (-5) ? +2

d. +4 + (-3) ? +2   **e.** -4 + (-7) ? +2   **f.** -3 + (-7) ? +3

Answers to Selected Questions

3a. -5	**3b.** -9	**5a.** 4	**5b.** -5
7a. 8	**7b.** 10	**9a.** -1	**9b.** -4

Why Do We Need to Know How to Use the Rules For Addition of Integers?
It is useful to know and use the rules for integer addition especially when the integers are large instead of using counters. For example, it will be difficult to use counters to add integers involving 300 and -450.

It is possible to use the rules for integer addition or a number line to add integers when the integers are large, as shown in the following examples.

Example 13

Using the rule for adding integers, find +261 + (-200)

Solution

+ (- becomes -, and so that, +261 + (-200) = +261 - 200 = +61 = 61. Notice that +261 - 200 = +61 = 61, when the rule for integer addition for adding a negative integer to a positive integer is used as in Example 3. Recall that absolute values are used in the rule.

Example 14

Using the rule for adding integers, find -261 + (-300).

Solution

From the solution of Example 2, +(- becomes -, therefore, -261 + (-300) = -261 - 300 = -561. Notice that -261 - 300 = -561, when the rule for adding a negative integer to another negative integer is used as in Example 2. Recall that absolute values are used in the rule.

Example 15

Use the number line to find the sum of 300 + (-450).

Solution

Step 1: Draw a number line, and start at 0 and go 300 units in the positive direction (right) as shown.

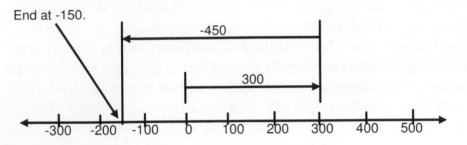

Step 2: From point 300 go 450 in the negative direction (left) as shown. You end at -150, making, 300 + (-450) = -150.

The notes and the generous worked examples have provided me with conceptual understanding and computational fluency to do my homework.

Exercise

1. Use the rule to find the following sums. Hint: See Example 13.

a. +340 + (-329) =   **b**. -450 + (+200) =   **c**. -701 + (+204) =

d. +528 + (-224) =   **e**. -178 + (+464) =   **f**. +379 + (-580) =

2. Use the rule to find the following sums. Hint: See Example 14.

a. -492 + (-321) =   **b**. -209 + (-164) =   **c**. -342 + (-201) =

d. -239 + (-101) =   **e**. -341 + (-244) =   **f**. -464 + (-100) =

3 Use a number line to find the sum of the following numbers. Hint: See Example 15.

a. 250 + (-200) =   **b**. 100 + (-400) =   **c**. 381 + (-250) =

d. 98 + (-164) =   **e**. 88 + (-238) =   **f**. 238 + (-108) =

Challenge Questions

4. Find the sum of the following numbers.

a. 340 + (-264) =   **b**. -277 + (-341)   **c**. +516 + (-201) =

d. -168 + (-295) =   **e**. 255 + (-179) =   **f**. +209 + (-304) =

Answers to Selected Questions

1a. 11   **2a**. -813   **3a**. 50

SUBTRACTING INTEGERS

The subtraction problems can be solved by using counters as shown in Example 1.

Example 1

Find 5 - 2

Solution

Step 1: Place 5 positive counters on a mat.

$\oplus \oplus \oplus \oplus \oplus$

Step 2: Since subtraction is the opposite of addition, remove 2 of the positive counters from the mat to represent subtracting 2.

Remove 2 of the positive counters.

$\oplus \oplus \oplus \oplus \oplus$ = 5 - 2

Step 3: Count the positive counters remaining on the mat.

$\oplus \oplus \oplus$ = 5 - 2 = 3

There are 3 positive counters left on the mat and meaning, 5 - 2 = 3.

Rule 1: **To subtract a smaller positive number from a bigger positive number, subtract the smaller number from the bigger number.**

Example 2

Find 2 - 6.

Solution

Step 1: Place 2 positive counters on a mat.

$\oplus \oplus$ = 2

Step 2: To subtract 6, we must remove 6 positive counters. But we cannot remove 6 positive counters because there are not 6 positive counters on the mat. We must add 6 zero pairs to the mat, and then we can remove 6 positive counters.

$\oplus \oplus$

$\ominus \ominus \ominus \ominus \ominus \ominus$ (6 negative and 6 positive counters form 6 zero pairs.)

$\oplus \oplus \oplus \oplus \oplus \oplus$ ← Remove these 6 positive counters.

Step 3: Pair the positive and negative counters. Remove all zero pairs.

$\oplus \oplus$

$\ominus \ominus \ominus \ominus \ominus \ominus$ = -4

Step 4: The number of the negative counters that remains on the mat is 4, therefore, 2 - 6 = -4

Rule 2: Considering Examples 1 and 2, **to subtract one positive number from another positive number, subtract the smaller absolute value of the numbers from the bigger absolute value, and then attach the sign of the bigger absolute value number.**

In Example 2, the bigger absolute value number is 6 and the smaller absolute value number is 2. Using the rule, 2 - 6 becomes 6 - 2 = 4, and then a negative sign is attached to the 4 because the sign of the bigger absolute value number is -. So we can write 2 - 6 = -4.

Example 3
Use counters to find -5 - 3
Solution
Step 1: Place 5 negative counters on the mat to represent -5.

$\ominus \ominus \ominus \ominus \ominus$ = -5

Step 2: To subtract 3 we must remove 3 positive counters, but we cannot remove 3 positive counters because there are none on the mat. Therefore, we must add 3 zero pairs to the mat. We can now remove 3 positive counters. Note that we cannot remove something that we do not have.

$\ominus \ominus \ominus \ominus \ominus$ = $\ominus \ominus \ominus \ominus \ominus$

$\ominus \ominus \ominus$ $\quad$ = $\ominus \ominus \ominus$

$\oplus \oplus \oplus$ $\quad \leftarrow$ Remove these 3 positive counters.

Step 3: There are 8 negative counters remaining on the mat and this represents -8. Therefore, -5 - 3 = -8.

Rule 3: Considering the answer for Example 3, **to subtract a positive number 3 from a negative number -5, add the absolute values of the numbers together (5 + 3 = 8) and attach negative sign the sum**, for example -8. Note that it is sometimes necessary to add zero pairs in order to subtract. When zero pairs are added, the value of the integers on the mat does not change. Note also that the absolute value of -5 is 5 and the absolute value of 3 is 3.

Example 4 (Subtraction problems involving two negative integers).
Use counters to find -6 - (-2).
Solution
Step 1: Place 6 negative counters on the mat to represent -6.

$\ominus \ominus \ominus \ominus \ominus \ominus$ = -6

Step 2: Remove 2 negative counters from the mat to represent subtracting -2.

Remove these 2 negative counters.

$\nearrow \nearrow$

$\ominus \ominus \ominus \ominus \ominus \ominus$ = $\ominus \ominus \ominus \ominus$ = -4

Step 3: There are 4 negative counters left on the mat and this represents -4.
Therefore, -6 - (-2) = -4.
Notice that -6 - (-2) = -4 is possible only when - (- becomes +, so that -6 - (-2) becomes -6 + 2 = -4.

Rule 4: Considering Example 4, **to subtract one negative number from another, subtract the smaller absolute value number (2) from the bigger absolute**

value number (6) and attach the sign of the bigger absolute value number (6) to the subtraction or difference (-4).

Considering example 4, the absolute value of -6 is 6 and the absolute value of -2 is 2.

The notes and the generous worked examples have provided me with conceptual understanding and computational fluency to do my homework.

Exercise

1. Find the difference. You may use counters.
   Hint: See Example 1 or Rule 1.
   a. 6 - 2   **b.** 5 - 3   **c.** 7 - 4   **d.** 6 - 2

2. Find the difference. You may use counters.
   Hint: See Example 2 or Rule 2.
   a. 2 - 4   **b.** 3 - 5   **c.** 3 - 7   **d.** 1 - 5

3. Use counters to find the following.
   Hint: See Example 3 or Rule 3.
   a. -4 - 2 =   **b.** -6 - 4 =   **c.** -5 - 4 =   **d.** -2 - 3 =
   e. -1 - 2 =   **f.** -4 - 4 =   **g.** -7 - 3 =   **h.** -2 - 1 =

4. Use counters to find the following:
   Hint: See Example 4 or Rule 4.
   a. -1 - (-4) =   **b.** -7 - (-3) =   **c.** -2 - (-5) =   **d.** -8 - (-2)=   **e.** -8 - (-5) =
   f. -3 - (-4) =   **g.** -3 - (-3) =   **h.** -10 - (-10) =   **i.** -8 - (-9) =

Challenge Questions

5. Find the difference.
   a. 3 - 5 =   **b.** 3 - (-5) =   **c.** -4 - (-8) =   **d.** -8 - (-8) =   **e.** 6 - 4 =
   f. -6 - 8 =   **g.** 0 - (-6) =   **h.** 7 - (-3) =   **i.** -5 - (-7) =   **j.** -6 - 6 =
   k. 4 - (-4) =   **l.** 1 - 7 =   **m.** -3 - (-4) =   **n.** -5 - (-6) =   **o.** -2 - (-2) =

Answers to Selected Questions

1a. 4   **2a.** -2   **3a.** -6   **4a.** 3

REAL WORLD APPLICATIONS - WORD PROBLEMS
Subtracting Integers

Example 1

The temperature in New York at 7:00 A.M. was -2^{0}F and at 2:00 P.M., the temperature was 5^{0}F. Find the change in the temperature.

Solution

To find the change in the temperature, subtract the starting temperature (-2^{0}F) from the ending temperature (5^{0}F) as shown:

$$5 - (-2) = 5 + 2 \qquad \text{Note: } - (- = +$$
$$= 7^0F$$

Therefore the change in the temperature = 7^{0}F.

─────────────────────────────

The notes and the generous worked examples have provided me with conceptual understanding and computational fluency to do my homework.

Exercises

1. On December 25 at 6:00 A.M. the temperature was -8^{0}F and at 12:30 P.M., the temperature was 10^{0}F. What is the change in temperature? Hint: See Example 1.

2. On December 24, 2004 the temperature of a certain city was -1^{0}F and 8 hours later, the temperature was −7^{0}F. What was the change in the temperature? Hint: Set up as follow: Change in temperature = -7 - (-1) and also see Example 1.

Challenge Questions

3. At 12:00 P.M. on January 6, 2005 the temperature was -2^{0}F, and at 7:00 P.M. the temperature was -3^{0}F. What is the change in the temperature?

4. The temperature of a certain village on December 28,1997 was -6^{0}F and about 10 hours later, the temperature was -3^{0}F. What is the change in the temperature?

MULTIPLYING INTEGERS

What is multiplication? Multiplication is repeated addition. The symbol for multiplication is $\times$. For example, 6×3 means $3 + 3 + 3 + 3 + 3 + 3$.

Example 1

Model the multiplication of 6×3 using counters.

Step 1: 6×3 means 6 sets of 3 positive counters. Put these counters on the mat.

$$\oplus \oplus \oplus \quad \oplus \oplus \oplus \quad \oplus \oplus \oplus$$
$$\oplus \oplus \oplus \quad \oplus \oplus \oplus \quad \oplus \oplus \oplus$$

Step 2: Find the number of counters on the mat. There are 18 positive counters on the mat. Therefore, $6 \times 3 = 18$.

Rule 1: **To multiply a positive number by another positive number, just multiply the two numbers together as in Example 1.**

Example 2

Use counters to find $5 \times (-2)$

Solution

Step 1: $5 \times (-2)$ means 5 sets of 2 negative counters as shown on the mat.

$$\ominus \ominus \quad \ominus \ominus \quad \ominus \ominus \quad \ominus \ominus \quad \ominus \ominus$$

Step 2: There are 10 negative counters on the mat, making $5 \times (-2) = -10$

Rule 2: **To multiply a positive number by a negative number just multiply the two numbers together and attach a negative sign to the product as shown in Example 2**, **Step 2**. Note also that $\times$ (- becomes a multiplication with a negative symbol attach to the product as in Example 2, Step 2.

Example 3

Use counters to find -2×4

Solution

Step 1: Using the fact that -2 is the opposite of 2, -2×4 means to remove 2 sets of 4 positive counters. However, we cannot remove 2 sets of 4 positive counters because there are none to remove. We must first add 2 sets of 4 zero pairs, and then we can remove 2 sets of 4 positive counters.

Two sets of 4 zero pairs of counters	Remove 2 sets of 4 positive counters.	
↓ ↓	↑ ↑	
$\oplus \ominus$ $\oplus \ominus$	$\oplus \ominus$ $\oplus \ominus$	$\ominus$ $\ominus$
$\oplus \ominus$ $\oplus \ominus$ =	$\oplus \ominus$ $\oplus \ominus$ =	$\ominus$ $\ominus$
$\oplus \ominus$ $\oplus \ominus$	$\oplus \ominus$ $\oplus \ominus$	$\ominus$ $\ominus$
$\oplus \ominus$ $\oplus \ominus$	$\oplus \ominus$ $\oplus \ominus$	$\ominus$ $\ominus$

Step 2: Find the number of the counters remaining on the mat. There are 8 negative counters remaining on the mat and this represents -8. Therefore, $-2 \times 4 = -8$.

Rule 3: **To multiply a negative number by a positive number, just multiply the two numbers and attach a negative symbol to the product as in Example 3, Step 2.**

Special note: To multiply a negative integer by another integer, remove as many sets of positive counters as possible as in Example 3, Step 1.

Example 4

Use counters to find -3(-2).

Solution

Step 1: Using the fact that -3 is the opposite of 3, -3(-2) means to remove 3 sets of 2 negative counters but there are none to remove. Therefore, we must first add 3 sets of 2 zero pairs and then we can remove 3 sets of 2 negative counters.

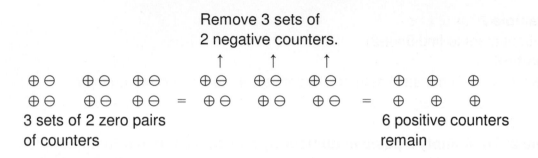

Remove 3 sets of
2 negative counters.

3 sets of 2 zero pairs
of counters

6 positive counters
remain

Step 2: Find the number of the remaining counters on the mat. There are 6 positive counters that remain on the mat, and this represents +6 or 6, and therefore, -3(-2) = 6.

Rule 4: **To multiply one negative number by another negative number, just multiply the two numbers together and their product must be positive as shown in example 4, step 2.**

Summary of the Signs of the Rules for Multiplying Integers

Considering Examples 1 to 4, when multiplying two numbers that have the same signs, the sign of the product of the numbers is positive. For example, -2(-3) = +6 = 6, and 2(3) = +6 = 6.

Considering Examples 1 to 4, when multiplying two numbers that have different signs, the sign of the product of the numbers is negative. For example, -2(3) = -6, and 2(-3) = -6.

The notes and the generous worked examples have provided me with conceptual understanding and computational fluency to do my homework.

Exercises

1. Explain what is meant by multiplication.
2. Use counters to multiply the following. Hint: See Example 1. You may use Rule 1.
   a. 3×2 **b.** 4×3 **c.** 2×5 **d.** 5×4
3. Use counters to find the following. Hint: See Example 2. You may use Rule 2.
   a. $3 \times (-2)$ **b.** $4 \times (-3)$ **c.** $3 \times (-5)$ **d.** $4 \times (-2)$
4. Use counters to find the following. Hint: See Example 3. You may Use Rule 3.

a. -3 × 4   b. -2 × 5   c. -4 × 3   d. -5 × 2

e. -3 × 3   f. -5 × 6   g. -2 × 6   h. -6 × 3

5. Use counters to find the followings. Hint: See Example 4. You may use Rule 4.

a. -2(-4)   **b.** -4(-4)   **c.** -3(-3)   **d.** -5(-3)

e. -4(-2)   **f.** -3(-2)   **g.** -4(-5)   **h.** -2(-5)

6. Solve questions 2 to 5 using just the rules.

Challenge Questions

7. Find the following products using the rules of multiplications.

a. -6(-6) =   **b.** -8 × 6 =   **c.** 7 × (-3) =   **d.** 9 × 4 =

e. -5(-5) =   **f.** 7 × 3 =   **g.** -3 × 8 =   **h.** (-7) =

i. 3 × (-7) =   **j.** -3 × (-7) =   **k.** -3(5) =   **l.** -4 × (-9) =

Answers to Selected Questions

2a. 6   **3a.** -6   **4a.** -12   **5a.** 8   **7k.** -15

Cumulative Review

Find each product, sum or difference.

1. -6 + 10 =   **2.** -8 - (-3) =   **3.** -3 + (-4) =

4. 7 - (-4) =   **5.** -7 × 3 =   **6.** -4 - (-3) =

7. 8 - (-2) =   **8.** -5 × (-2) =   **9.** 6(-3) =

10. Replace each ? with =, < or > to make a true statement. Review the chapter/section on Number Line.

a. 4 ? -2   **b.** -4 ? -3   **c.** -3 ? 0

d. -1 ? -1   **e.** -2 ? -1   **f.** 0 ? -1

11. Which problem does not have -4 as its answer?

A. 8 - 12

B. -1 + (-3)

C. 2 - 6

D. -2(-2)

E. 2(-2)

Answer to Selected Questions

10a. 4 > -2   **10c.** -3 < 0   **10d.** -1 = -1

DIVIDING INTEGERS

What is division? Division is separating a quantity into equal-sized groups. For example, 3 girls want to share 9 apples equally, how can this be done?

Step 1: Put 9 counters on a mat, and let 9 counters represent the 9 apples.

⊕ ⊕ ⊕ ⊕ ⊕ ⊕ ⊕ ⊕ ⊕

Step 2: Separate the 9 counters into 3 equal-sized groups.

⊕ ⊕ ⊕
⊕ ⊕ ⊕
⊕ ⊕ ⊕

There are 3 equal groups of 3 positive counters each, and therefore,
$9 \div 3 = 3$. Each girl will receive 3 apples.

Example 1
Use counters to find $-12 \div 4$
Solution
Step 1: Put 12 negative counters on the mat to represent -12.

⊖ ⊖ ⊖ ⊖ ⊖ ⊖ ⊖ ⊖ ⊖ ⊖ ⊖ ⊖

Step 2: Separate the 12 counters into 4 equal-sized groups.

⊖ ⊖ ⊖ ⊖
⊖ ⊖ ⊖ ⊖
⊖ ⊖ ⊖ ⊖
  4 equal-sized groups.

There are 4 equal-sized groups of 3 negative counters each and meaning
  $-12 \div 4 = -3$
Rule 1: From Example 1, **when a negative integer is divided by a positive integer, the quotient is negative**.

Working Backward to Solve Division Problems
Multiplication is the opposite of division. We can therefore, work backward by using multiplication to solve division problems by using the logic of "**what number multiplied by the divisor equals to the dividend**". Examples 2 to 5 will explain how we can divide integers by working backward. Review the section on multiplication of integers and knowing the multiplication tables will be helpful.

Example 2
Find $12 \div 3$.
Solution
To find $12 \div 3$, think of what number times 3 equals to 12?

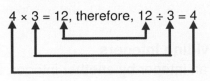

$4 \times 3 = 12$, therefore, $12 \div 3 = 4$

Rule 2: From Example 2, **when a positive integer is divided by a positive integer the quotient is positive**.

Example 3
Find $-8 \div (-2)$.
Solution
To find $-8 \div (-2)$, think of what number times -2 equals to -8?

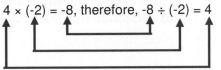

$4 \times (-2) = -8$, therefore, $-8 \div (-2) = 4$

Rule 3: From Example 3, **when a negative integer is divided by a negative integer the quotient is positive**.

Example 4
Find $-15 \div 3$.
Solution
To find $-15 \div 3$, think of what number multiplied by 3 equals to -15?

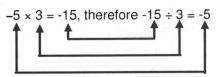

$-5 \times 3 = -15$, therefore $-15 \div 3 = -5$

Rule 4: From Example 4, **when a negative integer is divided by a positive integer, the quotient is negative**.

Example 5
Find $15 \div (-3)$.
Solution
To find $15 \div (-3)$, think of what number multiplied by -3 equals to 15?

$-5 \times (-3) = 15$, therefore $15 \div (-3) = -5$

Rule 5: From Example 5, **when a positive integer is divided by a negative integer**

the quotient is negative.

Summary of the Signs of the Rules for Dividing Integers

Considering Examples 1 to 5, when dividing an integer by another integer, that have the same signs, the sign of the quotient (answer) is positive. For example, $-6 \div -2 = 3$, and $6 \div 2 = 3$.

Considering examples 1 to 5, when dividing an integer by another integer, that have different signs, the sign of the quotient (answer) is negative. For example, $-6 \div 2 = -3$, and $6 \div (-2) = -3$.

The notes and the generous worked examples have provided me with conceptual understanding and computational fluency to do my homework.

Exercises

1. Division is the opposite of multipli_____.

2. Use counters to find the following. Hint: See Example 1. **You may use Rule 1**.

   a. $-9 \div 3 =$ **b**. $-10 \div 2 =$ **c**. $-4 \div 2 =$ **d**. $-6 \div 3 =$

   e. $-15 \div 5 =$ **f**. $-18 \div 3 =$ **g**. $-24 \div 8 =$ **i**. $36 \div 6 =$

   k. $-28 \div 4 =$ **l**. $-50 \div 10 =$ **m**. $-44 \div 11 =$ **n**. $-14 \div 7 =$

3. Work backward by using multiplication to solve the following division problems. Hint: See Example 2. **You may use Rule 2**.

   a. $15 \div 5 =$ **b**. $12 \div 6 =$ **c**. $28 \div 4 =$ **d**. $16 \div 4 =$

   e. $18 \div 9 =$ **f**. $21 \div 3 =$ **g**. $24 \div 3 =$ **h**. $48 \div 6 =$

4. Work backward by using multiplication to solve the following division problems. Hint: See Example 3. **You may use Rule 3**.

   a. $-12 \div (-2) =$ **b**. $-8 \div (-4) =$ **c**. $-10 \div (-5) =$ **d**. $-21 \div (-3) =$

   e. $-30 \div (-6) =$ **f**. $-18 \div (-3) =$ **g**. $-28 \div (-4) =$ **h**. $-9 \div (-3) =$

5. Work backward by using multiplication to solve the following division problems. Hint: See Example 4. **You may use Rule 4**.

   a. $-4 \div 2 =$ **b**. $-6 \div 3 =$ **c**. $-9 \div 3 =$ **d**. $-16 \div 4 =$

   e. $-20 \div 5 =$ **f**. $-21 \div 7 =$ **g**. $-36 \div 3 =$ **h**. $-12 \div 6 =$

6. Work backward by using multiplication to solve the following division problems. Hint: See Example 5. **You may use Rule 5**.

   a. $21 \div (-3) =$ **b**. $12 \div (-4.) =$ **c**. $28 \div (-4) =$ **d**. $16 \div (-4) =$

   e. $36 \div (-6) =$ **f**. $18 \div (-3) =$ **g**. $10 \div (-2) =$ **h**. $14 \div (-7) =$

Answers to Selected Questions

2a. -3	**2b**. -5	**3a**. 3	**3b**. 2	**4a**. 6
4b. 2	**5a**. -2	**5b**. −2	**6a**. -7	**6b**. -3

Challenge Questions

7 Find each quotient.

    a. -32 ÷ 4 =   **b.** 21 ÷ (-3) =   **c.** -33 ÷ (-11) =   **d.** 24 ÷ 8 =

    e. -15 ÷ 3 =   **f.** -6 ÷ (-6) =   **g.** -36 ÷ (-4) =   **h.** 35 ÷ (-7) =

8 Find the value of a ÷ b if a = -2 and b = -1. Hint: Substitute a = -2 and b = -1 in the expression a ÷ b, and then divide.

Cumulative Review Exercises.

1. Solve the following problems.

    a. -5 + (-4) =   **b.** -3 + (+3) =   **c.** +2 + 6 =   **d.** -4 ÷ (-2) =

    e. 8 ÷ (-4) =   **f.** 27 + (-7) =   **g.** -3 + 8 =   **h.** -6 - (-3) =

    i. -3 - 4 =   **j.** 4 × (-3) =   **k.** -2 × 7 =   **l.** -1 + (-1) =

    m. 4 - 6 =   **n.** -4(-2) =   **o.** -5 - 3 =   **p.** -2 × (-3) =

    q. -8 - (-2) =   **r.** -16 ÷ 4 =   **s.** -16 ÷ (-4) =   **t.** 10 - (-4) =

6. Compare and write <, > or = for ?

    a. +3 + (-2) ? -3   **b.** -1 + (+7) ? 6   **c.** -1 + (-1) ? 0   **d.** +3 + (-3) ? +1

FRACTIONS

A fraction can be considered a "part of something." A fraction may be defined as a "part of a unit." An apple may be considered one whole or a unit and if some part of the apple is eaten, then the remaining apple is no more a unit, but a part of the whole apple, which is called a **fraction** of the whole apple.

Fraction of the apple

Whole apple = I unit ⟶   ⟵ **This part of the apple is removed**

(Note: A unit = 1 whole)

A fraction consists of two numbers separated by a fraction bar as shown below.

Assume that half of the apple is eaten, then it means that the apple is divided into two parts and one part of it has been eaten. This statement can be written as half of the apple has been eaten, and the fraction half is written as: $\frac{1}{2}$

Numerator

Fraction bar ⟶ $\frac{1}{2}$ ⟵ **Denominator**

The numerator indicates how many equal parts are being considered, or how many parts are represented in the fraction. Since the apple is divided into two equal parts and one part is eaten, then we are considering one out of the two equal parts.
The denominator indicates how many equal parts the whole is divided into. The apple is divided into two equal parts.
A fraction therefore, tells us that:
(**a**) The top number (numerator) indicates how many parts are represented or considered by a fraction.
(**b**) The bottom number (denominator) indicates into how many parts the unit has been divided.

Group Exercise

The materials needed for this exercise are oranges and knives.
This exercise is to demonstrate how to divide a whole into two halves. The class should be divided into pairs of students and with the supervision of the teacher and the parents, each pair of students should put an orange onto a plate. The teacher should give one student per group a knife to cut the orange into approximately two equal parts. These two equal parts of the whole orange are referred to as "one half of a whole orange" as shown in the diagram.

One whole orange   **One half of a whole orange.**   **One half of a whole orange.**

Each member of the group should be given one half of the whole orange to be eaten in order to remember one whole orange can be cut into two equal halves and the two equal halves can be shared by the two students in each group. Also, if we add the two halves of the oranges together, we should get the original whole orange.

UNDERSTANDING FRACTIONS WITH MORE DIAGRAMS

The diagrams below show an egg that is divided into two equal parts.

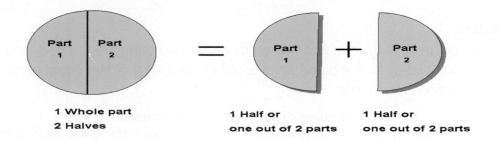

The diagrams below show a special colored cake that is divided into three equal parts and one part can be written in a fraction form as $\dfrac{1}{3}$.

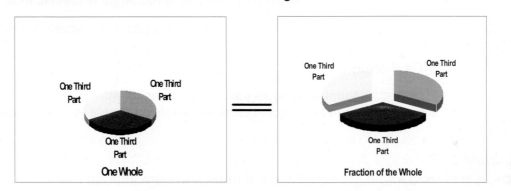

If we are considering two equal parts of the cake out of the total three equal parts, then it can be written in a fraction form as $\dfrac{2}{3}$.

Example 1

How many equal parts are the rectangles divided into?

(a) 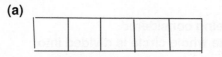 **(b)** 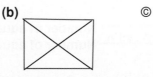 ©

Solution

(**a**) The rectangle is divided into 5 equal parts.

(**b**) The rectangle is divided into 4 equal parts.

(**c**) The rectangle is divided into 3 equal parts.

343

Example 2
Write the shaded or colored part as a fraction of each rectangle.

(a)   (b)   ©

Solution

(**a**) The rectangle is divided into five equal parts. Two parts are shaded, and therefore, two parts are being considered out of a total of five equal parts.
The fraction is therefore,

$$\frac{2}{5}$$ 2 ← Number of equal parts being considered.
5 ← Number of equal parts the whole rectangle is divided into.

(**b**) The rectangle is divided into four equal parts. Three parts are shaded, and therefore, three out of the total of four equal parts are being considered.
The fraction is therefore,

$$\frac{3}{4}$$ 3 ← Number of equal parts being considered.
4 ← Number of equal parts the whole rectangle is divided into.

(**c**) The rectangle is divided into three equal parts. Two parts are shaded, and therefore, two out of the total three equal parts are being considered.
The fraction is therefore,

$$\frac{2}{3}$$ 2 ← Number of equal parts being considered.
3 ← Number of equal parts the whole rectangle is divided into.

Example 3
A circle is divided into eight equal parts. If three parts are shaded black,
(**a**) What fraction is shaded black?
(**b**) What fraction is not shaded black?

Solution

(**a**) The circle is divided into eight equal parts, and 3 equal parts out of the total of 8 equal parts are shaded black.
Therefore, the fraction shaded black is,

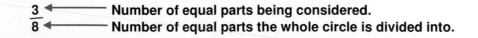

$$\frac{3}{8}$$ 3 ← Number of equal parts being considered.
8 ← Number of equal parts the whole circle is divided into.

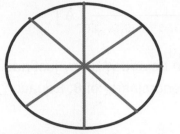 =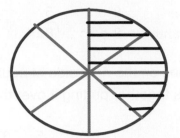

The circle is divided into 8 parts.   **3 out of 8 parts are shaded black.**

(**b**) Since 3 equal parts of the circle is shaded black, the circle is divided into 8 equal parts, the number of equal parts of the circle that are not shaded black is

$$8 - 3 = 5$$

Therefore, the fraction of the circle that is not shaded black is,

$\dfrac{5}{8}$ ◄——— **Number of equal parts being considered.**
◄——— **Number of equal parts the whole circle is divided into.**

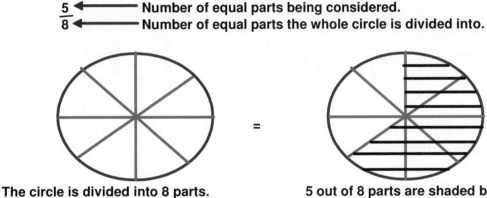

The circle is divided into 8 parts.   **5 out of 8 parts are shaded black.**

Critical Thinking

1. From the solution of Example **3**, note that the circle is divided into eight equal parts and one part is one-eighth of the circle and it is written in a fraction form as $\dfrac{1}{8}$.

2. In Example **3(a)**, three-eighths of the circle is shaded black and five-eighths is not shaded black. Three-eighths is written in a fraction form as $\dfrac{3}{8}$, 5-eigths is written in a fraction form as $\dfrac{5}{8}$ and 8-eigths is written as $\dfrac{8}{8}$.

Using Example **3(b)** solution, we can then add up fractions with the same denominator as shown:

$$8\text{-eigths} = 5\text{-eigths} + 3\text{-eigths}$$

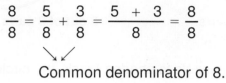

$$\frac{8}{8} = \frac{5}{8} + \frac{3}{8} \ \underline{\hspace{2cm}} \ [A]$$

The fractions on the right side of equation [A] can be added up by just adding the numerators together putting it over the common denominator of 8. Equation [A] then becomes:

$$\frac{8}{8} = \frac{5}{8} + \frac{3}{8} = \frac{5 + 3}{8} = \frac{8}{8}$$

Common denominator of 8.

In Example **3(b)**, note that 8-eigths of the circle is the same as 1 whole circle and the 8-eigths can be written as $\frac{8}{8}$. Therefore, $\frac{8}{8}$ = 1 whole circle. We conclude by stating that whenever the top number of a fraction is the same as the bottom number, then the fraction = 1. Examples are: $\frac{1}{1} = 1$, $\frac{2}{2} = 1$, $\frac{3}{3} = 1$, $\frac{4}{4} = 1$, $\frac{5}{5} = 1$, $\frac{6}{6} = 1$,...

Example 4

There are 24 students in a class in a certain school. If 13 of the students are girls,
(**a**) What fraction of the students are girls?
(**b**) What fraction of the students are boys?
Solution
(**a**) Total number of students = 24
Number of girls = 13

The fraction of girls = $\dfrac{13}{24}$

$$= \frac{13}{24} \quad \swarrow \text{Number of parts of the whole class being considered.}$$
$$\swarrow \text{Number of the students in the whole class.}$$

(**b**) Total number of students = 24
Number of girls = 13
Number of boys = Total number of students − Number of girls.
$$= 24 - 13 = 11$$

The fraction of boys = $\dfrac{11}{24}$

$$= \frac{11}{24} \quad \swarrow \text{Number of parts of the whole class being considered.}$$
$$\swarrow \text{Number of students in the whole class.}$$

Example 5

Mary had 11 out of 12 of her mathematics test questions correct.

(**a**) What fraction did she have correct?

(**b**) What fraction did she have wrong?

Solution

(**a**) Total number of questions = 12

Number of correct questions = 11

Therefore, the fraction correct $= \dfrac{11}{12}$

$= \dfrac{11}{12}$ ⟋Number of questions considered to be correct.

⟋Total number of questions.

(**b**) Total number of questions = 12

Number of questions that are correct = 11

The number of wrong questions =

Total number of questions - Number of correct questions.

$= 12 - 11 = 1$

The fraction of the wrong questions $= \dfrac{1}{12}$ ⟋Number of wrong questions.

⟋Total number of questions.

Group Exercise

The class should be divided into four teams, Team A, Team B, Team C, and Team D. The class may be divided into more teams if needed. With the supervision of a teacher or a parent, each team should order a pizza which should be divided into 8 equal parts.

(The pizza is shown on the next page.)

347

Team A   Team B   Team C

Team D

1. Team A should remove 5 parts of the pizza to share. What fraction of the pizza is shared and what fraction remains?
2. Team B should remove 7 parts of the pizza to share. What fraction of the pizza is shared and what fraction remains?
3. Team C should remove 6 parts of the pizza to share. What fraction of the pizza is shared and what fraction remains?
4. Team D should remove 4 parts of the pizza to share. What fraction of the pizza is shared and what fraction remains?

Each team should copy and complete Table 1.

Table 1, Team _____

Equal parts of pizza	Parts shared	Part remains	Fraction shared	Fraction Remains

Each team should post Table 1 on the blackboard, and then report their answers to the class.

The notes and the generous worked examples have provided me with conceptual understanding and computational fluency to do my homework.

Exercises

Hint: For the solutions to questions 1 - 9, see the preceding notes/information.

1. What is a fraction?

2. A fraction represents a ———————

3. The top number of a fraction is called ——————

4. The bottom number of a fraction is called ——————

5. The top number of a fraction tells us about ——————

6. The bottom number of a fraction tells us about ——————-

7. If the numerator of a fraction is the same as the denominator, the fraction is equal to ——-

8. If a whole apple is divided into seven equal parts, the bottom number of the fraction will be ———

9. If a circle is divided into five equal parts and 2 parts are removed,
  (a) What fraction is removed?
  (b) What fraction remains?

10 Write the fraction of the shaded or the colored areas. Hint: See Example **3**.

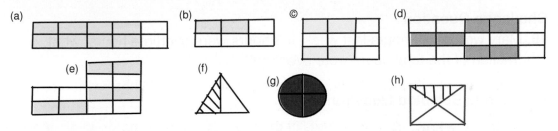

(a) (b) © (d)

(e) (f) (g) (h)

11. If a whole unit, such as a whole circle is divided into ten equal parts, the bottom number of the fraction is _____

12. Write four separate fractions which are equal to 1 or represent a whole unit. Hint: Read the section under "Critical thinking."

13. John had 7 out of 10 mathematics problems correct.
  (a) What fraction of the questions did John have correct?
  (b) What fraction of the questions did John have wrong? Hint: See example 5.

14. There are 20 students in a class. If 3 students were absent one day,
  (a) what fraction were absent?
  (b) what fraction were present? Hint: See Example **4**.

15. Mary bought 12 cookies and she gave away 8 of them.
  (a) What fraction did she give away?
  (b) What fraction remained? Hint: See Example **3**.

16. The school team won 5 out of the last 13 games.
  (a) What fraction of the games did they win?
  (b) What fraction of the games did they loose? Hint: See Example **5**.

17. If a fraction is written as $\frac{3}{7}$, into how many parts has the unit been divided?

  Hint: See Example **2**.

18. In the picture, what part of the pizza is removed? What part of the picture remains? Hint: See Example 3.

The pizza is divided into 8 parts.

=

The part of the pizza that remains.

The part of the pizza that is removed.

Challenge Question

19. Mary worked 48 hours last week. If 8 hours were overtime hours, what fraction of the total hours were overtime?

Answers to Selected Questions

14(a) $\dfrac{3}{20}$ **16(a)** $\dfrac{5}{13}$

FRACTIONS AS A PART OF A SET

Quick Cumulative Review

Using the graph of blue, pink, green, and yellow rings:

1. How many pink rings are in the graph?

2. How many more blue rings are there in the graph than green rings?

3. Which colors of the rings have the same number of rings?

4. Which color has the greatest number of rings?

5. Which color has the least number of rings?

6. Which color is your favorite and why?

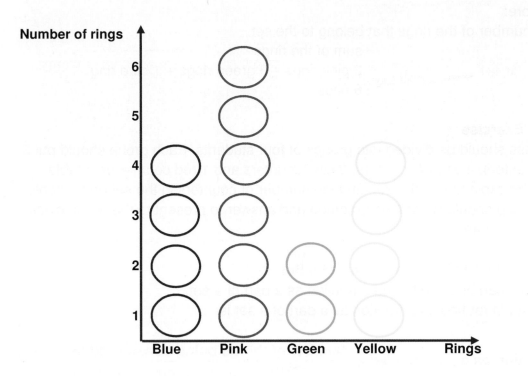

What is a Set?

Recall that we have already discussed fractions as a part of a whole. It is also possible to write fractions as a part of a set. Therefore, a fraction is a number that stands for a part of a whole or a part of a set. A set is things that belong to the same group and all the things that belong to the same group form one whole and can be considered as one. For example, the female students and the male students in grade 5 belong to the same group or belong to the same class or belong to the same set known as students. The female students form a fraction of the class or a fraction of the set or a fraction of the whole. The male students also form a fraction of the class or a fraction of the set or a fraction of the whole. The number of female students and the number of male students form the whole set. **A set is therefore, the sum or the total of things that belong to the same group or a common group.**

Example 1

There are 2 pink rings, 3 green rings, and 1 blue ring. How many rings are in the set?

Solution

The pink rings, green rings and the blue ring belong to the same group or a common group known as rings. We have already discussed that a set is the sum of the total of things that belong to the same group or a common group.

Therefore:

The number of the rings that belong to the set

= sum of the rings

= 2 pink rings + 3 green rings + 1 blue ring

= 6 rings

Group Exercise

The class should be divided into groups of four students. Each group should put 3 blue counters, 4 yellow counters, 2 blue counters and 1 red counter on a table. Using the explanation of a set, find the number of counters in the set on the table. Each group should record their method and answer to present to the whole class within 10 minutes.

How to Find a Fraction as a Part of a Set

A formula can be used to find a fraction as a part of a set.

The formula for finding a fraction as a part of a set is:

$$\textbf{A fraction as a part of a set} = \frac{\textbf{Number of things being considered in the set}}{\textbf{Total Number of things in the set}}$$

The formula simply means that we are considering and **comparing a certain number of things in the set to the total number of things in the set**.

Example 2

There are 3 blue balls and 1 red ball on the table.

a. What fraction of the set is blue balls?

b. What fraction of the set is red balls?

Solution

We can use the formula for finding the fraction as a part of a set to find the fraction of the blue balls as a part of a set of all the balls as shown:

a. The fraction of the blue balls as a part of a set

$$= \frac{\text{Number of things being considered in the set}}{\text{Total Number of things in the set}}$$

$$= \frac{\text{Number of blue balls in the set}}{\text{Total number of balls in the set}}$$

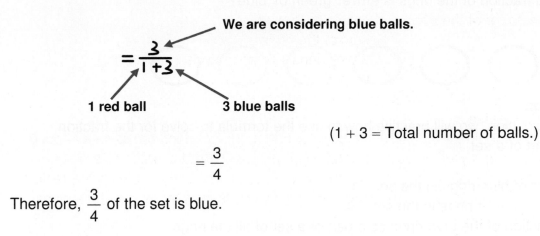

We are considering blue balls.

$$= \frac{3}{1+3}$$

1 red ball   **3 blue balls**

(1 + 3 = Total number of balls.)

$$= \frac{3}{4}$$

Therefore, $\frac{3}{4}$ of the set is blue.

b. We can use the formula for finding the fraction as a part of a set to find the fraction of the red balls as a part of a set of all the balls as shown:

The fraction of red balls as a part of a set

$$= \frac{\text{Number of things being considered in the set}}{\text{Total Number of things in the set}}$$

$$= \frac{\text{Number of red balls in the set}}{\text{Total number of balls in the set}}$$

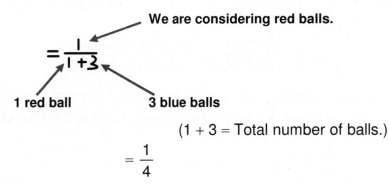

We are considering red balls.

$$= \frac{1}{1+3}$$

1 red ball   **3 blue balls**

(1 + 3 = Total number of balls.)

$$= \frac{1}{4}$$

Therefore, $\frac{1}{4}$ of the set is red.

Example 3
The diagram represents pink, green and blue rings.
a. What fraction of the rings is blue?
b. What fraction of the rings is pink?
c. What fraction of the rings is green?
d. What fraction of the rings is either pink or green?
e. What fraction of the rings is either pink or blue?

353

f. What fraction of the rings is either green or blue?

Solution

In this solution, we will practise how to use the formula to solve for the fraction as a part of a set.

a.

Number of blue rings in the set = 1.

Total number of rings in the set = 6.

The fraction of the blue rings as a part of a set of all the rings

$$= \frac{\text{Number of blue rings in the set}}{\text{Total number of rings in the set}}$$

$$= \frac{1}{6}$$

Therefore, the fraction of the blue rings as a part of a set of all the rings is $\frac{1}{6}$.

b.

Number of pink rings in the set = 2

Total number of the rings in the set = 6.

The fraction of the pink rings as a part of a set of all the rings

$$= \frac{\text{Number of pink rings in the set}}{\text{Total number of rings in the set}}$$

$$= \frac{2}{6}$$

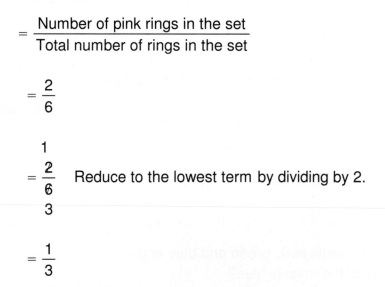

$$= \frac{\overset{1}{\cancel{2}}}{\underset{3}{\cancel{6}}} \qquad \text{Reduce to the lowest term by dividing by 2.}$$

$$= \frac{1}{3}$$

Therefore, the fraction of the pink rings as a part of a set of all the rings is $\frac{1}{3}$.

c.

Number of green rings in the set = 3.

354

Total number of rings in the set = 6.
The fraction of the green rings as a part of a set of all the rings

$$= \frac{\text{Number of green rings in the set}}{\text{Total number of rings in the set}}$$

$$= \frac{3}{6}$$

$$= \frac{\overset{1}{\cancel{3}}}{\underset{2}{\cancel{6}}}$$ Reduce to the lowest term by dividing by 3.

$$= \frac{1}{2}$$

Therefore, the fraction of the green rings as a part of a set of all the rings is $\frac{1}{2}$.

d.
Number of pink rings = 2.
Number of green rings = 3.
Number of either pink or green rings in the set
= Number of pink rings + number of green rings.
= 2 + 3
= 5

The fraction of either pink or green rings as a part of the set of all the rings

$$= \frac{\text{Number of either pink or green rings in the set}}{\text{Total number of rings in the set}}$$

╱ Number of either pink or green rings in the set.

$$= \frac{5}{6}$$

╲ Total number of rings in the set.

Therefore, the fraction of either pink or green rings as a part of a set of all the rings
is $\frac{5}{6}$.

e.
Number of pink rings in the set = 2.
Number of blue rings in the set = 1.

Number of either pink or blue rings in the set
$$= \text{Number of pink rings} + \text{number of blue rings.}$$
$$= 2 + 1$$
$$= 3$$
The fraction of either pink or blue rings as a part of a set of all the rings

$$= \frac{\text{Number of either pink or blue rings in the set}}{\text{Total number of rings in the set}}$$

↙ Number of either pink or blue rings in the set.
$$= \frac{3}{6}$$
↖ Total number of rings in the set.

$$= \frac{\overset{1}{\cancel{3}}}{\underset{2}{\cancel{6}}} \qquad \text{Reduce to the lowest term by dividing by 3.}$$

$$= \frac{1}{2}$$

Therefore, the fraction of either pink or blue rings as a part of a set of all the rings is $\frac{1}{2}$.

f.
Number of green rings in the set = 3.
Number of blue rings in the set = 1.
Number of either green or blue rings in the set
$$= \text{Number of green rings} + \text{number of blue rings.}$$
$$= 3 + 1$$
$$= 4$$
The fraction of either green or blue rings as a part of a set of all the rings

$$= \frac{\text{Number of either green or blue rings in the set}}{\text{Total number of rings in the set}}$$

↙ Number of either green or blue rings in the set.
$$= \frac{4}{6}$$
↖ Total number of rings in the set.

$$= \frac{\frac{4}{6}}{\frac{3}{2}} \quad \text{Reduce to the lowest term by dividing by 2.}$$

$$= \frac{2}{3}$$

Therefore, the fraction of either green or blue rings as a part of a set of all the rings is $\frac{2}{3}$.

Example 4

The Science Club of a middle school consists of 3 boys and 7 girls.

a. What fraction of the club members are boys?

b. What fraction of the club members are girls?

Solution

Both the girls and the boys belong to the Science Club.

The total number of the club members is the set of all the members of the club.

a.

Therefore, we can use the formula for finding the fraction as a part of a set to find the fraction of the boys as a part of a set of the total club members as shown:

The fraction of the boys as a part of a set of club members

$$= \frac{\text{Number of things being considered in the set}}{\text{Total number of things in the set}}$$

$$= \frac{\text{Number of boys in the club}}{\text{Total number of club members}}$$

We are considering boys in the club.

$$= \frac{3}{3 + 7}$$

3 boys ↗   ↖ 7 girls

$$= \frac{3}{10}$$

Therefore, $\frac{3}{10}$ of the club members are boys.

b.

Similar to the solution of 4a, we can use the formula for finding the fraction as a part of a set to find the fraction of the girls as a part of a set of the total club members as shown:

The fraction of the girls as a part of a set of the total club members

$$= \frac{\text{Number of things being considered in the set}}{\text{Total number of things in the set}}$$

$$= \frac{\text{Number of girls in the club}}{\text{Total number of club members}}$$

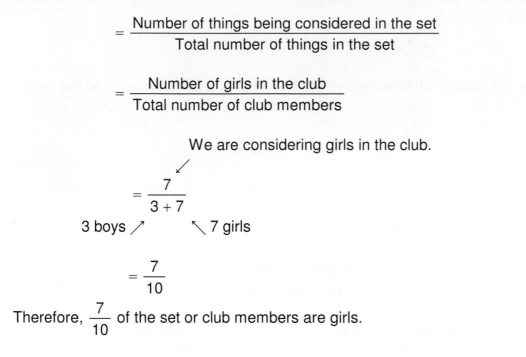

We are considering girls in the club.

$$= \frac{7}{3+7}$$

3 boys ↗   ↖ 7 girls

$$= \frac{7}{10}$$

Therefore, $\frac{7}{10}$ of the set or club members are girls.

The notes and the generous worked examples have provided me with conceptual understanding and computational fluency to do my homework.

Exercises

1. Explain what is meant by a set.

2. Explain what is meant by a fraction as a part of a set.

3. Give two examples of sets.

4. There is 1 red ball, 4 blue balls and 2 green balls. What is the number of balls in the set?

Hint: See Example 1.

5. What is the formula for finding a fraction as part of a set?

6. Use the diagram of rings to answer the questions.

   a. What is the fraction of the green rings?

   b. What is the fraction of the blue ring?

Hint: See Example 2.

7. Use the diagram of rings to answer the questions.
   a. What is the fraction of the pink rings?
   b. What is the fraction of the blue ring?
   Hint: See Example 2

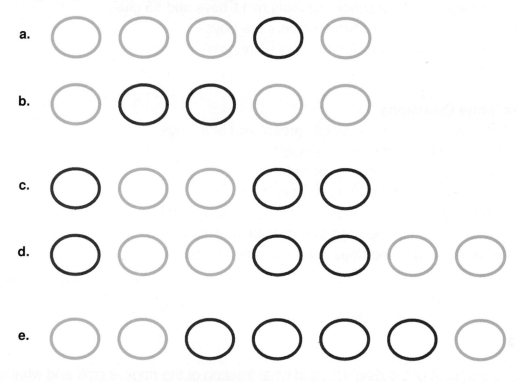

8. In each set of the diagram, find what fraction of the rings is blue and what fraction of the rings is green? Hint: See Example 2.

   a.

   b.

   c.

   d.

   e.

9. The diagram represents pink, green and blue rings.
   a. What fraction of the rings is blue?
   b. What fraction of the rings is pink?
   c. What fraction of the rings is green?
   d. What fraction of the rings is either pink or green?
   e. What fraction of the rings is either pink or blue?
   f. What fraction of the rings is either green or blue?

   Hint: See Example 3.
10. The diagram represents pink, green, and blue rings.
   a. What fraction of the rings is blue?
   b. What fraction of the rings is pink?

c. What fraction of the rings is green?

d. What fraction of the rings is either pink or green?

e. What fraction of the rings is either pink or blue?

f. What fraction of the rings is either green or blue?

Hint: See Example 3.

11. The Glee Club of a school consists of 11 boys and 15 girls.

a. What fraction of the club members are boys?

b. What fraction of the club members are girls?

Hint: See Example 4.

Challenge Questions

12. The diagram represents pink, green, and blue rings.

a. What fraction of the rings is blue?

b. What fraction of the rings is pink?

c. What fraction of the rings is green?

d. What fraction of the rings is either pink or green?

e. What fraction of the rings is either pink or blue?

f. What fraction of the rings is either green or blue?

13. In each set of the diagram, find what fraction of the rings is pink and what fraction of the rings is green? Hint: See Example 2.

a.

b.

c.

d.

e.

Answers to Selected Questions

6a. $\dfrac{2}{3}$ **7a.** $\dfrac{2}{3}$ **8a.** $\dfrac{1}{5}$ is blue, and $\dfrac{4}{5}$ is green **9a.** $\dfrac{2}{5}$ **10a.** $\dfrac{2}{7}$

ADDITION OF FRACTIONS
ADDITION OF FRACTIONS THAT HAVE THE SAME DENOMINATORS

Rule: To add fractions that have the same denominators, add the numerators and put the sum or addition of the numerators over the same (common) denominator.

Example 1

Add the following:

(a) $\dfrac{1}{6} + \dfrac{2}{6} + \dfrac{1}{6}$

(b) $\dfrac{1}{7} + \dfrac{2}{7} + \dfrac{3}{7}$

Solution

(**a**) The numerators are 1, 2, and 1. The denominator of each fraction is 6.

Step 1: Add the numerators: $1 + 2 + 1 = 4$

Step 2: Put the addition (sum) of the numerators over the same denominator as shown: $\dfrac{4}{6}$

Step 3: Therefore, $\dfrac{1}{6} + \dfrac{2}{6} + \dfrac{1}{6} = \dfrac{4}{6}$.

(**b**) The numerators are 1, 2, and 3. The denominator of each fraction is 7.

Step 1: Add the numerators: $1 + 2 + 3 = 6$

Step 2: Put the addition (sum) of the numerators over the same common denominator as shown: $\dfrac{6}{7}$

Step 3: Therefore, $\dfrac{1}{7} + \dfrac{2}{7} + \dfrac{3}{7} = \dfrac{6}{7}$

Example 2
Add the following:

(a) $\dfrac{2}{9} + \dfrac{1}{9} + \dfrac{4}{9} + \dfrac{3}{9} + \dfrac{5}{9}$ (b) $\dfrac{3}{12} + \dfrac{2}{12} + \dfrac{1}{12} + \dfrac{4}{12}$ (c) $\dfrac{3}{24} + \dfrac{2}{24} + \dfrac{4}{24} + \dfrac{5}{24}$

Solution
(a) The numerators are 2, 1, 4, 3, and 5. The denominator of each fraction is 9.
Step 1: Add the numerators: $2 + 1 + 4 + 3 + 5 = 15$
Step 2: Put the addition (sum) of the numerators over the same common

denominator as shown: $\dfrac{15}{9}$.

Step 3: Therefore, $\dfrac{2}{9} + \dfrac{1}{9} + \dfrac{4}{9} + \dfrac{3}{9} + \dfrac{5}{9} = \dfrac{15}{9}$

This book will later discuss how to handle fractions such as how to reduce to the lowest terms and improper fractions.
(b) The numerators are 3, 2, 1, and 4. The denominator of each fraction is 12.
Step 1: Add the numerators: $3 + 2 + 1 + 4 = 10$
Step 2: Put the addition (sum) of the numerators over the same common

denominator as shown: $\dfrac{10}{12}$

Step 3: Therefore, $\dfrac{3}{12} + \dfrac{2}{12} + \dfrac{1}{12} + \dfrac{4}{12} = \dfrac{10}{12}$

(c) The numerators are 3, 2, 4 and 5. The denominator of each fraction is 24.
Step 1: Add the numerators: $3 + 2 + 4 + 5 = 14$
Step 2: Put the addition (sum) of the numerators over the same common

denominator as shown: $\dfrac{14}{24}$

Step 3: Therefore, $\dfrac{3}{24} + \dfrac{2}{24} + \dfrac{4}{24} + \dfrac{5}{24} = \dfrac{14}{24}$

Example 3

Eric needs $\dfrac{5}{12}$ foot, $\dfrac{7}{12}$ foot, $\dfrac{11}{12}$ foot, and $\dfrac{8}{12}$ foot of lumber to complete a project. How many feet of the lumber does Eric need?

Solution

The fractions of the lumber are $\dfrac{5}{12}, \dfrac{7}{12}, \dfrac{11}{12},$ and $\dfrac{8}{12}.$

Total feet of lumber needed $= \dfrac{5}{12} + \dfrac{7}{12} + \dfrac{11}{12} + \dfrac{8}{12}$

The numerators are 5, 7, 11, and 8. The denominator of each fraction is 12.

   Step 1: Add the numerators: $5 + 7 + 11 + 8 = 31$

   Step 2: Put the addition (sum) of the numerators over the same common

   denominator as shown: $\dfrac{31}{12}$

   Step 3: Therefore, the total feet of lumber needed

$$= \dfrac{5}{12} + \dfrac{7}{12} + \dfrac{11}{12} + \dfrac{8}{12} = \dfrac{31}{12} \text{ feet.}$$

Example 4

Nicholas bought the following weights of cheese: $\dfrac{6}{16}$ pound, $\dfrac{8}{16}$ pound, $\dfrac{9}{16}$ pound, and $\dfrac{11}{16}$ pound. What was the total weight of cheese that Nicholas bought?

Solution

The fractions of the cheese are:

$$\dfrac{6}{16}, \dfrac{8}{16}, \dfrac{9}{16}, \text{ and } \dfrac{11}{16}$$

The total weight of the cheese $= \dfrac{6}{16} + \dfrac{8}{16} + \dfrac{9}{16} + \dfrac{11}{16}$

The numerators are 6, 8, 9, and 11. The denominator of each fraction is 16.

Step 1: Add the numerators: $6 + 8 + 9 + 11 = 34$

Step 2: Put the addition (sum) of the numerators over the same common

   denominator as shown: $\dfrac{34}{16}$

Step 3: Therefore, the total weight of the cheese $= \dfrac{6}{16} + \dfrac{8}{16} + \dfrac{9}{16} + \dfrac{11}{16} = \dfrac{34}{16}$

Critical Thinking

To add fractions is really finding out how many parts are there in all the fractions to be added. For example, in Example **2(c)**, **we are really finding out how many 24^{ths} there are in all the fractions to be added**.

_____

The notes and the generous worked examples have provided me with conceptual understanding and computational fluency to do my homework.

Exercises

Add the following. Hint: See Examples 1 and 2.

(1) $\dfrac{1}{4} + \dfrac{2}{4} + \dfrac{1}{4}$

(2) $\dfrac{1}{5} + \dfrac{3}{5}$

(3) $\dfrac{1}{8} + \dfrac{3}{8} + \dfrac{4}{8}$

(4) $\dfrac{3}{11} + \dfrac{4}{11} + \dfrac{1}{11} + \dfrac{2}{11}$

(5) $\dfrac{1}{10} + \dfrac{3}{10} + \dfrac{6}{10} + \dfrac{4}{10}$

(6) $\dfrac{4}{13} + \dfrac{2}{13} + \dfrac{4}{13} + \dfrac{5}{13}$

(7) $\dfrac{3}{17} + \dfrac{2}{17} + \dfrac{1}{17} + \dfrac{6}{17}$

(8) $\dfrac{5}{15} + \dfrac{1}{15} + \dfrac{4}{15} + \dfrac{3}{15}$

(9) $\dfrac{5}{16} + \dfrac{1}{16} + \dfrac{3}{16} + \dfrac{4}{16}$

(10) $\dfrac{7}{27} + \dfrac{6}{27}$

(11) $\dfrac{2}{31} + \dfrac{5}{31} + \dfrac{7}{31}$

(12) $\dfrac{10}{41} + \dfrac{6}{41} + \dfrac{8}{41}$

(13) $\dfrac{11}{45} + \dfrac{1}{45} + \dfrac{13}{45}$

(14) $\dfrac{7}{35} + \dfrac{2}{35} + \dfrac{10}{35}$

(15) $\dfrac{9}{40} + \dfrac{6}{40} + \dfrac{13}{40}$

(16) $\dfrac{3}{28} + \dfrac{4}{28} + \dfrac{6}{28}$

(17) $\dfrac{2}{9} + \dfrac{4}{9}$

(18) $\dfrac{4}{15} + \dfrac{7}{15}$

(19) Joshua needs $\dfrac{1}{6}$ foot, $\dfrac{2}{6}$ foot, $\dfrac{3}{6}$ foot, and $\dfrac{4}{6}$ foot of wood to complete his project. How many feet of wood does Joshua need? Hint: See Example **3**.

(20) Samuel bought $\dfrac{17}{36}$ yard, $\dfrac{28}{36}$ yard, $\dfrac{25}{36}$ yard, and $\dfrac{33}{36}$ yard of fabric for his school project. How many yards did Samuel buy? Hint: See Example **3**.

(21) Mary bought the following weights of cheese: $\dfrac{9}{16}$ pound, $\dfrac{5}{16}$ pound, $\dfrac{7}{16}$ pound, and $\dfrac{13}{16}$ pound. What was the total weight of cheese that Mary bought? Hint: See Example **4**.

(20) Rose made a cake for her friend. She mixed $\frac{3}{6}$ cup of milk, $\frac{3}{6}$ cup of sugar, $\frac{3}{6}$ cup of shortening, and $\frac{3}{6}$ cup of flour. How many cups did she mix? Hint: See Example 4.

Challenge Question

(21) Karen cut off the following pieces of wood: $\frac{4}{9}$ foot, $\frac{7}{9}$ foot, $\frac{5}{9}$ foot, and $\frac{8}{9}$ foot. How many feet of wood did she cut?

Answers to Selected Questions

(1) $\frac{4}{4} = 1$, **(19)** $\frac{10}{6} = 1\frac{4}{6} = 1\frac{2}{3}$ feet

TYPES OF FRACTIONS

New Terms
Proper fraction, **improper fraction** and **mixed fractions**

The three types of fractions are:
1. **Proper fraction**
2. **Improper fraction**
3. **Mixed fraction**

A proper fraction is a fraction where the numerator is less than the denominator. Some examples of proper fractions are: $\frac{1}{2}, \frac{3}{4}, \frac{5}{12}, \frac{99}{100}$, and $\frac{199}{200}$.

An improper fraction is a fraction where the numerator is greater than the denominator. Some examples of improper fractions are: $\frac{7}{4}, \frac{8}{3}, \frac{11}{4}, \frac{12}{7}$, and $\frac{250}{199}$.

A mixed fraction contains both a whole number and a fractional part.
Some examples of mixed fractions are: $1\frac{1}{2}, 2\frac{3}{4}, 3\frac{4}{5}, 4\frac{12}{13}$, and $5\frac{1}{6}$.

RAISING FRACTIONS AND LOWERING FRACTIONS.

New term
Equivalent fractions

Equivalent fractions are fractions that have the same values or fractions that represent the same part of a whole.

Group Class Exercise
Divide the class into four groups. Each group should be given three pages of 11 x 8 paper, a ruler and a pencil.

Step 1: Each group should sketch a rectangle with dimensions of 8 inches by 4 inches.

A rectangle is a four sided figure as shown →

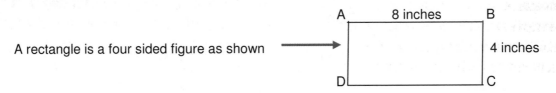

Label the rectangle ABCD. Let AB and DC be the lengths of the rectangle. Each group should mark point E between A and B such that E should be 4 inches from A. Mark point F between D and C so that F should be 4 inches from D. With a pencil and a ruler, draw a line from E to F.

Note that rectangle EBCF is $\frac{1}{2}$ of rectangle ABCD.

Step 2: Measure and mark the point G between A and E such that G is 2 inches from A. Measure and mark point H between D and F so that H is 2 inches from D. Use a pencil and a ruler to draw a line from G to H. Measure and mark point I between E and B so that I is 2 inches from E. Measure and mark point J between F and C so that J is 2 inches from F. Use a pencil and a ruler to draw a line from I to J. Note that rectangle ABCD is divided into 4 equal parts and rectangle EBCF is:

$$\frac{2}{4} \text{ of rectangle ABCD.}$$

Step 3: Measure and mark point K between A and D so that point K is 2 inches from A. Measure and mark point L between B and C so that L is 2 inches from B. Use a pencil and a ruler to draw a line from K to L. Note that rectangle ABCD is divided into 8 equal parts and rectangle EBCF is:

$$\frac{4}{8} \text{ of rectangle ABCD.}$$

Summary:

Step 1: Shows that rectangle EBCF = $\dfrac{1}{2}$ of rectangle ABCD.

Step 2: Shows that rectangle EBCF = $\dfrac{2}{4}$ of rectangle ABCD.

Step 3: Shows that rectangle EBCF = $\dfrac{4}{8}$ of rectangle ABCD.

Conclusion: Rectangle EBCF = $\dfrac{1}{2} = \dfrac{2}{4} = \dfrac{4}{8}$ of rectangle ABCD, and these

fractions are known as **equivalent fractions**. Equivalent fractions are fractions that represent the same part of a whole.

.

How are Equivalent Fractions Obtained?

Rule 1: Equivalent fractions are obtained by multiplying both the denominator and the numerator by the same number.

For example, the fraction $\dfrac{1}{3}$ can be changed to $\dfrac{2}{6}$ by multiplying both the

numerator and the denominator by 2 as shown: $\dfrac{1}{3} = \dfrac{1}{3} \times \dfrac{2}{2} = \dfrac{2}{6}$

Critical Thinking

By multiplying both the numerator and the denominator by 2, we are actually

multiplying $\dfrac{1}{3}$ by 1 because $\dfrac{2}{2} = 1$, and multiplying $\dfrac{1}{3}$ by a fraction of $\dfrac{2}{2}$ which is

equal to 1 does not change the value of $\dfrac{1}{3}$, but only changes the original

fraction to an equivalent fraction of $\dfrac{2}{6}$. When $\dfrac{1}{3}$ is changed to $\dfrac{2}{6}$ without changing

the value of $\dfrac{1}{3}$ is called raising $\dfrac{1}{3}$ to $\dfrac{2}{6}$, and the fraction with the bigger

denominator or numerator is called the higher equivalent. In this case, the higher

equivalent is $\dfrac{2}{6}$.

Rule 2: Multiplying both the numerator and the denominator by the same number will not change the value of the fraction.

Example 1

Raise $\dfrac{1}{5}$ to a higher equivalent that has a denominator of 20.

Solution

The problem can be written as: $\dfrac{1}{5} = \dfrac{?}{20}$

367

Using Rule 1, which states that equivalent fractions are obtained by multiplying both the denominator and the numerator by the same number, let us find what number is multiplied by the denominator 5 to obtain 20.

$$\frac{1}{5} = \frac{?}{20}$$

The denominator of 5 is multiplied by 4 to obtain a higher equivalent denominator of 20, and the numerator of 1 should also be multiplied by the same number 4 to obtain a higher equivalent numerator of 4 as shown:

$$\text{Therefore, } \frac{1}{5} = \frac{4}{20} \leftarrow \text{Higher equivalent fraction}$$

The higher equivalent $= \frac{4}{20}$, and this may also be obtained by simply multiplying the numerator and the denominator by 4 as shown:

$$\frac{1}{5} \times \frac{4}{4} = \frac{4}{20} \leftarrow \text{Higher equivalent fraction}$$

Example 2

Raise $\frac{2}{7}$ to a higher equivalent that has a numerator of 6.

Solution

The problem can be written as: $\frac{2}{7} = \frac{6}{?}$

Using Rule 1, let us find what number is multiplied by the numerator 2 to obtain the higher equivalent numerator of 6. The numerator 2 is multiplied by 3 to obtain the higher equivalent numerator of 6, and therefore, the denominator of 7 should also be multiplied by 3 to obtain the higher equivalent denominator of 21 as shown below:

$$\frac{2}{7} = \frac{6}{21} \leftarrow \text{Higher equivalent fraction}$$

The higher equivalent $= \frac{6}{21}$, and this may also be obtained simply by multiplying the numerator and the denominator of $\frac{2}{7}$ by 3 as shown:

$$\frac{2}{7} \times \frac{3}{3} = \frac{6}{21} \leftarrow \text{Higher equivalent fraction}$$

Example 3

Copy and complete to make a true statement:

(a) $\dfrac{2}{6} = \dfrac{10}{?}$ **(b)** $\dfrac{3}{?} = \dfrac{6}{8}$ **(c)** $\dfrac{?}{4} = \dfrac{12}{16}$

Solution

(a) Using Rule 1, let us find what number is multiplied by the numerator 2 to obtain the higher equivalent numerator of 10. The numerator 2 is multiplied by 5 to obtain the higher equivalent numerator of 10, and therefore, the denominator of 6 should also be multiplied by 5 to obtain the higher equivalent denominator of 30 as shown:

$$\frac{2}{6} = \frac{10}{30} \leftarrow \text{Higher equivalent fraction}$$

The higher equivalent fraction is $\dfrac{10}{30}$, and this can also be obtained simply by multiplying the denominator and the numerator by 5 as shown:

$$\frac{2}{6} \times \frac{5}{5} = \frac{10}{30} \leftarrow \text{Higher equivalent fraction}$$

(b) Let us find the number that is used to divide the numerator of 6 in order to obtain the lower equivalent numerator of 3. The numerator of 6 is divided by 2 in order to obtain the lower equivalent numerator of 3, and therefore, the denominator of 8 should also be divided by the same number 2 in order to obtain the lower equivalent denominator of 4 as shown:

$$\text{Lower equivalent fraction} \rightarrow \frac{3}{4} = \frac{6}{8}$$

The lower equivalent is $\dfrac{3}{4}$, and this can also be obtained by dividing the numerator and the denominator of the higher equivalent fraction of $\dfrac{6}{8}$ by 2 as shown:

$$\text{Lower equivalent fraction} \rightarrow \frac{3}{4} = \frac{6 \div 2}{8 \div 2}$$

(c) Let us find the number that is used to divide the higher equivalent denominator of 16 in order to obtain a lower equivalent denominator 4. The higher equivalent denominator of 16 is divided by 4 in order to obtain the lower equivalent denominator of 4, and therefore, the numerator of 12 should also be divided by the same number 4 to obtain the lower equivalent numerator of 3 as shown:

$$\text{Lower equivalent fraction} \rightarrow \frac{3}{4} = \frac{12}{16}$$

The lower equivalent fraction $= \dfrac{3}{4}$, and this can also be obtained simply by dividing the numerator and the denominator of the higher equivalent of $\frac{12}{16}$ by 4 as shown:

$$\text{Lower equivalent fraction} \rightarrow \frac{3}{4} = \frac{12 \div 4}{16 \div 4}$$

Critical Thinking

1. Changing from any fraction to a higher equivalent fraction involves the multiplication of the numerator and the denominator by the same number.

2. Changing from any fraction to a lower equivalent fraction involves the division of the numerator and the denominator by the same number which is the same common factor. We will learn more about common factors later.

REAL WORLD APPLICATIONS - WORD PROBLEMS
Equivalent Fractions

Example 4

Mary made a pizza and she cut it into 8 slices. If she ate $\frac{1}{4}$ of the pizza, how many slices did she eat?

Solution

8 slices of pizza is the whole pizza. Therefore, the solution can be set up as shown:

$$\frac{1}{4} = \frac{?}{8}$$

Let us find the number which multiplied the lower equivalent denominator of 4 to obtain the higher equivalent denominator of 8. The lower equivalent denominator of 4 is multiplied by 2 in order to obtain the higher equivalent denominator of 8, therefore, the lower equivalent numerator of 1 should also be multiplied by the same number of 2 in order to obtain a higher equivalent numerator of 2 as shown:

$$\frac{1}{4} = \frac{2}{8} \searrow$$

This is the number of slices eaten by Mary.

Mary eats 2 slices of the pizza, and this can also be solved simply by multiplying the denominator and the numerator of the lower equivalent fraction of $\frac{1}{4}$ by 2 as shown:

$$\frac{1}{4} \times \frac{2}{2} = \frac{2}{8} \searrow$$

Mary ate 2 slices of the pizza.

370

The notes and the generous worked examples have provided me with conceptual understanding and computational fluency to do my homework.

Exercise

1. What is meant by equivalent fractions?

2. How are equivalent fractions obtained?

3. Write the equivalence of $\dfrac{1}{4}$ by raising the denominator to 24. Hint: See Example 1.

4. Write the equivalence of $\dfrac{3}{7}$ by raising the numerator to 12. Hint: See Example 2.

5. Copy and complete to make a true statement. Hint: See Example 3.

   (a) $\dfrac{2}{10} = \dfrac{?}{40}$ (b) $\dfrac{1}{8} = \dfrac{?}{32}$ (c) $\dfrac{6}{7} = \dfrac{36}{?}$ (d) $\dfrac{?}{27} = \dfrac{1}{3}$ (e) $\dfrac{5}{6} = \dfrac{25}{?}$

6. Raise $\dfrac{2}{3}$ to a higher equivalent fraction that has a denominator of 15. Hint: See Example 1.

7. Copy and complete to make true statements. Hint: See Example 3.

   (a) $\dfrac{1}{6} = \dfrac{?}{12}$ (b) $\dfrac{2}{8} = \dfrac{?}{24}$ (c) $\dfrac{?}{36} = \dfrac{2}{6}$ (d) $\dfrac{4}{?} = \dfrac{12}{9}$

   (e) $\dfrac{?}{14} = \dfrac{3}{7}$ (f) $\dfrac{5}{15} = \dfrac{1}{?}$ (g) $\dfrac{12}{?} = \dfrac{36}{9}$ (h) $\dfrac{?}{7} = \dfrac{15}{21}$

8. John made a pizza and cut it into 12 slices. If he ate $\dfrac{1}{4}$ of the pizza, how many slices did he eat? Hint: See Example 4.

9. In a class of 25 students, $\dfrac{2}{5}$ are girls. How many students are girls? Hint: The whole class has 25 students . Set up as shown: $\dfrac{2}{5} = \dfrac{?}{25}$, and then solve it.

Challenge Questions

8. Complete each pair of equivalent fractions.

   (a) $\dfrac{1}{4} = \dfrac{?}{12}$ (b) $\dfrac{2}{?} = \dfrac{12}{18}$ (c) $\dfrac{3}{8} = \dfrac{?}{24}$

   (d) $\dfrac{?}{21} = \dfrac{9}{7}$ (e) $\dfrac{5}{35} = \dfrac{15}{?}$ (f) $\dfrac{11}{77} = \dfrac{1}{?}$

(g) $\dfrac{24}{36} = \dfrac{6}{?}$ **(h)** $\dfrac{20}{60} = \dfrac{?}{120}$ **(i)** $\dfrac{?}{30} = \dfrac{8}{10}$

9. Write an equivalent fraction for each fraction below. You may choose to raise or lower the equivalent fraction.

(a) $\dfrac{1}{2}$ **(b)** $\dfrac{1}{3}$ **(c)** $\dfrac{2}{7}$ **(d)** $\dfrac{2}{5}$ **(e)** $\dfrac{7}{10}$

(f) $\dfrac{3}{7}$ **(g)** $\dfrac{6}{12}$ **(h)** $\dfrac{11}{22}$ **(i)** $\dfrac{24}{25}$ **(j)** $\dfrac{21}{34}$

Answers to Selected Questions

3. $\dfrac{6}{24}$ **5(a).** 8   **9(a).** $\dfrac{1}{2} \times \dfrac{2}{2} = \dfrac{2}{4}$

MULTIPLES, LEAST COMMON MULTIPLE, COMMON DENOMINATORS, AND LEAST COMMON DENOMINATOR

1. MULTIPLES

The multiples of a whole number are the product of that number and any other whole number except zero.

Example 1
(a) What are the multiples of 5?
(b) What are the multiples of 3?
Solution:
(a) The multiples of 5 are: $5 \times 1 = 5$, $5 \times 2 = 10$, $5 \times 3 = 15$, $5 \times 4 = 20$, $5 \times 5 = 25$, . . .
Therefore the multiples of 5 are: 5, 10, 15, 20, 25,...
(b) The multiples of 3 are: $3 \times 1 = 3$, $3 \times 2 = 6$, $3 \times 3 = 9$, $3 \times 4 = 12$, $3 \times 5 = 15$, $3 \times 6 = 18$, $3 \times 7 = 21$, ...
Therefore, the multiples of 3 are: 3, 6, 9, 12, 15, 18, 21, . . .

2. LEAST COMMON MULTIPLES
Rule 1: The least common multiple (LCM) of two or more numbers is the least or the smallest multiple that is common to all the numbers.
Rule 2: The least common multiple (LCM) of two or more numbers can be found by listing the multiples of each number in order from the smallest to the greatest until a multiple that is common to all the numbers is obtained.

Example 2

What is the least common multiple (LCM) of 3 and 4?

Solution

The multiples of 3 are: $3 \times 1 = 3$
$$3 \times 2 = 6$$
$$3 \times 3 = 9$$
$$3 \times 4 = 12 \rightarrow (LCM)$$
$$3 \times 5 = 15$$
$$3 \times 6 = 18$$

Therefore, the multiples of 3 are: 3, 6, 9, 12, 15, 18, . . .

The multiples of 4 are: $4 \times 1 = 4$
$$4 \times 2 = 8$$
$4 \times 3 = 12 \rightarrow$ Stop here because 12 also appears as a multiple of 3, and 12 is therefore the least common multiple of 3 and 4.

Therefore, the multiples of 4 are: 4, 8, 12, . . .

↑
LCM

The LCM = 12

Note that Rule 2 is used in solving this problem.

Example 3

What is the least common multiple of 4 and 6?

Solution

The multiples of 4 are: $4 \times 1 = 4, 4 \times 2 = 8, 4 \times 3 = 12, 4 \times 4 = 16, 4 \times 5 = 20, . . .$
Therefore, the multiples of 4 are: 4, 8, 12, 16, 20, . . .
The multiples of 6 are: $6 \times 1 = 6, 6 \times 2 = 12, . . .$

↑
Stop here because 12 also appears as a multiple of 4 and therefore, 12 is the least common multiple (LCM) of 4 and 6.

The LCM = 12

Note that Rule 2 is used in solving this problem.

Example 4

Find the least common multiple (LCM) of 6 and 7.

Solution

The multiples of 6 are: $6 \times 1 = 6, 6 \times 2 = 12, 6 \times 3 = 18, 6 \times 4 = 24, 6 \times 5 = 30,$
$$6 \times 6 = 36, 6 \times 7 = 42, 6 \times 8 = 48, . . .$$
The multiples of 6 are: 6, 12, 18, 24, 30, 36, 42, 48, . . .

The multiples of 7 are: $7 \times 1 = 7, 7 \times 2 = 14, 7 \times 3 = 21, 7 \times 4 = 28, 7 \times 5 = 35,$
$\qquad 7 \times 6 = 42$
$\qquad\qquad\qquad \uparrow$
$\qquad\qquad\qquad$ Stop here because 42 also appears as a multiple
$\qquad\qquad\qquad$ of 6 and so, 42 is the least common multiple
$\qquad\qquad\qquad$ of 6 and 7.

The LCM is 42
Note that Rule 2 is used to solve this problem.

Example 5
Given that the multiples of 4 are: 4, 8, 12, 16, 20, 24, 28, 32, . . . and given that
the multiples of 6 are: 6, 12, 18, 24, 30, 36, . . ., explain why although 24 is
a common multiple of 4 and 6, 24 is not the least common multiple (LCM) of 4
and 6.
Solution
The multiples of 4 are: 4, 8, 12, 16, 20, 24, 28, 32, . . .
The multiples of 6 are: 6, 12, 18, 24, 30, 36, . . .
By observing the multiples of 4 and 6 above, 24 appears as one of the multiples of
4 and 6. It can also be observed that 12 is one of the multiples of 4 and 6 but 12 is
the smallest number that is the multiple of both 4 and 6 and therefore, 12 is the
least common multiple (LCM) of 4 and 6 and 24 is just one of the common
multiples of 4 and 6.

Example 6
Find the least common multiple of 6, 9, and 12.
Solution
The multiples of 6 are: $6 \times 1 = 6, 6 \times 2 = 12, 6 \times 3 = 18, 6 \times 4 = 24, 6 \times 5 = 30,$
$\qquad\qquad 6 \times 6 = 36, 6 \times 7 = 42, . . .$
The multiples of 9 are: $9 \times 1 = 9, 9 \times 2 = 18, 9 \times 3 = 27, 9 \times 4 = 36,$
$\qquad\qquad\qquad\qquad\qquad\qquad \uparrow$
$\qquad\qquad\qquad\qquad$ Stop here because 36 is also one of
$\qquad\qquad\qquad\qquad$ the multiples of 6.
The multiples of 12 are: $12 \times 1 = 12, 12 \times 2 = 24, 12 \times 3 = 36,$
$\qquad\qquad\qquad\qquad\qquad \uparrow$
$\qquad\qquad\qquad\qquad$ Stop here because 36 is also one of the multiples
$\qquad\qquad\qquad\qquad$ of 6 and 9. Since 36 is the smallest multiple which
$\qquad\qquad\qquad\qquad$ is common to 6, 9, and 12, 36 is the least common
$\qquad\qquad\qquad\qquad$ multiple (LCM) of 6, 9, and 12.
The LCM is 36.

The notes and the generous worked examples
have provided me with conceptual understanding
and computational fluency to do my homework.

Exercises

1. Explain what is meant by a multiple of a number?
2. List the first eight multiples of each number. Hint: See Examples **1** and **2**.
   (**a**) 5   (**b**) 8   (**c**) 9   (**d**) 4   (**e**) 10   (**f**) 11   (**g**) 12
3. Explain what is meant by the least common multiple of two or more numbers?
4. Find the least common multiple of each set of numbers. Hint: See Examples **2**, **3** and **4**.
   (**a**) 2 and 7   (**b**) 3 and 7   (**c**) 4 and 7   (**d**) 5 and 7   (**e**) 6 and 8

   (**f**) 7 and 8   (**g**) 5 and 9   (**h**) 7 and 9   (**i**) 12 and 8   (**j**) 12 and 48

   (**k**) 10 and 7   (**l**) 11 and 4   (**m**) 13 and 4   (**n**) 7 and 4   (**o**) 5 and 7
5. Given that the multiples of 5 are: 5, 10, 15, 20, 25, 30, 35, 40, 45, 50, 55, 60, . . .,
   and the multiples of 6 are: 6, 12, 18, 24, 30, 36, 42, 48, 54, 60, . . . ,
   explain why 60 cannot be the least common multiple (LCM) of 5 and 6. Hint: See
   Example **5**.
6. Find the least common multiple (LCM) of each set of numbers. Hint: See
   Example **6**.
   (**a**) 3, 4, and 6   (**b**) 4, 8, and 24   (**c**) 3, 5, and 6   (**d**) 3, 11, and 33

   (**e**) 4, 7, and 14   (**f**) 9, 4, and 6   (**g**) 6, 9, and 4   (**h**) 6, 5, and 4.
7. Explain the difference between the common multiples of two or more numbers and
   the least common multiple of two or more numbers. Hint: See Example **5**.

3. COMMON DENOMINATORS

A common denominator is when two or more fractions have the same denominator.

Considering the fractions $\frac{1}{12}$, $\frac{5}{12}$, $\frac{7}{12}$, and $\frac{11}{12}$, the denominator 12 is common to all

the fractions of $\frac{1}{12}$, $\frac{5}{12}$, $\frac{7}{12}$, and $\frac{11}{12}$, and therefore, the common denominator is 12.

The **usefulness of the common denominator** will be discussed fully under
comparing fractions.

4. LEAST COMMON DENOMINATORS

The least common denominator of two or more fractions is the least common

multiple (LCM) of their denominators. Hint: Review the topic under the Least Common Multiple (LCM) to fully understand the least common multiple (LCM) of numbers.

Example 1

Find the least common denominator of $\frac{1}{3}$ and $\frac{2}{7}$.

Solution

The denominators of $\frac{1}{3}$ and $\frac{2}{7}$ are 3 and 7.

The multiples of 3 are: $3 \times 1 = 3$, $3 \times 2 = 6$, $3 \times 3 = 9$, $3 \times 4 = 12$, $3 \times 5 = 15$, $3 \times 6 = 18$, $3 \times 7 = 21$, $3 \times 8 = 24$, . . .

Therefore, the multiples of 3 are: 3, 6, 9, 12, 15, 18, 21, 24, . . .

The multiples of 7 are: $7 \times 1 = 7$, $7 \times 2 = 14$, $7 \times 3 = 21$, . . .

↑

Stop here because 21 is the smallest number which also appears as a multiple of 3. Therefore, 21 is the least common denominator of $\frac{1}{3}$ and $\frac{2}{7}$.

Example 2

Find the least common denominator of $\frac{2}{5}$ and $\frac{7}{9}$.

Solution

The denominators of $\frac{2}{5}$ and $\frac{7}{9}$ are 5 and 9 .

The multiples of 5 are: $5 \times 1 = 5$, $5 \times 2 = 10$, $5 \times 3 = 15$, $5 \times 4 = 20$, $5 \times 5 = 25$, $5 \times 6 = 30$, $5 \times 7 = 35$, $5 \times 8 = 40$, $5 \times 9 = 45$, $5 \times 10 = 50$, . . .

Therefore, the multiples of 5 are: 5, 10, 15, 20, 25, 30, 35, 40, 45, 50, . . .

The multiples of 9 are: $9 \times 1 = 9$, $9 \times 2 = 18$, $9 \times 3 = 27$, $9 \times 4 = 36$, $9 \times 5 = 45$, . . .

↑

Stop here because 45 is the smallest number which also appears as a multiple of 5. Therefore, 45 is the least common denominator of $\frac{2}{5}$ and $\frac{7}{9}$.

Example 3

Find the least common denominator of $\frac{2}{3}$, $\frac{3}{4}$, and $\frac{5}{9}$.

Solution

The denominators of $\frac{2}{3}$, $\frac{3}{4}$, and $\frac{5}{9}$ are 3, 4 and 9.

The multiples of 3 are: $3 \times 1 = 3$, $3 \times 2 = 6$, $3 \times 3 = 9$, $3 \times 4 = 12$, $3 \times 5 = 15$,

$3 \times 6 = 18$, $3 \times 7 = 21$, $3 \times 8 = 24$, $3 \times 9 = 27$, $3 \times 10 = 30$,

$3 \times 11 = 33$, $3 \times 12 = 36$, $3 \times 13 = 39$, . . .

Therefore the multiples of 3 are: 3, 6, 9, 12, 15, 18, 24, 27, 30, 33, (36), 39, . . .

The multiples of 4 are: $4 \times 1 = 4$, $4 \times 2 = 8$, $4 \times 3 = 12$, $4 \times 4 = 16$, $4 \times 5 = 20$,

$4 \times 6 = 24$, $4 \times 7 = 28$, $4 \times 8 = 32$, $4 \times 9 = 36$, . . .

↑

Stop here because 36 is the smallest number that also appears as a multiple of 3 and the third denominator which is 9 can divide 36 evenly (without a remainder). Note also that 12 and 24 appear as multiples of both 3 and 4 but we cannot choose neither 12 nor 24 as the least common multiple of 3, 4 and 9 because 9 cannot divide neither 12 nor 24 evenly (without a remainder). Note that 12 and 24 are not multiples of 9. Therefore, the least common multiple of 3, 4, and 9 is 36 and the least common denominator of $\frac{2}{3}$, $\frac{3}{4}$,

and $\frac{5}{9}$ is 36.

Note 1: The best common denominator is the LCM of the denominator.

Note 2: Knowing the multiplication tables from 1 to 12 is very helpful in detecting quickly that $9 \times 4 = 36$ or 9 can divide into 36 evenly (without a remainder).

The notes and the generous worked examples have provided me with conceptual understanding and computational fluency to do my homework.

Exercises

1. What is the best common denominator?

2. Explain why knowing the multiplication tables from 1 to12 is very helpful in determining the LCM and the LCD.

3. List the multiplication tables that you know.

4. Explain what is meant by the least common denominator (LCD).

5. Explain what is meant by the least common multiple (LCM).

6. Find the least common denominator of the following: Hint: See Examples **1** and **2**.

(a) $\frac{1}{3}$ and $\frac{2}{5}$ (b) $\frac{3}{4}$ and $\frac{5}{6}$ (c) $\frac{1}{2}$ and $\frac{2}{5}$ (d) $\frac{2}{3}$ and $\frac{1}{7}$

(e) $\dfrac{2}{7}$ and $\dfrac{2}{5}$ **(f)** $\dfrac{1}{4}$ and $\dfrac{3}{7}$ **(g)** $\dfrac{3}{5}$ and $\dfrac{3}{7}$ **(h)** $\dfrac{2}{3}$ and $\dfrac{5}{8}$

(i) $\dfrac{5}{8}$ and $\dfrac{5}{7}$ **(j)** $\dfrac{5}{6}$ and $\dfrac{5}{7}$ **(k)** $\dfrac{5}{6}$ and $\dfrac{5}{9}$ **(l)** $\dfrac{2}{9}$ and $\dfrac{5}{12}$

(m) $\dfrac{4}{9}$ and $\dfrac{1}{4}$ **(n)** $\dfrac{5}{7}$ and $\dfrac{4}{9}$ **(o)** $\dfrac{2}{11}$ and $\dfrac{7}{12}$ **(p)** $\dfrac{2}{3}$ and $\dfrac{3}{8}$

7. Find the least common denominator of the following. Hint: See Examples **1**, **2**, and **3**.

   (a) $\dfrac{2}{3}$, $\dfrac{1}{4}$, and $\dfrac{1}{2}$ **(b)** $\dfrac{3}{4}$, $\dfrac{1}{5}$, and $\dfrac{3}{10}$ **(c)** $\dfrac{1}{3}$, $\dfrac{2}{7}$, and $\dfrac{2}{21}$

   (d) $\dfrac{3}{4}$, $\dfrac{5}{6}$, and $\dfrac{1}{2}$ **(e)** $\dfrac{2}{7}$, $\dfrac{2}{9}$, and $\dfrac{2}{3}$ **(f)** $\dfrac{5}{6}$, $\dfrac{1}{3}$, and $\dfrac{5}{8}$

   (g) $\dfrac{2}{9}$, $\dfrac{1}{6}$, and $\dfrac{1}{4}$ **(h)** $\dfrac{3}{5}$, $\dfrac{1}{2}$, and $\dfrac{3}{4}$ **(i)** $\dfrac{7}{8}$, $\dfrac{2}{9}$, and $\dfrac{1}{6}$

ADDITION OF FRACTIONS THAT HAVE UNLIKE DENOMINATORS

Rule 1

In order to add fractions, follow these three steps:

Step 1: First find a common denominator.

Step 2: Change each given fraction to an equivalent fraction that has the same denominator.

Step 3: Add the numerators of the equivalent fractions and write the sum of the numerators of the equivalent fraction over the common equivalent denominator.

Note: The larger or largest denominator in the question can be used as the equivalent common denominator which is the same as the least common denominator.

Example 1

Find $\dfrac{1}{2} + \dfrac{1}{4}$

Solution

Step 1: Find the common denominator. The common denominator is 4 because the denominator of $\frac{1}{2}$ which is 2 can divide evenly into the denominator of $\frac{1}{4}$ which is 4 (without a remainder). This is an example where the larger or largest denominator in the question can at times be used as the equivalent common denominator which is the same as the least common denominator.

$$\frac{1}{2} = \frac{?}{4} \quad \diagup \text{Equivalent common denominator}$$

$$\frac{1}{4} = \frac{1}{4} \quad \diagup \text{Equivalent common denominator}$$

Step 2: Write an equivalent fraction for $\frac{1}{2}$ by multiplying $\frac{1}{2}$ by $\frac{2}{2}$ as shown:

$$\frac{1}{2} \times \frac{2}{2} = \frac{2}{4} \rightarrow \text{Equivalent fraction.}$$

$$\frac{1}{4} \times \frac{1}{1} = \frac{1}{4} \rightarrow \text{Equivalent fraction.}$$

We do not need to find the equivalent of $\frac{1}{4}$ because the denominator of 4 is already being used as the equivalent common denominator. Now, $\frac{2}{4}$ and $\frac{1}{4}$ have a common denominator of 4.

Step 3: Add the numerators of the equivalent fractions and write the sum of the numerators over the common denominator.

$$\frac{2+1}{4} = \frac{3}{4} \quad \begin{matrix} \diagup \text{Sum of the equivalent numerators} \\ \diagup \text{Common equivalent denominator (LCD).} \end{matrix}$$

Therefore, $\frac{1}{2} + \frac{1}{4} = \frac{3}{4}$

Example 2

Find $\frac{2}{3} + \frac{1}{4}$

Solution

Step 1: Find the least common denominator. Review the section on Least Common Denominator. The denominators are 3 and 4, but in this case, 4 cannot be the common factor because 3 cannot divide into 4 evenly (without a remainder). In this case, the least common denominator (LCD) is $3 \times 4 = 12$. Note that both 3 and 4 can divide into 12 evenly (without a remainder).

$$\frac{2}{3} = \frac{?}{12} \quad \diagup \text{Least common denominator.}$$

$$\frac{1}{4} = \frac{?}{12} \quad \diagup \text{Least common denominator.}$$

Step 2: Write equivalent fractions. Hint: Refer to the section on Equivalent Fractions.

$$\frac{2}{3} = \frac{2}{3} \times \frac{4}{4} = \frac{8}{12} \quad \leftarrow \text{Equivalent fraction.}$$

$$\frac{1}{4} = \frac{1}{4} \times \frac{3}{3} = \frac{3}{12} \quad \leftarrow \text{Equivalent fraction.}$$

Now, $\dfrac{8}{12}$ and $\dfrac{3}{12}$ have a common denominator of 12.

Step 3: Add the numerators of the equivalent fractions and write the sum of the numerators over the equivalent common denominator.

$$\diagup \text{Sum of the numerators of the equivalent fractions}$$
$$\frac{8+3}{12} = \frac{11}{12}$$
$$\diagdown \text{Common equivalent denominator (LCD).}$$

Therefore, $\dfrac{2}{3} + \dfrac{1}{4} = \dfrac{11}{12}$

Example 3

Find $\dfrac{2}{5} + \dfrac{3}{7}$

Solution

Step 1: Find the least common denominator. Refer to the Least Common Denominator section. The denominators are 5 and 7, but in this case, 5 cannot divide evenly into seven (without a remainder). In this case, the common denominator is $5 \times 7 = 35$.
Note that both 5 and 7 can divide evenly into 35 (without a remainder).

$$\frac{2}{5} = \frac{?}{35} \quad \diagup \text{Least common denominator.}$$

$$\frac{3}{7} = \frac{?}{35} \;\diagup \text{Least common denominator.}$$

Step 2: Write equivalent fractions. Hint: Refer to the section on Equivalent Fractions.

$$\frac{2}{5} \times \frac{7}{7} = \frac{14}{35} \;\leftarrow \text{Equivalent fraction}$$

$$\frac{3}{7} \times \frac{5}{5} = \frac{15}{35} \;\leftarrow \text{Equivalent fraction}$$

Now, $\frac{14}{35}$ and $\frac{15}{35}$ have a common denominator of 35.

Step 3: Add the numerators of the equivalent fractions and write the sum of the numerators over the common denominator.

$$\frac{14 + 15}{35} = \frac{29}{35} \;\diagup \text{Sum of the numerators of the equivalent fractions}$$

$\diagdown$ Common equivalent denominator (LCD)

Therefore, $\dfrac{2}{5} + \dfrac{3}{7} = \dfrac{29}{35}$

Example 4

Find $\dfrac{3}{5} + \dfrac{2}{25}$

Solution

Step 1: Find the least common denominator. Review the section on Least Common Denominators. The denominators are 5 and 25. In this case, 5 can divide into 25 evenly (without any remainder), and therefore, the least common denominator is 25. Note that both 5 and 25 can divide evenly into 25 (without any remainder).

$$\frac{3}{5} = \frac{?}{25} \;\diagup \text{Least common denominator}$$

$$\frac{2}{25} = \frac{?}{25} \;\diagup \text{Least common denominator}$$

Step 2: Write the equivalent fractions. Hint: Review the section on Equivalent Fractions.

$$\frac{3}{5} \times \frac{5}{5} = \frac{15}{25} \quad \leftarrow \text{Equivalent fraction}$$

$$\frac{2}{25} \times \frac{1}{1} = \frac{2}{25} \quad \leftarrow \text{Equivalent fraction}$$

We do not have to write an equivalent fraction for $\frac{2}{25}$ because the

denominator of 25 is already the common equivalent denominator for $\frac{3}{5}$.

Now, $\frac{15}{25}$ and $\frac{2}{25}$ have a common denominator of 25.

Step 3: Add the numerators of the equivalent fractions and write the sum of the numerators of the equivalent fraction over the equivalent common denominator.

Sum of the numerators of equivalent fractions

$$\frac{15+2}{25} = \frac{17}{25}$$

Common equivalent denominator (LCD)

Therefore, $\frac{3}{5} + \frac{2}{25} = \frac{17}{25}$

Example 5

Find $\frac{2}{3} + \frac{2}{4} + \frac{2}{6}$

Solution

Step 1: Find the least common denominator. Review the section on the Least Common Denominator. The denominators are 3, 4, and 6. Although 3 can divide into 6 evenly (without a remainder), 4 cannot divide into 6 evenly (without a remainder), and therefore, 6 cannot be the common denominator. Look for the least number that can be divided by 3, 4, and 6 evenly (without a remainder) and that number is 12. Therefore, the common denominator is 12.

$$\frac{2}{3} = \frac{?}{12} \quad \text{Least common denominator}$$

$$\frac{2}{4} = \frac{?}{12} \quad \text{Least common denominator}$$

$$\frac{2}{6} = \frac{?}{12} \quad \diagup \text{Least common denominator}$$

Step 2: Write the equivalent fractions. Hint: Review the section on Equivalent fractions.

$$\frac{2}{3} \times \frac{4}{4} = \frac{8}{12} \leftarrow \text{Equivalent fraction}$$

$$\frac{2}{4} \times \frac{3}{3} = \frac{6}{12} \leftarrow \text{Equivalent fraction}$$

$$\frac{2}{6} \times \frac{2}{2} = \frac{4}{12} \leftarrow \text{Equivalent fraction}$$

Step 3: Add the numerators of the equivalent fractions and then write the sum of the numerators of the equivalent fractions over the equivalent common denominator.

$$\diagup \text{Sum of the numerators of the equivalent fractions.}$$

$$\frac{8 + 6 + 4}{12} = \frac{18}{12}$$

$$\diagdown \text{Common equivalent denominator (LCD).}$$

Therefore, $\dfrac{2}{4} + \dfrac{2}{6} = \dfrac{18}{12}$

The notes and the generous worked examples have provided me with conceptual understanding and computational fluency to do my homework.

Exercises

1. Find the sum. Hint: See Examples **1** and **4**.

   a. $\dfrac{3}{10} + \dfrac{1}{5}$ **b.** $\dfrac{1}{4} + \dfrac{5}{16}$ **c.** $\dfrac{1}{3} + \dfrac{2}{9}$ **d.** $\dfrac{2}{4} + \dfrac{1}{8}$

2. Find the sum. Hint: See Examples **2** and **3**.

   a. $\dfrac{3}{4} + \dfrac{1}{6}$ **b.** $\dfrac{2}{7} + \dfrac{1}{2}$ **c.** $\dfrac{1}{3} + \dfrac{2}{4}$ **d.** $\dfrac{2}{6} + \dfrac{3}{10}$

3. Find the sum. Hint: See Example **5**.

   a. $\dfrac{3}{5} + \dfrac{1}{3} + \dfrac{2}{15}$ **b.** $\dfrac{1}{2} + \dfrac{3}{4} + \dfrac{2}{3}$ **c.** $\dfrac{1}{4} + \dfrac{3}{5} + \dfrac{3}{10}$ **d.** $\dfrac{3}{4} + \dfrac{1}{2} + \dfrac{5}{6}$

Challenge Questions

Find the sum.

4. $\dfrac{3}{4} + \dfrac{2}{3}$ **5.** $\dfrac{3}{5} + \dfrac{4}{3} + \dfrac{7}{30}$ **6.** $\dfrac{5}{18} + \dfrac{5}{6} + \dfrac{2}{3}$ **7.** $\dfrac{2}{7} + \dfrac{2}{3} + \dfrac{1}{21}$

Answers to Selected Questions

1a. $\dfrac{5}{10}$ or $\dfrac{1}{2}$ **2a.** $\dfrac{11}{12}$

REAL WORLD APPLICATIONS - WORD PROBLEMS
Addition of Fractions That Have Unlike Denominators

Example 6

Mary walked $\dfrac{3}{4}$ mile to the market and $\dfrac{1}{3}$ mile to school. How many miles did she walk?

Solution

Total miles walked $= \dfrac{3}{4} + \dfrac{1}{3}$

Step 1: Find the least common denominator. Review the section on Least Common Denominator. The denominators are 4 and 3. In this case, since 3 cannot divide into 4 evenly (without a remainder), 4 cannot be the common denominator. The least common denominator is $3 \times 4 = 12$. Note that the least number that both 4 and 3 can divide into evenly (without a remainder) is 12.

$$\dfrac{3}{4} = \dfrac{?}{12} \quad \nearrow \text{Least common denominator}$$

$$\dfrac{1}{3} = \dfrac{?}{12} \quad \nearrow \text{Least common denominator}$$

Step 2: Write equivalent fractions. Refer to the section under Equivalent Fractions.

$$\dfrac{3}{4} = \dfrac{3}{4} \times \dfrac{3}{3} = \dfrac{9}{12} \leftarrow \text{Equivalent fraction}$$

$$\dfrac{1}{3} = \dfrac{1}{3} \times \dfrac{4}{4} = \dfrac{4}{12} \leftarrow \text{Equivalent fraction}$$

Step 3: Add the numerators of the equivalent fractions and write the sum of the numerators of the equivalent fractions over the equivalent common denominator of 12.

$$\frac{9 + 4}{12} = \frac{13}{12}$$

↙ Sum of the numerators of the equivalent fractions

↙ Equivalent common fraction (LCD)

Example 7

John needs $\frac{3}{8}$ yard, $\frac{1}{3}$ yard and $\frac{1}{6}$ yard of wood to do a school project. How many yards of wood is needed for the project?

Solution

Total yards needed for the project = $\frac{3}{8} + \frac{1}{3} + \frac{1}{6}$

Step 1: Find the least common denominator.

The denominators are 8, 3, and 6. The least common denominator (LCD) or the lowest number that can be divided by denominators 8, 3, and 6 evenly (without a remainder) is 24. Example: $8 \times 3 = 24$ and $6 \times 4 = 24$. Notice also that 8 is the largest denominator but 3 and 6 cannot divide into 8 evenly (without a reminder) and therefore the LCD is 24.

$$\frac{3}{8} = \frac{?}{24}$$ ↙ least common denominator

$$\frac{1}{3} = \frac{?}{24}$$ ↙ least common denominator

$$\frac{1}{6} = \frac{?}{24}$$ ↙ least common denominator

Step 2: Write equivalent fractions. Review the section under Equivalent Fractions.

$$\frac{3}{8} \times \frac{3}{3} = \frac{9}{24}$$ ← Equivalent fraction.

$$\frac{1}{3} \times \frac{8}{8} = \frac{8}{24}$$ ← Equivalent fraction.

$$\frac{1}{6} \times \frac{4}{4} = \frac{4}{24}$$ ← Equivalent fraction.

Step 3: Add the numerators of the equivalent fractions and write the sum of the numerators of the equivalent fractions over the equivalent common denominator as shown:

$$\frac{9+8+4}{24} = \frac{21}{24}$$

Sum of the numerators of the equivalent fractions.

Equivalent common denominator which is the same as the LCD.

The notes and the generous worked examples have provided me with conceptual understanding and computational fluency to do my homework.

Exercises

(**1**) John needs the following pieces of lumber to finish a project: $\frac{5}{7}$ foot, $\frac{3}{14}$ foot, and $\frac{3}{7}$ foot. How many feet of lumber does he need? Hint: See Example **6**.

(**2**) Rose walked $\frac{3}{8}$ mile to the library, $\frac{3}{4}$ mile to school. How many miles did she walk altogether? Hint: See Example **6**.

(**3**) Jane walked $\frac{3}{4}$ mile to school, $\frac{1}{6}$ mile to the market, and $\frac{2}{3}$ mile to the football game. How many miles did she walk altogether? Hint: See Example **7**.

(**4**) A class needs the following lengths of fabric for an experiment: $\frac{2}{5}$ foot, $\frac{3}{10}$ foot, and $\frac{17}{20}$ foot. How many feet of fabric are needed altogether? Hint: see Example **7**.

Challenge Questions

(**5**) Nick would like to bake a cake by adding $\frac{3}{5}$ cup of milk, $\frac{2}{3}$ cup of chocolate, $\frac{1}{2}$ cup of flour, and $\frac{1}{4}$ cup of sugar. How many cups would he need? Hint: Review how to find LCD.

Perform the following operations:

(**6**) $\frac{9}{16} + \frac{3}{8}$ (**7**) $\frac{15}{16} + \frac{1}{4}$ (**8**) $\frac{5}{7} + \frac{3}{14}$ (**9**) $\frac{5}{6} + \frac{1}{3}$ (**10**) $\frac{17}{21} + \frac{2}{7}$

(**11**) $\frac{3}{4} + \frac{2}{3}$ (**12**) $\frac{2}{3} + \frac{2}{9}$ (**13**) $\frac{2}{9} + \frac{7}{18}$ (**14**) $\frac{1}{5} + \frac{7}{15}$ (**15**) $\frac{2}{3} + \frac{1}{3}$

(**16**) $\frac{9}{28} + \frac{2}{7}$ (**17**) $\frac{3}{20} + \frac{2}{5}$ (**18**) $\frac{1}{5} + \frac{2}{10} + \frac{3}{20}$ (**19**) $\frac{2}{5} + \frac{3}{30} + \frac{11}{20}$

(20) $\dfrac{4}{5} + \dfrac{3}{20} + \dfrac{13}{20}$ (21) $\dfrac{3}{8} + \dfrac{3}{16} + \dfrac{7}{32}$ (22) $\dfrac{3}{4} + \dfrac{3}{8} + \dfrac{1}{5}$ (23) $\dfrac{3}{8} + \dfrac{2}{5}$

(24) $\dfrac{1}{3} + \dfrac{3}{8} + \dfrac{5}{12}$ (25) $\dfrac{1}{6} + \dfrac{2}{3} + \dfrac{5}{8}$ (26) $\dfrac{2}{7} + \dfrac{1}{4} + \dfrac{3}{14}$ (27) $\dfrac{5}{7} + \dfrac{3}{4}$

Answers to Selected Questions

1. $\dfrac{19}{14}$ 3. $\dfrac{19}{12}$ 6. $\dfrac{15}{16}$ 9. $\dfrac{7}{6}$

(**Note**: We will learn how to change fractions to mixed fractions later.)

ADDITION OF MIXED FRACTIONS

Types of fractions are:
Proper fraction
Improper fraction
Mixed fraction

A proper fraction is a fraction that has a numerator which is less than the denominator.

Examples of proper fractions are: $\dfrac{1}{4}, \dfrac{2}{4}, \dfrac{2}{3}$, and $\dfrac{14}{15}$.

An improper fraction is a fraction that has a numerator which is greater than the denominator.

Examples of improper fractions are: $\dfrac{4}{3}, \dfrac{12}{9}, \dfrac{15}{12}$, and $\dfrac{38}{25}$.

A mixed fraction is a fraction that contains both a whole number and a fraction.
Examples of mixed fractions are:

whole number↘   ↗fraction
$1\dfrac{1}{2}, \quad 2\dfrac{2}{5}, \quad 5\dfrac{7}{9}$, and $11\dfrac{7}{8}$.

As stated above, a mixed fraction is a fraction that contains both a whole number and a fraction, and therefore, mixed fractions are added up in three steps as shown:

Step 1 : **Add the whole numbers.**
Step 2 : **Add the fractions.**
Step 3 : **Combine the sum (addition) of the whole numbers in step 1 and the sum (addition) of the fractions in step 2 into a final sum.**

Example 1

Add: $2\dfrac{1}{3} + 1\dfrac{1}{6}$

Solution

(**Notice** that in Step 1, an imaginary line | separates the whole numbers from the fractions so that we can work on the whole numbers and the fractions separately.)

Step 1: Add the whole numbers first.

$\downarrow$

$2|\ \dfrac{1}{3}$

$1|\ \dfrac{1}{6}$

$\overline{3}$

addition of whole numbers

Step 2: Add the fractions second. (Review Addition of Fractions) In order to add fractions, find the LCD.

Determine LCD. Write equivalent fractions, and then add the fractions.

$2|\ \dfrac{1}{3} = \dfrac{}{6}$ ∕LCD

$1|\ \dfrac{1}{6} = \dfrac{}{6}$ ∕LCD

$\overline{3}$

$2|\ \dfrac{1}{3} \times \dfrac{2}{2} = \dfrac{2}{6}$

$1|\ \dfrac{1}{6} \times \dfrac{1}{1} = \dfrac{1}{6}$

$\overline{3}$

$\dfrac{3}{6}$

addition of fractions.

Step 2: Combine the sum (addition) of the whole numbers in Step 1 and the sum (addition) of the fractions in Step 2, into a final sum as shown:

From Step 1 ∕$3 + \dfrac{3}{6} = 3\dfrac{3}{6}$

∕ ＼Final sum
From Step 2

Example 2

Add: $4\dfrac{2}{3} + 10\dfrac{1}{4}$

Solution

(**Notice** that in Step 1, an imaginary line | separates the whole numbers from the fractions so that we can work on the whole numbers and the fractions separately.)

Step 1: Add the whole numbers first.
↓

Step 2: Add fractions second.
(Review Addition of Fractions)
In order to add fractions, find the LCD.
↙
Determine LCD.

Write equivalent fractions, and then add the fractions.
↓

$$4\mid \dfrac{2}{3}$$

$$10\mid \dfrac{1}{4}$$

$$\overline{}$$
$$14$$

$$4\mid \dfrac{2}{3} = \dfrac{}{12} \swarrow\text{LCD}$$

$$10\mid \dfrac{1}{4} = \dfrac{}{12} \swarrow\text{LCD}$$

$$\overline{}$$
$$14 \qquad \nwarrow\text{LCD}$$

$$4\mid \dfrac{2}{3} \times \dfrac{4}{4} = \dfrac{8}{12}$$

$$10\mid \dfrac{1}{4} \times \dfrac{3}{3} = \dfrac{3}{12}$$

$$\overline{}$$
$$14$$

$$\overline{}$$
$$\dfrac{11}{12}$$

↖ Addition of whole numbers ↗

↗ Addition of fractions

Step 3: Combine the sum (addition) of the whole numbers in Step 1 and the sum (addition) of the fractions in Step 2 into the final sum as shown:

From Step 1 ↗ $14 + \dfrac{11}{12} = 14\dfrac{11}{12}$ ↙ Final sum

↖ From Step 2

Example 3

Add: $11\dfrac{3}{4} + 4\dfrac{1}{8} + 2\dfrac{1}{2}$

Solution

(**Notice** that in Step 1, an imaginary line | separates the whole numbers from the fractions so that we can work on the whole numbers and the fractions separately.)

Step 1: Add the whole numbers first.

↓

Step 2: Add the fractions second.
(Review Addition of Fraction)
In order to add fractions, find the LCD.
Determine LCD.
Write equivalent fractions, and then add the fractions.

↓

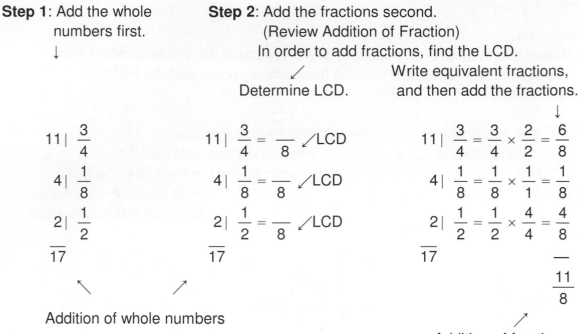

$$11| \frac{3}{4}$$

$$4| \frac{1}{8}$$

$$2| \frac{1}{2}$$

$$\overline{17}$$

$$11| \frac{3}{4} = \frac{}{8} \quad \text{LCD}$$

$$4| \frac{1}{8} = \frac{}{8} \quad \text{LCD}$$

$$2| \frac{1}{2} = \frac{}{8} \quad \text{LCD}$$

$$\overline{17}$$

$$11| \frac{3}{4} = \frac{3}{4} \times \frac{2}{2} = \frac{6}{8}$$

$$4| \frac{1}{8} = \frac{1}{8} \times \frac{1}{1} = \frac{1}{8}$$

$$2| \frac{1}{2} = \frac{1}{2} \times \frac{4}{4} = \frac{4}{8}$$

$$\overline{17}$$

$$\overline{\frac{11}{8}}$$

Addition of whole numbers

Addition of fractions

Review how to change an improper fraction such as $\frac{11}{8}$ into a mixed number such as $1\frac{3}{8}$.

Step 3: Combine the sum (addition) of the whole numbers in Step 1 and the sum (addition) of the fractions in Step 2 into the final sum as shown:

From Step 1 $\nearrow 17 + 1\frac{3}{8} = 18\frac{3}{8}$

↗ From Step 2

↖ Final sum

Example 4

Add: $\frac{2}{9} + 6\frac{2}{3} + 20\frac{8}{36}$

Solution

(**Notice** that in Step 1, an imaginary line | separates the whole numbers from the fractions so that we can work on the whole numbers and the fractions separately.)

Step 1: Add the whole numbers first.

Step 2: Add the fractions second. (Review Addition of Fractions) In order to add fractions find the LCD.

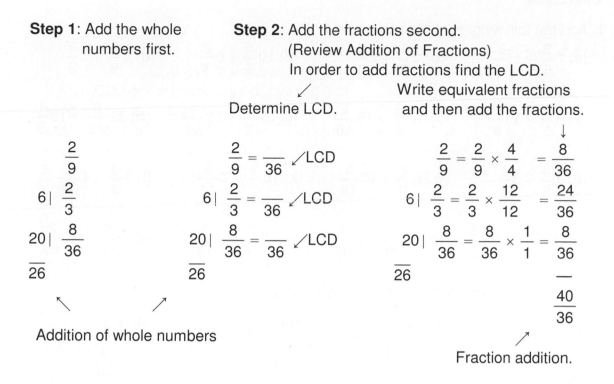

Determine LCD.

Write equivalent fractions and then add the fractions.

$$\frac{2}{9}$$

$$6 \mid \frac{2}{3}$$

$$20 \mid \frac{8}{36}$$

$$\overline{26}$$

$$\frac{2}{9} = \frac{}{36} \quad \diagup LCD$$

$$6 \mid \frac{2}{3} = \frac{}{36} \quad \diagup LCD$$

$$20 \mid \frac{8}{36} = \frac{}{36} \quad \diagup LCD$$

$$\overline{26}$$

$$\frac{2}{9} = \frac{2}{9} \times \frac{4}{4} = \frac{8}{36}$$

$$6 \mid \frac{2}{3} = \frac{2}{3} \times \frac{12}{12} = \frac{24}{36}$$

$$20 \mid \frac{8}{36} = \frac{8}{36} \times \frac{1}{1} = \frac{8}{36}$$

$$\overline{\quad}$$

$$\frac{40}{36}$$

Addition of whole numbers

Fraction addition.

(**Note**: Review how to change improper fractions such as $\frac{40}{36}$ into a mixed fraction such as $1\frac{4}{36}$).

Example: $\frac{40}{36} = 1\frac{4}{36}$

(**Note**: Review how to reduce fractions, $\frac{4}{36}$ can be reduced to $\frac{1}{9}$ by dividing both numerator and denominator by 4.

Step 3: Combine the sum (addition) of the whole numbers in Step 1 and the sum (addition) of the fractions in Step 2 into the final sum as shown:

Final sum

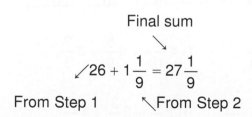

$$\diagup 26 + 1\frac{1}{9} = 27\frac{1}{9}$$

From Step 1 $\diagdown$From Step 2

Exercises

1. Add the following. Hint: See Example **1**

(a) $7\dfrac{2}{5} + 1\dfrac{3}{10}$ (b) $3\dfrac{1}{4} + 2\dfrac{3}{8}$ (c) $10\dfrac{5}{6} + 8\dfrac{2}{3}$ (d) $5\dfrac{5}{9} + 7\dfrac{2}{3}$

(e) $9\dfrac{1}{3} + 10\dfrac{2}{9}$ (f) $17\dfrac{2}{8} + 15\dfrac{2}{16}$ (g) $2\dfrac{11}{12} + 13\dfrac{1}{24}$ (h) $32\dfrac{3}{12} + 15\dfrac{1}{3}$

(i) $7\dfrac{5}{8} + 3\dfrac{1}{4}$ (j) $35\dfrac{7}{9} + 40\dfrac{5}{18}$ (k) $10\dfrac{3}{7} + 7\dfrac{3}{14}$ (l) $9\dfrac{3}{8} + 4\dfrac{7}{24}$

(m) $17\dfrac{2}{5} + 22\dfrac{16}{25}$ (n) $16\dfrac{3}{9} + 2\dfrac{5}{36}$ (o) $6\dfrac{2}{3} + 8\dfrac{5}{12}$ (p) $5\dfrac{3}{5} + 11\dfrac{2}{15}$

2. Add the following. Hint: See Examples **1** and **2**.

(a) $10\dfrac{3}{7}$ (b) $17\dfrac{3}{5}$ (c) $3\dfrac{3}{4}$ (d) $8\dfrac{3}{9}$

     $7\dfrac{3}{14}$ $11\dfrac{2}{10}$ $27\dfrac{5}{12}$ $7\dfrac{4}{18}$

(e) $19\dfrac{4}{5} + 4\dfrac{2}{3}$ (f) $22\dfrac{3}{4} + 7\dfrac{1}{16}$ (g) $31\dfrac{5}{12} + 1\dfrac{3}{4}$ (h) $20\dfrac{2}{7} + 11\dfrac{2}{21}$

(i) $3\dfrac{3}{12} + 6\dfrac{2}{3}$ (j) $5\dfrac{3}{8} + 2\dfrac{2}{24}$ (k) $7\dfrac{5}{7} + \dfrac{11}{14}$ (l) $7\dfrac{5}{7} + 2\dfrac{2}{14}$

(m) $11\dfrac{9}{11} + 3\dfrac{15}{22}$ (n) $6\dfrac{7}{33} + 4\dfrac{10}{11}$ (o) $5\dfrac{3}{7} + 6\dfrac{4}{21}$ (p) $9\dfrac{3}{4} + 6\dfrac{4}{5}$

3. Add the following. Hint: See Examples **3** and **4**.

(a) $4\dfrac{2}{3} + 3\dfrac{3}{4} + 7\dfrac{5}{12}$ (b) $3\dfrac{4}{7} + 4\dfrac{4}{21} + 6\dfrac{5}{7}$ (c) $5\dfrac{3}{5} + 2\dfrac{7}{10} + 1\dfrac{7}{20}$

(d) $9\dfrac{5}{16} + 1\dfrac{7}{8} + 8\dfrac{3}{4}$ (e) $7\dfrac{2}{3} + 4\dfrac{4}{9} + 2\dfrac{5}{18}$ (f) $4\dfrac{7}{18} + 9\dfrac{5}{9} + 3\dfrac{2}{3}$

(g) $29\dfrac{1}{4} + 10\dfrac{5}{12} + 6\dfrac{3}{8}$ (h) $2\dfrac{3}{7} + 22\dfrac{11}{21} + 1\dfrac{1}{42}$ (i) $2\dfrac{3}{4} + 3\dfrac{3}{8} + 4\dfrac{1}{2}$

(j) $6\dfrac{2}{3} + 4\dfrac{1}{4} + 7\dfrac{5}{6}$ (k) $5\dfrac{2}{3} + 7\dfrac{1}{4} + 2\dfrac{5}{6}$ (l) $4\dfrac{5}{8} + 4\dfrac{9}{16} + 2\dfrac{27}{32}$

(m) $3\dfrac{1}{3} + 4\dfrac{5}{6} + 10\dfrac{5}{8}$ **(n)** $2\dfrac{11}{16} + 1\dfrac{21}{64} + 3\dfrac{3}{4}$ **(o)** $4\dfrac{6}{7} + \dfrac{3}{14} + 2\dfrac{5}{28}$

(p) $\dfrac{3}{5} + 7\dfrac{7}{25} + \dfrac{49}{50}$ **(q)** $2\dfrac{2}{5} + 2\dfrac{2}{3} + 1\dfrac{1}{5}$ **(r)** $1\dfrac{3}{4} + 2 + 2\dfrac{3}{5}$

4. Add the following. Hint: See Examples **3** and **4**.

(a) $\begin{array}{r} 3\frac{3}{4} \\ 4\frac{3}{8} \\ 7\frac{1}{2} \\ \hline \end{array}$ **(b)** $\begin{array}{r} 5\frac{3}{4} \\ \frac{4}{5} \\ 12\frac{1}{2} \\ \hline \end{array}$ **(c)** $\begin{array}{r} 9\frac{2}{3} \\ \frac{1}{4} \\ \frac{5}{6} \\ \hline \end{array}$ **(d)** $\begin{array}{r} 7\frac{4}{5} \\ 5\frac{12}{15} \\ 8\frac{5}{6} \\ \hline \end{array}$ **(e)** $\begin{array}{r} 5\frac{1}{3} \\ 30\frac{5}{8} \\ 7\frac{5}{6} \\ \hline \end{array}$

(f) $\begin{array}{r} 4\frac{19}{28} \\ 20\frac{5}{7} \\ 3\frac{9}{14} \\ \hline \end{array}$ **(g)** $\begin{array}{r} 7\frac{2}{3} \\ 8\frac{4}{5} \\ 5\frac{7}{10} \\ \hline \end{array}$ **(h)** $\begin{array}{r} 2\frac{3}{4} \\ 7\frac{5}{8} \\ 12\frac{3}{5} \\ \hline \end{array}$ **(i)** $\begin{array}{r} 24\frac{31}{32} \\ 7\frac{9}{16} \\ 12\frac{3}{8} \\ \hline \end{array}$ **(j)** $\begin{array}{r} 10\frac{1}{2} \\ 7\frac{3}{8} \\ 5\frac{3}{4} \\ \hline \end{array}$

(k) $\begin{array}{r} 4\frac{2}{3} \\ 6\frac{3}{4} \\ 7\frac{5}{6} \\ \hline \end{array}$ **(l)** $\begin{array}{r} 7\frac{5}{6} \\ 8\frac{7}{12} \\ 5\frac{3}{4} \\ \hline \end{array}$ **(m)** $\begin{array}{r} 4\frac{1}{3} \\ \frac{5}{6} \\ 3\frac{1}{4} \\ \hline \end{array}$ **(n)** $\begin{array}{r} 22\frac{1}{2} \\ 3\frac{2}{3} \\ 2\frac{5}{12} \\ \hline \end{array}$ **(o)** $\begin{array}{r} 5\frac{1}{7} \\ 6\frac{3}{14} \\ 4\frac{3}{4} \\ \hline \end{array}$

Answers to Selected Questions

1(a) $8\dfrac{7}{10}$ **2(a)** $17\dfrac{9}{14}$ **3(a)** $15\dfrac{5}{6}$ **3(o)** $7\dfrac{7}{28} = 7\dfrac{1}{4}$ **4(a)** $14\dfrac{13}{8} = 15\dfrac{5}{8}$

REAL WORLD APPLICATIONS - WORD PROBLEMS
Addition of Mixed Fractions

Example 1

If I traveled $40\frac{1}{4}$ miles, $13\frac{1}{8}$ miles, and $15\frac{7}{24}$ miles in one day, what is the total number of miles that I traveled?

Solution

The total number of miles traveled $= 40\frac{1}{4} + 13\frac{1}{8} + 15\frac{7}{24}$

(**Notice** that in Step 1, an imaginary line | separates the whole numbers from the fractions so that we can work on the whole numbers and fractions separately.)

Step 1: Add the whole numbers first.

$40| \dfrac{1}{4}$

$13| \dfrac{1}{8}$

$15| \dfrac{7}{24}$

$\overline{68}$

Addition of whole numbers

Step 2: Add the fractions second. (Review Addition of Fractions) In order to add fractions, find the LCD.

Determine LCD.

$40| \dfrac{1}{4} = \dfrac{}{24}$ ⟋LCM

$13| \dfrac{1}{8} = \dfrac{}{24}$ ⟋LCM

$15| \dfrac{7}{24} = \dfrac{}{24}$ ⟋LCM

$\overline{68}$

Write the equivalent fractions, and then add the fractions.

$40| \dfrac{1}{4} \times \dfrac{6}{6} = \dfrac{6}{24}$

$13| \dfrac{1}{8} \times \dfrac{3}{3} = \dfrac{3}{24}$

$15| \dfrac{7}{24} \times \dfrac{1}{1} = \dfrac{7}{24}$

$\dfrac{\overline{16}}{24}$

Addition of fractions

Notice that $\dfrac{16}{24}$ can be reduced to $\dfrac{2}{3}$ by dividing the numerator and the denominator of $\dfrac{16}{24}$ by 8.

Step 3: Combine the sum (addition) of the whole numbers in Step 1 and the sum (addition) of the fractions in Step 2 into the final sum as shown:

From Step 1 ⟋$68 + \dfrac{2}{3} = 68\dfrac{2}{3}$ miles

From Step 2   Final sum

Example 2:

Mary bought $8\dfrac{1}{2}$ pounds of pears, $3\dfrac{2}{3}$ pounds of apples, and $4\dfrac{5}{6}$ pounds of cherries.
How many pounds of fruit did she buy?
Solution

The total number of pounds of fruit bought by Mary $= 8\dfrac{1}{2} + 3\dfrac{2}{3} + 4\dfrac{5}{6}$

(**Notice** that in Step 1, an imaginary line | separates the whole numbers from the fractions so that we can work on the whole numbers and the fractions separately.)

Step 1: Add the whole
      numbers first

Step 2: Add the fraction second.
      (Review fraction addition)
      In order to add fractions, find the LCD.
      Write the equivalent fractions,
      Determine the LCD.   and then add the fractions.

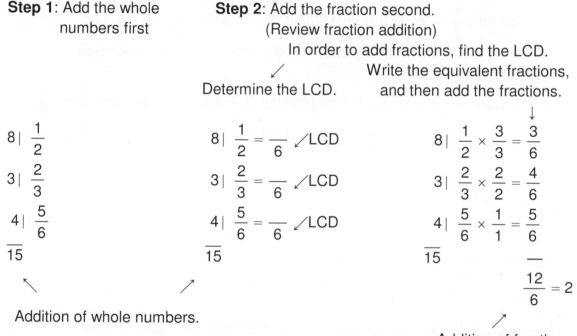

Addition of whole numbers.

Addition of fractions.

Step 3: Combine the sum (addition) of the whole numbers in Step 1 and the sum
      (addition) of the fractions in Step 2 into the final sum as shown:

$$\overset{\text{Final sum}}{15 + 2 = 17}$$

From step 1.   From step 2
Mary bought 17 pounds of fruits.

395

The notes and the generous worked examples have provided me with conceptual understanding and computational fluency to do my homework.

Exercises

1. A school project needs $6\frac{2}{3}$ inches, $8\frac{1}{2}$ inches and $4\frac{5}{12}$ inches of pipe. How many inches of pipe is needed? Hint: See Example **2**.

2. John needs $3\frac{2}{3}$ feet, $7\frac{1}{4}$ feet, and $2\frac{3}{4}$ feet of wood for a school project. How many feet of wood is needed by John for the total project? Hint: See Example **2**.

3. Rose walked $1\frac{1}{2}$ miles to the Post Office, $1\frac{5}{7}$ miles to the cinema, and $1\frac{3}{14}$ miles to the market. How many miles did she walk altogether? Hint: See Example **1**.

4. A baker used $3\frac{2}{3}$ dozen of eggs on Monday, $2\frac{3}{4}$ dozen on Tuesday, and $3\frac{1}{6}$ dozen on Wednesday for various mixes. How many dozen of eggs did the baker use? Hint: See Example **2**.

Challenge Questions

5. A plumber needs $8\frac{2}{3}$ inches, $6\frac{1}{6}$ inches, and $9\frac{1}{24}$ inches of pipe. What is the total length of the pipe that the plumber needs?

6. Rose bought three packages of meat weighing $6\frac{1}{5}$ pounds, 10 pounds, and $15\frac{2}{15}$ pounds. What was the total weight of the three packages of meat?

SUBTRACTION OF FRACTIONS

Rule 1: In order to subtract fractions, follow the three steps as follow:
Step 1: First find the least common denominator (LCD).
Step 2: Change each fraction to an equivalent fraction that has the same least common denominator (LCD).
Step 3: Subtract the numerators and write the difference of the numerators over the least common denominator (LCD).

Rule 2: The large or largest denominator in the question can, at times, be used as the least common denominator.

Rule 3: Knowing the multiplication tables from 1 to 12 will help to quickly identify the least common denominator (LCD).

Example 1

Subtract: $\dfrac{1}{2} - \dfrac{1}{4}$

Solution

Step 1: Find the least common denominator which is 4 because the denominator

of $\dfrac{1}{2}$ which is 2 can divide evenly (without any remainder) the denominator

of $\dfrac{1}{4}$ which is 4. Notice that rule 2 is being used.

$$\frac{1}{2} = \frac{\ }{4} \quad \checkmark \text{ least common denominator (LCD)}$$

$$\frac{1}{4} = \frac{\ }{4} \quad \checkmark \text{ least common denominator (LCD)}$$

Step 2: Write equivalent fractions. Review the section on Equivalent Fractions.

$$\frac{1}{2} = \frac{1}{2} \times \frac{2}{4} = \frac{2}{4} \leftarrow \text{ Equivalent fraction}$$

$$-\frac{1}{4} = -\frac{1}{4} \times \frac{1}{1} = -\frac{1}{4} \leftarrow \text{ Equivalent fraction}$$

Step 3: Subtract the numerators of the equivalent fractions and write the difference of the numerators of the equivalent fractions over the least common denominator (LCD) or over the common equivalent denominator to get the final difference as shown:

$$\overset{\diagup \text{Difference of the numerators of the equivalent fraction}}{\frac{2-1}{4} = \frac{1}{4}}$$

$\diagdown$ Common equivalent denominator or LCD

Example 2

Subtract: $\dfrac{3}{4} - \dfrac{2}{5}$

Solution

Step 1: Find the least common denominator. In order to find the LCD, we should find the least number that can be divided by both the denominators 4 and

5 evenly (without any remainder).

The multiples of 4 are:

$4 \times 1 = 4, 4 \times 2 = 8, 4 \times 3 = 12, 4 \times 4 = 16, 4 \times 5 = 20, 4 \times 6 = 24, \ldots$

Therefore the multiples of 4 are: 4, 8, 12, 16, 20, 24, . . .

The multiples of 5 are:

$5 \times 1 = 5, 5 \times 2 = 10, 5 \times 3 = 15, 5 \times 4 = 20, . \quad . \quad .$

$\downarrow$

Stop here because 20 appears as a multiple of 4. Since 20 is the smallest number that appears as the multiple of both 4 and 5, 20 is the LCD.

$\dfrac{3}{4} = \dfrac{}{20}$ ⟋LCD   Observe both sides of the equation, the denominator 4

must be multiplied by 5 in order to obtain the equivalent denominator of 20, and therefore, the numerator of 3 must also be multiplied by 5 to obtain 15 as shown in Step 2.

$-\dfrac{2}{5} = -\dfrac{}{20}$ ⟋LCD   Observe both sides of the equation, the denominator 5

must be multiplied by 4 in order to obtain the equivalent denominator of 20, and therefore, the numerator of 2 must also be multiplied by 4 to obtain an equivalent numerator of 8 as shown in Step 2.

Step 2: Write equivalent fractions. Review the section on Equivalent Fractions.

$$\dfrac{3}{4} = \dfrac{3}{4} \times \dfrac{5}{5} = \dfrac{15}{20} \leftarrow \text{Equivalent fraction}$$

$$-\dfrac{2}{5} = -\dfrac{2}{5} \times \dfrac{4}{4} = -\dfrac{8}{20} \leftarrow \text{Equivalent fraction}$$

Step 3: Subtract the numerators of the equivalent fractions and write the difference of the numerators of the equivalent fractions over the least common denominator (LCD) or over the common equivalent denominator of 20 to get the final difference as shown:

⟋Difference of the numerators of the equivalent fractions

$$\dfrac{15 - 8}{20} = \dfrac{7}{20}$$

⟍Denominator of the common equivalent fraction or LCD

Example 3

Subtract: $\dfrac{2}{3} - \dfrac{1}{7}$

Solution

Step 1: Find the LCD.

In order to find the LCD, we should find the least number that can be divided by both the denominators 3 and 7 evenly (without a remainder) by using multiples.

The multiples of 3 are:

$3 \times 1 = 3,\ 3 \times 2 = 6,\ 3 \times 3 = 9,\ 3 \times 4 = 12,\ 3 \times 5 = 15,\ 3 \times 6 = 18,\ 3 \times 7 = 21,$
$3 \times 8 = 24,\ \ldots$

Therefore, the multiples of 3 are: 3, 6, 9, 12, 15, 18, 21, 24, . . .

The multiples of 7 are:

$7 \times 1 = 7,\ 7 \times 2 = 14,\ 7 \times 3 = 21,\ . \ . \ . \ . \ . \ . \ .$

$\downarrow$

Stop here because 21 also appears as a multiple of 3. Since 21 appears as the smallest number that appears as a multiple of 3 and 7, 21 is the LCD.

$$\frac{2}{3} = \frac{}{21}\ \diagup \text{LCD}$$

Observe both sides of the equation above. The denominator 3 must be multiplied by 7 in order to obtain the equivalent denominator (LCD) of 21, and the numerator of 2 must also be multiplied by 7 to obtain 14 as shown in Step 2.

$$-\frac{1}{7} = -\frac{}{21}\ \diagup \text{LCD}$$

Observe both sides of the equation above. The denominator of 7 must be multiplied by 3 in order to obtain the equivalent denominator (LCD) of 21, and the numerator of 1 must also be multiplied by 3 in order to obtain the equivalent numerator of 3 as shown in Step 2.

Step 2: Write equivalent fractions. Review the section on Equivalent Fractions.

$$\frac{2}{3} \times \frac{7}{7} = \frac{14}{21}\ \leftarrow \text{Equivalent fraction}$$

$$-\frac{1}{7} \times \frac{3}{3} = -\frac{3}{21}\ \leftarrow\text{Equivalent fraction}$$

Step 3: Subtract the numerators of the equivalent fractions and write the difference of the numerators of the equivalent fractions over the least common equivalent denominator (LCD) to get the final difference as shown:

Difference of the numerators of the equivalent fractions

$$\frac{14-3}{21} = \frac{11}{21} \quad \text{Common equivalent denominator or the LCD}$$

Example 4

Solve: $\dfrac{5}{6} - \dfrac{3}{8}$

Solution

Step 1: Find the LCD.

In order to find the LCD, we should find the least common number that can be divided by both 6 and 8 evenly (without a remainder) by using multiples. The multiples of 6 are:

$6 \times 1 = 6, 6 \times 2 = 12, 6 \times 3 = 18, 6 \times 4 = 24, 6 \times 5 = 30, \ldots$

Therefore, the multiples of 6 are: 6, 12, 18, 24, 30, . . .

The multiples of 8 are:

$8 \times 1 = 8, 8 \times 2 = 16, 8 \times 3 = 24, \ldots$

↓

Stop here because 24 also appears as a multiple of 6. Since 24 appears as the smallest number that appears as a multiple of both 6 and 8, 24 is the LCD.

$$\frac{5}{6} = \frac{}{24} \quad \text{LCD}$$

Observe both sides of the equation above. The denominator 6 must be multiplied by 4 in order to obtain the equivalent denominator (LCD) of 24, and the numerator of 5 must also be multiplied by 4 to obtain 20 as shown in Step 2.

$$-\frac{3}{8} = -\frac{}{24} \quad \text{LCD}$$

Observe both sides of the equation above. The denominator of 8 must be multiplied by 3 in order to obtain the equivalent denominator (LCD) of 24, and the numerator of 3 must also be multiplied by 3 in order to obtain the equivalent numerator of 9 as shown in Step 2.

Step 2: Write equivalent fractions. Review the topic on Equivalent Fractions.

$$\frac{5}{6} = \frac{5}{6} \times \frac{4}{4} = \frac{20}{24} \quad \leftarrow \text{Equivalent fraction.}$$

$$-\frac{3}{8} = -\frac{3}{8} \times \frac{3}{3} = -\frac{9}{24} \leftarrow \text{Equivalent fraction.}$$

Step 3: Subtract the numerators of the equivalent fractions and write the difference of the numerators of the equivalent fractions over the least common denominator (LCD) or over the common equivalent denominator to get the final difference as shown:

$$\overset{\displaystyle\diagup\text{Difference of the numerators of the equivalent fractions}}{\frac{20-9}{24} = \frac{11}{24}}$$

$\diagdown$ Common equivalent denominator or LCD

The notes and the generous worked examples have provided me with conceptual understanding and computational fluency to do my homework.

Exercises

1. State the three steps for doing subtraction.

2. What is meant by LCD?

3. Subtract the following. Hint: See Example **1**.

(a) $\dfrac{3}{4} - \dfrac{1}{8}$ (b) $\dfrac{7}{8} - \dfrac{3}{16}$ (c) $\dfrac{4}{5} - \dfrac{2}{10}$ (d) $\dfrac{5}{6} - \dfrac{3}{12}$ (e) $\dfrac{8}{9} - \dfrac{2}{3}$

4. Subtract the following. Hint: See Examples **2**, **3**, and **4**.

(a) $\dfrac{4}{5} - \dfrac{1}{4}$ (b) $\dfrac{5}{6} - \dfrac{1}{8}$ (c) $\dfrac{3}{5} - \dfrac{1}{3}$ (d) $\dfrac{4}{5} - \dfrac{3}{7}$ (e) $\dfrac{2}{3} - \dfrac{1}{7}$

(f) $\dfrac{2}{3} - \dfrac{2}{4}$ (g) $\dfrac{5}{7} - \dfrac{3}{8}$ (h) $\dfrac{4}{5} - \dfrac{2}{3}$ (i) $\dfrac{5}{6} - \dfrac{3}{8}$ (j) $\dfrac{3}{4} - \dfrac{1}{3}$

(k) $\dfrac{5}{8} - \dfrac{1}{3}$ (l) $\dfrac{2}{3} - \dfrac{1}{5}$ (m) $\dfrac{5}{6} - \dfrac{3}{4}$ (n) $\dfrac{4}{5} - \dfrac{3}{4}$ (o) $\dfrac{7}{8} - \dfrac{1}{5}$

Challenge Questions

(a) $\dfrac{10}{11} - \dfrac{2}{3}$ (b) $\dfrac{5}{7} - \dfrac{1}{6}$ (c) $\dfrac{5}{7} - \dfrac{4}{14}$ (d) $\dfrac{9}{10} - \dfrac{3}{5}$ (e) $\dfrac{1}{6} - \dfrac{3}{4}$

Answers to Selected Questions

3(a) $\dfrac{5}{8}$ 3(c) $\dfrac{6}{10}$ or $\dfrac{3}{5}$ 4(a) $\dfrac{11}{20}$ 4(c) $\dfrac{4}{15}$

REAL WORLD APPLICATIONS - WORD PROBLEMS
Subtraction of Fractions

Example 1

Rose bought $\dfrac{3}{4}$ pound of sugar and she used $\dfrac{3}{16}$ pound for baking. How much sugar was left?

Solution

The amount of sugar left is $\dfrac{3}{4}$ - $\dfrac{3}{16}$.

The subtraction is done just like the previous examples under the heading Subtraction of Fraction

Step 1: Find the LCD.

In order to find the LCD, we should find the least common number that can be divided by both the denominators of 4 and 16 evenly (without a remainder) by using multiples.

The multiples of 4 are:

$4 \times 1 = 4, 4 \times 2 = 8, 4 \times 3 = 12, 4 \times 4 = 16, 4 \times 5 = 20, 4 \times 6 = 24, \ldots$

Therefore, the multiples of 4 are:

4, 8, 12, 16, 20, 24, . . .

The multiples of 16 are:

$16 \times 1 = 16, \ldots$

↓

Stop here because 16 also appears as a multiple of 4. Since 16 appears as the smallest number that appears as the multiple of 4 and 16,16 is the LCD. [Shortcut: By knowing the multiplication tables, $4 \times 4 = 16$ therefore, 4 can divide into 16 evenly (without any remainder), and therefore, we can know mentally that the LCD of 4 and 16 is 16.]

$$\dfrac{3}{4} = \dfrac{}{16}$$

↖

LCD

Observe both sides of the equation above. The denominator of 4 must be multiplied by 4 in order to obtain the equivalent denominator of 16, and the numerator of 3 must also be multiplied by 4 to obtain 12 as shown in Step 2.

$$-\frac{3}{16} = -\frac{}{16}$$

$$\nwarrow$$
$$\text{LCD}$$

Observe both sides of the equation above. The denominator of 16 at the left side of the equation is the same as the denominator of 16 at the right side of the equation, and he numerator of 3 on the left hand side of the equation must be the same (3) at the right side of the equation as shown in Step 2.

Step 2: Write equivalent fractions. Review the section on Equivalent Fractions.

$$\frac{3}{4} \times \frac{4}{4} = \frac{12}{16} \leftarrow \text{Equivalent fraction.}$$

$$-\frac{3}{16} \times \frac{1}{1} = -\frac{3}{16} \leftarrow \text{Equivalent fraction.}$$

Step 3: Subtract the numerators of the equivalent fractions and write the difference of the numerators of the equivalent fractions over the least common denominator (LCD) or over the common equivalent denominator to get the final difference as shown:

Difference of the numerators of the equivalent fraction

$$\nearrow$$

$$\frac{12 - 3}{16} = \frac{9}{16} \text{ pound of sugar}$$

$$\nwarrow$$

Common equivalent denominator or LCD

$\frac{9}{16}$ pound of sugar was left.

Example 2

A company bought $\frac{3}{4}$ ton of drinking water and used up $\frac{1}{2}$ ton. How much of the drinking water is left. (**Notice** that this problem is solved without detailed explanation as in Example 1. The student may see Example 1 for the similar detailed explanation.)

Solution

The amount of the drinking water left is $\frac{3}{4} - \frac{1}{2}$.

Step 1: Find the LCD.

Since the denominator 2 can divide 4 evenly (without a remainder), 4 is the LCD of 2 and 4.

$$\frac{3}{4} = \frac{}{4} \quad \swarrow \text{LCD}$$

$$-\frac{1}{2} = -\frac{}{4} \quad \swarrow \text{LCD}$$

Step 2: Write equivalent fractions. Review the sections on Equivalent Fractions.

$$\frac{3}{4} \times \frac{1}{1} = \frac{3}{4} \quad \leftarrow \text{Equivalent fraction}$$

$$-\frac{1}{2} \times \frac{2}{2} = -\frac{2}{4} \quad \leftarrow \text{Equivalent fraction}$$

Step 3: Subtract the numerators of the equivalent fractions and write the difference of the numerators of the equivalent fractions over the least common denominator (LCD) to get the final difference as shown:

Difference of the numerators of the equivalent fractions

$$\frac{3-2}{4} = \frac{1}{4} \text{ ton of drinking water}$$

LCD or the common denominator of the equivalent fractions.

Example 3

Samuel bought $\frac{3}{4}$ pound of beef and ate $\frac{3}{8}$ pound for lunch. How much of the beef is left ?

Solution

(For similar detailed explanation, see Example 1.)

The amount of beef left is $\frac{3}{4} - \frac{3}{8}$

Step 1: Find the LCD.

Since denominator of 4 can divide the denominator of 8 evenly (without any remainder), 8 is the LCD of 4 and 8.

$$\frac{3}{4} = \frac{}{8} \quad \swarrow \text{LCD}$$

$$-\frac{3}{8} = -\frac{}{8} \quad \swarrow \text{LCD}$$

Step 2: Write equivalent fractions. Review the sections on Equivalent Fractions.

$$\frac{3}{4} \times \frac{2}{2} = \frac{6}{8} \quad \leftarrow \text{Equivalent fractions}$$

$$-\frac{3}{8} \times \frac{1}{1} = -\frac{3}{8} \quad \leftarrow \text{Equivalent fractions}$$

Step 3: Subtract the numerators of the equivalent fractions and write the difference over the least common denominator (LCD) or over the common denominator of the equivalent fraction to get the final difference as shown:

Difference of the numerators of the equivalent fractions

$$\frac{6-3}{8} = \frac{3}{8} \quad \text{pound of beef}$$

LCD or the common denominator of the equivalent fractions

$\frac{3}{8}$ pound of the beef is left.

Example 4

Joshua bought $\frac{7}{8}$ of a yard of material for a school project. If he only used $\frac{5}{6}$ of a yard, how much material was left?

Solution

(For similar detailed explanation, see Example 1.)

The material left is $\frac{7}{8} - \frac{5}{6}$.

Step 1: Find the LCD.

The denominators of the fractions are 8 and 6, however, 6 cannot divide 8 evenly (without any remainder), and therefore, 8 cannot be the LCD for 6 and 8.

Shortcut to find any LCD: Multiply the denominators together, then reduce the product of the denominators to the smallest number that can be divided by the denominators evenly (without any remainder), and **this smallest number is the LCD**. To find the LCD of 8 and 6, multiply 8 and 6 which is 48, then reduce 48 to the smallest number that can be divided by both 8 and 6 evenly (without a remainder) if possible. 48 can be reduced to 24 by dividing 48 by 2, and knowing from the " Multiplication Table" that $6 \times 4 = 24$ and $8 \times 3 = 24$, 24 is the least number that can be divided evenly (without a remainder), and therefore, 24 is the LCD.

$$\frac{7}{8} = \frac{}{24} \diagup \text{LCD}$$

$$-\frac{5}{6} = -\frac{}{24} \diagup \text{L CD}$$

Step 2: Write equivalent fractions. Review the sections on Equivalent Fractions.

$$\frac{7}{8} \times \frac{3}{3} = \frac{21}{24} \leftarrow \text{Equivalent fractions}$$

$$-\frac{5}{6} \times \frac{4}{4} = -\frac{20}{24} \leftarrow \text{Equivalent fractions}$$

Step 3: Subtract the numerators of the equivalent fractions and write the difference of the numerators of the equivalent fractions over the least common denominator (LCD) or over the common equivalent denominator to get the final difference shown:

$$\frac{21-20}{24} = \frac{1}{24} \text{ of a yard of material was left.}$$

The notes and the generous worked examples have provided me with conceptual understanding and computational fluency to do my homework.

Exercises

1. Samuel used $\frac{3}{4}$ cup of sugar and $\frac{1}{2}$ cup of milk to bake some cakes. How much more sugar than milk did he use? (Hint: Samuel used $\frac{3}{4} - \frac{1}{2}$ cup more of sugar than milk.) Hint: See Examples **1** to **4**.

2. John bought $\frac{6}{7}$ ton of coal and used up $\frac{1}{2}$ ton. How much coal was left? Hint: See Examples **1** to **4**.

3. Nick bought $\frac{3}{5}$ pound of beef and ate $\frac{1}{4}$ pound for lunch. How much of the beef was left? Hint: See Examples **1** to **4**.

4. John bought $\frac{7}{9}$ of a yard of material for a school project. If he only used $\frac{1}{4}$ of a yard, how much material was left? Hint: See Examples **1** to **4**.

5. Karen is $\frac{9}{10}$ meter tall and Mabel is $\frac{4}{5}$ meter tall. How much taller is Karen?

Hint: See Examples **1** to **4**.

6. A bag contained $\frac{9}{10}$ pound of salt. If $\frac{2}{8}$ pound were used, how much of the salt remained? Hint: See Examples **1** to **4**.

7. Rose had $\frac{5}{6}$ yard of fabric. If she used $\frac{3}{4}$ yard, how much fabric is left?

Hint: See Examples **1** to **4**.

SUBTRACTION OF MIXED NUMBERS

Subtraction often involves the technique known as **borrowing**. **Borrowing** is necessary when subtracting a larger digit number from a smaller digit number. You will learn about the technique of borrowing later in this chapter.

In the subtraction of mixed numbers, subtract the fractions first, and then subtract the whole numbers, see Example **3**.

The steps for subtracting mixed numbers are:
Step 1: **Arrange the mixed numbers, one under the other and find the LCD.**
Step 2: **Write equivalent fractions.**
Step 3: **Subtract the equivalent fractions first by subtracting the numerators and put the difference over the equivalent denominator and if borrowing of a whole number is necessary, do so.**
Step 4: **Subtract the whole numbers and combine the subtraction of whole numbers and the subtraction of the equivalent fractions into the final answer.**

Example 1
Subtract: $3\frac{5}{8} - 2\frac{5}{16}$

Solution
(**Notice** that in Step 1, an imaginary line | separates the whole numbers from the fractions so that we can work on the whole numbers and the fractions separately.)

Step 1: Arrange the mixed numbers, one under the other and find the LCD.
(Review the section on LCD)

$$3 \,|\, \frac{5}{8} = \frac{}{16} \;\diagup\; \text{LCD}$$

$$-\,2 \,|\, \frac{5}{16} = -\frac{}{16} \;\diagup\; \text{LCD}$$

8 can divide evenly into 16 (without any remainder) and therefore, 16 is the LCD of 8 and 16.

Step 2: Write equivalent fractions.

From Step 1, the denominator of $\frac{5}{8}$ which is 8 must have been multiplied by 2 to get the equivalent denominator of 16, and therefore, both the numerator and the denominator of $\frac{5}{8}$ in Step 2 should be multiplied by 2 as shown:

$$3 \,|\, \frac{5}{8} \times \frac{2}{2} = \frac{10}{16} \quad \leftarrow \text{Equivalent fraction}$$

From Step 1, the denominator of $\frac{5}{16}$ which is 16 must have been multiplied by 1 to get the equivalent denominator of 16 and therefore, both the numerator and the denominator of $\frac{5}{16}$ in Step 2 should be multiplied by 1 as shown:

$$2 \,|\, \frac{5}{16} \times \frac{1}{1} = \frac{5}{16} \quad \leftarrow \text{Equivalent fraction.}$$

Step 3: Subtract the equivalent fractions first by subtracting the numerators and put the difference over the equivalent denominator and if "borrowing" of a whole number is necessary, do so. (**Note**: "Borrowing" of a whole number is not needed in this case because $\frac{5}{16}$ is less than $\frac{10}{16}$.)

$$3 \,|\, \frac{5}{8} \times \frac{2}{2} = \frac{10}{16} \quad \leftarrow \text{Equivalent fraction}$$

$$-\,2 \,|\, \frac{5}{16} \times \frac{1}{1} = -\frac{5}{16} \quad \leftarrow \text{Equivalent fraction}$$

$$\frac{10-5}{16} = \frac{5}{16} \quad \diagup \text{Difference of the equivalent numerators}$$

$$\diagdown \text{Equivalent denominator}$$

Step 4: Subtract the whole numbers and combine the subtraction of the whole numbers and the subtraction of the equivalent fractions into the final answer. (**Notice** that an imaginary line | separates the whole numbers from the fractions so that we can work on the whole numbers and fractions separately.)

$$3| \quad \frac{5}{8} \times \frac{2}{2} = \quad \frac{10}{16}$$

$$-2| \quad \frac{5}{16} \times \frac{1}{1} = -\frac{5}{16}$$

$$\overline{1}$$

Subtraction of whole numbers.

/Difference of the equivalent numerators

$$\frac{10-5}{16} = \frac{5}{16}$$

\Equivalent denominator

Combine the whole number which is 1 and the fraction which is $\frac{5}{16}$ into a final answer of $1\frac{5}{16}$.

Therefore, $3\frac{5}{8} - 2\frac{5}{16} = 1\frac{5}{16}$

Example 2

Subtract: $7\frac{3}{4} - 5\frac{1}{5}$

Solution

Step 1: Arrange the mixed numbers, one under the other and find the LCD.

$$7| \quad \frac{3}{4} = \frac{}{20} \quad \text{/LCD}$$

$$-5| \quad \frac{1}{5} = -\frac{}{20} \quad \text{/LCD}$$

Multiply the denominators 4 and 5 to obtain the LCD of 20. Note that 20 is the smallest number that can be divided by both 4 and 5 evenly (without any remainder).

Step 2: Write equivalent fractions.

From Step 1, the denominator of 4 must have been multiplied by 5 to get the equivalent denominator of 20, and therefore, both the numerator and the denominator of $\frac{3}{4}$ in Step 2 should be multiplied by 5 as shown:

$$7| \quad \frac{3}{4} \times \frac{5}{5} = \frac{15}{20} \quad \leftarrow \text{Equivalent fraction}$$

From Step 1, the denominator of $\frac{1}{5}$ which is 5 must have been multiplied by 4 to get the equivalent denominator of 20, and therefore, both the numerator and the denominator of $\frac{1}{5}$ in Step 2 should be multiplied by 4 as shown:

$$-5 \mid \frac{1}{5} \times \frac{4}{4} = -\frac{4}{20} \quad \leftarrow \text{Equivalent fraction}$$

Step 3: Subtract the equivalent fractions first by subtracting the numerators of the equivalent fractions and put the difference over the equivalent denominator, and if "borrowing" of a whole number is necessary, do so. (**Note** that borrowing of a whole number is not needed in this case because $\frac{4}{20}$ is less than $\frac{15}{20}$.)

$$7 \mid \frac{3}{4} \times \frac{5}{5} = \frac{15}{20} \quad \leftarrow \text{Equivalent fraction}$$

$$-5 \mid \frac{1}{5} \times \frac{4}{4} = -\frac{4}{20} \quad \leftarrow \text{Equivalent fraction}$$

$$\underline{\qquad\qquad} \quad \nearrow \text{Difference of the equivalent numerators}$$

$$\frac{15-4}{20} = \frac{11}{20}$$

$$\nwarrow \text{Equivalent denominator or the denominator}$$
$$\text{of the equivalent fraction}$$

Step 4: Subtract the whole numbers and combine the subtraction of the whole numbers and the subtraction of the equivalent fractions into the final answer as shown:

$$7 \mid \frac{3}{4} \times \frac{5}{5} = \frac{15}{20}$$

$$-5 \mid \frac{1}{5} \times \frac{4}{4} = -\frac{4}{20}$$

$$\overline{2} \qquad\qquad \underline{\qquad\qquad} \quad \nearrow \text{Difference of the equivalent numerators.}$$

$$\frac{15-4}{20} = \frac{11}{20}$$

$\nearrow$

Subtraction of whole numbers (7 - 5 = 2.)

Combine the whole number 2 and the fraction $\frac{11}{20}$ into a final answer $2\frac{11}{20}$.

Therefore, $7\frac{3}{4} - 5\frac{1}{5} = 2\frac{11}{20}$.

Example 3

Subtract: $10\frac{2}{5} - 3\frac{5}{6}$

Solution

Step 1: Arrange the mixed numbers, one under the other and find the LCD.

$$10\mid \frac{2}{5} = \frac{\ }{30}\ \diagup LCD$$

(Multiply the denominators 5 and 6 to obtain the LCD of 30. Note that 30 is the smallest number that can

$$-3\mid \frac{5}{6} = -\frac{\ }{30}\ \diagup LCD$$

be divided by both 5 and 6 evenly (without remainder.)

Step 2: Write equivalent fractions.

From Step 1, the denominator 5 must have been multiplied by 6 to get the equivalent denominator of 30 and therefore, both the numerator and the denominator of $\frac{2}{5}$ in Step 2 should be multiplied by 6 as shown:

$$10\mid \frac{2}{5} \times \frac{6}{6} = \frac{12}{30} \quad \leftarrow\text{Equivalent fraction}$$

From Step 1 the denominator of $\frac{5}{6}$ which is 6 must have been multiplied by 5 to get the equivalent denominator of 30, and therefore, both the numerator and the denominator of $\frac{5}{6}$ in Step 2 should be multiplied by 5 as shown:

$$-3\mid \frac{5}{6} \times \frac{5}{5} = -\frac{25}{30} \quad \leftarrow\text{Equivalent fraction}$$

Step 3: Subtract the equivalent fraction first by subtracting the numerators and put the difference over the equivalent denominator, and if "**borrowing**" of a whole number is necessary, do so (Note that "borrowing" of a whole number from 10 is necessary because $\frac{23}{30}$ is greater than $\frac{12}{30}$.) Notice in Step 2 that the numerator of $\frac{25}{30}$ which is 25 is bigger than the numerator of $\frac{12}{30}$ which is 12. Since 25 cannot be taken from 12, borrow 1 from 10 and change 10 to 9. Put the **borrowed** 1 in front of $\frac{12}{30}$, to get the mixed number $1\frac{12}{30}$ as shown:

$$\overset{9}{10}\mid \frac{2}{5} \times \frac{6}{6} = 1\frac{12}{30} \quad \leftarrow \text{Mixed number}$$

$$-3\mid \frac{5}{6} \times \frac{5}{5} = -\frac{25}{30} \quad \leftarrow \text{ Equivalent fraction}$$

Change $1\frac{12}{30}$ to an improper fraction:

Rule: To change a mixed fraction to an improper fraction, multiply the denominator by the whole number, then add the numerator and put the addition over the denominator.

To change $1\frac{12}{30}$ to an improper fraction, multiply 30 by 1 and then add 12

and put the addition over 30. ($1\frac{12}{30}$ becomes $\frac{30 \times 1 + 12}{30} = \frac{42}{30}$.)

Replace $1\frac{12}{30}$ in Step 3 with $\frac{42}{30}$ in the problem and subtract $\frac{25}{30}$ from $\frac{42}{30}$.
Then subtract the whole numbers and combine the two results into a final answer as shown:

$$
\begin{array}{l}
\overset{9}{\cancel{10}}\mid \dfrac{2}{5} \times \dfrac{6}{6} = 1\dfrac{12}{30} \rightarrow \dfrac{42}{30} \\[2mm]
-3\mid \dfrac{5}{6} \times \dfrac{5}{5} = \qquad -\dfrac{25}{30} \\[1mm]
\hline
9-3
\end{array}
$$

$9 - 3 = 6$

$\dfrac{42 - 25}{30} = \dfrac{17}{30}$ ⟋Difference of equivalent numerators

⟍Difference of the whole number

Combine the whole number and the final fraction to obtain the final answer $6\frac{17}{30}$.

Therefore, $10\frac{2}{5} - 3\frac{5}{6} = 6\frac{17}{30}$.

.

Special Note to the Student

The method for solving Example **3** is long, but Example **3** provides a logical detailed method of solving the problem so that the students can understand the detailed logic of the mathematics. Once the detailed logic is understood, the student does not need to write detailed explanations during actual problem solving in class or during test. See Example **6** for a shortcut method involving "borrowing" to be used to solve problems and also Example **5** shows a shortcut method which does not involve "borrowing."

Example 4

Subtract: $10\dfrac{2}{5} - 3\dfrac{5}{6}$

Note that Example **4** is the same problem as Example **3**, however, Example **4** shows an alternate solution method to that of Example **3** where the whole number borrowed is changed to an equivalent fraction that has the common denominator as shown in Step 3.

Solution

Step 1: Find the LCD as in Step 1 of Example 3.

$$10\mid \frac{2}{5} = \frac{}{30} \quad \diagup\text{LCD}$$

$$-3\mid \frac{5}{6} = -\frac{}{30} \quad \diagup\text{LCD}$$

Step 2: Find the equivalent fraction as in Step 2 of Example 3.

$$10\mid \frac{2}{5} \times \frac{6}{6} = \frac{12}{30} \quad \leftarrow \text{Equivalent fraction}$$

$$-3\mid \frac{5}{6} \times \frac{5}{5} = -\frac{25}{30} \quad \leftarrow \text{Equivalent fraction}$$

Step 3: From Step 2, it can be seen that since $\dfrac{25}{30}$ is bigger than $\dfrac{12}{30}$, we cannot subtract the numerator of $\dfrac{25}{30}$ which is 25 from the numerator of $\dfrac{12}{30}$ which is 12. Therefore, as in Example **3**, we have to borrow 1 from the whole number of 10. The borrowed 1 should be written as an equivalent fraction that has a common denominator of 30. The borrowed 1 then becomes: $1 = \dfrac{30}{30}$. (Recall that the value of any fraction which has the same number as the numerator and the denominator is 1.) Add the borrowed $\dfrac{30}{30}$ to $\dfrac{12}{30}$ and then subtract as already done in Example **3** as shown:

$$
\overset{9}{10}\mid \frac{2}{5} \times \frac{6}{6} = \frac{12}{30} + \frac{30}{30} \qquad \frac{42}{30}
$$

$\diagup$Addition of numerators

$$-3 \mid \frac{5}{6} \times \frac{5}{5} = -\frac{25}{30} \qquad \rightarrow \quad -\frac{25}{30}$$

$$\overline{9 \cdot 3}$$

$$9 - 3 = 6$$

↙ Subtraction of numerators

$$\frac{42 - 25}{30} = \frac{17}{30} \leftarrow \text{Final fraction.}$$

↖ Whole number subtraction

Combine the whole number which is 6 and the final fraction which is $\frac{17}{30}$ to

obtain the final answer $6\frac{17}{30}$.

Therefore, $10\frac{2}{5} - 3\frac{5}{6} = 6\frac{17}{30}$

Example 5

Subtract: $15\frac{3}{4} - 5\frac{5}{9}$ (See Examples **1** and **2** for sample detailed solutions.)

Solution

$$15 \mid \frac{3}{4} \times \frac{9}{9} = \frac{27}{36}$$

↖ LCD

$$-5 \mid \frac{5}{9} \times \frac{4}{4} = -\frac{20}{36} \quad \text{↙ LCD}$$

$$\overline{10}$$

↗

$$\frac{27 - 20}{36} = \frac{7}{36} \leftarrow \text{Final fraction}$$

↙ Subtraction of the denominators

Subtraction of
whole numbers

Combine the final fraction and the whole number to get the final answer $10\frac{7}{36}$.

Therefore, $15\frac{3}{4} - 5\frac{5}{9} = 10\frac{7}{36}$.

Note: It is recommended that the method of solution used for Example **5** should
be used in solving homework problems without the detailed explanations.

Example 6

Subtract: $13\frac{1}{2} - 8\frac{5}{8}$ (See Example **4** for sample detailed solution method.)

Solution

$$13 \mid \frac{1}{2} \times \frac{4}{4} = \frac{4}{8} \quad \text{↙ LCD}$$

$$-8|\ \frac{5}{8} \times \frac{1}{1}\ =-\frac{5}{8}\ \diagup\text{LCD}$$

$\frac{5}{8}$ is bigger than $\frac{4}{8}$, so we have to borrow 1 from 13 and the 1 is added to $\frac{4}{8}$ as $\frac{8}{8}$ as shown:

$$12 \qquad\qquad\qquad\qquad \diagup\text{This is the same as 1 added to } \frac{4}{8}.$$

$$13|\ \frac{1}{2} \times \frac{4}{4} = \frac{4}{8} + \frac{8}{8} = \frac{12}{8}$$

$$-8|\ \frac{5}{8} \times \frac{1}{1} \qquad\qquad =-\frac{5}{8}$$

$$\overline{\quad 12 - 8 \quad} \qquad\qquad \overline{\qquad\qquad}\ \diagup\text{Subtraction of numerators}$$

$$12 - 8 = 4 \qquad\qquad\qquad \frac{12-5}{8} = \frac{7}{8} \leftarrow \text{Final fraction}$$

$$\nwarrow$$

Whole number subtraction

Combine the whole number and the final fraction to obtain the final answer $4\frac{7}{8}$.

Therefore, $13\frac{1}{2} - 8\frac{5}{8} = 4\frac{7}{8}$

Note: It is recommended that the method of solution of Example 6 should be used in homework and tests without the detailed explanations.

Example 7

Subtract: $1 - \frac{2}{7}$

Solution

Step 1: Change the whole number 1 into an equivalent fraction that has the same denominator as that of $\frac{2}{7}$ which is 7. Therefore, $1 = \frac{7}{7}$. (Recall that any fraction which has the same number as both the numerator and the denominator has a value of 1.)

Therefore, $1 - \frac{2}{7}$ becomes $\frac{7}{7} - \frac{2}{7}$

Step 2: Subtract the numerators and put the difference over the common denominator of 7 as shown:

$$\frac{7}{7} - \frac{2}{7} = \frac{7-2}{7} = \frac{5}{7}.$$

Example 8

Subtract: $1 - \dfrac{13}{49}$

Solution

Step 1: Change the whole number 1 into an equivalent fraction that has the same denominator as that of $\dfrac{13}{49}$ which is 49. Therefore, $1 = \dfrac{49}{49}$. (Recall that any fraction which has the same number as both the denominator and the numerator has a value of 1.)

Therefore, $1 - \dfrac{13}{49}$ becomes $\dfrac{49}{49} - \dfrac{13}{49} = \dfrac{36}{49}$.

Step 2: Subtract the numerators and put the difference over the common denominator of 49 as shown:

$$\dfrac{49}{49} - \dfrac{13}{49} = \dfrac{49 \text{ - } 13}{49} = \dfrac{36}{49}.$$

The notes and the generous worked examples have provided me with conceptual understanding and computational fluency to do my homework.

Exercises

1. Subtract (Hint: See Examples **7** and **8**.)

(a) $1 - \dfrac{2}{5}$ (b) $1 - \dfrac{1}{4}$ (c) $1 - \dfrac{1}{10}$ (d) $1 - \dfrac{8}{9}$

(e) $1 - \dfrac{4}{7}$ (f) $1 - \dfrac{1}{6}$ (g) $1 - \dfrac{3}{11}$ (h) $1 - \dfrac{17}{18}$

(i) $1 - \dfrac{99}{100}$ (j) $1 - \dfrac{28}{44}$ (k) $1 - \dfrac{77}{78}$ (l) $1 - \dfrac{49}{74}$

(m) $1 - \dfrac{99}{200}$ (n) $1 - \dfrac{47}{64}$ (o) $1 - \dfrac{38}{65}$ (p) $1 - \dfrac{24}{37}$

2. Subtract (Hint: See Example **1**.)

(a) $3\dfrac{3}{4} - 1\dfrac{1}{8}$ (b) $7\dfrac{3}{4} - 5\dfrac{1}{6}$ (c) $5\dfrac{5}{6} - 3\dfrac{5}{12}$ (d) $8\dfrac{8}{9} - 2\dfrac{2}{9}$

(e) $4\dfrac{2}{3} - 2\dfrac{5}{12}$ **(f)** $10\dfrac{11}{12} - 3\dfrac{5}{6}$ **(g)** $3\dfrac{8}{9} - 1\dfrac{7}{9}$ **(h)** $6\dfrac{4}{5} - 2\dfrac{3}{10}$

(i) $8\dfrac{9}{12} - 3\dfrac{1}{3}$ **(j)** $12\dfrac{3}{4} - 7\dfrac{5}{16}$ **(k)** $6\dfrac{17}{18} - 2\dfrac{2}{9}$ **(l)** $28\dfrac{6}{7} - 2\dfrac{3}{14}$

(m) $9\dfrac{17}{21} - 3\dfrac{2}{7}$ **(n)** $13\dfrac{5}{6} - 4\dfrac{7}{18}$ **(o)** $56\dfrac{11}{15} - 6\dfrac{7}{30}$ **(p)** $10\dfrac{5}{6} - 2\dfrac{7}{24}$

(q) $110\dfrac{5}{8} - 90\dfrac{3}{64}$ **(r)** $94\dfrac{7}{9} - 64\dfrac{7}{36}$ **(s)** $32\dfrac{4}{5} - 19\dfrac{2}{15}$ **(t)** $6\dfrac{5}{6} - 2\dfrac{7}{24}$

3. Subtract (Hint: See Examples **2** and **5**.)

(a) $4\dfrac{2}{3} - 2\dfrac{1}{5}$ **(b)** $8\dfrac{4}{5} - 5\dfrac{1}{3}$ **(c)** $6\dfrac{3}{5} - 1\dfrac{1}{4}$ **(d)** $12\dfrac{1}{2} - 3\dfrac{2}{5}$

(e) $7\dfrac{2}{3} - 4\dfrac{1}{4}$ **(f)** $11\dfrac{7}{8} - 9\dfrac{1}{3}$ **(g)** $47\dfrac{4}{5} - 23\dfrac{2}{7}$ **(h)** $45\dfrac{2}{3} - 33\dfrac{3}{7}$

4. What is the rule for changing a mixed fraction into an improper fraction?

5. Subtract (Hint: See Example **1**).

(a) $10\dfrac{11}{12}$ **(b)** $4\dfrac{7}{8}$ **(c)** $12\dfrac{5}{6}$ **(d)** $9\dfrac{6}{7}$
$\quad\;\; -3\dfrac{5}{6}$ $\quad -2\dfrac{1}{4}$ $\quad -6\dfrac{7}{12}$ $\quad -6\dfrac{2}{7}$

(e) $11\dfrac{11}{12}$ **(f)** $28\dfrac{15}{16}$ **(g)** $5\dfrac{1}{2}$ **(h)** $29\dfrac{6}{7}$
$\quad\;\; -6\dfrac{1}{6}$ $\quad -17\dfrac{3}{8}$ $\quad -2\dfrac{1}{4}$ $\quad -3\dfrac{10}{21}$

6. Subtract (Hint: See Examples **2** and **5**.)

(a) $18\dfrac{2}{3}$ **(b)** $7\dfrac{4}{5}$ **(c)** $10\dfrac{11}{12}$ **(d)** $72\dfrac{3}{4}$
$\quad -5\dfrac{1}{5}$ $\quad -2\dfrac{2}{3}$ $\quad -6\dfrac{3}{5}$ $\quad -35\dfrac{2}{7}$

(m) $27\dfrac{4}{5}$ **(n)** $14\dfrac{6}{7}$ **(o)** $7\dfrac{7}{8}$ **(f)** $10\dfrac{3}{4}$
$\quad -7\dfrac{1}{3}$ $\quad -3\dfrac{2}{3}$ $\quad -2\dfrac{4}{9}$ $\quad -2\dfrac{1}{3}$

7. Subtract (Hint: See Examples **3, 4,** and **6.**)

(a) $10\frac{2}{3} - 4\frac{4}{5}$ (b) $4\frac{2}{7} - 2\frac{15}{21}$ (c) $7\frac{1}{6} - 4\frac{2}{3}$ (d) $11\frac{3}{5} - 2\frac{9}{10}$

(e) $15\frac{3}{11} - 7\frac{15}{22}$ (f) $41\frac{1}{2} - 2\frac{7}{9}$ (g) $7\frac{3}{7} - 5\frac{4}{5}$ (h) $8\frac{1}{5} - 2\frac{2}{3}$

(i) $7\frac{2}{7} - 5\frac{2}{3}$ (j) $8\frac{3}{11} - 5\frac{2}{3}$ (k) $9\frac{2}{3} - 4\frac{7}{8}$ (l) $15\frac{2}{5} - 4\frac{2}{3}$

(m) $9\frac{1}{6} - 7\frac{3}{4}$ (n) $12\frac{2}{7} - 8\frac{16}{21}$ (o) $25\frac{1}{16} - 5\frac{7}{8}$ (p) $24\frac{2}{5} - 8\frac{14}{15}$

Challenge Questions

8. Subtract

(a) $14\frac{2}{9} - 2\frac{3}{4}$ (b) $5\frac{7}{12} - 3\frac{5}{6}$ (c) $7\frac{2}{3} - 2\frac{1}{8}$ (d) $4\frac{5}{18} - 1\frac{1}{6}$

(e) $6\frac{23}{24} - 2\frac{1}{3}$ (f) $14\frac{1}{4} - 6\frac{5}{8}$ (g) $17\frac{4}{5} - 1\frac{3}{10}$ (h) $29\frac{2}{9} - 9\frac{7}{18}$

Answers to Selected Questions

1(a) $\frac{3}{5}$ 2(a) $2\frac{5}{8}$ 3(a) $2\frac{7}{15}$ 5(a) $7\frac{1}{12}$ 7(a) $5\frac{13}{15}$

REAL WORLD APPLICATIONS - WORD PROBLEMS
Subtraction of Mixed Numbers

Example 1

After roasting $15\frac{1}{2}$ pounds of beef, the beef weighed $12\frac{7}{8}$ pounds. How much less did the beef weigh after roasting?

Solution

(**Notice** that in Step 1, an imaginary line | separates the whole numbers from the fractions so that we can work on the whole numbers and the fractions separately.)

The beef is $15\frac{1}{2} - 12\frac{7}{8}$ pounds less after roasting. (Refer to Examples **4** under the topic Subtraction of Mixed Numbers for a detailed sample solution.)

$15\dfrac{1}{2} - 12\dfrac{7}{8}$ is solved as shown:

$15\,|\quad \dfrac{1}{2} \times \dfrac{4}{4} = \dfrac{4}{8}$ ← Equivalent fraction

$12\,|\quad \dfrac{7}{8} \times \dfrac{1}{1} = \dfrac{7}{8}$ ← Equivalent fraction

$\dfrac{7}{8}$ is bigger than $\dfrac{4}{8}$, so we have to borrow 1 from 15 and add the 1 to $\dfrac{4}{8}$.

$\overset{14}{}$ ⟋This is adding the 1 borrowed from 15 here.

$\cancel{15}\,|\quad \dfrac{1}{2} \times \dfrac{4}{4} = \dfrac{4}{8} + \dfrac{8}{8} \rightarrow \dfrac{12}{8}$

$-\,12\,|\quad \dfrac{7}{8} \times \dfrac{1}{1} = \dfrac{7}{8} \qquad \rightarrow \dfrac{7}{8}$

$\rule{2cm}{0.4pt}$ $\rule{2cm}{0.4pt}$ ⟋Difference of the equivalent numerators.

$14 - 12 = 2$ $\qquad\qquad \dfrac{12-7}{8} = \dfrac{5}{8}$

↖

Subtraction of whole numbers

Therefore $15\dfrac{1}{2} - 12\dfrac{7}{8} = 2\dfrac{5}{8}$ pounds.

Example 2

A painter had $12\dfrac{1}{4}$ gallons of paint. If he used $8\dfrac{2}{3}$ gallons of paint, how much paint is left?

Solution

The gallons of paint left $= 12\dfrac{1}{4} - 8\dfrac{2}{3}$. (Refer to Example **3**, under the topic Subtraction of Mixed Numbers for a detailed sample solution.)

$12\dfrac{1}{4} - 8\dfrac{2}{3}$ is solved as shown:

$12\,|\quad \dfrac{1}{4} \times \dfrac{3}{3} = \dfrac{3}{12}$ ← Equivalent fraction

$-\,8\,|\quad \dfrac{2}{3} \times \dfrac{4}{4} = \dfrac{8}{12}$ ← Equivalent fraction

$\dfrac{8}{12}$ is larger than $\dfrac{3}{12}$, so we have to borrow 1 from 12 and add the 1 to $\dfrac{3}{12}$ as shown:

$$1 \text{ which is borrowed from 12.}$$

$$11$$
$$\downarrow$$

$$12 \mid \dfrac{1}{4} \times \dfrac{3}{3} = 1\dfrac{3}{12} \;\rightarrow\; \dfrac{15}{12} \quad \leftarrow \text{Change mixed fraction to improper fraction.}$$

$$-8 \mid \dfrac{2}{3} \times \dfrac{4}{4} = \dfrac{8}{12} \;\rightarrow\; \dfrac{8}{12}$$

$$\underline{} \qquad\qquad \underline{} \;\;\nearrow \text{Difference in the numerators.}$$

$$11 - 8 = 3 \qquad\qquad \dfrac{15 - 8}{12} = \dfrac{7}{12}$$

$$\nwarrow$$

Subtraction of whole numbers

Therefore, $12\dfrac{1}{4} - 8\dfrac{2}{3} = 3\dfrac{7}{12}$ gallons.

(**Notice** that an imaginary line | separates the whole numbers from the fractions so that we can work on the whole numbers and the fractions separately.)

Example 3

John had $12\dfrac{1}{3}$ cups of flour and he used $5\dfrac{4}{5}$ cups to prepare food for his friends.

How many cups of flour were left?

Solution

The cups of flour left $= 12\dfrac{1}{3} - 5\dfrac{4}{5}$. (Refer to the example under the topic Subtraction

of Mixed Numbers for the detailed sample solution.)

$12\dfrac{1}{3} - 5\dfrac{4}{5}$ is solved as shown:

$$12 \mid \dfrac{1}{3} \times \dfrac{5}{5} = \dfrac{5}{15} \quad \leftarrow \text{Equivalent fractions}$$

$$-5 \mid \dfrac{4}{5} \times \dfrac{3}{3} = -\dfrac{12}{15} \quad \leftarrow \text{Equivalent fraction}$$

$\dfrac{12}{15}$ is larger than $\dfrac{5}{15}$, so we have to borrow 1 from 12 and add the 1 to $\dfrac{5}{15}$ as shown:

This is the 1 added to $\dfrac{5}{15}$

11

$12| \dfrac{1}{3} \times \dfrac{5}{5} = 1\dfrac{5}{15} \rightarrow \dfrac{20}{15}$ ← Change the mixed fraction to an improper fraction.

$-5| \dfrac{4}{5} \times \dfrac{3}{3} = \dfrac{12}{15} \rightarrow -\dfrac{12}{15}$

$11 - 5 = 6$ $\dfrac{20-12}{15} = \dfrac{8}{15}$ ← Difference of the numerators.

Subtraction of whole numbers

Therefore, $12\dfrac{1}{3} - 5\dfrac{4}{5} = 6\dfrac{8}{15}$ cups of flour.

The notes and the generous worked examples have provided me with conceptual understanding and computational fluency to do my homework.

Exercises

1. After roasting $14\dfrac{1}{2}$ pounds of turkey, the turkey weighed $9\dfrac{2}{3}$ pounds. How much less did the turkey weigh after roasting? Hint: See Example **1**.

2. If a painter had $7\dfrac{1}{6}$ gallons of paint and he used up $3\dfrac{7}{8}$ gallons of the paint. How much paint is left? Hint: See Example **2**.

3. Nick had $15\dfrac{3}{4}$ cups of flour and if he used $2\dfrac{5}{6}$ cups to prepare cakes, how many cups of flour is left? Hint: See Example **3**.

Challenge Questions

4. John weighed $260\dfrac{2}{5}$ pounds. After going on a diet, he lost $70\dfrac{1}{2}$ pounds. What was John's weight after dieting?

5. Joshua had $6\dfrac{1}{2}$ dozen eggs and he used $2\dfrac{4}{5}$ dozen. How many dozen eggs were left?

6. Mary bought $20\dfrac{1}{2}$ feet of board for her school project. If she cut off $5\dfrac{5}{8}$ feet for the project, how many feet of board were left?

7. Joanna had $18\frac{2}{3}$ yards of ribbon. If she used $11\frac{7}{8}$ yards, how much ribbon did she have left?

Answers to Selected Questions

1. $4\frac{5}{6}$ pounds   3. $12\frac{11}{12}$ cups

SUBTRACTION OF A FRACTION FROM A WHOLE NUMBER

Example 1

Subtract: $1 - \frac{2}{3}$

Solution

Before a fraction can be subtracted from a whole number,

Step 1: Change the whole number 1 into an equivalent fraction that has the same denominator as that of $\frac{2}{3}$ which is 3. Therefore, $1 = \frac{3}{3}$. (Recall that any fraction which has the same number as both the numerator and the denominator has a value of 1.)

$$1 - \frac{2}{3} \text{ becomes } \frac{3}{3} - \frac{2}{3}$$

Step 2: Subtract the numerators and put the difference over the common denominator of 3.

$$\frac{3}{3} - \frac{2}{3} = \frac{1}{3}$$

Example 2

Subtract: $2 - \frac{2}{3}$

Solution

Step 1: Before a fraction can be subtracted from a whole number, 1 should be taken from the whole number and changed to an equivalent fraction that has the same denominator as the fraction which is being subtracted from the whole number. 2 can be written as $1 + 1$ and then, 1 can be changed to an equivalent fraction as follows:

$$2 - \frac{2}{3} = 1 + 1 - \frac{2}{3}$$

$$= 1 + \frac{3}{3} - \frac{2}{3} \quad \left(\text{Note: } \frac{3}{3} = 1 \right)$$

↑

Equivalent fraction

Step 2: Subtract the numerators of the fractions and put the difference over the common denominator of 3.

$$1 + \frac{3}{3} - \frac{2}{3} = 1 + \frac{3 - 2}{3}$$

$$= 1 + \frac{1}{3}$$

$$= 1\frac{1}{3} \quad \text{Combine the whole number and the fraction.}$$

Example 3

Subtract: $6 - \frac{3}{4}$

Solution

Step 1: Before a fraction can be subtracted from a whole number, 1 should be taken from the whole number and changed to an equivalent fraction that has the same denominator as the fraction which is being subtracted from the whole number. 6 can be written as $5 + 1$, and then, 1 can be changed to an equivalent fraction as shown:

$$6 - \frac{3}{4} = 5 + 1 - \frac{3}{4}$$

$$= 5 + \frac{4}{4} - \frac{3}{4} \qquad \left(\textbf{Note: } \frac{4}{4} = 1 \right)$$

↑

Equivalent fraction

Step 2: Subtract the numerators of the fractions and put the difference over the common denominator of 4.

$$5 + \frac{4}{4} - \frac{3}{4} = 5 + \frac{4 - 3}{4}$$

$$= 5 + \frac{1}{4}$$

$$= 5\frac{1}{4} \qquad \text{Combine the fraction and the whole number.}$$

The notes and the generous worked examples have provided me with conceptual understanding and computational fluency to do my homework.

Exercises

1. Subtract. Hint: See Example **1**.

(a) $1 - \dfrac{4}{8}$

(b) $1 - \dfrac{9}{10}$

(c) $1 - \dfrac{3}{6}$

(d) $1 - \dfrac{7}{8}$

(e) $1 - \dfrac{2}{9}$

(f) $1 - \dfrac{4}{11}$

(g) $1 - \dfrac{1}{12}$

(h) $1 - \dfrac{3}{5}$

(i) $1 - \dfrac{2}{19}$

(j) $1 - \dfrac{3}{4}$

(k) $1 - \dfrac{7}{12}$

(l) $1 - \dfrac{1}{99}$

(m) $1 - \dfrac{49}{50}$

(n) $1 - \dfrac{1}{39}$

(o) $1 - \dfrac{8}{9}$

(p) $1 - \dfrac{1}{64}$

(q) $1 - \dfrac{7}{49}$

(r) $1 - \dfrac{5}{16}$

(s) $1 - \dfrac{3}{25}$

(t) $1 - \dfrac{5}{6}$

(u) $1 - \dfrac{5}{14}$

(v) $1 - \dfrac{7}{11}$

(w) $1 - \dfrac{4}{7}$

(x) $1 - \dfrac{99}{200}$

2. Subtract. Hint: See Examples **2** and **3**.

(a) $7 - \dfrac{8}{9}$

(b) $2 - \dfrac{4}{11}$

(c) $8 - \dfrac{3}{5}$

(d) $10 - \dfrac{4}{9}$

(e) $12 - \dfrac{3}{7}$

(f) $4 - \dfrac{1}{9}$

(g) $9 - \dfrac{2}{7}$

(h) $3 - \dfrac{2}{11}$

(i) $10 - \dfrac{2}{5}$

(j) $5 - \dfrac{3}{8}$

(k) $6 - \dfrac{5}{12}$

(l) $10 - \dfrac{2}{5}$

(m) $90 - \dfrac{4}{5}$

(n) $64 - \dfrac{4}{9}$

(o) $3 - \dfrac{2}{9}$

(p) $28 - \dfrac{3}{7}$

(q) $12 - \dfrac{5}{12}$

(r) $15 - \dfrac{3}{5}$

(s) $11 - \dfrac{2}{30}$

(t) $9 - \dfrac{3}{16}$

(u) $8 - \dfrac{3}{7}$ (v) $15 - \dfrac{1}{15}$ (w) $12 - \dfrac{4}{9}$ (x) $14 - \dfrac{5}{8}$

Challenge Questions

3. Subtract:

(a) $200 - \dfrac{19}{20}$ (b) $4 - \dfrac{19}{100}$ (c) $1 - \dfrac{6}{7}$ (d) $1 - \dfrac{3}{8}$

Answers to Selected Questions

1(a) $\dfrac{4}{8}$ **2**(a) $6\dfrac{1}{9}$

(We will learn about how to reduce fractions to the lowest terms later.)

MULTIPLYING FRACTIONS

A fraction is made up of a numerator, a denominator, and a fraction bar as shown:

$\dfrac{2}{5}$ ╱ numerator
    ← fraction bar
    ╲ denominator

The fraction bar is a line that separates the numerator and the denominator.

Rule 1: To multiply fractions, multiply all the numerators together and multiply all the denominators together and then put the product of the numerators over the product of the denominators and if it is possible to reduce to the **lowest terms**, do so.

Example 1

Multiply: $\dfrac{2}{5} \times \dfrac{3}{4}$

Solution

Step 1: Multiply all the numerators together and multiply all the denominators together and then put the product of the numerators over the product of the denominators as shown:

$$\dfrac{2}{5} \times \dfrac{3}{4} = \dfrac{6}{20}$$

425

Step 2: Reduce $\dfrac{6}{20}$ to the lowest term by dividing both the numerator and the denominator of $\dfrac{6}{20}$ by the same number, and in this case 2 is the largest number that can divide evenly into 6 and 20 evenly without a remainder as shown:

$$\overset{3}{\underset{10}{\dfrac{6}{20}}} = \dfrac{3}{10} \qquad \text{Divide the numerator and the denominator by 2.}$$

Therefore, $\dfrac{2}{5} \times \dfrac{3}{4} = \dfrac{3}{10}$

Special Explanation

Note that Example **1** could have been solved differently by reducing $\dfrac{2}{5} \times \dfrac{3}{4}$ in Step 1 by dividing both the numerator and the denominator by 2 because 2 can divide the numerator 2 and the denominator 4.

Rule 2: In order to simplify the multiplication of fractions, divide any numerator and any denominator by the same number, and this is called canceling.

$$\dfrac{2}{5} \times \dfrac{3}{4} \text{ becomes } \dfrac{\overset{1}{2}}{5} \times \dfrac{3}{\underset{2}{4}} \qquad \text{Divide numerator and denominator by 2.}$$

$$\dfrac{1 \times 3}{5 \times 2} = \dfrac{3}{10} \qquad \text{This is the same answer for Example 1.}$$

Example 2

Multiply: $\dfrac{3}{7} \times \dfrac{5}{6}$

Solution

Step 1: Since 3 can divide evenly into the numerator 3 and the denominator 6 (without a remainder), divide the numerator and the denominator by 3. Rule 2 can be used here as shown:

$$\frac{3}{7} \times \frac{5}{6} = \frac{3}{7} \times \frac{\overset{1}{5}}{\underset{2}{6}}$$ Divide the numerator and the denominator by 3.

$$= \frac{1 \times 5}{7 \times 2} = \frac{5}{14}$$ Multiply the numerators and multiply the

denominators and put the product of the numerator over the product of the denominator which is Rule 1.

Note: Since in Example 2, both the numerator and the denominator are divided by 3, and we can no more reduce $\frac{5}{14}$, Step 2 is not necessary in this case.

Recommendation

It is recommended that during the multiplication of fractions, the student should divide the numerators and the denominators by the same numbers if possible first before multiplying all the numerators and also multiplying all the denominators, and then put the product of the numerators over the product of the denominators.

Example 3

Multiply: $\frac{5}{12} \times \frac{4}{15}$

Solution

Step 1: Since 5 is the largest number that divides the numerator 5 and the denominator 15 evenly (without a remainder) and also, 4 is the largest number that divides the numerator 4 and the denominator 12 evenly (without a remainder), Rule 2 can be used here as shown:

$$\frac{\overset{1}{5}}{\underset{3}{12}} \times \frac{\overset{1}{4}}{\underset{3}{15}}$$ Divide both numerators and denominators by 5 and 4.

$(5 \div 5 = 1, 15 \div 5 = 3, 4 \div 4 = 1, 12 \div 4 = 3)$

$$= \frac{1}{3} \times \frac{1}{3}$$ Since we can no longer reduce $\frac{1}{3} \times \frac{1}{3}$, multiply the

numerators and multiply the denominators and put the product of the numerators over the product of the denominators as shown:

$$= \frac{1 \times 1}{3 \times 3} = \frac{1}{9}$$

Example 4

Multiply: $\dfrac{5}{6} \times \dfrac{7}{9}$

Solution

Step 1: Since there is no number that can divide both the numerators and the denominators evenly (without a remainder), we can only multiply all the numerators, and then multiply all the denominators and put the product of the numerators over the denominators as shown:

$$\frac{5}{6} \times \frac{7}{9} = \frac{5 \times 7}{6 \times 9} \qquad \text{Rule 1 is used here.}$$

$$= \frac{35}{54}$$

Example 5

Multiply: $\dfrac{12}{15} \times \dfrac{3}{8} \times \dfrac{4}{9}$

Solution

Step 1: Since the numerators and the denominators can be divided by 2, 3, and 4, the fractions should be reduced by dividing by 2, 3, and 4 before the numerators should be multiplied together and the denominators multiplied together, and then put the product of the numerators over the product of the denominators as shown:

$$\overset{\overset{1}{\underset{}{}} }{\underset{}{}}$$

$$\overset{4 \qquad 1 \qquad 2}{\underset{5 \qquad 2 \qquad 3}{\dfrac{\cancel{12}}{\cancel{15}} \times \dfrac{\cancel{3}}{\cancel{8}} \times \dfrac{\cancel{4}}{\cancel{9}}}}$$

$$\underset{1}{}$$

$(12 \div 3 = 4,\ 15 \div 3 = 5,\ 4 \div 4 = 1,\ 8 \div 4 = 2)$

$(2 \div 2 = 1,\ 4 \div 2 = 2)$

$(3 \div 3 = 1,\ 9 \div 3 = 3)$

Rule 2 is being used here.

$$= \frac{1}{5} \times \frac{1}{1} \times \frac{2}{3}$$

$$= \frac{1 \times 1 \times 2}{5 \times 1 \times 3} = \frac{2}{15} \qquad \text{Rule 1 is used here.}$$

Exercises

1. Multiply (Hint: See Example **2**.)

(a) $\dfrac{4}{7} \times \dfrac{5}{8}$ (b) $\dfrac{5}{7} \times \dfrac{2}{10}$ (c) $\dfrac{1}{3} \times \dfrac{3}{4}$ (d) $\dfrac{3}{5} \times \dfrac{5}{7}$

(e) $\dfrac{2}{5} \times \dfrac{1}{6}$ (f) $\dfrac{2}{3} \times \dfrac{1}{2}$ (g) $\dfrac{4}{7} \times \dfrac{14}{15}$ (h) $\dfrac{3}{4} \times \dfrac{5}{6}$

(i) $\dfrac{3}{49} \times \dfrac{7}{10}$ (j) $\dfrac{2}{9} \times \dfrac{27}{29}$ (k) $\dfrac{2}{12} \times \dfrac{7}{9}$ (l) $\dfrac{3}{11} \times \dfrac{22}{23}$

(m) $\dfrac{3}{7} \times \dfrac{77}{78}$ (n) $\dfrac{2}{3} \times \dfrac{3}{5}$ (o) $\dfrac{3}{4} \times \dfrac{4}{5}$ (p) $\dfrac{5}{6} \times \dfrac{7}{15}$

(q) $\dfrac{4}{5} \times \dfrac{7}{12}$ (r) $\dfrac{3}{7} \times \dfrac{4}{15}$ (s) $\dfrac{5}{7} \times \dfrac{21}{22}$ (t) $\dfrac{2}{33} \times \dfrac{11}{13}$

(u) $\dfrac{21}{22} \times \dfrac{3}{7}$ (v) $\dfrac{10}{18} \times \dfrac{6}{13}$ (w) $\dfrac{27}{30} \times \dfrac{7}{9}$ (x) $\dfrac{45}{46} \times \dfrac{1}{15}$

(y) $\dfrac{50}{51} \times \dfrac{7}{25}$ (z) $\dfrac{42}{50} \times \dfrac{3}{12}$ (a1) $\dfrac{7}{17} \times \dfrac{3}{14}$ (b1) $\dfrac{4}{9} \times \dfrac{12}{13}$

2. Multiply (Hint: See Example **3**.)

(a) $\dfrac{3}{4} \times \dfrac{2}{9}$ (b) $\dfrac{9}{10} \times \dfrac{2}{3}$ (c) $\dfrac{4}{5} \times \dfrac{5}{8}$ (d) $\dfrac{3}{7} \times \dfrac{14}{15}$

(e) $\dfrac{5}{6} \times \dfrac{3}{5}$ (f) $\dfrac{2}{5} \times \dfrac{5}{6}$ (g) $\dfrac{4}{7} \times \dfrac{7}{8}$ (h) $\dfrac{3}{8} \times \dfrac{4}{6}$

(i) $\dfrac{2}{5} \times \dfrac{10}{12}$ (j) $\dfrac{3}{5} \times \dfrac{10}{18}$ (k) $\dfrac{2}{3} \times \dfrac{24}{28}$ (l) $\dfrac{4}{5} \times \dfrac{15}{24}$

(m) $\dfrac{2}{9} \times \dfrac{3}{4}$ (n) $\dfrac{3}{16} \times \dfrac{4}{9}$ (o) $\dfrac{2}{5} \times \dfrac{15}{16}$ (p) $\dfrac{2}{5} \times \dfrac{20}{22}$

(q) $\dfrac{4}{11} \times \dfrac{22}{24}$ **(r)** $\dfrac{3}{4} \times \dfrac{8}{9}$ **(s)** $\dfrac{3}{4} \times \dfrac{12}{27}$ **(t)** $\dfrac{2}{11} \times \dfrac{33}{34}$

(u) $\dfrac{5}{7} \times \dfrac{14}{15}$ **(v)** $\dfrac{5}{6} \times \dfrac{12}{15}$ **(w)** $\dfrac{3}{8} \times \dfrac{24}{27}$ **(x)** $\dfrac{2}{9} \times \dfrac{18}{20}$

3. Multiply (Hint: See Example **4**.)

(a) $\dfrac{3}{4} \times \dfrac{3}{7}$ **(b)** $\dfrac{7}{22} \times \dfrac{5}{8}$ **(c)** $\dfrac{1}{4} \times \dfrac{5}{6}$ **(d)** $\dfrac{2}{5} \times \dfrac{3}{5}$

(e) $\dfrac{2}{7} \times \dfrac{3}{5}$ **(f)** $\dfrac{3}{7} \times \dfrac{2}{5}$ **(g)** $\dfrac{2}{9} \times \dfrac{11}{15}$ **(h)** $\dfrac{1}{8} \times \dfrac{5}{7}$

(i) $\dfrac{2}{3} \times \dfrac{3}{5}$ **(j)** $\dfrac{7}{8} \times \dfrac{9}{11}$ **(k)** $\dfrac{5}{6} \times \dfrac{5}{7}$ **(l)** $\dfrac{3}{4} \times \dfrac{5}{7}$

(m) $\dfrac{2}{5} \times \dfrac{3}{5}$ **(n)** $\dfrac{1}{7} \times \dfrac{3}{4}$ **(o)** $\dfrac{2}{11} \times \dfrac{2}{3}$ **(p)** $\dfrac{5}{6} \times \dfrac{7}{8}$

4. Multiply (Hint: See Example **5**.)

(a) $\dfrac{2}{3} \times \dfrac{6}{5} \times \dfrac{15}{18}$ **(b)** $\dfrac{2}{7} \times \dfrac{21}{22} \times \dfrac{11}{12}$ **(c)** $\dfrac{3}{4} \times \dfrac{4}{9} \times \dfrac{4}{16}$

(d) $\dfrac{5}{6} \times \dfrac{3}{15} \times \dfrac{2}{7}$ **(e)** $\dfrac{7}{9} \times \dfrac{18}{21} \times \dfrac{3}{4}$ **(f)** $\dfrac{4}{5} \times \dfrac{10}{12} \times \dfrac{3}{7}$

(g) $\dfrac{4}{5} \times \dfrac{15}{24} \times \dfrac{2}{3}$ **(h)** $\dfrac{1}{3} \times \dfrac{2}{3} \times \dfrac{9}{10}$ **(i)** $\dfrac{3}{4} \times \dfrac{16}{17} \times \dfrac{1}{6}$

(j) $\dfrac{2}{7} \times \dfrac{5}{6} \times \dfrac{14}{15}$ **(k)** $\dfrac{4}{7} \times \dfrac{14}{16} \times \dfrac{2}{3}$ **(l)** $\dfrac{4}{9} \times \dfrac{18}{19} \times \dfrac{19}{20}$

(m) $\dfrac{2}{3} \times \dfrac{4}{5} \times \dfrac{3}{8}$ **(n)** $\dfrac{5}{8} \times \dfrac{6}{7} \times \dfrac{14}{15}$ **(o)** $\dfrac{2}{3} \times \dfrac{9}{10} \times \dfrac{4}{9}$

Challenge Questions
5. Multiply:

(a) $\dfrac{3}{5} \times \dfrac{15}{16}$ **(b)** $\dfrac{3}{4} \times \dfrac{8}{9}$ **(c)** $\dfrac{1}{5} \times \dfrac{3}{5}$ **(d)** $\dfrac{3}{5} \times \dfrac{15}{18}$

(e) $\dfrac{4}{9} \times \dfrac{5}{8} \times \dfrac{3}{15}$

(f) $\dfrac{2}{11} \times \dfrac{3}{4} \times \dfrac{22}{24}$

(g) $\dfrac{3}{5} \times \dfrac{7}{12} \times \dfrac{5}{14}$

(h) $\dfrac{2}{7} \times \dfrac{3}{5} \times \dfrac{10}{9}$

(i) $\dfrac{4}{7} \times \dfrac{14}{15}$

(j) $\dfrac{2}{5} \times \dfrac{4}{7}$

(k) $\dfrac{2}{7} \times \dfrac{14}{15}$

(l) $\dfrac{5}{7} \times \dfrac{3}{4}$

(m) $\dfrac{2}{7} \times \dfrac{3}{7}$

(n) $\dfrac{2}{3} \times \dfrac{3}{4} \times \dfrac{4}{5}$

(o) $\dfrac{2}{5} \times \dfrac{2}{27} \times \dfrac{15}{16}$

(p) $\dfrac{3}{4} \times \dfrac{3}{4}$

Answers to Selected Questions

1(a) $\dfrac{5}{14}$ **2(a)** $\dfrac{1}{6}$ **3(a)** $\dfrac{9}{28}$ **4(a)** $\dfrac{2}{3}$

REAL WORLD APPLICATIONS - WORD PROBLEMS
Multiplying Fractions

In mathematics, "**of**" means to multiply.

Example 1

Mary won $\dfrac{3}{5}$ of a million dollars in a lottery. If she pays $\dfrac{1}{3}$ of the money in federal taxes, how much of her prize:

(a) is paid to the federal government?

(b) will remain after taxes?

Solution

(a) $\dfrac{1}{3}$ of the money is used to pay taxes.

$\dfrac{1}{3}$ of $\dfrac{3}{5}$ of a million dollars is used to pay taxes.

In mathematics "**of**" means to multiply.

Therefore, $\dfrac{1}{3}$ of $\dfrac{3}{5} = \dfrac{1}{3} \times \dfrac{3}{5}$

431

$$1$$
$$= \frac{1}{\underset{1}{3}} \times \frac{3}{5} \qquad \text{Divide the numerator and the denominator by 3.}$$

$$= \frac{1 \times 1}{1 \times 5}$$

$$= \frac{1}{5} \text{ of a million dollars is used to pay the taxes.}$$

(b) The total money won $= \dfrac{3}{5}$ of a million dollars.

The money used to pay taxes $= \dfrac{1}{5}$ of a million dollars.

Therefore, the money that remains $= \dfrac{3}{5} - \dfrac{1}{5}$

(Review topics on Subtraction of Fractions.)

$$\frac{3}{5} - \frac{1}{5} = \frac{3-1}{5} \qquad \text{Since the denominators of } \frac{3}{5} \text{ and } \frac{1}{5} \text{ are the same,}$$

subtract the numerators and put the difference over 5.

$$= \frac{2}{5} \text{ of a million dollars remained.}$$

Example 2

A truck had a load of $\dfrac{11}{12}$ ton of goods. If $\dfrac{3}{11}$ of the goods were delivered,

(a) what part of a ton of the goods were delivered?
(b) what part of the ton of goods remained?

Solution

(a) Total load of goods $= \dfrac{11}{12}$ ton

$\dfrac{3}{11}$ of the goods were delivered.

Therefore, $\dfrac{3}{11}$ of $\dfrac{11}{12}$ ton of goods were delivered.

In mathematics "**of**" means to multiply.

$$\frac{3}{11} \text{ of } \frac{11}{12} = \frac{3}{11} \times \frac{11}{12}$$

$$1 \qquad 1$$

$$= \frac{\overset{1}{\cancel{3}}}{\cancel{11}} \times \frac{\overset{1}{\cancel{11}}}{\underset{4}{12}}$$

(Divide the numerators and the denominators by 3 and 11.) $(3 \div 3 = 1, 12 \div 3 = 4, 11 \div 11 = 1)$

$$= \frac{1 \times 1}{1 \times 4}$$

$$= \frac{1}{4} \text{ ton of the goods were delivered.}$$

(b) Total load of the goods $= \dfrac{11}{12}$ ton

Load of goods delivered $= \dfrac{1}{4}$ ton

The remaining ton of goods $= \dfrac{11}{12} - \dfrac{1}{4}$

Step 1: Find the LCD of $\dfrac{11}{12}$ and $\dfrac{1}{4}$ (Review topics on Subtraction of Fractions.)

The LCD of $\dfrac{11}{12}$ and $\dfrac{1}{4}$ is 12 because it is the least number/denominator

that both 4 and 12 can divide evenly into (without a remainder).

$$\frac{11}{12} = \frac{}{12} \;\diagup \text{LCD}$$

$$-\frac{1}{4} = -\frac{}{12} \;\diagup \text{LCD}$$

Step 2: Write equivalent fractions.

$$\frac{11}{12} \times \frac{1}{1} = \frac{11}{12} \;\leftarrow \text{Equivalent fractions}$$

$$-\frac{1}{4} \times \frac{3}{3} = -\frac{3}{12} \;\leftarrow \text{Equivalent fractions}$$

Step 3: Subtract the numerators of the equivalent fractions and write the difference of the numerators over the least common denominator (LCD) to get the final difference.

$$\frac{11}{12} \times \frac{1}{1} = \frac{11}{12}$$

$$-\frac{1}{4} \times \frac{3}{3} = -\frac{3}{12}$$

$$\frac{11-3}{12} = \frac{8}{12} \text{ ton of goods remained.}$$

Note: $\frac{8}{12}$ should be reduced to the lowest term by dividing both the numerator and the denominator by 4 as shown:

$$\frac{8}{12} = \frac{\overset{2}{\cancel{8}}}{\underset{3}{\cancel{12}}} = \frac{2}{3} \text{ ton of goods remained.}$$

Example 3

Mary bought $\frac{9}{10}$ pound of beef and she used $\frac{1}{2}$ of the beef.

(**a**) What fraction of a pound did she use?
(**b**) What fraction of a pound remained?
Solution

(**a**) Total weight of the beef = $\frac{9}{10}$ pound.

$\frac{1}{2}$ pound of the beef was used.

Therefore, $\frac{1}{2}$ of $\frac{9}{10}$ of the beef was used.

In mathematics "**of** " means to multiply.

$$\frac{1}{2} \text{ of } \frac{9}{10} = \frac{1}{2} \times \frac{9}{10} \qquad \text{We cannot reduce to the lowest terms.}$$

$$= \frac{1 \times 9}{2 \times 10} \qquad \text{(The numerators are multiplied together and the}$$

denominators are multiplied together because there is no number that can divide both the numerator and the denominator evenly (without a remainder.)

434

$$= \frac{9}{20} \text{ pound of beef was used.}$$

(b) Total weight of the beef $= \dfrac{9}{10}$ pound

The weight of beef used $= \dfrac{9}{20}$ pound

Therefore the weight of beef that remains is equal to

$$\frac{9}{10} - \frac{9}{20} \quad \text{(Review the topic on Subtraction of Fractions.)}$$

Step 1: Find the LCD.

The LCD for $\dfrac{9}{10}$ and $\dfrac{9}{20}$ is 20 because 20 is the least number that can be divided by 10 and 20 evenly (without a remainder).

$$\frac{9}{10} = \frac{}{20} \quad \swarrow \text{LCD}$$

$$-\frac{9}{20} = -\frac{}{20} \quad \swarrow \text{LCD}$$

Step 2: Write equivalent fractions.

$$\frac{9}{10} \times \frac{2}{2} = \frac{18}{20} \quad \leftarrow \text{Equivalent fractions}$$

$$-\frac{9}{20} \times \frac{1}{1} = -\frac{9}{20} \quad \leftarrow \text{Equivalent fractions}$$

Step 3: Subtract the numerators of the equivalent fractions and write the difference of the numerators over the least common denominator (LCD) to get the final difference.

$$\frac{9}{10} \times \frac{2}{2} = \frac{18}{20}$$
$$-\frac{9}{20} \times \frac{1}{1} = -\frac{9}{20}$$

$$\frac{18-9}{20} = \frac{9}{20} \text{ pound of the beef remained.}$$

Example 4

A boxer earned $\dfrac{8}{9}$ of a million dollars. If the agent of the boxer gets $\dfrac{3}{21}$ of the

boxer's earnings, what fraction of a million did the agent get?
Solution

Total money earned by the boxer $= \dfrac{8}{9}$ of a million dollars.

$\dfrac{3}{21}$ of the boxer's earnings was received by the agent.

Therefore, $\dfrac{3}{21}$ of $\dfrac{8}{9}$ of a million dollars was received by the agent.

In mathematics, "**of**" means to multiply.

Therefore, $\dfrac{3}{21}$ of $\dfrac{8}{9} = \dfrac{3}{21} \times \dfrac{8}{9}$

$$= \dfrac{\overset{1}{\cancel{3}}}{21} \times \dfrac{8}{\underset{3}{\cancel{9}}} \qquad \text{Divide the numerator and denominator by 3.}$$

$$(3 \div 3 = 1, 9 \div 3 = 3)$$

$$= \dfrac{1 \times 8}{21 \times 3}$$

$$= \dfrac{8}{63} \text{ of a million was received by the agent.}$$

Example 5

Rose can mow her lawn in $\dfrac{8}{9}$ of an hour. How long will it take two people to do

the same job assuming that each of the two people works at the same rate as Rose?
Solution

Time taken by 1 person (Rose) to mow the lawn $= \dfrac{8}{9}$ of an hour.

Time taken by 2 people to mow the lawn $= \dfrac{1}{2}$ of the time taken by 1 person.

$$= \dfrac{1}{2} \text{ of the time taken by Rose.}$$

In mathematics, "**of**" means multiplication

$$= \dfrac{1}{2} \text{ of } \dfrac{8}{9} = \dfrac{1}{2} \times \dfrac{8}{9}$$

$$= \dfrac{1}{2} \times \dfrac{\overset{4}{\cancel{8}}}{\underset{1}{\cancel{9}}} \qquad \text{(Divide numerator and the}$$

$$\text{denominator by 2.)}$$

$$= \frac{1 \times 4}{1 \times 9}$$

$$= \frac{4}{9} \text{ of an hour.}$$

The notes and the generous worked examples have provided me with conceptual understanding and computational fluency to do my homework.

Exercises

1. John won $\frac{6}{7}$ of a million dollars in a lottery. If he pays $\frac{1}{3}$ of the money in federal taxes, how much of his prize:
   (a) Is paid to the federal government?
   (b) Will remain?
   Hint: See Example **1**.

2. Mary won $\frac{5}{6}$ of a million dollars in a lottery. Assume that she paid $\frac{4}{15}$ of the money in federal taxes, how much of her prize:
   (a) Is paid to the federal government?
   (b) Will remain?
   Hint: See Example **1**.

3. A truck had a load of $\frac{9}{10}$ ton of goods. If $\frac{5}{6}$ of the goods were delivered,
   (a) what part of a ton of the goods were delivered?
   (b) what part of a ton of the goods remained?
   Hint: See Example **2**.

4. A truck had a load of $\frac{7}{8}$ ton of sand. If $\frac{4}{21}$ of the sand was delivered,
   (a) what part of a ton of the sand was delivered?
   (b) what part of a ton of the sand remained?
   Hint: See Example **2**.

5. Rose bought $\frac{3}{4}$ pound of ham and she used $\frac{1}{3}$ of the ham.
   (a) What fraction of a pound did she use?
   (b) What fraction of a pound remained?
   Hint: See Example **3**.

6. Assume that a school district bought $\frac{3}{4}$ ton of rice for the year. If $\frac{1}{6}$ of the rice

has been used,
(**a**) what fraction of a ton was used?
(**b**) what fraction of a ton remained?
Hint: See Example **3**.

7. A coach earned $\dfrac{5}{12}$ of a million dollars. If the trainer of the team gets $\dfrac{3}{10}$ of the coach's earnings, what fraction of a million did the trainer get?
Hint: See Example **4**

8. Frank can mow a lawn in $\dfrac{7}{9}$ of an hour. How long will it take 2 people to mow the same lawn, assuming that each of the two people works at the same rate as Frank? Hint: See Example **5**.

Challenge Questions

9. Nick can rake a lawn of leaves in $\dfrac{7}{12}$ of an hour. How long will it take three people to rake the same lawn, assuming that each of the three people works at the same rate as Nick?

MULTIPLICATION OF FRACTIONS AND WHOLE NUMBERS

Rule 1: To multiply fractions and whole numbers, write the whole numbers as fractions by dividing the whole numbers by 1. (Example: The fraction form of the whole number 9 is $\dfrac{9}{1}$.)

Rule 2: Before multiplying all the numerators and also multiplying all the denominators reduce the fractions to the lowest terms by dividing the numerators, and the denominators by the same number evenly (without a remainder) if possible.

Rule 3: Multiply the numerators and then multiply the denominators.

Rule 4: Change the answer (which is an improper fraction) to a mixed number by dividing the numerator by the denominator. (For example, the improper fraction $\dfrac{12}{5}$ can be written as $2\dfrac{2}{5}$ as a mixed number.)

Example 1

Multiply: $4 \times \dfrac{3}{4}$

Solution

Step 1: Change the whole number 4 to a fraction. See Rule 1.

$$4 = \frac{4}{1}$$

Therefore, $4 \times \dfrac{3}{4} = \dfrac{4}{1} \times \dfrac{3}{4}$

Step 2: Reduce the fractions to the lowest terms by dividing the numerators and the denominators by the same number evenly (without a remainder) if possible. See Rule 2.

Therefore, $\dfrac{4}{1} \times \dfrac{3}{4} = \dfrac{\overset{1}{4}}{1} \times \dfrac{3}{\underset{1}{4}}$ $(4 \div 4 = 1)$.

Step 3: Multiply the numerators and then multiply the denominators. See Rule 3.

From Step 2, $\dfrac{1}{1} \times \dfrac{3}{1} = \dfrac{1 \times 3}{1 \times 1} = \dfrac{3}{1} = 3$

Therefore, $4 \times \dfrac{3}{4} = 3$

Example 2

Solve the question in Example 1 without showing the detailed explanations. Use a shortcut method.

Solution

Shortcut: $4 \times \dfrac{3}{4} = \dfrac{4}{1} \times \dfrac{3}{4}$

$= \dfrac{\overset{1}{4}}{1} \times \dfrac{3}{\underset{1}{4}}$

$= \dfrac{1 \times 3}{1 \times 1} = \dfrac{3}{1} = 3$

Example 3

Multiply: $12 \times \dfrac{3}{4}$

Solution

Step 1: Change the whole number 12 to a fraction. See Rule 1.

$$12 = \frac{12}{1}$$

Therefore, $12 \times \dfrac{3}{4} = \dfrac{12}{1} \times \dfrac{3}{4}$

Step 2: Reduce the fractions to the lowest terms by dividing the numerators and the denominators by the same number evenly (without a remainder), if possible. See Rule 2.

Therefore, $\dfrac{12}{1} \times \dfrac{3}{4} = \dfrac{\overset{3}{12}}{1} \times \dfrac{3}{\underset{1}{4}}$ $(12 \div 4 = 3, 4 \div 4 = 1)$.

Step 3: Multiply the numerators, and then multiply the denominators. See Rule 3.

From Step 2, $\dfrac{3}{1} \times \dfrac{3}{1} = \dfrac{3 \times 3}{1 \times 1} = \dfrac{9}{1} = 9$

Therefore, $12 \times \dfrac{3}{4} = 9$

Example 4

Solve the question in Example 3 without showing any detailed explanations. Use a shortcut method.

Solution

$12 \times \dfrac{3}{4} = \dfrac{12}{1} \times \dfrac{3}{4}$

$= \dfrac{\overset{3}{12}}{1} \times \dfrac{3}{\underset{1}{4}}$

$= 9$

Example 5

Use multiplication to explain what all the shaded areas of the models represent?

440

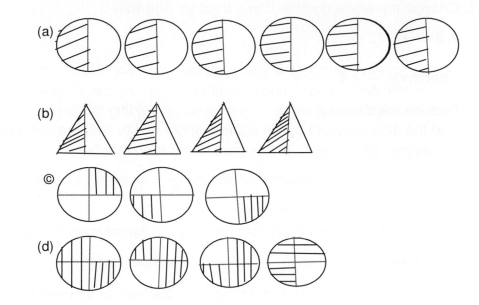

Solution

(**a**) Each shaded area shows $\frac{1}{2}$ of a circle.

There are 6 circles.

Therefore, the shaded area $= 6 \times \frac{1}{2}$ circles.

(**b**) Each shaded area shows $\frac{1}{2}$ of a triangle.

There are 4 triangles.

Therefore, the shaded area $= \frac{1}{2} \times 4$ triangles.

(**c**) Each shaded area shows $\frac{1}{4}$ of a circle.

There are 3 circles.

Therefore, the shaded area $= \frac{1}{4} \times 3$ circles.

(**d**) Each shaded area shows $\frac{3}{4}$ of a circle.

There are 4 circles.

Therefore, the shaded area $= 4 \times \frac{3}{4}$ circle.

Example 6

Multiply: $\frac{3}{5} \times 6$

Solution

441

Step 1: Change the whole number 6 to a fraction. See Rule 1.

$$6 = \frac{6}{1}$$

Therefore, $\frac{3}{5} \times 6 = \frac{3}{5} \times \frac{6}{1}$

Step 2: Reduce the fractions to the lowest terms by dividing the numerators and the denominators by the same number evenly (without a remainder) if possible. See Rule 2 . In this case, there is no number that can divide the numerators and the denominators of $\frac{3}{5} \times \frac{6}{1}$ evenly (without a remainder), therefore, go to Step 3.

Step 3: Multiply the numerators and then multiply the denominators. See Rule 3.

From Step 2, $\frac{3}{5} \times \frac{6}{1} = \frac{3 \times 6}{5 \times 1} = \frac{18}{5}$ ← Improper fraction

Step 4: Change the answer (which is an improper fraction) to a mixed number by dividing the numerator by the denominator. See Rule 4.

$$\frac{18}{5} = 3\frac{3}{5} \quad \text{(Note: } 18 \div 5 = 3 \text{ remainder 3, which is written as } 3\frac{3}{5}.\text{)}$$

Therefore, $\frac{3}{5} \times 6 = 3\frac{3}{5}$

Example 7

Solve the question in Example 6 without showing the detailed explanations. Use a shortcut method.

Solution

$$\frac{3}{5} \times 6 = \frac{3}{5} \times \frac{6}{1}$$

$$= \frac{3 \times 6}{5 \times 1}$$

$$= \frac{18}{5}$$

$$= 3\frac{3}{5}$$

Example 8

Find the product: $8 \times \frac{1}{3} \times 12 \times \frac{3}{4}$

Solution

Note: Find the product means to multiply.

Step 1: Change the whole numbers 8 and 12 to fractions. See Rule 1.

The fraction form of $8 = \dfrac{8}{1}$

The fraction form of $12 = \dfrac{12}{1}$

Therefore, $8 \times \dfrac{1}{3} \times 12 \times \dfrac{3}{4} = \dfrac{8}{1} \times \dfrac{1}{3} \times \dfrac{12}{1} \times \dfrac{3}{4}$

Step 2: Reduce the fractions to the lowest terms by dividing the numerators and the denominators by the same number evenly (without a remainder), if possible. See Rule 3.

$$\dfrac{\overset{2}{8}}{1} \times \dfrac{1}{\underset{1}{3}} \times \dfrac{12}{1} \times \dfrac{\overset{1}{3}}{\underset{1}{4}} \qquad (8 \div 4 = 2,\ 4 \div 4 = 1,\ 3 \div 3 = 1)$$

Step 3: Multiply the numerators, and then multiply the denominators. See Rule 3.

From Step 2, $\dfrac{2}{1} \times \dfrac{1}{1} \times \dfrac{12}{1} \times \dfrac{1}{1} = \dfrac{2 \times 1 \times 12 \times 1}{1 \times 1 \times 1 \times 1} = \dfrac{24}{1} = 24$

Example 9

Solve the question in Example 8 without showing the detailed explanations. Use the shortcut method.

Solution

Shortcut:

$$8 \times \dfrac{1}{3} \times 12 \times \dfrac{3}{4} = \dfrac{8}{1} \times \dfrac{1}{3} \times \dfrac{12}{1} \times \dfrac{3}{4}$$

$$= \dfrac{\overset{2}{8}}{1} \times \dfrac{1}{\underset{1}{3}} \times \dfrac{12}{1} \times \dfrac{\overset{1}{3}}{\underset{1}{4}}$$

$$= 24$$

The notes and the generous worked examples have provided me with conceptual understanding and computational fluency to do my homework.

Exercises

1. Multiply the following. Hint: See Examples **1** and **3**.

(a) $12 \times \dfrac{1}{6}$

(b) $3 \times \dfrac{2}{3}$

(c) $15 \times \dfrac{2}{5}$

(d) $25 \times \dfrac{3}{5}$

(e) $14 \times \dfrac{2}{7}$

(f) $9 \times \dfrac{2}{3}$

(g) $6 \times \dfrac{2}{3}$

(h) $4 \times \dfrac{1}{4}$

(i) $16 \times \dfrac{3}{4}$

(j) $22 \times \dfrac{2}{11}$

(k) $21 \times \dfrac{3}{7}$

(l) $14 \times \dfrac{2}{7}$

(m) $18 \times \dfrac{5}{6}$

(n) $16 \times \dfrac{1}{4}$

(o) $12 \times \dfrac{1}{3}$

(p) $8 \times \dfrac{1}{4}$

(q) $18 \times \dfrac{2}{9}$

(r) $15 \times \dfrac{2}{3}$

(s) $12 \times \dfrac{3}{4}$

(t) $27 \times \dfrac{2}{3}$

(u) $36 \times \dfrac{5}{6}$

2. Solve questions **1(a)** to **1(u)** without showing detailed explanations. Use shortcut method. Hint: See Example **2** and **4**.

3. Multiply the following. Hint: See Example **6**.

(a) $\dfrac{3}{5} \times 6$

(b) $\dfrac{1}{4} \times 9$

(c) $\dfrac{3}{7} \times 3$

(d) $\dfrac{2}{3} \times 8$

(e) $\dfrac{2}{7} \times 4$

(f) $\dfrac{2}{9} \times 7$

(g) $\dfrac{1}{9} \times 14$

(h) $\dfrac{3}{7} \times 8$

(i) $\dfrac{2}{9} \times 11$

(j) $\dfrac{3}{5} \times 22$

(k) $\dfrac{3}{7} \times 5$

(l) $\dfrac{4}{5} \times 24$

(m) $\dfrac{3}{5} \times 24$

(n) $\dfrac{2}{7} \times 18$

(o) $\dfrac{3}{11} \times 30$

(p) $\dfrac{3}{4} \times 25$

4. Solve questions **3(a)** to **3(o)** without showing any detailed explanations. Use a shortcut method. Hint: See Example **7**.

5. Multiply: Hint: See Example **8**.

(a) $12 \times \dfrac{1}{4} \times 3 \times \dfrac{1}{3}$

(b) $\dfrac{2}{5} \times 15 \times \dfrac{2}{3}$

(c) $4 \times \dfrac{2}{5} \times \dfrac{5}{8}$

(d) $\frac{2}{7} \times 14 \times 2 \times \frac{3}{4}$ **(e)** $3 \times 4 \times \frac{2}{9} \times 6$ **(f)** $\frac{3}{4} \times 12 \times \frac{2}{5} \times 10$

(g) $\frac{3}{7} \times \frac{21}{27} \times 3 \times 2$ **(h)** $\frac{4}{5} \times \frac{2}{3} \times 6$ **(i)** $\frac{3}{5} \times \frac{2}{7} \times 35$

(j) $\frac{2}{9} \times 27 \times \frac{1}{4}$ **(k)** $\frac{2}{3} \times \frac{3}{4} \times \frac{6}{7} \times \frac{14}{18}$ **(l)** $\frac{3}{5} \times \frac{10}{12} \times \frac{3}{4}$

(m) $\frac{7}{8} \times \frac{3}{21} \times \frac{4}{9} \times 36$ **(n)** $\frac{3}{5} \times \frac{10}{11} \times \frac{22}{27}$ **(p)** $\frac{2}{7} \times \frac{5}{6} \times 14 \times \frac{2}{3}$

Challenge Questions

6. Find the product:

(a) $\frac{2}{3} \times 24$ **(b)** $24 \times \frac{5}{6}$ **(c)** $\frac{1}{3} \times 15$ **(d)** $\frac{2}{7} \times 5$

(e) $12 \times \frac{2}{3}$ **(f)** $14 \times \frac{3}{7}$ **(g)** $\frac{3}{5} \times 6$ **(h)** $3 \times \frac{7}{8}$

(i) $7 \times \frac{3}{21}$ **(j)** $\frac{2}{7} \times 10$ **(k)** $30 \times \frac{3}{5}$ **(l)** $\frac{3}{5} \times 20$

(m) $9 \times \frac{5}{8}$ **(n)** $\frac{4}{9} \times 7$ **(o)** $\frac{2}{5} \times 25$ **(p)** $\frac{4}{9} \times 27$

(q) $9 \times \frac{2}{3}$ **(r)** $16 \times \frac{3}{4}$ **(s)** $10 \times \frac{3}{4} \times \frac{2}{5} \times 6$

(t) $7 \times 3 \times \frac{5}{12} \times \frac{2}{21}$ **(u)** $\frac{2}{15} \times 8 \times \frac{5}{6} \times \frac{3}{4}$ **(v)** $\frac{2}{5} \times \frac{1}{3} \times \frac{2}{3}$

Answers to Selected Questions

1(a) 2   **3(a)** $\frac{18}{5}$ **5(a)** 3

REAL WORLD APPLICATIONS - WORD PROBLEMS
Multiplication of Fractions and Whole Numbers

Example 1

Given that $\frac{k}{3} \times 9 = 21$, find k.

Solution

Setup: Let us work on the left side of the equation which is $\frac{k}{3} \times 9$ to determine how 21 is obtained at the right side of the equation.

Step 1: Consider the left hand of the equation which is $\frac{k}{3} \times 9$ as the multiplication of a fraction by a whole number where $\frac{k}{3}$ is the fraction and 9 is the whole number. Recall that under the topic, Multiplication of Fractions and Whole Numbers, to multiply fractions by whole numbers, write the whole numbers as fractions by dividing the whole numbers by 1. Therefore, 9 can be written as the fraction $\frac{9}{1}$.

Therefore, the left side of the equation which is $\frac{k}{3} \times 9 = \frac{k}{3} \times \frac{9}{1}$

Step 2: Reduce the left side of the equation which is $\frac{k}{3} \times \frac{9}{1}$ to the lowest terms by dividing both the numerator and the denominator by the same number evenly (without remainder) if possible. In this case, both the numerator and the denominator can be divided by 3 as shown:

$$\frac{k}{3} \times \frac{\overset{3}{\cancel{9}}}{1} = \frac{k}{\underset{1}{\cancel{3}}} \times \frac{\cancel{9}}{1}$$

$$= \frac{k}{1} \times \frac{3}{1}$$

Step 3: Multiply all the numerators together, and then multiply all the denominators together as shown:

$$\frac{k}{1} \times \frac{3}{1} = \frac{3k}{1}$$

$$= 3k$$

Therefore, the left side of the equation which is $\frac{k}{3} \times 9$ is simplified to become 3k.

Step 4: Compare the simplified form of the left side of the equation, which is 3k to the right side of the equation which is 21.
Therefore:
$$3k = 21$$
We have to think of a number that can be multiplied by 3 to obtain 21, and that number is 7.
Therefore, k = 7.

Check your answer

$$3k = 21$$
$$3 \times 7 = 21 \qquad \text{Substitute } k = 7$$
$$21 = 21 \qquad \text{Since the left side of the equation which is 21 is}$$
equal to the right side of the equation, which is 21, then k = 7 is a correct answer.

Example 2
Solve the question in Example 1 without showing detailed explanations. Use the shortcut method.
Solution

$$\frac{k}{3} \times 9 = 21$$

$$\frac{k}{\underset{1}{3}} \times \frac{\overset{3}{9}}{1} = 21$$

$$3k = 21$$
$$3 \times 7 = 21$$
Therefore, k = 7

Critical Thinking
The shortcut method is recommended for homework, class exercises and tests, however the detailed explanation method is to provide the students with the necessary mathematical logic for understanding the true concepts.

Example 3
Find the value of z in the equation $\frac{1}{3} \times z = 4$

Solution

Setup: Let us work on the left side of the equation which is $\frac{1}{3} \times z$ to determine how 4 is obtained at the right side of the equation.

Step 1: Consider the left side of the equation which is $\frac{1}{3} \times z$ as a multiplication of a fraction by a whole number where $\frac{1}{3}$ is a fraction and z is the whole number.

Recall that under the topic Multiplication of Fractions and Whole Numbers, to multiply fractions by whole numbers write the whole numbers as fractions by dividing the whole numbers by 1.

Therefore, z can be written as a fraction as $\frac{z}{1}$.

Therefore, the left side of the equation which is:

$$\frac{1}{3} \times z = \frac{1}{3} \times \frac{z}{1}$$

Step 2: Reduce the left side of the equation which is $\frac{1}{3} \times \frac{z}{1}$ to the lowest terms by dividing both the numerator and the denominator by the same number evenly (without a remainder) if possible.

In this case, both the numerator and the denominator cannot be divided by the same number evenly (Note: We do not know the value of z yet.) Go to Step 3.

Step 3: Multiply all the numerators together, and then multiply all the denominators together as shown:

$$\frac{1}{3} \times \frac{z}{1} = \frac{1 \times z}{3 \times 1}$$

$$= \frac{z}{3}$$

Therefore, the left side of the equation is simplified to become $\frac{z}{3}$.

Step 4: Compare the simplified form of the left side of the equation, which is $\frac{z}{3}$ to the right side of the equation, which is 4.

Therefore: $\frac{z}{3} = 4$

We have to think of a number that can be divided by 3 to obtain 4 and that number is 12. Therefore, z = 12.

Check your answer

$$\frac{z}{3} = 4$$

$$\frac{12}{3} = 4 \qquad \text{Substitute } z = 12$$

$$\frac{\overset{4}{\cancel{12}}}{\underset{1}{\cancel{3}}} = 4$$

$4 = 4 \qquad$ Since the left side of the equation is equal to 4 and the right side of the equation is also equal to 4, then, $z = 12$ is a correct answer.

Example 4

Solve the equation in Example 3 without showing detailed explanations. Use a shortcut method.

Solution

$$\frac{1}{3} \times z = 4$$

$$\frac{1}{3} \times \frac{z}{1} = 4$$

$$\frac{z}{3} = 4$$

$$\frac{12}{3} = 4$$

Therefore, $z = 12$

Check your answer

$$\frac{z}{3} = 4$$

$$\frac{12}{3} = 4 \qquad \text{Substitute } z = 12$$

$$4 = 4$$

Example 5

Find k in the equation $\frac{2}{k} \times 9 = 6$

Solution

Setup: Let us work on the left side of the equation, which is $\frac{2}{k} \times 9$ to determine how 6 on the right of the equation is obtained.

Step 1: Consider the left side of the equation, which is $\frac{2}{k} \times 9$ as a multiplication of a fraction by a whole number, where $\frac{2}{k}$ is the fraction and 9 is the whole number.

Recall that under the topic Multiplication of Fractions and Whole Numbers, to multiply fractions by whole numbers write the whole numbers as fractions by dividing the whole numbers by 1.

So, 9 can be written as a fraction as $\frac{9}{1}$.

Therefore, the left side of the equation which is:

$$\frac{2}{k} \times 9 = \frac{2}{k} \times \frac{9}{1}$$

Step 2: Reduce the left hand side of the equation which is $\frac{2}{k} \times \frac{9}{1}$ to the lowest terms by dividing the numerators and denominators by the same number evenly (without a remainder). Since we do not know the value of k yet, we cannot divide numerators and the denominators evenly (without a remainder.) Go to Step 3.

Step 3: Multiply all the numerators together and then multiply all the denominators together as shown:

$$\frac{2}{k} \times \frac{9}{1} = \frac{2 \times 9}{k \times 1}$$

$$= \frac{18}{k}$$

Therefore, the left side of the equation, which is $\frac{2}{k} \times \frac{9}{1}$ is simplified to become $\frac{18}{k}$.

Step 4: Compare the simplified form of the left side of the equation, which is $\frac{18}{k}$ to the right side of the equation, which is 6.

Therefore, $\frac{18}{k} = 6$

We have to think of a number that can divide 18 in order to obtain 6. The number is 3.

Therefore, k = 3.

Check your answer

$$\frac{18}{k} = 6$$

$$\frac{18}{3} = 6 \qquad \text{Substitute } k = 3$$

$$6 = 6 \qquad \text{Therefore, } k = 3 \text{ is a correct answer.}$$

Example 6

Solve the question in Example 5 without showing detailed information. Use a shortcut method.

Solution

$$\frac{2}{k} \times 9 = 6$$

$$\frac{2}{k} \times \frac{9}{1} = 6$$

$$\frac{18}{k} = 6, \qquad \frac{18}{3} = 6$$

Therefore, $k = 3$

_____

The notes and the generous worked examples have provided me with conceptual understanding and computational fluency to do my homework.

Exercises

1. Solve for k in the following equations. (Hint: See Examples **1** and **2**.) Check your answer.

(a) $\frac{k}{2} \times 10 = 5$ (b) $\frac{k}{4} \times 12 = 9$ (c) $\frac{k}{5} \times 15 = 6$ (d) $\frac{k}{6} \times 24 = 20$

(e) $\frac{k}{3} \times 9 = 6$ (f) $\frac{k}{7} \times 21 = 12$ (g) $\frac{k}{8} \times 64 = 24$ (h) $\frac{k}{9} \times 18 = 10$

(i) $\frac{k}{10} \times 30 = 27$ (j) $\frac{k}{6} \times 60 = 20$ (k) $\frac{k}{5} \times 25 = 15$ (l) $\frac{k}{3} \times 24 = 16$

2. Solve for k in the following equations. (Hint: See Examples **3** and **4**.) Check your answer.

(a) $\dfrac{1}{3} \times k = 5$ **(b)** $\dfrac{2}{3} \times k = 4$ **(c)** $\dfrac{1}{4} \times k = 12$ **(d)** $\dfrac{2}{5} \times k = 4$

(e) $\dfrac{1}{5} \times k = 6$ **(f)** $\dfrac{1}{7} \times k = 6$ **(g)** $\dfrac{1}{6} \times k = 6$ **(h)** $\dfrac{1}{7} \times k = 2$

(i) $\dfrac{1}{10} \times k = 10$ **(j)** $\dfrac{1}{8} \times k = 2$ **(k)** $\dfrac{1}{6} \times k = 3$ **(l)** $\dfrac{1}{9} \times k = 9$

3. Solve for k in the following equations. (Hint: See Examples **5** and **6**.) Check your answer.

(a) $\dfrac{2}{k} \times 9 = 3$ **(b)** $\dfrac{2}{k} \times 6 = 2$ **(c)** $\dfrac{1}{k} \times 20 = 5$ **(d)** $\dfrac{1}{k} \times 28 = 4$

(e) $\dfrac{1}{k} \times 12 = 3$ **(f)** $\dfrac{1}{k} \times 12 = 4$ **(g)** $\dfrac{1}{k} \times 15 = 3$ **(h)** $\dfrac{1}{k} \times 15 = 5$

(i) $\dfrac{1}{k} \times 24 = 8$ **(j)** $\dfrac{3}{k} \times 6 = 3$ **(k)** $\dfrac{1}{k} \times 24 = 6$ **(l)** $\dfrac{1}{k} \times 24 = 4$

(m) $\dfrac{1}{k} \times 18 = 6$ **(n)** $\dfrac{1}{k} \times 18 = 3$ **(o)** $\dfrac{1}{k} \times 16 = 4$ **(p)** $\dfrac{1}{k} \times 6 = 2$

Challenge Questions

4. Solve for k in the following equations:

(a) $\dfrac{k}{5} \times 5 = 5$ **(b)** $\dfrac{2}{3} \times k = 6$ **(c)** $4 = \dfrac{2}{4} \times k$ **(d)** $\dfrac{1}{2k} \times 8 = 1$

5. Solve for w in the following equations:

(a). $w \times \dfrac{3}{4} = 9$ **(b).** $\dfrac{3}{5w} \times 15 = 27$ **(c)** $\dfrac{w}{7} = 11$ **(d)** $4w = 16$

Answers to Selected Questions

1(a) 1   **1(d)** 5   **1(g)** 3   **2(b)** 6   **2(d)** 10   **3(a)** 6   **3(f)** 3   **3(n)** 6

Example 7

Solve for k in the equation:

$$\dfrac{3}{7} \times k = 3$$

Solution

Setup: Let us work on the left side of the equation, which is $\frac{3}{7} \times k$ to determine how 3 on the right side of the equation is obtained.

Step 1: Consider the left side of the equation, which is $\frac{3}{7} \times k$ as a multiplication

of a fraction by a whole number where $\frac{3}{7}$ is the fraction and k is the whole number. Recall that under the topic Multiplication of Fractions and Whole Numbers, to multiply fractions by whole numbers write the whole numbers as fractions by dividing the whole numbers by 1.

Therefore, k can be written as a fraction as: $\frac{k}{1}$.

Therefore, the left side of the equation, which is:

$$\frac{3}{7} \times 3 = \frac{3}{7} \times \frac{k}{1}$$

Step 2: Reduce the left side of the equation, which is $\frac{3}{7} \times \frac{k}{1}$ to the lowest

terms by dividing the numerators and the denominators by the same number evenly (without a remainder.) In this case, there is no number that can divide both the numerators and the denominators evenly (without a remainder) and the value of k is not known yet. Go to Step 3.

Step 3: Multiply all the numerators together, and then multiply all the denominators together as shown:

$$\frac{3}{7} \times \frac{k}{1} = \frac{3 \times k}{7 \times 1}$$

$$= \frac{3k}{7}$$

Therefore, $\frac{3k}{7} = 3$

We have to think of a number that can be divided by 7 in order to obtain 3 on the right side of the equation. The number is 21, because $21 \div 7 = 3$. (Note: Knowing the multiplication tables is very helpful in determining that $7 \times 3 = 21$ and, therefore, $21 \div 7 = 3$, Therefore, the number that can be divided by 7 in order to obtain 3 is 21.)

We can write $3k = 21$.

$$3k = 21 \text{ ————————— } [A]$$

Using equation $[A]$, the number that can be multiplied by 3 to obtain 21 is 7. Therefore,

$$k = 7 \,.$$

Check your answer:

$$\frac{3}{7} \times k = 3$$

$$\frac{3}{7} \times 7 = 3$$ Substitute k = 7, then the numerator 7 can divide the

denominator 7 such that 3 = 3.

3 = 3 Therefore, the answer k = 7 is correct.

Example 8
Solve the question in Example 7 without showing detailed explanations.
Solution

$$\frac{3}{7} \times k = 3$$

$$\frac{3k}{7} = 3$$

$$\frac{3 \times 7}{7} = 3 \quad \text{Therefore, } k = 7$$

The notes and the generous worked examples have provided me with conceptual understanding and computational fluency to do my homework.

Exercises
1. Solve for k in the following equations. (Hint: See Examples **7** and **8**.) Check your answer.

(a) $\frac{4}{7} \times k = 4$ (b) $\frac{3}{9} \times k = 3$ (c) $\frac{2}{3} \times k = 6$ (d) $\frac{3}{4} \times k = 6$

(e) $\frac{3}{5} \times k = 6$ (f) $\frac{4}{7} \times k = 8$ (g) $\frac{3}{9} \times k = 6$ (h) $\frac{5}{6} \times k = 10$

Challenge Questions
2. Solve for p in the following equations.

(a) $\frac{3}{8} \times p = 9$ (b) $p \times \frac{3}{4} = 12$ (c) $21 = \frac{3}{7} \times p$ (d) $\frac{5}{4} \times p = 20$

Answers to Selected Questions
1(a) 7 **1(e)** 10

REAL WORLD APPLICATIONS - WORD PROBLEMS
Finding a Number When a Fractional Part of it is known

Explanation

Given that there are 12 students in a science class, which represent $\frac{1}{4}$ of the number of the students in the class. Find the total number in the class.

This means 12 students $= \frac{1}{4} \times$ Total number of students

$$12 \text{ students} = \frac{1 \times \text{Total number of students}}{4}$$

$$12 \text{ students} = \frac{\text{Total number of students}}{4}$$

Let us think of a number that can be divided by 4 to obtain 12. The number is 48. Therefore, the total number of students in the class is 48. Therefore, the multiplication problem involving 12 students $= \frac{1}{4} \times$ Total number of students can be changed to the division problem as shown:

$$12 \div \frac{1}{4} = ?$$

$$12 \div \frac{1}{4} = 12 \times \frac{4}{1} \quad \text{(To divide a number by a fraction, invert or flip}$$

the fraction and change the division sign to a multiplication sign. Review reciprocals.)

$$= 48 \text{ students}$$

We can therefore establish a rule to find a number when a fractional part of it is known as shown:

Rule: To find a number when a fractional part of the number is known, divide the known part by the fraction. The quotient is the unknown number.

Example 1

Given that 5 students in a class went to the zoo last week and this represents $\frac{1}{5}$ of the students in the class. Find the total number of students in the class.
Solution

455

Using the rule, the total number of students in the class is:

$$5 \div \frac{1}{5}$$

$$5 \div \frac{1}{5} = 5 \times \frac{5}{1}$$ (When dividing by a fraction, invert or flip the fraction

and change the division sign to a multiplication sign. Review the section on Reciprocals.)

$$= \frac{5 \times 5}{1}$$

$$= 25$$

There are 25 students in the class.

Example 2

Mary saves $80 of her earnings each week. If this is $\frac{3}{5}$ of her earnings, what is her weekly total earnings?

Solution

Using the rule, the total weekly earnings is:

$$80 \div \frac{3}{5}$$

$$80 \div \frac{3}{5} = 80 \times \frac{5}{3}$$ (When dividing by a fraction, invert or flip the

fraction and change the division sign to a multiplication sign. Review reciprocals.)

$$= \frac{80 \times 5}{3}$$

$$= \frac{400}{3}$$

$$= 133.33$$ You may use a calculator.

Therefore, the total weekly earnings is $133. 33.

Check your answer:

$$\text{Savings per week} = \frac{3}{5} \times 133. 33 = \frac{400}{5}$$

$$= \$80 \text{ which is given in the original question.}$$

Therefore, the total weekly earnings of $133.33 is correct.

Example 3

If $\frac{3}{8}$ of a number is 24, find the number.

Solution

Using the rule, the number is:

$$24 \div \frac{3}{8}$$

$$24 \div \frac{3}{8} = 24 \times \frac{8}{3}$$ (When dividing by a fraction, invert or flip the fraction and change the division sign to a multiplication sign. Review reciprocals.)

$$= 24 \times \frac{8}{\overset{3}{\underset{1}{3}}}$$ Divide the numerator and the denominator by 3.

$$= 8 \times \frac{8}{1}$$

$$= 64$$

Therefore, the number is 64

Check your answer

$$\frac{3}{8} \text{ of the unknown number} = 24$$

$$\frac{3}{8} \times 64 = 24$$ Substitute 64 for the unknown number.

$$\frac{3}{\underset{1}{8}} \times \overset{8}{64} = 24$$ Divide the numerator and the denominator by 8.

$$\frac{3}{1} \times 8 = 24$$

$$24 = 24$$

The answer 64 is correct because the left side is equal to the right side of the equation.

Example 4

$\dfrac{5}{8}$ of what number is 40?

Solution

Using the Rule,

$$\text{Number} = 40 \div \dfrac{5}{8}$$

$$40 \div \dfrac{5}{8} = 40 \times \dfrac{8}{5} \qquad \text{Review the topic, Dividing a Number By a Fraction.}$$

$$= 40 \times \dfrac{\overset{8}{\cancel{40}}}{\underset{1}{\cancel{5}}} \qquad \text{Divide the numerator and the denominator by 5.}$$

$$= 8 \times \dfrac{8}{1}$$

$$= 64$$

The number is 64

Check your answer:

$$\dfrac{5}{8} \text{ of an unknown number} = 40$$

$$\dfrac{5}{8} \text{ of } 64 = 40 \qquad \text{Substitute 64 for the unknown number.}$$

$$\dfrac{5}{\underset{1}{\cancel{8}}} \times \overset{8}{\cancel{64}} = 40$$

$$\dfrac{5}{1} \times 8 = 40$$

$$40 = 40$$

Since the left and the right sides of the equations are equal, the unknown number which is 64 is correct.

The notes and the generous worked examples have provided me with conceptual understanding and computational fluency to do my homework.

Exercises

1. Given that 5 students of a class visited the zoo last term, which is $\frac{1}{4}$ of the class, find the total number of students in the class. (Hint: See Example **1**.) Check your answer.

2. Nancy saved $10, 000.00 a year which represents $\frac{2}{5}$ of her salary. What is her total salary? (Hint: See Example **2**.) Check your answer.

3. $\frac{4}{7}$ of a number is 28. What is the number? (Hint: See Example **3**.) Check your answer.

4. Given that in a hospital, there are 64 female nurses. If the female nurses represent $\frac{4}{7}$ of the total nurses at the hospital, what is the total number of nurses at the hospital? (Hint: See Example **1**.). Check your answer.

5. John spent $30, 000. 00 last year, which represents $\frac{3}{4}$ of his salary. What is the salary of John? (Hint: See Example **2**). Check your answer.

6. 40 is $\frac{4}{7}$ of what number? (Hint: See Example 4.) Check your answer.

Challenge Questions

7. Mary withdrew $20.00 from the bank and if this withdrawal represents $\frac{2}{5}$ of her total savings, how much money did she have at the bank?

8. 27 is $\frac{3}{4}$ of what number?

9. Ten members of a club went to see a football game. If the number of the club members that went to the football game represents $\frac{2}{5}$ of the total club members, what is the total number of club members?

Answers to Selected Questions

(1) 20   (3) 49   (6) 70

MORE REAL WORLD APPLICATIONS - WORD PROBLEMS
Finding a Number When a Fractional Part of it is Known

Example 1

A stadium has 40, 000 general admission seats. Find the total number of seats if this represents $\frac{2}{3}$ of the seats in the stadium.

Solution

Using the rule, the total number of seats is $40,000 \div \frac{2}{3}$.

$$40,000 \div \frac{2}{3} = 40,000 \times \frac{3}{2}$$ (When dividing by a fraction, invert or flip the fraction and change the division sign to a multiplication sign. Review the topic: Dividing a Number By a Fraction.)

$$= \overset{20,000}{\cancel{40,000}} \times \frac{3}{\underset{1}{\cancel{2}}}$$ Divide the numerator and denominator by 2.

$$= 20,000 \times \frac{3}{1}$$
$$= 60,000 \text{ seats.}$$

Example 2

The price of a shirt is reduced by $10.00. If the reduction was $\frac{5}{7}$ of the original price, what was the original price of the shirt?

Solution

Using the rule, the original price of the shirt is $10 \div \frac{5}{7}$

$$10 \div \frac{5}{7} = 10 \times \frac{7}{5}$$ (When dividing by a fraction, invert or flip the fraction and change the division sign to a multiplication sign. Review the topic: Dividing a Number By a Fraction.)

$$= 10 \times \frac{\overset{2}{\cancel{7}}}{\underset{1}{\cancel{5}}}$$ Divide the numerator and the denominator by 5.

$$= 2 \times \frac{7}{1}$$

$$= \$14.00$$

The original price of the shirt is $14.00.

Example 3

A school baseball team won 16 games. If they won $\frac{2}{3}$ of the games played,

what was the total number of games played?

Solution

Using the rule, the total number of games played is $16 \div \frac{2}{3}$

$$16 \div \frac{2}{3} = 16 \times \frac{3}{2}$$ (When dividing by a fraction, invert or flip the fraction and change the division sign to a multiplication sign. Review the topic: Dividing a Number By a Fraction.)

$$= \overset{8}{\cancel{16}} \times \frac{3}{\underset{1}{\cancel{2}}}$$ Divide the numerator and the denominator by 2.

$$= 8 \times \frac{3}{1}$$

$$= 24$$

The total number of games won was 24.

_____

The notes and the generous worked examples have provided me with conceptual understanding and computational fluency to do my homework.

Exercises

1. A stadium has 25,000 general admission seats. Find the total number of seats if this represents $\frac{5}{7}$ of the stadium seats. (Hint: See Example 1.)

2. If the price of a shirt is reduced by $8.00 and if this reduction represents $\frac{2}{5}$ of the

original price of the shirt, what was the original price of the shirt?
(Hint: See Example **2**.)

3. A school baseball team won 20 games. If the school won $\frac{5}{7}$ of the games played, what was the total number of games played? (Hint: See Example **3**.)

Challenge Question

4. Regis received 450 votes for school president. If this represents $\frac{5}{8}$ of all the votes, how many students voted in the election?

FRACTIONAL PARTS

Rule: To find what fractional part one number is of another number, write a fraction with the partial amount as the numerator and the total amount as the denominator.

Example 1
What fractional part of 50 is 5?
Solution

Using the rule, the fractional part is $\dfrac{\text{partial amount}}{\text{Total amount}} = \dfrac{5}{50}$

$$\frac{5}{50} = \frac{\overset{1}{5}}{\underset{10}{50}}$$ Divide the numerator and the denominator by 5.

$$= \frac{1}{10}$$

The fractional part $= \dfrac{1}{10}$

Check your answer
Fractional part of 50 = 5

Therefore, $\dfrac{1}{10} \times 50 = 5$ (The fractional part is $\dfrac{1}{10}$ and "**of**" means multiplication.)

$$\frac{\overset{5}{1}}{10} \times 50 = 5$$

$$\frac{1}{\underset{1}{1}} \times 5 = 5$$

$$5 = 5$$

Since the left side and right side of the equation are the same (5), the fractional part $\frac{1}{10}$ is correct.

Example 2

James has $50.00 and if he spent $15.00, what fractional part of his money did he spend?

Solution

Using the rule, the fractional part of the money that he spent is $\dfrac{\text{Amount spent}}{\text{Total amount}} = \dfrac{15}{50}$

$$= \frac{\overset{3}{15}}{\underset{10}{50}} \qquad \textbf{(Reduce the fraction to the lowest terms} \text{ by dividing the numerator and the denominator by 5.)}$$

$$= \frac{3}{10}$$

Therefore, the fractional part which has been spent is $\dfrac{3}{10}$.

The notes and the generous worked examples have provided me with conceptual understanding and computational fluency to do my homework.

Exercises

1. Find the fractional part of the following: (Hint: See Example **1**.)

   (**a**) 6 is what part of 18?   (**b**) 3 is what part of 9?
   (**c**) 4 is what part of 12?   (**d**) 5 is what part of 15?
   (**e**) 11 is what part of 44?   (**f**) 8 is what part of 24?
   (**g**) 4 is what part of 32?   (**h**) 7 is what part of 21?
   (**i**) 7 is what part of 35?   (**j**) 9 is what part of 45?
   (**k**) 5 is what part of 65?   (**l**) 8 is what part of 64?
   (**m**) 3 is what part of 24?   (**n**) 4 is what part of 36?

(**o**) 15 is what part of 60?   (**p**) 10 is what part of 80?

(**q**) 30 is what part of 80?   (**r**) 25 is what part of 75?

2. If a student got 75 out of 100 questions correct, what fraction was correct? (Hint: See Example **2**.)

3. A student had $100.00 and he spent $75.00 on books. What fraction of the money was spent on books? (Hint: See Example **2**.)

4. There are 18 boys in a class of 34 students. What part of the class is boys? (Hint: See Example **2**.)

Challenge Questions

5. If 4 students are absent in a class of 24 students, what fractional part of the class is absent?

6. If a 26 year old student spent 6 years in college, what part of the student's life was spent in college?

7. 100 is what part of 500?

Answers to Selected Questions

1(a) $\dfrac{1}{3}$ **1(g)** $\dfrac{1}{8}$ **1(p)** $\dfrac{1}{8}$ **(5)** $\dfrac{1}{6}$

CUMULATIVE REVIEW – FRACTIONS

1. Change the following improper fractions to mixed numbers.

(**a**) $\dfrac{12}{3}$ (**b**) $\dfrac{10}{4}$ (**c**) $\dfrac{11}{4}$ (**d**) $\dfrac{28}{7}$ (**e**) $\dfrac{32}{5}$ (**f**) $\dfrac{48}{5}$

2. Change the following mixed numbers to improper fractions.

(**a**) $1\dfrac{3}{5}$ (**b**) $2\dfrac{2}{7}$ (**c**) $4\dfrac{1}{7}$ (**d**) $7\dfrac{1}{9}$ (**e**) $5\dfrac{3}{4}$ (**f**) $8\dfrac{3}{5}$

3. Arrange each set of fractions in descending order of value.

(**a**) $\dfrac{4}{5}, \dfrac{6}{7}$ (**b**) $\dfrac{2}{3}, \dfrac{2}{5}$ (**c**) $\dfrac{2}{7}, \dfrac{3}{8}$ (**d**) $\dfrac{3}{4}, \dfrac{4}{5}$

(**e**) $\dfrac{2}{3}, \dfrac{4}{6}, \dfrac{3}{5}$ (**f**) $\dfrac{1}{5}, \dfrac{2}{7}, \dfrac{5}{14}$ (**g**) $\dfrac{2}{5}, \dfrac{3}{6}, \dfrac{2}{3}$ (**h**) $\dfrac{1}{4}, \dfrac{1}{5}$

4. Divide: Reduce the answer to the lowest terms.

(**a**) $\dfrac{2}{3} \div \dfrac{3}{8}$ (**b**) $\dfrac{4}{5} \div \dfrac{3}{5}$ (**c**) $\dfrac{5}{7} \div \dfrac{5}{14}$ (**d**) $\dfrac{2}{5} \div \dfrac{3}{10}$

5. Multiply: Reduce to the lowest terms.

(a) $\dfrac{2}{5} \times \dfrac{3}{4}$ **(b)** $\dfrac{3}{8} \times \dfrac{4}{9}$ **(c)** $\dfrac{3}{5} \times \dfrac{15}{21}$ **(d)** $\dfrac{2}{7} \times \dfrac{49}{50}$

(e) $\dfrac{2}{3} \times \dfrac{2}{5} \times \dfrac{3}{4}$ **(f)** $\dfrac{1}{4} \times \dfrac{2}{7} \times \dfrac{3}{4}$ **(g)** $\dfrac{2}{5} \times \dfrac{1}{5} \times \dfrac{2}{3}$ **(h)** $\dfrac{1}{5} \times \dfrac{2}{3} \times \dfrac{3}{4}$

6. Subtract: Reduce to the lowest terms.

(a) $\dfrac{3}{4} - \dfrac{1}{3}$ **(b)** $\dfrac{7}{9} - \dfrac{5}{18}$ **(c)** $\dfrac{7}{8} - \dfrac{5}{24}$ **(d)** $\dfrac{2}{3} - \dfrac{5}{15}$

7. Add and change the answers to mixed numbers.

(a) $\dfrac{2}{5} + \dfrac{1}{5} + \dfrac{4}{5} + \dfrac{3}{5}$ **(b)** $\dfrac{5}{8} + \dfrac{7}{8} + \dfrac{3}{8} + \dfrac{1}{8}$

(c) $\dfrac{5}{7} + \dfrac{4}{5}$ **(d)** $\dfrac{4}{8} + \dfrac{3}{4}$ **(e)** $\dfrac{1}{4} + \dfrac{5}{7}$

8. Change each fraction to a higher equivalent fraction that has the given denominator.

(a) $\dfrac{3}{10} = \dfrac{}{100}$ **(b)** $\dfrac{5}{25} = \dfrac{}{100}$ **(c)** $\dfrac{5}{8} = \dfrac{}{64}$

(d) $\dfrac{4}{7} = \dfrac{}{21}$ **(e)** $\dfrac{8}{9} = \dfrac{}{27}$ **(f)** $\dfrac{3}{7} = \dfrac{}{49}$

9. Add: Reduce to the lowest terms.

(a) $\dfrac{2}{3}$ **(b)** $\dfrac{1}{4}$ **(c)** $\dfrac{2}{5}$ **(d)** $\dfrac{5}{12}$

$\dfrac{4}{5}$ $\dfrac{3}{4}$ $\dfrac{2}{3}$ $\dfrac{2}{3}$

$\dfrac{1}{2}$ $\dfrac{2}{3}$ $\dfrac{7}{15}$ $\dfrac{3}{4}$

10. Subtract: Reduce to the lowest terms.

(a) $21 - 17\dfrac{2}{5}$ **(b)** $40 - 12\dfrac{1}{4}$ **(c)** $14 - 10\dfrac{5}{7}$

11. Add: Reduce to the lowest terms.

(a) $2\dfrac{2}{3}$ **(b)** $3\dfrac{1}{3}$ **(c)** $4\dfrac{2}{3}$ **(d)** $\dfrac{2}{5}$

$1\dfrac{1}{4}$ 4 $2\dfrac{1}{4}$ $\dfrac{3}{4}$

$1\dfrac{1}{4}$ $2\dfrac{3}{4}$ 8 $\dfrac{2}{20}$

12. Divide: Reduce to the lowest terms.

(a) $\dfrac{3}{4} \div \dfrac{3}{4}$ **(b)** $6\dfrac{4}{5} \div \dfrac{2}{5}$ **(c)** $3\dfrac{1}{2} \div 1\dfrac{3}{4}$ **(d)** $\dfrac{3}{4} \div \dfrac{3}{8}$

(e) $7\dfrac{3}{6} \div 5$ **(f)** $10 \div 2\dfrac{2}{5}$

13. Find the unknown number.

  (a) $\dfrac{2}{3}$ of what number is 90?   **(b)** $\dfrac{1}{4}$ of what number is 24?

  (c) $\dfrac{3}{7}$ of what number is 36?   **(d)** $\dfrac{3}{5}$ of what number is 15?

14. Find the fractional parts.
  (a) 3 is what part of 15?   **(b)** 4 is what part of 24?
  (c) 20 is what part of 60?   **(d)** 5 is what part of 50?

15. Reduce the following to the lowest term
  (a) $\dfrac{4}{12}$ **(b)** $\dfrac{5}{45}$ **(c)** $\dfrac{24}{60}$ **(d)** $\dfrac{36}{72}$ **(e)** $\dfrac{18}{72}$

MULTIPLICATION OF FRACTIONS, WHOLE NUMBERS, AND MIXED NUMBERS

Rule 1: To multiply whole numbers by mixed numbers or to multiply mixed numbers by whole numbers, change both the mixed numbers and the whole numbers to improper fractions.

Rule 2: To change a whole number to an improper fraction, write the whole number over the number 1 as the denominator.

Example 1

Write the following as improper fractions:

(a) 3   **(b)** 4   **(c)** 17   **(d)** 100

Solution

(a) The improper fraction of $3 = \dfrac{3}{1}$ (Use Rule 2)

(b) The improper fraction of $4 = \dfrac{4}{1}$ (Use Rule 2)

(c) The improper fraction of $17 = \dfrac{17}{1}$ (Use Rule 2)

(d) The improper fraction of $100 = \dfrac{100}{1}$ (Use Rule 2)

Rule 3: **To change a mixed number to an improper fraction, multiply the denominator by the whole number, add the numerator to the product, and then write the sum over the denominator.**

Example 2

Write the following mixed numbers as improper fractions:

(a) $4\dfrac{3}{11}$ **(b)** $3\dfrac{3}{4}$ **(c)** $10\dfrac{4}{7}$

Solution

(a) Using Rule 3, multiply 11 by 4, add 3 to the product (the product of 11 and 4) and write the sum over 11.

Therefore, $4\dfrac{3}{11} = \dfrac{11 \times 4 + 3}{11} = \dfrac{47}{11}$

The improper fraction of $4\dfrac{3}{11}$ is $\dfrac{47}{11}$.

(b) Using Rule 3, multiply 4 by 3, add 3 to the product (the product of 4 and 3) and write the sum over 4

Therefore, $3\dfrac{3}{4} = \dfrac{4 \times 3 + 3}{4} = \dfrac{15}{4}$

The improper fraction of $3\dfrac{3}{4}$ is $\dfrac{15}{4}$.

(c) Using Rule 3, multiply 7 by 10, add 4 to the product (the product of 7 and 10) and write the sum over 7.

Therefore, $10\dfrac{4}{7} = \dfrac{7 \times 10 + 4}{7} = \dfrac{74}{7}$

The improper fraction of $10\dfrac{4}{7}$ is $\dfrac{47}{7}$.

Example 3

Multiply: $4 \times 7\dfrac{3}{5}$

Solution

Step 1: Change both the whole number 4 and the mixed fraction $7\dfrac{3}{5}$ to improper

467

fractions and multiply the improper fractions. (See Rule 1)

The improper fraction of $4 = \dfrac{4}{1}$ 　　　　　　　　　　(See Rule 2)

The improper fraction of $7\dfrac{3}{5} = \dfrac{7 \times 5 + 3}{5} = \dfrac{38}{5}$ 　　(See Rule 3)

Write the multiplication of both improper fractions as shown:

$$\dfrac{4}{1} \times \dfrac{38}{5}$$

Step 2: Reduce the improper fractions to the lowest terms by dividing both the numerators and the denominators by the same numbers if possible.

Note that in this example, $\dfrac{4}{1} \times \dfrac{38}{5}$

there are no numbers that can divide both the numerators and the denominators evenly (without a remainder), go to Step 3.

Step 3: Multiply the numerators together and multiply the denominators together and put the product of the numerators over the product of the denominators.

$$\dfrac{4}{1} \times \dfrac{38}{5} = \dfrac{4 \times 38}{1 \times 5}$$

$$= \dfrac{152}{5}$$

Step 4: Change the improper fraction $\dfrac{152}{5}$ in Step 3 to mixed numbers by dividing the numerator by the denominator.

$$\dfrac{152}{5} = 30\dfrac{2}{5} \qquad (152 \div 5 = 30 \text{ remainder } 2 = 30\dfrac{2}{5})$$

Therefore, $4 \times 7\dfrac{3}{5} = 30\dfrac{2}{5}$

Example 4

Multiply: $3 \times 4\dfrac{2}{3}$

Solution

Step 1: Change both the whole number 3 and the mixed fraction $4\dfrac{2}{3}$ to improper fractions and multiply the improper fractions. (See Rule 1)

The improper fraction of $3 = \dfrac{3}{1}$ (See Rule 2)

The improper fraction of $4\dfrac{2}{3} = \dfrac{4 \times 3 + 2}{3}$ (See Rule 3)

$$= \dfrac{14}{3}$$

Write the multiplication of both improper fractions as shown:

$$\dfrac{3}{1} \times \dfrac{14}{3}$$

Step 2: Reduce the improper fractions to the lowest terms by dividing both the numerators and the denominators by the same number or numbers if possible.

$$\overset{1}{\underset{1}{\dfrac{3}{1}}} \times \dfrac{14}{\underset{1}{3}}$$ Divide both the numerator and the denominator by 3.

Note: $3 \div 3 = 1$

Step 3: Multiply the numerators together and multiply the denominators together and put the product of the numerators over the product of the denominators.

From Step 2, $\dfrac{1}{1} \times \dfrac{14}{1} = \dfrac{1 \times 14}{1 \times 1}$

$$= \dfrac{14}{1}$$

$$= 14$$

Example 5

Multiply: $2\dfrac{2}{10} \times 5$

Solution

Step 1: Change both the fraction $2\dfrac{2}{10}$ and the whole number 5 to improper fractions and multiply the improper fractions.   (See Rule 1)

The improper fraction of $2\dfrac{2}{10} = \dfrac{10 \times 2 + 2}{10}$ (See Rule 3)

$$= \dfrac{22}{10}$$

The improper fraction of $5 = \dfrac{5}{1}$ (See Rule 2)

Write the multiplication of both improper fractions as shown:

$$\dfrac{22}{10} \times \dfrac{5}{1}$$

Step 2: Reduce the improper fractions to the lowest terms by dividing both the numerators and the denominators by the same number or numbers if possible.

$$\overset{\overset{11}{\cancel{22}}}{\underset{\underset{1}{\cancel{10}}}{}} \times \overset{\overset{1}{\cancel{5}}}{\underset{\underset{1}{\cancel{1}}}{}} \qquad (\,5 \div 5 = 1,\ 10 \div 5 = 2,\ 2 \div 2 = 1,\ 22 \div 2 = 11)$$

$$= \dfrac{11}{1} \times \dfrac{1}{1}$$

Step 3: Multiply the numerators together and multiply the denominators together and put the product of the numerators over the product of the denominators.

$$\text{From Step 2, } \dfrac{11}{1} \times \dfrac{1}{1} = \dfrac{11 \times 1}{1 \times 1}$$

$$= \dfrac{11}{1}$$

$$= 11$$

Example 6

Multiply: $21 \times 2\dfrac{3}{14} \times 4$

Solution

Step 1: Change the whole number 21, the mixed number $2\dfrac{3}{14}$ and the whole number 4 to improper fractions and multiply all the improper fractions. (See Rule 1)

The improper fraction of $21 = \dfrac{21}{1}$ (See Rule 2)

The improper fraction of $2\frac{3}{14} = \frac{14 \times 2 + 3}{14}$ (See Rule 3)

$$= \frac{31}{14}$$

The improper fraction of $4 = \frac{4}{1}$ (See Rule 2)

Write the multiplication of all the improper fractions as shown:

$$\frac{21}{1} \times \frac{31}{14} \times \frac{4}{1}$$

Step 2: Reduce the improper fractions to the lowest terms by dividing the numerators and the denominators by the same number or numbers if possible.

$$\frac{\overset{3}{\cancel{21}}}{1} \times \frac{31}{\underset{2}{\cancel{14}}} \times \frac{\overset{2}{\cancel{4}}}{\underset{1}{1}} \qquad (21 \div 7 = 3,\ 14 \div 7 = 2,\ 2 \div 2 = 1,\ 4 \div 2 = 2)$$

$$= \frac{3}{1} \times \frac{31}{1} \times \frac{2}{1}$$

Step 3: Multiply the numerators together and multiply the denominators together and put the product of the numerators over the product of the denominators.

From step 2, $\dfrac{3}{1} \times \dfrac{31}{1} \times \dfrac{2}{1} = \dfrac{3 \times 31 \times 2}{1 \times 1 \times 1}$

$$= \frac{186}{1}$$

$$= 186$$

Example 7

Multiply: $2\frac{1}{2} \times 3\frac{1}{5}$

Solution

Step 1: Change the mixed number $2\frac{1}{2}$ and the mixed number $3\frac{1}{5}$ to improper fractions and multiply the improper fractions.　　(See Rule 1)

The improper fraction of $2\frac{1}{2} = \dfrac{2 \times 2 + 1}{2}$　　　　(See Rule 3)

$$= \frac{5}{2}$$

The improper fraction of $3\frac{1}{5} = \dfrac{5 \times 3 + 1}{5}$　　　　(See Rule 3)

$$= \frac{16}{5}$$

Write the multiplication of the improper fractions as shown:

$$\frac{5}{2} \times \frac{16}{5}$$

Step 2: Reduce the improper fractions to the lowest terms by dividing the numerators and the denominators by the same number or numbers if possible.

$$\overset{1}{\underset{1}{\frac{5}{2}}} \times \overset{8}{\underset{1}{\frac{16}{5}}} \qquad (2 \div 2 = 1,\ 16 \div 2 = 8,\ 5 \div 5 = 1)$$

$$= \frac{1}{1} \times \frac{8}{1}$$

Step 3: Multiply the numerators together and multiply the denominators together and put the product of the numerators over the product of the denominators.

From step 2, $\dfrac{1}{1} \times \dfrac{8}{1} = \dfrac{1 \times 8}{1 \times 1}$

$$= \frac{8}{1}$$

$$= 8$$

Example 8

Multiply: $2\dfrac{3}{4} \times 3\dfrac{1}{6} \times 2\dfrac{2}{11}$

Solution

Step 1: Change the mixed numbers $2\dfrac{3}{4}$, $3\dfrac{1}{6}$ and $2\dfrac{2}{11}$ to improper fractions and

multiply the improper fractions.   (See Rule 1)

The improper fraction of $2\dfrac{3}{4} = \dfrac{4 \times 2 + 3}{4}$ (See Rule 3)

$$= \dfrac{11}{4}$$

The improper fraction of $3\dfrac{1}{6} = \dfrac{6 \times 3 + 1}{6}$ (See Rule 3)

$$= \dfrac{19}{6}$$

The improper fraction of $2\dfrac{2}{11} = \dfrac{11 \times 2 + 2}{11}$ (See Rule 3)

$$= \dfrac{24}{11}$$

Write the multiplication of the improper fractions as shown:

$$\dfrac{11}{4} \times \dfrac{19}{6} \times \dfrac{24}{11}$$

Step 2: Reduce the improper fractions to the lowest terms by dividing the numerators and the denominators by the same number or numbers if possible.

$$\dfrac{\overset{1}{\cancel{11}}}{\underset{1}{\cancel{4}}} \times \dfrac{19}{\underset{1}{\cancel{6}}} \times \dfrac{\overset{\overset{1}{\cancel{6}}}{\cancel{24}}}{\underset{1}{\cancel{11}}} \quad (\; 11 \div 11 = 1, \; 4 \div 4 = 1, \; 24 \div 4 = 6, \; 6 \div 6 = 1 \;)$$

Step 3: Multiply the numerators together and multiply the denominators together and put the product of the numerators over the product of the denominators.

From Step 2, $\dfrac{1}{1} \times \dfrac{19}{1} \times \dfrac{1}{1} = \dfrac{1 \times 19 \times 1}{1 \times 1 \times 1}$

$$= \dfrac{19}{1}$$

$$= 19$$

Example 9

Multiply: $2\dfrac{1}{6} \times 4\dfrac{3}{4} \times 1\dfrac{1}{19} \times 3\dfrac{1}{5}$

Solution

Step 1: Change the mixed numbers $2\dfrac{1}{6}, 4\dfrac{3}{4}, 1\dfrac{1}{19},$ and $3\dfrac{1}{5}$ to improper fractions.

(See Rule 1)

The improper fraction of $2\dfrac{1}{6} = \dfrac{6 \times 2 + 1}{6}$ (See Rule 3)

$$= \dfrac{13}{6}$$

The improper fraction of $4\dfrac{3}{4} = \dfrac{4 \times 4 + 3}{4}$ (See Rule 3)

$$= \dfrac{19}{4}$$

The improper fraction of $1\dfrac{1}{19} = \dfrac{19 \times 1 + 1}{19}$ (See Rule 3)

$$= \dfrac{20}{19}$$

The improper fraction of $3\dfrac{1}{5} = \dfrac{5 \times 3 + 1}{5}$ (See Rule 3)

$$= \dfrac{16}{5}$$

Write the multiplication of all the improper fractions as shown:

$$\dfrac{13}{6} \times \dfrac{19}{4} \times \dfrac{20}{19} \times \dfrac{16}{5}$$

Step 2: Reduce the improper fractions to the lowest terms by dividing the numerators and the denominators by the same numbers if possible.

$$\frac{\overset{1}{\cancel{13}}}{\underset{3}{\cancel{6}}} \times \frac{\overset{1}{\cancel{19}}}{\underset{1}{\cancel{4}}} \times \frac{\overset{\overset{2}{\cancel{10}}}{\cancel{20}}}{\underset{1}{\cancel{19}}} \times \frac{\overset{4}{\cancel{16}}}{\underset{1}{\cancel{5}}} \qquad (19 \div 19 = 1, 6 \div 2 = 3, 20 \div 2 = 10,)$$

$$(5 \div 5 = 1, 10 \div 5 = 2, 4 \div 4 = 1, 16 \div 4 = 4)$$

$$= \frac{13}{3} \times \frac{1}{1} \times \frac{2}{1} \times \frac{4}{1}$$

Step 3: Multiply the numerators together and multiply the denominators together and put the product of the numerators over the product of the denominators.

$$\text{From Step 2, } \frac{13}{3} \times \frac{1}{1} \times \frac{2}{1} \times \frac{4}{1} = \frac{13 \times 1 \times 2 \times 4}{3 \times 1 \times 1 \times 1}$$

$$= \frac{104}{3}$$

Step 4: Change the improper fraction $\frac{104}{3}$ in Step 3 to mixed numbers by dividing the numerator by the denominator.

$$\frac{104}{3} = 34\frac{2}{3} \qquad (104 \div 3 = 34 \text{ remainder } 2 = 34\frac{2}{3})$$

Example 10

Multiply: $3\frac{1}{4} \times 4 \times 2\frac{2}{13} \times 2$

Solution

Step 1: Change the mixed number $3\frac{1}{4}$, the whole number 4, the mixed number $2\frac{2}{13}$ and the whole number 2 to improper fractions.   (See Rule 1)

$$\text{The improper fraction of } 3\frac{1}{4} = \frac{4 \times 3 + 1}{4} \qquad \text{(See Rule 3)}$$

$$= \frac{13}{4}$$

The improper fraction of $4 = \dfrac{4}{1}$ (See Rule 2)

The improper fraction of $2\dfrac{2}{13} = \dfrac{13 \times 2 + 2}{13}$ (See Rule 3)

$$= \dfrac{28}{13}$$

The improper fraction of $2 = \dfrac{2}{1}$ (See Rule 2)

Write the multiplication of the improper fractions as shown:

$$\dfrac{13}{4} \times \dfrac{4}{1} \times \dfrac{28}{13} \times \dfrac{2}{1}$$

Step 2: Reduce the improper fractions to the lowest terms by dividing the numerators and the denominators by the same number or numbers if possible.

$$\dfrac{\overset{1}{\cancel{13}}}{\underset{1}{\cancel{4}}} \times \dfrac{\overset{1}{\cancel{4}}}{1} \times \dfrac{28}{\underset{1}{\cancel{13}}} \times \dfrac{2}{1} \qquad (13 \div 13 = 1,\ 4 \div 4 = 1)$$

$$= \dfrac{1}{1} \times \dfrac{1}{1} \times \dfrac{28}{1} \times \dfrac{2}{1}$$

Step 3: Multiply the numerators together and multiply the denominators together and put the product of the numerators over the product of the denominators.

From Step 2, $\dfrac{1}{1} \times \dfrac{1}{1} \times \dfrac{28}{1} \times \dfrac{2}{1} = \dfrac{1 \times 1 \times 28 \times 2}{1 \times 1 \times 1 \times 1}$

$$= \dfrac{56}{1}$$

$$= 56$$

Recommendation

Examples 1 to 10 show the detailed methods of solving the problems in order to provide the students with the logic needed in solving similar problems. Once the students master the skills of the problem solving, the detailed solution is not needed in doing homework, class exercises, or tests. The understanding of the logic of the problem solving is very important, and then the student can use shortcuts in solving similar problems.

It is recommended that after the students master the logic of the problem solving, during homework, class exercises or tests, the students should begin solving the problems starting from step 2, without showing detailed solutions as shown in Example 11.

Example 11

Multiply: $4\dfrac{1}{5} \times 1\dfrac{4}{11} \times 2\dfrac{3}{4} \times 2$

Solution

$$\overset{3}{\underset{1}{\dfrac{21}{5}}} \times \overset{1}{\underset{1}{\dfrac{\cancel{15}}{\cancel{11}}}} \times \overset{1}{\underset{2}{\dfrac{\cancel{11}}{4}}} \times \dfrac{2}{1} = \dfrac{63}{2} = 31\dfrac{1}{2}$$

The notes and the generous worked examples have provided me with conceptual understanding and computational fluency to do my homework.

Exercises

1. How do you change a whole number to an improper fraction? (Hint: See Rule 2)
2. How do you change a mixed number to an improper fraction? (Hint: See Rule 3)
3. Write the following as improper fractions: (a) 2,   (b) 4,   (c) 13 ,   (d) 200. (Hint: See Example **1**).
4. How do you change a mixed number to an improper fraction? (Hint: See Rule 3)
5. Write the following mixed numbers as improper fractions: (Hint: See Example **2**) Reduce to the lowest terms.

   (a) $2\dfrac{1}{2}$ (b) $7\dfrac{3}{4}$ (c) $10\dfrac{3}{4}$ (d) $4\dfrac{5}{6}$ (e) $7\dfrac{1}{7}$ (f) $5\dfrac{3}{5}$

6. Multiply the following whole numbers and mixed numbers: (Hint See Example **3**) Reduce to the lowest terms.

   (a) $6 \times 1\dfrac{7}{5}$ (b) $2 \times 2\dfrac{2}{3}$ (c) $3 \times 3\dfrac{2}{5}$ (d) $5 \times 2\dfrac{1}{4}$

   (e) $4 \times 2\dfrac{2}{3}$ (f) $4 \times 3\dfrac{1}{7}$ (g) $6 \times 2\dfrac{2}{7}$ (h) $2 \times 2\dfrac{1}{9}$

7. Multiply the following whole numbers and mixed numbers: (Hint: See Example **4**) Reduce to the lowest terms.

   (a) $4 \times 3\dfrac{1}{4}$ (b) $6 \times 2\dfrac{1}{6}$ (c) $5 \times 3\dfrac{2}{5}$

(d) $7 \times 2\frac{2}{7}$ **(e)** $3 \times 4\frac{1}{3}$ **(f)** $2 \times 3\frac{1}{2}$

(g) $3 \times 4\frac{2}{3}$ **(h)** $8 \times 2\frac{3}{8}$ **(i)** $5 \times 2\frac{3}{5}$

8. Multiply the following whole numbers and mixed numbers: (Hint: See Example **5**). Reduce to the lowest terms.

(a) $3\frac{1}{3} \times 3$ **(b)** $2\frac{1}{2} \times 2$ **(c)** $3\frac{1}{4} \times 4$ **(d)** $2\frac{2}{5} \times 5$

(e) $4\frac{1}{2} \times 2$ **(f)** $3\frac{3}{4} \times 4$ **(g)** $5\frac{1}{5} \times 5$ **(h)** $2\frac{1}{6} \times 6$

9. Multiply the following whole numbers and a fraction: (Hint: See Example **6**) Reduce to the lowest terms.

(a) $3 \times 4\frac{2}{3} \times 4$ **(b)** $2 \times 6\frac{1}{2} \times 3$ **(c)** $4 \times 2\frac{2}{3} \times 6$

(d) $4 \times 3\frac{3}{4} \times 2$ **(e)** $5 \times 2\frac{2}{5} \times 3$ **(f)** $3 \times 4\frac{1}{3} \times 2$

(g) $5 \times 3\frac{1}{5} \times 4$ **(h)** $7 \times 2\frac{5}{7} \times 3$ **(i)** $4 \times 3 \times 3\frac{3}{4}$

10. Multiply the following mixed numbers: (Hint: See Example **7**) Reduce to the lowest terms.

(a) $3\frac{1}{3} \times 2\frac{1}{5}$ **(b)** $2\frac{2}{3} \times 1\frac{2}{4}$ **(c)** $3\frac{1}{3} \times 2\frac{2}{5}$

(d) $2\frac{1}{4} \times 2\frac{2}{3}$ **(e)** $1\frac{2}{5} \times 2\frac{1}{7}$ **(f)** $2\frac{2}{3} \times 3\frac{3}{4}$

(g) $4\frac{1}{2} \times 2\frac{2}{3}$ **(h)** $5\frac{3}{5} \times 4\frac{2}{7}$ **(i)** $1\frac{3}{4} \times 2\frac{2}{3}$

11. Multiply the following mixed numbers: (Hint: See Example **8**) Reduce to the lowest terms.

(a) $2\frac{1}{2} \times 4\frac{1}{6} \times 2\frac{2}{5}$ **(b)** $3\frac{2}{3} \times 2\frac{3}{11} \times 3\frac{1}{2}$

(c) $4\dfrac{2}{3} \times 2\dfrac{1}{7} \times 3\dfrac{1}{5}$

(d) $3\dfrac{1}{4} \times 2\dfrac{2}{7} \times 1\dfrac{1}{13}$

(e) $2\dfrac{1}{3} \times 4\dfrac{1}{2} \times 2\dfrac{1}{7}$

(f) $3\dfrac{1}{3} \times 1\dfrac{1}{2} \times 2\dfrac{4}{10}$

(g) $5\dfrac{3}{4} \times 2\dfrac{2}{5} \times 1\dfrac{1}{23}$

(h) $1\dfrac{3}{4} \times 2\dfrac{2}{7} \times 2\dfrac{2}{5}$

12. Multiply the following mixed numbers: (Hint: See Example **9**)
 Reduce to the lowest terms.

(a) $1\dfrac{1}{6} \times 2\dfrac{1}{5} \times 1\dfrac{1}{11} \times 2\dfrac{1}{7}$

(b) $2\dfrac{1}{7} \times 3\dfrac{1}{5} \times 4\dfrac{3}{4} \times 1\dfrac{1}{3}$

(c) $2\dfrac{1}{3} \times 6\dfrac{2}{5} \times 3\dfrac{1}{3} \times 2\dfrac{1}{2}$

(d) $4\dfrac{2}{3} \times 1\dfrac{3}{7} \times 2\dfrac{1}{6} \times 2\dfrac{2}{5}$

(e) $3\dfrac{2}{3} \times 4\dfrac{3}{4} \times 1\dfrac{1}{11} \times 2\dfrac{5}{6}$

(f) $7\dfrac{1}{7} \times 1\dfrac{4}{10} \times 3\dfrac{1}{5} \times 4\dfrac{3}{4}$

(g) $2\dfrac{2}{3} \times 3\dfrac{3}{5} \times 4\dfrac{1}{6} \times 7\dfrac{1}{3}$

(h) $4\dfrac{1}{2} \times 9\dfrac{2}{7} \times 4\dfrac{3}{5} \times 2\dfrac{3}{9}$

13. Multiply the following whole numbers and mixed numbers:
 (Hint: See Example **10**). Reduce your answers to the lowest terms if needed.

(a) $2\dfrac{1}{2} \times 3 \times 4\dfrac{4}{5} \times 2$

(b) $3\dfrac{1}{3} \times 3 \times 1\dfrac{1}{10} \times 4$

(c) $3\dfrac{1}{4} \times 9 \times 1\dfrac{1}{6} \times 2$

(d) $1\dfrac{3}{7} \times 14 \times 2\dfrac{2}{3} \times 3$

(e) $2 \times 4\dfrac{1}{3} \times 2\dfrac{1}{2} \times 3$

(f) $1\dfrac{1}{3} \times 4\dfrac{2}{7} \times 14 \times 2$

(g) $5 \times 2\dfrac{1}{2} \times 3\dfrac{1}{5} \times 2$

(h) $3\dfrac{1}{3} \times 2\dfrac{1}{7} \times 3 \times 2$

Challenge Questions

14. Multiply: Reduce to the lowest terms.

(a) $8 \times 3\dfrac{3}{4}$

(b) $1\dfrac{1}{3} \times 6\dfrac{1}{4} \times 1\dfrac{3}{5} \times 2\dfrac{1}{2}$

(c) $12 \times 5\dfrac{1}{6}$

(d) $4 \times 3\dfrac{2}{3} \times 3$

(e) $4\frac{2}{3} \times 5\frac{1}{7}$

(f) $3\frac{2}{3} \times 2\frac{1}{5} \times 2\frac{1}{7}$

(g) $2\frac{1}{2} \times 1\frac{3}{5} \times 6$

(h) $5\frac{1}{5} \times 1\frac{1}{13} \times 2 \times 2\frac{4}{7}$

(i) $3\frac{1}{3} \times 1\frac{1}{5} \times 4\frac{1}{6}$

(j) $5 \times 2\frac{2}{5} \times 2\frac{1}{4}$

Answers to Selected Questions

5(a) $\frac{5}{2}$ **6(a)** $14\frac{2}{5}$ **7(a)** 13   **8(a)** 10   **9(a)** 56

10(a) $7\frac{1}{3}$ **11(a)** 25   **12(a)** 6   **13(a)** 72

Cumulative Review

1. Simplify:

   a. $32 \div 4 \times 2 =$ **b**. $32 \times 4 \div 2 =$ **c**. $7 + 3 \times 2 =$

   d. $2 - 1 + 2 =$ **e**. $17 - 5 \times 3 =$ **f**. $3.97 \times 3 =$

   g. $7.38 \times 2.3 =$ **h**. $5^2 - 3^2 \times 2^2 =$ **i**. $6^2 \times 2 =$

REAL WORLD APPLICATIONS - WORD PROBLEMS
Multiplication of Fractions, Whole Numbers, and Mixed Numbers

Example 1

John needs $4\frac{3}{5}$ yards of material for a school project. How many yards of material will he need for 4 projects, assuming that each project requires the same amount of material?

Solution

1 school project needs $4\frac{3}{5}$ yards of material.

4 school projects will need $4 \times 4\frac{3}{5}$ yards of material.

We need to multiply 4 by $4\frac{3}{5}$ to obtain the amount of material needed.

Step 1: Change the whole number 4 and the mixed number $4\frac{3}{5}$ to improper fractions and multiply the improper fractions. (See Rule 1)

The improper fraction of $4 = \dfrac{4}{1}$ (See Rule 2)

The improper fraction of $4\dfrac{3}{5} = \dfrac{5 \times 4 + 3}{5}$ (See Rule 3)

$$= \dfrac{23}{5}$$

Write the multiplication of both of the improper fractions as shown:

$$\dfrac{4}{1} \times \dfrac{23}{5}$$

Step 2: Reduce the improper fractions to the lowest terms by dividing both the numerators and the denominators by the same number or numbers if possible.

Note that in this example, $\dfrac{4}{1} \times \dfrac{23}{5}$, there are no numbers that can divide

both the numerators and the denominators evenly (without a remainder.)

Step 3: Multiply the numerators together and multiply the denominators together and put the product of the numerators over the product of the denominators.

$$\dfrac{4}{1} \times \dfrac{23}{5} = \dfrac{4 \times 23}{1 \times 5}$$

$$= \dfrac{92}{5}$$

Step 4: Change the improper fraction $\dfrac{92}{5}$ in Step 3 to mixed numbers by dividing the numerator by the denominator.

$$\dfrac{92}{5} = 18\dfrac{2}{5} \qquad (92 \div 5 = 18 \text{ remainder } 2 = 18\dfrac{2}{5})$$

Therefore, $18\dfrac{2}{5}$ yards of material will be needed for the 4 projects.

Example 2

A ground beef patty weighs $\dfrac{1}{3}$ pound. How many pounds will 24 ground beef patties weigh?

Solution

1 ground beef patty weighs $\dfrac{1}{3}$ pound.

24 ground beef patties will weigh $24 \times \dfrac{1}{3}$ pounds.

We have to multiply 24 by $\frac{1}{3}$ to obtain the weight of the 24 ground beef patties.

Step 1: Change the number 24 to an improper fraction and multiply the improper fraction by $\frac{1}{3}$. (See Rule 1)

The improper fraction of $24 = \frac{24}{1}$ (See Rule 2, under Multiplication of Fractions, Whole and Mixed Numbers.)

Write the multiplication of the improper fraction $\frac{24}{1}$ and $\frac{1}{3}$ as shown:

$$\frac{24}{1} \times \frac{1}{3}$$

Step 2: Reduce the improper fraction $\frac{24}{1}$ and the proper fraction $\frac{1}{3}$ to the lowest terms by dividing the numerators and the denominators by the same number or numbers if possible.

$$\overset{8}{\underset{1}{\frac{24}{1}}} \times \frac{1}{\underset{1}{3}} \qquad (24 \div 3 = 8, \ 3 \div 3 = 1)$$

$$= \frac{8}{1} \times \frac{1}{1}$$

Step 3: Multiply the numerators together and multiply the denominators together and put the product of the numerators over the product of the denominators.

From Step 2, $\frac{8}{1} \times \frac{1}{1} = \frac{8 \times 1}{1 \times 1}$

$$= \frac{8}{1}$$

$$= 8$$

Therefore, 24 patties will weigh 8 pounds.

Example 3

Karen's overtime pay is $10\frac{1}{2}$ dollars per hour. How much overtime pay did she earn for $8\frac{3}{4}$ hours. (Note: $10\frac{1}{2}$ dollars = \$10.50)

Solution

Overtime pay for 1 hour = $10\frac{1}{2}$ dollars.

Overtime pay for $8\frac{3}{4}$ hours = $8\frac{3}{4} \times 10\frac{1}{2}$ dollars.

We have to multiply $8\frac{3}{4}$ by $10\frac{1}{2}$ to obtain the amount of overtime earned in $8\frac{3}{4}$ hours. (See Rule 1)

Step 1: Change the mixed numbers $8\frac{3}{4}$ and $10\frac{1}{2}$ to improper fractions and multiply the improper fractions.

$$\text{The improper fraction of } 8\frac{3}{4} = \frac{4 \times 8 + 3}{4} \quad \text{(See Rule 3 under Multiplication}$$

$$= \frac{35}{4} \quad \text{of Fractions, Whole and Mixed}$$

Numbers.)

$$\text{The improper fraction of } 10\frac{1}{2} = \frac{2 \times 10 + 1}{2} \quad \text{(See Rule 3 under Multiplication}$$

of Fractions, Whole and Mixed

$$= \frac{21}{2} \quad \text{Numbers.)}$$

Write the multiplication of the improper fractions $\frac{35}{4}$ and $\frac{21}{2}$ as shown:

$$\frac{35}{4} \times \frac{21}{2}$$

Step 2: Reduce the improper fractions to the lowest terms by dividing the numerator and the denominator by the same number or numbers if possible.

Note that in this example, $\frac{35}{4} \times \frac{21}{2}$, there are no numbers that can divide both the numerators and the denominators evenly (without a remainder.)

Step 3: Multiply the numerators together and multiply the denominators together and put the product of the numerators over the product of the denominators.

$$\frac{35}{4} \times \frac{21}{2} = \frac{35 \times 21}{4 \times 2}$$

$$= \frac{735}{8}$$

Step 4: Change the improper fraction $\frac{735}{8}$ in Step 3 to mixed numbers by dividing the numerator by the denominator if needed.

$$\frac{735}{8} = 91\frac{7}{8} \quad (735 \div 8 = 91 \text{ remainder } 7 = 91\frac{7}{8})$$

Therefore, Karen earned $91\frac{7}{8}$ dollars for $8\frac{3}{4}$ hours of overtime.

Example 4

Nick needs $12\frac{1}{4}$ feet of lumber for his school project. How many feet of lumber does

Nick need in order to complete $10\frac{2}{5}$ of the same project? (Hint: The solution of this example does not show the detailed solution steps. It is recommended that after the student masters the logic of the detailed solution steps, the student should use shortcuts to solve homework, class exercises and tests as shown in this solution. It is recommended that the student should set up the solution initially, and then use Step 2 and Step 3 in solving the problem as shown in this example.

Solution

Initial setup:

1 school project requires $12\frac{1}{4}$ feet of lumber.

$10\frac{2}{5}$ school projects will require $10\frac{2}{5} \times 12\frac{1}{4}$ feet of lumber.

Shortcut Step:

$10\frac{2}{5}$ school projects will require $10\frac{2}{5} \times 12\frac{1}{4}$ feet of lumber.

$$10\frac{2}{5} \times 12\frac{1}{4} = \frac{52}{5} \times \frac{49}{4}$$

$$= \frac{\overset{13}{\cancel{52}}}{5} \times \frac{49}{\underset{1}{\cancel{4}}} \quad (52 \div 4 = 13, 4 \div 4 = 1).$$

$$= \frac{13 \times 49}{5} = \frac{637}{5} = 127\frac{2}{5}$$

Therefore, $10\frac{2}{7}$ school projects will require $127\frac{2}{5}$ feet of lumber.

Example 5

A fabric material sells at $3. 25 per yard. How much will $2\frac{2}{13}$ yards cost? (Hint:

$3.25 may be written as $3\frac{1}{4}$. Note that $0.25 = \frac{25}{100} = \frac{1}{4}$. $25 \div 25 = 1$,

$100 \div 25 = 4$, hence $\frac{25}{100} = \frac{1}{4}$ and therefore, $3.25 = 3\frac{1}{4}$.) Solve this problem

without showing the detailed solutions.

Solution

Initial setup:

1 yard of the fabric material sells at $3.25.

$2\frac{2}{13}$ yards of the fabric material will cost $2\frac{2}{13} \times 3.25$ dollars.

Shortcut setup:

$2\frac{2}{13}$ yards of the fabric material will cost $2\frac{2}{13} \times 3.25$ dollars.

$$2\frac{2}{13} \times 3\frac{1}{4} = \frac{28}{13} \times \frac{13}{4}$$

$$= \frac{\overset{7}{\cancel{28}}}{\underset{1}{\cancel{13}}} \times \frac{\overset{1}{\cancel{13}}}{\underset{1}{\cancel{4}}}$$

$$= 7$$

Therefore, $2\frac{2}{13}$ yards of the fabric will cost $7.00.

_____

The notes and the generous worked examples have provided me with conceptual understanding and computational fluency to do my homework.

Exercises

1. If Rose, needs $6\frac{2}{5}$ yards of a material for a school project, how many yards of the

material will she need for 15 projects assuming that each project requires the same amount of material? (Hint: See Example **1**)

2. Given that a ground beef patty weighs $\frac{2}{3}$ pounds, how many pounds will 30

ground beef patties weigh? (Hint: See Example **2**)

3. John's overtime pay is $12\frac{2}{3}$ dollars per hour. How much overtime pay did he earn for $4\frac{1}{2}$ hours? (Hint: See Example **3**)

4. Karen needs $16\frac{1}{4}$ feet of lumber for her school project. How many feet of lumber does she need to complete $3\frac{1}{5}$ of the same project? (Hint: See Example **4**, use shortcut method to solve this problem.)

5. If a fabric material sells at $5.75 per yard, how much will $2\frac{2}{23}$ yards cost? (Hint: See Example **5**, use the shortcut method to solve this problem. $5.75 may be written as $5\frac{3}{4}$. Note: $0.75 = \frac{75}{100} = \frac{3}{4}$)

Answers to Selected Questions
4. 52 feet.   **5**. $12.00

DIVISION OF FRACTIONS

New words: **Divisor**, **Quotient** and **Dividend**.

Quick Review
Invert: **To invert is to turn upside down.** Therefore, **to invert a fraction means that the numerator which is at the top will change to the bottom and the denominator which is at the bottom will change to the top.**

If $\frac{1}{4}$ is inverted, it becomes $\frac{4}{1}$. If $\frac{3}{5}$ is inverted, it becomes $\frac{5}{3}$.

If $\frac{99}{100}$ is inverted, it becomes $\frac{100}{99}$. If $\frac{25}{4}$ is inverted, it becomes $\frac{4}{25}$.

Reciprocal: To find the **reciprocal** of a number is the same as to **invert** the number.

Rule 1: **To divide by fractions, invert the divisor which is the second fraction and change the division sign to a multiplication sign.**

The **reciprocal** of any number or fraction is the same as to divide 1 by the number or by the fraction.

Therefore, the reciprocal of $7 = \dfrac{1}{7}$, _____ Case 1.

The **reciprocal** of $\dfrac{3}{5} = \dfrac{1}{\dfrac{3}{5}}$

$$= 1 \div \dfrac{3}{5} = 1 \times \dfrac{5}{3} \qquad \text{Using rule 1.}$$

$$= \dfrac{5}{3} \qquad \text{_____ Case 2.}$$

Considering cases 1 and 2, to invert a number or a fraction is the same as to find the reciprocal of the number.

Example 1

Divide: $\dfrac{3}{4} \div \dfrac{1}{8}$

Solution

Step 1: Use Rule 1, which states that " to divide fractions, invert the divisor which is the second fraction and change the division sign to a multiplication sign."

$\dfrac{3}{4} \div \dfrac{1}{8}$ then becomes $\dfrac{3}{4} \times \dfrac{8}{1}$ (Note that $\dfrac{1}{8}$ is inverted to become $\dfrac{8}{1}$ and the division sign changes to a multiplication sign.)

Step 2: Reduce the fractions to the lowest terms by dividing the numerators and the denominators by the same numbers if possible.

$$\dfrac{3}{4} \times \dfrac{8}{1} = \dfrac{3}{\underset{1}{4}} \times \dfrac{\overset{2}{8}}{1} \qquad (8 \div 4 = 2, \ 4 \div 4 = 1)$$

$$= \dfrac{3}{1} \times \dfrac{2}{1}$$

Step 3: Multiply the numerators together and multiply the denominators together and put the product of the numerator over the product of the denominator.

From Step 2, $\dfrac{3}{1} \times \dfrac{2}{1} = \dfrac{3 \times 2}{1 \times 1}$

$$= \dfrac{6}{1}$$

$$= 6$$

Example 2

Divide: $\dfrac{3}{8} \div \dfrac{3}{4}$.   Check your answer.

Solution

Step 1: Use Rule 1

$\dfrac{3}{8} \div \dfrac{3}{4}$ then becomes $\dfrac{3}{8} \times \dfrac{4}{3}$ (Note that $\dfrac{3}{4}$ is inverted to become $\dfrac{4}{3}$ and the $\div$ changes to $\times$.)

Step 2: Reduce the fractions to the lowest terms by dividing the numerators and the denominators by the same numbers if possible.

$$\dfrac{3}{8} \times \dfrac{4}{3} = \dfrac{\overset{1}{3}}{\underset{2}{8}} \times \dfrac{\overset{1}{4}}{\underset{1}{3}} \qquad (4 \div 4 = 1,\ 8 \div 4 = 2,\ 3 \div 3 = 1)$$

$$= \dfrac{1}{2} \times \dfrac{1}{1}$$

Step 3: Multiply the numerators together and multiply the denominators together and put the product of the numerators over the product of the denominators.

From Step 2, $\dfrac{1}{2} \times \dfrac{1}{1} = \dfrac{1 \times 1}{2 \times 1}$

$$= \dfrac{1}{2}$$

Check answer

From Example 2, $\dfrac{3}{8} \div \dfrac{3}{4} = \dfrac{1}{2}$

Dividend↘   ↙Divisor

$$\dfrac{3}{8} \div \dfrac{3}{4} = \dfrac{1}{2}$$

↖Quotient

The quotient, which is the answer after the division, multiplied by the divisor should equal the dividend.

Quotient × Divisor = Dividend ————————— [A].

Substitute $\dfrac{1}{2}$ for Quotient, $\dfrac{3}{4}$ for Divisor and $\dfrac{3}{8}$ for Dividend in equation [A].

Equation [A] then becomes $\dfrac{1}{2} \times \dfrac{3}{4} = \dfrac{3}{8}$

$$\dfrac{1 \times 3}{2 \times 4} = \dfrac{3}{8}$$

$$\dfrac{3}{8} = \dfrac{3}{8} \quad\text{———————— [B]}$$

Since the left side of the equation [B] is the same as the right side of equation [B] which is $\dfrac{3}{8}$, the answer $\dfrac{1}{2}$ in Step 3 is correct. We can create Rule 2.

Rule 2: Quotient × Divisor = Dividend

Divisor: For example, if $\dfrac{3}{4} \div \dfrac{1}{8}$, $\dfrac{1}{8}$ is the divisor.

If $\dfrac{7}{9} \div \dfrac{2}{5}$, $\dfrac{2}{5}$ is the divisor.

If $\dfrac{11}{12} \div \dfrac{3}{8}$, $\dfrac{3}{8}$ is the divisor.

Therefore, **the divisor is the number by which a dividend is divided**. The number to be divided is the **dividend**, as shown:

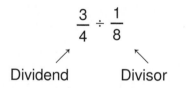

$$\dfrac{3}{4} \div \dfrac{1}{8}$$

Dividend   Divisor

Quotient is the number that results from the division of one number by another. Dividend is a quantity to be divided.

Relationship Among Dividend, Divisor, and Quotient
Let us investigate the relationship among the Dividend, Divisor and Quotient by by using the fact that $8 \div 2 = 4$ as shown:

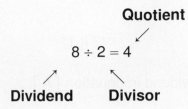

Quotient

$$8 \div 2 = 4$$

Dividend   **Divisor**

Therefore, **(a) Dividend ÷ Divisor = Quotient**

          or

       (b) Quotient × Divisor = Dividend. This statement will be useful in checking some answers to some questions later.

Example 3

Divide: $\dfrac{5}{8} \div \dfrac{3}{16}$. Check the answer.

Do not show any detailed method. Although the examples are intentionally designed to provide the students with detailed explanations including mathematical logic, it is recommended that the students use shortcuts in solving homework, class exercises and tests as much as possible as shown in Example **3**.

Solution

Shortcut:

$$\frac{5}{8} \div \frac{3}{16} = \frac{5}{8} \times \frac{16}{3}$$

$$= \frac{5}{\underset{1}{8}} \times \frac{\overset{2}{16}}{3} \qquad \text{(Divide numerator and the denominator by 8.)}$$

$$= \frac{10}{3} \qquad \text{(10 ÷ 3 = 3, remainder 1, } = 3\frac{1}{3}\text{)}$$

$$= 3\frac{1}{3}$$

Check answer

Quotient × Divisor = Dividend

$$3\frac{1}{3} \times \frac{3}{16} = \frac{5}{8}$$

$$\frac{10}{3} \times \frac{3}{16} = \frac{5}{8} \qquad (3\frac{1}{3} = \frac{10}{3})$$

$$\frac{\overset{5}{\cancel{10}}}{\underset{1}{3}} \times \frac{\overset{1}{\cancel{3}}}{\underset{8}{16}} = \frac{5}{8} \qquad \text{(Divide the numerator and the denominator by 2 and 3).}$$

$$\frac{5}{8} = \frac{5}{8} \qquad\qquad\qquad [A]$$

Left side of equation $[A]$ is equal to the right side of equation $[A]$, therefore, the answer $3\frac{1}{3}$ is correct.

_____

The notes and the generous worked examples have provided me with conceptual understanding and computational fluency to do my homework.

Exercises

1. How are fractions divided? (Hint: See Rule 1)

2. Explain the following:

(**a**) Divisor

(**b**) Quotient

(**c**) Dividend.

(**d**). State the relationship among the Divisor, Quotient, and Dividend.

3. Divide the following fractions: (Hint: See Example **1**)

(**a**) $\dfrac{1}{4} \div \dfrac{3}{8}$ (**b**) $\dfrac{4}{5} \div \dfrac{4}{5}$ (**c**) $\dfrac{6}{7} \div \dfrac{3}{7}$ (**d**) $\dfrac{1}{3} \div \dfrac{5}{6}$

(**e**) $\dfrac{2}{5} \div \dfrac{1}{5}$ (**f**) $\dfrac{5}{12} \div \dfrac{3}{4}$ (**g**) $\dfrac{2}{3} \div \dfrac{4}{5}$ (**h**) $\dfrac{5}{6} \div \dfrac{5}{6}$

4. Divide the following fractions and check your answer. (Hint: See Examples 2 and 3)

(**a**) $\dfrac{4}{5} \div \dfrac{9}{10}$ (**b**) $\dfrac{2}{7} \div \dfrac{8}{21}$ (**c**) $\dfrac{11}{12} \div \dfrac{22}{24}$ (**d**) $\dfrac{3}{16} \div \dfrac{4}{9}$

(**e**) $\dfrac{3}{7} \div \dfrac{6}{21}$ (**f**) $\dfrac{7}{15} \div \dfrac{7}{10}$ (**g**) $\dfrac{5}{64} \div \dfrac{5}{8}$ (**h**) $\dfrac{4}{9} \div \dfrac{5}{18}$

(**i**) $\dfrac{5}{4} \div \dfrac{5}{16}$ (**j**) $\dfrac{5}{81} \div \dfrac{10}{9}$ (**k**) $\dfrac{3}{16} \div \dfrac{7}{8}$ (**l**) $\dfrac{9}{10} \div \dfrac{3}{5}$

(**m**) $\dfrac{3}{4} \div \dfrac{4}{5}$ (**n**) $\dfrac{11}{12} \div \dfrac{11}{24}$ (**o**) $\dfrac{3}{5} \div \dfrac{3}{10}$ (**p**) $\dfrac{3}{4} \div \dfrac{5}{6}$

Challenge Questions

5. (**a**) $\dfrac{1}{3} \div \dfrac{1}{24}$ (**b**) $\dfrac{11}{12} \div \dfrac{11}{24}$ (**c**) $\dfrac{4}{5} \div \dfrac{3}{10}$ (**d**) $\dfrac{6}{49} \div \dfrac{3}{7}$

(e) $\dfrac{5}{64} \div \dfrac{5}{8}$ **(f)** $\dfrac{16}{25} \div \dfrac{4}{15}$ **(g)** $\dfrac{3}{7} \div \dfrac{3}{14}$ **(h)** $\dfrac{2}{9} \div \dfrac{2}{3}$

Answers to Selected Questions

3(a) $\dfrac{2}{3}$ **4(a)** $\dfrac{8}{9}$ **5(a)** 8

REAL WORLD APPLICATIONS - WORD PROBLEMS
Division of Fractions

Example 1

How many $\dfrac{1}{8}$ yard pieces of pipe can be cut from a length of pipe measuring $\dfrac{19}{24}$ yard? Check your answer.

Solution

Setup: The number of $\dfrac{1}{8}$ yard pieces of pipe that can be cut from a length of $\dfrac{19}{24}$ yard of pipe

$$= \dfrac{19}{24} \div \dfrac{1}{8}$$

Step 1: Use Rule 1, under Division of Fractions.

$$\dfrac{19}{24} \div \dfrac{1}{8} = \dfrac{19}{24} \times \dfrac{8}{1} \quad \text{(Note } \dfrac{1}{8} \text{ changes to } \dfrac{8}{1} \text{ and} \div \text{ changes to } \times.)$$

Step 2: Reduce the fractions to the lowest terms by dividing the numerators and the denominators by the same number or numbers if possible.

$$\dfrac{19}{24} \times \dfrac{8}{1} = \dfrac{19}{\underset{3}{24}} \times \dfrac{\overset{1}{8}}{1} \quad (24 \div 8 = 3, 8 \div 8 = 1)$$

$$= \dfrac{19}{3} \times \dfrac{1}{1}$$

Step 3: Multiply the numerators together and multiply the denominators together and put the product of the numerators over the product of the denominators.

492

From Step 2, $\dfrac{19}{3} \times \dfrac{1}{1} = \dfrac{19 \times 1}{3 \times 1}$

$$= \dfrac{19}{3}$$

Step 4: Change the improper fraction of $\dfrac{19}{3}$ to a mixed fraction by dividing the numerator by the denominator if needed.

$$\dfrac{19}{3} = 6\dfrac{1}{3} \qquad (19 \div 3 = 6 \text{ reminder } 1, = 6\dfrac{1}{3})$$

Therefore, $6\dfrac{1}{3}$ pieces of $\dfrac{1}{8}$ yard of pipe can be cut.

Check the answer

Quotient × Divisor = Dividend

$$6\dfrac{1}{3} \times \dfrac{1}{8} = \dfrac{19}{24}$$

$$\dfrac{19}{3} \times \dfrac{1}{8} = \dfrac{19}{24} \qquad (6\dfrac{1}{3} = \dfrac{19}{3})$$

$$\dfrac{19 \times 1}{3 \times 8} = \dfrac{19}{24}$$

$$\dfrac{19}{24} = \dfrac{19}{24} \qquad\qquad\qquad [A]$$

Since the left side of the equation $[A]$ is equal to the right side of the equation $[A]$, the answer $6\dfrac{1}{3}$ is correct.

Example 2

How many $\dfrac{1}{8}$ hours are there in $\dfrac{17}{24}$ hours? Check your answer. Use the shortcut to solve this problem.

Solution

Setup: The number of $\dfrac{1}{8}$ hour $= \dfrac{17}{24} \div \dfrac{1}{8}$

Shortcut: $\dfrac{17}{24} \div \dfrac{1}{8} = \dfrac{17}{24} \times \dfrac{8}{1}$

$$= \frac{17}{\underset{3}{24}} \times \frac{\overset{1}{8}}{1} \qquad (24 \div 8 = 3, 8 \div 8 = 1)$$

$$= \frac{17}{3}$$

$$= 5\frac{2}{3} \qquad (17 \div 3 = 5 \text{ remainder } 2, = 5\frac{2}{3})$$

Therefore, there are $5\frac{2}{3}$ of $\frac{1}{8}$ hours in $\frac{17}{24}$ hours.

Check answer

Quotient × Divisor = Dividend

$$5\frac{2}{3} \times \frac{1}{8} = \frac{17}{24}$$

$$\frac{17}{3} \times \frac{1}{8} = \frac{17}{24}$$

$$\frac{17 \times 1}{3 \times 8} = \frac{17}{24}$$

$$\frac{17}{24} = \frac{17}{24} \text{ —————————— [A]}$$

Since the left side of equation [A] is equal to the right side of equation [A] which is $\frac{17}{24}$, the answer is correct.

Example 3

How many periods of 10 minutes are there in $\frac{3}{4}$ of an hour? Use the shortcut method in solving the problem. (Hint: 10 minutes $= \frac{10}{60}$ hour $= \frac{1}{6}$ hour.)

Note: 60 minutes = 1 hour.

Solution

Setup: The number of $\frac{1}{6}$ hour in $\frac{3}{4}$ hour

$$= \frac{3}{4} \div \frac{1}{6}$$

494

Shortcut:

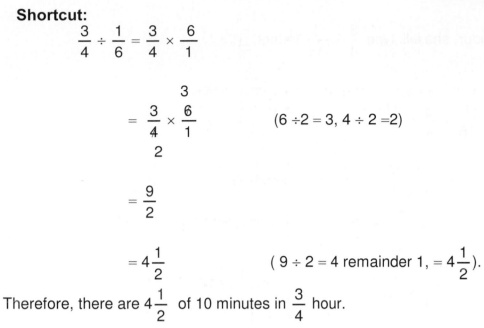

$$\frac{3}{4} \div \frac{1}{6} = \frac{3}{4} \times \frac{6}{1}$$

$$= \frac{3}{4} \times \frac{\overset{3}{6}}{\underset{2}{1}} \qquad (6 \div 2 = 3, \; 4 \div 2 = 2)$$

$$= \frac{9}{2}$$

$$= 4\frac{1}{2} \qquad (\, 9 \div 2 = 4 \text{ remainder } 1, = 4\frac{1}{2}\,).$$

Therefore, there are $4\frac{1}{2}$ of 10 minutes in $\frac{3}{4}$ hour.

Critical Thinking

Before any division is done, the unit of the dividend and the unit of the divisor must be the same. In Example 3 for example, we cannot divide $\frac{3}{4}$ hour by 10 minutes because we cannot divide hours by minutes, but we are able to divide $\frac{3}{4}$ hour by $\frac{1}{6}$ hour because both the unit of the dividend and the unit of the divisor are the same (hour.)

Example 4

Mary takes an average of 4 minutes to type a letter. How many similar letters can she type in $\frac{3}{4}$ hour? (Hint: Write 4 minutes as a fraction of an hour, and then reduce the fraction to the lowest term.) Use the shortcut method to solve the problem.

Solution

Setup: First write 4 minutes as a fraction of an hour.

$$60 \text{ minutes} = 1 \text{ hour}$$

$$4 \text{ minutes} = \frac{4}{60} \text{ hour} \qquad \text{(Reduce } \frac{4}{60} \text{ to the lowest term, } 4 \div 4 = 1$$

$$= \frac{1}{15} \text{ hour} \qquad 60 \div 4 = 15.)$$

In $\frac{1}{15}$ hour, 1 letter was typed.

In $\dfrac{3}{4}$ hour, she will type $\dfrac{3}{4} \div \dfrac{1}{15}$ letters.

Shortcut:

$$\frac{3}{4} \div \frac{1}{15} = \frac{3}{4} \times \frac{15}{1}$$

$$= \frac{3 \times 15}{4 \times 1}$$

$$= \frac{45}{4}$$

$$= 11\frac{1}{4}$$

Therefore, Mary will type $11\dfrac{1}{4}$ letters in $\dfrac{3}{4}$ hour.

Example 5

Anthony has $\dfrac{11}{12}$ gallon of drinking water. How many pint-size containers does he have? (Hint: 8 pints = 1 gallon)

Setup: Write 1 pint as a fraction of a gallon.

$$8 \text{ pints} = 1 \text{ gallon}$$

$$1 \text{ pint} = \frac{1}{8} \text{ gallon}$$

The number of pint-size containers in $\dfrac{11}{12}$ gallons $= \dfrac{11}{12} \div \dfrac{1}{8}$

Shortcut: $\dfrac{11}{12} \div \dfrac{1}{8} = \dfrac{11}{12} \times \dfrac{8}{1}$

$$= \frac{11}{\overset{}{\underset{3}{12}}} \times \frac{\overset{2}{8}}{1} \qquad (8 \div 4 = 2,\ 12 \div 4 = 3)$$

$$= \frac{11 \times 2}{3 \times 1}$$

$$= \frac{22}{3}$$

$$= 7\frac{1}{3}$$

Therefore, Anthony has $7\frac{1}{3}$ pint-size containers of drinking water.

The notes and the generous worked examples have provided me with conceptual understanding and computational fluency to do my homework.

Exercises

1. How many $\frac{1}{6}$ yard pieces of wood can be cut from a length of wood measuring $\frac{5}{6}$ yard. Check your answer. (Hint: See Example **1**)

2. How many $\frac{1}{6}$ hours are there in $\frac{19}{24}$ hour? Check your answer.

(Hint: See Example **2**) Use the shortcut method to solve this problem.

3. How many periods of 15 minutes are there in $\frac{11}{12}$ of an hour? (Hint: 15 minutes $= \frac{15}{60}$ hour $= \frac{1}{4}$ hour. Note that 60 minutes = 1 hour). Use the shortcut method to solve this problem. (Hint: See Example **3**)

4. Nick takes an average of 5 minutes to type a letter. How many similar letters can he type in $\frac{7}{12}$ hour? Check your answer. (Hint See Example **4**)

(Hint: 5 minutes $= \frac{5}{60}$ hour $= \frac{1}{12}$ hour. Note that 60 minutes = 1 hour).

Use the shortcut method to solve the problem.

5. Samuel has $\frac{7}{8}$ gallon of syrup. How many pint-size containers does he have?

(Hint: 8 pints = 1 gallon. See Example **5**) Use the shortcut method to solve the problem.

Answers Selected Questions
(**1**). 5 pieces of wood.   (**4**). 7 letters.

DIVISION BY MIXED NUMBERS

Rule 1: To divide a mixed number by another mixed number, change the

mixed numbers to improper fractions, invert the divisor and change the division sign to a multiplication sign.

Rule 2: To change a mixed number to an improper fraction, multiply the denominator by the whole number, add the numerator to the product and then write the sum over the denominator.

Example 1

Divide: $4\dfrac{1}{3} \div 1\dfrac{1}{6}$

Solution

Step 1: Change the mixed numbers $4\dfrac{1}{3}$ and $1\dfrac{1}{6}$ to improper fractions. (See Rule 1)

The improper fraction of the mixed number

$$4\frac{1}{3} = \frac{3 \times 4 + 1}{3} = \frac{13}{3}$$
(See Rule 2 and also Rule 3 under Multiplication of Fractions, Whole, and Mixed Numbers.)

The improper fraction of the mixed number

$$1\frac{1}{6} = \frac{6 \times 1 + 1}{6} = \frac{7}{6}$$
(See Rule 2 and also Rule 3 under Multiplication of Fractions, Whole, and Mixed Numbers,)

Therefore, $4\dfrac{1}{3} \div 1\dfrac{1}{6} = \dfrac{13}{3} \div \dfrac{7}{6}$

Step 2: Invert the divisor and change the $\div$ sign to $\times$ sign. (Note: $\dfrac{7}{6}$ is the divisor)

$\dfrac{13}{3} \div \dfrac{7}{6}$ from Step 1 becomes $\dfrac{13}{3} \times \dfrac{6}{7}$ ($\dfrac{7}{6}$ is inverted to become $\dfrac{6}{7}$ and $\div$ sign is changed to $\times$ sign.) (See Rule 1)

Step 3: Reduce the fractions to the lowest terms by dividing the numerators and the denominators by the same number or numbers if possible.

$$\frac{13}{3} \times \frac{6}{7} = \frac{13}{\overset{}{\underset{1}{3}}} \times \frac{\overset{2}{6}}{7} \qquad (6 \div 3 = 2,\ 3 \div 3 = 1)$$

Step 4: Multiply the numerators together and multiply the denominators together and put the product of the numerators over the product of the denominators.

$$\frac{13}{1} \times \frac{2}{7} = \frac{13 \times 2}{1 \times 7}$$

$$= \frac{26}{7} \qquad (26 \div 7 = 3 \text{ remainder } 5, = 3\frac{5}{7})$$

$$= 3\frac{5}{7}$$

Example 2

Solve the question in Example 1 without showing any detailed steps. (Hint: This is the shortcut method of problem solving. It is recommended that once the student understands the logic of the detailed solution, the students may use the shortcut method for homework, class exercises and tests.)

Solution

Divide: $4\frac{1}{3} \div 1\frac{1}{6}$ (Question from Example **1**)

Shortcut

$$4\frac{1}{3} \div 1\frac{1}{6} = \frac{13}{\underset{1}{3}} \times \frac{\overset{2}{6}}{7}$$

$$= \frac{26}{7} = 3\frac{5}{7}$$

Example 3

Divide: $2\frac{2}{3} \div 7\frac{1}{2}$

Solution

Step 1: Change the mixed numbers $2\frac{2}{3}$ and $7\frac{1}{2}$ to improper fractions. (See Rule 1)

The improper fraction of the mixed number

$$2\frac{2}{3} = \frac{3 \times 2 + 2}{3} = \frac{8}{3}$$ (See Rule 2 and also Rule 3 under Multiplication of Fractions, Whole, and Mixed Numbers.)

The improper fraction of the mixed number

$$7\frac{1}{2} = \frac{2 \times 7 + 1}{2} = \frac{15}{2}$$ (See Rule 2 and also Rule 3 under

Multiplication of Fractions, Whole, and
Mixed Numbers.)

Therefore, $2\frac{2}{3} \div 7\frac{1}{2} = \frac{8}{3} \div \frac{15}{2}$

Step 2: Invert the divisor and change the ÷ sign to × sign. (Note: $\frac{15}{2}$ is the divisor)

$\frac{8}{3} \div \frac{15}{2}$ from Step 1 becomes $\frac{8}{3} \times \frac{2}{15}$ ($\frac{15}{2}$ is inverted to become $\frac{2}{15}$

and ÷ sign is changed to × sign.)
(See Rule 1)

Step 3: Reduce the fractions to the lowest terms by dividing the numerators and
the denominators by the same number or numbers if possible. In this case,
there is no number that can divide both the numerators and denominators of
$\frac{8}{3} \times \frac{2}{15}$ evenly (without a remainder.)

Step 4: Multiply the numerators together and multiply the denominators together
and put the product of the numerators over the product of the denominators
as the final answer.

$$\frac{8}{3} \times \frac{2}{15} = \frac{8 \times 2}{3 \times 15} = \frac{16}{45}$$

Example 4
Solve the question in Example **3** without showing any detailed explanations.
Solution
The question in Example **3** is to divide: $2\frac{2}{3} \div 7\frac{1}{2}$

Shortcut method:

$$2\frac{2}{3} \div 7\frac{1}{2} = \frac{8}{3} \times \frac{2}{15}$$

$$= \frac{16}{45}$$

Example 5

Divide: $6\dfrac{2}{3} \div 3\dfrac{1}{5}$

Solution

Step 1: Change the mixed numbers $6\dfrac{2}{3}$ and $3\dfrac{1}{5}$ to improper fractions.

(See Rule 1).

The improper fraction of the mixed number

$6\dfrac{2}{3} = \dfrac{3 \times 6 + 2}{3} = \dfrac{20}{3}$ (See Rule 2 and also Rule 3 under Multiplication

of Fractions, Whole, and Mixed Numbers.)

The improper fraction of the mixed number

$3\dfrac{1}{5} = \dfrac{5 \times 3 + 1}{5} = \dfrac{16}{5}$ (See Rule 2 and also Rule 3 under Multiplication

of Fractions, Whole, and Mixed Numbers.)

Therefore, $6\dfrac{2}{3} \div 3\dfrac{1}{5} = \dfrac{20}{3} \div \dfrac{16}{5}$

Step 2: Invert the divisor and change the $\div$ sign to $\times$ sign. (Note: $\dfrac{16}{5}$ is the divisor.)

$\dfrac{20}{3} \div \dfrac{16}{5}$ from Step 1 becomes $\dfrac{20}{3} \times \dfrac{5}{16}$ ($\dfrac{16}{5}$ is inverted to become

$\dfrac{5}{16}$ and $\div$ sign changes to $\times$ sign.)

(See Rule 1.)

Step 3: Reduce the fractions to the lowest terms by dividing the numerators and the denominators by the same number or numbers if possible.

$\dfrac{20}{3} \times \dfrac{5}{16} = \dfrac{\overset{5}{\cancel{20}}}{3} \times \dfrac{5}{\underset{4}{\cancel{16}}}$ ($20 \div 4 = 5$, $16 \div 4 = 4$)

Step 4: Multiply the numerators together and multiply the denominators together and put the product of the numerators over the product of the denominators.

$\dfrac{5}{3} \times \dfrac{5}{4} = \dfrac{5 \times 5}{3 \times 4}$

$$= \frac{25}{12}$$

Step 5: Change the improper fraction $\frac{25}{12}$ to mixed numbers.

$$\frac{25}{12} = 2\frac{1}{12} \qquad (25 \div 12 = 2 \text{ remainder } 1, \ = 2\frac{1}{12})$$

Example 6

Solve the question in Example **5** without showing any detailed explanations.
(Hint: Use the shortcut method.)

Solution

The question in Example **5** is Divide: $6\frac{2}{3} \div 3\frac{1}{5}$

Solution

$$6\frac{2}{3} \div 3\frac{1}{5} = \frac{\overset{5}{\cancel{20}}}{3} \times \frac{5}{\underset{4}{\cancel{16}}}$$

$$= \frac{25}{12}$$

$$= 2\frac{1}{12}$$

Critical Link

When a fraction is being divided by another fraction, once the divisor is inverted and the ÷ sign changes to × sign, the question becomes multiplication of fractions. There are many examples of solutions of multiplications of fractions under the topic Multiplication of Fractions.

The notes and the generous worked examples have provided me with conceptual understanding and computational fluency to do my homework.

Exercises

1. Divide the following: Reduce to the lowest terms. (Hint: See Example 1.)

(a) $3\frac{1}{2} \div 1\frac{3}{4}$ 　　　　**(b)** $2\frac{2}{5} \div 1\frac{1}{5}$ 　　　　**(c)** $7\frac{1}{2} \div 2\frac{1}{2}$

(d) $4\frac{2}{3} \div 1\frac{5}{7}$ **(e)** $5\frac{1}{3} \div 1\frac{1}{3}$ **(f)** $6\frac{1}{2} \div 3\frac{1}{4}$

(g) What is the rule or the process for dividing a mixed number by another mixed number?

2. Divide the following using the shortcut method. (Hint: See Example **2**.)
   Reduce to the lowest terms.

   (a) $6\frac{2}{3} \div 1\frac{2}{3}$ **(b)** $3\frac{1}{3} \div 1\frac{2}{3}$ **(c)** $4\frac{1}{2} \div 1\frac{1}{2}$

   (d) $4\frac{2}{3} \div 2\frac{1}{3}$ **(e)** $4\frac{2}{3} \div 2\frac{2}{6}$ **(f)** $3\frac{1}{2} \div 1\frac{3}{4}$

3. Divide the following: Reduce to the lowest terms. (Hint: See Example **3**.)

   (a) $4\frac{1}{3} \div 10\frac{1}{2}$ **(b)** $2\frac{2}{7} \div 3\frac{3}{8}$ **(c)** $1\frac{1}{2} \div 2\frac{2}{3}$

   (d) $3\frac{1}{4} \div 9\frac{3}{7}$ **(e)** $5\frac{1}{2} \div 6\frac{1}{5}$ **(f)** $4\frac{2}{5} \div 6\frac{1}{3}$

4. Divide the following using shortcut method. (Hint: See Example **4**.)
   Reduce to the lowest terms.

   (a) $2\frac{1}{2} \div 3\frac{2}{3}$ **(b)** $1\frac{3}{7} \div 2\frac{3}{8}$ **(c)** $4\frac{2}{3} \div 5\frac{4}{5}$

   (d) $2\frac{3}{5} \div 5\frac{1}{3}$ **(e)** $2\frac{1}{5} \div 4\frac{1}{3}$ **(f)** $3\frac{2}{3} \div 5\frac{2}{5}$

5. Divide the following: Reduce to the lowest terms. (Hint: See Example **5**.)

   (a) $4\frac{1}{2} \div 2\frac{1}{2}$ **(b)** $3\frac{3}{5} \div 1\frac{2}{3}$ **(c)** $5\frac{1}{3} \div 2\frac{2}{3}$

   (d) $6\frac{2}{3} \div 1\frac{1}{4}$ **(e)** $8\frac{3}{4} \div 1\frac{2}{5}$ **(f)** $7\frac{1}{5} \div 2\frac{1}{4}$

6. Divide the following: (Hint: See Example **6**.)
   Solve Exercises **5(a)** to **5(f)** without showing any detailed explanations. Use the shortcut method. Reduce to the lowest terms.

Answers to Selected Questions

1(a) 2   **2(a)** 4   **3(a)** $\frac{26}{63}$ **3(b)** $\frac{128}{189}$ **3(f)** $\frac{66}{95}$

4(a) $\frac{15}{22}$ **4(c)** $\frac{70}{87}$ **5(a)** $1\frac{4}{5}$ **5(d)** $5\frac{1}{3}$

REAL WORLD APPLICATIONS - WORD PROBLEMS
Division by Mixed Numbers

Example 1

A rod is $8\frac{3}{4}$ meters long. How many pieces of rod measuring $1\frac{1}{4}$ meters can

the length of the $8\frac{3}{4}$ meters of rod be cut into?

Solution

Setup: The number of the pieces of rod measuring $1\frac{1}{4}$ meters that can be cut from

the $8\frac{3}{4}$ meters of rod $= 8\frac{3}{8} \div 1\frac{1}{4}$

(Note: We are required to find how many $1\frac{1}{4}$ meters are contained in $8\frac{3}{4}$

meters.)

Step 1: Change the mixed numbers $8\frac{3}{4}$ and $1\frac{1}{4}$ to improper fractions. (See Rule 1.)

The improper fraction of the mixed number

$8\frac{3}{4} = \frac{4 \times 8 + 3}{4} = \frac{35}{4}$ (See Rule 2 and also Rule 3 under Multiplication

of Fractions, Whole, and Mixed Numbers.)

The improper fraction of the mixed number

$1\frac{1}{4} = \frac{4 \times 1 + 1}{4} = \frac{5}{4}$ (See Rule 2 and also Rule 3 under Multiplication

of Fractions, Whole, and Mixed Numbers.)

Therefore, $8\frac{3}{4} \div 1\frac{1}{4} = \frac{35}{4} \div \frac{5}{4}$

Step 2: Invert the divisor and change the ÷ sign to × sign (Note: $\frac{5}{4}$ is the divisor.)

$\frac{35}{4} \div \frac{5}{4}$ from Step 1 becomes $\frac{35}{4} \times \frac{4}{5}$ (Note: $\frac{5}{4}$ is inverted to become

$\frac{4}{5}$ and the ÷ sign is changed to × sign.) (See Rule 1.)

Step 3: Reduce the fractions in $\frac{35}{4} \times \frac{4}{5}$ to the lowest terms by dividing the

numerators and the denominators by the same number or numbers if possible.

$$\frac{35}{4} \times \frac{4}{7} = \frac{\overset{7}{\cancel{35}}}{4} \times \frac{\cancel{4}}{\underset{1}{\cancel{5}}} \underset{1}{}$$

$$(35 \div 5 = 7, 5 \div 5 = 1, 4 \div 4 = 1)$$

Step 4: Multiply the numerators together and multiply the denominators together and put the product of the numerators over the product of the denominators.

$$\frac{7}{1} \times \frac{1}{1} = \frac{7 \times 1}{1 \times 1}$$

$$= \frac{7}{1}$$

$$= 7$$

Therefore, 7 pieces of rod measuring $1\frac{1}{4}$ meters can be cut from $8\frac{3}{4}$ meters.

Example 2

Solve the question in Example **1** without showing any detailed explanations, and we refer to this as a shortcut method.

Solution

Setup: Number of $1\frac{1}{4}$ meters of rod $= 8\frac{3}{4} \div 1\frac{1}{4}$

Solve: $\quad \frac{35}{4} \div \frac{5}{4} = \frac{35}{4} \times \frac{4}{5}$

$$= \frac{\overset{7}{\cancel{35}}}{\underset{1}{\cancel{4}}} \times \frac{\cancel{4}}{\underset{1}{\cancel{5}}}$$

$$= 5$$

Therefore, 5 pieces of rod measuring $1\frac{1}{4}$ meters can be cut from the $8\frac{3}{4}$ meters of rod.

Example 3

Given that it takes $\frac{2}{3}$ yard of a fabric to make a baby's shirt, how many similar shirts can be made with $10\frac{2}{3}$ yards?

Solution

Setup: The number of $\frac{2}{3}$ yard of shirts that can be made with $10\frac{2}{3}$ yards of fabric

is $10\frac{2}{3} \div \frac{2}{3}$ (Note: We are to find how many $\frac{2}{3}$ are contained in $10\frac{2}{3}$.)

Step 1: Change the mixed number $10\frac{2}{3}$ to an improper fraction. (See Rule 1.)

The improper fraction for the mixed number $10\frac{2}{3}$

$= \dfrac{3 \times 10 + 2}{3} = \dfrac{32}{3}$ (See Rule 2 and also rule 3 under Multiplication of

Fractions, Whole, and Mixed Numbers.)

Therefore, $10\frac{2}{3} \div \frac{2}{3} = \dfrac{32}{3} \div \dfrac{2}{3}$

Step 2: Invert the divisor and change the $\div$ sign to $\times$ sign. (Note: $\frac{2}{3}$ is the divisor,)

$\dfrac{32}{3} \div \dfrac{2}{3}$ from Step 1 becomes $\dfrac{32}{3} \times \dfrac{3}{2}$ (Note: $\frac{2}{3}$ is inverted to become $\dfrac{3}{2}$

and the $\div$ sign changes to the $\times$ sign.)
(See Rule 1.)

Step 3: Reduce the fractions in $\dfrac{32}{3} \times \dfrac{3}{2}$ to the lowest terms by dividing the

numerators and the denominators by the same number or numbers if possible.

$$\dfrac{32}{3} \times \dfrac{3}{2} = \dfrac{\overset{16}{\cancel{32}}}{\underset{1}{\cancel{3}}} \times \dfrac{\overset{1}{\cancel{3}}}{\underset{1}{\cancel{2}}}$$ $(32 \div 2 = 16, 2 \div 2 = 1, 3 \div 3 = 1)$

Step 4: Multiply the numerators together and multiply the denominators together and put the product of the numerators over the product of the denominators.

$$\dfrac{16}{1} \times \dfrac{1}{1} = \dfrac{16 \times 1}{1 \times 1}$$

$$= \dfrac{16}{1}$$

$$= 16$$

Therefore, 16 of $\frac{2}{3}$ yard of shirts can be made from $10\frac{2}{3}$ yards of fabric.

Example 4

Solve the question in Example **3** without showing any detailed explanations.
(**Note**: We refer to this method of solution as the shortcut method.)
Solution

Setup: The number of $\frac{2}{3}$ yard of shirts that can be made with $10\frac{2}{3}$ yards of

fabric $= 10\frac{2}{3} \div \frac{2}{3}$

Solve:

$$10\frac{2}{3} \div \frac{2}{3} = \frac{\overset{16}{\cancel{32}}}{\underset{1}{\cancel{3}}} \times \frac{\overset{1}{\cancel{3}}}{\underset{1}{\cancel{2}}}$$
Divide by 3 and 2. ($32 \div 2 = 16$ and $3 \div 3 = 1$)

$$= \frac{16 \times 1}{1 \times 1}$$
$$= 16$$

Therefore, 16 of $\frac{2}{3}$ of shirts can be made with $10\frac{2}{3}$ yards of fabric.

_____

The notes and the generous worked examples have provided me with conceptual understanding and computational fluency to do my homework.

Exercises

1. A pole is $9\frac{1}{3}$ feet long .How many pieces of the pole measuring $2\frac{1}{3}$ feet can be cut from the $9\frac{1}{3}$ feet long of the pole? (Hint: See Example **1**.)

2. Solve question 1 using the shortcut method. (Hint: See Example **2**.)

3. John bought a tape, which is $12\frac{4}{5}$ yards long. If he needs 8 pieces of tape measuring $1\frac{3}{5}$ yards for his school project, is $12\frac{4}{5}$ yards of tape enough for his project? (Hint: Find how many $1\frac{3}{5}$ are contained in $12\frac{4}{5}$. See Example **1**.)

4. Mrs. Aggor is making matching outfits for a school band. If a matching outfit requires $1\frac{3}{5}$ yards of fabric, and she bought $11\frac{1}{5}$ yards of fabric, how many similar outfits could she make? (Hint: Find how many $1\frac{3}{5}$ are contained in $11\frac{1}{5}$. See Example **1**.)

5. Solve question 4 without showing any detailed explanations. (Hint: See Example **2**.)

6. Eric used $3\frac{1}{5}$ feet of wire for a school project. How many similar school projects could he make from $12\frac{4}{5}$ feet of wire? (See Example **1** or **2**.)

7. Solve question 6 without showing any detailed explanations. (Hint: See Example **2**.)

Challenge Questions

8. Given that it takes $\frac{9}{10}$ of a yard of fabric to make a baby's shirt, how many similar shirts can be made from $12\frac{3}{5}$ yards of fabric?

9. How many pieces of $2\frac{3}{4}$ meters of wire can be cut from $27\frac{1}{2}$ meters of wire?

Answer to Selected Questions

1. 4	**4.** 7	**8.** 14

DIVISION OF A WHOLE NUMBER BY A MIXED NUMBER AND DIVISION OF A MIXED NUMBER BY A WHOLE NUMBER

Rule 1: **To divide a whole number by a mixed number or to divide a mixed number by a whole number, change both the mixed number and the whole number to improper fractions, invert the divisor and change the ÷ sign to × sign.**

Rule 2: **To change a mixed number to an improper fraction, multiply the denominator by the whole number, add the numerator to the product, and then write the sum over the denominator.**

Rule 3: **To change a whole number to an improper fraction, write the whole number over the number 1 as the denominator.**

Example 1

Divide: $8 \div 1\frac{1}{3}$

Solution

Step 1: Change 8 and $1\frac{1}{3}$ to improper fractions. (See Rule 1.)

The improper fraction of $8 = \frac{8}{1}$ (See Rule 3 and also Rule 2 under Multiplication of Fractions, Whole, and

Mixed Numbers.)

The improper fraction of $1\frac{1}{3} = \frac{3 \times 1 + 1}{3} = \frac{4}{3}$ (See Rule 2 and also

Rule 3 under Multiplication of Fractions, Whole, and Mixed Numbers.)

Therefore, $8 \div 1\frac{1}{3} = \frac{8}{1} \div \frac{4}{3}$

Step 2: Invert the divisor and change the $\div$ sign to $\times$ sign. (Note: $\frac{4}{3}$ is the divisor.)

$\frac{8}{1} \div \frac{4}{3}$ from Step 1 becomes: $\frac{8}{1} \times \frac{3}{4}$ (Note: $\frac{4}{3}$ is inverted to become $\frac{3}{4}$

and $\div$ sign change to $\times$ sign.)
(See Rule 1.)

Step 3: Reduce the fractions in $\frac{8}{1} \times \frac{3}{4}$ to the lowest terms by dividing the

numerators and the denominators by the same number or numbers if possible.

$$\frac{8}{1} \times \frac{3}{4} = \frac{\overset{2}{\cancel{8}}}{1} \times \frac{3}{\underset{1}{\cancel{4}}} \qquad (8 \div 4 = 2,\ 4 \div 4 = 1)$$

$$= \frac{2}{1} \times \frac{3}{1}$$

Step 4: Multiply all the numerators and multiply all the denominators and put the product of the numerators over the product of the denominators.

$$\frac{2}{1} \times \frac{3}{1} = \frac{2 \times 3}{1} = \frac{6}{1}$$

$$= 6$$

Therefore, $8 \div 1\frac{1}{3} = 6$

Example 2
Solve the question in Example **1** without showing any detailed solution methods. Use the shortcut method.
Solution

$$8 \div 1\frac{1}{3} = \frac{\overset{2}{\cancel{8}}}{1} \times \frac{3}{\underset{1}{\cancel{4}}}$$

509

$$= 6$$

Example 3

Divide: $3\dfrac{5}{8} \div 4$

Solution

Step 1: Change $3\dfrac{5}{8}$ and 4 to improper fractions. (See Rule 1.)

The improper fraction of $3\dfrac{5}{8} = \dfrac{8 \times 3 + 5}{8} = \dfrac{29}{8}$ (See Rule 2 and also Rule

3 under Multiplication of Fractions, Whole, and Mixed Numbers.)

The improper fraction of $4 = \dfrac{4}{1}$ (See Rule 3 and also Rule 2 under

Multiplication of Fractions, Whole, and Mixed Numbers.)

Therefore, $3\dfrac{5}{8} \div 4 = \dfrac{29}{8} \div \dfrac{4}{1}$

Step 2: Invert the divisor and change the $\div$ sign to $\times$ sign. (Note: $\dfrac{4}{1}$ is the divisor.)

$\dfrac{29}{8} \div \dfrac{4}{1}$ from Step 1 becomes $\dfrac{29}{8} \times \dfrac{1}{4}$ (Note: $\dfrac{4}{1}$ is inverted to become $\dfrac{1}{4}$

and the $\div$ sign changes to $\times$ sign.)
(See Rule 1.)

Step 3: Reduce the fractions in $\dfrac{29}{8} \times \dfrac{1}{4}$ to the lowest terms by dividing the

numerators, and denominators by the same number or numbers if possible. In this case, there is no number that can divide the numerators and the denominators evenly (without a remainder.)

Step 4: Multiply all the numerators and multiply all the denominators and put the product of the numerators over the product of the denominators.

$$\frac{29}{8} \times \frac{1}{4} = \frac{29 \times 1}{8 \times 4} = \frac{29}{32}$$

Therefore, $3\dfrac{5}{8} \div 4 = \dfrac{29}{32}$

Example 4

Solve the question in Example 3 without showing any detailed explanations.
Use the shortcut method.

Solution

$$3\frac{5}{8} \div 4 = \frac{29}{8} \times \frac{1}{4} = \frac{29}{32}$$

Example 5

Divide: $7\frac{1}{7} \div 7$

Solution

Step 1: Change $7\frac{1}{7}$ and 7 to improper fractions. (See Rule 1.)

The improper fraction of $7\frac{1}{7} = \frac{7 \times 7 + 1}{7} = \frac{50}{7}$ (See Rule 2 and also Rule

3 under Multiplication of
Fractions, Whole, and Mixed
Numbers.)

The improper fraction of $7 = \frac{7}{1}$ (See Rule 3 and also Rule 2 under

Multiplication of Fractions, Whole, and
Mixed numbers.)

Therefore, $7\frac{1}{7} \div 7 = \frac{50}{7} \div \frac{7}{1}$

Step 2: Invert the divisor and change the $\div$ sign to $\times$ sign.   (Note: $\frac{7}{1}$ is the divisor.)

$\frac{50}{7} \div \frac{7}{1}$ from Step 1 becomes $\frac{50}{7} \times \frac{1}{7}$ (Note: $\frac{7}{1}$ is inverted to become $\frac{1}{7}$

and $\div$ sign changes to $\times$ sign.)
(See Rule 1.)

Step 3: Reduce the fraction in $\frac{50}{7} \times \frac{1}{7}$ to the lowest terms by dividing the

numerators and the denominators by the same number or numbers if possible.
In this case, there is no number that can divide the numerators and the
denominators evenly (without a remainder.)

Step 4: Multiply all the numerators and multiply all the denominators and put the
product of the numerators over the product of the denominators.

$$\frac{50}{7} \times \frac{1}{7} = \frac{50 \times 1}{7 \times 7} = \frac{50}{49}$$

Step 5: Change $\dfrac{50}{49}$ to a mixed fraction, by dividing the numerator by the denominator.

$$\dfrac{50}{49} = 1\dfrac{1}{49} \qquad (50 \div 49 = 1 \text{ remainder } 1, = 1\dfrac{1}{49}.)$$

Therefore, $7\dfrac{1}{7} \div 7 = 1\dfrac{1}{49}$

Example 6
Solve Example **5** without showing any detailed solutions.
Use the shortcut method.
Solution

$$7\dfrac{1}{7} \div 7 = \dfrac{50}{7} \times \dfrac{1}{7} = \dfrac{50}{49} = 1\dfrac{1}{49} \quad \text{(See Steps 4 and 5 in Example 5.)}$$

The notes and the generous worked examples have provided me with conceptual understanding and computational fluency to do my homework.

Exercises
1. Divide the following whole numbers by the mixed numbers. (Hint: See Example **1**.)

(a) $3 \div 1\dfrac{1}{2}$ (b) $16 \div 2\dfrac{2}{3}$ (c) $12 \div 2\dfrac{2}{3}$ (d) $10 \div 2\dfrac{1}{2}$

(e) $14 \div 2\dfrac{1}{3}$ (f) $18 \div 1\dfrac{2}{4}$ (g) $24 \div 1\dfrac{1}{3}$ (h) $18 \div 4\dfrac{1}{2}$

2. Solve question **1(a)** to **1(h)** using the shortcut method. (Hint: See Example **2**.)
3. Divide the following mixed numbers by the whole numbers. (Hint: See Examples **3** and **5**.)

(a) $4\dfrac{1}{2} \div 2$ (b) $9\dfrac{1}{3} \div 2$ (c) $4\dfrac{2}{3} \div 2$ (d) $10\dfrac{2}{3} \div 8$

(e) $5\dfrac{1}{3} \div 4$ (f) $12\dfrac{1}{2} \div 5$ (g) $3\dfrac{1}{2} \div 14$ (h) $4\dfrac{1}{2} \div 18$

4. Solve questions **3(a)** to **3(h)** using the shortcut method. (Hint: See Example **4**.)
5. Divide the following mixed numbers and whole numbers. (Hint: See Examples **1**, **3**, and **5**.)

(a) $4 \div 1\dfrac{1}{2}$ (b) $7\dfrac{1}{2} \div 5$ (c) $8 \div 3\dfrac{1}{3}$ (d) $64 \div 2\dfrac{2}{3}$

(e) $6\dfrac{2}{5} \div 8$ **(f)** $12 \div 2\dfrac{2}{4}$ **(g)** $9\dfrac{1}{3} \div 8$ **(h)** $27 \div 2\dfrac{1}{4}$

(i) $8\dfrac{1}{3} \div 5$ **(j)** $6 \div 1\dfrac{1}{3}$ **(k)** $3\dfrac{1}{3} \div 5$ **(l)** $4\dfrac{4}{5} \div 8$

6. Solve questions **5(a)** to **5(l)** using the shortcut methods. (Hint: See Examples **2**, **4**, and **6**.)

Challenge Questions

7. Divide the following mixed numbers and whole numbers.

(a) $5 \div 2\dfrac{1}{2}$ **(b)** $9\dfrac{1}{3} \div 7$ **(c)** $36 \div 2\dfrac{1}{2}$ **(d)** $17 \div 1\dfrac{1}{2}$

Answers to Selected Questions

1(a) 2   **1(c)** $4\dfrac{1}{2}$ **1(g)** 18   **2(b)** 6   **2(d)** 4

2(f) 12   **2(h)** 14   **5(a)** $2\dfrac{2}{3}$ **5(c)** $2\dfrac{2}{5}$ **5(h)** 12

REAL WORLD APPLICATIONS - WORD PROBLEMS

Division of a Whole Number by a Mixed Number and Division of a Mixed Number by a Whole Number

Example 1

A store used $3\dfrac{3}{4}$ yards of material to make a dress. How many dresses can be made with 60 yards of material?

Solution

Setup: The number of $3\dfrac{3}{4}$ yards in 60 yards = $60 \div 3\dfrac{3}{4}$

Step 1: Change 60 and $3\dfrac{3}{4}$ to improper fractions. (See Rule 1.)

The improper fraction of $60 = \dfrac{60}{1}$.   (See Rule 3.)

The improper fraction of $3\dfrac{3}{4} = \dfrac{4 \times 3 + 3}{4} = \dfrac{15}{4}$.   (See Rule 2.)

Therefore, $60 \div 3\dfrac{3}{4}$ becomes $\dfrac{60}{1} \div \dfrac{15}{4}$.

Step 2: Invert the divisor and change ÷ sign to × sign. (Note: $\dfrac{15}{4}$ is the divisor.)

$\dfrac{60}{1} \div \dfrac{15}{4}$ from step 1 becomes: $\dfrac{60}{1} \times \dfrac{4}{15}$. (Note: $\dfrac{15}{4}$ is inverted to

become $\dfrac{4}{15}$ and the ÷ sign changes to × sign.) (See Rule 1.)

Step 3: Reduce the fraction in $\dfrac{60}{1} \times \dfrac{4}{15}$ to the lowest terms by dividing the

numerators and the denominators by the same number or numbers if possible.

$$\dfrac{60}{1} \times \dfrac{4}{15} = \dfrac{\overset{\overset{4}{\cancel{12}}}{\cancel{60}}}{1} \times \dfrac{4}{\underset{\underset{1}{\cancel{3}}}{\cancel{15}}} \qquad (60 \div 5 = 12, \; 15 \div 5 = 3, \; 12 \div 3 = 4, \; 3 \div 3 = 1)$$

Step 4: Multiply all the numerators together and multiply all the denominators together and put the product of the numerators over the product of the denominators.

$$\dfrac{4}{1} \times \dfrac{4}{1} = \dfrac{4 \times 4}{1 \times 1} = 16$$

Therefore, 16 dresses can be made from 60 yards of material.

Example 2

Solve Example **1** without showing detailed solution information. Use the shortcut method.

Solution

The number of $3\dfrac{3}{4}$ yards in 60 yards $= 60 \div 3\dfrac{3}{4}$

$$= 60 \div 3\dfrac{3}{4} = \dfrac{\overset{\overset{4}{\cancel{12}}}{\cancel{60}}}{1} \times \dfrac{4}{\underset{\underset{1}{\cancel{3}}}{\cancel{15}}} \qquad (60 \div 5 = 12, \; 15 \div 5 = 3, \; 12 \div 3 = 4, \; 3 \div 3 = 1)$$

$$= 4 \times 4 = 16$$

Therefore, 16 dresses can be made from 60 yards of material.

Exercises

1. Mary used $1\dfrac{2}{3}$ ounces of honey to make a loaf of bread. How many similar loaves can she make from a 60-ounce jar of honey? (Hint: See Example **1**.)

2. The Johnson family wants to know how many pieces of fence of length $3\dfrac{1}{3}$ yards is needed to fence around their garden, which has a total length of 200 yards. Is the Johnson's family correct by stating that 62 pieces of $3\dfrac{1}{3}$ yards are needed for the project? (Hint: See Example 1.)

COMPARISON OF FRACTIONS

New Terms: Ascending Order and Descending Order

Two or more fractions can be compared to find their magnitude in ascending or descending order. **Ascending order** of magnitude means that the fractions are arranged from the lowest to the highest. **Descending order** of magnitude means that the fractions are arranged from the highest to the lowest.

Rule 1: **To compare, write fractions in ascending or descending order of magnitude of two or more fractions, change all the fractions to equivalent fractions (with the same denominator.)**

Once the equivalent fractions are written, the value of each numerator of the equivalent fraction determines how large or small each fraction is. The larger the numerator of the equivalent fraction, the larger that specific fraction and the smaller the numerator of the equivalent fraction, the smaller that specific fraction.

Critical Thinking

Two or more fractions can be compared by arranging the equivalent fractions in ascending or descending order.

Example 1

Which fraction is greater, $\dfrac{3}{5}$ or $\dfrac{3}{4}$?

Solution

Step 1: Using Rule 1, Change the fractions $\dfrac{3}{5}$ and $\dfrac{3}{4}$ to equivalent fractions. The LCD of $\dfrac{3}{5}$ and $\dfrac{3}{4}$ is 20. Hint: See Examples under the topics Subtraction of Fractions or Addition of Fractions. For example, $5 \times 4 = 20$ and 5 and 4 can divide evenly into 20 (without a remainder.)

$$\frac{3}{5} = \frac{}{20} \nearrow \text{LCD}$$

$$\frac{3}{4} = \frac{}{20} \nearrow \text{LCD}$$

Step 2: Find the equivalent fractions. Review Equivalent Fractions.

$$\frac{3}{5} = \frac{3}{5} \times \frac{4}{4} = \frac{12}{20} \leftarrow \text{Equivalent fraction}$$

$$\frac{3}{4} = \frac{3}{4} \times \frac{5}{5} = \frac{15}{20} \leftarrow \text{Equivalent fraction}$$

Step 3: Compare the equivalent fractions.

Comparing the equivalent fractions $\frac{12}{20}$ and $\frac{15}{20}$, $\frac{15}{20} > \frac{12}{20}$ because the numerator 15 is greater than the numerator 12.

Therefore, $\frac{3}{4} > \frac{3}{5}$ The symbol $>$ means greater than.

Example 2
Solve Example **1** without showing any detailed solutions.

Shortcut: The LCD of $\frac{3}{5}$ and $\frac{3}{4}$ is 20. Find the equivalent fractions.

$$\frac{3}{5} = \frac{3}{5} \times \frac{4}{4} = \frac{12}{20} \leftarrow \text{Equivalent fraction}$$

$$\frac{3}{4} = \frac{3}{4} \times \frac{5}{5} = \frac{15}{20} \leftarrow \text{Equivalent fraction}$$

By comparing equivalent fractions, $\frac{15}{20} > \frac{12}{20}$ because the numerator 15 is greater

than the numerator 12. Therefore, $\frac{3}{4} > \frac{3}{5}$.

Example 3
Arrange the fractions in ascending and descending order of magnitude.

$$\frac{2}{3}, \frac{3}{4}, \frac{4}{5}$$

Solution

Step 1: Using Rule 1, change the fractions $\frac{2}{3}$, $\frac{3}{4}$, and $\frac{4}{5}$ to equivalent fractions.

The LCD of the fractions $\frac{2}{3}$, $\frac{3}{4}$, and $\frac{4}{5}$ is 60. (For example, $3 \times 4 \times 5 = 60$. Multiply all the denominators together to obtain the LCD.)

$$\frac{2}{3} = \frac{}{60} \quad \nearrow \text{LCD}$$

$$\frac{3}{4} = \frac{}{60} \quad \nearrow \text{LCD}$$

$$\frac{4}{5} = \frac{}{60} \quad \nearrow \text{LCD}$$

Step 2: Find the equivalent fractions. (Review topics on Equivalent Fractions.)

$$\frac{2}{3} = \frac{2}{3} \times \frac{20}{20} = \frac{40}{60} \quad \leftarrow \text{Equivalent fraction}$$

$$\frac{3}{4} = \frac{3}{4} \times \frac{15}{15} = \frac{45}{60} \quad \leftarrow \text{Equivalent fraction}$$

$$\frac{4}{5} = \frac{4}{5} \times \frac{12}{12} = \frac{48}{60} \quad \leftarrow \text{Equivalent fraction}$$

Step 3: Compare the equivalent fractions

$$\frac{40}{60}, \frac{45}{60}, \text{ and } \frac{48}{60}$$

$\frac{40}{60} < \frac{45}{60} < \frac{48}{60}$ because the numerator 40 is less than the numerator 45 and the numerator 45 is less than the numerator 48.)

Therefore, the ascending (increasing) order is: $\frac{2}{3}$, $\frac{3}{4}$, and $\frac{4}{5}$.

Therefore, the descending (decreasing) order is: $\frac{4}{5}$, $\frac{3}{4}$, and $\frac{2}{3}$.

Example 4

Solve Example **3**, without showing any detailed explanations. Use the shortcut method.
Solution
Shortcut:

The LCD for $\frac{2}{3}$, $\frac{3}{4}$ and $\frac{4}{5}$ is 60.

Write equivalent fractions:

$$\frac{2}{3} = \frac{2}{3} \times \frac{20}{20} = \frac{40}{60} \leftarrow \text{Equivalent fraction}$$

$$\frac{3}{4} = \frac{3}{4} \times \frac{15}{15} = \frac{45}{60} \leftarrow \text{Equivalent fraction}$$

$$\frac{4}{5} = \frac{4}{5} \times \frac{12}{12} = \frac{48}{60} \leftarrow \text{Equivalent fraction}$$

By comparing equivalent fractions, the ascending order is $\frac{2}{3}$, $\frac{3}{4}$, and $\frac{4}{5}$ and the descending order is $\frac{4}{5}$, $\frac{3}{4}$, and $\frac{2}{3}$.

The notes and the generous worked examples have provided me with conceptual understanding and computational fluency to do my homework.

Exercise

1. Explain how fractions can be compared (Hint: See Rule 1.)
2. Which of the following pairs of fractions is greater?. (Hint: See Example **1**)

   (a) $\frac{3}{7}$ and $\frac{2}{5}$ **(b)** $\frac{1}{4}$ and $\frac{2}{5}$ **(c)** $\frac{2}{5}$ and $\frac{3}{8}$

   (d) $\frac{3}{5}$ and $\frac{4}{7}$ **(e)** $\frac{2}{7}$ and $\frac{1}{5}$ **(f)** $\frac{4}{5}$ and $\frac{3}{4}$

3. Solve questions **2(a)** to **2(f)** without showing a detailed solution method. Use the shortcut method. (Hint: See Example 2.)
4. Arrange the following fractions in ascending and descending orders.
   (Hint: See Example **3**.)

   (a) $\frac{2}{3}$, $\frac{4}{7}$, $\frac{8}{21}$ **(b)** $\frac{2}{5}$, $\frac{3}{8}$, $\frac{3}{4}$ **(c)** $\frac{4}{9}$, $\frac{1}{3}$, $\frac{1}{4}$

   (d) $\frac{1}{5}$, $\frac{2}{7}$, $\frac{8}{35}$ **(e)** $\frac{1}{3}$, $\frac{2}{5}$, $\frac{4}{15}$ **(f)** $\frac{2}{3}$, $\frac{3}{4}$, $\frac{4}{5}$

5. Solve questions **4(a)** to **4(f)** without showing a detailed solution method. Use the shortcut method. (Hint: See Example 4.)

518

Challenge Questions

6. Arrange the following fractions in ascending and descending orders.

    (a) $\dfrac{1}{4}, \dfrac{2}{3}, \dfrac{5}{6}$ **(b)** $\dfrac{3}{5}, \dfrac{4}{7}$ **(c)** $\dfrac{3}{5}, \dfrac{2}{3}$ **(d)** $\dfrac{4}{7}, \dfrac{8}{14}, \dfrac{5}{7}$

Answers to Selected Questions

2(a) $\dfrac{3}{7}$ **4(a)** Ascending order is $\dfrac{8}{21}, \dfrac{4}{7}, \dfrac{2}{3}$ Descending order is $\dfrac{2}{3}, \dfrac{4}{7}, \dfrac{8}{21}$

CHAPTER 18

METRIC AND CUSTOMARY SYSTEMS OF UNITS

Understanding Measures

When the early humans changed from hunters to farmers, they needed to measure the size of their farms. The first units of length were based on the human body parts such as the length of the palm and the length of a finger. For example, the people of Ghana in West Africa use the distance from the tip of the left middle finger to the tip of the right middle finger of an adult as approximately 6 feet or 2 yards. (3 feet = 1 yard). People do not have the same body size, and therefore each of the measures using body parts differed considerably. In order to avoid confusion, measures were made standard so that everybody would use the same standards.

    The National Bureau of Standards in Washington D.C. determines the units on rulers or measuring tapes. When you measure something with a ruler or a tape measure, you are actually comparing it with these standard units.

    The two main systems of measurements are the Customary and the Metric systems. The Customary system is also known as the English system. The metric system is used in most countries and the metric system is also known as SI which stands for System International.

METRIC SYSTEM

Metric Length

The metric unit is named after the unit of length, the meter, because the metric units of length are based on the meter. The diagram shows a part of the metric length of a ruler in centimeters. The distance between any small division = 1 millimeter (mm) and 10 millimeters (mm) = 1 centimeter (cm). Note carefully that when you take a ruler, the type of the units at any edge of the ruler is indicated such as centimeter (cm) or inch (in.).

Let us measure the length of an eraser as shown in the diagram.

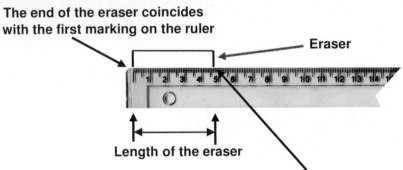

The length of the ruler is **4 centimeters and 6 millimeters**.

To measure the length of an eraser or any object, one of the edges of the eraser or the object should coincide with the first marking on the ruler, and then read the marking on the ruler that coincides with the other edge of the eraser or the object. This method of measuring the length of any object is very useful in solving many exercises later.

Benchmark

A benchmark is an object whose measure is already known and we can then use the object to estimate the lengths of other objects. For example if we know the length of your mathematics textbook, we can then use the textbook as a benchmark to measure the length of the top of your desk at school. We should then record the length of your desk in "mathematics textbook lengths."

Team Exercise

1. Use a ruler to measure the length of your mathematics textbook to the nearest millimeter (for example, the measurement could be 10 centimeters and 4 millimeters.)
2. Now use the length of the mathematics textbook to estimate the length of the top of your desk.
3. Record the length of the top of your desk in "mathematics textbook lengths."

For example, your record could be $3\frac{1}{3}$ mathematics textbook lengths.

4. Now use a ruler to measure the length of the top of your desk.
5. Which unit is more convenient to use in measuring the length of the top of your desk? (Length of the mathematics textbook or using a ruler.) Explain your answer.

Team Exercise

Each team should measure the following objects and then select the most appropriate measure. (Hint: It is more convenient to use a measuring tape to measure longer distances or objects.)

Object to be measured.	Measurements
1. The length of your classroom door.	**a.** 1 meter **b.** $2\frac{1}{2}$ meters **c.** 50 meters
2. The thickness of a quarter.	**a.** 2 centimeters **b.** 35 cm **c.** 1 millimeters
3. The length of a new pencil.	**a.** 1 meter **b.** 35 cm **c.** 19 cm
4. The length of a dollar bill.	**a.** $15\frac{1}{2}$ cm **b.** 2 cm **c.** 1 m
5. The width of a dollar bill.	**a.** $2\frac{1}{2}$ m **b.** $6\frac{1}{2}$ cm **c.** 12 cm

6. Track events are measured in meters. Each team should record two track events in meters.
7. Each team should use a measuring tape to measure the length and width of the classroom. What unit would be the most appropriate for measuring the length and the width of the classroom? (a) meters (b) centimeters (c) millimeters.
    Hint: The largest feasible unit is the correct answer.
8. What unit would be the most appropriate for measuring the length of a postage stamp?
    (a) meters (b) centimeters (c) millimeters. Hint: The largest feasible unit is the correct answer.
9. Explain why the length of the chalkboard should be expressed in meters instead of millimeters?
10. Select the correct answer
    a. Your classroom door is about 92 cm, 92 m, or 92 km wide.
    b. The thickness of a dime is about 1 kg, 1 cm, or 1 mm.
    c. The width of an index fingernail is about 1 mm, or 1 cm or 1 km.
    d. The height of a kitchen counter is about 90 km, 90 m, or 90 cm.
    e. The width of a quarter is about 1 mm, 1 cm, or 1 m
Each team should report their answers to the whole class.

Group Exercises/Exercises

Use the method of measuring the length of the eraser to measure the length of each line with a ruler. Record your answers in centimeters and milliliters. (Group Exercises: 1 - 4, Exercises: 5 - 10)

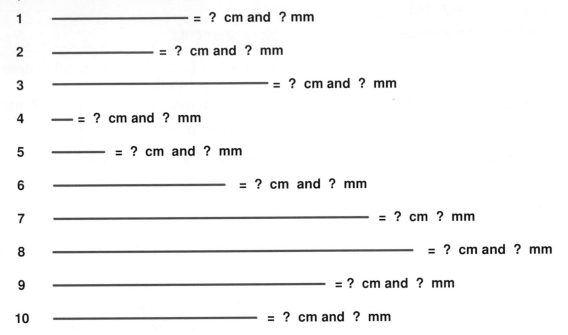

1 —————————— = ? cm and ? mm

2 ——————— = ? cm and ? mm

3 ——————————————— = ? cm and ? mm

4 —— = ? cm and ? mm

5 ————— = ? cm and ? mm

6 ——————————— = ? cm and ? mm

7 ———————————————— = ? cm ? mm

8 ————————————————— = ? cm and ? mm

9 ————————————— = ? cm and ? mm

10 ———————————— = ? cm and ? mm

Metric Units of Length

10 millimeters (mm) = 1 centimeter (cm)
100 centimeters (cm) = 1 meter (m)
1,000 meters (m) = 1 kilometer (km)

Look at the metric equations involving millimeters, centimeters, meters, and kilometers. **Note** that the metric system is easy to use because the units of measurements are related by the powers of 10. For example, to change different size units you just divide or multiply by 10, 100, or 1,000. The prefixes **milli-**, **centi-**, **deci-**, **deka-**, **hecto-**, and **Kilo-** shows how the measures are related to the basic unit which is the meter. For example;

a. milli - means "thousandth" therefore, 1 **milli**meter is .001 or $\frac{1}{1000}$ of a meter.

b. Centi - means "hundredth" therefore, 1 **centi**meter is .01 or $\frac{1}{100}$ of a meter.

c. Kilo - means "one thousand " and therefore, 1 Kilometer means 1000 meters.

Table of Metric Prefixes - Based on the meter

Prefix	Meaning
milli-	one thousandth or .001 or $\dfrac{1}{1000}$
centi-	one hundredth or .01 or $\dfrac{1}{100}$
deci-	one tenth or .1 or $\dfrac{1}{10}$
basic unit (meter)	1
deka	ten or 10
hecto-	one hundred or 100
kilo-	one thousand or 1000

The prefixes that are in the bold type are most commonly used units of measurement.

Table of Metric Units

Unit	Abbreviation	Equivalent
millimeter	**mm**	.001 m, .01 dm, **.1 cm**
centimeter	**cm**	.01 m, .1 dm, **10 mm**
decimeter	dm	.1m, 10 cm, 100 mm
meter	**m**	10 dm, **100 cm, 1,000 mm**, .1 dam, .01 hm, .001 km
dekameter	dam	10 m, .1 hm, .01 km
hectometer	hm	100 m, 10 dam, .1 km
kilometer	**km**	**1,000 m**, 100 dam, 10 hm

The prefixes that are in the bold type are most commonly used units of measurement.

Converting Between the Metric Units

There are two ways to convert between the metric units as follows:
(a). by multiplying by .001, .01, .1, 10, 100, or 1,000 as applicable.
(b). by multiplying or dividing by 10, 100, or 1000 as applicable.

Rule 1: To change a smaller unit to a larger unit follow the following two steps:
Step 1: Find how many smaller units are contained in one unit of the larger unit.
Step 2: **Divide** the given number of smaller units by the number you have determined in step 1.

Rule 2: To change a larger unit to a smaller unit follow the following two steps:

Step 1: Find how many smaller units are **contained** in one unit of the larger unit.

Step 2: **Multiply** the given number of larger units by the number you have determined in Step 1.

Example 1

How many centimeters are there in 200 millimeters?

Solution

We are converting from millimeters to centimeters and therefore, we are converting from a smaller unit to a larger unit. Therefore, we can use **Rule 1** as shown:

Step 1: 10 mm = 1 cm

Step 2: Therefore, 200 mm = 200 mm ÷ 10 mm = $\dfrac{200}{10} = \dfrac{\overset{20}{\cancel{200}}}{\underset{1}{\cancel{10}}} = 20$ cm.

Example 2

Solve: 25 cm = ? mm

Solution

We are converting from centimeters to millimeters, and therefore, we are converting from a larger unit to a smaller unit. Therefore, we can use **Rule 2** as follows:

Step 1: I cm = 10 mm

Step 2: Therefore, 25 cm = 25 × 10 mm = 250 mm.

Example 3

Solve:15 m = ? cm.

Solution

We are converting from meters to centimeters, and therefore, we are converting from a larger unit to a smaller unit. Therefore, we can use **Rule 2** as follows:

Step 1: 1 m = 100 cm.

Step 2: Therefore, 15 m = 15 × 100 cm = 1500 cm.

Example 4

Solve: ? m = 250 cm.

Solution

We are converting from centimeters to meters, and therefore, we are converting from a smaller unit to a larger unit. Therefore, we can use **Rule 1** as shown:

Step 1: 1m = 100 cm

Step 2: Therefore, $\dfrac{250}{100}$ m = 250 cm.

represented by 5.5 cm?

Solution

Setup: Change 5.5 cm to millimeters, and then find how many 10 mm
(10 mm = 1 cm) are contained in 5.5 cm. Finally, multiply 78 km by the
number of 10 mm in 5.5 cm.

Step 1: Change the 5.5 cm to millimeters as shown:
1 cm =10 mm (See the section on "Metric units of Length.")
Therefore, 5.5 cm = 5.5 × 10 mm = 55 mm.   (Review decimal multiplication.)

Step 2: Find the number of 10 mm that are contained in the 55 mm as shown:

$$\textbf{Divide } 55 \text{ mm by } 10 = 55 \div 10 = \frac{55}{10} = 5.5$$

Step 3: Find the kilometers represented by 5.5 cm on the map as shown:
Multiply 78 km by 55 = 78 km × 55 = 429 km.

Therefore, 5.5 cm on the map represents 429 km.

The notes and the generous worked examples have provided me with conceptual understanding and computational fluency to do my homework.

Exercises

1. Eric runs 3.8 kilometers every day. How many meters does he run in a week?
Hint: See Example 1.

2. How many meters are contained in $\frac{3}{5}$ kilometers? Hint: See Example 2.

3. Susan has a wire that measures .95 meters long. If her school project requires many
lengths of the wire measuring 30 millimeters, how many lengths can she cut from
the .95 meter long wire. Hint: See Example 3.

4. Given that the scale on a certain map is 5 mm = 74 km, how many kilometers are
represented by 7.2 cm? Hint: See Example 3.

Challenge Question

5. How many meters are contained in $\frac{2}{5}$ km?

Add and Subtract Measurements
Example 1
Copy and complete.
2 m + 150 cm = ? cm

Solution

Change the 2 m to centimeters by multiplying 2 m by 100 because 1 m = 100 cm
(See the section on "Metric Units of Length") and then add as shown:

```
  12 m   9 cm
-  8 m   5 cm
   4 m   4 cm
```

━━━━━━━━━━━━━━━━━━━ **The notes and the generous worked examples have provided me with conceptual understanding and computational fluency to do my homework.**

Exercises

1. Copy and complete. Hint: See Example 1.

    a. 4 m + 125 cm =? cm   **b.** 1 m + 85 cm = ? cm

    c. 6 m + 201 cm = ? cm   **d.** 3 m + 111 cm = ? cm

2. Copy and complete. Hint: See Example 2.

    a. 4 m + 300 cm = ? m   **b.** 1 m + 100 cm = ? m

    c. 2 m + 500 cm = ? m   **d.** 3 m + 200 cm = ? m

3. Copy and complete. Hint: See Example 3.

    a. 3 cm + 4 mm + 12 mm + 2 cm =

    b. 7 mm + 1 cm + 3 mm + 4 cm =

    c. 10 cm + 6 mm + 4 cm + 12 mm =

    d. 12 mm + 5 cm + 5 mm + 2 cm =

4. Solve: See Example 4.

    a.   4 km   200 m   **b.**   3 km   700 m   **c.**   5 km   98 m
       -1 km   400 m   - 2 km   800 m   - 3 km   100 m

5. Solve: Hint: See Example 5.

    a. 3 cm 4 mm - 1 cm 6 mm =

    b. 2 cm 5 mm - 1 cm 7 mm =

    c. 6 cm 8 mm - 2 cm 9 mm =

    d. 12 cm 6 mm - 9 cm 7 mm =

6. Solve: Hint: See Example 6.

    a.   10 m   8 cm   **b.**   2 m   5 cm   **c.**   4 m   7 cm
       - 5 m   3 cm   - 1 m   2 cm   - 2 m   5 cm

Challenge Questions

7. Copy and complete.

    a. 9 cm + 4 mm + 2 cm + 8 mm =

    b. 4 cm 3 mm - 2 cm 9 mm =

    c. 6 cm 7 mm - 5 cm 5 mm =

    d. 3 m + 600 cm = ? m

    e. 10 m + 150 cm = ? cm

8. Solve:

   a.   12 km   700 m   **b.**   2 cm   9 mm   **c.**   6 m + 700 cm = ? m

        - 2 km   800 m   + 5 cm   5 mm

Answers to Selected Questions

1a. 525 cm   **2a.** 7 m   **3a.** 6 cm 6 mm   **4a.** 2 km 800 m

CUSTOMARY UNITS OF LENGTH

The Customary unit of length are the inch, foot, yard, and mile.

    12 inches (in.) = 1 foot (ft)

         3 feet (ft) = 1 yard (yd)

   5,280 feet (ft) = 1 mile (mi)

    1,760 yards = 1 mile

Detailed Customary Units of Length table

Unit	Abbreviation	Equivalence
inch	in.	12 in. = 1 foot
foot	ft	1 ft = 12 in., 3 ft = 1 yard, 5,280 ft = 1 mile
yard	yd	1 yd = 3 ft, 1 yd = 36 in., 1,760 yd = 1 mile

Example 1

How many inches are in 5 feet?

Solution

We are to find 5 feet = how many inches.

Note: **To change from a larger unit (for example feet) to a smaller unit, (for example inches), multiply as shown:**

    Number of feet × Number of inches in 1 foot = Number of inches.

Number of feet × **Number of inches in 1 foot = Number of inches**

      5   ×   12   =   60 inches.

There are 60 inches in 5 feet.

When we compare feet to inches, the feet is a bigger unit. Using the rule, to change a bigger unit to a smaller unit, we must multiply.

$$1 \text{ ft}^2 = 144 \text{ in.}^2 \qquad \text{See table}$$
$$\text{Therefore, } 2 \text{ ft}^2 = 2 \times 144 \qquad \text{Using the rule, we must multiply.}$$
$$= 288 \text{ in.}^2$$

Example 3

Change 4 yd² to square feet.

Solution

When we compare yards to feet, the yard is a bigger unit. Using the rule, to change a bigger unit to a smaller unit, we must multiply.

$$1 \text{ yd}^2 = 9 \text{ ft}^2 \qquad \text{See the table.}$$
$$\text{Therefore, } 4 \text{ yd}^2 = 4 \times 9 \qquad \text{Using the rule, we must multiply.}$$
$$= 36 \text{ ft}^2$$

Example 4

Change $5\dfrac{2}{3}$ yd² to square feet

Solution

When we compare yards to feet, the yard is a bigger unit. Using the rule, to change a bigger unit to a smaller unit, we must multiply.

$$1 \text{ yd}^2 = 9 \text{ ft}^2 \qquad \text{See the table.}$$
$$\text{Therefore, } 5\dfrac{2}{3} \text{ yd}^2 = 5\dfrac{2}{3} \times 9 \text{ ft}^2 \qquad \text{Using the rule, must multiply.}$$
$$= \dfrac{17}{3} \times 9 \text{ ft}^2 \qquad \text{Review fractions.}$$
$$= \dfrac{17}{\overset{}{\underset{1}{3}}} \times \overset{3}{9} \text{ ft}^2 \qquad \text{Divide by 3.}$$
$$= 17 \times 3 \text{ ft}^2$$
$$= 51 \text{ ft}^2$$

Example 5

Change 63 square feet to square yards.

Solution

When we compare feet and yard, feet is the smaller unit. Using the rule, changing from the smaller unit to the bigger unit, we must divide.

$$9 \text{ ft}^2 = 1 \text{ yd}^2 \qquad \text{See the table.}$$
$$\text{Therefore, } 63 \text{ ft}^2 = 63 \div 9 \qquad \text{Using the rule, we must divide.}$$

$$= 7 \text{ yd}^2$$

Exercises

1. Change the following square inches to square feet. Hint: See Example 1.
  a. 432 in.^{2} **b**. 720 in.^{2}

2. Change the following square feet to square inches. Hint: See Example 2.
  a. 3 ft^2 **b**. 8 ft^2 **c**. 10 ft^2 **d**. 12 ft^2

3. Change the following square yards to square feet. Hint: See Example 3.
  a. 3 yd^2 **b**. 7 yd^2 **c**. 10 yd^2 **d**. 6 yd^2

4. Change the following square yards to square feet. Hint: See Example 4.
  a. $4\dfrac{1}{3}$ yd^2 **b**. $6\dfrac{2}{3}$ yd^2 **c**. $7\dfrac{1}{3}$ yd^2 **d**. $3\dfrac{2}{3}$ yd^2

5. Change the following square feet to square yards. Hint: See Example 5.
  a. 18 ft^2 **b**. 90 ft^2 **c**. 45 ft^2 **d**. 72 ft^2

Challenge Questions

5. Change the following square yards to square feet
  a. $2\dfrac{2}{3}$ yd^2 **b**. 1 yd^2 **c**. 11 yd^2

6. Change the following square inches to square feet.
  a. 144 in^2 **b**. 576 in^2

7. Change the following square feet to square inches.
  a. 4 ft^2 **b**. 7 ft^2 **c**. 8 ft^2

8. Change the following square feet to square yards.
  a. 27 ft^2 **b**. 36 ft^2 **c**. 45 ft^2 **d**. 9 ft^2

Answers to Selected Questions.
  1a. 3 ft^2 **2a**. 432 in^2 **3a**. 27 ft^2

REAL WORLD APPLICATIONS - WORD PROBLEMS
Customary Units of Square Measures

Example 1
A room has 99 square feet of floor space. How many square yards of tiles is needed for the floor assuming that there will be no waste of the tiles.
Solution
When we compare feet to yard, the yard is a bigger unit. Using the rule, to change from smaller unit to bigger unit, we must divide.

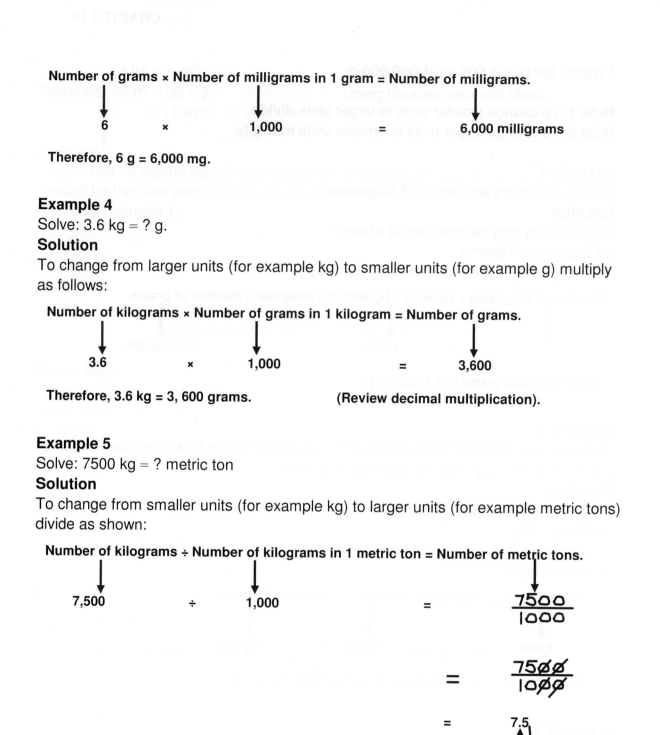

Number of grams × Number of milligrams in 1 gram = Number of milligrams.

6 × 1,000 = 6,000 milligrams

Therefore, 6 g = 6,000 mg.

Example 4
Solve: 3.6 kg = ? g.
Solution
To change from larger units (for example kg) to smaller units (for example g) multiply as follows:

Number of kilograms × Number of grams in 1 kilogram = Number of grams.

3.6 × 1,000 = 3,600

Therefore, 3.6 kg = 3, 600 grams.   (Review decimal multiplication).

Example 5
Solve: 7500 kg = ? metric ton
Solution
To change from smaller units (for example kg) to larger units (for example metric tons) divide as shown:

Number of kilograms ÷ Number of kilograms in 1 metric ton = Number of metric tons.

7,500 ÷ 1,000 = $\frac{7500}{1000}$

$= \frac{75\not0\not0}{10\not0\not0}$

$= 7.5$

Therefore, 7,500 kg = 7.5 metric tons

Example 6
Compare and write =, < or > for ?
3 metric tons ? 2,500,000 g
Solution
Setup: The first step in comparing numbers is to change the numbers to the same

units before comparing.

Step 1: Change 3 metric tons to grams. To change from larger units (for example metric tons) to smaller units (for example grams) multiply as shown:

Number of metric tons × Number of grams in 1 metric tons = Number of grams.

| 3 | × | 1,000,000 | = | 3,000,000 g |

Therefore, 3 metric tons = 3,000,000 g.

But 3,000,000 g is greater than 2,500,00 g. Therefore, 3 metric tons > 2,500,000 g.

The notes and the generous worked examples have provided me with conceptual understanding and computational fluency to do my homework.

Exercises

1. Select the correct answer. The metric mass is based on:

   a. inches   **b**. meter   **c**. gram   **d**. kilogram

2. How many grams are there in the following? Hint: See Example 1.

   a. 6 kg   **b**. 2 kg   **c**. 1.5 kg   **d**. 3 kg

3. If the mass of 1 tablet of a medication is 500 mg, what is the weight of the tablet in grams? Hint: See Example 2.

4. Replace ? with the number that makes the statement true. Hint: See Example 3.

   a. 2 g = ? mg   **b**. 4 g = ? mg   **c**. 3 g = ? mg

5. Solve the following: Hint: See Example 4.

   a. 4.2 kg = ? g   **b**. 2.3 kg = ? g   **c**. 1.5 kg = ? g

6. Solve: Hint: See Example 5.

   a. 2,500 kg = ? metric tons   **b**. 3,300 kg = ? metric tons
   c. 1,100 kg = ? metric tons   **d**. 6,200 kg = ? metric tons

7. Compare and write =, < or > for ? Hint: See Example 6.

   a. 2 metric tons ? 2,000,000 g   **b**. 4 metric tons ? 3,900,000 g
   c. 3 metric tons ? 3,100,000 g   **d**. 5 kg ? 4,900 g

Challenge Questions

8. Solve:

   a. 4 metric tons = ? kg   **b**. 8 g = ? mg   **c**. 5000 g = ? kg.
   d. 3,000,000g =? metric tons   **e**. 4,500 mg = ? g.

CUSTOMARY UNITS OF WEIGHT

The basic unit of mass in the Customary System is the pound.

16 ounces (oz) =1 pound (lb)

2,000 pounds =1 ton (T)

Example 1

Solve: 40 oz = ? lb

To change from smaller units (for example, ounces) to larger units (for example pound), divide as shown:

Number of ounces ÷ Number of ounces in 1 pound = Number of pounds.

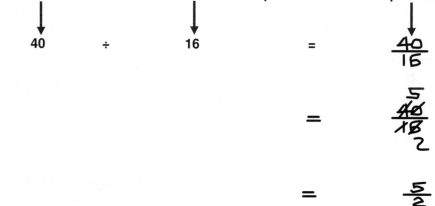

Therefore, 40 oz = $2\frac{1}{2}$ lb.

Example 2

Solve: 4lb = ? oz.

Solution

To change from larger units (for example, pounds) to smaller units (for example ounces), multiply as shown:

Number of pounds × Number of ounces in 1 pound = Number of ounces.

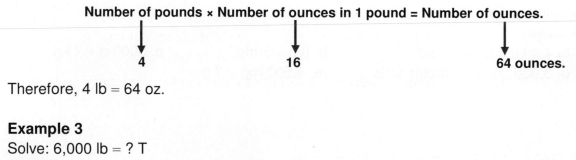

Therefore, 4 lb = 64 oz.

Example 3

Solve: 6,000 lb = ? T

Solution

To change from smaller units (for example, pounds) to larger units (for example tons), divide as shown:

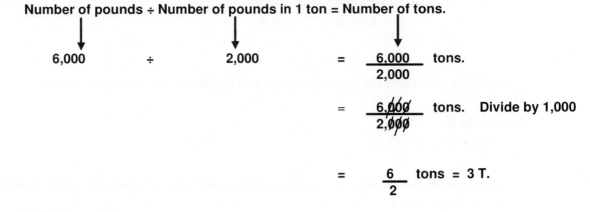

Number of pounds ÷ Number of pounds in 1 ton = Number of tons.

$$6,000 \quad ÷ \quad 2,000 \quad = \quad \frac{6,000}{2,000} \text{ tons.}$$

$$= \quad \frac{6,\cancel{000}}{2,\cancel{000}} \text{ tons.} \quad \text{Divide by 1,000}$$

$$= \quad \frac{6}{2} \text{ tons} = 3 \text{ T.}$$

Therefore, 6,000 lb = 3 T

Example 4

Solve: 4 T = ? lb

Solution

To change from larger units (for example, tons) to smaller units (for example pounds), multiply as shown:

Number of tons × Number of pounds in 1 ton = Number of pounds.

$$4 \quad × \quad 2,000 \quad = \quad 8,000 \text{ pounds}$$

Therefore, 4 T = 8,000 lb.

REAL WORLD APPLICATION - WORD PROBLEMS
Customary Units of Weight

Example 5

How many 100-pound bags of potatoes can be obtained from a ton of potatoes?

Solution

Setup: Change a ton of potatoes to pounds of potatoes and then divide by 100 pounds. To change from larger units (for example, tons) to smaller units (for example pounds), multiply as shown:

Number of tons × Number of pounds in 1 ton = Number of pounds.

$$1 \quad × \quad 2,000 \quad = \quad 2,000 \text{ pounds.}$$

Therefore, there are 2000 lb in 1 ton.

To find how many 100-pound bags of potatoes are contained in the 2000 lb of potatoes, divide 2000 lb by 100 lb as shown:

$$\frac{2{,}000 \text{ lb}}{100 \text{ lb}} = \frac{2{,}000 \cancel{\text{ lb}}}{100 \cancel{\text{ lb}}}$$ Divide by 100.

$$= 20$$

Therefore, there are 20-pound bags of potatoes in a ton of the potatoes.

Example 6

How much would 48 ounces of candy cost at $4.00 per pound?

Solution

Setup: Let us find how many pounds are there in 48 ounces, and then multiply the number of pounds in 48 ounces by $4.00 to obtain the cost of 48 ounces of the candy as shown:

To change from smaller units (for example, ounces) to larger units (for example pounds), divide as shown:

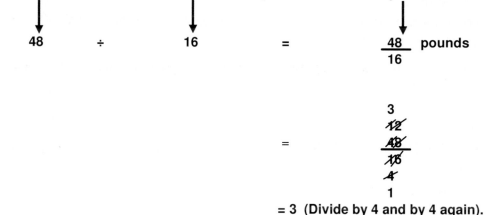

Number of ounces ÷ Number of ounces in 1 pound = Number of pounds.

$$48 \qquad ÷ \qquad 16 \qquad = \qquad \frac{48}{16} \text{ pounds}$$

$$= \frac{\overset{3}{\cancel{12}}\;\overset{}{\cancel{48}}}{\underset{\underset{1}{\cancel{4}}}{\cancel{16}}}$$

= **3 (Divide by 4 and by 4 again).**

Therefore, there are 3 pounds in 48 ounces.

If 1 lb of the candy costs $4.00, then 3 lb of the candy will cost 3 × $4.00 = $12.00.

The notes and the generous worked examples have provided me with conceptual understanding and computational fluency to do my homework.

Exercises

1. The basic unit of mass in the Customary System is the_____.

2. Solve: Hint: See Example 1.

   a. 32 oz = ? lb   **b**. 24 oz = ? lb   **c**. 8 oz = ? lb   **d**. 48 oz = ? lb

3. Solve: Hit: See Example 2.

a. 2 lb = ? oz   **b.** 5 lb = ? oz   **c.** 10 lb = ? oz   **d.** 7 lb = ? oz

4. Solve: Hint: See Example 3.

   a. 2000 lb = ? T   **b.** 1000 lb = ? T   **c.** 4000lb = ? T   **d.** 8000 lb = ? T

5. Solve: Hint: See Example 6.

   a. 2 T = ? lb   **b.** 6 T = ? lb   **c.** 3 T = ? lb   **d.** 5 T = ? lb

6. Solve: Hint: See Example 5.

How many 50-pound bags of rice can be obtained from 2 tons of rice?

7. Solve: Hint: See Example 6.

How much would 32 ounces of candy cost at $3.00 per pound?

Challenge Questions

8. Solve: **a.** 6 lb = ? oz   **b.** 40 oz = ? lb   **c.** 10 T = ? lb   **d.** 5000 lb = ? t

Answers to Selected Questions

2a. 2 lb   **3a.** 32 oz   **4a.** 1 T   **5a.** 4000 lb

METRIC CAPACITY AND CUSTOMARY CAPACITY

METRIC CAPACITY

The basic unit in measuring liquid is the liter. The metric units of capacity are:

1,000 millimeters (ml) = 1 liter (L)

250 milliliters = 1 metric cup

4 metric cups = 1 liter

1,000 liters = 1 kilometer (KL)

Team Project

The class should be divided into four teams. (Each team should bring the big, bigger and the biggest empty containers of milk, orange juice and soda drink from the super market to the class.) Each team should sketch and complete the chart using the labels on the containers.

Example 5

Compare. Write <, > or = for ? in the question.

a. 4,000 L ? 3 kL

b. 2 L ? 9 metric cups

Solution

a. In order to compare two quantities, we must change both quantities to the **same units** first before comparing. In this case, let us change kL to L first as follows:

To change from larger units (such as kL) to smaller units (such as L), multiply as shown:

Number of kL × Number of liters in 1 kL = Number of kL.

| 3 | × | 1000 | = | 3,000 |

Therefore, there are 3,000 liters in 3 kL.

We can now compare the 4,000 L and the 3,000 L because 3,000 L and 4,000 L have the same units. Since 4,000 L is greater than 3,000 L, we can write:

4,000 L > 3,000 L, and therefore, 4,000 L > 3 kL.

(Note: We have already showed that 3kL = 3,000 L.)

b. In order to compare two quantities, we must change both quantities to the same units first before comparing them. In this case, let us change 2L to metric cups first as shown:

To change from larger units (such as liters) to smaller units (such as metric cups) we multiply as shown:

Number of liters × Number of metric cups in 1 liter = Number of metric cups.

| 2 | × | 4 | = | 8 metric cups. |

Therefore, there are 8 metric cups in 2 L.

Now, we can compare the 8 metric cups and the 9 metric cups because the 8 metric cups and the 9 metric cups have the same units. Since 8 metric cups is less than 9 metric cups we can write:

8 metric cups < 9 metric cups. Therefore, we can write:

2 L < 9 metric cups (Note: We have already showed that 2 L = 8 metric cups).

REAL WORLD APPLICATIONS - WORD PROBLEMS
Metric Capacity

Example 6

How many bottles each holding 150 milliliters of orange juice can be filled from a plastic container that holds 4.5 liters of the orange juice?

Solution

Change the 150 milliliters and 4.5 liters to the same unit, and then divide 4.5 liters by 150 milliliters. Let us change 4.5 liters to milliliters as shown:

Number of liters × Number of milliliters in 1 liter = Number of milliliters.

$$4.5 \quad × \quad 1,000 \quad = \quad 4500.0 \text{ milliliters.}$$

Therefore, there are 4,500 milliliters in 4.5 liters.
Let us find how many 150 milliliters are contained in 4,500 milliliters by dividing 4,500 milliliters by 150 milliliters as shown:

$$\frac{4,500}{150} = \frac{4,500}{150}$$ Divide the numerator and the denominator by 10.

$$= \frac{\overset{90}{\cancel{450}}}{\underset{3}{\cancel{15}}}$$ Divide the numerator and the denominator by 5.

$$= \frac{\overset{30}{\cancel{90}}}{\underset{1}{\cancel{3}}}$$ Divide the numerator and the denominator by 3.

$$= 30$$

Therefore, 30 bottles each holding 150 milliliters of orange juice can be filled from a plastic container that holds 4.5 liters of orange juice.

Example 7

Five engineers drank a total of 4 L of water. If each engineer drank an equal amount of water, how many milliliters did each engineer drink?

Solution

Step 1: Change 4 L to milliliters as shown:

To change from larger units (such as liters) to smaller units (such as milliliters) we should multiply as shown:

Number of liters × Number of milliliters in 1 liter = Number of milliliters.

$$4 \quad × \quad 1,000 \quad = \quad 4000 \text{ milliliters.}$$

Therefore, there are 4000 milliliters in 4 liters.

Step 2: To find the amount of water that each engineer drank, find the average amount of water that each engineer drank by dividing 4000 milliliters by 5

Example 1

What is the length of time between 7:15 A.M. and 10:50 A.M.?

Solution

Use Rule 1 to solve the question as shown:

```
  10 hr    50 min
-  7 hr    15 min
_____
   3 hr    35 min
```

Therefore, the length of time between 7:15 A.M. and 10:50 A.M. is 3 hr and 35 minutes.

Example 2

Find the length of time between 2:50 P.M. and 10:23 P.M.

Solution

Use Rule 1 to solve the question as shown:

```
  10 hr    23 min
-  2 hr    50 min
```

We cannot subtract 50 minutes from 23 minutes, and therefore, we have to borrow 1 hr from 10 hr and this 1 hr becomes 60 minutes (see Table 1), and we then add the 60 minutes to the 23 minutes to obtain 83 minutes, and the 10 hours is therefore reduced to 9 hours, and then subtract as shown:

```
    9       83
  10 hr    23 min
-  2 hr    50 min
_____
   7 hr    33 min
```

Therefore, the length of the time between 2:50 P.M. and 10:23 P.M. is 7 hr 33 min.

Example 3

The school day of the Accra Middle School starts at 8:10 A.M and ends at 2:51 P.M. How long is the school day?

Solution

Use Rule 2 to solve the question as shown:

Step 1: Subtract to find the length of the time from 8:10 A.M. to 12:00 noon.

```
  12 hr    00 min
-  8 hr    10 min
_____
```

We cannot subtract 10 minutes from 00 minutes, and therefore, we have to borrow 1 hour from 12 hours, and this 1 hr is 60 minutes (see Table 1), and we then add the 60 minutes to the 00 minutes to become 60 minutes and the 12 hours is therefore, reduced to 11 hours, and then we subtract as shown:

$$
\begin{array}{rr}
11 & 60 \\
\cancel{12}\ \text{hr} & \cancel{00}\ \text{min} \\
-\ 8\ \text{hr} & 10\ \text{min} \\
\hline
3\ \text{hr} & 50\ \text{min}
\end{array}
$$

Step 2: 2:51 P.M. is 2 hours and 51 minutes after 12:00 noon.

Step 3: Add the two intervals found in Steps 1 and 2 as shown:

$$
\begin{array}{rr}
3\ \text{hr} & 50\ \text{min} \\
+\ 2\ \text{hr} & 51\ \text{min} \\
\hline
5\ \text{hr} & 101\ \text{min}
\end{array}
$$

Note that 101 minutes is more than 60 minutes and 60 minutes is equal to one hour. Divide 101 minutes by 60 to obtain the hours and minutes that are contained in 101 minutes as shown:

$$
\begin{array}{r}
\textbf{1 hr remainder 41 minutes} \\
60\overline{)\textbf{101 minutes}} \\
\underline{-\ 60} \\
41
\end{array}
$$

Therefore, 5 hr 101 min can be written as:

$$
\begin{array}{rr}
5\ \text{hr} & \\
+\ 1\ \text{hr} & 41\ \text{min} \\
\hline
6\ \text{hr} & 41\ \text{min}
\end{array}
$$

Therefore, the school day is 6 hours and 41 minutes.

Example 4

Find the length of the interval between 9:45 P.M. and 4:10 A.M.

Solution

Use Rule 2 to solve the question as shown:

Step 1: Subtract to find the length of the time from 9:45 P.M. to 12:00 midnight.

$$
\begin{array}{rr}
12\ \text{hr} & 00\ \text{min} \\
-\ 9\ \text{hr} & 45\ \text{min}
\end{array}
$$

We cannot subtract 45 minutes from 00 minutes, and therefore, we borrow 1 hour from 12 hours and this 1 hour is 60 minutes and we add the 60 minutes to 00 minutes to obtain 60 minutes and the 12 hours is reduced to 11 hours and we then subtract as shown:

$$
\begin{array}{rr}
11 & 60 \\
\cancel{12}\ \text{hr} & \cancel{00}\ \text{min} \\
-\ 9\ \text{hr} & 45\ \text{min} \\
\hline
2\ \text{hr} & 15\ \text{min}
\end{array}
$$

Step 2: 4:10 A.M. is 4 hours and 10 minutes after 12 midnight.

Step 3: Add the two intervals found in steps 1 and 2 as shown:

$$
\begin{array}{rr}
2\ \text{hr} & 15\ \text{min} \\
+\ 4\ \text{hr} & 10\ \text{min} \\
\hline
6\ \text{hr} & 25\ \text{min}
\end{array}
$$

Therefore, the interval between 9:45 P.M and 4:10 A.M. is 6 hr 25 min.

Example 5

How many hours are in 3 days?

Solution

To change from larger units such as days to smaller units such as hours, multiply as shown:

Number of days × Number of hours in 1 day = Number of hours.

| 3 | × | 24 | = | 72 hours |

Therefore, there are 72 hours in 3 days.

Example 6

How many weeks are in 28 days?

Solution

To change from smaller units such as days to larger units such as weeks, divide as shown:

Number of days ÷ Number of days in 1 week = Number of weeks.

| 28 | ÷ | 7 | = | 4 weeks |

Therefore, there are 4 weeks in 28 days.

Exercises

1. State the rule that is used in finding the length of the time interval between two given times that are both A.M. or both P.M. Hint:See Rule 1.

2. State the rule that is used in finding the length of the time interval between two given times when one is A.M. and the other is P.M. Hint: See Rule 2.

3. Find the length of the interval between the two given times. Hint: See Example 1.
  a. 7:30 A.M. to 11:46 A.M.   **b**. 6:14 A.M. to 10:34 A.M.
  c. 9:47 A.M. to 10:59 A.M.   **d**. 10:01 A.M. to 11:09 A.M.

4. Find the length of the interval between the two given times. Hint: See Example 2.
  a. 6:30 P.M. to 9:40 P.M.   **b**. 4:10 P.M. to 8:30 P.M.
  c. 7:20 A.M. to 10:45 A.M.   **d**. 8:15 A.M. to 11:35 A.M.

5. Find the length of the interval between the two given times. Hint: See Example 3.
  a. 10:30 A.M. to 3:15 P.M.   **b**. 9:00 A.M. to 2:30 P.M.
  c. 7:40 A.M. to 2:45 P.M.   **d**. 8:07 A.M. to 5:45 P.M.

6. Find the length of the interval between the two given times. Hint: See Example 4.
  a. 10:30 P.M. to 2:30 A.M.   **b**. 7:00 P.M. to 4:00 A.M.
  c. 8:18 P.M. to 8:19 A.M.   **d**. 11:20 P.M. to 1:40 A.M.

7. Solve: (Hint: See Example 5).
  a. How many hours are in 6 days?   **b**. How many hours are in 2 days?

8. Solve: (Hint: See Example 6).
  a. How many weeks are in 21 days?   **b**. How many weeks are in 35 days?

Challenge Questions

9. Find the length of the interval between the two given times.
  a. 11:15 P.M. to 3:00 A.M.   **b**. 5:20 A.M. to 10:30 A.M.
  c. 7:48 A.M. to 11:57 A.M.   **d**. 1:31 P.M. to 9:20 P.M.
  e. 7:25 A.M. to 4:15 P.M.   **f**. 9:00 A.M. to 11:30 A.M.
  g. 6:18 A.M. to 11:30 A.M.   **h**. 2:40 P.M. to 3:15 A.M.

Answers to Selected Questions

3a. 4 hr 16 min   **4a**. 3 hr 10 min   **5a**. 4 hr 45 min.   **6a**. 4 hr 0 min

PROBABILITY

Cumulative Review
1. 8 + 9 =   **2.** 12 + 9 =   **3.** 11 - 8 =   **4.** 7 × 2 =
5. 12 ÷ 3 =   **6.** 23 - 14 =   **7.** 24 ÷ 6 =   **8.** 13 - 7 =

9. 11   **10.**   26   **11.** 31   **12.**   8
× 2   + 25   - 13   × 4

13. 18 ÷ 6 =   **14.** 24 ÷ 3 =   **15.** 12 + 8 =   **16.** 19 - 12 =

17. 27   **18.**   17   **19.**   39   **20.**   18
× 3   + 18   - 13   × 4

21. 48 ÷ 3 =   **22.** 24 ÷ 8 =   **23.** 12 + 38 =   **24.** 36 - 17 =

25. 14   **26.**   23   **27.** 19   **28.**   12
× 5   + 27   - 15   × 3

29. 48 - 17 =   **30.** 20 ÷ 4 =   **31.** 16 + 38 =   **32.** 28 - 16 =

New Terms: **probability, outcome, experiment**

Probability is sometimes used in decision making. For example, if two friends want to go to either a movie or a football game together, but they are not sure if they should go to the movie first or the football game, then they may use coin flipping for decision making. There must be established rules before the coin is flipped, such as, if a head appears, they should go to the movie first and if a tail appears, they should go to the football game first.

Class Exercise
1. Give reasons why you think that coin flipping for decision making is not fair.
2. Give reasons why you think that coin flipping for decision making is fair

.

Group Exercise
In a soccer game, a coin toss is used to decide which team gets to select on which direction of the field it wants to play towards on the first play of the game.
Let us divide the class into two soccer teams of Team A and Team B. Each team should toss a coin 10 times and record the results using the tally table as

shown:

Team A and Team B Sample Chart

Trials	Heads tally	Tails tally
1st trial		
2nd trial		
3rd trial		
4th trial		
5th trial		
6th trial		
7th trial		
8th trial		
9th trial		
10th trial		
Total trials		
Fraction	$\dfrac{\text{Number of Heads}}{\text{Sum of total trials of heads and tails}} = \dfrac{?}{10}$	

Add up the results for the heads and tails. Find the fraction of the heads by using the formula :

$$\text{Fraction of the heads} = \frac{\text{Number of heads}}{\text{Number of trials}} = \frac{?}{10}$$

Find the fraction of the tails by using the formula:

$$\text{Fraction of the tails} = \frac{\text{Number of tails}}{\text{Number of trials}} = \frac{?}{10}$$

Conclusions of the Group Exercise

1. The group exercise is an example of an **experiment**. Therefore, the toss of a coin is an experiment.
2. The result of the experiment is the **outcome**. Therefore, the results of the number of heads and tails during the toss of the coin is the outcome.
3. The fraction of heads is actually the chances of obtaining a head when the coin is tossed 10 times, and this is known as the **probability** of obtaining a head.
4. The fraction of tails is actually the chances of obtaining a tail when the coin is tossed 10 times, and this is known as the **probability** of obtaining a tail.
5. From the group exercise, what is the fraction of heads? What is the probability of obtaining a head?
6. From the group exercise, what is the fraction of tails? What is the probability of obtaining a tail?
7. The outcomes of Team A and Team B should not necessarily be the same.

8. Note that the probability that Team A and Team B have found are fractions, for example, $\dfrac{?}{10}$. However, the probability can be expressed in **decimal** and **percent** also. Each group should change the fractional probability to decimal and percent probability (review the section on Decimal and Percent.)

9. When a coin was tossed, it was equally likely for either a head or a tail to occur. When outcomes have the same chance of occurring, they are said to be **equally likely**.

10. In the group exercise, we tossed the coin 10 times. It is possible to toss the coin more than 10 times, such as 20, 40, 100, or 200 times. Note that **the more we repeat the experiment, the closer we are to the true value of the probability**.

Experimental Probability

Experimental probability can be found by repeating an experiment many times and observing the results, as we did with the group exercise.

The formula for finding the experimental probability is given as shown:

$$\text{Experimental probability (outcome)} = \frac{\text{number of outcomes}}{\text{number of times the experiment was repeated}}$$

The experimental probability is sometimes called the **relative frequency**.

Example 1

A coin was tossed 45 times and 25 heads occurred.

(a) What is the experimental probability of obtaining heads? Express your answer as a fraction, a decimal, and a percent. Round your answer to the nearest hundredth.

(b) What is the experimental probability of obtaining tails? Express your answer as a fraction, a decimal, and a percent. Round your answer to two decimal places.

Solution

The number of times the coin was tossed $= 45$
The number of times the heads occurred $= 25$

$$\text{Experimental probability of heads} = \frac{\text{number of times heads occurred}}{\text{number of times the coin was tossed}}$$

$$= \frac{25}{45} \quad \text{This is the fractional form.}$$

$$= \frac{\overset{5}{25}}{\underset{9}{45}} \quad \text{Reduce to the lowest term by dividing by 5.}$$

$$= \frac{5}{9}$$ This is the probability in the fractional form, reduced to the lowest term.

To change the probability of $\frac{5}{9}$ to decimal, divide 5 by 9 as shown:

$$
\begin{array}{r}
.555 \\
9\overline{)50} \\
-45 \\
\hline
050 \\
-45 \\
\hline
050 \\
-45 \\
\hline
05
\end{array}
$$

The decimal probability is .56 to the nearest hundredth. (Review the section on decimal fractions.)

The decimal probability of .56 can be changed to a percent form by moving the decimal point in .56 two decimal places or two digits to the right which is the same as multiplying .56 by 100 as shown:

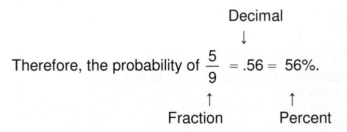

Move the decimal point two decimal places to the right.

Decimal
↓

Therefore, the probability of $\frac{5}{9}$ = .56 = 56%.

↑   ↑

Fraction   Percent

(b) The coin was tossed 45 times and the outcome in each toss was either a head or a tail. Since the heads occurred 25 times, then the number of tails is 45 − 25 = 20.

$$\text{Experimental probability of tails} = \frac{\text{Number of times tails occurred}}{\text{Number of times the coin was tossed.}}$$

$$= \frac{20}{45} \quad \text{This is the fractional form.}$$

$$= \frac{\overset{4}{\cancel{20}}}{\underset{9}{\cancel{45}}} \quad \text{Reducing to the lowest term by dividing by 5.}$$

$$= \frac{4}{9} \quad \text{This is the probability in the fractional form,}$$

reduced to the lowest term.

To change the probability of $\frac{4}{9}$ to a decimal form, divide 4 by 9 as shown:

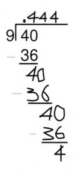

The decimal probability = .44 to the nearest hundredth.

The decimal probability of .44 can be changed to a percent by moving the decimal point in .44 two decimal places or two digits to the right which is the same as multiplying .44 by 100 as shown:

$$.44 = .44 = 44\%$$

Move the decimal point two places to the right.

Decimal
↓

Therefore, the probability of $\frac{4}{9}$ = .44 = 44%

↑   ↑

Fraction   Percent

Example 2

What is the probability of getting a tail when a coin is tossed?

Solution

We can use the tree diagram to solve the problem as follows with H representing a head and T representing a tail when a coin is tossed once.

a head and T representing a tail when a coin is tossed once.

A coin

There is one successful outcome of a tail or a T out of two possible outcomes of H or T as shown in the diagram. There are two possible outcomes, which are a head or a tail when a coin is tossed.

The probability of getting a tail when a coin is tossed

$$= \frac{\text{Number of successful outcomes}}{\text{Number of possible outcomes}} = \frac{1}{2}$$

Special Note: The probability of getting a tail is $\frac{1}{2}$ and this can also be expressed in a decimal form as .5 and in percent form as 50%. This means that the probability of getting a head $=100\% - 50\% = 50\%$ (The total probability $= 100\%$ or 1). We can then say that there is a **fifty-fifty chance** of getting a head or a tail when a coin is tossed.

Example 3

(a) Using T_1 and T_2 for tails and H_1 and H_2 for heads, show all the possible outcomes of tossing a coin twice by drawing a tree diagram.

(b) How is the tree diagram read? Write the possible outcomes.

(c) Explain the possible outcomes in terms of probability.

Solution

(a) The tree diagram is shown as shown:

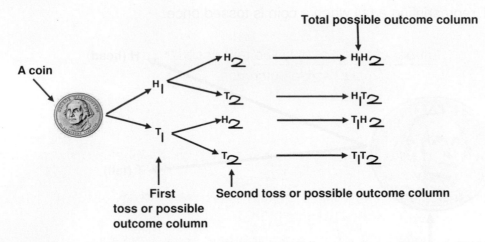

First toss or possible outcome column

Second toss or possible outcome column

(b) The tree diagram is read by following each branch from left to right. Using this idea and starting from the top of the tree diagram, the possible outcomes are: H_1H_2, H_1T_2, T_1H_2, and T_1T_2.

(c) There are 4 possible outcomes which are H_1H_2, H_1T_2, T_1H_2, and T_1T_2.

Exactly two heads or H_1H_2 occurred one time out of the 4 outcomes, and therefore the probability of obtaining exactly two heads

$$= \frac{\text{Number of times } H_1H_2 \text{ occurred}}{\text{Total possible outcomes}}$$

$$= \frac{1}{4}$$

The probability that at least one head occurred is 3 times in H_1H_2, H_1T_2, and T_1H_2 out of 4 possible outcomes of H_1H_2, H_1T_2, T_1H_2, and T_1T_2 is:

$$= \frac{\text{Number of times that at least one head occurred}}{\text{Total possible outcomes}}$$

$$= \frac{3}{4} \quad \text{(At least one head occurred 3 times in } H_1H_2, H_1T_2, \text{ and } T_1H_2\text{).}$$

The probability that at least one tail occurred 3 times in H_1T_2, T_1H_2, and T_1T_2 out of 4 possible outcomes of H_1H_2, H_1T_2, T_1H_2, and T_1T_2

$$= \frac{\text{Number of times at least one tail occurred}}{\text{Total possible outcomes}}$$

$$= \frac{3}{4}$$

The probability of exactly two tails or T_1T_2 occurred one time out of the 4 possible outcomes of H_1H_2, H_1T_2, T_1H_2, and T_1T_2

$$= \frac{\text{Number of times exactly two tails occurred}}{\text{Total possible outcomes}}$$

$$= \frac{1}{4}$$

The probability of no tails occurring is the same as the probability of exactly two heads occurring because there is no T_1 or T_2 in H_1H_2.

The probability of no heads occurring is the same as the probability of exactly two tails occurring because there is no H_1 or H_2 in T_1T_2.

Special Note: Tossing two coins once is the same as tossing one coin twice.

Group Exercise

Recall that experimental probability is sometimes called relative frequency. Let us find out how we can use relative frequency to find the probability. The class should select one person as the recorder to record the month in which every student in the class was born on a frequency table as shown:

Months	Jan	Feb	Mar	Apr	May	June	July	Aug	Sept	Oct	Nov	Dec
Frequency												

Frequency here means how many students are born in each month.
Sum of the frequencies = Total number of students in the class.
Let us answer a few questions.
(a) What is the fraction of the students who were born in January?

$$\text{The fraction of the students who were born in January} = \frac{\text{Frequency for January}}{\text{Sum of the frequencies}}$$

$$= \frac{\text{No. of students born in January}}{\text{Total number of students}}$$

Using your frequency table, find the fraction of the students who were born in January. How do you think that we can interpret this fraction? We can interpret this fraction by stating that the probability of selecting a student at random from the class that was born in January.

(b) Similarly, we can find the probability of selecting a student at random that was born in August as shown:
Probability of selecting a student at random that was born in August =

$$\frac{\text{Frequency of students born in August}}{\text{Sum of the frequencies}} = \frac{\text{No. of students born in August}}{\text{Total number of students in the class}}$$

Using your frequency table, find the probability that if a student is selected at random from the class, that student was born in August.

(c) Similarly using your frequency table, find the probability that if a student is selected at random, the student was born in: (1) June, (2) December, (3) April, (4) October.

Note: **Random** selection means that the selection is from a population without being biased. Population means a group , such as a group of students in a class or the total number of students is a population of students.

Exercises

1. Explain what is meant by probability.
2. Explain what is meant by an experiment and an outcome of an experiment.
3. Explain what is meant by the probability of obtaining a head.
4. Explain what is meant by "an outcome is equally likely."
5. The more we repeat the experiment, the closer we are to the true value of the probability. True or False?
6. What is the formula for finding experimental probability?.
7. The experimental probability is sometimes called relative frequency. True or False?
8. A coin was tossed 10 times and 3 heads occurred.
   (a) What is the experimental probability of obtaining a head. Express your answer in a fraction, a decimal, and a percent. Hint: See Example **1**.
   (b) What is the experimental probability of obtaining a tail? Express your answer in a fraction, a decimal, and a percent. Hint: See Example 1.
9. A coin was tossed 15 times and 5 tails occurred.
   (a) What is the probability of obtaining a tail? Express your answer in a fraction, a decimal, and a percent. Hint: See Example **1**.
   (b) What is the probability of obtaining a head? Express your answer in a fraction, a decimal, and a percent. Hint: See Example **1**.
10. Explain why a coin is tossed, there is a fifty-fifty chance of obtaining a head or a tail? Hint: See Example **2**.
11. Draw a tree diagram when a coin is tossed twice.
   (a) From your diagram, what are the possible outcomes?
   (b) What is the probability of obtaining exactly 2 tails?
   (c) What is the probability of obtaining exactly 2 heads?
   Hint: See Example **3**.

THEORETICAL PROBABILITY

Theoretical probability is when the probability of an event is found without doing an experiment.

A set of outcomes for a particular experiment is known as an **event**.

$$\text{Theoretical probability of an event} = \frac{\text{Number of outcomes in the event}}{\text{Total number of possible outcomes}}$$

Example 1

What is the theoretical probability that in the spinner below, the pointer will:

(a) land on 2?   (b) land on an even number?

(c) land on an odd number?   (d) land on a prime number?

Solution

(a) There is one outcome of 2 out of a total of 4 possible outcomes of 1, 2, 3, and 4 when the pointer lands on 2. Therefore, the theoretical probability that the spinner

$$\text{will land on 2} = \frac{\text{Number of the number 2 outcomes}}{\text{Total number of possible outcomes}}$$

$$= \frac{1}{4}$$

(b) The even numbers on the spinner are 2 and 4, and that means, there will be two outcomes of even numbers out of a possible of 4 outcomes of 1, 2, 3, and 4. Therefore, the theoretical probability that the spinner will land on an even number

$$= \frac{\text{Number of even number outcomes}}{\text{Total number of possible outcomes}}$$

$$= \frac{2}{4}$$

$$= \frac{\overset{1}{2}}{\underset{2}{4}} \quad \text{Reduce to the lowest term by dividing by 2.}$$

571

$$= \frac{1}{2}$$

(c) The odd numbers on the spinner are 1 and 3, that means, there will be two outcomes of odd numbers out of a total of 4 possible outcomes of 1,2,3, and 4. Therefore, the theoretical probability that the spinner will land on an odd number

$$= \frac{\text{Number of odd number outcomes}}{\text{Total number of possible outcomes}}$$

$$= \frac{2}{4}$$

$$= \frac{\frac{1}{2}}{\frac{4}{2}} \quad \text{Reduce to the lowest term by dividing by 2.}$$

$$= \frac{1}{2}$$

(d) A prime number is a number that has exactly two factors, which are 1 and the number itself. Out of the numbers 1, 2, 3, and 4 on the spinner, only 2 and 3 are prime numbers. Therefore, two out of four numbers are prime numbers. Therefore, there will be two outcomes of prime numbers out of the possible 4 outcomes of 1, 2, 3, and 4.

$$\text{Theoretical probability of a prime number} = \frac{\text{Number of prime number outcomes}}{\text{Total number of possible outcomes}}$$

$$= \frac{2}{4}$$

$$= \frac{\frac{1}{2}}{\frac{4}{2}} \quad \text{Reduce to the lowest term by dividing by 2}$$

$$= \frac{1}{2}$$

Example 2

Find the theoretical probability of each event .

(a) The spinner stops on C.

(b) The spinner stops on a vowel.

Solution

(a) There is one letter which is C out of a possible 8 letters.

$$\text{The theoretical probability of event C} = \frac{\text{Number of outcomes of C}}{\text{Total number of possible outcomes}}$$

$$= \frac{1}{8}$$

(b) All the vowels in the English language are a, e, i, o, and u. The vowels on the spinner are A, O and U, therefore, there are 3 vowels out of the 8 possible letters on the spinner.

The theoretical probability that the spinner stops on a vowel

$$= \frac{\text{Number of outcomes of a vowel}}{\text{Total number of possible outcomes}}$$

$$= \frac{3}{8}$$

0 AND 1 PROBABILITY VALUES

A probability of 0 is an event that cannot happen, and it is, therefore, an **impossible event**. A probability of 1 is an event that must happen, and it is, therefore a **certain event**. Some events are either impossible or certain. For example if, a bag contains only 10 green apples, the probability of drawing a green apple is $\frac{10}{10}$ which is 1.

The event of drawing a green apple is certain to occur because no other types of apples are in the bag and therefore, no other result is possible. An event which is certain to occur has a probability of 1.

Using the same bag of green apples, the event of drawing a red apple is impossible because the bag contains no red apples. Therefore, the probability of drawing a red apple is $\frac{0}{10} = 0$. An **impossible event has a probability of 0**.

Some more examples of impossible events are:

(a) obtaining an outcome of 7 from a single roll of a die because the maximum number on a die is 6, and so the outcome of a 7 will never occur. The number of outcomes of a 7 is 0 out of the possible outcomes of 6. Therefore, the probability of obtaining a 7 is $\dfrac{0}{6} = 0$. Obtaining an outcome of a 7 is impossible.

(b) A spinner has the numbers 1, 2, 3, 4, and 5. The probability of obtaining an outcome of a 9 out of 5 possible outcomes is 0 because there is no 9 on the spinner. Obtaining an outcome of a 9 is impossible.

Group Exercise

Decide if the following events are impossible or certain:

(a) A spinner has the numbers 1, 2, 3, 4, 5, 6, 7, and 8. What is the probability of the pointer stopping on 10?

(b) A bag has 6 black pens. What is the probability of drawing a red pen? What is the probability of drawing a black pen?

(c) The probability of obtaining a 10 from the roll of a single die.

Extreme Values of Probability

The extreme values of probability are 0 and 1 where an impossible event is 0 and an event certain to happen is 1. The probability of all other events is between 0 and 1. The extreme values of probability means the minimum and the maximum values of probability.

Example 3

Plot the probability of an impossible event, certain event, a 50-50 chance event, an equally likely event, 0% chance of an event and 100% chance of an event.

Solution

Since the extreme values of probability are 0 and 1, probabilities can be plotted on the part of a number line between 0 and 1 as shown:

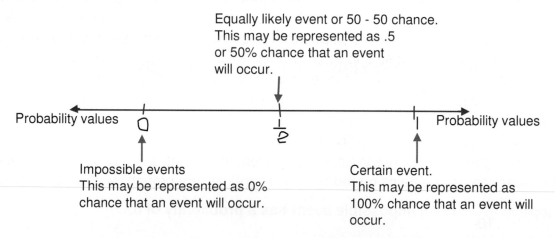

Comparing the Values of Probability

Since an event which is certain to happen has a probability of 1 and an impossible event has a probability of 0, an event which has a probability value close to 1 has a better chance of occurring than an event that has a probability value that is close to 0.

Rule: Given the probability values of many events, the event that has the highest probability value has the best chance of occurring and the event that has the lowest probability value has the least chance of occurring.

If the value of an event is close to 0, it is likely that the **event will not occur**.
If the value of an event is close to 1, it is likely that the **event will occur**.

Group Exercise

1. Using the rule, select the event which has the best chance of occurring and the least chance of occurring and explain your choices.

(a) Event A has the probability of .4 of occurring, event B has the probability of .2 of occurring and event C has the probability of .9 of occurring.

(b) Event A has the probability of $\frac{3}{4}$ of occurring, event B has the probability of $\frac{1}{4}$ of occurring and event C has the probability of $\frac{4}{4}$ of occurring.

(c) Event A has the probability of $\frac{1}{2}$ of occurring, event B has the probability of $\frac{1}{4}$ of occurring and event C has the probability of $\frac{1}{3}$ of occurring. Hint: Change all the fractions of the probabilities to have the **same** least common denominator (LCD), and then you will be able to compare the fractions (numerators). (Hint: Refer to the sections/chapter on fractions.) You may also change all the fractions to decimals and then compare the decimals. (Hint: Refer to the section/chapter on decimals.)

(d) Event A has an 80% chance of occurring, event B has a 20% chance of occurring, and event C has a 100% chance of occurring.

2. Discuss five examples of impossible events and five examples of certain events in everyday life. The class should be divided into 8 groups for the discussion and each group should record their five examples and report them to the class.

Example 4

A spinner is divided into 8 sections. If the pointer is spun, find the theoretical probability that it will land on:

(a) a number 3   (b) an even number   (c) an odd number
(d) a prime number   (e) a number 9   (f) a number greater than 8
(g) a number which is not a 6   (h) a number less than 5
(i) a number greater than 3

Indicate the probabilities of the events on a number line.

Solution

These solutions may be considered by some students to be long, but this example is designed to show the students various ways to solve the problem and also to enable the students to logically compare many solution methods.

(a) There is only one number 3 out of the total number of 8. Therefore, the probability of landing on the number 3 out of 8 numbers can be represented as shown:

$$\text{The the theoretical probability of landing on 3} = \frac{\text{Number of outcomes of 3}}{\text{Total number of possible outcomes}}$$

$$= \frac{1}{8}$$

(b) An even number is a number that can be divided by 2. The spinner has 4 even numbers which are 2, 4, 6, and 8 out of a total of 8 numbers on the spinner. Therefore, the probability of landing on an even number can be represented as shown:

The theoretical probability of landing on an even number

$$= \frac{\text{Number of even number outcomes}}{\text{Total number of possible outcomes}}$$

$$= \frac{4}{8}$$

$$= \frac{\overset{1}{\cancel{4}}}{\underset{2}{\cancel{8}}} \quad \text{Reduce to the lowest term by dividing by 4}$$

$$= \frac{1}{2}$$

(c) An odd number is a number that cannot be divided by 2. The spinner has 4 odd numbers which are 1, 3, 5, and 7 out of a total of 8 numbers on the spinner. Therefore, the probability of landing on an odd number can be represented as shown:

The theoretical probability of landing on an odd number

$$= \frac{\text{Number of odd number outcomes}}{\text{Total number of possible outcomes}}$$

$$= \frac{4}{8}$$

$$= \frac{\overset{1}{\cancel{4}}}{\underset{2}{\cancel{8}}} \quad \text{Reducing to lowest term by dividing by 4.}$$

$$= \frac{1}{2}$$

(d) A prime number is a number that has exactly two factors, which are 1 and the number itself. There are four prime numbers on the spinner, which are 2, 3, 5, and 7 out of the total of 8 numbers on the spinner. Therefore, the probability of landing on a prime number can be represented as shown:

Theoretical probability of landing on a prime number

$$= \frac{\text{Number of outcomes of a prime number}}{\text{Total number of possible outcomes}}$$

$$= \frac{4}{8}$$

$$= \frac{\overset{1}{\cancel{4}}}{\underset{2}{\cancel{8}}} \quad \text{Reduce to the lowest term by dividing by 4.}$$

$$= \frac{1}{2}$$

(e) There is no number 9 on the spinner, so it is impossible for the pointer to land on number 9. The impossible events have the probability of 0.

(f) There is no number greater than 8, so it is impossible for the pointer to land on a number greater than 8. The impossible events have the probability of 0.

(g) The total number of numbers on the spinner is 8. If the pointer will not land on 6, then the pointer will land on the other 7 remaining numbers of 1, 2, 3, 4, 5, 7, and 8 out of the total number of 8 on the spinner. The probability that the pointer will not land on the number 6 can be represented as:

$$\text{Theoretical probability of not landing on 6} = \frac{\text{Number of outcomes of not landing on 6}}{\text{Total possible outcomes}}$$

$$= \frac{7}{8}$$

(h) The numbers on the spinner which are less than 5 are 1, 2, 3, and 4. Therefore, there are 4 numbers that are less than 5 out of the total number of 8 numbers on the spinner. The probability that the pointer will land on a number less than 5 can be represented as:

Theoretical probability of landing on a number less than 5

$$= \frac{\text{Number of outcomes that are less than 5}}{\text{Total possible outcomes}}$$

$$= \frac{4}{8}$$

$$= \frac{\overset{1}{\cancel{4}}}{\underset{2}{\cancel{8}}} \quad \text{Reduce to the lowest term by dividing by 4.}$$

$$= \frac{1}{2}$$

(i) The numbers on the spinner which are greater than 3 are 4, 5, 6, 7, and 8. There are a total of five numbers that are greater than 3 out of the total number of 8 on the spinner.

Theoretical probability of landing on a number which is greater than 3

$$= \frac{\text{Number of outcomes} > 3}{\text{Total possible outcomes}}$$

$$= \frac{5}{8}$$

The probabilities of the events are indicated on the number line using assigned solution numbers.

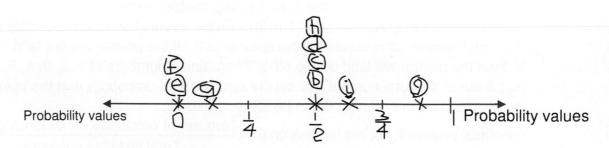

578

Example 5
(a) Find the theoretical probability of the outcome of B. Give your answer in a
fraction, a decimal, and a percent form.
(b) Find the experimental probability of the outcome of B.
(c) Find the experimental probability of the outcome of A.
(d) Find the experimental probability of the outcome of C.
(e) Find the experimental probability of the outcome of D.

Outcome	Number of spins
A	8
B	2
C	7
D	3
Total	20

This diagram is used to find the theoretical
probability because the data on the spinner
is obtained without conducting any
experiment.

This diagram is used to find the
experimental probability because
the data in the diagram is got from
conducting the experiment.

Solution
(a) The spinner is divided into 4 equal sections labelled A, B, C, and D. Section B is 1
out of the 4 equal parts of the spinner.

$$\text{Theoretical probability of outcome of B} = \frac{\text{Number of outcomes of B}}{\text{Total number of possible outcomes}}$$

$$= \frac{1}{4} \text{ (Fraction form of the probability).}$$

The decimal form of the theoretical probability of $\frac{1}{4}$ can be obtained by dividing 1

by 4 as shown:

$$
\begin{array}{r}
.25 \\
4\overline{)10} \\
8 \\
\overline{20} \\
20 \\
\overline{00}
\end{array}
$$

The decimal form of the theoretical probability of $\frac{1}{4}$ = .25

The decimal form of the theoretical probability of .25 can be changed to a percent by
moving the decimal point 2 places or two digits to the right, and attaching the
percent sign (%), which is the same as multiplying by 100 as shown:

579

$$.25 = .25. = 25\%$$

Therefore, the theoretical probability of $\dfrac{1}{4}$ = .25 = 25%

(b) The number of spins that give the outcomes of B are 2 out of the total of 20 spins.

Experimental probability of outcome of B = $\dfrac{\text{Number of spins that give outcomes of B}}{\text{Total number of possible spins}}$

$$= \dfrac{2}{20}$$

$$= \dfrac{\overset{1}{\cancel{2}}}{\underset{10}{\cancel{20}}} \qquad \text{Reduce to the lowest term by dividing by 2.}$$

$$= \dfrac{1}{10}$$

(c) The number of spins that give the outcomes of A are 8 out of the total of 20 spins.

Experimental probability of outcome of A = $\dfrac{\text{Number of spins that give outcomes of A}}{\text{Total number of possible spins}}$

$$= \dfrac{8}{20}$$

$$= \dfrac{\overset{2}{\cancel{8}}}{\underset{5}{\cancel{20}}} \qquad \text{Reduce to the lowest term by dividing by 4.}$$

$$= \dfrac{2}{5}$$

(d) The number of spins that give the outcomes of C are 7 out of the total of 20 spins.

Experimental probability of outcome of C = $\dfrac{\text{Number of spins that give outcomes of C}}{\text{Total number of possible spins}}$

$$= \dfrac{7}{20}$$

(e) The number of spins that give the outcomes of D are 3 out of the total of 20 spins.

580

Experimental probability of outcome of D = $\dfrac{\text{Number of spins that give outcomes of D}}{\text{Total number of possible spins}}$

$$= \frac{3}{20}$$

Example 6

A die is a small solid cube marked on each face from one to six spots or dots.

←——This is a die.

A die was rolled 10 times. On 2 of the rolls, the outcome was three dots on the die.
(a) What is the experimental probability of rolling a three?
   Give your answer as a fraction, a decimal, and a percent.
(b) How many rolls was the outcome not showing the side with three dots? What is the experimental probability of not rolling the side with three dots?
(c) Based on the experimental probabilities that you have found, and suppose the die is rolled 100 times, about how many times do you expect to roll a side:
   (i) with three dots?
   (ii) without three dots?

Solution

Note that this is an experimental probability because the event was repeated, for example, it was repeated 10 times.
(a) The outcome of the three dots on the die is 2 out of 10 total possible rolls.
   Experimental probability of the outcome of rolling a three

$$= \frac{\text{Number of outcomes of rolling a three on a side}}{\text{Total number of possible rolls or outcomes}}$$

$$= \frac{2}{10}$$

$$= \frac{\overset{1}{\cancel{2}}}{\underset{5}{\cancel{10}}} \qquad \text{Reduce to the lowest term by dividing by 2.}$$

$$= \frac{1}{5}$$

The experimental probability of $\dfrac{1}{5}$ can be expressed as a decimal by dividing 1 by 5 as shown:

$$5\overline{)10}^{.2}$$
$$-\underline{10}$$
$$00$$

Therefore, the decimal form of the experimental probability of $\dfrac{1}{5}$ = .2

The decimal form of the experimental probability of .2 can be expressed as a percent by moving the decimal point two places or two digits to the right and attaching the percent sign (%) which is the same as multiplying by 100 as shown:

Write a zero here as a place holder.

$$.2 = .20 = 20\%$$

Therefore, the experimental probability of $\dfrac{1}{5}$ = .2 = 20%

(b) The die was rolled 10 times. The outcome of the side with three dots was 2 and therefore, the number of rolls that the outcomes were not the side with three dots
   = 10 rolls - 2 rolls
   = 8 rolls

Experimental probability of not rolling the side with three dots

$$= \dfrac{\text{Number of outcomes without rolling a three}}{\text{Total number of possible rolls or outcomes}}$$

$$= \dfrac{8}{10}$$

$$= \dfrac{\overset{4}{\cancel{8}}}{\underset{5}{\cancel{10}}} \qquad \text{Reduce to the lowest term by dividing by 2.}$$

$$= \dfrac{4}{5}$$

(c)(i) From Example 6(c), the number of possible rolls = 100.
   Let the number of outcomes with three dots when the die is rolled 100 times = x. The experimental probability of the outcomes with the three dots when the die is rolled 100 times

$$= \dfrac{\text{Number of outcomes with a three when the die is rolled 100 times}}{\text{Number of possible rolls}}$$

$$= \frac{x}{100} \quad\rule{6cm}{0.4pt}\text{[A]}$$

From the solution of Example 6(a), the experimental probability of the outcome

of the side with the three dots $= \frac{1}{5}$ $\quad\rule{5cm}{0.4pt}$[B]

Equation [A] and equation [B] are equal because $\frac{x}{100}$ and $\frac{1}{5}$ are equivalent

fractions or equivalent ratios, therefore,

$$\frac{x}{100} = \frac{1}{5} \quad\rule{5cm}{0.4pt}\text{[C]}$$

(Review the section on Equivalent Fractions or Equivalent Ratios).
The cross products of equivalent fractions or ratios are equal, so

$$\frac{x}{100} \times \frac{1}{5}$$

Therefore, $5 \times x = 100 \times 1$

$\qquad 5x = 100$ $\quad\rule{5cm}{0.4pt}$[D]

Divide each side of equation [D] by 5 in order to obtain the value of x as shown:

$$\frac{\overset{x}{\cancel{5x}}}{\underset{1}{\cancel{5}}} = \frac{\overset{20}{\cancel{100}}}{\underset{1}{\cancel{5}}}$$

$x = 20$ outcomes of three dots.

(ii) From Example 6(c), the number of possible rolls = 100.

Let $y =$ "the number of times of outcomes with no side with three dots out of 100 possible rolls."

The experimental probability of not rolling the side with three dots out of 100 possible outcomes

$$= \frac{\text{Number of outcomes with no three dots when the die is rolled 100 times}}{\text{Total number of possible rolls}}$$

$= \frac{y}{100}$ $\quad\rule{5cm}{0.4pt}$[E]

From solution of Example 6(b), the experimental probability of not rolling the side

with three dots $= \frac{4}{5}$ $\quad\rule{5cm}{0.4pt}$[F]

Equation $[E]$ and equation $[F]$ are equal because $\dfrac{y}{100}$ and $\dfrac{4}{5}$ are equivalent fractions or ratios, and therefore,

$$\frac{y}{100} = \frac{4}{5}$$

(Review the section on Equivalent Fractions and Equivalent Ratios).
The cross products of equivalent fractions or ratios are equal, so

Therefore, $= 5 \times y = 4 \times 100$

$$5y = 400 \text{——————————————————}[G]$$

Divide each side of equation $[G]$ by 5 in order to obtain the value of y as shown:

$$\frac{5y}{5} = \frac{400}{5}$$

$$\underset{1}{\frac{\overset{y}{\cancel{5}y}}{\cancel{5}}} = \underset{1}{\frac{\overset{80}{\cancel{400}}}{\cancel{5}}} \quad \text{Divide each side of the equation by 5.}$$

$y = 80$ outcomes of not rolling a side with three dots.

Example 7

(Example 7 is intentionally designed to be long to provide the student with critical and logical methods of solving diverse problems.)
A die was thrown once.
(a) List the possible outcomes.
  From your possible outcomes in (a), what is the theoretical probability of rolling:
(b) an even number.   (c) an odd number.   (d) a number greater than 2.
(e) a number between 2 and 5. (f) a multiple of 3.   (g) not a multiple of 3.
(h) a prime number.   (i) not a prime number.

Solution

(a) A die has six sides and the sides are numbered from 1 to 6. When the die is thrown, any of the six sides can show up, so there are six possible outcomes, which are 1, 2, 3, 4, 5, and 6.
(b) The even numbers out of the total possible outcomes of 1, 2, 3, 4, 5 and 6 are 2, 4, and 6. There are three even numbers out of the total of 6 possible outcomes.
  The theoretical probability of obtaining an even number

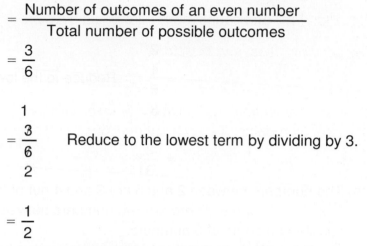

$$= \frac{\text{Number of outcomes of an even number}}{\text{Total number of possible outcomes}}$$

$$= \frac{3}{6}$$

$$= \frac{\overset{1}{\cancel{3}}}{\underset{2}{\cancel{6}}} \qquad \text{Reduce to the lowest term by dividing by 3.}$$

$$= \frac{1}{2}$$

(c) The odd numbers out of the total possible outcomes of 1, 2, 3, 4, 5, and 6 are 1, 3, and 5. Therefore, there are three odd numbers out of the total of 6 possible outcomes.

The theoretical probability of obtaining an odd number

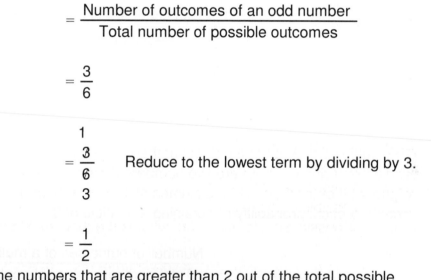

$$= \frac{\text{Number of outcomes of an odd number}}{\text{Total number of possible outcomes}}$$

$$= \frac{3}{6}$$

$$= \frac{\overset{1}{\cancel{3}}}{\underset{3}{\cancel{6}}} \qquad \text{Reduce to the lowest term by dividing by 3.}$$

$$= \frac{1}{2}$$

(d) The outcome of the numbers that are greater than 2 out of the total possible outcomes of 1, 2, 3, 4, 5, and 6 are 3, 4, 5, and 6. There are four numbers, which are greater than 2 out of the total possible outcome of 6 numbers. The theoretical probability of obtaining a number greater than 2

$$= \frac{\text{Number of outcomes greater than 2}}{\text{Total number of possible outcomes}}$$

$$= \frac{4}{6}$$

$$= \frac{\overset{2}{\cancel{4}}}{\underset{3}{\cancel{6}}}$$

Reduce to the lowest term by dividing by 2.

$$= \frac{2}{3}$$

(e) The numbers between 2 and 5 are 3 and 4 out of the total possible outcomes of 1, 2, 3, 4, 5, and 6. There are two numbers between 2 and 5 out of the total possible outcome of 6 numbers.

The theoretical probability of obtaining a number between 2 and 5

$$= \frac{\text{Number of outcomes of a number between 2 and 5}}{\text{Total number of possible outcomes}}$$

$$= \frac{2}{6}$$

$$= \frac{\overset{1}{\cancel{2}}}{\underset{3}{\cancel{6}}}$$

Reduce to the lowest term by dividing by 2.

$$= \frac{1}{3}$$

(f) The multiples of 3 out of the total numbers of possible outcomes of 1, 2, 3, 4, 5, and 6 are 3 and 6. There are two numbers (3 and 6) that are multiples of 3 out of the total of the 6 possible outcomes of 1, 2, 3, 4, 5, and 6.

The theoretical probability of obtaining a multiple of 3

$$= \frac{\text{Number of outcomes of a multiple of 3}}{\text{Total number of possible outcomes}}$$

$$= \frac{2}{6}$$

$$= \frac{\overset{1}{\cancel{2}}}{\underset{3}{\cancel{6}}}$$

Reduce to the lowest term by dividing by 2.

$$= \frac{1}{3}$$

(g) The numbers that are not multiples of 3 out of the total outcomes of 1, 2, 3, 4, 5, and 6 are 1, 2, 4, and 5. There are 4 numbers (1, 2, 4, and 5) that are not multiples of 3 out of a total of 6 possible outcomes.

The theoretical probability of obtaining a number that is not a multiple of 3

$$= \frac{\text{Number of outcomes that are not multiples of 3}}{\text{Total number of possible outcomes}}$$

$$= \frac{4}{6}$$

$$= \frac{\overset{2}{4}}{\underset{3}{6}} \qquad \text{Reduce to the lowest term by dividing by 2}$$

$$= \frac{2}{3}$$

(h) A prime number has exactly two factors which are 1 and the number itself. The prime numbers out of the total possible outcomes of 1, 2, 3, 4, 5, and 6 are 2, 3, and 5. There are 3 prime numbers (2, 3, and 5) out of the total possible outcomes of 6 numbers.

The theoretical probability of obtaining a prime number

$$= \frac{\text{Number of outcomes of a prime number}}{\text{Total number of possible outcomes}}$$

$$= \frac{3}{6}$$

$$= \frac{\overset{1}{3}}{\underset{2}{6}} \qquad \text{Reduce to the lowest term by dividing by 3.}$$

$$= \frac{1}{2}$$

(i) The numbers which are not prime numbers out of the total possible outcome of

1, 2, 3, 4, 5, and 6 are 1, 4, and 6. There are 3 numbers (1, 4, and 6), which are not prime numbers out of a total possible outcomes of 6 numbers.

The theoretical probability of not getting a prime number

$$= \frac{\text{Number of outcomes which are not a prime number}}{\text{Total number of possible outcomes}}$$

$$= \frac{3}{6}$$

$$= \frac{\overset{1}{\cancel{3}}}{\underset{2}{\cancel{6}}} \quad \text{Reduce to the lowest term by dividing by 3.}$$

$$= \frac{1}{2}$$

Exercises

1. Explain what is meant by (a) theoretical probability, (b) an event.
2. How do you find the theoretical probability of an event?
3. What is the theoretical probability that if you spin the spinner:

   (a). The pointer will land on 3?
   (b). The pointer will land on an even number?
   (c). The pointer will land on an odd number?
   (d). The pointer will land on a prime number?
   Hint: See example 1.

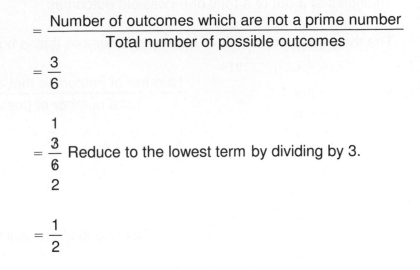

4. Find the theoretical probability of each event:

   (a). The spinner will stop on E.
   (b). The spinner will stop on a vowel.
   Hint: See example 2.

5. Explain (a) an impossible event, (b) equally likely event, (c) certain event.
   Hint: See Example 3.
6. The probability of an event A occurring is .6, B occurring is .9, C occurring is .5, and D occurring is .2. By comparing the probability values, which event is most likely to occur and which event is least likely to occur? Hint: See the section under "Comparing the Values of Probability."
7. Find the theoretical probability that the pointer will land on:

(a). a number 10.
(b). a number 0.
(c). an odd number.
(d). an even number.
(e). a number less than 3.
(f). a prime number.
Indicate the probabilities on a number line.
Hint: See example 4.

8. (a) Find the theoretical probability of outcome of Y.
   Give your answer as a fraction, a decimal, and a percent.
   (b) Find the experimental probability of the outcome of W.
   (c) Find the experimental probability of the outcome of Z.
   (d) Find the experimental probability of the outcome of Y.
   (e) Find the experimental probability of the outcome of X.
   Hint: See Example **5**.

Outcome	Number of spins
W	3
X	6
Y	8
X	4

9. A die was rolled 20 times. On 4 of the rolls the outcome was a 2.
   (a) What is the experimental probability of rolling a 2?
   Give your answer as a fraction, a decimal, and a percent.
   (b) How many rolls was the outcome not showing a 2? What is the experimental
   probability of not rolling a 2?
   (c) Based on the experimental probabilities that you have found and suppose the
   die is rolled 100 times, about how many times do you expect to roll a side:
      (i) with a 2?
      (ii) without a 2?
   Hint: See Example **6**.

10. A die was thrown once.
   (a) List the possible outcomes.
   From your possible outcomes in (a), what is the theoretical probability of
   obtaining:
   (b) an odd number?   (c) an even number?
   (d) a number greater than 4?   (e) a number between 3 and 6?
   (f) a multiple of 2?   (g) not a multiple of 2?
   (h) a prime number?   (i) not a prime number?
   Hint: See Example **7**.

Challenge Questions

11. Using the spinner, what is the probability in fractions, decimals and percent of:

       (a). Obtaining a number less than 30.
       (b). Obtaining a number between 15 and 35.
       (c). Obtaining an even number?
       (d). Obtaining an odd number?
       (e). Obtaining a number greater than 60.

12. A bag contains 3 green balls and 7 yellow balls. If a ball is selected at random, what is the probability that the ball is: (a) green, (b) yellow, (c) not green, (d) not yellow?

Answers to Selected Questions

3a. $\dfrac{1}{3}$ **4a.** $\dfrac{1}{4}$ **7a.** 0

RELATIVE FREQUENCY

The relative frequency is how frequently a value appears relative to the total data set. The relative frequency can therefore be represented as percent of frequency or probability. The relative frequency table is a frequency table that has a column that shows how frequently a value appears relative to the total data set. The relative frequency column is a percent of frequency or probability. The formula for relative frequency is:

$$\text{Relative frequency} = \frac{\text{each frequency}}{\text{sum of all frequencies}}$$

Example 1
The table shows the result of the survey of the favorite month of the year of some students.
a. Make a relative frequency table for the data.
b. What is the least popular month of the year?
c. How many more people choose December rather than November?
d. How many people took part in the survey?
e. If 2 more students choose December, how many total people would have chosen December?
f. Which month had the highest relative frequency and what is the value of the relative frequency?
g. What month had the least relative frequency, and what is the value of the relative

frequency?

h. What is the probability that a randomly selected student will choose November as a favorite month?

i. Find the probability that a student selected at random had February, September, or November as a favorite month.

j. How many more people chose November rather than February?

Month	Number of students
January	4
February	2
March	3
April	5
May	1
June	2
July	4
August	5
September	4
October	4
November	6
December	20

Solution

a. The relative frequency table includes a column that shows how frequently each month appears relative to the total number of times that all the months appear as shown in the table:

(The relative frequency table is shown on the next page.)

Month	Number of Students	Relative frequency
January	4	$\dfrac{\text{Frequency}}{\text{Total frequency}} = \dfrac{4}{60} = 0.0\overline{6} = 6.\overline{6}\%$
February	2	$\dfrac{\text{Frequency}}{\text{Total frequency}} = \dfrac{2}{60} = 0.0\overline{3} = 3.\overline{3}\%$
March	3	$\dfrac{\text{Frequency}}{\text{Total frequency}} = \dfrac{3}{60} = 0.05 = 5\%$
April	5	$\dfrac{\text{Frequency}}{\text{Total frequency}} = \dfrac{5}{60} = 0.08\overline{3} = 8.\overline{3}\%$
May	1	$\dfrac{\text{Frequency}}{\text{Total frequency}} = \dfrac{1}{60} = 0.01\overline{6} = 1.\overline{6}\%$
June	2	$\dfrac{\text{Frequency}}{\text{Total frequency}} = \dfrac{2}{60} = 0.0\overline{3} = 3.\overline{3}\%$
July	4	$\dfrac{\text{Frequency}}{\text{Total frequency}} = \dfrac{4}{60} = 0.0\overline{6} = 6.\overline{6}\%$
August	5	$\dfrac{\text{Frequency}}{\text{Total frequency}} = \dfrac{5}{60} = 0.08\overline{3} = 8.\overline{3}\%$
September	4	$\dfrac{\text{Frequency}}{\text{Total frequency}} = \dfrac{4}{60} = 0.0\overline{6} = 6.\overline{6}\%$
October	4	$\dfrac{\text{Frequency}}{\text{Total frequency}} = \dfrac{4}{60} = 0.0\overline{6} = 6.\overline{6}\%$
November	6	$\dfrac{\text{Frequency}}{\text{Total frequency}} = \dfrac{6}{60} = 0.1 = 10\%$
December	20	$\dfrac{\text{Frequency}}{\text{Total frequency}} = \dfrac{20}{60} = 0.\overline{3} = 33.\overline{3}\%$
Total	60	

b. The least popular month is May because May had the least frequency of 1 or the least relative frequency of $0.01\overline{6}$.

c. There are 20 - 6 = 14 more people that chose December than November.

d. The number of the people that took part in the survey is the sum of the frequencies which is 60.

e. The number of students that chose December is 20 and if 2 more people chose December, the new total for December would be 20 + 2 = 22 people.

f. The month that has the highest relative frequency is December and the value of this relative frequency is $0.\overline{3}$.

g. May has the least relative frequency of $0.01\overline{6}$.

h. The relative frequency for November is 0.1, and therefore, there is a 0.1 probability that a randomly selected student will pick November as his favorite month.

i. Let event A = February as favorite month, let event B = September as favorite month, let event C = November as favorite month. Assume that events A, B, and C are mutually exclusive. (Hint: Review the MathMasters Series on mutually exclusive events).

P(A or B or C) = P(A) + P(B) + P(C)

$\qquad\qquad$ = 0.03 + 0.06 + 0.1 $\qquad$ Where P(A) = 0.03, P(B) = 0.06 and P(C) = 0.1.

$\qquad\qquad \approx 0.19$

The probability that a student had randomly selected February, September or November as a favorite month is approximately 0.19.

Note that P(A) is the probability of event A occurring, P(B) is the probability of event B occurring and P(C) is the probability of event C occurring. Hint: Review the chapter on probability in the MathMasters Series.

j. Number of students that chose November = 6 and the number of students that chose February = 2. Therefore, 6 - 2 = 4 more people chose November than February.

Special Note
Example 1 is long but it is intentionally designed to show the students the possible types of questions that could be asked involving relative frequency.

Example 2
The table shows the result of students' survey. The survey shows how many hours students stayed at the library in a week.

Hours	Frequency
1	2
2	5
3	11
4	6
5	5
6	1

a. Make a relative frequency table for the data.

b. Use the relative frequencies obtained in Example 2a to find the probability that a randomly selected student will stay in the library for 6 hours.

c. Use the relative frequencies obtained in the solution of Example 2a to estimate the probability that a randomly selected student will stay in the library for 4 or more hours.

Solution
a. The relative frequency table is shown as shown:

Hours	Frequency	Relative Frequency
1	2	$\text{Relative Frequency} = \dfrac{\text{Frequency}}{\text{Total Frequency}} = \dfrac{2}{30} = 0.0\overline{6} \text{ or } 6.\overline{6}\%$
2	5	$\text{Relative Frequency} = \dfrac{\text{Frequency}}{\text{Total Frequency}} = \dfrac{5}{30} = 0.1\overline{6} \text{ or } 16.\overline{6}\%$
3	11	$\text{Relative Frequency} = \dfrac{\text{Frequency}}{\text{Total Frequency}} = \dfrac{11}{30} = 0.3\overline{6} \text{ or } 36.\overline{6}\%$
4	6	$\text{Relative Frequency} = \dfrac{\text{Frequency}}{\text{Total Frequency}} = \dfrac{6}{30} = 0.2 \text{ or } 20\%$
5	5	$\text{Relative Frequency} = \dfrac{\text{Frequency}}{\text{Total Frequency}} = \dfrac{5}{30} = 0.1\overline{6} \text{ or } 16.\overline{6}\%$
6	1	$\text{Relative Frequency} = \dfrac{\text{Frequency}}{\text{Total Frequency}} = \dfrac{1}{30} = 0.0\overline{3} \text{ or } 3.\overline{3}\%$
Total	30	

b. From the solution of Example 2a, the relative frequency for a student staying in the library for 6 hours is $0.0\overline{3}$ or $3.\overline{3}\%$ and therefore, the probability that a randomly selected student will stay in the library for 6 hours is $0.0\overline{3}$ or $3.\overline{3}\%$.

c. Let event A = 4 hours, event B = 5 hours and event C = 6 hours. Assume that events A, B, and C are mutually exclusive. (Hint: Review the section on mutually exclusive events under probability in the MathMasters Series). Note that from the question, staying in the library 4 or more hours means that we have to consider the events involving 4, 5, or 6 hours.

$P(A \text{ or } B \text{ or } C) = P(A) + P(B) + P(C)$

$\qquad\qquad = 0.2 + 0.1\overline{6} + 0.0\overline{3}$ Where $P(A) = 0.2$, $P(B) = 0.1\overline{6}$, and $P(C) = 0.0\overline{3}$.

$\qquad\qquad \approx 0.39$

The probability that a student selected at random stayed in the library for 4 or more hours is approximately 0.39 or about 39%.

Exercises

1. Explain relative frequency.

2. The table shows the survey of students involving their favorite animals.
   Hint: See Example 1.

Animals	Number of students
Lion	3
Dog	10
Elephant	1
Gorilla	2
Zebra	4

a. Make a relative frequency table for the data.

b. How many students took part in the survey?

c. What is the least popular animal?

d. Which animal has the highest relative frequency?

e. How many more students like the dog than the zebra?

f. Which animal had the least relative frequency?

g. What is the probability that a randomly selected student will choose a dog as a favorite animal?

h. Find the probability that a student selected at random will choose a lion, an elephant or a zebra as a favorite animal?

3. Find the relative frequency of each set of data or each set of table. Hint: See Examples 1 and 2.

Favorite days

a.

Day	Number of students
Monday	1
Tuesday	3
Wednesday	2
Thursday	2
Friday	6
Saturday	11
Sunday	5

Favorite animals

b.

Animals	Number of students
Lion	2
Zebra	8
Tiger	1
Gorilla	5
Elephant	2
Flamingo	3

Test scores

c.

Marks	Number of students
50 - 60	2
61 - 70	5
71 - 80	12
81 - 90	4
91 - 100	3

Challenge Questions

4. The table shows the list of the majors of the students in the Supporters Club. Find the probability that a randomly selected student is an engineering major or undecided.

Major	Number of students
English	8
Biology	12
Engineering	10
Chemistry	7
Undecided	9

CUMULATIVE AND RELATIVE CUMULATIVE FREQUENCY

New Terms: **Cumulative frequency** and **relative cumulative frequency**

Cumulative frequency is the sum of all the frequencies of all the data values that are less than a given value. The cumulative frequency for a class is the sum of all the frequencies for that class and all the previous classes.

Relative cumulative frequency is the cumulative frequency divided by the total number of the data values or the total sum of the frequencies.

$$\text{Relative cumulative frequency} = \frac{\text{Cumulative frequency}}{\text{Sum of all the frequencies}}$$

How to find cumulative frequencies

Table 1 shows that the cumulative frequency is obtained by writing the first original frequency of 3 in the first column of the cumulative frequency, the second cumulative frequency of 7 is obtained by adding the first and the second frequencies together (3 + 4 = 7), the third cumulative frequency of 16 is obtained by adding the first, the second and the third frequencies together (3 + 4 + 9 = 16), and so on.

Table 1

Time (s)	Frequency	Cumulative Frequency
5 - 14	3	3
15 - 24	4	3 + 4 = 7
25 - 34	9	3 + 4 + 9 =16
35 - 44	8	3 + 4 + 9 + 8 = 24
45 - 54	1	3 + 4 + 9 + 8 + 1 = 25
55 - 64	6	3 + 4 + 9 + 8 + 1 + 6 = 31

Example 1

The table shows how long a number of balloons stayed on a post.

a. Create a cumulative frequency table.

b. How many balloons stayed on the post no more than 64 seconds?

Time (s)	Frequency
25 - 34	5
35 - 44	2
45 - 44	7
55 - 64	6
65 - 74	3

Solution

a. Create a cumulative frequency table as shown below.

Time (s)	Frequency	Cumulative frequency
25 - 34	5	5
35 - 44	2	$5 + 2 = 7$
45 - 54	7	$5 + 2 + 7 = 14$
55 - 64	6	$5 + 2 + 7 + 6 = 20$
65 - 74	3	$5 + 2 + 7 + 6 + 3 = 23$

b. The cumulative frequency table shows, 20 balloons stayed on the post no more than 64 seconds or 20 balloons stayed on the post for 64 seconds or less.

Example 2

The table shows the range of students' test scores with the associated number of students who scored in that range or frequency.

a. Find the relative frequency of the test scores in the 81 - 85 range.

b. What is the cumulative frequency of the test scores less than 76?

c. Find the relative cumulative frequency of test scores less than 81.

Test scores	61 - 65	66 - 70	71 - 75	76 - 80	81 - 85	86 - 90	91 - 95	96 - 100
Frequency	2	4	8	6	5	9	2	3

Solution

a. The formula for relative frequency is:

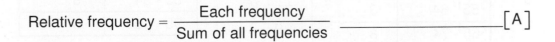

$$\text{Relative frequency} = \frac{\text{Each frequency}}{\text{Sum of all frequencies}} \qquad\qquad [A]$$

The sum of all the frequencies = $2 + 4 + 8 + 6 + 5 + 9 + 2 = 39$.

The frequency for the range of 81 - 85 test score is 5.

Substitute "each frequency" = 5 and sum of all the frequencies = 39 into equation

[A] as shown:

$$\text{Relative frequency} = \frac{\text{Each frequency}}{\text{Sum of all frequencies}}$$

$$= \frac{5}{39}$$

Each frequency or frequency for the range of

81 - 85 = 5 and the sum of all the frequencies = 39.

$$\approx 0.14$$

b. To find the cumulative frequency of the test scores less than 76, add the frequencies of all the test scores less than 76 as follows:

$2 + 4 + 8 = 14$ Recall that the cumulative frequency is the sum of all the frequencies of all the data values that are less than a given value.

c. Relative cumulative frequency of the test scores less than 81

$$= \frac{\text{Cumulative frequency of the test scores less than 81}}{\text{Sum of all frequencies}}$$

$$= \frac{2 + 4 + 8 + 6}{2 + 4 + 8 + 6 + 5 + 9 + 2 + 3}$$

$$= \frac{20}{39}$$

$$\approx 0.51$$

Exercises

1. Explain cumulative frequency.

2. Describe how you could find the cumulative frequency.

3. Create a cumulative frequency table for each of the tables. Hint: See Example 1.

a.

Age (years)	Frequency
15 - 24	2
25 - 34	1
35 - 44	5
45 - 54	4
55 - 64	3
65 - 74	8

b.

Test scores	Frequency
55 - 64	3
65 - 74	2
75 - 84	1
85 - 94	8
95 - 100	6

Test scores	Frequency
10 - 19	2
20 - 29	4
30 - 39	7
40 - 49	1
50 - 59	3
60 - 69	2

c.

4. The frequency table shows the frequency of each range of height of students selected at random for a survey.

    a. What is the cumulative frequency of the students' heights less than 5 ft 6 in?
       Hint: See Example 1b and Example 2b.

    b. What is the cumulative frequency of the students' height less than 6 ft?
       Hint: See Example 1b and Example 2b.

    c. What is the relative frequency of the students' height in the 5 ft 6 in. - 5 ft 11 in. range? Hint: See Example 2a.

    d. What is the relative frequency of the students' heights in the 4 ft 6 in. - 4 ft 11 in. range? Hint: See Example 2a.

    e. Find the relative cumulative frequency of the students' heights less than 6 ft.
       Hint: See Example 2c.

    f. What is the relative cumulative frequency of the students' height less than 5 ft?
       Hint: See Example 2c.

Students' heights	Frequency
4 ft - 4 ft 5 in.	3
4 ft 6 in. - 4 ft 11 in.	5
5 ft - 5 ft 5 in.	7
5 ft 6 in. - 5 ft 11 in.	3
6 ft - 6 ft 5 in.	2

Challenge Question

5. The table shows the test scores for students who are randomly selected for a survey.

Test score	61 - 65	66 - 70	71 - 75	76 - 80	81 - 85	86 - 90	91 - 95	96 - 100
Frequency	1	3	5	4	2	6	8	2

    a. What is the relative frequency of the students' test scores in the 86 - 90 range?

    b. What is the cumulative frequency of the students' test scores less than 91?

    c. What is the cumulative frequency of the students' test scores less than 81?

    d. What is the relative frequency of the students' test scores in the 76 - 80 range?

    e. Find the relative cumulative frequency of the students' test scores less than 96.

    f. Find the relative cumulative frequency of the students' test scores less than 76.

Answers to Selected Questions
4a. Cumulative frequency less than 5 ft 6 in. = 3 + 5 + 7 = 15.

CHAPTER 22

GRAPHS

Cumulative Review
1. 13 + 8 =   **2.** 12 ÷ 4 =   **3.** 16 - 8 =   **4.** 8 × 3 =
5. 25 ÷ 5 =   **6.** 21 - 12 =   **7.** 30 ÷ 6 =   **8.** 17 - 8 =

9. 24   **10.** 14   **11.** 35   **12.** 19
  × 3   + 19   - 13   × 4

13. 48 ÷ 3 =   **14.** 24 ÷ 8 =   **15.** 12 + 38 =   **16.** 36 - 17 =
17. 2.9 + 3.7 =   **18.** 5.6 × 4 =   **19.** 2.5 × 3.4 =   **20.** 24.7 - 1.6 =

21. $\dfrac{2}{3} \times \dfrac{1}{5} =$ **22.** $\dfrac{2}{3} \div \dfrac{2}{5} =$ **23.** $\dfrac{3}{4} - \dfrac{1}{5} =$ **24.** $2\dfrac{1}{3} + 3\dfrac{3}{4} =$

New Terms: frequency table, at least, at most, fewer than, relative frequency

Interpreting Data

Frequency Table
A **frequency table** is a table that shows the number of times each event occurs.

  Note that in the tally column in example 1, the 5th time of an event is indicated by
  crossing the previous 4 events as follows: ̶I̶I̶I̶I̶ .

Example 1
The frequency table shows the number of subjects studied by students in grade 11
at the Peki Secondary school in Ghana.

Number of subjects studied by students		
Number of subjects studied	Number of students. Tally	Number of students. Frequency
9	1111	4
8	~~1111~~ ~~1111~~ 11	12
7	~~1111~~ 1	6
6	111	3
5	11	2

a. How many students studied 8 subjects?

b. How many students studied at least 7 subjects?

c. How many students studied 6 or more subjects?

d. How many students studied at most 7 subjects?

e. How many students were in the survey?

f. What percent of the students studied 6 subjects?

g. What percent of the students studied fewer than 6 subjects?

h. What percent of the students studied at least 7 subjects?

i. What percent of the students studied at most 7 subjects?

j. What is the relative frequency of the students that studied 5 subjects?

k. If a student is selected at random, what is the probability that the student studied 9 subjects?

Solution

a. The frequency column shows that 12 students studied 8 subjects.

b. "**At least 7 subjects**" means 7 or more subjects. Therefore, the number of students that studied at least 7 subjects is the sum of the frequencies of the students that studied 7, 8, and 9 subjects which = 6 + 12 + 4 = 22 students.

c. The number of students that studied 6 or more subjects is the sum of the frequencies of the students that studied 6, 7, 8, and 9 subjects which = 3 + 6 + 12 + 4 = 25 students.

d. "**At most 7 subjects**" means 7 or less subjects. Therefore, the number of students that studied at most 7 subjects is the sum of the frequencies of the students that studied 7, 6, and 5 subjects which = 6 + 3 + 2 = 11 students.

e. The number of the students in the survey is the sum of the total frequency which
$$= 4 + 12 + 6 + 3 + 2 = 27 \text{ students.}$$

f. Percent of students that studied 6 subjects

$$= \frac{\text{Number that studied 6 subjects}}{\text{Total number of students}} \times 100 \quad \text{(Hint: Review the section on Percent.)}$$

$$= \frac{3}{27} \times 100 \qquad (\frac{\text{Part}}{\text{Total}} \times 100 = \text{Percent of the total.})$$

$$= \frac{\frac{1}{3}}{\frac{27}{9}} \times 100 \qquad \text{Divide by 3.}$$

$$= \frac{100}{9} = 11\frac{1}{9}\% \qquad \text{Divide by 9.}$$

g. Those who studied **fewer than** 6 subjects means those who studied 5 subjects.
The number of students that studied 5 subjects = 2

h. Percent of the students that studied **at least** 7 subjects

$$= \frac{\text{Number that studied at least 7 subjects}}{\text{Total number of students}} \times 100 \quad \text{(Review the section on Percent).}$$

$$= \frac{22}{27} \times 100 \qquad \text{(From solution (b) 22 students studied at least 7 subjects)}$$

$$(\frac{\text{part}}{\text{Total}} \times 100 = \text{percent of total}).$$

$= 81.48\%$ You many use a calculator.

i. Percent of students that studied **at most** 7 subjects

$$= \frac{\text{Number of students that studied at most 7 subjects}}{\text{Total number of students}} \times 100$$

Review the section on Percent.

$$= \frac{11}{27} \times 100 \qquad (\frac{\text{Part}}{\text{Total}} \times 100 = \text{Percent of the total}).$$

(From solution **d**, the number of the students that studied at most 7 subjects is 11).

$= 40.74\%$ You may use a calculator.

j. The relative frequency of an event

$$= \frac{\text{Frequency of the event.}}{\text{Total frequencies}}, \text{ therefore,}$$

the **relative frequency** of the students that studied 5 subjects

$$= \frac{\text{Frequency of the students that studied 5 subjects}}{\text{Total frequencies}}$$

$$= \frac{2}{27}$$

k. Probability that a student selected studied 9 subjects

$$= \frac{\text{Number of students that studied 9 subjects}}{\text{Total number of students}}$$

(Review the section on Probability).

$$= \frac{4}{27}$$

Bar Graph

A bar graph is a graph in which the height of the vertical bars represent the frequencies or values assigned to each activity. The bars are spaced evenly and they may be drawn vertically or horizontally. A bar graph is drawn from a frequency table.

Example 2

Use the bar graph to answer the following question:

Students' test scores in percent.

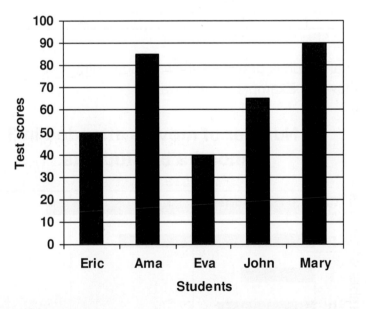

a. Who did the best in the test?
b. Who did the poorest in the test?
c. How many more marks did Mary have than Erica?
d. Who scored 10% more marks than Eva?

e. What is the range of the scores?

Solution

a. Mary had the highest score of 90%, and therefore, Mary did the best in the test.

b. Eva had the lowest score of 40%, and therefore Eva did poorest in the test.

c. Mary's score was 90%, and Eric's score was 50%, and therefore, Mary has 40% or (90% - 50%) more marks than Eric.

d. Eric scored 50%, and Eva scored 40%, and therefore, Eric scored 10% or (50% - 40%) more marks than Eva.

e. The range of the scores:

$$= \text{Greatest score - Least score}$$
$$= 90\% - 40\%$$
$$= 50\%$$

Example 3

Use the frequency table to draw a bar graph on graph paper. Hint: Recall that the bar graph is spaced evenly and may be drawn vertically or horizontally.

Number of movies attended in 3 months by students		
Number of movies	Number of students. Tally	Number of students. Frequency
3	~~IIII~~ ~~IIII~~ 1	11
2	~~IIII~~ 111	8
1	111	3
0	1111	4

Solution

The horizontal bar graph is drawn as shown below. Hint: You may draw the vertical bar graph as shown in Example **2** if you want.

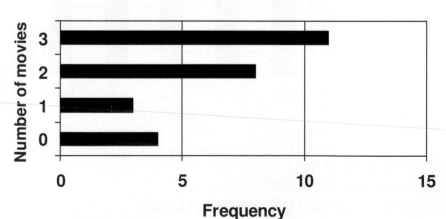

Number of movies attended in 3 months by students.

Hint: It is best to draw graphs on a graph or grid paper.

Multiple Bar Graph

A multiple bar graph consists of two or more component bar columns or graphs which are evenly spaced and the heights of the component bars represent the frequencies or values assigned to each activity. Like a bar graph, the multiple bar graph can be vertical or horizontal.

Test scores of two schools in percent		
Year	School A	School B
2000	95	80
2001	85	90
2002	95	95

a. Which school had the better score in 2000?

b. In which year were the performance of schools A and B the same?

Solution

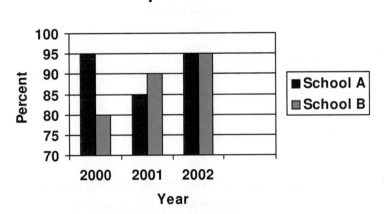

Test scores of two schools in percent.

The graph shows a vertical multiple bar graph. The component bar column or graph are evenly spaced and the heights of the component bar columns represent the frequencies or values assigned to each activity.

a. School A had a better score than school B because school A had a higher score of 95% in 2000 whereas school B has a score of 80%.

b. The performance of the schools A and B were the same in 2002 because both schools had the same score of 95%. Hint: It is best to draw graphs on graph paper or grid paper.

Histogram

A histogram is a bar graph which does not have any space between the bars.
Like the bar graph, a histogram can be vertical or horizontal.

Example 5

Some school districts in Ghana were surveyed to find the number of goals scored by the soccer teams during the year. A frequency table is made with intervals of 10 goals.

Goals	Frequency of the school district
0 - 9	3
10 - 19	4
20 - 29	2
30 - 39	0
40 - 49	1
50 - 59	3

a. Draw a histogram of the frequency table.

b. From the survey, how many school districts scored the highest number of goals?

c. How many school districts took part in the survey?

d. How many school districts scored the least number of goals?

e. If a school district is selected at random,

    (i) what is the probability that its goals are between 10 - 19?

    (ii) what is the probability that its goals are between 30 -39?

  Hint: Review the section on probability.

Solution

a. The histogram of the frequency table is drawn. Hint: It is best to draw a graph on a paper or grid paper.

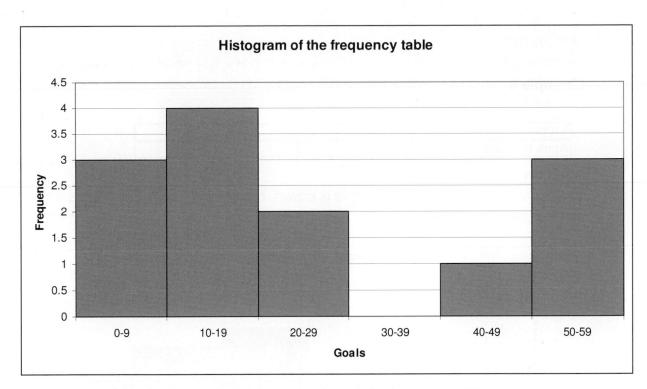

b. Three schools scored the highest number of goals between 50 - 59 goals.

c. The number of the school districts that took part in the survey

$$= \text{sum of the frequencies}$$
$$= 3 + 4 + 2 + 0 + 1 + 3$$
$$= 13 \text{ school districts.}$$

d. Three schools scored the least goals in the interval of 0 - 9 goals.

e(i). The number of school districts that have goals between 10 - 19 is 4. The total number of school districts that took part in the survey is the sum of the frequencies which is ($3 + 4 + 2 + 0 + 1 + 3 = 13$).

The probability of selecting a school district that has goals between 10 - 19

$$= \frac{\text{Number of school districts that have goals between 10 - 19}}{\text{Total number of schools}}.$$

$$= \frac{4}{13}$$

e(ii). The number of school districts that have goals between 30 - 39 is 0. The total number of school districts that took part in the survey is the sum of the frequencies which is ($3 + 4 + 2 + 0 + 1 + 3 = 13$). Therefore, the number of school districts that has goals between 30 - 39

$$= \frac{\text{Number of school districts that have goals between 30 - 39}}{\text{Total number of school districts}}$$

$$= \frac{0}{13} = 0$$

Example 6

Use the frequency table to draw a histogram.

Students	Joe	Mary	Eric	Ben	Eli
Ages in years	6	7	10	9	8

Solution

The histogram of the frequency table is drawn. Hint: It is best to draw graphs on graph paper or grid paper.

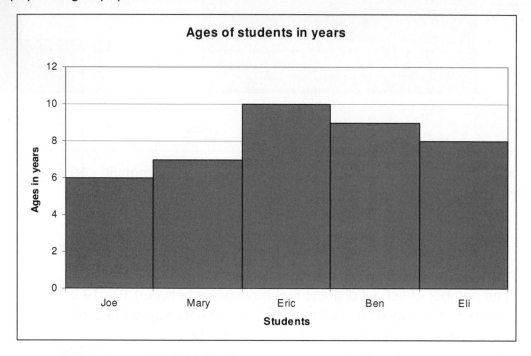

Line Graphs

Line graphs are ordered pairs from a data in a table and the ordered pairs are plotted on a grid or graph paper and the points of the plotted ordered pairs are connected with lines. What is the line graph used for? **The line graph is used to find or estimate one of the ordered pairs if the other ordered pair is known.**

Example 7

Make a line graph of the given data.

Months	1	2	3	4	5	6	7
Savings in dollars	10	15	10	8	5	20	30

Solution

Use the ordered pairs of the data to plot each point, for example, the first set of the data is the savings in the first month which is $10 which may be written as a pair of data as (months, dollars) or (1,10) where 1 is the first month's savings and 10 is $10 saved in the first month. Similarly, the other sets of data or ordered pairs of data are (2, 15), (3, 10), (4, 8), (5, 5), (6, 20), and (7, 30). To plot the points using the ordered pairs of data, first draw the axis for the savings for the months horizontally and draw the axis for the savings vertically and then for the first ordered pair of data (1,10), locate 1 which represents the first month on the horizontal axis and locate the 10 which represent the $10 on the vertical axis. Where (1,10) meet is the required point to be plotted. Similarly, you can plot the points of the remaining ordered pairs of data. (Hint: See how to plot points under the chapter on "Coordinate Geometry.") Connect the points with lines to form a line graph as shown.

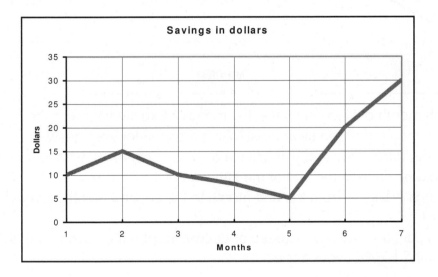

When a line in a line graph goes up from left to right, it shows that there is **an increase in the data**. When a line in a line graph goes down from left to right, it shows that there is **a decrease in the data**. When a line in a line graph is horizontal (for example between two points,) it shows that there is **no change in the data**. The **trend** in the data is the increase or decrease in the data.

Example 8
Use the line graph to answer each question (**a** to **d**.)

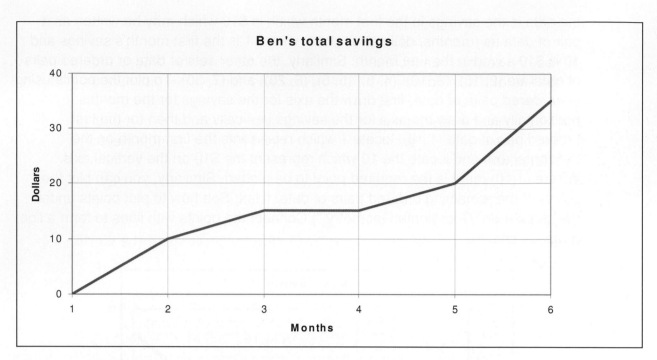

Ben's total savings

a. During which month did Ben not save any money? Explain your answer.

b. During which month did Ben save most? Give reasons for your answer.

c. If Ben is saving his money to buy a calculator which costs $70, what percent of the money did he save at the end of the fifth week?

d. Did the savings increase from the first month to the second month? Explain your answer.

e. In Example 7, did the savings increase or decrease from the second month to the third month? Explain your answer.

Solution

a. Ben did not save any money during the third month because the line graph during the third month is horizontal which means that there was no increment of savings in the third month.

b. Ben saved most in the fifth month because the line graph during the fifth month is the steepest which shows the greatest savings of $35 - $20 = $15.

c. The total money saved at the end of the fifth month is $35. Therefore, the percent of the amount saved is:

$$= \frac{35}{70} \times 100 \qquad (\frac{\text{Part}}{\text{Total}} \times 100 = \text{Percent of the total}).$$

$$= \frac{\overset{5}{\cancel{35}}}{\underset{7}{\cancel{70}}} \times \cancel{100} \qquad \text{Divide by 10 and 7.}$$

$$= 5 \times 10 = 50\%$$

d. Yes, the savings has increased from the first month to the second month because, the line of the line graph between the first and second months went up from left to right.

e. The savings has decreased from the second month to the third month because the line of the line graph between the second and the third months went down from left to right.

Circle Graph

A circle graph is data shown in a circle using the sectors of the circle proportionally.

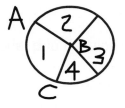

In this circle graph, the area 1, 2, 3, and 4 represent sectors. For example, the sector ABC is represented by area 1.

Example 9

If Mary spends her monthly income according to the circle graph, find:

a. How much she spends on rent?

b. How much she spends on food?

c. How much more does she spend on the rent than food monthly?

d. On which item does she spend the least amount of money?

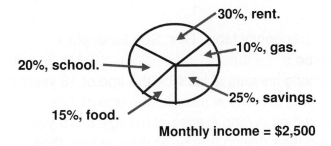

Monthly income = $2,500

Solution

a. She spent 30% of $2,500 on rent,

$$= \frac{30}{100} \times \$2,500 \quad \text{(Express 30\% as } \frac{30}{100} \text{ and "of" is the same as}$$

multiplication). Hint: Review the section on Percent.

611

$$= \frac{30}{100} \times \$2{,}500 \qquad \text{Divide by 100 by canceling the two zeros.}$$

$$= 30 \times \$25$$
$$= \$750.$$

b. She spends 15% of $2,500 on food,

$$= \frac{15}{100} \times \$2{,}500 \qquad \text{(Express 15\% as } \frac{15}{100} \text{ and "of" is the same as}$$

multiplication.) Hint: Review the section on Percent.

$$= \frac{15}{100} \times \$2{,}500 \qquad \text{Divide by 100 by canceling the zeros}$$

$$= 15 \times \$25 = \$375$$

c. From the solution of **a**, she spends $750 on rent, from the solution of **b**, she spends $375 on food, and therefore, she spends

$$\$750 - \$375 \text{ more on rent than food.}$$
$$= \$375$$

d. She spends the least amount of money on gas because the percent of gas is the lowest percent among the items that she spends money on.

━━━━━━━━━━━ The notes and the generous examples have provided
━━━━━━━━━━━ me with the conceptual understanding and the
computational fluency to do my homework.

Exercises

1. Answer the questions by using the frequency table. Hint: See Example 1.
   a. How many students were surveyed?
   b. How many students had their driving lessons at least by the age of 18 years?
   c. How many students had their driving lessons at most by the age of 17 years?
   d. What percent of the students had their driving license at the age of 18 years?
   e. What percent of the students had their driving license at the age less than 18 years?
   f. What percent of the students had their driving license at the age of at least 17 least?
   g. What is the relative frequency of the students who had their driving license at the age of 19 years.
   h. If a student is selected at random, what is the probability that the student is 16 years old?

Student's age of obtaining a license.		
Age	Tally	Frequency
16	~~++++~~ ~~++++~~ 11	12
17	~~++++~~ 111	8
18	~~++++~~	5
19	111	3

2. Describe a bar graph.

3. Use the bar graph to answer the following questions:

    a. Who did the best in the test?

    b. Who did the poorest on the test?

    c. How many more marks did student D have than student A?

    d. Which student had 25% more marks than student A?

    e. What is the range of scores?

  Hint: See Example **2**.

Test scores of students A, B, C, and D in percent.

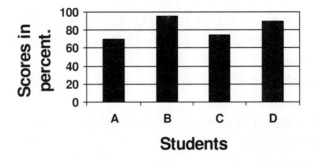

Students

4. Use the frequency table to draw a bar graph on a graph paper.
    Hint: See Example **3**.

Number of movies attended in 3 months by students		
Number of movies.	Number of students. Tally	Number of students. Frequency
4	~~++++~~ 11	7
3	1111	4
2	~~++++~~ 111	8
1	~~++++~~	5
0	11	2

5. Describe a multiple bar graph.

6. Use the table to draw a multiple bar graph.

Year	Test scores of two schools A and B in percent.	
	School A	School B
2002	88	92
2003	79	80
2004	95	95
2005	98	97

(a) Which school had the better score in 2004?

(b) In which year were the scores of schools A and B the same?

Hint: See Example **4**.

7. Describe a histogram.

8. Use the data in the table to draw a histogram.

Goals (soccer)	Frequency of schools.
0 - 9	2
10 - 19	5
20 - 29	3
30 - 39	0
40 - 49	4
50 - 59	7
60 - 69	1

a. How many schools scored the highest number of goals?

b. How many schools took part in the survey?

c. How many schools scored the least number of goals?

d. If a school is selected at random, what is the probability that the school's goals were between 50 - 59?

e. If a school is selected at random, what is the probability that the school's goals were between 20 - 29?

f. If a school is selected at random, what is the probability that the school's goals were between 30 - 39?

Hint: See Example **5**.

9. Use the frequency table to draw a histogram.

Students	Nick	Rose	Josh	Sam	Eric
Ages in years.	12	14	10	15	8

Hint: See Example **6**.

10. Describe a line graph. What is a **trend** in a line graph?

11. Make a line graph of the given data.

Weeks	1	2	3	4	5	6
Savings in dollars.	12	8	13	9	10	11

Hint: See Example **7**.

12. Use the line graph to answer each question.

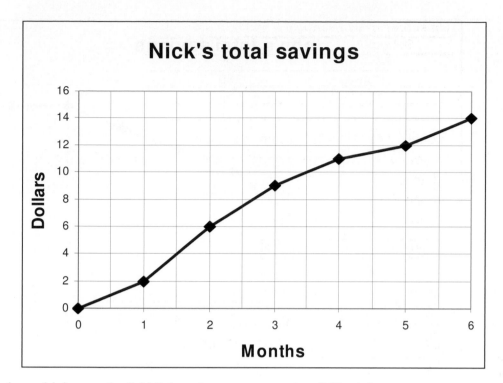

Nick's total savings

a. During which month did Nick not save any money? Explain your answer.

b. During which month did Nick save the most?
   Explain you answer.

c. If Nick is saving his money to buy a calculator which costs $21, what percent of the money did he save by the end of the sixth month?
   Hint: See Example **8**.

13. Describe a circle graph.

14. If Nick spends his monthly income according to the circle graph, find:

   a. How much he spent on insurance?

   b. How much he spent on school?

   c. How much more does he spend on school than on insurance monthly?

   d. On which item does he spend the least amount of money?

   Hint: See Example **9**.

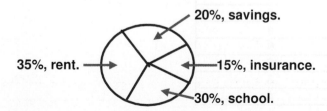

Challenge Questions

15. Use the line graph to answer each question.

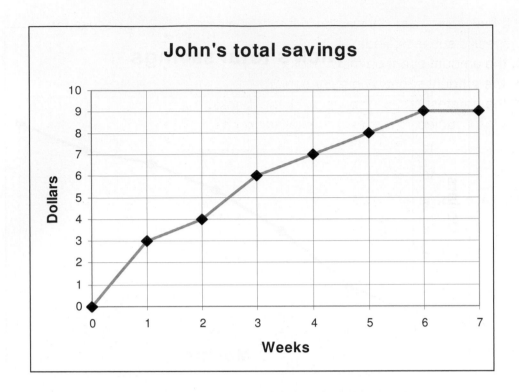

John's total savings

(**a**) If John is saving his money to buy a toy that costs $12.00, what percent of the money did he save by the end of the seventh week?

(**b**) During which week did he save most?
Explain your answer.

(**c**) During which week did he not save any money? Explain your answer?

16. Make a line graph of the given data.

Weeks	1	2	3	4	5	6	7
Savings in dollars.	5	8	4	10	9	7	5

17. Use the data in the table to draw a histogram.

Goals (soccer)	Frequency of schools.
0 - 9	7
10 - 19	5
20 - 29	6
30 - 39	4
40 - 49	0
50 - 59	3
60 - 69	8
70 - 79	4

a. If a school is selected at random, what is the probability that the school scored between 50 - 59 goals?

b. How many schools scored the most goals?

c. If a school is selected at random, what is the probability that the school scored between 40 - 49 goals?

18. If the circle graph shows how a bookstore spent $2000 on books for specific subjects, find:

   a. the amount spent on math books.

   b. the amount spent on history books.

   c. the greatest amount spent on history books.

   d. which subject is the least money spent on?

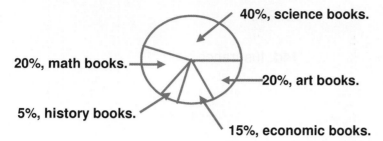

40%, science books.

20%, math books.

20%, art books.

5%, history books.

15%, economic books.

19. Use the bar graph to answer the following questions.

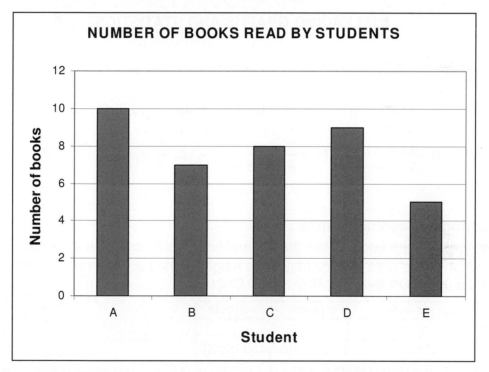

NUMBER OF BOOKS READ BY STUDENTS

   a. Which student read the most books?

   b. What is the range of the number of books read?

   c. How many more books did student A read than student E?

   d. What fraction of the total books in the survey was read by student D?

Hint: Fraction of books read by student D = $\dfrac{\text{Number of books read by student D}}{\text{Total number of books}}$

   e. What percent of the books was read by student D?

617

Hint: Percent of books read by student D = $\dfrac{\text{Number of books read by student D}}{\text{Total number of books.}} \times 100$

Answers to Selected Questions

1a. 28 students   **1h**. $\dfrac{3}{7}$ **6b**. 2004

8f. 0   **12c**. $66\dfrac{2}{3}\%$ **14d**. Insurance

MISLEADING GRAPHS AND STATISTICS

Cumulative Review:
Solve or simplify:

1. $3x = 18$ **2**. $\dfrac{3x}{4} = 9$ **3**. $27 = 9y$ **4**. $6w - 2(2w - 8) = -4$

5. Simplify **a**. $\dfrac{3}{4} - \dfrac{3}{8} =$ **b**. $4\dfrac{1}{3} \div \dfrac{2}{13} =$ **c**. $\dfrac{5}{7} \times \dfrac{14}{15} =$ **d**. $\dfrac{2}{3} + 3\dfrac{2}{5} =$

Identifying Misleading Graphs
Sometimes graphs such as bar graphs and histograms can give a misleading impression of the data they display if the height of the bars are not proportional to the values they represent.

Example 1
Draw a line graph of the data in the table using:
a. a vertical scale of 5 units.
b. a vertical scale of 1 unit, and then, go to **c**.
c. compare line graph **a** and **b**. What is your conclusion?
   The savings is in dollars.

Week	1	2	3	4	5
Savings	2	3	5	8	9

Solution
a. A line graph with a vertical scale of 5 units is shown below.

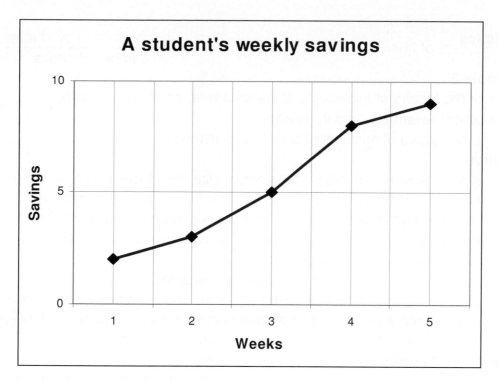

b. A line graph with a vertical scale of 1 unit is shown below.

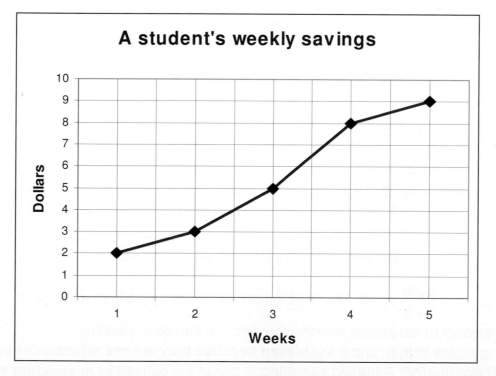

c. By changing the vertical scale of the line graph from 5 units as in **a**, to 1 unit as in **b**, the data values seem large in **b**. It can be concluded that the vertical scale of a line graph can be changed or adjusted to make the data values seem larger or smaller.

Statistics

Example 2

Some of the factors of misleading statistics are: **a**. small sample size,
b. period of the sample, and **c**. average.
Explain the factors of misleading statistics as listed in **a**, **b**, and **c**.

Solution

a. Small sample size: The bigger the sample size, the closer we are to the true value of the statistics. For example, if two students are selected randomly, and both of them had an A in chemistry, it does not necessarily mean that every student in the school had an A in chemistry, because the school has over 800 students whose grades we do not know.

b. The period of the sample: For example, the weather may affect the outcome of a sampling if one sampling is done in the Winter and the other is done in the Summer. Another example is when one sampling is done during the low sale season and the other sampling is done during the high sale season. The period or season of certain sampling can be misleading.

c. When average is used: An average does not show the true picture of the individual data that form the sample. For example, the sample of the ages of 5 people are 10 years, 12 years, 11 years, 10 years, and 95 years. The average age of the five people is

$$= \frac{\text{Sum of ages}}{\text{Total ages}}$$

$$= \frac{10 + 12 + 11 + 10 + 95}{5}$$

$$= \frac{138}{5} = 27\frac{2}{5} \text{ years.}$$

Although the average age is $27\frac{2}{5}$ years, only one person out of five whose age is greater than $27\frac{2}{5}$ years. Note that although the average is high, the age of the majority of the people is rather low and this can be misleading.

The samples in **a**, **b**, and **c** are **biased because they are not representative of each population**. A **biased sampling** is one of the **causes of misleading statistics**.

Example 3

A business had 6 employees with the following salaries: $14,000, $15,000, $13,000, $14,000, $120,000 (owner), $10,000. "Employment available, average salary

$31,000" was the owner's advertisement . It is therefore, not likely that the salary of a new employee would be $31,000. The advertisement is misleading noting that only the owner had a huge salary of $120, 000.

Example 4
If the total revenue of market A during the three months in the summer was $400,000 and the total revenue of market B in the winter was $800,000,
a. Will it be misleading to compare the revenues of markets A and B?
b. What is the correct method of comparing the revenues of markets A and B?
Solution
a. Yes, it is misleading to compare the revenues of markets A and B because the revenues were measured at two different seasons of the year which are winter and summer and that during the busy shopping season of winter, the revenue of market B is greater than the revenue of market A in the summer.
b. The correct method of comparing the revenues of markets A and B is to measure the revenue for both markets at the same season.

Example 5
a. If a car dealership claims that out of a survey of 10 customers, 5 of them are satisfied with their cars, and the dealership's ad states: "5 out of 10 customers are satisfied with their cars", is this ad misleading?
b. What is the correct way of doing the survey?
Solution
a. Yes, the ad is misleading because the sample size of 10 customers is too small. The sample size of 10 customers is not representative of the population of the customers who bought cars from the dealership. The dealership has many more customers than 10.
b. The correct method of doing the survey is to include all the customers who bought vehicles from the dealership in the survey and that will enable the dealership to know the total number of people who are satisfied with their vehicles.

Exercises
1. It can be concluded that the vertical scale of a line graph can be changed or adjusted to make changes in the data values seem larger or smaller.
True or false? Explain. Hint: See Example 1.
2. "Five out of seven students scored 90% in the math test".
a. How many students are in the sample?
b. Can you say that the number of students in the sample is representative of the student population?

c. Is the statement misleading? Hint: See Examples **2a** and **5**.

3. A school newspaper is comparing the total revenue of two stores, P-mart and J-Mart. If the total revenue of P-Mart from May 1st to August 1st is compared to the total revenue for J-Mart from October 1st to January 1st, do you think that the comparison is misleading? Explain your answer. Hint: See Examples 2b and 4.

Challenge Questions

4. A biased sampling is one of the causes of misleading statistics. True or false? Explain.

5. Comparing the total summer revenue of one super market to the total winter revenue of another super market is misleading statistics. True or false? Explain.

6. Explain how the average revenue for twelve months of a supermarket could be misleading statistics.

7. Explain how a vertical scale of a line graph can be adjusted to make changes in a data value seem larger or smaller.

CHAPTER 23

COORDINATE SYSTEM

INTRODUCTION
New Terms: **coordinate system**, **coordinate plane**, **x-axis**, **y-axis**, **origin**, **quadrants**, **ordered pair**, **x-coordinate**, **y-coordinate**.

The **coordinate system** or the **coordinate plane** is formed by two perpendicular and intersecting number lines called the x-axis and the y-axis. The horizontal number line is called the x-axis and the vertical number line is called the y-axis. The point where the two number lines intersect is called the **origin** and the origin has a coordinate of (**0**, **0**). The coordinate of a point is an **ordered pair of numbers** such that the first number is related to a point on the x-axis and the second number is related to a point on the y-axis. The x-axis, y-axis, and the origin are shown in the diagram.

Example 1

Describe how to find the coordinates of the ordered pair of point A.

Solution

Step 1: Find the x-coordinate first. From point A, imagine a perpendicular line on the x-axis and this imaginary perpendicular line meets the x-axis at point 3, and therefore, the first coordinate of the ordered pair is 3.

Step 2: Find the y-coordinate second. From point A, imagine a perpendicular line on the y-axis and this imaginary perpendicular line meets the y-axis at point 4, and therefore, the second coordinate of the ordered pair is point 4.

Step 3: Combine the first coordinate of the ordered pair which is 3 with the second coordinate of the ordered pair which is 4 to form the **coordinates of the ordered pair of the point A as (3, 4)**.

Special notes

1. In general, the coordinates of the ordered pair of any point may be written as (x, y) where x, which is always the first pair refers to a number on the x-axis and y which is always the second pair refers to a number on the y-axis.

2. How can the coordinates of a point be read? The coordinates of a point can be read by moving along the x-axis to read the first coordinate and then moving along the y-axis to read the second coordinate.

Exercises

1. Find the coordinates of the ordered pair of point B in the diagram.

Hint: See Example **1**.

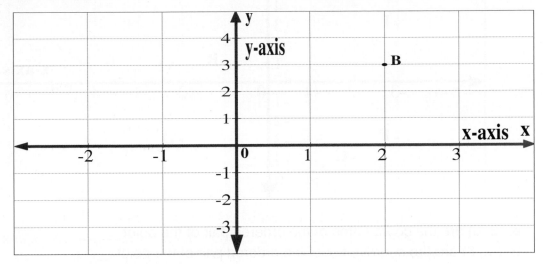

2. Find the coordinates of the ordered pair of the point C in the diagram.

Hint: See Example 1.

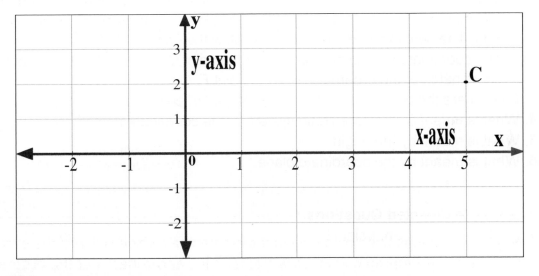

3. Using the diagram, copy and complete the sentences.

Hint: See Example **1**, Step **3**.

a. (2, 6) are the coordinates of the ordered pair of the point _____.

b. (-2, 6) are the coordinates of the ordered pair of the point _____.
   Hint: The negative x-coordinates are at the left side of the origin.

c. (_, _) are the coordinates of the ordered pair of point C.

d. The coordinate of the ordered pair of the point E is (5, -5) and (_, _) are the coordinates of the ordered pair of the point D.
   Hint: The negative y-coordinates are below the origin.

e. The coordinates of the ordered pair of the point G is (-2, -4) and (_, _) are the coordinates of the ordered pair of the point F.

f. (1, 1) are the coordinates of the ordered pair of point B.

4. What is meant by the coordinate system or the coordinate plane?

5. What is meant by the origin?

6. What is meant by the coordinate plane.

Answers to Selected Questions

1. (2, 3)   **3b.** point H

Critical thinking: What is the importance of the coordinates of a point? The coordinates of a point show how far and in which direction to move horizontally along the x-axis and then vertically along the y-axis on the coordinate plane.

Graphing on the Coordinate Plane

We can graph the coordinates of the ordered pair of any point by moving along the x-axis until we are at the x-coordinate of the required ordered pair. Then we continue by moving perpendicularly to the x-axis until we meet the imaginary perpendicular line from the y-coordinate of the ordered pair which is on the y-axis. The point where the imaginary perpendicular line from the x-coordinate of the ordered pair meet the imaginary perpendicular line from the y-coordinate of the ordered pair is the point or the graph of the point.

Example 1

Graph the point (3, 5).

Solution

Move along the x-axis from the origin (0, 0) until you are at the coordinate of the first required ordered pair which is 3, then you move perpendicular to the x-axis (imaginary) until you meet the imaginary perpendicular line from point 5 on the y-axis. Where the imaginary perpendicular line from the x-axis coincide with the imaginary perpendicular line from the y-axis is the point (3, 5).

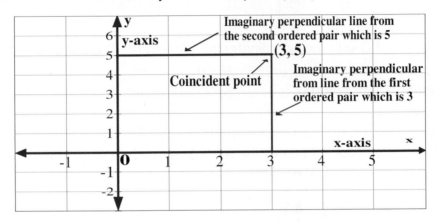

Importance of the Sign of the Coordinates

1. If the first coordinate is negative, then move along the x-axis is toward the left side of the origin (0, 0), but if the sign is positive, then the move is towards the right of the origin (0, 0).

2. If the second coordinate is negative, then move along the y-axis is below the origin (0, 0)

Example 2

Graph the point (-3, 4).

Solution

Move along the x-axis from the origin (0, 0) until you are at the x-coordinate of -3 and then move perpendicularly to the x-axis until you coincide with the imaginary perpendicular line from the point 4 on the y-axis. Where the imaginary perpendicular lines from the x-coordinate of -3 and the y-coordinate of 4 meet is the coordinate of the ordered pair of the point (-3, 4) or the graph of the point.

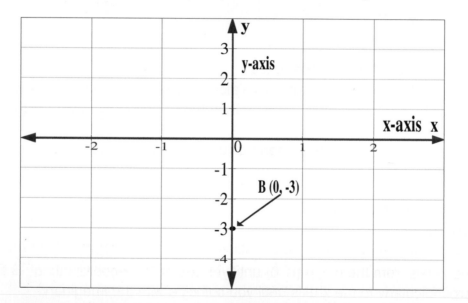

Imaginary perpendicular line from the second ordered pair which is 4

(-3, 4)

Imaginary perpendicular line from the first ordered pair which is -3

y-axis

x-axis

Example 3

a. Graph the points B and C with the coordinates (0, -3) and (2, 0) respectively on the same diagram.

b. Draw a line through points B and C.

Solution

a. To graph the point B(0, -3), from the x-coordinate of 0 on the x-axis, move perpendicularly to the x-axis until you come to the y-coordinate of -3 and this point will have the coordinates of (0, -3) as shown in the diagram.

To graph the point C(2, 0), move along the x-axis from the origin (0, 0) until you are at the x-coordinates of 2 but y = 0 on the x-axis and this mean that the y-coordinate of 0 is on the x-axis therefore, the point (2, 0) is the graph of point C as shown in the diagram.

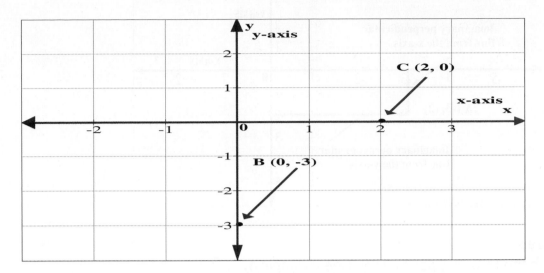

b. Draw a line through the points B(0, -3) and C(2, 0).

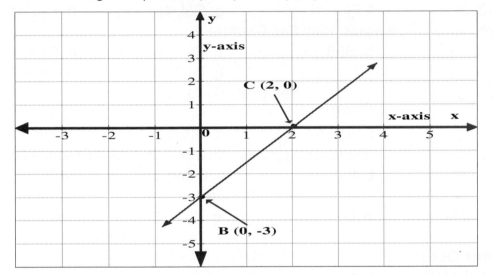

Example 4
Graph the point A with coordinates (-3, -2).
Solution
Move along the x-axis from the origin (0, 0) until you are at the x-coordinate of the ordered pair which is -3 and then move perpendicularly to the x-axis until you meet the imaginary perpendicular line from the point -2 on the y-axis. This meeting point are the coordinates of the ordered pair (-3,-2) or the graph of the point (-3, -2).

Exercises

1. Graph the following points. Hint: See Example **1**.

   a. A(2, 1)　　　　**b**. B(3, 1)　　　　**c**. C(4, 1)　　　　**d**. D(2, 1)

   e. E(2, 2)　　　　**f**. F(-1, 1)　　　　**g**. G(4, 4)　　　　**h**. H(2, 4)

2. Graph the following points. Hint: See Example **2**.

   a. A(-2, 1)　　　　**b**. B(-3, 4)　　　　**c**. C(-1, 2)　　　　**d**. D(-4, 1)

   e. E(-2, 2)　　　　**f**. F(-1, 1)　　　　**g**. G(-2, 3)　　　　**h**. H(-3, 1)

3. Graph the following points. Hint: See Example **3a**.

   a. A(0, -2)　　　　**b**. B(0, -1)　　　　**c**. C(0, -4)　　　　**d**. D(0, -5)

   e. E(1, 0)　　　　**f**. F(3, 0)　　　　**g**. G(5, 0)　　　　**h**. H(6, 0)

4. Using question 3, join the following points with a line. Hint: See Example **3b**.

   a. A and E　　　　**b**. B and F　　　　**c**. C and G　　　　**d**. D and H

5. Graph the following points. Hint: See Example **4**.

   a. A(-1, -1)　　　　**b**. B(-3, -2)　　　　**c**. C(-2, -3)　　　　**d**. D(-1, -4)

Challenge Questions

6. Graph the following points.

   a. A(0, 4)　　　　**b**. B(1, 4)　　　　**c**. C(0, -6)　　　　**d**. D(-3, -3)

7. Graph the three points (1, 2), (3, 1), and (1, 3).

   Join the three points to form a triangle.

Quadrants

Quadrants are the four areas that the x-axis and the y-axis divide the coordinate system into as shown in Figure 1.

Figure 1

Critical Thinking

Using Figure 1:

1. The coordinates of the point A are (5, 2) which are positive and the point A is located in the quadrant 1, and therefore, any point that has both positive x-coordinate and y-coordinates is in quadrant 1.

2. The coordinates of the point B are (-2, 3) which shows that the x-coordinate is negative and the y-coordinate is positive and the point B is located in the quadrant 2. Therefore, any point that has a negative x-coordinate and a positive y-coordinate is located in the quadrant 2.

3. The coordinates of the point C are (-3, -4) which shows that both the x-coordinate and the y-coordinate are negative and the point C is located in the quadrant 3. Therefore, any point that has a negative x-coordinate and a negative y-coordinate is located in the quadrant 3.

4. The coordinates of the point D are (3, -2) which shows that the x-coordinate is positive and the y-coordinate is negative and the point D is located in the quadrant 4. Therefore, any point that has a positive x-coordinate and a negative y-coordinate is located in the quadrant 4.

Team Exercises

Using the notes under "Critical Thinking,"

1. In which quadrant is the graph of the following ordered pairs located?
   a. (-1, -3)   **b**. (3, -1)   **c**. (-2, 3)   **d**. (4, 3).

2. in which quadrant is a graph of the ordered pair located when both coordinates are negative?

3. in which quadrant is a graph of the ordered pair located when both coordinates are positive?

Cumulative Review

1. Draw a number line and use dots to locate the integers on it. Then list the integers

from the greatest to the smallest.

10, 2, -3, -8, 6, 0, and -1

2. Solve:

a. $\dfrac{2}{3} \div \dfrac{1}{6} =$ **b.** $2\dfrac{1}{4} - 1\dfrac{1}{2} =$ **c.** $\dfrac{7}{9} \times \dfrac{12}{4} =$ **d.** $\dfrac{3}{4} + \dfrac{2}{3} =$

REAL WORLD APPLICATIONS - WORD PROBLEMS
Coordinate System

Example 1

Mary started walking from the origin (0, 0). If she went 4 units to the right on the x-axis and then went 3 units down what are the coordinates of the final location of Mary?

Solution

Mary walked 4 units from the origin (0, 0) to the right on the x-axis, and therefore, her location is 4 units to the right. She then went 3 units down and her position on the y-axis is -3. The coordinates of her location are (4, -3) as shown in the diagram.

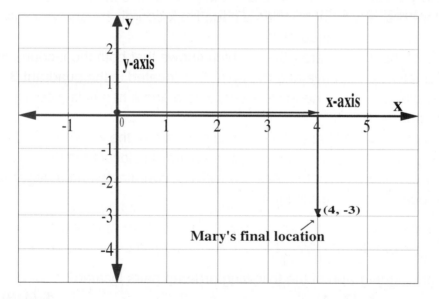

Example 2

John started walking from the origin. If he moved 6 units to the left and then 5 units up what are the coordinates of John?

Solution

John moved 6 units to the left from the origin, and therefore the x-coordinate of his location is -6. He then moved 5 units up, and therefore, his y-coordinate is 5. The coordinates of his location are (-6, 5) as shown in the diagram.

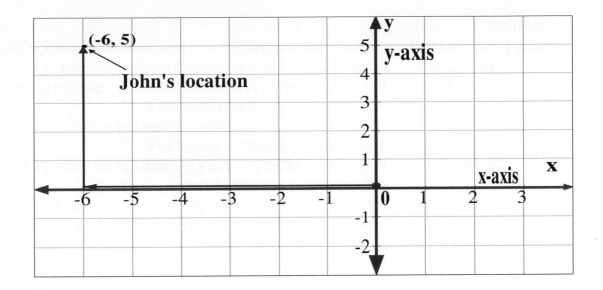

Exercises

1. Eric started at the origin and moved 5 units to the right and then 5 units down. What are the coordinates of Eric? Hint: See Example 1.

2. Start at the origin, move 1 unit to the left and then 4 units up. What are the coordinates of the location? Hint: See Example 2.

Graphing of Equations

An equation is a mathematics statement which indicates that one expression is equivalent to another expression. An example of an equation is $y = 2x + 2$.

How Can We Graph An Equation?

1. In the previous section under "Graphing on the coordinate plane" we learned that we can graph a point if we know the x and the y coordinates.

2. Similarly in order to graph an equation of a line, we need to find at least two sets of the values of the x and y coordinates of the equation by giving a value to x (usually starting from 0 and finding the corresponding value of y as shown in Example 1.

3. Using the values of the x and y coordinates, we can write the ordered pairs to be graphed.

4. Make the graph by:
   a. Plotting each ordered pair on a coordinate plane
   b. Connect all the points by using a straight line
   c. Put arrows at both ends of the line to show that the line continues in both directions.

Example 1

Graph the equation $y = x$ on a coordinate plane.

Solution

Step 1: Pick values for x (usually starting from 0) and then find the corresponding values for y by substituting the value for x into the given equation y = x.

when x = 0, y = 0   Note, when you put x = 0 into the equation y = x, then the equation becomes y = 0.

when x = 1, y = 1   Note, when you put x = 1 into the equation y = x, then the equation becomes y = 1.

when x = 2, y = 2   Note, when you put x = 2 into the equation y= x, then the equation becomes y = 2.

Therefore, the ordered pairs of the coordinates are (0, 0), (1, 1), and (2, 2).

Step 2: Plot the ordered pairs of the coordinates on a coordinate plane and draw a line through the points.

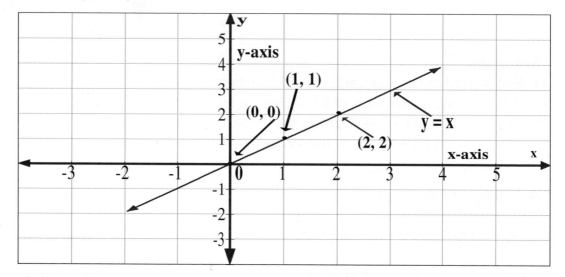

The graph shows the equation y = x.

Example 2

Graph the equation y = x + 1 on a coordinate plane.

Solution

Step 1: Pick values for x (usually starting from 0) and then find the corresponding values for y by substituting the values for x in the given equation y = x + 1.

When x = 0, y = 0 + 1 = 1.   Note, when you put x = 0 into the equation y = x + 1, the equation becomes y = 0 + 1 = 1. Therefore, when x = 0, y = 1.

When x = 1, y = 1 + 1 = 2   Note, when you put x = 1 into the equation y = x + 1, the equation becomes y = 1 + 1 = 2. Therefore, when x = 1, y = 2.

When x = 2, y = 2 + 1 = 3   Note, when you put x = 2 into the equation y = x + 1, the equation becomes y = 2 + 1 = 3. Therefore, when x = 1, y = 3.

Therefore, the ordered pairs of the coordinates are (0, 1), (1, 2), and (2, 3).

Step 2: Plot the ordered pairs on a coordinate plane and draw a line through the points.

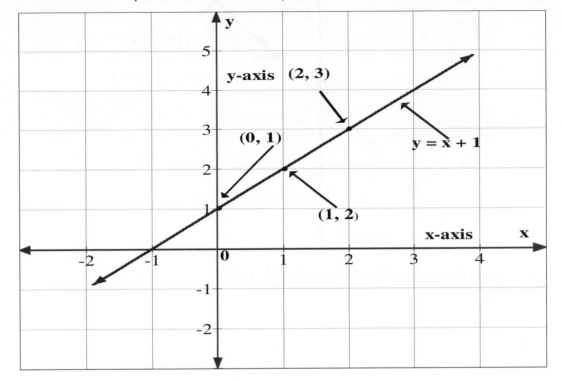

The graph shows the equation y = x + 1.

Example 3

Graph the equation y = 2x + 3.

Solution

Step 1: Pick values for x (usually starting from 0), and then find the corresponding values for y.

When x = 0, y = 2 × 0 + 3 = 3   Note, when you put x = 0 into the equation y = 2x + 3, the equation becomes y = 2 × 0 + 3 = 3. Therefore, when x = 0, y = 3.

When x = 1, y = 2 × 1 + 3 = 5   Note, when you put x = 1 into the equation y = 2x + 3, the equation becomes y = 2 × 1 + 3 = 5. So, when x = 1, y = 5.

When x = 2, y = 2 × 2 + 3 = 7   Note, when you put x = 2 into the equation y = 2x + 3, the equation becomes y = 2 × 2 + 3 = 7. Therefore, when x = 2, y = 7.

Therefore, the ordered pair of the coordinates are (0, 3), (1, 5), and (2, 7).

Step 2: Plot the ordered pairs of the coordinates on a coordinate plane and draw a line through the points.

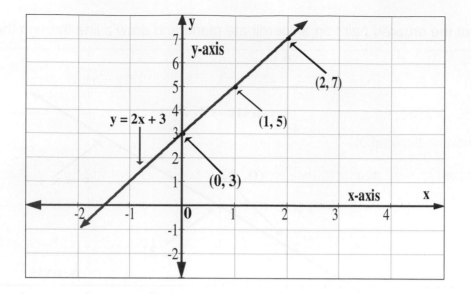

The graph shows the equation y = 2x + 3

Exercises

1 Graph the following equations Hint: See Example **1**.

    a. y = 2x   **b**. y = 3x   **c**. y = 4x   **d**. y = 5x

2. Graph the following equations. Hint: See Example **2**.

    a. y = x + 2   **b**. y = x + 3   **c**. y = x + 5   **d**. y = x + 4

3. Graph the following equations. Hint: See Example **3**.

    a. y = 2x + 2   **b**. y = 3x + 1   **c**. y = 4x + 1   **d**. y = 2x - 1

Challenge Questions

4. Graph the following equations.

    a. y = 3x - 1   **b**. y = 2x + 3   **c**. y = 3x + 2   **d**. y = 2x - 2

5. A real world application of the ordered pair of numbers may be the temperature corresponding to each day as shown in the table.

Day	1	2	3	4	5	6
Temperature (°F)	4	-2	6	0	-3	2

Let the day be on the x-coordinate and the temperature be on the y-coordinate and graph each ordered point. Hint: the first coordinate may be written as (1, 4).

Mixed Review

1. The sum of the measures of two angles of a triangle is 101⁰. What is the measure of the third angle?

2. The sum of the measures of three angles of a quadrilateral is 300⁰. What is the measure of the fourth angle?

3. The sum of the angles on a line except an angle labelled A is 155⁰. What is the measure of angle A?

4. Solve for x:

   a. 5x - 3 = 3x + 7   **b**. $\dfrac{3x}{8} = \dfrac{3}{4}$ **c**. $90^0 + 3x = 180^0$

5. Find 20% of $200

6. What is the reciprocal of $\dfrac{2}{5}$?

7. A square swimming pool has an area of 100 m². Find the perimeter of the swimming pool.

8. Simplify:

   a. $\dfrac{4}{5} \div \dfrac{3}{20}$ **b**. $\dfrac{5 \times 3 \times 4 \times 2}{3 \times 20 \times 2 \times 3}$ **c**. 20 ÷ 4 - 2   **d**. 20 - 4 ÷ 2

SLOPE OF A LINE

The slope of a line is the ratio: $\dfrac{\text{Vertical change}}{\text{Horizontal change}} = \dfrac{\text{Change in y distance}}{\text{Change in x distance}} = \dfrac{\text{rise}}{\text{run}}$

where the "rise" is the number of units moved up or down and the "run" is the number of units moved to the left or right.

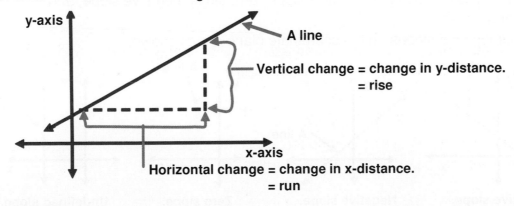

Types of Slopes
The four types of slopes are positive, zero, negative, and undefined slopes.
The four types of slopes may be described as shown:
a. An upward slope (↗) has a positive slope.
b. A horizontal slope (→) has a zero slope.

c. A downward slope (↘) has a negative slope.

d. A vertical slope (↓) has an undefined slope.

Students may be able to remember the four types of slopes if they can recall the slopes sketch below. Let us call this slopes sketch the "Aggor slopes sketch."

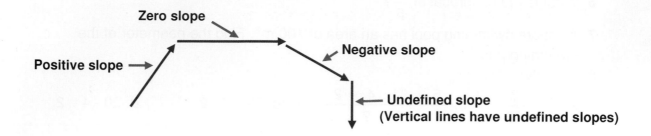

Hint: Example 3 explained mathematically positive, zero, negative, and undefined slopes.

Example 1

a. Name the four types of slopes.

b. Sketch the four types of slopes on a coordinate plane.

c. Describe a line with a positive slope.

d. Describe a line with a negative slope.

e. Describe a line with q zero slope.

f. Describe a line with an undefined slope.

Solution

a. The four types of slopes are positive slope, zero slope, negative slope, and undefined slopes.

b. The four types of slopes on the coordinate plane are as shown:

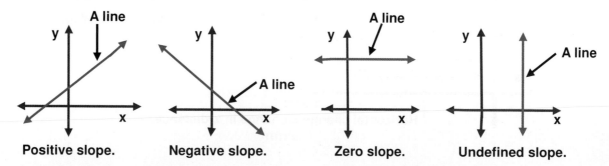

c. A line with a positive slope goes up in the direction from left to right. Hint: See the positive slope diagram in the Solution **b.**

d. A line with a negative slope goes down from the direction of left to right. Hint: See the negative slope diagram in the Solution **b.**

e. A line with a zero slope is parallel to the horizontal or the x axis. Hint: See the diagram of the line with a zero slope in the Solution **b.**

f. A line with an undefined slope is parallel to the y axis or it is vertical. Hint: See the diagram of the line with the undefined slope in the Solution **b**.

Example 2

What is the slope of the line that passes through the points $(x_1, y_1,)$ and (x_2, y_2)?

Solution

The line is sketched with the points as shown below.

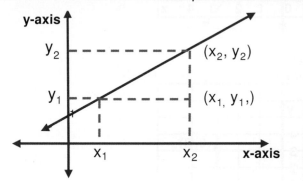

The slope of a line is the ratio: $\dfrac{\text{Vertical change}}{\text{Horizontal change}} = \dfrac{\text{change in y-distance}}{\text{change in x-distance}}$

$$= \frac{\text{rise}}{\text{run}} = \frac{y_2 - y_1}{x_2 - x_1}$$

Note: The formula for finding the slope of a line is:

$$\textbf{Slope} = \frac{\textbf{Vertical change}}{\textbf{Horizontal change}} = \frac{\textbf{change in y-distance}}{\textbf{change in x-distance}} = \frac{\textbf{rise}}{\textbf{run}} = \frac{y_2 - y_1}{x_2 - x_1}$$

Example 3

Using slope $= \dfrac{y_2 - y_1}{x_2 - x_1}$, show that:

a. Figure 1 has a positive slope.

b. Figure 2 has a negative slope.

c. Figure 3 has a zero slope.

d. Figure 4 has an undefined slope.

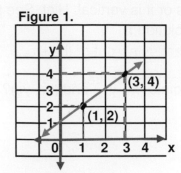

Figure 1.

Figure 2

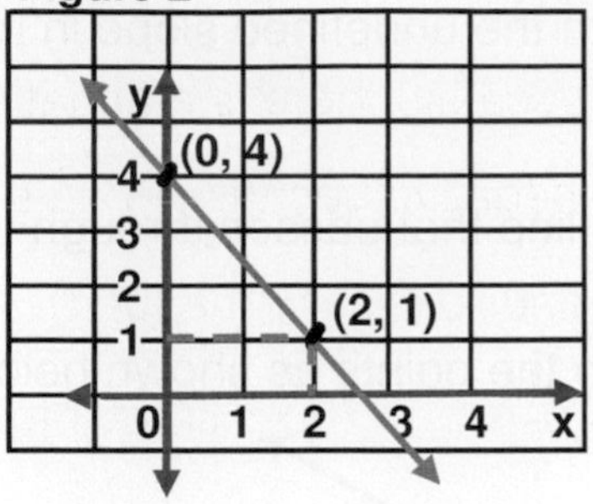

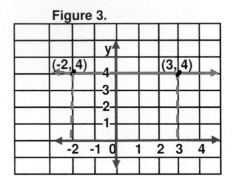

Figure 3.

Figure 4.

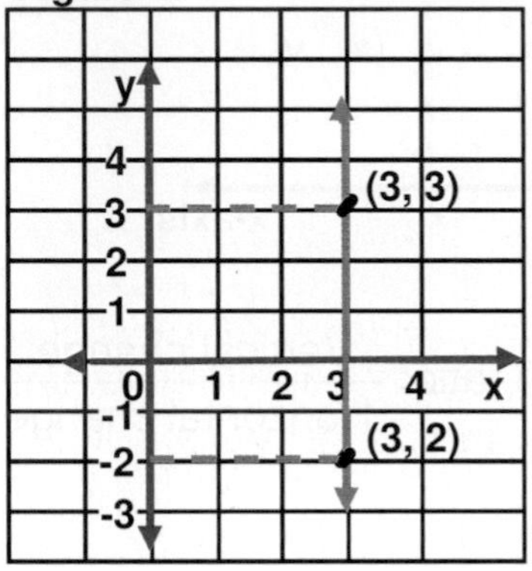

Solution

a. Let (x_1, y_1) be $(1, 2)$ and let (x_2, y_2) be $(3, 4)$.

$$\text{Slope} = \frac{y_2 - y_1}{x_2 - x_1} = \frac{4 - 2}{3 - 1}$$

Substitute 4 for y_2, 2 for y_1, 3 for x_2, and 1 for x_1.

$$= \frac{2}{2}$$

$4 - 2 = 2,\ 3 - 1 = 2$

$$= 1$$

The slope is positive because the sign in front of the slope, which is 1 is positive, although a positive symbol is not written in front of the slope 1. (The slope is positive because 1 is a positive number.)

b. Let (x_1, y_1) be $(2, 1)$ and let (x_2, y_2) be $(0, 4)$.

$$\text{Slope} = \frac{y_2 - y_1}{x_2 - x_1} = \frac{4 - 1}{0 - 2}$$

Substitute 4 for y_2 1 for y_1 0 for x_2, and 2 for x_1.

$$= \frac{3}{-2}$$

$4 - 1 = 3,\ 0 - 2 = -2$

$$= -1\frac{1}{2}$$

The slope is negative because there is a negative symbol in front of the slope as $-1\frac{1}{2}$. (The slope is negative because $-1\frac{1}{2}$ is a negative number.)

c. Let (x_1, y_1) be $(-2, 4)$ and let (x_2, y_2) be $(3, 4)$.

$$\text{Slope} = \frac{y_2 - y_1}{x_2 - x_1} = \frac{4 - 4}{3 - (-2)}$$ Substitute 4 for y_2, 4 for y_1, x_2 for 3, and x_1 for -2.

$$= \frac{0}{3 + 2}$$ $4 - 4 = 0$, $3 - (-2) = 3 + 2$. Note that $-(-2$ becomes $+2$.

$$= \frac{0}{5}$$ $3 + 2 = 5$

$$= 0$$ Zero divided by any number is zero.

The slope is 0 because the value of the slope is 0

d. Let (x_1, y_1) be $(3, -2)$ and let (x_2, y_2) be $(3, 3)$.

$$\text{Slope} = \frac{y_2 - y_1}{x_2 - x_1} = \frac{3 - (-2)}{3 - 3}$$ Substitute 3 for y_2 -2 for y_1, 3 for x_2, and 3 for x_1.

$$= \frac{3 + 2}{0}$$ $3 - (-2) = 3 + 2$, $3 - 3 = 0$. Note that $-(-2$ becomes $+2$.

$$= \frac{5}{0}$$ A number divided by 0, the result is undefined.

$$= \text{undefined slope. A number divided by 0, the result is undefined.}$$

How to Find the Slope When Two Points are Given

Example 4

Find the slope of the line that passes through $(3, 6)$ and $(5, 2)$.

Solution

The formula for the slope of a line that passes through the points (x_1, y_1) and (x_2, y_2) is:

$$\text{Slope} = \frac{y_2 - y_1}{x_2 - x_1}$$

To find the slope of a line when two ordered pairs of points (x_1, x_2) and (y_1, y_2) are given, use the formula:

$$\text{Slope} = \frac{y_2 - y_1}{x_2 - x_1}$$

Let (x_1, y_1) be (3, 6) ad let (x_2, y_2) be (5, 2).

$$\text{Slope} = \frac{y_2 - y_1}{x_2 - x_1} = \frac{2 - 6}{5 - 3}$$ Substitute 2 for y_2, 6 for y_1, 5 for x_2, and 3 for x_1.

$$= \frac{-4}{2}$$ $2 - 6 = -4, \; 5 - 3 = 2$

$$= -2$$ $-4 \div 2 = -2$

The slope of the line is -2.

Example 5

Find the slope of the line that passes through (-3, -2) and (0, 4).

Solution

The formula for the slope of a line that passes through the points (x_1, y_1) and (x_2, y_2) is:

$$\text{Slope} = \frac{y_2 - y_1}{x_2 - x_1}$$

Let (x_1, y_1) be (-3, -2) and let (x_2, y_2) be (0, 4).

$$\text{Slope} = \frac{y_2 - y_1}{x_2 - x_1} = \frac{4 - (-2)}{0 - (-3)}$$ Substitute 4 for y_2, -2 for y_1, 0 for x_2, and -3 for x_1.

$$= \frac{4 + 2}{0 + 3}$$ $-(-2) = +2$, and $-(-3) = +3$.

$$= \frac{6}{3}$$ $4 + 2 = 6$ and $0 + 3 = 3$

$$= 2$$ $6 \div 3 = 2.$

The slope of the line is 2.

How to Find the Slope From a Graph

Example 6

Use the graph to find the slope of the line by:

a. Using the formula, Slope $= \dfrac{y_2 - y_1}{x_2 - x_1}$

b. Using the formula, Slope $= \dfrac{\text{rise}}{\text{run}}$

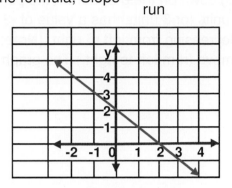

Solution

a. Select two points on the line and then use the slope formula to find the slope as follows:

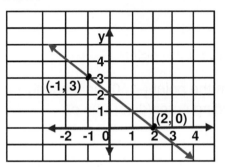

Let the two points selected on the line be (2, 0) and (-1, 3).
Let (x_1, y_1) be (-1, 3) and let (x_2, y_2) be (2, 0).

$$\text{Slope} = \frac{y_2 - y_1}{x_2 - x_1} = \frac{0 - 3}{2 - (-1)} \qquad \text{Substitute 0 for } y_2, \text{ 3 for } y_1, \text{ 2 for } x_2, \text{ and -1 for } x_1.$$

$$= \frac{0 - 3}{2 + 1} \qquad \text{Note: } - (- = +, \text{ so } 2 - (-1) = 2 + 1$$

Hint: See the chapter on "Subtraction of Integers."

$$= \frac{-3}{3} \qquad -3 \div 3 = -1$$

$$= -1 \qquad -3 \div 3 = -1$$

b. Use the same graph as in the solution of Example 6a. Select the same two points on the line as in the graph of the solution of Example 6a.

To find the slope by using the formula, Slope = $\dfrac{\text{rise}}{\text{run}}$, we have to count square units (or units) on the graph that represent "rise" and "run."

We can count 3 square units (or 3 units) down on the graph from the point (-1, 3) to the x-axis as the rise. This 3 square units (or 3 units) has a value of -3 because the y value of the line on the graph is decreasing from left to right. (**Note**: Lines that have negative slopes go down as you move from left to right.) The graph is modified to show the rise and the run.

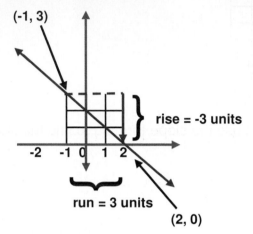

We can also count 3 square units (or units) from the point (-1, 0) horizontally to the point (2, 0) as the run. (Hint: See the preceding notes/diagrams on Slope = $\dfrac{\text{rise}}{\text{run}}$.)

Substitute rise = -3 square units (or units) and run = 3 square units (or units) into the equation:

$$\text{Slope} = \frac{\text{rise}}{\text{run}} \text{ to obtain the slope as shown:}$$

$$\text{Slope} = \frac{\text{rise}}{\text{run}} = \frac{-3}{3}$$

$$= -1 \qquad\qquad\qquad -3 \div 3 = -1$$

How to Identify Parallel Lines by Using Other Slopes

Note: Parallel lines have equal slopes.

Example 7

Is the line AB that passes through the points (1, 1) and (-2, 2) parallel to the line DC that passes through the points (1, 3) and (-2, 4)?

(The line AB can be written as $\overleftrightarrow{AB}$, and the line DC can also be written as $\overleftrightarrow{DC}$.)

Solution

If the line AB is parallel to the line DC, then the line AB and the line DC must have the same slope because parallel lines have equal slopes. For line AB, let (x_1, y_1) be (1, 1) and (x_2, y_2) be (-2, 2).

Slope of the line AB $= \dfrac{y_2 - y_1}{x_2 - x_1} = \dfrac{2 - 1}{-2 - 1}$ Substitute 2 for y_2, 1 for y_1, -2 for x_2,

and 1 for x_1.

$= \dfrac{1}{-3}$ $2 - 1 = 1, -2 - 1 = -3$

$= -\dfrac{1}{3}$

For the line DC, let (x_1, y_1) be (1, 3) and (x_2, y_2) be (-2, 4).

Slope of the line DC $= \dfrac{y_2 - y_1}{x_2 - x_1} = \dfrac{4 - 3}{-2 - 1}$ Substitute 4 for y_2, 3 for y_1, -2 for x_2,

and 1 for x_1.

$= \dfrac{1}{-3}$ $4 - 3 = 1, -2 - 1 = -3$

$= -\dfrac{1}{3}$

Since the lines AB and DC have the same slope of $-\dfrac{1}{3}$, they are parallel.

Example 8

Determine if the line AB that passes through the points (4, 2) and (7, -1) and the line DC that passes through the points (5, 3) and (4, 3) are parallel or not.

Solution

If the line AB is parallel to the line DC, then their slopes must be equal. Let us find if their slopes are equal or not.

For the line AB, let (x_1, y_1) be (4, 2) and let (x_2, y_2) be (7, -1).

For the line DC, let (x_1, y_1) be (5, 3) and let (x_2, y_2) be (4, 3).

Slope of the line AB $= \dfrac{y_2 - y_1}{x_2 - x_1} = \dfrac{-1 - 2}{7 - 4}$ Substitute -1 for y_2, 2 for y_1, 7 for x_2, and 4 for x_1.

$= \dfrac{-3}{3}$ $-1 - 2 = -3, 7 - 4 = 3$

$$= -1 \qquad\qquad -3 \div 3 = -1$$

Slope of the line DC $= \dfrac{y_2 - y_1}{x_2 - x_1} = \dfrac{3 - 3}{4 - 5}$ Substitute 3 for y_2, 3 for y_1, 4 for x_2, and 5 for x_1.

$$= \dfrac{0}{-1} \qquad\qquad 3 - 3 = 0,\ 4 - 5 = -1$$

$$= 0 \qquad\qquad \text{0 divided by any number is 0.}$$

The slope of the line AB is -1 and the slope of line DC is 0. Since the slopes of the line AB and the line DC are not equal, then the line AB and the line DC are not parallel.

How to Identify Perpendicular Lines by Using Their Slopes

Two lines are perpendicular to each other if the product of their slopes is **-1**, and that is, their slopes are negative reciprocals of each other. For an example, if two lines are **perpendicular**, and the slope of the first line is **m**, then the slope of the second line should be $-\dfrac{1}{m}$.

Note that the product of the two slopes $= \mathbf{m} \times (-\dfrac{1}{\mathbf{m}})$

$$= \overset{1}{\cancel{\mathbf{m}}} \times (-\dfrac{1}{\underset{1}{\cancel{\mathbf{m}}}}) \qquad\qquad \text{Divide.}$$

$$= 1 \times (-\dfrac{1}{1})$$

$$= 1 \times (-1) \qquad\qquad -\dfrac{1}{1} = -1$$

$$= -1$$

Example 9

Determine if the line AB that passes through the points (1, 1) and (4, 0) is perpendicular to the line DC that passes through the points (1, 1) and (2, 4).

Solution

Two lines are perpendicular to each other if the product of their slopes is -1, and that is their slopes are negative reciprocals of each other. Let us find the slopes of the line AB and the line DC, and then check if the product of their slopes is -1 or not.

For the line AB, let (x_1, y_1) be (1, 1) and let (x_2, y_2) be (4, 0).

Slope of the line AB $= \dfrac{y_2 - y_1}{x_2 - x_1} = \dfrac{0 - 1}{4 - 1}$ Substitute 0 for y_2, 1 for y_1, 4 for x_2, and 1 for x_1.

$$= \dfrac{-1}{3}$$ $0 - 1 = -1$, $4 - 1 = 3$

$$= -\dfrac{1}{3}$$

For the line DC, let (x_1, y_1) be $(1, 1)$ and let (x_2, y_2) be $(2, 4)$.

Slope of the line DC $= \dfrac{y_2 - y_1}{x_2 - x_1} = \dfrac{4 - 1}{2 - 1}$ Substitute 4 for y_2, 1 for y_1, 2 for x_2, and 1 for x_1.

$$= \dfrac{3}{1}$$ $4 - 1 = 3$, $2 - 1 = 1$

$$= 3$$

The slope of the line AB $= -\dfrac{1}{3}$ and the slope of the line DC is 3. Note that $-\dfrac{1}{3}$ and 3 are negative reciprocal of each other and therefore the line AB and the line DC are perpendicular to each other.

Additionally, the product of the slopes of the line AB and the line DC is -1 as shown below.

$$= -\dfrac{1}{3} \times 3$$

$$= -\dfrac{1}{3} \times 3 = -\dfrac{3}{3} = -1$$

Since the product of the slopes of the line AB and the line DC is -1, then the line AB is perpendicular to the line DC.

Example 10

Show that the line AB that passes through the points $(6, 2)$ and $(4, 1)$ and the line DC that passes through the points $(4, 8)$ and $(9, 3)$ are not perpendicular to each other.

Solution

To show that the line AB is not perpendicular to the line DC, we need to show that the slopes of the line AB and the line DC are not negative reciprocal of each other, and that means the product of their slopes is not equal to -1.

For the line AB, let (x_1, y_1) be $(6, 2)$ and let (x_2, y_2) be $(4, 1)$.

Slope of the line AB $= \dfrac{y_2 - y_1}{x_2 - x_1} = \dfrac{1 - 2}{4 - 6}$

Substitute 1 for y_2, 2 for y_1, 4 for x_2, and 6 for x_1.

$$= \dfrac{-1}{-2}$$

$1 - 2 = -1$, $4 - 6 = -2$

$$= \dfrac{1}{2}$$

$\dfrac{-1}{-2} = \dfrac{1}{2}$, the negative symbols cancel out.

Considering the line DC, let (x_1, y_1) be (4, 8) and let (x_2, y_2) be (9, 3).

Slope of the line DC $= \dfrac{y_2 - y_1}{x_2 - x_1} = \dfrac{3 - 8}{9 - 4}$

Substitute 3 for y_2, 8 for y, 9 for x_2, and

4 for x_1.

$$= \dfrac{-5}{5}$$

$3 - 8 = -5$, $9 - 4 = 5$

$$= -1$$

$-5 \div 5 = -1$

The slope of the line AB is $\dfrac{1}{2}$ and the slope of the line DC $= -1$. Since the slope of the line AB is not a negative reciprocal of the slope of the line DC, then the line AB is not perpendicular to the line DC.

Or we can state that since the product of the slopes of the line AB and the line DC (which is $\dfrac{1}{2} \times -1 = -\dfrac{1}{2}$) is not equal to -1, then the line AB and the line DC are not perpendicular to each other.

Example 11
Sketch (a) parallel lines (b) perpendicular lines.
Solution
The parallel lines and the perpendicular lines are sketched as shown.

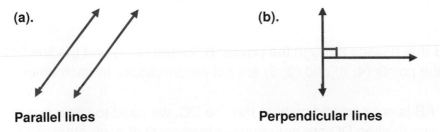

(a).   (b).

Parallel lines   Perpendicular lines

Exercises
1. What is the slope of a line? Hint: See the notes.
2. What are the four types of slopes? Hint: See Example 1.

3a. Sketch the four types of slopes. Hint: See Example 1.

3b. Label each slope of the line as undefined, zero, positive and negative.
Hint: See the notes.

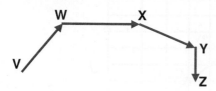

4. The slope of a line = $\dfrac{y_2 - y_1}{x_2 - x_1}$. Is this true or false? Hint: See Example 2

5. a. Vertical change = change in y distance = rise. True or false?

b. Horizontal change = change in x distance = run. True or false?

c. Rise is the number of units moved up or d_____.

d. Run is the number of units moved to the left or r_____.

e The slope of a line is the ratio:

$$\frac{\text{Vertical change}}{\text{horizontal change}} = \frac{\text{Change in y distance}}{\text{Change in x distance}} = \frac{\text{rise}}{\text{run}}, \text{true or false?}$$

Hint: See the notes.

6. Describe the slope of the line x at the top of the mountain and the slopes of the two lines Y and Z at the sides of the mountain. Hint: See the notes.

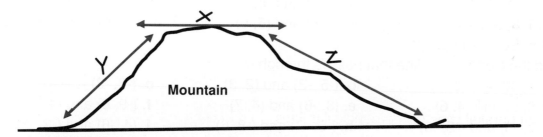

Mountain

7. Do the following slopes appear to be zero, positive, negative or undefined?
Hint: See Example 1.

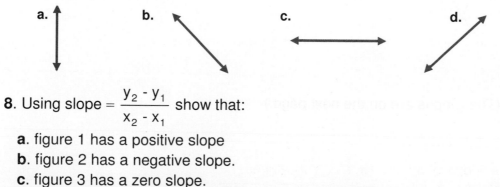

a.　　　　b.　　　　c.　　　　d.

8. Using slope = $\dfrac{y_2 - y_1}{x_2 - x_1}$ show that:

a. figure 1 has a positive slope

b. figure 2 has a negative slope.

c. figure 3 has a zero slope.

d. figure 4 has an undefined slope.

Hint: See Example 3.

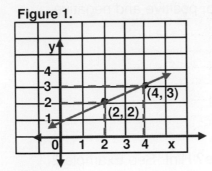

Figure 1.

Figure 2

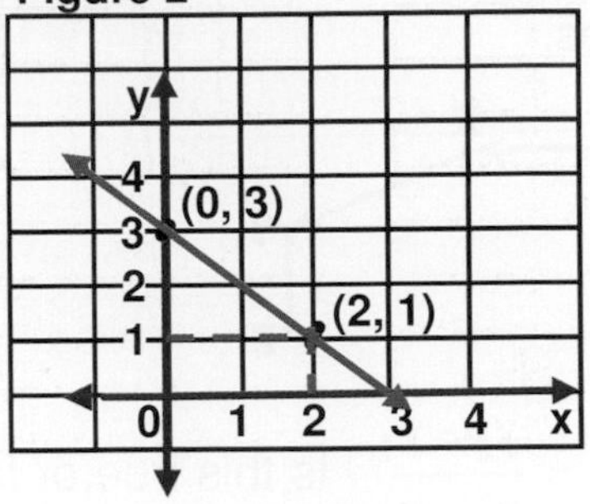

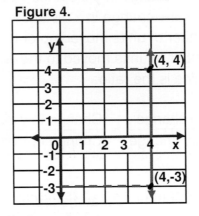

Figure 3.

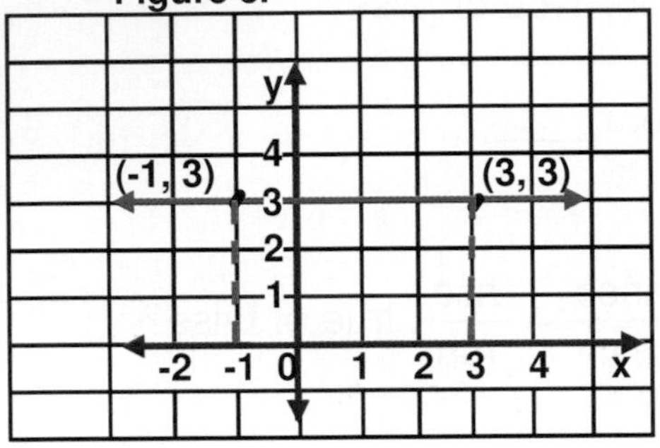

Figure 4.

9. Find the slope of the line that passes through:

    a. (2, 4) and (6, 3)   **b**. (3, 5) and (5, 2)   **c**. (3, 4) and (5, 1)

    d. (5, 6) and (4, 2)   **e**. (7, 8) and (6, 5)   **f**. (8, 10) and (6, 5)

    Hint: See Example 4

10. Find the slope of the line that passes through:

    a. (-4, -2) and (0, 5)   **b**. (-5, -3) and (2, 3)   **c**. (-6, -3) and (3, 2)

    d. (-8, 5) and (4, 6)   **e**. (8, -6) and (4, 7)   **f**. (-9, 6) and (4, -5)

    g. (-7, -3) and (-5, -6)   **h**. (-5, -7) and (-8, 6)   **i**. (4, -6) and (-2, -3)

    Hint: See Example 5.

11. Use the graphs to find the slope of each line. Hint: See Example 6.

(The graphs are on the next page.)

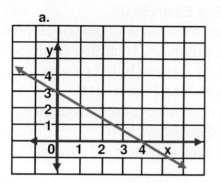

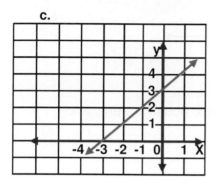

12. Complete the statement. Parallel lines have the s_____ slopes.
    Hint: See the notes.

13. Complete the statement. If line X is parallel to line Y, then line X and line Y must
    have the same s____ because parallel lines have eq_____- slopes.
    Hint: See Example 7.

14. Lines that are parallel have the same slope. True or false? Hint: See Example 7.

15. Determine if line A that passes through (4, 9) and (-3, -5) is parallel to line B that
    passes through (1, 9) and (-1, 5). Hint: See Example 7.

16. Determine if line X that passes through (-2, 0) and (1, 3) is parallel to line Z that
    passes through (-1, -2) and (3, 2). Hint: See Example 7.

17. Determine if line A that passes through (0, 0) and (1, 2) is parallel to the line that
    passes through (1, 0) and (2, 2). Hint: See Example 7.

18. If the slope of the line X and the line Z are not equal, then the line X and the line Z
    are not parallel. True or false? Hint: See Example 8.

19. Determine if line A that passes through (1, 1) and (2, -1) is parallel to line B that
    passes through (-4, 0) and (2, -2). Hint: See Example 8.

20. Determine if the line A that passes through (1, 2) and (4, 6) is parallel to the line B
    that passes through the points (2, 3) and (-3, 1). Hint: See Example 8.

21. Two lines are perpendicular to each other if the products of their slopes is _____,
    and that their slopes are n_____ reciprocals of each other. Complete the
    statement. Hint: See Example 9.

22. Determine if line P that passes through (1, 3) and (1, 1) is perpendicular to line
    that passes through (-2, 1) and (1, 1). Hint: See Example 9.

23. Determine if the line A that passes through (2, 2) and (0, 0) is perpendicular to the

line B that passes through (3, 1) and (1, 3). Hint: See Example 9.

24. If the slope of the line A is not a negative reciprocal of the slope of the line B, then line A is not p——— to the line B. Complete the statement. Hint: See Example 10.

25. Show that line A that passes through (3, 4) and (6, 1) and line B that passes through (-2, -2) and (2, 2) are not perpendicular. Hint: See Example 10.

26. Show that line Y that passes through (-3, 1) and (-1, 4) is not perpendicular to line X that passes through (-1, -1) and (4, 3). Hint: See Example 10.

27. Which lines appear to be perpendicular and which lines appear to be parallel?

a.　　　　　　　　　　　　　　　　**b.**

Challenge Questions

28. In the diagram, which lines appear to have undefined, positive, zero, and negative slopes?

29. In the diagram, which lines appear to be parallel and which lines appear to be perpendicular?

30. Find the slope of the line that passes through:

    a. (5, 7) and (9, 2)　　　　**b.** (2, 7) and (9, 5)　　　　**c.** (-5, -3) and (2, 4)

    d. (-7, 3) and (4, -6)　　　**e.** (-2, -4) and (-3, -1)　　**f.** (-4, 7) and (0, 0)

    g. (-4, -3) and (-6, -2)　　**h.** (-5, 0) and (-1, -3)　　**i.** (0, 0) and (-1, -3)

31. Use the graph to find the slope of each line.

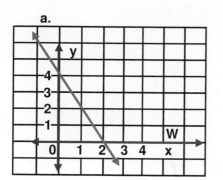

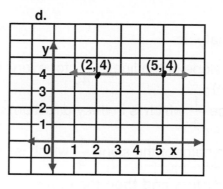

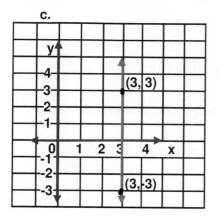

32. Determine if line A that passes through (1, 3) and (-2, 0) is parallel to line B that passes through (2, 2) and (-3, -3).

33. Determine if line Y that passes through (1, 2) and (-2, -4) is parallel to line X which passes through (2, 1) and (-1, -5).

34. Determine if line P that passes through (2, -4) and (3, 6) is parallel to line Q which passes through (1, 7) and (-3, 5).

35. Determine if line A that passes through (-4, 2) and (5, 3) is perpendicular to line that passes through (4, 0) and (3, 4).

36. Determine if line P that passes through (-3, 3) and (0, 0) is perpendicular to line Q that passes through (2, 2) and (-3, -3).

Answers to Selected Questions

8d. slope $= \dfrac{y_2 - y_1}{x_2 - x_1} = \dfrac{4 - (-3)}{4 - 4} = \dfrac{4 + 3}{0} = \dfrac{7}{0} =$ undefined.

9a. slope $= \dfrac{y_2 - y_1}{x_2 - x_1} = \dfrac{3 - 4}{6 - 2} = \dfrac{-1}{4} = -\dfrac{1}{4}$

10a. slope $= \dfrac{y_2 - y_1}{x_2 - x_1} = \dfrac{5 - (-2)}{0 - (-4)} = \dfrac{5 + 2}{4} = \dfrac{7}{4} = 1\dfrac{3}{4}$

30e. slope $= \dfrac{y_2 - y_1}{x_2 - x_1} = \dfrac{-1 - (-4)}{-3 - (-2)} = \dfrac{-1 + 4}{-3 + 2} = \dfrac{3}{-1} = -3$

How to Graph a Line Using a Point and a Slope

Example 12

Graph the line that passes through (1, 1) with slope of $\dfrac{1}{4}$

Solution
Step 1: Slope analysis

Since the slope of the line is $\dfrac{1}{4}$, for every 1 unit (this 1 unit is the numerator of the slope $\dfrac{1}{4}$ which is in the y-direction) up, move four units (this 4 units is the denominator of the slope $\dfrac{1}{4}$ which is in the x-direction) to the right.

Step 2: **Plot the points and then the graph.**

Plot the given point (1, 1). Then from the point (1, 1), move 4 units (this 4 units represent the denominator of the slope of $\dfrac{1}{4}$ which is in the x-direction) to the right and then move 1 unit (this 1 unit represents the numerator of the slope of $\dfrac{1}{4}$ which is in the y-direction) up and then plot the point (5, 2). Note that (1 + 4, 1 + 1) = (5, 2). Use a ruler to connect the two points (1, 1) and (5, 2) which is the graph of the required line. Hint: See diagram.

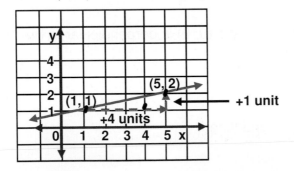

Example 13

Graph the line that passes through (2, 3) with a slope of $-\dfrac{1}{4}$.

Solution
Step 1: Slope analysis

Since the slope of the line is $-\frac{1}{4}$, for every 1 unit movement down, 4 units should be moved to the right, or, for every 1 unit movement up, move 4 units to the left. (Compare the Step 1 in Example 12 to the Step 1 in Example 13 and note the effect of the negative symbol in front of the slope in Step 1 of Example 13.)

Step 2: Plot the points and then the graph.

Plot the given point (2, 3). Then from the point (2, 3), move 4 units (this 4 units represent the positive denominator of the slope of $-\frac{1}{4}$) to the right and then

move 1 unit (this 1 unit represents the negative numerator of the slope of $-\frac{1}{4}$) down and then plot the point (6, 2). Note that (2 + 4, 3 - 1) = (6, 2). Use a ruler to connect the two points (2, 3) and (6, 2) which is the graph of the required line. Hint: See diagram.

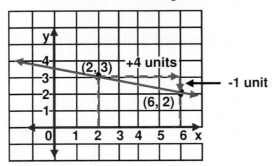

Exercises

1. Graph the line that passes through (3, 5) with a slope of $\frac{1}{3}$. Hint: See Example 12.

2. Graph the line that passes through (1, 3) with a slope of $-\frac{1}{4}$. Hint: See Example 13.

Challenge Questions

3. Graph the line that passes through (2, 6) with a slope of $\frac{1}{5}$.

4. Graph the line with a slope of $-\frac{1}{2}$ and passes through (-4, 3).

SLOPE-INTERCEPT FORM

New Terms: x-axis, y-axis, and slope-intercept form

How to Find the x-intercept and the y-intercept
The **x-intercept** of a line is the value of x at the point where the line crosses the
x-axis. **Note** that where the line crosses the x-axis, y = 0. The **y-intercept** of a line
is the value of y at where the line crosses the **y-axis**. **Note** that where the line
crosses the y-axis, x = 0. The diagram shows the x-intercept and the y-intercept.

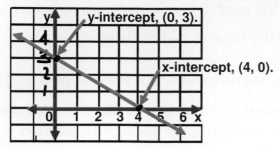

How to Graph Linear Equations by Finding the x-intercept and the y-intercept

Example 1
Find the x-intercept and the y-intercept of the line 2x + 2y = 8. Graph the equation.
Solution
Step 1: **Find the x-intercept and the y-intercept**.

Recall that at the x-axis, y = 0, therefore, **to find the x-intercept** substitute
y = 0 into the equation of the line which is 2x + 2y = 8 as shown:
When y = 0, 2x + 2y = 8 becomes 2x + 2(0) = 8

$$2x + 0 = 8 \qquad\qquad\qquad 2(0) = 0$$

$$2x = 8$$

$$\frac{2x}{2} = \frac{8}{2} \qquad \text{Divide each side of the equation by 2 in order to obtain the value of x.}$$

$$\frac{\overset{x}{\cancel{2x}}}{\underset{1}{2}} = \frac{\overset{4}{\cancel{8}}}{\underset{1}{2}}$$

$$x = 4$$

So, the x-intercept is 4 and the coordinates of the x-intercept are (4, 0). At the
x-intercept, y = 0. (See the graph in Step 2.)
Recall that at the y-axis, x = 0, (See the graph in Step 2.) so, **to find the y-intercept**
substitute x = 0 into the equation of the line which is 2x + 2y = 8 as shown:
When x = 0, 2x + 2y = 8 becomes 2(0) + 2y = 8

$$0 + 2y = 8$$
$$2y = 8$$

$$\frac{2x}{2} = \frac{8}{2}$$ Divide each side of the equation by 2 in order to obtain the value of x.

$$\frac{\overset{x}{\cancel{2x}}}{\underset{1}{\cancel{2}}} = \frac{\overset{4}{\cancel{8}}}{\underset{1}{\cancel{2}}}$$

$$x = 4$$

The y-intercept is 4 and the coordinates of the y-intercept are (0, 4). At the y-intercept, x = 0. (See the graph in Step 2.)

Step 2: **Use the intercepts to graph the equation**.

Plot the x-intercept of 4 and y-intercept of 4 on a graph and use a ruler to draw a line through the x-intercept and the y-intercept. This line is the required graph of the line 2x + 2y = 8.

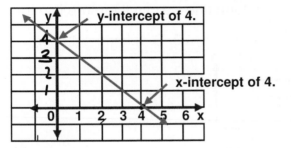

Slope-Intercept Form

The equation of a line can be written in the standard slope-intercept form which is **y = mx + b** where m is the slope and b is the y-intercept

Example 2

Use the **slope-intercept form** to find the slope and the y-intercept of the equation of the line:

    a. y = 8x + 3   **b.** y = -7x + 1   **c.** y = 3x - 5

Solution

a. If we compare y = 8x + 3 to the slope-intercept form of y = mx + b, we can conclude that y = 8x + 3 is already in the slope-intercept form and we can therefore, find the corresponding values for m and b as shown:

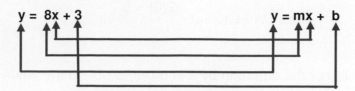

By comparing or matching the two equations above, m = 8 and b = 3. So the slope = m = 8 and the y-intercept = b = 3.

b. If we compare y = -7x + 1 to the slope-intercept form of y = mx + b, we can conclude that y = -7x + 1 is already in the slope-intercept form and we can therefore find the corresponding values for m and b as shown:

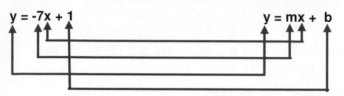

By comparing or matching the two equations above,
m = -7 and b = 1 therefore the slope = m = -7 and the y-intercept = b = 1.

c. If we compare y = 3x - 5 to the slope intercept form of y = mx + b, we can conclude that y = 3x - 5 is already in the slope-intercept form and we can therefore find the corresponding values for m and b as shown:

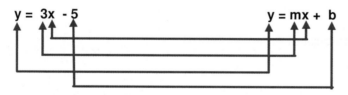

By comparing or matching the two equations above,
m = 3 and b = -5 therefore the slope = m = 3 and the y-intercept = b = - 5.

Example 3
The equation of the line in Example 1 is 2x + 2y = 8.
a. Write the equation of the line 2x + 2y = 8 in the slope-intercept form.
b. Find the slope of the line and the y-intercept.

Solution
a. The slope-intercept form is y = mx + b where m is the slope and b is the y-intercept. We need to write the equation 2x + 2y = 8 in the slope-intercept form such that y will have no number attached to it as a coefficient. We want y to be by itself at the left side of the equation as shown:

2x + 2y = 8

2x - 2x + 2y = 8 - 2x   Subtract 2x from both sides of the equation such that 2y will remain at the left side of the equation.

2x - 2x + 2y = -2x + 8

2y = -2x + 8   2x - 2x = 0

$$\frac{2y}{2} = \frac{-2x + 8}{2}$$ Divide each side of the equation by 2 in order to obtain y by itself.

$y = -x + 4$ $\frac{2y}{2} = y$ and $\frac{-2x + 8}{2} = -x + 4$

$y = -1x + 4$ which is in the slope-intercept form of $y = mx + b$. Note that $-x = -1x$.

b. From the solution of **a**, $y = -1x + 4$ which is in the slope-intercept form of $y = mx + b$, where $m = -1$ and $b = 4$ by comparing the equation $y = -1x + 4$ to the slope-intercept form of $y = mx + b$ as shown:

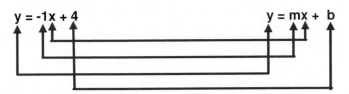

The slope of the line $= m = -1$ and the y-intercept of the line $= b = 4$.

Example 4

Using the slope-intercept form, find the slope and the y-intercept of:

a. $y = x$

b. $2x = 3y$

Solution

a. Rewrite the equation $y = x$ to show similar parts of the slope-intercept form of $y = mx + b$ as shown:

$y = x$ becomes $y = 1x + 0$ 1 is in the place of m and 0 is in the place of b.

Note that $x = 1x$.

We can now compare or match $y = 1x + 0$ with the slope-intercept form as shown:

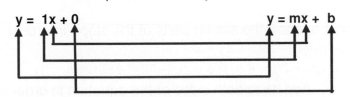

By comparing or matching the two equations above, the slope $= m = 1$ and the intercept on the y-axis$= b = 0$

b. Rewrite the equation $2x = 3y$ to show similar parts of the slope-intercept form, so you can compare the equation of the formula $y = mx + b$ to the given equation.

$2x = 3y$

$3y = 2x$ Reverse the equation so that y will be on the left side of the equation.

$$\frac{3y}{3} = \frac{2x}{3}$$ Divide both sides of the equation by 3 in order to obtain the value for y.

$$\frac{\cancel{3}^1 y}{\cancel{3}} = \frac{2x}{3} \qquad \text{Divide by 3.}$$

$$y = \frac{2}{3}x$$

$$y = \frac{2}{3}x + 0 \qquad \text{Add the 0 to obtain the slope-intercept form of } y = mx + b.$$

We can now compare $y = \dfrac{2}{3}x + 0$ to the slope-intercept form of $y = mx + b$ as shown:

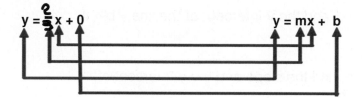

By comparing or matching the two equations above, the slope $= m = \dfrac{2}{3}$ and the y-intercept $= b = 0$.

Example 5

Write the equation -2y - 4x = 4 in the slope-intercept form, and then find the slope and the y-intercept.

Solution

Rewrite the equation -2y - 4x = 4 to show the similar parts of the slope-intercept form as shown:

-2y - 4x = 4

-2y - 4x + 4x = 4x + 4   Add 4x to both sides of the equation in order to eliminate the -4x at the left side of the equation.

-2y + 0 = 4x + 4   -4x + 4x = 0

-2y = 4x + 4

$$\frac{-2y}{-2} = \frac{4x}{-2} + \frac{4}{-2} \qquad \text{Divide both sides of the equation by -2 in order to obtain the value of y.}$$

$$\begin{array}{ccc} y & -2x & -2 \\ \dfrac{-2y}{-2} = & \dfrac{4x}{-2} + & \dfrac{4}{-2} \\ 1 & 1 & 1 \end{array}$$

y = -2x - 2   4x ÷ (-2) = -2x and 4 ÷ (-2) = -2

We can now compare or match the equation y = - 2x - 2 to the slope-intercept form of y = mx + b as shown:

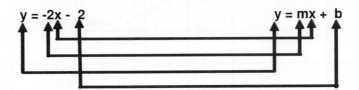

By comparing or matching the two equations above, the slope = m = -2 and the y-intercept = b = -2.

How to Use the Slope-intercept Form to Construct the Graph of an Equation

Example 5a

Use the slope-intercept form to construct a graph of each equation

a. y = 2x + 5.   **b.** $y = \dfrac{2x}{3} + 3$

Solution

a. Step 1: Find the rise, run, and the y-intercept.

The slope-intercept form is y = mx + b

$$= (\dfrac{rise}{run})x + b \qquad\qquad\qquad [A].$$

Recall that slope = m = $\dfrac{rise}{run}$, substitute m = $\dfrac{rise}{run}$.

The equation y = 2x + 5 can be written in the form of equation $[A]$ as shown:

$$y = (\dfrac{2}{1}) x + 5 \qquad\qquad\qquad [B],$$

where $\dfrac{2}{1} = \dfrac{rise}{run}$. Note: $\dfrac{2}{1} = 2$ such that m is not changed

Equation $[B]$ shows that the rise = 2, the run = 1, and the y-intercept = b = 5. This y-intercept should be the first point on the graph. Locate the y-intercept on graph paper, and draw the **run** and the **rise** to locate the second point.

Since the y-intercept or b is 5, measure or count 5 units up from the origin (0, 0) on the y-axis and graph a point. This point has coordinates of (0, 5), see Figure 1.

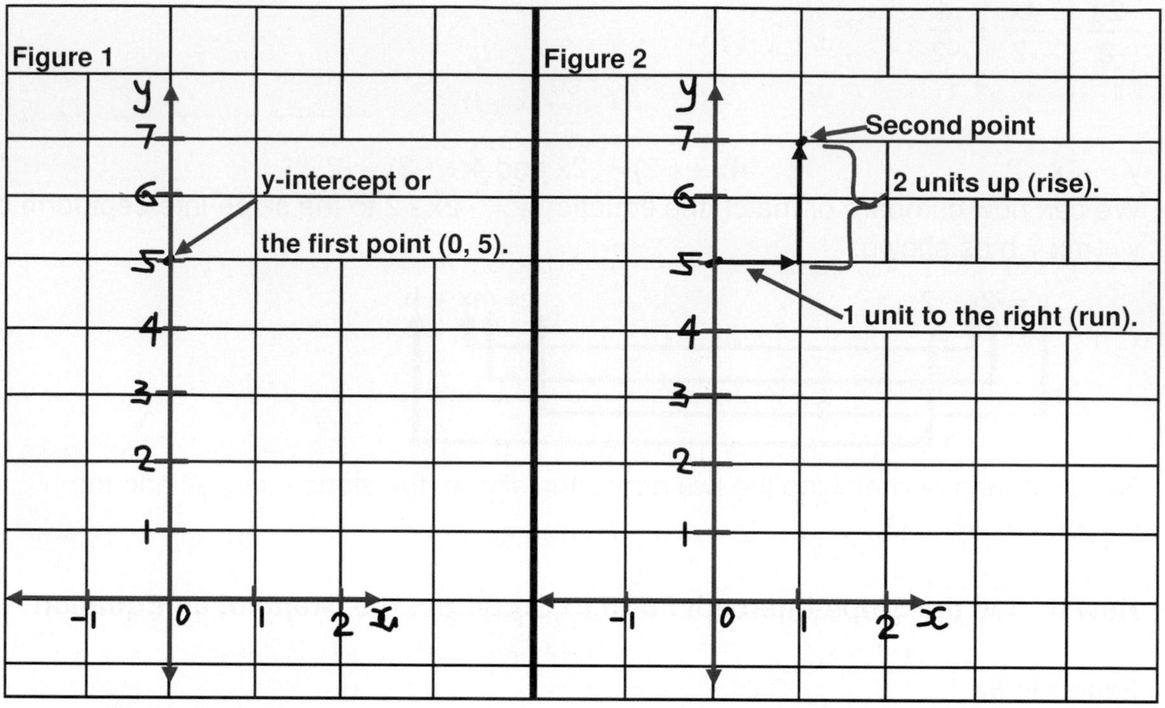

Figure 1 / **Figure 2**

Since the run is 1, from this initial point of (0, 5), draw 1 unit to the right and since the rise is 2, draw 2 units up and then graph the second point, see Figure 2.

Step 3: Draw a line through the y-intercept which is the first point and the second point to obtain the graph of y = 2x + 5 as shown in Figure 3.

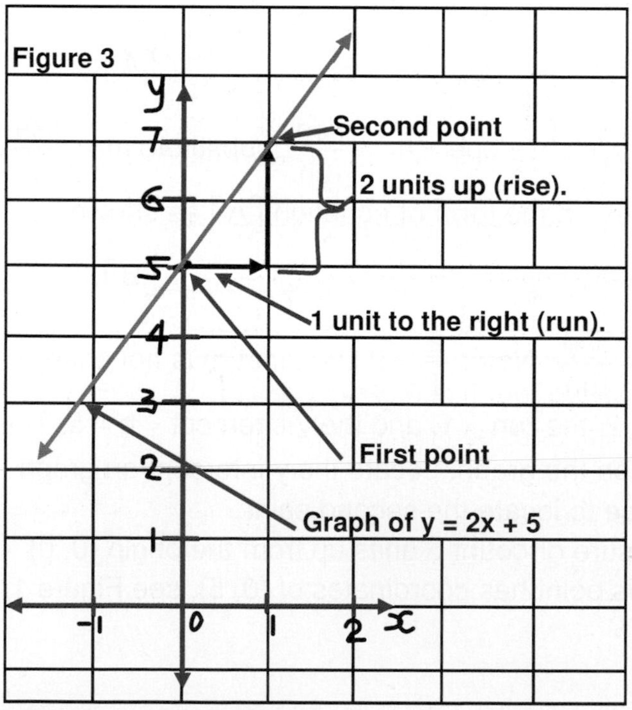

b. Step 1: Find the rise, run and the intercept.

The slope-intercept form is $y = mx + b$

$$= (\frac{rise}{run})x + b \underline{\hspace{5cm}} [C]$$

Recall that slope $= m = \dfrac{rise}{run}$, substitute $m = \dfrac{rise}{run}$.

Similarly, the equation $y = \dfrac{2x}{3} + 3$ can be written in the form of equation $[C]$ as shown:

$$y = (\frac{2}{3})x + 3 \underline{\hspace{4cm}} [D], \text{ where } \frac{2}{3} = \frac{rise}{run} = m.$$

Equation $[D]$ shows that the rise = 2, the run = 3, and the y-intercept is 3 and this y-intercept should be the first point drawn on the graph.

Step 2: Locate the y-intercept on graph paper, draw the run and the rise to locate the second point.

Since the y-intercept or b is 3, measure or count 3 units up from the origin (0, 0) on the y-axis and graph a point and this point has coordinates of (0, 3) as shown in Figure 4.

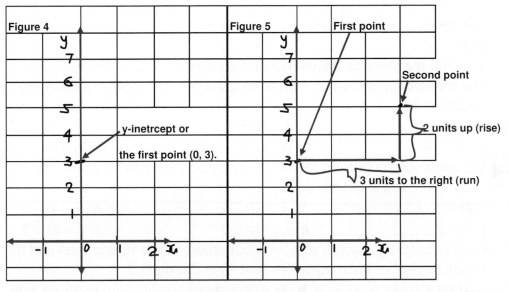

Since the run = 3, from this initial point of (0, 3) draw 3 units to the right and since the rise is 2, draw 2 units up, and then draw the second point as shown in Figure 5.

Step 3: Draw a line through the first and the second points. This line is the graph of $y = \dfrac{2}{3}x + 3$ as shown in Figure 6.

Figure 6

First point

Second point

2 units up (rise)

3 units to the right (run)

Graph of $y = \frac{2x}{3} + 3$

Exercises

1. Explain what is meant by x-intercept and y-intercept.

2. Find the x-intercept and y-intercept of each line. Graph each equation. Hint: See Example 1.

   a. $2x + y = 3$ **b.** $x + 2y = 4$ **c.** $2x + 2y = 3$

   d. $2x + 3y = 4$ **e.** $2x + 2y = 4$ **f.** $3y + 2x = 4$

3. Use the slope-intercept form to find the slope and the y-intercept of the equation of each line. Hint: See Example 2.

   a. $y = 2x + 4$ **b.** $y = -3x + 2$ **c.** $y = 4x - 3$

   d. $y = 3x - 2$ **e.** $y = -4x + 3$ **f.** $y = 2x + 2$

4. Write the equation of each line in the slope-intercept form, and then find the slope and the y-intercept of each equation. Hint: See Example 3.

   a. $2x + 3y = 4$ **b.** $3x + 2y = 5$ **c.** $2y + x = 4$

   d. $x + y = 2$ **e.** $2x - 4y = 8$ **f.** $-3x + y = 2$

5. Using the slope-intercept form, find the slope and the y-intercept of each equation. Hint: See Example 4.

   a. $y = 2x$ **b.** $2y = x$ **c.** $3y = 2x$

   d. $2y = 2x$ **e.** $3y = x$ **d.** $2y = 3x$

6. Write each equation in the slope-intercept form and then find the slope and the y-intercept. Hint: See Example 5.

   a. $-2y - 3x = 4$ **b.** $-2y - 2x = 3$ **c.** $-2y + 3x = 3$

   d. $-y - 2x = 3$ **e.** $-2x + 3y = 4$ **f.** $-3y - 2x = 6$

7. Construct the graph of each equation by using the slope and the y-intercept.

Hint: See Example 5a.

a. $y = 2x + 3$

b. $y = \dfrac{3}{4}x + 2$

c. $y = \dfrac{4}{3}x + 2$

d. $y = 3x - 3$

e. $y = 3x - 1$

f. $y = 2x + 5$

Challenge Questions

8. Identify the x-intercept and the y-intercept. Use the intercepts to draw each line.

a. $y = 3x + 4$

b. $y = 6x - 1$

c. $y = -2x + 3$

d. $y = 8x - 5$

e. $y = -4x + 3$

f. $y = -3x + 4$

9. Construct the graph of each equation by using the slope and the y-intercept.
Hint: See Example 5a.

a. $y = 2x + 4$

b. $y = \dfrac{3}{5}x - 2$

c. $y = 3x + 2$

d. $y = 4x - 2$

e. $y = \dfrac{3}{2}x + 4$

f. $y = 2x + 1$

10. Write an equation in the slope-intercept form for each line that fits each description.

   a. The line that crosses the y-axis at 2 and has a slope of 3.
   Hint: Where the line crosses the y-axis is the y-intercept.

   b. The line that crosses the y-axis at -2 and has a slope of 4.
   Hint: Where the line crosses the y-axis is the y-intercept.

   c. The line that crosses the y-axis at -3 and has a slope of -5.
   Hint: Where the line crosses the y-axis is the y-intercept.

   d. The line that contains the origin and has a slope of 3.
   Hint: The origin has coordinates of (0, 0), and therefore, the y-intercept = 0.

   e. The line that contains the origin and has a slope $\dfrac{3}{5}$.

   Hint: The origin has coordinates of (0, 0), and therefore, the y-intercept = 0.

   f. The line contains the origin and has a slope of -3.
   Hint: The origin has coordinates of (0, 0), and therefore, the y-intercept = 0

11. Using the slope intercept form, find the slope and the y-intercept of each equation

a. $y = -3x + 4$

b. $y = -2x$

c. $y = \dfrac{3x}{4} + 1$

d. $y = -x - 4$

e. $y = -\dfrac{2x}{5}$

f. $y = 2 + 3x$

g. $y = \dfrac{x}{4} + 5$

h. $y = 7$ (Hint: See the chapter on horizontal lines).

i. $x = 3$ (Hint: See the chapter on vertical lines)

j. $y = 6 - x$.

Answer to Selected Questions (Partial answer)

2a. y-intercept = 3 and x-intercept = $\dfrac{3}{2}$

3a. Slope = 2 and y-intercept = 4

4a. $y = \dfrac{-2x}{3} + \dfrac{4}{3}$

How to Write the Equation of the Line That Passes Through Two Given Points in a Slope-intercept Form

Example 6

Find the equation of the line that passes through (-2, 5) and (3, -4) in the slope-intercept form.

Solution

Step 1: Find the slope. Let this slope be m.

Let (x_1, y_1) be (-2, 5) and let (x_2, y_2) be (3, -4).

$$\text{Slope} = m = \dfrac{y_2 - y_1}{x_2 - x_1} \qquad \text{Slope formula.}$$

$$= \dfrac{-4 - 5}{3 - (-2)}$$

$$= \dfrac{-9}{3 + 2} \qquad -4 - 5 = -9 \text{ and } -(-2) = 2.$$

$$= \dfrac{-9}{5}$$

Step 2: Find the y-intercept which is b.

Substitute the slope of $\dfrac{-9}{5}$ in step 1 and either the point (-2, 5) or (3, -4) into the slope-intercept form of $y = mx + b$ in order to obtain b as shown:

$$y = mx + b \underline{\hspace{6cm}} [A]$$

$$5 = \dfrac{-9}{5}(-2) + b \qquad \text{Substitute (-2, 5) and } m = \dfrac{-9}{5} \text{ in to equation } [A].$$

$$5 = \dfrac{18}{5} + b \qquad -9(-2) = 18$$

$$5 - \dfrac{18}{5} = \dfrac{18}{5} - \dfrac{18}{5} + b \qquad \text{Subtract } \dfrac{18}{5} \text{ from both sides of the equation in}$$

order to obtain only b at the right side.

666

$5 - \dfrac{18}{5} = 0 + b$

$\dfrac{18}{5} - \dfrac{18}{5} = 0$

$\dfrac{5}{1} - \dfrac{18}{5} = b$

$\dfrac{25 - 18}{5} = b$

LCD (least common denominator) is 5.

$\dfrac{7}{5} = b$

$25 - 18 = 7$

We can now write the equation of the line using $\dfrac{-9}{5}$ for m and $\dfrac{7}{5}$ for b as shown:

$y = \dfrac{-9}{5}m + \dfrac{7}{5}$

POINT - SLOPE FORM

The **point-slope form** of an equation of a line enables us to find the equation of a line given one point and the slope. The **point-slope form** of an equation of a line that passes through (x_1, y_1) with a slope m is $\mathbf{y - y_1 = m(x - x_1)}$.

Let us find how we can obtain the piont-slope form of an equation:
Recall that the slope of a line passing through the points (x_1, y_1) and (x_2, y_2) is:

$\text{Slope} = \dfrac{y_2 - y_1}{x_2 - x_1}$

$m = \dfrac{y_2 - y_1}{x_2 - x_1}$

Substitute m for slope.

$m(x_2 - x_1) = \dfrac{y_2 - y_1}{x_2 - x_1}(x_2 - x_1)$

Multiply both sides of the equation by $(x_2 - x_1)$ in order to eliminate $x_2 - x_1$ as a denominator.

$m(x_2 - x_1) = \dfrac{y_2 - y_1}{\overset{1}{\cancel{x_2 - x_1}}}(\overset{1}{\cancel{x_2 - x_1}})$

Divide by $(x_2 - x_1)$. Note: $(x_2 - x_1) \div (x_2 - x_1) = 1$

$m(x_2 - x_1) = y_2 - y_1$ —————————————————————[A]

Reverse equation [A] as follows:

$y_2 - y_1 = m(x_2 - x_1)$ and this equation is in the **point-slope form** of the equation of a line which is $y - y_1 = m(x - x_1)$ where y_2 is replaced by y and x_2 is replaced by x.

It is important to note that the point-slope form of the equation of a line, which is $y - y_1 = m(x - x_1)$, is used to solve many problems.

How to Use the Point-slope Form of the Equation of a Line to Identify the Slope of the Line and the Point the Line Passes Through

Example 1

Use the point-slope form of the equation of a line to identify the slope of the line and the point the line passes through.

$$y - 2 = 3(x + 4)$$

Solution

The equation of the line is $y - 2 = 3(x + 4)$. The equation of the point slope form of a line is $y - y_1 = m(x - x_1)$ where m is the slope and the line passes through the point (x_1, y_1). Compare or match the equation of the line $y - 2 = 3(x + 4)$ with the point-slope form of the equation of the line which is $y - y_1 = m(x - x_1)$ as shown:

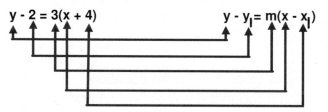

By comparing or matching the two equations as shown above, $-2 = -y_1$, $3 = m$, and $4 = -x_1$.

If $-2 = -y_1$, then $2 = y_1$ Multiply both sides of the equation by -1 in order to eliminate the negative symbol in front of y.
                                                 Note: $-2(-1) = 2$ and $(-y)(-1) = y$

If $4 = -x_1$, then $-4 = x_1$ Multiply each side of the equation by -1 in order to eliminate the negative symbol in front of x_1.

The slope of the line $= m = 3$, and the line passes through the point (x_1, y_1) which is (-4, 2).

Example 2

Use the point-slope form of the equation of a line to identify the slope of the line and the point the line passes through.

$$y - 6 = -\frac{4}{5}(x - 12)$$

Solution

The equation of the line is $y - 6 = -\frac{4}{5}(x - 12)$.

The equation of the point-slope form of a line is $y - y_1 = m(x - x_1)$ where m is the slope and the line passes through the point (x_1, y_1). Compare or match the equation of the line $y - 6 = -\frac{4}{5}(x - 12)$ with the point-slop form of the equation of the line which is $y - y_1 = m(x - x_1)$ as shown:

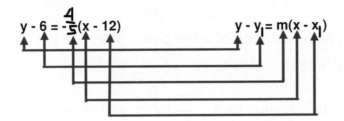

By comparing or matching the two equations as shown above, $-6 = -y_1$, $\frac{-4}{5} = m$, and $-12 = -x_1$.

If $-6 = -y_1$, then $6 = y_1$ Multiply both sides of the equation by -1 in order to eliminate the negative symbol in front of y_1.
     Note: $-6(-1) = 6$ and $-y_1(-1) = y_1$

If $-12 = -x_1$ then $12 = x_1$ Multiply each side of the equation by -1 in order to eliminate the negative symbol in front of x_1.
     Note: $-12(-1) = 12$ and $-x_1(-1) = x_1$.

The slope of the line $= m = -\frac{4}{5}$, and the line passes through the point (x_1, y_1) which is (12, 6).

How to Write the Point-slope Form of an Equation of a Line That Passes Through a Given Point With a Given Slope

Example 3
Write the point-slope form of the equation of a line that passes through (3, 2) with a slope of 5.
Solution
The point-slope form of the equation of a line passing through (x_1, y_1) with a slope m is:

$$y - y_1 = m(x - x_1) \text{———————————————-[A]}$$

Therefore, the slope of the equation of a line passing through (3, 2) with a slope of 5 is:

$$y - 2 = 5(x - 3)$$ Substitute 2 for y_1, 3 for x_1, and 5 for m into equation [A].

Example 4

Write the point-slope form of the equation of a line that passes through (-4, 6) with a slope of $-\frac{3}{8}$.

Solution

The point-slope form of the equation of a line passing through (x_1, y_1) with a slope m is:

$$y - y_1 = m(x - x_1)\text{————————————————}[B].$$

Therefore, the point-slope form of the equation of a line passing through (-4, 6) with a slope of $-\frac{3}{8}$ is:

$$y - 6 = -\frac{3}{8}[x - (-4)]$$ Substitute 6 for y_1, $\frac{-3}{8}$ for m, and -4 for x_1 into equation [B].

$$y - 6 = -\frac{3}{8}(x + 4)$$ **Note**: $-(-4) = +4$

Exercises

1. The point-slope form of the equation of a line that passes through (x_1, y_1) with a slope m is _____ .

2. Use the point-slope form of each equation to identify the slope of the line and the point the line passes through. Hint: See Examples 1 and 2.

   a. $y - 5 = 3(x - 4)$ **b.** $y - 2 = -4(x - 3)$ **c.** $y - 1 = 9(x + 6)$

   d. $y + 3 = 7(x - 4)$ **e.** $y + 5 = \frac{4}{5}(x + 1)$ **f.** $y - 2 = \frac{-3}{7}(x + 4)$

   g. $y - 3 = \frac{-2}{5}(x - 8)$ **h.** $y - 3 \cdot 5 = -2 \cdot 4(x - 8)$ **i.** $y - 2 = -6(x + 3)$

3. Write the point-slope form of the equation of a line with the given slope that passes through the given points. Hint: See Examples 3 and 4.

   a. slope = 4, point is (2, 7)   **b.** slope = -2, point is (-2, 3)

   c. slope = 1, point is (5, 6)   **d.** slope = $\frac{3}{7}$, point is (6, -3)

   e. slope = $-\frac{1}{9}$, point is (-2, 5)   **f.** slope = 12, point is (7, 2)

Challenge Questions

4. Use the point-slope form of each equation to identify the slope of the line and the point the line passes through.

a. $y - 10 = 4(x - 12)$ **b.** $y + 2 = \dfrac{-7}{8}(x - 4 \cdot 5)$

5. Write the point-slope form of the equation of the line with the given slope that passes through the given points.
   a. slope $= 13$, point is $(3, 16)$ **b.** slope $= -3$, point is $(-2, -5)$

PARALLEL AND PERPENDICULAR LINES

How to Write the Point-slope Form of the Equation of a Line that is Parallel to a Given Line and Passes Through a Given Point

Example 1
Write the point-slope form of the equation of a line that is parallel to $y = 5x - 2$ and passes through $(3, -4)$.
Solution
We need the slope and the point that the line passes through to write the point-slope form of the equation of the line. It is given that the line passes through $(3,-4)$, and therefore, we need to find the slope of the line.

To find the slope of the line:
It is given that the line is parallel to $y = 5x - 2$, and $y = 5x - 2$ is in the **slope-intercept form** of $y = mx + b$ where m is the slope and the y-intercept is b. By comparing or matching the two equations $y = 5x - 2$ and $y = mx + b$, the slope of $y = 5x - 2$ is 5 as shown:

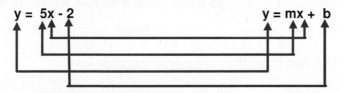

Recall that the line that is parallel to $y = 5x - 2$ **must also have a slope of 5 because parallel lines have the same slope**.

Let us write the equation of a line which has slope of 5 and passes through $(3, -4)$.
Recall that the **point-slope** of an equation of a line with slope m and passes through (x_1, y_1) is:
$$y - y_1 = m(x - x_1). \underline{\hspace{6cm}}[A]$$
Similarly the point-slope of an equation of a line with slope of 5 and passes through $(3, -4)$ is:

671

$$y - (-4) = 5(x - 3)$$ 　　　Substitute m = 5, x_1 = 3, and y_1 = -4 into equation [A].

$$y + 4 = 5(x - 3)$$ 　　　**Note**: -(-4) = 4.

How to Write the Point-slope Form of the Equation of the Line Which is Perpendicular to a Given Line and Passes Through a Given Point.

Example 2
Write the **point-slope form** of the equation of a line that is perpendicular to y = -8x and passes through (-2, -6).

Solution
We need the slope and the point that the line passes through to write the point-slope form of the equation of the line. It is given that the line passes through (-2, -6), and therefore, we need to find the slope of the line.

To find the slope of the line:
It is given that the line is perpendicular to y = -8x, and y = -8x is in the slope-intercept form (if we add zero to the equation, see the diagram.) of y = mx + b where m is the slope and y-intercept is b. By comparing or matching the two equations, y = -8x and y = mx + b, the slope of the line is -8 and the y-intercept = 0 as shown:

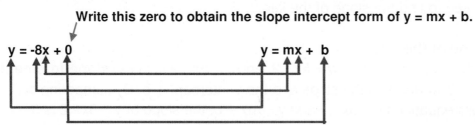

Write this zero to obtain the slope intercept form of y = mx + b.

y = -8x + 0 　　　　　　　　　　　y = mx + b

Recall that the line that is perpendicular to y = -8x must have **a slope which is a negative reciprocal of -8**, which is $-\dfrac{1}{-8} = \dfrac{1}{8}$, 　　　Note: $-\dfrac{1}{-8} = \dfrac{-1}{-8} = \dfrac{1}{8}$.

or the product of the slopes of the two lines that are perpendicular = -1.

For example, $-8 \times \dfrac{1}{8} = -\overset{-1}{\cancel{8}} \times \dfrac{1}{\cancel{8}}$ 　　　　　Divide by 8.

$$= -1$$ 　　　　　**Note**: Review Reciprocals.

The slope of the line that is perpendicular to y = -8x is $\dfrac{1}{8}$.

Let us write the equation of a line which has a slope of $\dfrac{1}{8}$ and passes

through (-2, -6).

Recall that the point-slope form of an equation of a line with a slope m and passes through (x_1, y_1) is:

$$y - y_1 = m(x - x_1) \text{——————————————[B]}$$

Similarly, the point-slope of an equation of a line with a slope $\dfrac{1}{8}$ and passes through

(-2, -6) is:

$$y - (-6) = \frac{1}{8}[x - (-2)]$$

$$y + 6 = \frac{1}{8}(x + 2) \qquad\qquad \text{Note: } -(-6) = 6 \text{ and } -(-2) = 2.$$

Exercises

Write the point-slope form of the equation of each of the lines described:

1. The line parallel to $y = 4x + 3$ and passes through (3, -5). Hint: See Example 1.
2. The line parallel to $y = 5x - 4$ and passes through (6, 4). Hint: See Example 1.
3. The line parallel to $y = -7x + 2$ and passes through (-4, -2). Hint: See Example 1.
4. The line perpendicular to $y = -5x + 1$ and passes through (-3, -2).
   Hint: See Example 2.
5. The line perpendicular to $y = -9x - 4$ and passes through (4, 3).
   Hint: See Example 2.
6. The line perpendicular to $y = 3x + 10$ and passes through (1, -4).
   Hint: See Example 2.

Challenge Questions

Write the point-slope form of the equation of each of the lines described:

7. The line parallel to $y = 8x + 4$ and passes through (2, -5).
8. The line perpendicular to $y = -5x + 8$ and passes through (-7, 4).
9. The line parallel to $y = -10x - 2$ and passes through (-6, 2).
10. The line perpendicular to $y = 12x - 7$ and passes through (-3, 4).

Answers to Selected Questions

1. $y + 5 = 4(x - 3)$ **4.** $y + 2 = \dfrac{1}{5}(x + 3)$

SCATTER PLOTS

New Terms: scatter plot, correlation, positive correlation, negative correlation,

no correlation, line of best fit

Scatter plots show relationships between two sets of data.
A **correlation** is when two variables are related in some way and the correlation describes the type of relationship between the two data sets.

The **three major types** of the correlations are:
1. **Positive correlation**
2. **Negative correlation**
3. **No correlation**

A **positive correlation** between two variables is when one variable (for example x) increases as the other variable (for example y) also increases. See Figure 1.
A **negative correlation** between two variables is when one variable (for example x) decreases as the other variable (for example y) increases. See Figure 2.
A **no correlation** between two variables is when the changes in one variable (for example x) do not affect the other variable (for example y). See Figure 3.

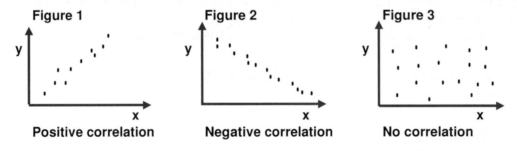

Figure 1	Figure 2	Figure 3
Positive correlation	Negative correlation	No correlation

Examples of three real-world variables that have positive correlations are:
1. Increase in the time (weeks) to exercise, results in increased weight loss. The variables here are time and "weight loss."
2. The more time it takes to snow, the more inches of snow will be on the ground. The variables here are time and "inches of snow."
3. More effective study time results in higher grades. The variables here are time and grades.

Group Exercises
The class may be divided into four teams.
1. Each team should list five real-world variables that have a negative correlation. Does an increase in one variable cause a decrease in the other variable?
2. Each team should list their five variables on the blackboard, and then explain them to the class.

Line of Best Fit

The line of best fit is the line which is drawn on the scatter plot such that the line is the closest to all the points on the scatter plot.

Estimating the Line of Best Fit

The line of best fit can be estimated by laying a ruler's edge over the scattered plot, and then adjusting the ruler until the ruler appears to be closest to all of the points. Use a pencil to draw the line along the edge of the ruler and this line is the line of best fit. The line of best fit is shown in Figure 4 and Figure 5.

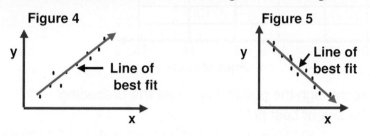

Strong and Weak Correlations

A strong correlation of two variables is when the points on the scatter plot are close together or when the points are close to the line of best fit. Figure 6 shows positive strong correlation and figure 8 shows negative strong correlation.

A weak correlation of two variables is when the points on the scatter plot are wide spread about the line of best fit. Figure 7 shows a weak positive correlation and figure 9 shows a negative weak correlation.

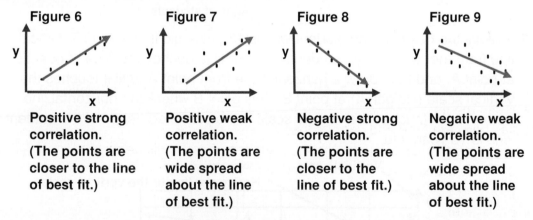

Using a Scatter Plot to Make Predictions

Example 1

Use the data to predict the height of a student who is 13 years old.

Heights (ft.)	5.4	5.5	6.0	5.0	5.0	6.4	6.0
Age of students (years)	11	12	14	12	11	14	15

Solution

Step 1: Indicate the ordered pair of the points (11, 5.4), (12, 5.5), (14, 6.0),

(12, 5.0), (11, 5.0), and (15, 5.8) on a graph paper as shown. This is the same as making a scatter plot of a data set.

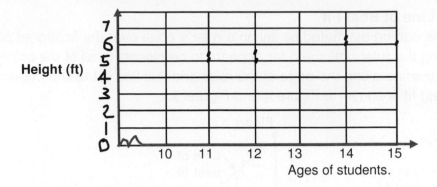

Step 2: Draw the line of best fit through the points. Hint: See the preceding notes on "estimating the line of best fit."

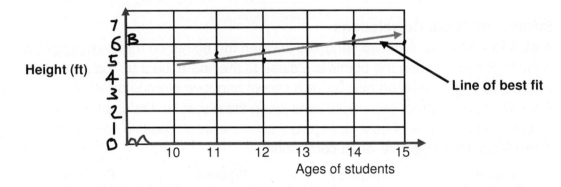

Step 3: Predict the height of the student who is 13 years old by drawing a vertical line from the "ages of the students" axis until it touches the "line of best fit" at point A, and then draw a horizontal line from point A until it touches the vertical scale (Height, ft) at point B. This point B where the horizontal line from point A touches the vertical scale is the predicted height of the student who is 13 years old.

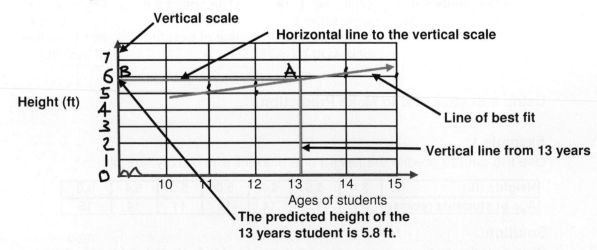

Exercises

1a. What is a correlation?

1b. What are the three major types of correlations?
Hint: See the preceding notes.

2a. Describe 2 positive correlations using a diagram.

2b. Describe 2 negative correlations using a diagram.

2c. Describe no correlation with a diagram.
Hint: See the preceding notes.

3a. Describe the "line of best fit".

3b. Describe how to estimate the "line of best fit". Hint: See preceding notes.

4. In your **own words**, explain what is meant by a strong correlation and a weak correlation using a diagram. Hint: See the preceding notes.

5. Explain how a scatter plot can be used to make predictions. Hint: See Example 1.

6. Use the data to predict the test grade for a student who studies:

(a). 8 hours.
(b). 4 hours.
©. 2 hours.
Hint: See Example 1.

Hours studied	10	5	7	6	12
Test grades	98	75	85	80	100

Challenge Questions

7. What is the difference between a strong correlation and a weak correlation?

8. What is the difference between a positive strong correlation and a negative strong correlation?

9. Use the data to predict the apparent temperature at (**a**) 30% humidity

(**b**) 90% humidity

Temperature due to humidity at room temperature of 70º F.						
Humidity (%).	0	20	40	60	80	100
Apparent temperature (ºF).	62	65	67	70	72	74

10. Use the data to predict the test grade for a student who studies:

(a). 6 hours.
(b). 10 hours.
©. 7 hours

Hours studied	5	2	3	9	12
Test grades	75	68	78	90	95

LINE OF BEST FIT

(Review the chapter on Coordinate Geometry before reading this chapter.)

The **line of best fit** is the line that is closest to all the points on a scatter plot such that about the same number of points are above the line as they are below the line.

Use of the Line of Best Fit
The line of best fit can be used to make **predictions** as shown in Example 1.

How to Estimate the Equation of a Line of Best Fit.
The steps for estimating the equation of a line of best fit are as follows:
Step 1: Find the means of the x-coordinate and y-coordinates and let the coordinates of the means be (x, y).
Step 2: Draw a line through (x, y) that appears to best fit the data such that about the same number of points are above the line as below the line.
Step 3: Estimate the coordinates of another point on the line.
Step 4: Find the equation of the line by finding the slope and then using the **point-slope form**.

Example 1

a. Plot the data and find the line of best fit.

b. Use the equation of the line of best fit to predict the value of y when x = 100.

x	3	1	2	7	6	8
y	3	2	5	10	6	10

Solution

a. The coordinates (x, y) for (3, 3), (1, 2), (2, 5), (7, 10), (6, 6), and (8,10) are plotted on graph paper as shown:

(The coordinates are located on the next page.)

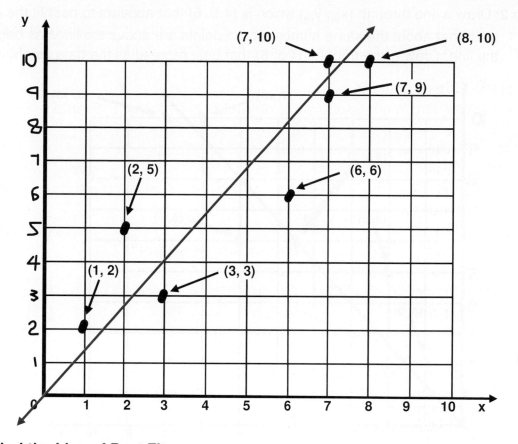

To Find the Line of Best Fit

Step 1: Find the means of the x-coordinates and the y-coordinates.

$$\text{Mean of the x-coordinates} = x_m = \frac{\text{Sum of x-coordinates}}{\text{Total number of x-coordinates.}}$$

$$= \frac{3 + 1 + 2 + 7 + 6 + 8}{6}$$

$$= \frac{27}{6} = 4.5$$

$$\text{Mean of y-coordinates} = y_m = \frac{\text{Sum of y-coordinates}}{\text{Total number of y-coordinates}}$$

$$= \frac{3 + 2 + 5 + 10 + 6 + 10}{6}$$

$$= \frac{36}{6}$$

$$= 6$$

Therefore, $(x_m, y_m) = (4.5, 6)$.

Step 2: Draw a line through (x_m, y_m) which is (4.5, 6) that appears to best fit the data such that about the same number of the points are above the lines as below the line. Draw a line through (4.5, 6) that best represents the data as shown:

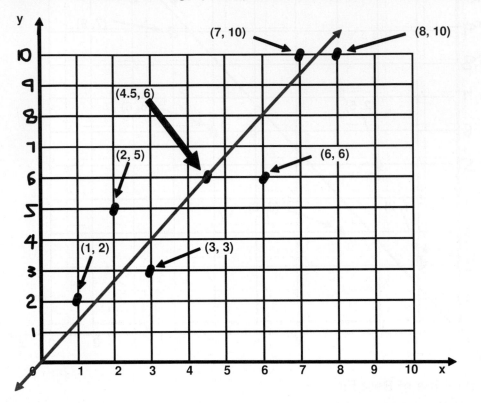

Step 3: Estimate the coordinates of another point on the line and then plot this second point on the line. The coordinates (3, 4) is another point on the line as shown:

(The coordinates (3, 4) are on the next page.)

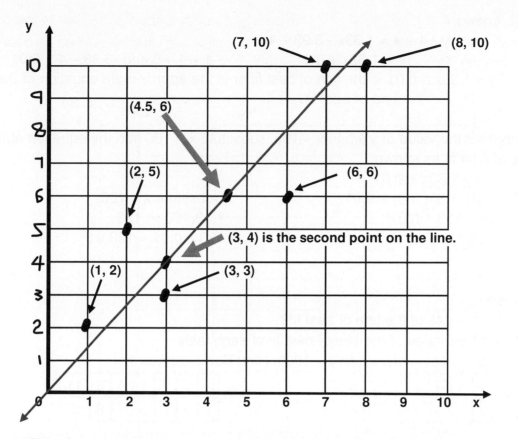

Step 4: Find the equation of the line by finding the slope and then using the point-slope form.

Let us use the two coordinates (3, 4) and (4.5, 6) to find the slope.

$$\text{Slope} = m = \frac{y_2 - y_1}{x_2 - x_1}$$

$$= \frac{6 - 4}{4.5 - 3} \qquad (x_1, y_1) = (3, 4) \text{ and } (x_2, y_2) = (4.5, 6).$$

$$= \frac{2}{1.5}$$

$$\approx 1.33 \qquad\qquad \text{You may use a calculator.}$$

Let us use the **point-slope form** to find the equation of the line of best fit as shown:

The equation of a line using the **point-slope form** is:

$$y - y_1 = m \,(x - x_1)$$

$$y - 4 \approx 1.33(x - 3) \qquad\qquad x_1 = 3,\ y_1 = 4,\ \text{and } m \approx 1.33$$

$$y - 4 \approx 1.33x - 3 \cdot 1.33$$

$$y - 4 \approx 1.33x - 3.99 \underline{\hspace{6cm}}[\text{A}]$$

Add 4 to both sides of equation $[\text{A}]$ in order to obtain the value of y as shown:

$$y - 4 + 4 \approx 1.33x - 3.99 + 4$$
$$y \approx 1.33x + 0.01 \qquad\qquad -4 + 4 = 0 \text{ and } -3.99 + 4 = 0.01.$$

$y \approx 1.33x + 0.01$ is the line of best fit or is the approximate equation of the line of best fit.

b. To predict the value of y when x = 100, substitute x = 100 into the equation of the line of best fit as shown:

$$y \approx 1.33x + 0.01$$
$$y \approx 1.33(100) + 0.01 \qquad\qquad \text{Substitute } x = 100.$$
$$y \approx 133 + 0.01 \qquad\qquad 1.33(100) = 133$$
$$y \approx 133.01 \qquad\qquad 133 + 0.01 = 133.01$$

Exercises

1. What is the use of the line of best fit?

2a. Find the equation of the line of best fit of each table.

2b. Predict the value of y when x = 1000. Hint: See Example 1.

1.

x	3	4	4	1	7	6
y	1	7	4	2	7	6

2.

x	5	7	1	4	8	11
y	5	7	3	7	8	12

3.

x	4	2	6	8	9	3	7	1
y	5	3	7	8	9	5	8	2

4.

x	0	3	5	6	7	8	10
y	3	3	6	9	7	8	11

5.

x	2	7	4	0	2	2
y	3	1	1	6	5	6

6.

x	4	6	9	0	3	7	8	9
y	1	8	11	5	7	3	8	9

Cumulative Review

1. The side of a square is 4 ft. What is the area of the square?

2. An equilateral triangle has a side of 10 cm.

    a. What is the area of the triangle?

    b. What is the perimeter of the triangle?

CHAPTER 25

CONGRUENT TRIANGLES

Cumulative Review

1. Describe how you would write 7.1723×10^6 in the standard notation. Hint: If you cannot solve this exercise, review the chapter on Scientific Notations.
2. Describe how you would write 0.01061 in the scientific notation. Hint: If you cannot solve this exercise, review the chapter on Scientific Notations.
3. The diameter of a circle is 14 cm.
   a. Find the radius of the circle.
   b. Find the area of the circle.
   Hint: Review the MathMasters Series for grade 6.
4. A side of a square figure is 5 ft.
   a. Find the perimeter of the square.
   b. Find the area of the square.
   Hint: Review the MathMasters Series for grade 6.
5. Describe how you would find the median of each data:
   a. 2, 10, 6, 13, 4   b. 4, 6, 3, 7   c. 6.6, 2, 8, 4.7, 1, 4.7
   Hint: If you cannot solve these exercises, review the section of the MathMasters Series on median.

Congruent Triangles
New Terms: congruent

Two triangles are **congruent** to each other if their corresponding sides and angles are equal. If $\triangle ABC$ and $\triangle XYZ$ are congruent, then the corresponding sides and angles are equal as follows:

Comparing Sides

$\overline{AB}$ corresponds to $\overline{XY}$, therefore $\overline{AB} = \overline{XY}$

$\overline{BC}$ corresponds to $\overline{YZ}$ therefore $\overline{BC} = \overline{YZ}$

$\overline{AC}$ corresponds to $\overline{XZ}$ therefore $\overline{AC} = \overline{XZ}$

Comparing Angles

$\angle A$ corresponds to $\angle X$ therefore $\angle A = \angle x$

$\angle B$ corresponds to $\angle Y$ therefore $\angle B = \angle Y$

$\angle C$ corresponds to $\angle Z$ therefore $\angle C = \angle Z$

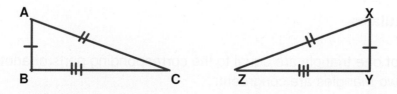

How to Determine the Corresponding Sides and the Corresponding Angles Between Two Triangles

Example 1

How could you determine the corresponding sides and the corresponding angles between two triangles?

Solutions

In order to determine the corresponding sides and the corresponding angles between two triangles, imagine that one triangle is put over the other triangle to coincide. The pairs of matching sides of both triangles are called a one-to-one correspondence and each pair of the matching sides form a specific corresponding side which are equal to one another. Similarly the pairs of matching angles of both triangles are called one-to-one correspondence and each pair of the matching angles form specific corresponding angles which equal to one another.

For example, $\triangle ABC$ is congruent to $\triangle DEF$, and therefore, if we imagine that we place $\triangle DEF$ over $\triangle ABC$ to coincide, the matching pairs of sides and angles are:

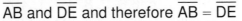

$\overline{AB}$ and $\overline{DE}$ and therefore $\overline{AB} = \overline{DE}$

$\overline{BC}$ and $\overline{DF}$ and therefore $\overline{BC} = \overline{DF}$

$\overline{AC}$ and $\overline{EF}$ and therefore $\overline{AC} = \overline{EF}$

$\angle A$ and $\angle E$ and therefore $\angle A = \angle E$

$\angle B$ and $\angle D$ and therefore $\angle B = \angle D$

$\angle C$ and $\angle F$ and therefore $\angle C = \angle F$

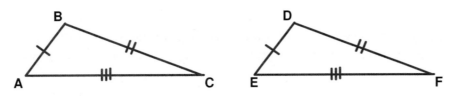

Congruence Postulate

The 3 basic congruence postulates that are used to prove that two triangles are congruent are:

1. **SSS** (side-side-side) Congruence Postulate

2. **SAS** (side-angle-side) Congruence Postulate

3. **ASA** (Angle-side-Angle) Congruence Postulate.

3 Congruence Postulates

1. SSS

If the three sides of one triangle are equal to the corresponding parts of another triangle then the two triangles are congruent.

2. SAS

If the two sides and the **included angle** of one triangle are equal to the corresponding parts of another triangle then the two triangles are congruent.

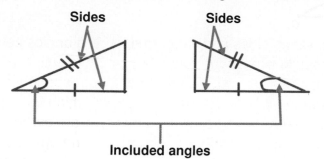

Note that in this particular case, included angle means that the angle is **between the two corresponding sides** of each triangle.

3. ASA

If two angles and the **included sides** of one triangle are equal to the corresponding parts of another triangle, then the triangles are congruent.

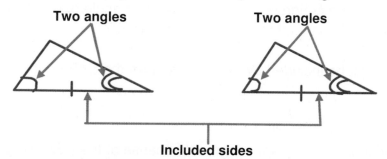

Note that in this particular case, included side means that the side is **between the two corresponding angles** of each triangle.

Critical Exclusions From the Congruence Postulate

The following are not Congruence Postulate.

1. AAA
2. SAA or AAS

Example 1

Draw a triangle and label its vertices A, B, and C.

a. Which sides include ∠B?

b. Which side of the triangle is included by ∠A and ∠B?

c. Which angle is included by sides $\overline{BC}$ and $\overline{AC}$?

d. Which angles include $\overline{AC}$?

Solution

Draw the △ABC.

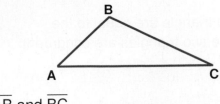

a. $\overline{AB}$ and $\overline{BC}$

b. $\overline{AB}$

c. $\angle C$

d. $\angle A$ and $\angle C$

Example 2

John says that two triangles are congruent if the three angles of one triangle are equal to the corresponding angles of the other. Is this correct?

Solution

No, because there is no AAA congruence postulate.

Example 3

Mary said that two triangles are congruent if two sides and an angle of one triangle are equal to the corresponding parts of the other. Is this correct?

Solution

No, because the angle must be included by the sides to form the SAS congruence postulate.

Example 4

Nick said that the two triangles shown are congruent because of the ASA congruence postulate. **Note** that the number of arcs and tick marks indicate the pairs of parts that are equal. Is this correct?

Solution

No, because the sides are not included by the angles.

Example 5

In each pair of triangles, the tick marks and the arcs identify equal parts. Write which congruence postulate that makes any pair of the triangles congruent, otherwise write "not congruent." Explain your answers as needed. The solutions to this example provide the students with useful road map with critical bench marks for solving problems.

a.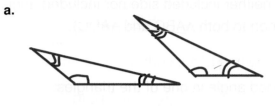

b.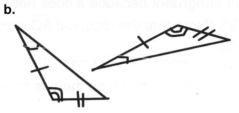

c.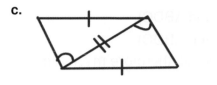

d.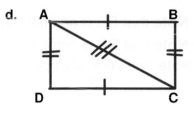

e.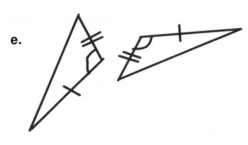

f.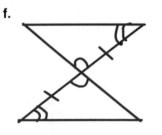

g.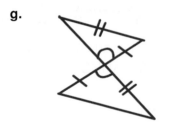

h.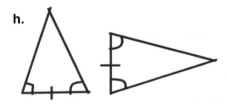

i.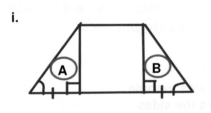

j.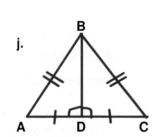

k.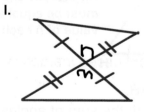

l.

Solution

5a. Not congruent, there is no AAA congruence postulate.

5b. SAS or ASA.

Writing Similar Figures and Congruent Figures Using Symbols

The symbol for a triangle is △.

1. We can write that triangle ABC is similar to triangle DEF by using the symbols as shown: △ABC ∽ △DEF

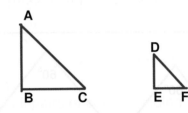

2. We can write that triangle PQW is congruent to triangle XYZ by using symbols as shown: △PQW ≅ △XYZ

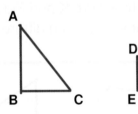

Group Discussion

Triangles ABC and triangles DEF are similar.

Similar polygons have corresponding angles and corresponding sides.

Note that when two figures are similar, for each part of one figure, there is a corresponding part on the other figure. To determine the corresponding angles and the corresponding sides of similar polygons, compare the shape of the polygons and then determine how each pair of angles and each pair of sides form corresponding parts as shown:

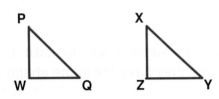

Corresponding Angles

∠A corresponds to ∠D

∠B corresponds to ∠E

∠C corresponds to ∠F

∠ is the symbol for angle.

Corresponding Sides

$\overline{AB}$ corresponds to $\overline{DE}$

$\overline{BC}$ corresponds to $\overline{EF}$

$\overline{AC}$ corresponds to $\overline{DF}$

Note that the angles in △ABC are congruent to the corresponding angles in △DEF and the length of the sides of △DEF are about twice the length of the corresponding sides in △ABC.

Conclusion: Note that in similar figures the **corresponding angles are congruent** (the same measure of angles), and the ratio of the lengths of the corresponding sides are **equal**.

Group Exercise

Given that △ABC is similar to △DEF, copy and complete the statements:

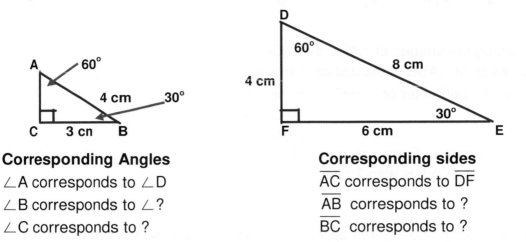

Corresponding Angles

∠A corresponds to ∠D

∠B corresponds to ∠?

∠C corresponds to ?

Corresponding sides

$\overline{AC}$ corresponds to $\overline{DF}$

$\overline{AB}$ corresponds to ?

$\overline{BC}$ corresponds to ?

Example 1

Given that the trapezoid ABCD is similar to the trapezoid EFGH, list all the pairs of the corresponding sides.

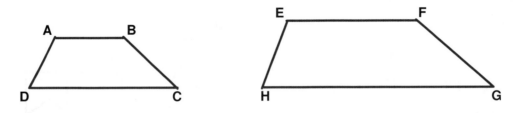

Solution

By comparing the shapes of the trapezoids ABCD and EFGH,

$\overline{AB}$ corresponds to $\overline{EF}$

$\overline{BC}$ corresponds to $\overline{FG}$

$\overline{CD}$ corresponds to $\overline{GH}$

$\overline{DA}$ corresponds to $\overline{HE}$

Example 2

Given that △ABC is congruent to △DEF,

a. What side of △DEF corresponds to side $\overline{AC}$?

b. What is the perimeter of △DEF ?

c. What is the length of $\overline{DF}$?

Smaller figure

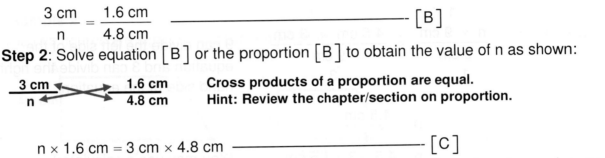

$$\frac{\overline{AB}}{\overline{IJ}} = \frac{\overline{AH}}{\overline{IP}} \qquad\qquad [A]$$

Smaller

Bigger figure

Bigger figure

(Note: It is very important to remember the order of the ratios such that for this specific example, the smaller figure value divides the bigger figure value on both sides of the equation $[A]$ as shown.)

From the figures, $\overline{AB} = 3$ cm, $\overline{IJ} = n$, $\overline{AH} = 1.6$ cm, and $\overline{IP} = 4.8$ cm.

Substitute $\overline{AB} = 3$ cm, $\overline{IJ} = n$, $\overline{AH} = 1.6$ cm, and $\overline{IP} = 4.8$ cm into equation $[A]$ as shown:

$$\frac{3 \text{ cm}}{n} = \frac{1.6 \text{ cm}}{4.8 \text{ cm}} \qquad\qquad [B]$$

Step 2: Solve equation $[B]$ or the proportion $[B]$ to obtain the value of n as shown:

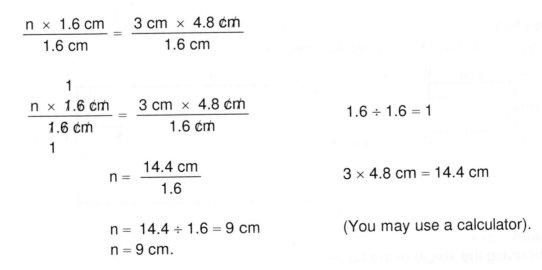

$$\frac{3 \text{ cm}}{n} \diagdown \diagup \frac{1.6 \text{ cm}}{4.8 \text{ cm}}$$

Cross products of a proportion are equal.
Hint: Review the chapter/section on proportion.

$$n \times 1.6 \text{ cm} = 3 \text{ cm} \times 4.8 \text{ cm} \qquad\qquad [C]$$

Divide both sides of equation $[C]$ by 1.6 cm in order to obtain the value of n as shown:

$$\frac{n \times 1.6 \text{ cm}}{1.6 \text{ cm}} = \frac{3 \text{ cm} \times 4.8 \text{ cm}}{1.6 \text{ cm}}$$

$$\frac{n \times 1.6 \,\cancel{cm}}{1.6 \,\cancel{cm}} = \frac{3 \text{ cm} \times 4.8 \,\cancel{cm}}{1.6 \,\cancel{cm}} \qquad\qquad 1.6 \div 1.6 = 1$$

$$n = \frac{14.4 \text{ cm}}{1.6} \qquad\qquad 3 \times 4.8 \text{ cm} = 14.4 \text{ cm}$$

$$n = 14.4 \div 1.6 = 9 \text{ cm} \qquad\qquad \text{(You may use a calculator)}.$$

$$n = 9 \text{ cm}.$$

Exercise

1. Each pair of figures are similar. Write and solve the proportion to find the length n.
   Hint: See Example 1.

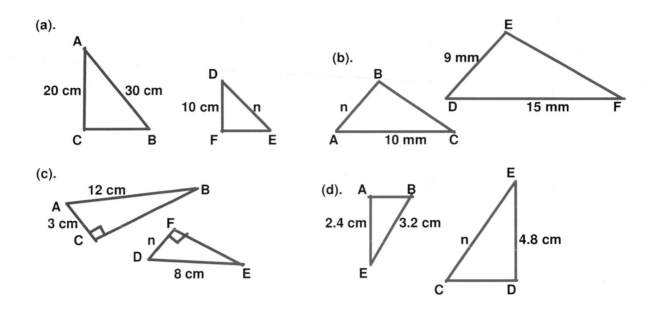

(a).
A
20 cm   30 cm
C   B

D
10 cm   n
F   E

(b).
E
9 mm
B
n
D   15 mm   F
A   10 mm   C

(c).
12 cm
A   B
3 cm
C
F
n
D
8 cm   E

(d).   A   B
2.4 cm   3.2 cm
E
E
n   4.8 cm
C   D

2. Each pair of figures are similar. Write and solve the proportion to find the length n.
Hint: See Example 2.

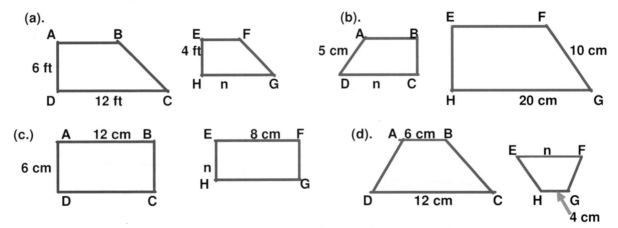

(a).
A   B
6 ft
D   12 ft   C
E   F
4 ft
H   n   G

(b).
A   B
5 cm
D   n   C
E   F
10 cm
H   20 cm   G

(c.)   A   12 cm   B
6 cm
D   C
E   8 cm   F
n
H   G

(d).   A 6 cm B
D   12 cm   C
E   n   F
H   G
4 cm

3. Each pair of figures are similar. Write and solve the proportion to find the length n.
Hint: See Example 3.

(The figures are located on the next page.)

SCALE DRAWINGS

What is a **scale drawing**? A **scale drawing** shows a real distance smaller than or longer than the real distance. When a scale drawing shows a real distance that is smaller than the real distance, is called a **reduction**. When a scale drawing shows a real distance that is longer than the real distance, is called an **enlargement**. A **map scale** is the ratio that compares the distance on a map to the actual distance.

Team Project 1
Goal of the project: To use a scale drawing and a map scale to find the actual distance between Peki and Hoe by using equivalent ratios.
Method:

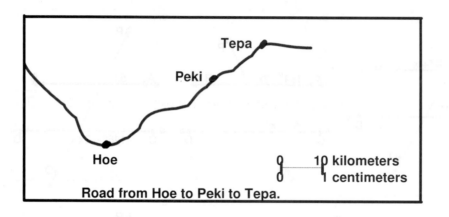

Road from Hoe to Peki to Tepa.

Step 1: **Read the map scale.**

The map shows the scale of 1 cm = 10 km, or $\dfrac{1 \text{ cm}}{10 \text{ km}}$.

Step 2: **Use a string to measure the distance from Peki to Hoe on the map**.
The distance between Peki and Hoe is marked on the string.

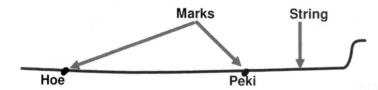

(**Note**: The distance from Hoe to Peki on the string is an approximate distance.)
Step 3: **Use a centimeter ruler to measure the distance between the two marks on the string as shown**.
The distance between the two marks on the string is about 5.2 cm.

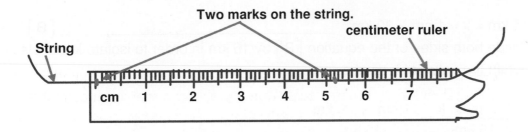

Two marks on the string.

centimeter ruler

String

cm 1   2   3   4   5   6   7

Step 4: **Use equivalent ratios to find the actual distance as shown**:

$$\frac{1}{10} = \frac{5.2}{k}$$

k is the actual distance in kilometers.

Hint: Review the chapter/section on equivalent ratios.

$1 \times k = 10 \times 5.2$ Cross multiply.

$k = 52$ km

Therefore, the distance from Peki to Hoe is 52 km.

Team Project 2

Goal of the project: To use the scale drawing and the map scale to find the actual distance between Peki and Tepa by using equivalent ratios. Use the map provided under Team Project 1. Use the same method as in Team Project 1 to find the distance between Peki and Tepa.

Example 1

Complete the map scale ratio table.

Map distance (cm)	1	?	5	?
Actual distance (km)	15	30	?	105

Solution

To find the map distance when the actual distance is 30 km.

Step 1: From the table, the map scale is 1 cm = 15 km or $\frac{1 \text{ cm}}{15 \text{ km}}$.

Step 2: When the actual distance is 30 km, let the map distance be k.

Step 3: Use equivalent ratios to find the map distance as shown:

$$\frac{1 \text{ cm}}{15 \text{ km}} = \frac{k}{30 \text{ km}} \qquad\qquad\qquad\qquad\qquad\qquad\text{[A]}$$

Step 4: Cross multiply equation $[A]$ because **cross products of equivalent ratios are equal** as shown:

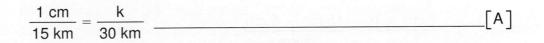

$$\frac{1 \text{ cm}}{15 \text{ km}} \quad\times\quad \frac{k}{30 \text{ km}}$$

15 km × k = 1 cm × 30 km _____[B]

Divide both sides of the equation [B] by 15 km in order to isolate k and also to obtain the value of k as shown:

$$\frac{15 \text{ km} \times k}{15 \text{ km}} = \frac{1 \text{ cm} \times 30 \text{ km}}{15 \text{ km}}$$

$$\frac{\overset{1}{\cancel{15 \text{ km}}} \times k}{\underset{1}{\cancel{15 \text{ km}}}} = \frac{1 \text{ cm} \times \overset{2}{\cancel{30 \text{ km}}}}{\underset{1}{\cancel{15 \text{ km}}}}$$

$$k = 1 \text{ cm} \times 2$$
$$k = 2 \text{ cm}$$

Therefore, when the actual distance = 30 km, the map distance = 2 cm.

To find the actual distance when the map distance is 5 cm.

Step 1: From the table, the map scale is 1 cm = 15 km or $\dfrac{1 \text{ cm}}{15 \text{ km}}$.

Step 2: When the map distance is 5 cm, let the actual distance be n.

Step 3: Use equivalent ratios to find the actual distance as shown:

$$\frac{1 \text{ cm}}{15 \text{ km}} = \frac{5 \text{ cm}}{n} \qquad\qquad\qquad\qquad\qquad [C]$$

Step 4: Cross multiply equation [C] because cross products of equivalent ratios are equal as shown:

$$\frac{1 \text{ cm}}{15 \text{ km}} \diagdown\!\!\!\diagup \frac{5 \text{ cm}}{n}$$

1 cm × n = 15 km × 5 cm. _____[D]

Divide both sides of equation [D] by 1 cm in order to obtain the value for n as shown:

$$\frac{1 \text{ cm} \times n}{1 \text{ cm}} = \frac{15 \text{ km} \times 5 \text{ cm}}{1 \text{ cm}}$$

$$\frac{\overset{1}{\cancel{1 \text{ cm}}} \times n}{\underset{1}{\cancel{1 \text{ cm}}}} = \frac{15 \text{ km} \times \overset{5}{\cancel{5 \text{ cm}}}}{\underset{1}{\cancel{1 \text{ cm}}}}$$

$$n = 15 \text{ km} \times 5$$
$$n = 75 \text{ km}$$

Therefore, when the map distance is 5 cm, the actual distance is 75 km.

To Find the Map Distance When the Actual Distance is 105 km

Step 1: From the table, the map scale is 1 cm =15 km or $\dfrac{1 \text{ cm}}{15 \text{ km}}$.

Step 2: When the map distance is 105 km, let the map distance be w.

Step 3: Use equivalent ratios to find the actual distance as shown:

$$\frac{1 \text{ cm}}{15 \text{ km}} = \frac{w}{105 \text{ km}} \underline{\hspace{6cm}}[E]$$

Step 4: Cross multiply equation [E] because cross products of equivalent ratios are equal as shown:

$$\frac{1 \text{ cm}}{15 \text{ km}} \bowtie \frac{w}{105 \text{ km}}$$

$$1 \text{ cm} \times 105 \text{ km} = 15 \text{ km} \times w \underline{\hspace{5cm}}[F]$$

Divide both sides of equation [F] by 15 km in order to isolate w and also to obtain the value of w as shown:

$$\frac{1 \text{ cm} \times 105 \text{ km}}{15 \text{ km}} = \frac{15 \text{ km} \times w}{15 \text{ km}}$$

$$\frac{1 \text{ cm} \times \overset{7}{\cancel{105}} \cancel{\text{km}}}{\underset{1}{\cancel{15}} \cancel{\text{km}}} = \frac{\overset{1}{\cancel{15}} \cancel{\text{km}} \times w}{\underset{1}{\cancel{15}} \cancel{\text{km}}}$$

$$1 \text{ cm} \times 7 = w$$
$$7 \text{ cm} = w$$

Therefore, when the actual distance is 105 km, the map distance is 7 cm.
Therefore, the completed table is:

Map Distance (cm)	1	2	5	7
Actual distance (km)	15	30	75	105

Example 2

Using the map, an inch ruler and the map scale, find the distance from Peki to Jawa to the nearest mile. Hint: Assume that the distance between any two cities is a straight line, and therefore, the distance can be measured directly with a ruler to the nearest inch.

Map of some cities.

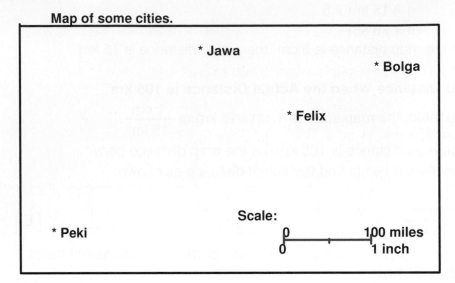

Solution

Step 1: Read the map scale.

The map shows a scale of 1 inch =100 miles or $\dfrac{1 \text{ inch}}{100 \text{ miles}}$.

Step 2: Use an inch ruler to measure the distance from Peki to Jawa on the map. The distance from Peki to Jawa on the map is approximately 2 inches to the nearest inch.

Step 3: When the map distance from Peki to Jawa is 2 inches, let the actual distance from Peki to Jawa be n.

Step 4: Use equivalent ratios to find the actual distance as shown:

$$\dfrac{1 \text{ inch}}{100 \text{ miles}} = \dfrac{2 \text{ inches}}{n} \hspace{2cm} [A]$$

Step 5: Cross multiply equation [A] because cross products of equivalent ratios are equal as shown:

$$1 \text{ in.} \times n = 100 \text{ miles} \times 2 \text{ in.} \hspace{2cm} [B]$$

Step 6: Divide both sides of the equation [B] by 1 in. in order to isolate n and also to obtain the value of n as shown:

$$\dfrac{1 \text{ in.} \times n}{1 \text{ in.}} = \dfrac{100 \text{ miles} \times 2 \text{ in.}}{1 \text{ in.}}$$

$$\frac{1 \text{ in.} \times n}{1 \text{ in.}} = \frac{100 \text{ miles} \times 2 \text{ in.}}{1 \text{ in.}}$$

$$n = 100 \text{ miles} \times 2$$
$$= 200 \text{ miles}$$

Therefore, the distance from Peki to Jawa is 200 miles.

Exercises

1. Explain what is meant by a scale drawing.

2. Explain what is meant by a map scale.

3. Copy and complete each ratio table. Hint: See Example **1**.

a.

Scale length (cm)	1	2	?	4
Actual length (km)	4	?	12	?

b.

Scale length (cm)	1	3	4	?
Actual length (km)	20	?	80	100

c.

Scale length (in.)	1	2	?	4
Actual length (ft)	5	?	15	?

4. Using the map in Example 2, find the:
   a. distance from Peki to Bolga.
   b. distance from Jawa to Bolga.
   Hint: See Example 2. The map distance should be to the nearest whole number. Assume that the road between any two cities is straight, and therefore, a ruler could be used to measure the map distance.

Challenge Questions

5. Copy and complete the ratio tables.

a.

Scale length (cm)	1	3	?
Actual length (km)	10	?	50

b.

Scale length (in.)	1	3	?	?
Actual length (ft)	4	?	24	48

6. Explain how to find the actual distance between two cities on a map.

CHAPTER 29

MEASUREMENT OF ANGLES

Quick Review

1. In the figure, given that $\overleftrightarrow{PQ}$ is a transversal and $\overleftrightarrow{XY}$ is parallel to $\overleftrightarrow{CD}$, find the measure of:
   a. Each obtuse angle.
   b. $\angle 5$.

c. Each acute angle.

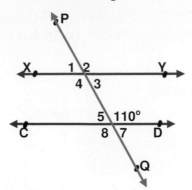

2. Change 125% to a fraction.
3. Find the next three terms of the sequence.

   3, 6, 9, 12, __, __, __.
4. Express the ratio 1 out of 5 as percent.
5. Explain what is meant by the probability of an event is:

   a. 0   **b.** 1   **c.** 50%   **d.** 100%

New Terms: **protractor**, **center of protractor**, **placement**

Example 1
(a) What instrument is used to measure angles?
(b) Describe a protractor.
Solution
(a) The instrument which is used to measure angles is the **protractor**.
(b) A protractor usually consist of a half circle or a half circular shape cut from transparent material or metal. A protractor is drawn below.

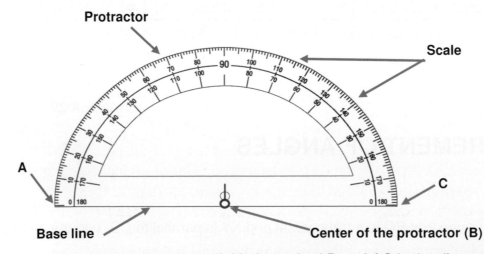

A protractor has a center and this is marked B and AC is the diameter of the protractor. The curved edge is divided and marked off equally in degrees from

722

0^0 to 180^0 in both clockwise and counterclockwise directions. This curved marked off section of the protractor is the scale of the protractor. AC is the base line of the protractor which is the same as the zero degree or 180^0 division line of the protractor.

Special Note

There are many styles of the protractors but they are all **used for measuring or drawing angles**.

Example 2

Describe how you would measure $\angle$AQB in the diagram, and then find the measurement of $\angle$AQB.

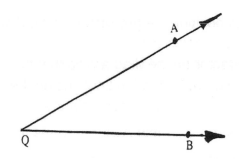

Solution

Place the protractor so that its **center** coincides with Q (which is the vertex of the angle) and its zero line (base line) should be lying along $\overrightarrow{QB}$ as shown in the diagram.

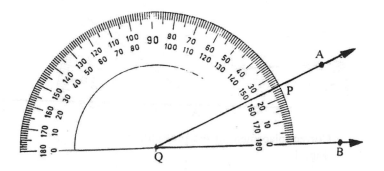

QA (which is the other side of the angle) then crosses the arc of the protractor at P. The ray QA should be lying along the degree scale at a point which indicates the number of degrees in the angle. From the diagram, the measure of $\angle$AQB is 25^0 because the ray QA is on the 25^0 scale mark of the protractor. (**Note** that it is always important to realize that the **center point of the protractor** must be placed at the point at which the angle is located and in this question the angle is located at point Q, and therefore, the protractor center coincided with point Q. The point Q is known as the vertex.)

35^0. Therefore, the measurement of angle A is 35^0 as shown in the next diagram.

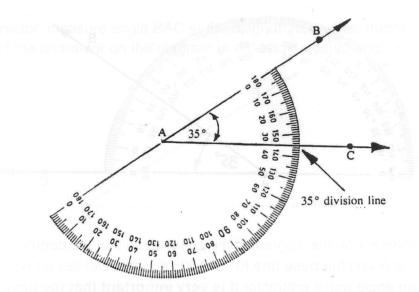

35° division line

Example 4

Describe how to draw an angle ABC which is 30^0, and then draw the angle ABC.

Solution

Note that when three letters of the alphabets are used to name an angle such as angle ABC or ∠ABC, the middle letter (in this case, B) is the vertex of the triangle and the angle is formed at the vertex of the triangle.

Draw a segment and label it BC, and note that the segment starts from B because B is the middle letter and the angle is formed at the middle letter as the vertex.

B   C

Note that the **center point** of the protractor must be placed at the point at which the angle is to be drawn. Since the angle is to be drawn at the point B, place the protractor such that its **center point** is on B and its 0^0 line (base line) is on the ray BC. Counting the number of degrees from the ray BC as 0^0, mark a point A on the paper at the desired degree reading on the scale of the protractor. From the question, the desired degree measurement is 30^0, and therefore, mark the point A at the 30^0 reading mark on the protractor scale.

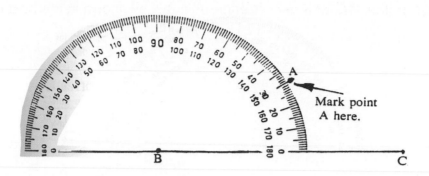

The protractor is removed and the ray BA is drawn with a pencil and a ruler to form the angle ABC with an angle measure of 30^0 as shown in the next diagram.

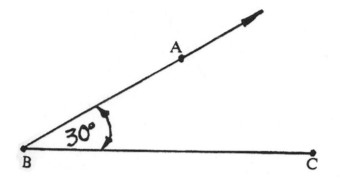

Example 5

Using a protractor, draw an angle BOA which is 60^0.

Solution

Note that when three letters of the alphabets are used to name an angle such as angle BOA or $\angle$ BOA, the middle letter of the alphabet (in this case, O), is the vertex of the triangle and the angle is formed at the vertex of the triangle.

Step 1: Draw the ray OA.

Note that the ray starts from O, because O is the middle letter of the alphabet and the angles are formed at the middle letter of the alphabets as the vertex.

Step 2: Put the protractor center on O with the 0^0 division mark of the protractor scale on ray OA, mark B at 60^0.

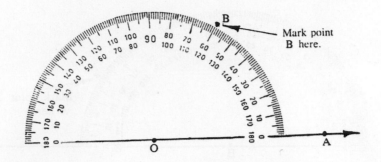

Mark point
B here.

Step 3: Remove the protractor and use a pencil and a ruler to draw the ray OB.
The $m\angle BOA = 60^0$.

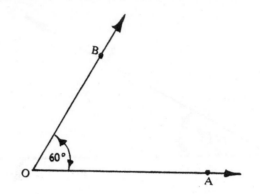

60°

Example 6

Using a protractor, a pencil and a ruler, draw $\angle ABC$ which is 140^0.

Solution

Step 1: Draw the $\overrightarrow{BC}$. Note that the ray starts from B because B is the middle letter of the alphabet in the $\angle ABC$, and therefore, B is the vertex.

Step 2: Put the protractor **center point** on B with the 0^0 division mark on the protractor on $\overrightarrow{BC}$ and then mark point A on the paper at 140^0 division scale marking on the protractor.

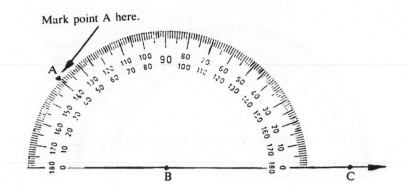

Mark point A here.

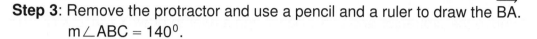

B   C

Step 3: Remove the protractor and use a pencil and a ruler to draw the $\overrightarrow{BA}$.
m∠ABC = 140⁰.

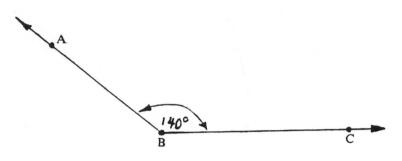

140°

B   C

Example 7

Using a protractor draw ∠XYZ which is 75⁰.

Solution

Step 1: Draw the $\overrightarrow{YZ}$. Note that the ray starts with Y because Y is the middle letter of the alphabets in the angle XYZ, and therefore, Y is the vertex of the angle XYZ.

Y   Z

Step 2: Put the protractor **center point** on point Y with the 0⁰ division mark (base line) on the protractor scale on $\overrightarrow{YZ}$, and then mark the point X on the paper at 75⁰ division scale marking.

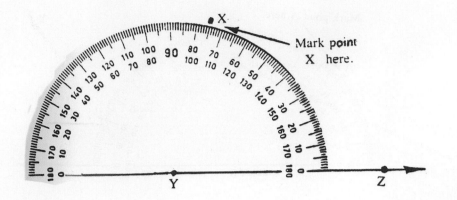

Mark point
X here.

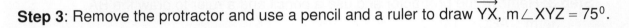

Step 3: Remove the protractor and use a pencil and a ruler to draw $\overrightarrow{YX}$, $m\angle XYZ = 75^0$.

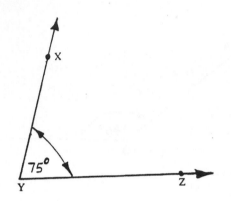

Exercises

1. The maximum scale reading on the protractor is 180^0. True or false? Hint: Look at the picture of the protractor.
2. The minimum scale reading on the protractor is 0^0 True or false? Hint: Look at the picture of the protractor.
3. Describe a protractor. Hint: See the notes.
4. What are protractors used for?
5. Describe how you would measure angle ABC.
6. Use a protractor to measure $\angle XYZ$ in each case.

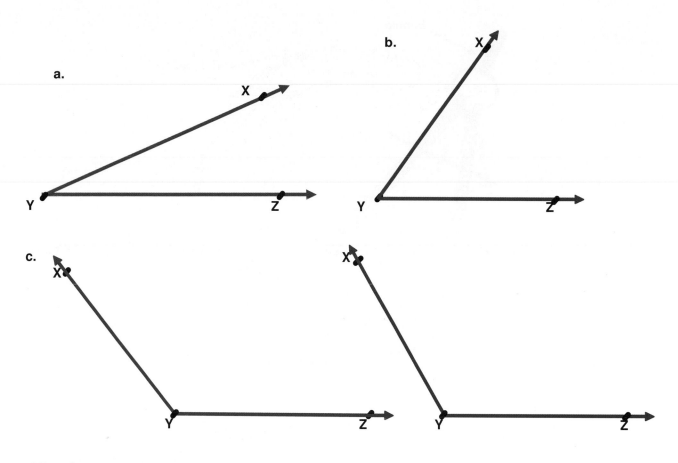

a.

b.

c.

Hint: See Examples 2 and 3.

7. Use a protractor, a pencil, and a ruler to draw the following angles.
   a. 90^0 **b**. 65^0 **c**. 15^0 **d**. 44^0
   e. 38^0 **f**. 77^0 **g**. 21^0 **h**. 88^0
   i. 110^0 **j**. 121^0 **k**. 134^0 **l**. 165^0
   Hint: See Examples 4 to 7.

CONSTRUCTION OF ANGLES

Note that a compass is not shown in the construction of angles in this chapter. The picture of the compass is shown below.

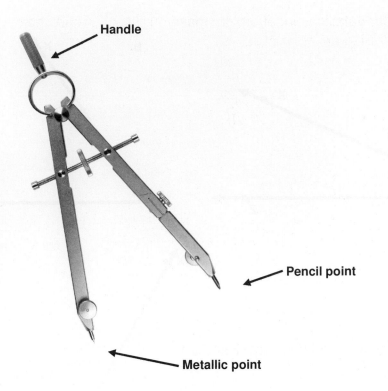

Handle

Pencil point

Metallic point

Example 1

Using a compass, construct an angle ABC which is 90^0.

Solution

Step 1: Draw $\overrightarrow{BC}$ and extend $\overline{CB}$ to E. Note that the ray BC starts with B because B is the letter that is in the middle of the angle ABC, therefore, B is the vertex of the angle ABC.

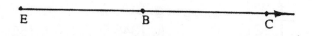

E   B   C

Step 2: Open the compass to about 3 cm and with the metallic point of the compass on point B mark an arc on $\overline{BE}$ at L, and then mark another arc with the same compass opening on $\overrightarrow{BC}$ at M.

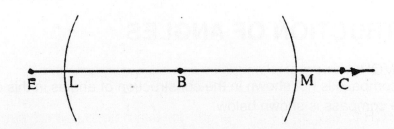

E   L   B   M   C

Step 3: With the metallic point of the compass on point L, and opening the compass beyond point B, mark an arc above point B. With the same compass opening and with the metallic point of the compass on point M, mark the second arc to intersect the first arc at point A.

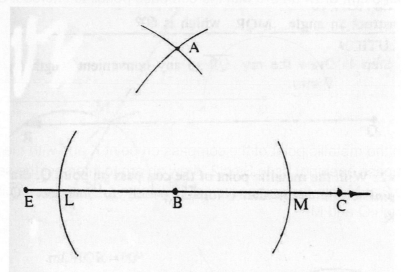

Step 4: Use a pencil and a ruler to draw $\overrightarrow{BA}$, the m$\angle$ABC = 90°.

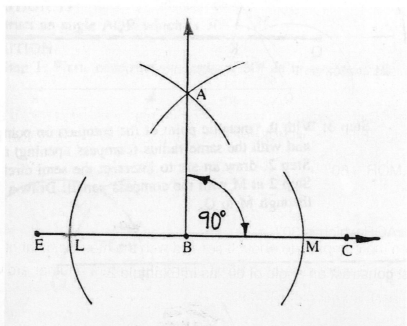

Example 2
Construct $\angle$MQR which should be 60°.
Solution

Step 1: Draw $\overrightarrow{QR}$ to any convenient length (for example to about 9 cm).

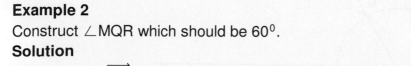

Step 2: With the metallic point of the compass on the point Q, and with a radius of about 3 cm, draw an arc with the compass pencil to intersect $\overrightarrow{QR}$ at K.

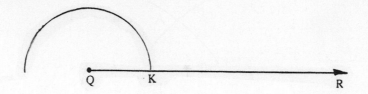

Step 3: With the metallic point of the compass on point K and with the same radius (compass opening) as in Step 2, draw an arc to intersect the semi circle in Step 2 at M with the compass pencil. Using a ruler and a pencil, draw a ray through Q and M.

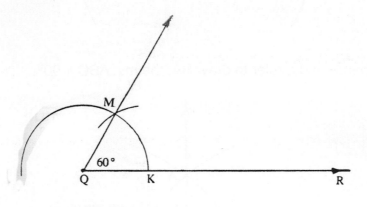

m∠MQR = 60⁰

Example 3
Construct ∠AQR which is 30⁰.
Solution
Step 1: First construct an angle of 60⁰ as in Example 2.

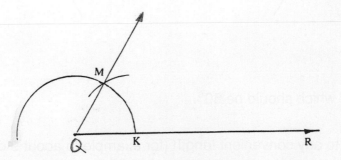

Step 2: With the metallic point of the compass on point K and opening the compass to M (or open the compass more than half of arc MK), draw an arc in front of

arc MK, and now with the metallic point of the compass on M and with the same radius (compass opening), draw an arc to intersect the first one at A.

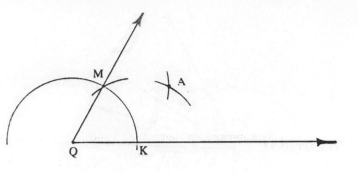

Step 3: Use a pencil and a ruler to draw $\overrightarrow{QA}$

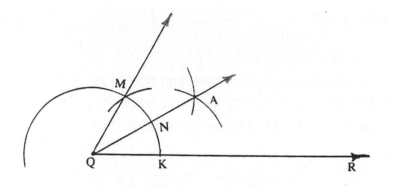

$m\angle AQR = 30^0$

Note: Also, $m\angle MQA = 30^0$ since $m\angle MQR = 60^0$.

Example 4
Construct an angle WQR which is 15^0.
Solution
Step 1: First construct an angle of 30^0 as in Example 3.

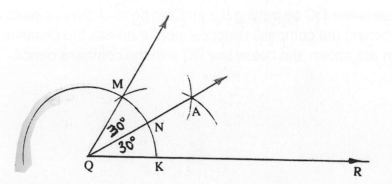

Step 2: With the metallic point of the compass on point K and opening the compass to N, draw an arc in front of the arc NK, use the same compass opening and with the metallic point of the compass on point N, draw another arc to

intersect the first arc at point W. (**Note**: The compass opening can be any convenient length which is more than half the length of arc NK.)

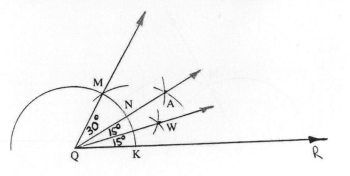

m∠WQR = 15⁰

$$m\angle WQR = 15^0$$

Note:
(a) Angle 30^0 can be constructed by bisecting 60^0 angle.
(b) Angle 15^0 can be constructed by bisecting angle 30^0.
(c) Angle $7\frac{1}{2}$ can be constructed by bisecting angle 15^0.

Example 5
Construct ∠ABC which is 45^0.
Solution
Step 1: First construct an angle of 90^0 as shown in Step 1.

(a) Draw a segment DC to any convenient length (for example about 8 cm).

D ————————————————————— C

(b) Bisect line DC by putting the metallic point of the compass on D and opening the compass distance more than half the distance of DC, mark an arc above and below line DC with the compass pencil.

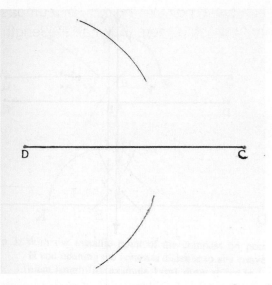

(c) With the metallic point of the compass on point C and keeping the same compass opening (distance) as in (b), draw an arc above and below line DC to intersect the arcs in (b) at point X and Y. Using a pencil and a ruler, draw a line through X and Y to intersect DC at B. $m\angle XBC$ is 90^0.

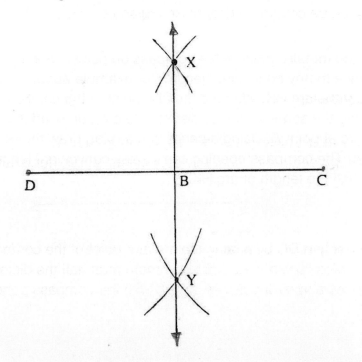

Step 2: With the metallic point of the compass on point B and with a convenient radius (for example about 1.5 cm) draw an arc to cut $\overline{BX}$ and $\overline{BC}$ at H and K respectively with the compass pencil.

737

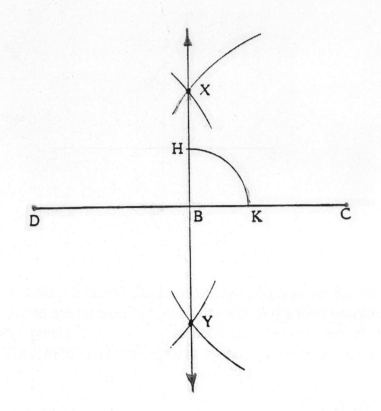

Step 3: With the metallic point of the compass on point H and opening the compass distance to any convenient length (for example about 3 cm), draw an arc in front of the arc HK. With the metallic point of the compass on point K and keeping the same compass distance (3 cm), draw another arc to intersect the first arc at point A. Using a pencil and a ruler, draw the ray BA.
(**Note**: The compass opening can be any convenient length which is more than half the length of arc HK.)

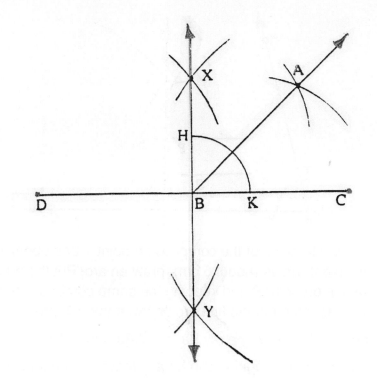

m∠ABC is 45⁰.

Example 6
Bisect ∠ABC which is 75⁰.
Solution
Step 1: Draw ∠ABC which is 75⁰ by using a protractor (See the chapter/section on "Measurement of Angles", Example 7 for the method.)

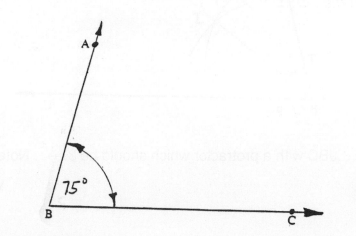

Step 2: With the metallic point of the compass on point B and opening the compass to a convenient length (about 1 cm) draw an arc to cut both $\overrightarrow{BA}$ and $\overrightarrow{BC}$ at T and P respectively.

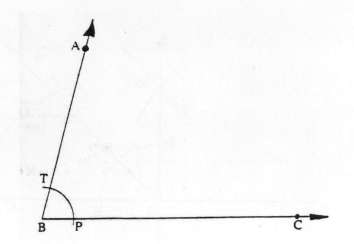

Step 3: With the metallic point of the compass on point T and opening the compass to a convenient radius (about 5 cm), draw an arc. Put the metallic point of the compass on point P and keeping the same compass opening, draw another arc to intersect the first arc at J with the compass pencil. Using a pencil and a ruler, draw the ray BJ. $m\angle ABJ = m\angle JBC = 37\frac{1}{2}^0$.

(**Note**:The compass opening can be any length which should be more than half the length of arc TP.)

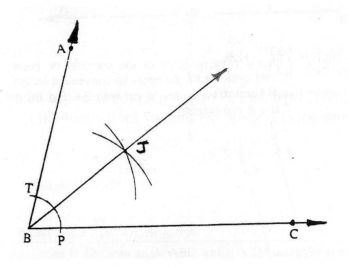

Check: Measure $\angle JBC$ with a protractor which should be $37\frac{1}{2}^0$. Note that the $\overrightarrow{BJ}$ bisects $\angle ABC$.

Example 7
Construct an angle with measure $y^0 + z^0$, given that $m\angle ACD = y^0$ and $m\angle FHJ = z^0$.
(**Note**: The radii of BC and CD of the arc BD and the radii of GH and HI of the arc GI are equal.)

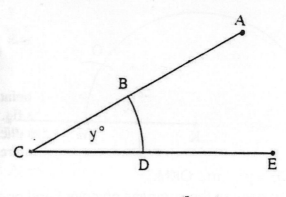

fig. 1

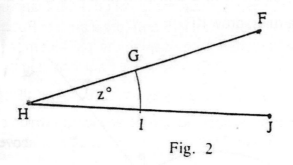

Fig. 2

Solution

Step 1: Draw a $\overrightarrow{KL}$ of a reasonable length (about 7 cm). With the metallic point of the compass on point K and with a radius of CD (as in question) draw an arc to meet the line KL at point M.

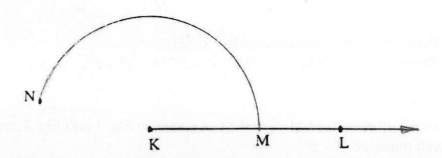

Step 2: Put the metallic point of the compass on point D and open the compass to point B (see Fig. 1), now with this compass on point M, mark an arc to cross the arc MN at O with the compass pencil.

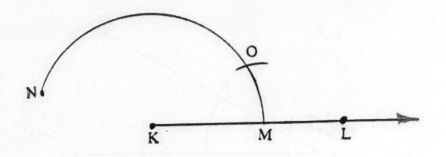

(**Note**: $m\angle BCE = y^0 = m\angle OKM$.)

Step 3: Put the metallic point of the compass on point I and open the compass to point G (see Fig. 2), and with this compass opening, put the metallic point of the compass on point O and draw an arc to cross arc MN at P. Using a pencil and a ruler, draw $\overrightarrow{KP}$.

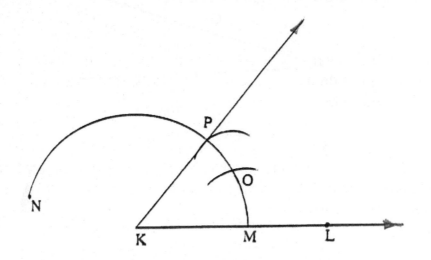

(Note: $m\angle PKO$ is equivalent to Fig. 2.)

Therefore, $m\angle PKM = m\angle BCD + m\angle GHI = y^0 + z^0$.

Example 8

Given angles of measures of y^0 and z^0 as shown in Fig. 1 and Fig. 2, construct an angle with measure $y^0 - z^0$

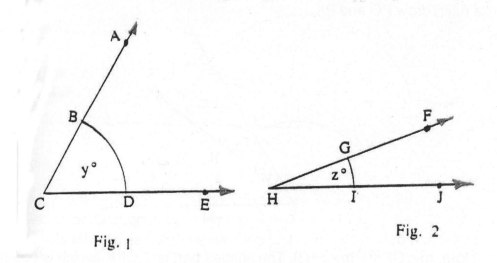

Fig. 1

Fig. 2

(**Note**: The radii BC and CD of the arc BD and the radii GH and HI of the arc GI are equal.)

Solution

Step 1: Draw a $\overline{PQ}$ of any reasonable length (about 5 cm). With the metallic point of the compass on point P and with the radius of BC draw an arc NM to meet the $\overline{PQ}$ at M.

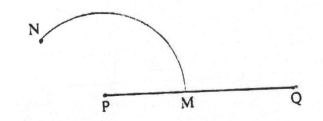

Step 2: Put the metallic point of the compass on point D and open the compass to point B in Fig 1. With this compass opening, put the metallic point of the compass on point M and mark an arc to cross arc MN at O.

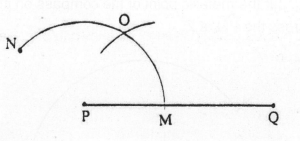

(**Note** that m∠ACE = y° = m∠OPM if $\overrightarrow{PO}$ were to be drawn.)

Step 3: Put the metallic point of the compass on point I and open the compass to point G. With this compass opening and with the metallic point of the compass on point O, draw an arc to cross arc MO at K. Using a pencil and

743

a ruler, draw $\overrightarrow{PO}$ and $\overrightarrow{PK}$.

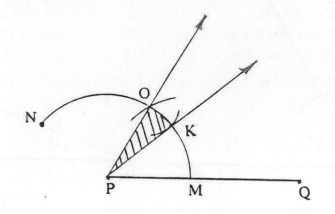

(**Note**: m∠OPK = m∠FHJ). The shaded part is ∠OPK (which is equal to ∠FHJ which is subtracted from ∠OPM (which is equal to ∠ACE). The remaining angle after this subtraction is ∠KPM which is $y^0 - z^0$.

Example 9
Given an angle of measure of x^0 below, construct an angle of $3x^0$.

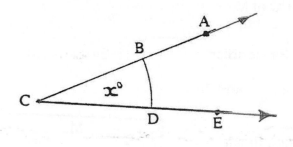

Solution
Step 1: Draw $\overline{PQ}$ with a length of about 5 cm. Put the metallic point of the compass on point C and open the compass to point D. With the same compass opening, put the metallic point of the compass on point P, and then draw an arc to cross the $\overline{PQ}$ at Z.

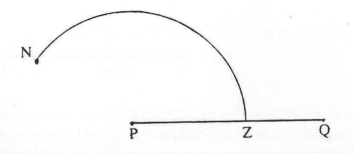

Step 2: Put the metallic point of the compass on point D and open the compass to

point B. With this compass opening, put the metallic point of the compass on point Z, and then mark an arc to intersect arc ZN at R. With the metallic point of the compass on point R and with the same compass opening, draw an arc to intercept the arc ZN at S. With the metallic point of the compass on point S, and with the same compass opening, draw the third arc which intercepts arc ZN at X. Using a pencil and a ruler, draw $\overrightarrow{PX}$.

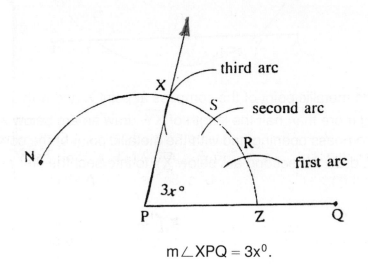

$$m\angle XPQ = 3x^0.$$

Construction of Perpendicular Lines, To Bisect a Segment, Construction of $22\frac{1}{2}^0$ and 135^0.

Example 10
What are perpendicular lines?
Solution
Two lines are perpendicular if they intersect to form a right angle. A right angle is an angle which has a measure of 90^0.

Example 11
Construct a perpendicular line from a point P to the segment AB.
Solution
Step 1: Mark a point P and below it draw a segment AB.

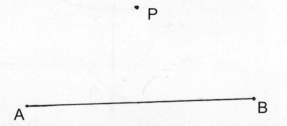

Step 2: With the metallic point of the compass on point P and with a radius of about 5 cm, draw an arc to cross $\overline{AB}$ at points X and Y.

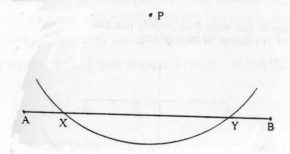

Step 3: With the metallic point of the compass at point X and with the compass opening more than half the length of $\overline{XY}$, draw an arc below $\overline{XY}$. With the same compass opening and with the metallic point of the compass on the point Y, draw the second arc below $\overline{XY}$ to intersect the first arc at point Q.

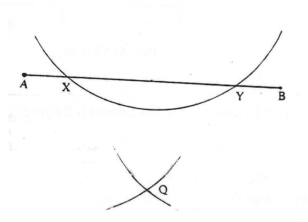

Step 4: Using a pencil and a ruler, draw the ray PQ. PQ is perpendicular to $\overline{AB}$.

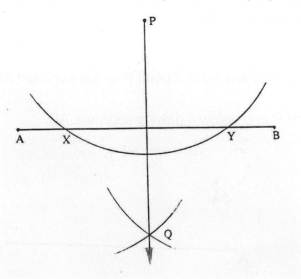

Example 12

Bisect $\overline{AB}$ which is 5 cm.

Solution

Step 1: Using a ruler and pencil, draw $\overline{AB}$ which is 5 cm long. To draw $\overline{AB}$ which is 5 cm long, put the ruler on the paper and draw a segment from the 0 marking along the centimeter scale to the 5 centimeter marking. Label the ends of the segments A and B. With the metallic point of the compass on point A and with the radius of the compass opening more than half of $\overline{AB}$, draw an arc above and below $\overline{AB}$.

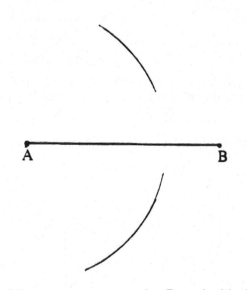

Step 2: With the metallic point of the compass on point B and with the same radius or compass opening as in Step 1, draw an arc above $\overline{AB}$ to cross the arc drawn in Step 1 at point X and also draw an arc below $\overline{AB}$ to cross the arc drawn in Step 1 at point Y.

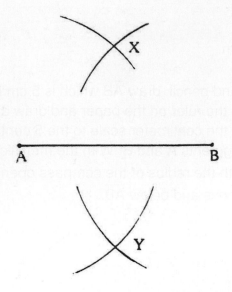

Step 3: Using a pencil and a ruler, draw the line XY to intersect $\overline{AB}$ at Z. Note that the point Z bisects $\overline{AB}$ and therefore $\overline{AZ} = \overline{ZB}$. We can also state that Z is the midpoint of $\overline{AB}$.

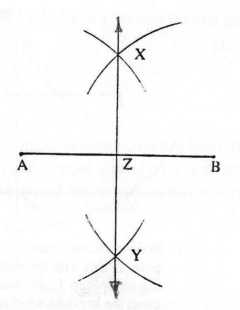

Example 13

Construct an angle of $22\frac{1}{2}^0$.

Solution

Step 1: Construct an angle of 90^0 (See Example 1 for the construction method.)

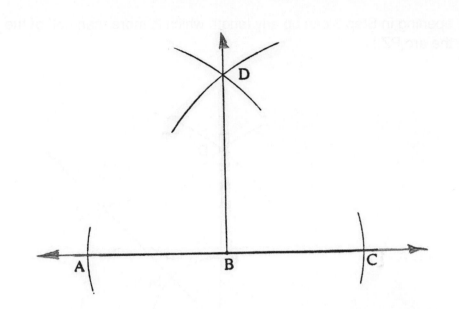

Step 2 Bisect the 90⁰ angle in Step 1 into two equal parts of 45⁰ as shown:
With the metallic point of the compass on point B and with a radius 5 cm or compass opening of 5 cm, draw an arc to cross $\overrightarrow{BC}$ at Z. With the same compass opening and still with the metallic point of the compass at point B, draw another arc to cross $\overrightarrow{BD}$ at P.

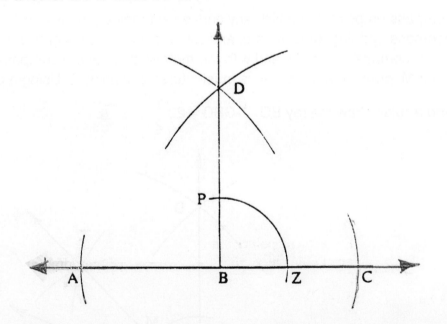

Step 3: With any convenient radius (about 6 cm) or any convenient compass opening, put the metallic point of the compass on point Z and draw an arc and with the same radius or with the same compass opening, put the metallic point of the compass at point P and draw an arc. Both arcs must intersect at point K. Using a pencil and a ruler, draw the ray BK. m∠KBC is 45⁰. Note that the $\overrightarrow{BK}$ crossed the arc PZ at M. (The convenient radius or the compass

749

opening in Step 3 can be any length which is more than half of the length of the arc PZ.)

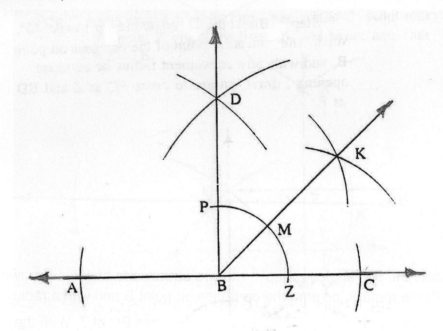

Step 4: Bisect $\angle$KBC which is 45^0 to get $22\frac{1}{2}^0$. With the metallic point of the compass on point Z and with any convenient radius (about 4 cm) or compass opening, draw an arc, and with the same radius or with the same compass opening, and with the metallic point of the compass at point M, draw an arc. Both arcs must intersect at point G. Using a pencil and a ruler, draw the ray BG. $\angle$GBC = $22\frac{1}{2}^0$.

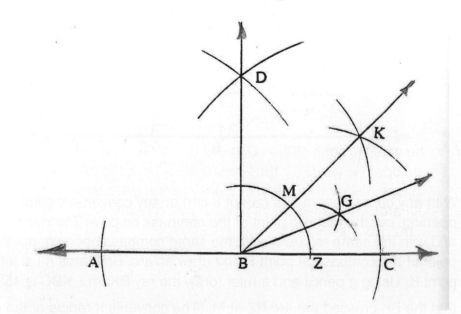